Publisher's Note

The book descriptions we ask booksellers to display prominently warn that this is an historic book with numerous typos or missing text; it is not indexed or illustrated.

The book was created using optical character recognition software. The software is 99 percent accurate if the book is in good condition. However, we do understand that even one percent can be an annoying number of typos! And sometimes all or part of a page may be missing from the book. Or the paper may be so discolored from age that it is difficult to read. We apologize and gratefully acknowledge Google's assistance.

After we re-typeset and design a book, the page numbers change so the old index and table of contents no longer work. Therefore, we usually remove them.

Our books sell so few copies that you would have to pay hundreds of dollars to cover the cost of proof reading and fixing the typos, missing text and index. Therefore, whenever possible, we let our customers download a free copy of the original typo-free scanned book. Simply enter the barcode number from the back cover of the paperback in the Free Book form at www.general-books. net. You may also qualify for a free trial membership in our book club to download up to four books for free. Simply enter the barcode number from the back cover onto the membership form on the same page. The book club entitles you to select from more than a million books at no additional charge. Simply enter the title or subject onto the search form to find the books.

If you have any questions, could you please be so kind as to consult our Frequently Asked Questions page at www. general-books.net/faqs.cfm? You are also welcome to contact us there.

General Books LLC™, Memphis, USA, 2012. ISBN: 9781235184468.

※ ※ ※ ※ ※ ※ ※ ※

PREFACE.

On the two principal philosophical Chinese systems, Confucianism and Taoism we are tolerably well informed by translations of the leading works and by systematical treatises. These two branches may be regarded as the most important, but it would be impossible to write a history of Chinese philosophy without paying special attention to the various heterodox philosophers, whose views do not agree with the current ideas of either Confucianists or Taoists. For that very reason they are often more interesting than the latter, being original thinkers, who disdain to resign themselves to merely iterating old stereotyped formulae. Many of their tenets remind us of similar arguments propounded by various philosophical schools of the West. I have called attention to the *Epicurean Yang Chu* and to the Chinese *Sophists* (vid. Journ. of Peking Orient. Soc, vol. IH, p. 203 and Journ. of China Branch of Royal Asiat. Soc, vol. XXXIV, p. 1) and now beg to place before the public a translation of the philosophical essays of *Wang Ch'ung,* whom we may well call a *Materialist*. As a first instalment I published, some years ago, a paper treating of *Wang Ch'ung's* ideas on Death and Immortality (Journ. oTCluna Branch of Royal Asiat. Soc, vol. XXXI, p. 40). My lecture on the Metaphysics of *Wang Ch'ung,* held in 1899 before the East Asiatic Section of the Congress of Orientalists at Rome, has not been printed, the manuscript having been lost by the secretaries of the Section.

Although he has much in common with the Confucianists and still more with the Taoists, *Wang Ch'ung's* philosophy does not lack originality. He is an Eclectic, and takes his materials from wherever it suits him, but he has worked it into an elaborate,.system such as did not exist before *Chu Hsi*. Like a true philosopher he has reduced the multiplicity of things to some few fundamental principles, by which he explains every phenomenon. One or two leading ideas pervade his philosophy as *"Leilmotives/"*

Lun-Heug. 1

The *Lun-Mng* is not a systematic digest of *Wang Ch'ung's* philosophy. Chinese philosophers like the Greeks before Aristotle have not yet learned the art of connecting their thoughts so as to form a complete system, in which each chapter is the logical sequence of the preceding one. But *Wang Ch'ung* has already made one step in this direction. Whereas the *Analects* and the works of *Mencius, Lieh Tse* and *Chuang Tse* are hardly anything else than collections of detached aphorisms, each chapter embracing the most heterogeneous subjects, each chapter of the *Lun-heng* is a real essay, the theme of which is given first and adhered to throughout. But there is not much connection between the separate essays.

These essays are not all of equal value. Some may perhaps interest a Chinese, but are not calculated to enlist our interest. For this reason I have not translated the whole work, but made a selection. It comprises the philosophical essays, and of the others the most characteristic, enabling the reader to form an adequate idea of the author and his peculiarities. My chief aim has been to set forth *Wang Ch'ung's* philosophy. The introduction contains a sketch of his system, which I have attempted to abstract from his writings.

Of the 84 essays of the *Lun-heng* I have translated 44. I have taken the liberty of arranging them more systematically than is done in the original, classing them under several heads as metaphysical, physical, critical, religious, and folklore. The division is not a strict one, because with many chapters it is doubtful, to which class they belong. Especially between metaphysics and physics it is difficult to draw a distinction, since purely physical questions are often treated metaphysically. From a table of contents of the *Lun-hbig* in its entirety the reader will learn the subject of those essays, which have not been translated, and by its help he can easily find the place, which each chapter takes in the original.

With the exception of the Autobiography and the two chapters on *Con/ucins* and *Mencius* translated by *Hutchinson* (China Review, vol. VII and VIII) the essays of *Wang Ch ung* have not been put into any European language before. A Chinese commentary to the *Lun-heng* does not exist. I hope that my translation may prove trustworthy. For any misunderstandings, which in Chinese and philosophical works particularly are unavoidable, I count upon the indulgence of my critics.

As far as lay in my power. I have endeavoured to trace the sources from which *Wang Ch ung* has quoted, which has not been an easy task, and I have added such explanatory notes as to enable even persons not knowing Chinese to understand the text. For the many proper names the index at the end of the volume will be of advantage.

'To my thinking, *Wang Ch'ung* is one of the most ingenious Chinese writers, a satirist like *Lucian* and an *esprit fort* like *Voltaire*, .whose *Lun-heng* well deserves the widest publicity.

INTRODUCTION.

L The Life of Wang Ch'ung.

The principal data of *Wang* ("/i'ung's life are furnished by his autobiography and by the biographical notice in chapter 79 p. 1 of the *Hou Han-shu*, the History of the Later *Han* Dynasty, which was written by *Fan Yeh* in the 5th cent. A.d. and commented on by Prince *Chang Huai Hsien* of the *T'ang* dynasty. There we read:

"*Wang Ch ung*, whose style was *Chung Jen*, was a native of *Shang-yil* in *K uei-chi*. His forefathers had immigrated from *Yuanch'ing* in the *Wei* circuit. As a bov he lost his lather and was commended in his village for his filial piety. Subsequently he repaired to the capital, where he studied at the academy.

The book of *Yuan SAan Sung* says that *Wang Ch'ung* was a very precocious youth. After having entered the academy, he composed an essay on six scholars on the occasion of the emperor visit-

ing the Imperial College.

His teacher was *Pan Piao* from *Fufeng*. He was very fond of extensive reading, but did not trouble much about paragraphs or sentences. His' family being poor, he possessed no books. Therefore he used to stroll about the marketplace and the shops in *Loyang* and read the books exposed there for sale. That which he had once read, he was able to remember and to repeat. Thus he had acquired a vast knowledge of the tenets of the various schools and systems. Having returned to his native place, he led a very solitary life as a teacher. Then he took office in the prefecture and was appointed secretary, but in consequence of frequent remonstrances with his superiors, disputes, and dissensions with his colleagues, he had to quit the service.

Wang Ch ung had a strong *penchant* for discussions. At the outset, his arguments would often appear rather queer, but his final conclusions were true and reasonable. Being convinced that the ordinary *savants* stuck too much to the letter, and thus would mostly lose the true meaning, he shut himself up for meditation, and no longer observed the ceremonies of congratulation or condolence. Everywhere near the door, the windows, and on the walls he had his knives and pens placed, with which he wrote the *Lun-hing* in 85 chapters containing over 200,000 words. *Yuan Shan Sung* says in his book that at first the *Lunheng* written by *Wang Ch'ung* was not current in the central provinces. When *T'sai Yung* came to *Wu*, he discovered it there, and used to read it secretly as a help to conversation. Afterwards *Wang Lang* became prefect of *K'uei-chi*, and likewise got into possession of the book. On his return to *Hsii-lma* his contemporaries were struck with the great improvement of his abilities. Some one remarked that, unless he had met with some extraordinary person, he must have found some extraordinary book. They made investigations, and found out that in fact it was from the *Lunheng* that he had derived this advantage. Thereupon the *Lun-heng* came into vogue. *Pao* P'v *Tse* relates that his con-

temporai ies grudged *T'sai Yung* the possession of a rare book. Somebody searched for it in the hiding place behind his curtains, and there in fact found the *Lun-heng*. He folded some chapters together in order to take them away, when *T'sai Yung* proposed to him that they should both keep the book, but not divulge its contents.

He explained the similarities and the diversities of the different classes of things, and settled the common doubts and errors of the time.

The governor *Tung Ch'in* made him assistant-magistrate. Later on he rose to the rank of a sub-prefect. Then he retired and returned home. A friend and fellow-countryman of his *Hsieh I Wu* addressed a memorial to the throne, in which he recommended *Wang Ch ung* for his talents and learning.

In the book of *Hsieh Ch eng* it is stated that in recommending *Wang Ch'ung*, *Hsieh I Wu* said that his genius was a natural gift and not acquired by learning. Even *Mendus* and *Sun t'hing* in former times, or *Yang Hsiung, Liu Hsiung*, or *See ma Ch'ien* more recently in the *Han* epoch could not surpass him.

Su Tsung commanded a chamberlain to summon *Wang Ch'ung* into his presence, but owing to sickness, he could not go. When he was nearly seventy years of age, his powers began to decline. Then he wrote a book on "Macrobiotics" in 16 chapters, and refraining from all desires and propensities, and avoiding all emotions, he kept himself alive, until in the middle of the *Yungyuan* period, when he died of an illness at his home."

By his own testimony *Wang Ch ung* was born in the third year of the *Chien-vti* cycle, *i. e.* in *Shang-gii-hsien*, the present *Shao-hsing-fu* of the province of *Chekiang*. His family had originally been residing in *Yuan-ch ing* — *Taming-fu* in *Chihli*. His father's name was *Wang Sung*. Owing to their violent temper his ancestors had several times been implicated in local feuds, which are still now of frequent occurrence in *Fukien* and *Chekiang*, and were compelled to change their domicile. *Wang Ch ung's* critics are scandalized at his coolly telling us that his great-grand-father behaved like a ruffian during a famine, killing and wounding his fel-low-people.

If *Wang Ch ung's* own description be true, he must have been a paragon in his youth. He never needed any correc-tion neither at the hands of his parents nor of his teachers. For his age he was exceptionally sedate and serious. When he was six years old, he received bis first instruction, and at the age of 8 be was sent to a public school. There the teacher explained to him the *Analects* and the *Shaking,* and he read 1,000 characters every day. When be bad mas-tered the Classics, one was astonished at the progress be made, so he nai'vely informs us. Of bis other attainments be speaks in the same strain and with the same conceit. The *Hon Ilan-shu* con-firms that he was a good son.

Having lost bis father very early, be entered the Imperial College at *Logang,* then the capital of *China.* His principal teacher was the historian *Pan Pian,* t he father of *Pan Kn,* author of the History of the Former *Han* dynasty. In *Loyang* he laid the foundation of the vast amount of knowledge by which he dis-tinguished himself later on, and became acquainted with the theories of the var-ious schools of thought, many of which be vigorously attacks in his writings. His aim was to grasp the general gist of what he read, and he did not care so much for minor details. The majority of the scholars of his time conversely would cling to the words and sentences and over these minutiae quite forget the whole. Being too poor to buy all the books required to satiate bis hunger for knowledge, be would saunter about in the marketplace and book-shops, and peruse the books exposed there for sale, having probably'made some sort of agreement with the booksellers, who may have taken an interest in the ardent student. His excellent memory was of great service to him, for be could re-member, even repeat what he had once read. At the same time his critical ge-nius developed. He liked to argue a point, and though his views often seemed paradoxical, bis opponents

could not but admit the justness of his arguments.

Having completed his studies, *Wang Ch ung* returned to his native place, where he became a teacher and lived a very quiet life. Subsequently he took of-fice and secured a small position as a secretary of a district, a post which he also filled under a military governor and a prefect. At last he was promoted to be assistantmagistrate of a department. He would have us believe that he was a very good official, and that his relations to his colleagues were excellent. The *Hon Han-shu,* on the other hand, tells us that he remonstrated so much with his superiors and was so quarrelsome, that he had to leave the service. This version seems the more probable of the two. *Wang Ch'ung* was much too inde-pendent, much too outspoken, and too clever to do the routine business well, which requires clerks and secretaries of moderate abilities, or to serve under su-periors, whom he surpassed by his tal-ents. 80 he devoted himself exclusively to his studies, lie lived in rather strait-ened circumstances, but supported his embarassments with philosophical equanimity and cheerfulness. "Although he was poor and had not au acre to dwell upon, his mind was freer than that of kings and dukes, and though he had no emoluments counted by pecks and bushels, he felt, as if he had ten thousand *chwig* to live upon. He en-joyed a tranquil happiness, but his de-sires did not run riot, and though he was living in a state of poverty, his energy was not broken. The study of ancient lit-erature was his debauchery, and strange stories his relish." He had a great admi-ration for superior men, and liked to as-sociate with people rising above medi-ocrity. As long as he was in office and well off, he had many friends, but most of them abandoned him, when he had retired into private life.

In A.d. 86 *Wang Ch'ung* emigrated into the province of *Anhvi,* where he was appointed sub-prefect, the highest post which he held, but two years only, for in 88 he gave up his official career, which had not been a brilliant one. The reason of his resignation this time seems

to have been ill health.

'So far *Wang Ch ung* had not suc-ceeded in attracting the attention of the emperor. An essay which he had com-posed, when the emperor had visited the college of *Loyang,* had passed unno-ticed. In the year 70, when parts of *Ho-nan* were suffering from a great dearth, *Wang Ch ung* presented a memorial to the Emperor *Chang Ti* in which he pro-posed measures to prohibit dissipation and extravagancies, and to provide for the time of need, but his suggestions were not accepted. He did not fare bet-ter with another anti-alcoholic memor-ial, in which he advocated the prohibi-tion of the use of spirits. When finally the Emperor became aware of *Wang Ch'ung,* it was too late. A friend and a countryman of his, *Hsieh I Wu* recom-mended him to the throne for his tal-ents and great learning, saying that nei-ther *Me1wius* or *Hsiln Tse* nor in the *Han* time *Yang Hsiung, Liu Hsiang* or *Sse Ma Chien* could outshine him. The Emperor *Chang Ti* (70—88 A.1i.) sum-moned him to his presence, but owing to his ill-health *Wang Chung* had to de-cline the honour. His state had impaired so much, that already in 89 he thought that his end had come. But the next two years passed, and he did not die. He found even the time to write a book on "Macrobiotics," which he put into prac-tice himself, observing a strict diet and avoiding all agitations in order to keep his vital fluid intact, until he expired in the middle of the *Yung-yuan* period (89-104) about the year 97. The exact year is not known.

2. The Works of Wang Ch'ung. *Wang Chung's* last work, the *Yang-hsing-shu* or *Macrobiotics* in 16 chapters, which he wrote some years before his death, has been mentioned. His first produc-tions were the *Chi-su-chieh-yi* "Cen-sures on Common Morals" in 12 chap-ters and the *Cheng-wu,* a book on Government, both preceding his princi-pal work, the *Luu-heng,* in which they are several times referred to in the two biographical chapters. *Wang Cliung* wrote his "Censures" as a protest against the manners of his time with a view to rouse the public conscience. He

was prompted to write this work by the heartlessness of his former friends, who abandoned him, when he was poor, and of the world in general. To be read and understood by the people, not the literati only, he adopted an easy and popular style. This appears to have been contrary to custom, for he thought it necessary to justify himself (p. 71).

The work on government owes its origin to the vain efforts of the Imperial Government of his time to administer the Empire. They did not see their way, being ignorant of the fundamental principles (p. 70). From the *Ching-wu* the territorial officials were to learn what they needed most in their administration, and the people should be induced "to reform and gratefully acknowledge the kindness of the government" (p. 90).

These three works: the Macrobiotics, the Censures on Morals, and the work on Government have all been lost, and solely the *Lun-hing* has come down to us. Whereas the *Chi-suchieh-yi* censures the common morals, the *Lun-hing* = *Disquisitions* tests and criticises the common errors and superstitions, the former being more ethical, the latter speculative. Many of these errors are derived from the current literature, classical as well as popular. *Wang Chung* takes up these books and points out where they are wrong. He avoids all wild speculations, which he condemns in others, so he says (p. 91). The *Lun-hing* is not professedly a philosophical work, intended to set forth a philosophical system, but in confuting and contesting the views of others, *Wang Ch'ung* incidentally develops his own philosophy. In this respect there is a certain resemblance with the *Theodicee* of Leibniz, which, strictly speaking, is a polemic against *Bagle. Wang Ch'ung's* aim in writing the *Lun-hing* was purely practical, as becomes plain from some of his utterances. "The nine chapters of the *Lun-heng* on Inventions, and the three chapters of the *Lun-hing* on Exaggerations, says he, are intended to impress people, that they must strive for truthfulness." Even such high metaphysical problems as that of immortality he regards from a practical point of

view. Otherwise he would not write, as he does:—" I have written the essays on Death and on the False Reports about Death to show that the deceased have no consciousness, and cannot become ghosts, hoping that, as soon as my readers have grasped this, they will restrain the extravagance of the burials and become economical" (p. 90).

From a passage (Chap. XXXVUI) to the effect that the reigning sovereign was continuing the prosperity of *Kuang Wu Ti* (25-57a.d.) and *Ming Ti* (58-75) it appears that the *Lun-hing* was written under the reign of the Emperor *Chang ti viz.* between 76 and 89 A.d. From another remark that in the *Chiang-jui* chapter (XXX) the auspicious portents, of the *Yuan-ho* and *Chang-ho* epochs (84-86 and 87-88) could not be mentioned, because of its being already completed, we may infer that the whole work was finished before 84. Thus it must date from the years 76-84 A.d.

The *Lun-heng* in its present form consists of 30 books comprising 85 chapters or separate essays. *Chien Lung's* Catalogue *(Sse-k u-chiian-shu-tsung-inu* chap. 120 p. 1) shows that we do not possess the *Lun-hing* in its entirety. In his autobiography *Wang ChUng* states that his work contains more than a hundred chapters (p. 78), consequently a number of chapters must have been lost. The 85 chapters mentioned above are enumerated in the index preceding the text, but of the 44th chapter "*Chao-chih*" we have merely the title, but not the text so, that the number of chapters really existing is reduced to 84. The chapters exceeding 85 must have already been lost in the first centuries, for we read in the *Hon Han-shu* of the 5th cent. A.d. that *Wang Ch'ung* wrote the LunMng in 85 chapters.

Some interesting data about the history of the text are furnished in another History of the Later *Han* Dynasty, the *Hon Han-shu* of *Yuan Shan Sung* of the *Chin* epoch (265-419 A.d.), who lived anterior to *Fan Yeh,* the author of the officially recognised History of the Later *Han. Yuan Shan Sung's* History was in 100 books (cf. *Li tai ming Mi-en lieh ni i shih hsing pu* chap. 44, p. 85 v.).

but it has not been incorporated into the Twenty-four dynastic Histories. *Yuan Shan Sung,* whose work is quoted by several critics, informs us that at first the *Lun-Mng* was only current in the southern provinces of China where *Wang Ch ung* had lived. There it was discovered by *T'sai Yung* (133-192 A. d.) a scholar of note from the north, but instead of communicating it to others, he kept it for himself, reading it secretly "as a help to conversation" *i. e.* he plundered the *Lun-Mng* to be able to shine in conversation. Another scholar, *Wang Lang* of the 2nd and 3d cent. A.d. is reported to have behaved in a similar way, when he became prefect of *K'uei-chi,* where he found the *Lun-heng.* His friends suspected him of having come into possession of an extraordinary book, whence he took his wisdom. They searched for it and found the *Lun-Mng,* which subsequently became universally known. The Taoist writer *Ko Hung* of the 4th cent, A.d., known as *Pao P'u Tse,* recounts that the *Lun-heng* concealed by *T sai Yung* was discovered in the same way. At all events *T'sai Yung* and *Wang Lang* seem to have been instru mental in preserving and transmitting the *Lun-heng.*

In the History of the *Sui* dynasty (580-618 A.d.), *Sui-shn* chap. 34 p. 7 v. , an edition of the *Lun-Mng* in 29 books is mentioned, whereas we have 30 books now. The commentary to this passage observes that under the *Liang* dynasty (502-556 A.d.) there was the *Tung-hsu* in 9 books and 1 book of Remarks written by *Ying Feng,* but that both works are lost. They seem to have been treatises on the *Lun-Mng,* of which there are none now left. The Catalogue of the Books in the History of the *T'ang* dynasty *Chien T'ang-shu* chap. 47 p. 8) has the entry:— "*Lun-Mng* 30 books."

At present the *Lun-heng* forms part of the well known collection of works of the *Han* and *Wei* times, the *Han Wei tsung-shu* dating from the *Ming* dynasty. The text of the *Lun-Mng* contained in the large collection of philosophical works, the *Tse shu po chia,* is only a reprint from the *Han Wei tsung-shu.* In his useful little biographical index, *Shu-mu-tang wen, Chang Chih Tung* records a separate edition of the *Lun-heng* printed under the *Ming* dynasty. I have not seen it and do not know, whether it is still to be found in the book-shops, and whether it differs from the current text. In the many quotations from the *Lun-heng* of the *laiping Yil lan* (9th cent, A.d.) there is hardly any divergence from the reading of our text. A commentary to the *Lunheng* has not been written.

In the appreciation of his countrymen *Wang Ch ung* does not rank very high. *Chao hung Wu* (12th cent, A.d.) opines that the" *Lun-heng* falls short of the elegant productions of the Former *Han* epoch. Another critic of the 12th cent., *Kao Sse Sun* is still more severe in his judgment. He declares the *Lun-heng* to be a medley of heterogeneous masses, written in a bad style, in which morality does not take the place it ought. After his view the *Lunheng* would have no intrinsic value, being nothing more than a "help to conversation." *Wang Po Hou* and others condemn the *Lun-heng* on account of the author's impious utterances regarding his ancestors and his attacks upon the Sage *Confucius*. That he criticised *Mencius* might be excused, but to dare to find fault with *Confucius* is an unpardonable crime. That mars the whole work.

In modern times a change of opinion in favour of *Wang Ch ung* seems to have taken place. In his Prefatory Notice to the *Lunheng, Yu Chun Hsi* pours down unrestricted praise upon him. "People of the *Han* period, he remarks, were fond of fictions and fallacies. *Wang (. 'h ung* pointed out whatever was wrong; in all his arguments he used a strict and thorough method, and paid special attention to meanings. Rejecting erroneous notions he came near the truth. Nor was he afraid of disagreeing with the worthies of old. Thus he furthered the laws of the State, and opened the eyes and ears of the scholars. People reading his books felt a chill at first, but then they repudiated all falsehood, and became just and good. They were set right, and discarded all crooked doctrines. It is as if somebody amidst a clamouring crowd

in the market-place lifts the scale: then the weights and prices of wares are equitably determined, and every strife ceases."

To a certain extent at least the *Ch'ien Lung* Catalogue does him justice, while characterising his strictures on *Confucius* and *Mencius* and his disrespect towards his forefathers as wicked and perverse, its critics still admit that in exposing falsehoods and denouncing what is base and low he generally hits the truth, and that by his investigations he has done much for the furtherance of culture and civilization. They conclude by saying that, although *Wang Ch'ung* be impugned by many, he will always have admirers.

I presume that most Europeans, untramelled by Chinese moral prejudices, will rather be among his admirers, and fall in with *Magers* speaking of *Wang Ch'ung* as "a philosopher, perhaps the most original and judicious among all the metaphysicians China has produced,... who in the writings derived from his pen, forming a work in thirty books, entitled Critical Disquisitions '*Lunlieng,*' handles mental and physical problems in a style and with a boldness unparallelled in Chinese literature" (*Reader's* Manual N. 795).

The first translator of the two chapters on *Confucius* and *Mencius* and of the autobiography, *Hutchinson*, says of the *Limiting:*—"The whole book will repay perusal, treating as it does of a wide range of subjects, enabling us to form some idea of the state of the Chinese mind at the commencement of the Christian era.

The subjects (treated) are well calculated to enlist the interest of the student and would most probably shed much light upon the history of Chinese Metaphysics" (China Review vol. VII, p. 40).

In my opinion *Wang Ch ung* is one of the greatest Chinese thinkers. As a speculative philosopher he leaves *Confucius* and *Mencius,* who are only moralists, far behind. He is much more judicious than *Lao Tse, Chuang Tse,* or *Me Ti.* We might perhaps place him on a level with *Chu Ilst,* the great philosopher of the *Sung* time, in point of abilities at least,

for their philosophies differ very much.

In most Chinese works *Wang Ch'ung* is placed among the Miscellaneous Writers or the Eclectics "*Tsa Chia,*" who do not belong to one single school, Confucianism, Mehism, or Taoism, but combine the doctrines of various schools. *Wang Ch ung* is treated as an Eclectic in the histories of the *Sui* dynasty and the *'Vang* dynasty, in *Ch'ien Lung's Catalogue,* and in the *Tse-slm-po-chia. Chang Chih Tung,* however, enumerates him among the Confucianists, and so does *Faber* (Doctrines of *Confucius* p. 31). Although he has not been the founder of a school, I would rather assign to him a place apart, to which his importance as a philosopher entitles him. It matters not that his influence has been very slight, and that the Chinese know so little of him. His work is hardly read, but is extensively quoted in dictionaries and cyclopedias. At any rate *Wang Ch'ung* is more of an Eclectic than a Confucianist. The Chinese qualify as "*Tsa Chia*" all those original writers whom they cannot place under any other head. *Wang Ch ung* seems to regard himself as a Confucianist. No other philosopher is more frequently mentioned hy him than *Confucius,* who, though he finds fault with him here and there, is still, in his eyes, *the Sage. Wang Ch ung* is most happy, when he can prove an assertion by quoting the authority of *Confucius.* This explains how he came to be classed by others with the Confucianists.

3. Wang Ch'ung's Philosophy.

At first sight *Wang Ch'ung's* philosophy might seem dualistic, for he recognises two principles, which are to a certain extent opposed to each other, the *Yang* and the *Yin* fluid. But. although the former, which is conceived as forming heaven as well as the human mind, be more subtle than the latter, from which the earth has been created, yet it is by no means immaterial. Both these principles have been evolved from Chaos, when the original fluid became differentiated and split into two substances, a finer one, *Yung,* and a coarser one, *Yin.* We do not find a purely spiritual or transcendent correlate to these two substances such *e. g.* as *Tao,* the all-embracing mystical force of the Taoists, or Li *"Reason,"* which in *Chu Ilst's* system rules over Matter "Ch'i," and thus makes this system truly dualistic. Even Fate, which takes such a prominent place in *Wang Ch ung's* philosophy, has been materialised by him, and it is hardly anything more than a sort of a natural law. We cannot be far wrong, if we characterise his philosophy as a materialistic monism.

Compared with western thought *Wang Ch'ung's* system bears some resemblance to the natural philosophy *of Epicurus* and *Lucretius.* In the East we find some kindred traits among the Indian materialists, the *Chdrvdkas. Epicurus* attaches great importance to physics. The knowledge of the natural causes of things shall be an antidote against superstitions. *Wang Chung* likewise takes a lively interest in all physical problems, and tries to base his arguments on experience, as far as possible. He wishes to explain all natural phenomena by natural causes. His method is quite modern. If he often falls into error nerertheless, it is not so much owing to bad reasoning as to the poor state of Chinese science at his time. He regards many things as proved by experience, which are not, and in spite of his radicalism has still too much veneration for the sayings of old classical authors. *Wang l h uug's* views agree, in many respects, with the Epicurean Physics, but not with its Euchemonology and Sensualism, his Ethics being totally different. Ethical Epicureanism has its representative in China in the pre-Christian philosopher *Yang Chu,* who seems to have concerned himself with Ethics exclusively, whereas *Wang Ch'ung* has especially devoted himself to the study of metaphysical and physical questions. The professed aim of the philosophy of *Epicurus* is human happiness. By delivering them from errors and superstitions he intends to render people happy. *Wang Chung* likewise hopes to do away with all inventions, fictions, and falsehoods, but in doing so he has truth, and not so much happiness in view. a) Metaphysics.

The pivots of *Wang Ch ung's* philosophy are Heaven and Earth, which have been formed of the two fluids, *Yang* and *Yin.* "The fluids of the *Yin* and *Yang,* he says, are the fluids of Heaven and Earth " (Chap. XXX). These two principles are not of *Wang Ch ung's* invention, they are met with in ancient Chinese literature, in the *Yiking* and the *Liki* for instance (see *Tchou Hi,* Sa Doctrine et son influence, par *S. Le Gall,* Changhai 1894, p. 35).

Earth is known to lIs, it has a material body like man (p. 93), but what are we to understand by Heaven? Is it a spirit, the Spirit of Heaven or God, or merely an expanse of air, the Blue Empyrean, or a substance similar to that of Earth? *Wang Ch ung* considers all these possibilities and decides in favour of the last. "Men are created by heaven, why then grudge it a body?" he asks. "Heaven is not air, but has a body on high and far from men" (Chap. XIX). "To him who considers the question, as we have done, it becomes evident that heaven cannot be something diffuse and vague." His reasons are that heaven has a certain distance from earth, which by Chinese mathematicians has been calculated at upwards of 60,000 Li, and that the constellations known as the solar mansions are attached to it. These arguments seem strange to us now, but we must bear in mind that the Greeks, the Babylonians, and the Jews held quite similar views, regarding heaven as an iron or a brazen vault, the "firmament" to which the sun, the moon, and the stars were fixed, or supposing even quite a number of celestial spheres one above the other, as *Aristotle* does.

With regard to the origin of the universe *Wang Ch'ung* simply adopts the old creation theory, on which he writes as follows:— "The commentators of the *Yiking* say that previous to the separation of the primogenial vapours, there was a chaotic and uniform mass, and the books of the Literati speak of a wild medley, and of air not yet separated. When it came to he separated, the pure elements formed heaven, and the impure ones, earth. According to the expositors of the *Yiking* and the writings

of the Literati the bodies of heaven and earth, when they first became separated, were still small, and they were not far distant from each other" *(lot: cit.).* In conformity with this view Heaven and Earth were originally one viz. air or vapour. This theory must be very old, for it is already alluded to in the *Liki,* and the Taoist philosopher *Lieh Tse* of the 5th cent, B.c, who gives the best exposition of it, seems to refer it to the sages of former times. The passage is so interesting, that I may be permitted to quote it in full:—

"The teacher *Lieh Tse* said:—The sages of old held that the *Yang* and the *Yin* govern heaven and earth. Now, form being born out of the formless, from what do heaven and earth take their origin? It is said:—There was a great evolution, a great inception, a great beginning, and a great homogeneity. During the great evolution, Vapours were still imperceptible, in the great inception Vapours originate, in the great beginning Forms appear, and during the great homogeneity Substances are produced."

"The state when Vapours, Forms, and Substances though existing were still undivided, is called Chaos, which designates the conglomeration and inseparability of things. 'They could not be seen though looked at, not be heard though listened to, and not be attained though grasped at,' therefore one speaks of (incessant) evolution. Evolution is not bound to any forms or limits."

"Evolution in its transformations produces one, the changes of one produce seven, the changes of seven produce nine. Nine is the climax, it changes again, and becomes one. With one forms begin to change."

"The pure and light matter becomes the heaven above, the turbid and heavy matter forms the earth below. The mixture of their fluids gives birth to man, and the vitalizing principle of heaven and earth creates all beings" *(Lieh Tse* I, 2).

In the *Liki* we read:—"Propriety must have sprung from the Great One. This by division became Heaven and Earth, and by transformation the *Yin* and the *Yang" (Legge's Liki.* Vol. I, p. 386).

It is curious to note the similarity of the Epicurean cosmogony with that of the ancient Chinese. *Lucretius* sings:—

"Quippe etenim primum terrai corpora qusque,
propterea quod erant gravia et perplexa,
coibant in medio atque imas capiebant omnia sedes;
quae quanto magis inter se perplexa coibant,
tarn magis expressere ea qsue mare sidera solem lunamque efficerent et magni mcenia mundi:
omnia enim magis haec e levibus atque rotundis seminibus multoque minoribu' sunt elementis quam tellus, ideo, per rara foramina, terras partibus erumpens primus se sustulit aether ignifer et multos secum levis abstulit ignis."
and further on:—

"Sic igitur terrse concreto corpore pondus constitit, atque omnis mundi quasi limus in imum confluxit gravis et subsedit funditus ut fapx;
inde mare, inde aer, inde aether ignifer ipse corporibus liquidis sunt omnia pura relicta et leviora aliis alia, et liquidissimus aether atque levissimus aerias super influit auras,
nec liquidum corpus turbantibus aeris auris commiscet."
(Lucr. V, 439-449; 485-493.)

The principle of division is the same:—the light primary bodies *Wang Ch'ung* and the Chinese cosmogonists term *Yang*, the heavy ones they designate by *Yin*. Only in respect of the line of demarcation the Epicureans and the Chinese differ, for, whereas the former regard earth alone as heavy and water, air and ether as light matter, the Chinese comprise earth and water under the term *Yin*, and air and fiery ether under *Yang*. From various utterances ot *Wang Ch ung* it would appear that he conceives the *Yang* as a fiery and the *Yin* as a watery element, in short that *Yang* is fire and *Yin* water. This would tolerably well account for the formation of the universe. Fire forms the sun, the moon, and the other luminaries of Heaven, while from water and its sediments Earth, the oceans, and the atmosphere are developed. "The solar fluid is identical with the heavenly fluid" (Chap.

XVI11), says *Wang Cliung,* and:—"Rain is *Yin,* and brightness *Yang,* and conversely cold is *Yin,* and warmth is *Yang*" (Chap. XXI).

The other attributes given by *Wang Ch'ung* to the *Yang* and the *Yin* principles are merely the qualities of fire and water. The *Yang,* the fiery ether or the solar fluid, is bright, *i. e.* light (Chap. XX), warm (Chap. XXI). dry (Chap. XVII), vivifying, and creative (Chap. XXI). The Yin, rain or water, is dark, cold, wet, and destructive (p. 111). By itself water possesses neither light nor warmth, and may well be called dark and cold.

There is not a strict separation of the fluids of Heaven and Earth, they often mix and permeate one another. Heaven as well as Earth enclose air (Chap. XIX). The immense mass of air forming the gaseous part of Heaven, which, as we have seen, is credited with a body, is called sky (p. 113).

Now, whereas Earth rests motionless in the centre of the world, Heaven revolves around it, turning from east to west. This movement is explained as the emission of the heavenly fluid which, however, takes place spontaneously. Spontaneity is another corner-stone of *Wang Ch ung's* system. It means that this movement is not governed by any intelligence or subservient to the purposes of any *spiritus rector,* but is solely regulated by its own inherent natural laws. The same idea is expressed in *Mddhavdcharya s Sarca-Darsana Sangraha: .*'The fire is hot, the water cold, refreshing cool the breeze of morn.
By whom came this variety? From their own nature was it born."
(Sarva-Darsana-Samgraha, translated by *E, B. Cowell* and *A. E. Gough,*

London 1882, 'p. 10.) *Wang Ch'ung* admits that he has adopted the principle of spontaneity from the Taoists, who however, have not sufficiently substantiated it by proofs (p. 97). He shows that Heaven cannot display a conscious activity like man, because such activity is evoked by desires and impulses, which require organs:—the eye, the mouth, etc. The heavenly fluid is not a human body with eyes and ears, but a formless

and insensible mass (p. 93). The observation of the natural growth of plants and of the regularity of other natural phenomena precluding the idea of special designed acts, has confirmed our philosopher in his belief in spontaneity. "The principle of Heaven is inaction," he says. "Accordingly in spring it does not do the germinating, in summer the growing, in autumn the ripening, or in winter the hiding of the seeds. When the *Yang* fluid comes forth spontaneously, plants will germinate and grow of themselves and, when the *Yin* fluid rises, they ripen and disappear of their own accord" (p. 99).

The movement of the *Yin* fluid is spontaneous likewise. "Heaven and Earth cannot act, nor do they possess any know

Lun-li£ng. 3 ledge" (p. 101). They are not inert, but their activity is unintentional and purposeless. Thus spontaneity is the law of nature.

From this point of view *Wang Ch'ung* characterises the fluid of Heaven as "placid, tranquil, desireless, inactive, and unbusied" (p. 93), all attributes ascribed by the Taoists to their Mundane Soul, *Tao.*

At all times Heaven has been personified and deified. With the Chinese as well as with us Heaven has become a synonym for God. *Wang Ch'ung* notices that human qualities have been attributed to him. We see in him the Father of Mankind, the Chinese an emperor, the "Supreme Ruler," *Shang Ti.* He lives in heaven like a king in his palace, and governs the world (Chap. XXII) meting out rewards and punishments to mankind, rewarding the virtuous (p. 160). and punishing the wicked (p. 104). He reprimands the sovereigns on earth for their misrule by means of extraordinary natural phenomena, and, unless they reform, visits them and their people with misfortune (p. 126). Thunder is his angry voice, and with his thunderbolt he strikes the guilty (Chap. XXII).

Regarding Heaven as nothing else than a substance, a pure and tenuous fluid without a mind, *Wang Ch ung* cannot but reject these anthropomorphisms.

Heaven has no mouth, no eyes: it does not speak nor act (p. 183), it is not affected by men (p. 110), does not listen to their prayers (p. 113), and does not reply to the questions addressed to it (p. 184).

By a fusion of the fluids of Heaven and Earth all the organisms on earth have been produced (p. 104). Man does not make an exception. In this respect Heaven and Earth are like husband aud wife, and can be regarded as the father and the mother of mankind (Chap. XX). The same idea has been enunciated by *Lucretius:* —

"Postremo pereunt imbres, ubi eos *pater atker*
in gremium *matris terrai* prsecipitavit:
at nitida-surgunt fruges, ramique virescunt arboribus, crescunt ipsse fetuque gravantnr."
(Lucr. I, 250-253.) and further on:—

"Denique ca»lesti sumus oiunes semine oriundi:
omnibus ille idem pater est, nnde alma liquentis umoris guttas mater cum terra recepit,
feta parit nitidas fruges arbustaque laeta,
et genus humanum parit, omnia saecula ferarum,
pallida cum pnebet. quibus omnes corpora pascunt et dulcem ducunt vitam prolemque propagant;
quapropter inerito maternum nomen adeptast."
(Lucr. II, 988-995.) *Wang Ch ung* compares the creation of man to the freezing of ice. He is the produce of the mixture and concretion or crystallization of the two primary fluids:—"During the chilly winter months the cold air prevails, and water turns into ice. At the approach of spring, the air becomes warm, and the ice melts to water. Man is born in the universe, as ice is produced so to speak. The *Yang* and the *Yin* fluids crystallize, and produce man. When his years are completed, and his span of life comes to its end, he dies and reverts to those fluids" p. 196).

The *Yin* forms the body, and the *Yang* produces the vital spirit and the mind. Both are identical, *Wang Chung* does not discriminate between the *anima* and the *animus:*—"That by which man is born are the *Yang* and the *Yin* fluids; the *Yin* fluid produces his bones and flesh, the *Yang* fluid the vital spirit. While man is alive, the *Yang* and *Yin* fluids are in order. Hence bones and flesh are strong, and the vital force is full of vigour. Through the vital force he has knowledge, and with his bones and flesh he displays strength. The vital spirit can speak, the body continues strong and robust. While bones and flesh and the vital spirit are entwined and linked together, they are always visible and do not perish" (Chap. XVIII).

Man is imbued with the heavenly or vital fluid at his birth. It is a formless mass like the yolk of an egg, before it is hatched, showing in this respect the nature of the primogenial vapours, from which it has been derived (p. 199). There is no difference between the vital forces of man and animals. They have the same origin. The vital fluid resides in the blood and the arteries, and is nourished and developed by eating and drinking (p. 194). It has to fulfil two difficult functions, to animate the body and keep it alive, and to form its mind. All sensations are caused by the vital fluid:—"When the vital fluid is thinking or meditating, it flows into the eyes, the mouth or the ears. When it flows into the eyes, the eyes see shapes, when it flows into the ears, the ears hear sounds, and, when it flows into the mouth, the mouth speaks something" (Chap. XVIII). *Wang Ch ung* imagines that all sensations are produced in their organs by the vital fluid, which must be the mental power as well, since it thinks and meditates. Insanity is defined as a disturbance of the vital force *end.).* There are no supernatural mental faculties and no prophets or sages knowing the future or possessing a special knowledge derived from any other source than the vital force (p. 61). It is also the will, which causes the mouth to speak. As such it determines the character, which in *Wang Chung's* belief depends npon its quantity (Chap. XXXI). As vital energy it modifies the length of human life, which ceases, as soon as this energy is used up (Chap. XXVII).

From what our author says about ghosts and spirits in particular, which consist of the *Yang* fluid alone without any *Yin,* we can infer that he conceived of the human soul also as an *aura,* a warm breath identical to a certain extent with the solar fluid.

It is easy to see, how the Chinese came to denote the body as *Yin* and the soul as *Yang*—I believe that these notions were already current at *Wang Chung's* time,'who only took them up. The body is formed of a much coarser stuff than the soul, consisting as it does of solid and liquid matter. Therefore they presume that it must have been produced from the heavier and grosser substance, the *Yin,* while the purer and lighter *Yang* formed the soul. A living body is warm, warmth is a quality of the *Yang* fluid, consequently the vital force must be *Yang.* The mind enlightens the body, the *Yang* fluid is light as well, ergo the mind is the *Yang* fluid. The last conclusion is not correct, the mind not being a material light, but a Chinese would not hesitate to use such an analogy: their philosophy abounds with such symbolism.

The ideas of the Epicureans on the nature of the soul agree very well with *Wang Chung's* views. According to *Epicurus* the soul is a tenuous substance resembling a breath with an admixture of some warmth, dispersed through the whole organism:— 'Xl cuJ/ua so-n in-T0fXspic,, mtp okov To aZpoiapa napianapxivov. wpoasfxsp-'aTO.Tov 8 7rvsii)uari *spfxov riva xpoiatv* Exovti *(Diog. Laert.* X, 63).

Elsewhere the soul is described as a mixture of four substances: a fiery, an aeriform, a pneumatical, and a nameless one, which latter is said to cause sensations:—*xpaia* Ex *Tirrapwy,* Sx *nciov nvpwoovc,,* Ex *noiov aspwoovc,,* Ex *noiov nvivpunxcv.* Ex *Ttraprov Tivoc,* axa *TovofJLCiaToV (Plnt. PloC.* IV, 3). *Lucretius* says that the soul consists of much finer atoms than those of water, mist or smoke, and that it is produced, grows, and ages together with the body *(Lucr.* III. 425-427, 444-445). When a man dies, a fine, warm, aura leaves his body (III, 232).

As regards man's position in nature *Wang Ch ung* asserts that he is the noblest and most intelligent creature, in which the mind of Heaven and Earth reach their highest development (Chap. XL1I1); still he is a creature like others, and there exists no fundamental difference between him and other animals (p. 202). *Wang Chung* likes to insist upon the utter insignificance of man, when compared with the immense grandeur of Heaven and Earth. It seems to have given him some satisfaction to put men, who are living on Earth, on a level with fleas and lice feeding upon the human body, for we find this drastic simile, which cannot have failed to hurt the feelings of many of his self-sufficient countrymen, repeated several times (p. 183, Chap. XXVI). In short, according to *Wang Ch ung* man does not occupy the exceptional position in the world which he uses to vindicate for himself. He has not been created on purpose, as nothing else has, the principle of nature being chance and spontaneity (p. 103). The world has not been created for the sake of man. "Some people," remarks *Wang Chung,* "are of opinion that Heaven produces grain for the purpose of feeding mankind, and silk and hemp to clothe them. That would be tantamount to making Heaven the farmer of man or his mulberry girl, it would not be in accordance with spontaneity " (p. 92). As an argument against the common belief that Heaven produces his creatures on purpose, he adduces the struggle for existence, for says *Wang Chung:*—" If Heaven had produced its creatures on purpose, he ought to have taught them to love each other, and not to prey upon and destroy one another. One might object that such is the nature of the five elements that, when Heaven creates all things, it imbues them with the fluids of the five elements, and that these fight together and destroy one another. But then Heaven ought to have filled its creatures with the fluid of one element only, and taught them mutual love, not permitting the fluids of the five elements to resort to strife and mutual destruction" (p. 104).

Here again *Wang Chung* is in perfect accord with the Epicureans. *Epicurus* asserts that nothing could be more preposterous than the idea that nature has been regulated with a view to the wellbeing of mankind or with any purpose at all. The world is not as it ought to be, if it had been created for the sake of man, for how could Providence produce a world so full of evil, where the virtuous so often are maltreated and the wicked. triumph? *(Zeller,* Philosophic der Griechen, III. Teil, 1. Abt., 1880, pp. 398 seq. and 428.)

The same sentiment finds expression in the following verses of the Epicurean poet:—

"Nam quamvis rerum ignorem primordia qua sint,
hoc tamen ex ipsis cseli rationibus ausim continnare aliisque ex rebus reddere multis,
nequaquam nobis divinitus esse creatam naturam mundi: tanta stat prsedita culpa."
(Lucr. II, 177-181 and V, 185-189.)

Although man owes his existence to the *Yang* and the *Yin* fluids, as we have seen, he is naturally born by propagation from his own species. Heaven does not specially come down to generate him. All the stories of supernatural births recorded in the Classics, where women were specially fecundated by the Spirit of Heaven, are inventions (p. 48). Human life lasts a certain time, a hundred years at most, then man dies (p. 46). A prolongation of life is impossible, and man cannot obtain immortality (p. 50):—"Of all the beings with blood in their veins, says our philosopher, there are none but are born, and of those endowed with life there are none but die. From the fact that they were born, one knows that they must die. Heaven and Earth were not born, therefore they do not die. Death is the correlate of birth, and birth the counterpart of death. That which has a beginning must have an end, and that which has an end, must necessarily have a beginning. Only that which is without beginning or end, lives for ever and never dies" (Chap. XX VIII).

To show that the human soul is not immortal and does not possess any personal existence after death *Wang Ch ung* reasons as follows:—During life the *Yang* fluid, t. e. the vital spirit or the soul, adheres to the body, by death it is dispersed and lost. By its own nature this fluid is neither conscious, nor intelligent, it has no will and does not act, for the principle of the *Yang* or the heavenly fluid is unconsciousness, inaction, and spontaneity. But it acquires mental faculties and becomes a soul by its temporary connection with a body. The body is the necessary substratum of intelligence, just as a fire requires a substance to burn. By death " that which harbours intelligence is destroyed, and that which is called intelligence disappears. The body requires the fluid for its maintenance, and the fluid the body to become conscious. There is no fire in the world burning quite of itself, how could there be an essence without a body, but conscious of itself" (p. 195). The state of the soul after death is the same as that before birth. "Before their birth men have no consciousness. Before they are born, they form part of the primogenial fluid, and when they die, they revert to it. This primogenial fluid is vague and diffuse, and the human fluid a part of it. Anterior to his birth, man is devoid of consciousness, and at his death he returns to this original state of unconsciousness, for how should he he conscious?" (p. 194.) *Wang Chung* puts forward a number of arguments against immortality. If there were spirits of the dead, they would certainly manifest themselves. They never do, consequently there are none (p. 193). Other animals do not become spirits after death, wherefore should man alone be immortal, for though the most highly organised creature, still he is a creature and falls under the general laws (p. 191). The vital spirit or soul is affected by external influences, it grows by nourishment, relaxes, and becomes unconscious by sleep, is deranged and partly destroyed by sickness, and the climax of sickness, death, which dissolves the body, should not affect it at all? (p. 196.)

At all times the dogma of immortality has been negatived by materialistic philosophers. The line of arguments of the Greek as well as the Indian materialists is very much akin to that of *Wang Oh iing. Epicurus* maintains that, when the body decays, the soul becomes scattered, and loses its faculties, which cannot be exercised in default of a body:— *xai flip xai otaXvcfxivov Tov Oov appoiaiaroc,-q* ilvx *diuaTTupiTau xai ovxtn* Sx«i xa; aura; Suvaiusi; *ovd xivsiraL, Ilut Ov6 alaprpiv* x=xrvjrat. ou *yap* oiov Ts Voeiv *awry* cuap-avopsi'rjv, *fxrj iv Tcvtw Tw ovarran xai Tcuc, xtrqaioi* -aureu; xp-'F'1, TM *areyaXfivTOL xai mpiixovra fxr rciavT r-i* otj *vvv ovaa.* si xavra; ra; xtv/)ffsi; *(Diog. Laert.* X, 65-66).

He adds that an immaterial essence can neither act nor suffer, and that it is foolish to say that the soul is incorporeal: — *To 6s* xsvov *ovn noiriaai Ovts na. $siv* Ouvarai.... *oi XtyovTsc, aawjj.aTov* sivai *rrv fxaratovatv.*

From the fact that the vital fluid is born with the body, that it grows, develops, and declines along with it, *Lucretius* infers that the fluid must also be dissolved simultaneously with the body, scattered into the air like smoke:—

"ergo dissolvi quoque convenit omnein animai naturam, ceu fumus, in altas aeris auras;

quandoquidem gigni pariter pariterque videmus crescere et, ut docui, simul sevo fessa fatisci."
(Lucr. III, 455-458.)

What *Wang Ch ung* asserts about the influence of sickness on the soul (p. 196), *Lucretius* expresses in the following pathetic verses:— "Quin etiam morbis in corporis avius errat ssepe animus: dementit enim deliraqne fatur, interdumque gravi lethargo fertur in altum aiternmnque soporein oculis nutuque cadenti; unde neque exaudit voces nec noscere voltus illorum potis est, ad vitam qui revocantes circutn stant lacrimis rorantes ora genasque, quare animuin quoque dissolvi fateare necessest, quandoquidem penetrant in eum contagia morbi." *(Lucr.* III, 463-471.)

The interaction of body and mind, which thrive only, as long as they are joined together, and both decay, when they have been separated, the poet de-

scribes as follows:—

"Denique corporis atque animi vivata potestas inter se coniuncta valent vitaque fruuntur:

nee sine corpore enim vitalis edere motus sola potest animi per se uatura nec autem cassum animi corpus durare et sensibus uti."
(Luer. m, 556-560.)

As the tree does not grow in the sky, as fish do not live on the fields, and as blood does not run in wood, thus the soul cannot reside anywhere else than in the body, not in the clods of earth, or in the fire of the sun, or in the water, or in the air *(Lucr.* V, 133-134) and, when the body dies, it must become annihilated likewise.

"Denique in aetliere non arbor, non aequore salso nubes esse queunt, nec pisces vivere in arvis,

nec cruor in lignis neque saxis sucus inesse.

certum ac dispositumst ubi quicquid crescat et insit.

sic animi natura nequit sine corpore oriri sola neque a nervis et sanguine longiter esse.''
(Ijucr. III, 781-786.)

"quare, corpus ubi interiit, periisse necessest confiteare animam distractain in corpore toto."
(Loc. cit. 795-796.)

Of the *Chdrvdkas* it is said by *Sankara* that "seeing no soul, but body, they maintain the non-existence of soul other than body."—" Thought, knowledge, recollection, etc. perceptible only where organic body is, are properties of an organized frame, not appartaining to exterior substances, or earth and other elements simple or aggregate, unless formed into such a frame."

"While there is body, there is thought, and sense of pleasure and pain, none when body is not, and hence, as well as from selfconsciousness it is concluded that self and body are identical. " *(H. T. Colebroke,* Miscellaneous Essays, vol. II, p. 428 seq.)

The dictum that everyone is the child of his time applies to *Wang Ch ung* also, free-thinker though he be. He has thrown over board a great many popular beliefs and superstitions, but he could

not get rid of all, and keeps a good deal. His veneration of antiquity and the sages of old is not unlimited, but it exists and induces him to accept many of their ideas, which his unbiassed eiitical genius would probably have rejected. Like the majority of his countrymen he believes in *Vate* and *Predestination.* However, his Fate is not Providence, for he does not recognise any Superior Being governing the world, and it has been considerably materialised. On a rather vague utterance of *Tse Hsia,* a disciple of *Confucius,* who probably never thought of the interpretation it would receive at the hands of *Wang Chung,* he builds his theory:—"Life and death depend on Destiny, wealth and honour come from Heaven" (Analects XII, 5). The destiny, says *Wang Ch ung,* which fixes the duration of human life, is the heavenly fluid, *i. e.* the vital force, with which man is imbued at his birth. This fluid forms his constitution. It can be exuberant, then the constitution is strong, and life lasts long; or it is scanty, then the body becomes delicate,' and death ensues early. This kind of Fate is after all nothing else than the bodily constitution (pp. 138 and 46). In a like manner is wealth and honour, prosperity and unhappiness transmitted in the stary fluid, with which men are likewise filled at their birth. "Just as Heaven emits its fluid, the stars send forth their effluence, which keeps amidst the heavenly fluid. Imbibing this fluid men are born, and live, as long as they keep it. If they obtain a fine one, they become men of rank, if a common one, common people. Their position may be higher or lower, and their wealth bigger or smaller" (p. 138). Consequently this sort of Fate determining the amount of happiness which falls to man's share during his life-time, depends on the star or the stars under which he has been born, and can be calculated by the astrologers. This science was flourishing at *Wang Ch'ung's* time and officially recognised. On all important occasions the court astrologers were consulted.

Now, Fate, whether it be the result of the vital force or of the stary fluid, is not always definitive. It may be altered or modified"by various circumstances, and only remains unchanged, if it be stronger than all antagonistic forces. As a rule "the destiny regulating man's lifetime is more powerful, than the one presiding over his prosperity" (p. 137). If a man dies suddenly, it is of no use that the stary fluid had still much happiness in store / for him. Moreover "the destiny of a State is stronger than that of individuals" (loc. cit.). Many persons are involved in the disaster of their country, who by Heaven were predetermined for a long and prosperous life.

The circumstances modifying man's original fate are often denoted as *Time,* Hesides *Wang (7i ung* distinguishes *Contingencies, Chances,* and *Incidents,* different names for almost the same idea (p. 142). These incidents may be happy or unhappy, they may tally with the original destiny or disagree with it, completely change it, or be repulsed. If an innocent man be thrown into jail, but is released again, this unlucky contingency was powerless against his favourable destiny; whereas, when hundreds or thousands perish together in a catastrophe "the disaster they met with was so paramount that their good fate and thriving luck could not ward it off" *(eod.).*

We see *Wang Ch ung's* Fate is not the inexorable decree of Heaven, the *ujxapixhr* of the Greeks, the *dira necessitas,* or the patristic predestination, being partly natural (vital fluid), partly supernatural (stary fluid), and partly chance.

Epicurus impugns fatalism, and so does *Me Ti* and his school on the ground that fatalism paralyzes human activity and is subvertive of morality. There were scholars at *Wang Chung's* time who attempted to mitigate the rigid fatalism by a compromise with selfdetermination. They distinguished three kinds of destiny:—the natural, the concomitant, and the adverse. Natural destiny is a destiny not interfered with by human activity. The concomitant destiny is a combination of destiny and activity both working in the same direction, either for the good or for the bad of the individual, whereas in the adverse destiny the two

forces work in opposite directions, but destiny gets the upper hand (p. 138). *Wang Ch'ung* repudiates this scholastic distinction, urging that virtue and wisdom, in short that human activity has no influence whatever on fate, a blind force set already in motion before the newborn begins to act (p. 141). There is no connection and no harmony between human actions and fate. Happiness is not a reward for virtue, or unhappiness a punishment for crimes. *Wang Ch'ung* adduces abundance of instances to show, how often the wise and the virtuous are miserable and tormented, while scoundrels thrive and flourish (Chap. XII). Therefore a wise man should lead a tranquil and quiet life, placidly awaiting his fate, and enduring what cannot be changed (p. 145).

In the matter of Fate *Wang Ch'ung* shares all the common prejudices of his countrymen. Fate, he thinks, can be ascertained by *astrology* and it can be foreseen from *physiognomies, omens, dreams,* and *apparitions* of ghosts and spirits. There are special *soi-disant* sciences for all these branches:—anthroposcopy, divination, oneiromancy, necromancy, etc.

Anthroposcopy pretends to know the fate not only from man's features and the lines of his skin (p. 47), but also from the osseous structure of the body and particularly from bodily abnormities (Chap. XXIY). Many such instances have been recorded in ancient Chinese books. Of features the physiognomists used to distinguish 70 different classes (p. 72). In accordance with this theory *Wang Ch ung* opines that the vital fluid, the bearer of destiny, finds expression in the forms and features of the body, and can be read by the soothsayers. He remarks that a person's character may likewise be determined from his features, but that no regular science for this purpose has been developed (Chap. XXIV).

Of *Omens* or *Portents* there are auspicious and inauspicious ones, lucky or unlucky auguries. Freaks of nature, and rare specimens, sometimes only existing in imagination, are considered auspicious *e.g. sweet dew* and *wine springs*

believed to appear in very propitious times, in the vegetable kingdom:—the *purple boletus,* and *auspicious grass,* in the animal kingdom: —the *phoenix,* the *unicorn,* the *dragon,* (he *tortoise,* and other fabulous animals (p. 56). *Wang Cluing* discourses at great length on the nature and the form of these auguries. They are believed to be forebodings of the rise of a wise emperor or of the birth of a sage, and harbingers of a time of universal peace. Those Sages are oftentimes distinguishable by a *halo* or an *aureole* above their heads. The Chinese historical works are full of such wonderful signs. But all these omens are by no means intentionally sent by Heaven, nor responses to questions addressed to it by man. They happen spontaneously and by chance (p. 186i, simultaneously with those lucky events, which they are believed to indicate. There exists, as it were, a certain natural harmony between human life and the forces of nature, manifested by those omens.

"Dreams, says *Wang Ch ung,* are visions. When good or bad luck are impending, the mind shapes these visions" (p. 215). He also declares that dreams are produced by the vital spirit (p. 200), which amounts to the same, for the mind is the vital fluid. In *Wang Ch ung's* time there already existed the theory still held at present by many Chinese that during a dream the vital spirit leaves the body, and communicates with the outer world, and that it is not before the awakening that it returns into the spiritless body. *Wang Ch'ung* combats this view, showing that dreams are images only, which have no reality. He further observes that there are direct and indirect dreams. The former directly show a future event, the latter are symbolical, and must be explained by the oneirocritics. *Wang Ch ung* denies the immortality of the soul, but at the same time he believes in Ghosts and-Spirits. His gbosts, however, are very poor figures, phantoms and semblances still less substantial than the Shades of Hades. They are unembodied apparitions, have no consciousness (p. 194), feel neither joy nor pain, and can cause neither good nor evil (Chap. XLII). They have human shape or are like mist and smoke (Chap. XLIV). The origin of ghosts and spirits is the same as that of the other manifestations of fate: features, omens, and dreams, namely the solar fluid and the vital force or *Yang*. "When the solar fluid is powerful, but devoid of the *Yin*, it can merely produce a semblance, but no body. Being nothing but the vital fluid without bones or flesh, it is vague and diffuse, and wlien it appears, it is soon extinguished again" (Chap. XVIII). Consequently ghosts and spirits possess the attributes of the solar fluid:—"The fluid of fire flickers up and down, and so phantoms are at one time visible, and another, not. A dragon is an animal resorting from the *Yang* principle, therefore it can always change. A ghost is the *Yang* fluid, therefore it now appears and then absconds. The *Yang* fluid is red, hence the ghosts seen by people, have all uniform crimson colour. Flying demons are *Yang*, which is fire. Consequently flying demons shine like fire. Fire is hot and burning, hence the branches and leaves of trees, on which these demons alight, wither and die" *(eod.)*. The solar fluid is sometimes poisonous, therefore a ghost being burning poison, may eventually kill somebody (Chap. XXIII).

Many other theories on ghosts were current at *Wang Chung's* time, one of which very well agrees with his system, to wit that in many cases ghosts are visions or hallucinations of sick people. Others were of opinion that ghosts are apparitions of the fluid of sickness, some held that they are the essence of old creatures. Another idea was that ghosts originally live in men, and at their deaths are transformed, or that they are spiritual beings not much different from man. According to one theory they would be the spirits of cyclical signs (Chap. XVIII).

According to *Wang Ch'ung's* idea ghosts and spirits are only one class of the many wonders and miracles happening between heaven and earth. "Between heaven and earth, he says, there are many wonders in words, in sound, and in writing. Either the miraculous fluid assumes a human shape, or a

man has it in himself, and performs the miracles. The ghosts, which appear, are all apparitions in human shape. Men doing wonders with the fluid in them, are sorcerers. Real sorcerers have no basis for what they say, and yet their lucky or unlucky prophecies fall from their lips spontaneously like the quaint sayings of boys. The mouth of boys utters those quaint sayings spontaneously, and the idea of their oration comes to wizards spontaneously. The mouth speaks of itself, and the idea comes of itself. Thus the assumption of human form by the miracles, and their sounds are spontaneous, and their words come forth of their own accord. It is the same thing in both cases" *(Inc. cit.)*. The miraculous fluid may also assume the shape of an animal like the big hog foreboding the death of Duke *Hstang* of *Cli ' i (eod.)*, or of an inanimate thing like the yellow stone into which *Chang Liang* was transformed (Chap. XXX).

b) Physics. *Wang Ch'ung* does not discriminate between a transcendental *Heaven* and a material *Skg*. He knows but one solid Heaven formed of the *Yang* fluid and filled with air.

This Heaven appears to us like an upturned bowl or a reclining umbrella, but that, says *Wang Ch'ung*, is an optical illusion caused by the distance. Heaven and Earth seem to be joined at the horizon, but experience shows us that that is not the case. *Wang Ch'ung* holds that Heaven is as level as Earth, forming a flat plain (Chap. XX).

Heaven turns from East to West round the Polar Star as a centre, carrying with it the Sun, the Moon, and the Stars. The Sun and the Moon have their own movements in opposite direction, from West to East, but they are so much slower than that of Heaven, that it carries them along all the same. He compares their movements to those of ants crawling on a rolling mill-stone *(eod.)*. *Plato* makes heaven rotate like a spindle. The planets take part in this movement of Heaven, but at the same time, though more slowly, move in opposite direction by means of the aqiovfluXoi forming the whirl *(Uberweg-Heinzr, Geschichte der Philosophic, vol. I, p.*

180).

Heaven makes in one day and one night one complete circumvolution of 365 degrees. One degree being calculated at 2,000 Li, the distance made by Heaven every 24 hours measures 730,000 Li. The sun proceeds only one degree = 2,000 Li, the Moon 13 degrees -26,000 Li. *Wang Cit'ung* states that this is the opinion of the Literati *(eod.)*. Heaven's movement appears to us very slow, owing to its great distance from Earth. In reality it is very fast. The Chinese mathematicians have computed the distance at upwards of 60,000 Li. The Taoist philosopher *Iluai Nan Tse* avers that it measures 50,000 Li (Chap. XIX).

The body of the Earth is still more solid than that of Heaven and produced by the *Yin* fluid. Whereas Heaven is in constant motion, the Earth does not move (Chap. XX). It measures 10,000 million square Li, which would be more than 2,500 million square-km., and has the shape of a rectangular, equilateral square, which is of course level. *Wang Ch'ung* arrives at these figures in the following way. The city of *Loyang* in *Ihnan* is by the Chinese regarded as the centre of the world and *Annam* or *Jihnan* as the country over which the sun in his course reaches the southernmost point. *Annam*, therefore would also be the southern limit of the Earth. The distance between *Logang* and *Annam* is 10,000 Li. Now, Chinese who have been in *Annam* have reported that the sun does not reach his south-point there, and that it must be still further south. *Wang Ch'ung* assumes that it might be 10,000 Li more south. Now *Logang,* though being the centre of the known world i. e. China, is not the centre of the Earth. The centre of the Earth must be beneath the Polar Star, the centre of Heaven. *Wang Ch'ung* supposes the distance between *Logang* and the centre of the Earth below the pole to be about 30,000 Li. The distance from the centre of the Earth to its southern limit, the south-point of the sun, thus measuring about 50,000 Li, the distance from the centre to the north-point must be the same. That would give 100,000 Li as the length of the Earth from north to south, and the same number can be assumed for the distance from east to west (Chap. XIX).

The actual world (China) lies in the south-east of the universe (Chap. XX). This peculiar idea may owe its origin to the observation that China lies south of the Polar Star, the centre of Heaven, and that at the east-side China is bordered by the ocean, whereas in the west the mainland continues.

Tsou Yen, a scholar of the 4th cent. n.o. has propounded the doctrine that there are Nine Continents, all surrounded by minor seas, and that China is but one of them, situated in the south-east. Beyond the Nine Continents there is still the Great Ocean. *Wang Ch ung* discredits this view, because neither the Great *Yü,* who is believed to have penetrated to the farthest limits of the Earth and to have written down his observations in the *Shan-hai-king,* nor *Huai Nan Tse,* who had great scholars and experts in his service, mention anything about different continents (Chap. XIX).

This Earth is high in the North-West and low in the SouthEast, consequently the rivers flow eastwards into the ocean (Chap. XX). This remark again applies only to China, which from the table land of Central Asia slopes down to the ocean, where all her big rivers flow.

Among; the celestial bodies the *Sun* is the most important. He is a star like the Moon and the Planets, consisting of fire. His diameter has been found to measure 1,000 Li. The Sun follows the movement of Heaven, but has his own at the same time. The common opinion that the sun and the other stars are round is erroneous. They only appear so by the distance. The Sun is fire, but fire is not round. The meteors that have been found, were not round. Meteors are stars, ergo the stars are not round *(loc. cit.).*

At noon, when the Sun is in the zenith, he is nearer to us than in the morning or the evening, because the perpendicular line from the zenith to the earth is shorter than the oblique lines, which must be drawn at sunrise or sunset. It is for this reason also that the sun is hottest, when he is culminating. That

the Sun in the zenith appears smaller than, when he rises or sets, whereas, being nearer then, he ought to be bigger, is because in bright daylight every fire appears smaller than in the darkness or at dawn *(eod.).*

This question has already been broached by *Lieh J'se* V, 9 who introduces two lads disputing about it, the one saying that the Sun must be nearer at sunrise, because he is larger then, the other retorting that at noon he is hottest, and therefore must be nearest at noon. *Confucius* is called upon to solve the problem, but cannot find a solution. *Wang Chung* is much nearer the truth than *Epicurus,* whose notorious argument on the size of the sun and the moon, is not very much to his credit. He pretends that the stars must be about the size, which they appear to us, because fires did not lose anything of their heat, or their size by the distance *(Diog. Laert.* X, 91), which is an evident misstatement. *Lucretius* repeats these arguments *(Luer.* V, 554-582).

The different lengths of day and night in winter and summer *Wang Chung* attributes to the shorter and longer curves described by the Sun on different days. In his opinion the Sun would take 16 different courses in heaven during the year. Other scholars speak of 9 only *(eod.).* *Wang Chung* is well acquainted with the winter and summer *Solstices* and the vernal and autumnal *Equinoxes (eod.).*

Whereas the *Sun* consists of fire, the *Moon* is water. Her apparent roundness is an illusion; water has no definite shape *(eod.).* Of the movement of the Moon we have already spoken. In Chinese natural philosophy the Moon is always looked upon as the opposite of the Sun. The Slm being the orb of day and light is *Yang,* fire, consequently the Moon, the companion of night and darkness, must be *Yin,* water. The Sun appears brilliant and hot like a burning fire, the Moon pale and cool like glistening water. What wonder that the ancient Chinese should have taken her for real water, for *Wang Chung* merely echoes the general belief.

In the matter of *Eclipses Wang*

Ch'ung does not fall in with the view of many of his time, to the effect that the Sun and the Moon over-shadow and cover one another, nor with another theory explaining the eclipses by the preponderance of either of the two fluids, the *Yin* or the *Yang,* but holds that by a spontaneous movement of their fluids the Sun or the Moon shrink for a while to expand again, when the eclipse is over. He notes that those eclipses are natural and regular phenomena, and that on an average an eclipse of the Sun occurs every 41 or 42 months, and an eclipse of the Moon every 180 days *(eod.).* *Epicurus* and *Lucretius* are both of opinion that the fading of the Moon may be accounted for in different ways, and that there would be a possibility that the Moon really decreases *i. e.* shrinks together, and then increases again *(Liog. Laert.* X, 95; *Lucr.* V, 719-724). *Wang Ch'ung* is aware that *ebb* and *high-tide* are caused by the phases of the Moon, and that the famous "Bore" at *Hangchou* is not an ebullition of the River, resenting the crime committed on *Wu Tse Hsil,* who was unjustly drowned in its waters (p. 48).

The *Stars* except the Five Planets, which have their proper movement, are fixed to Heaven, and turn round with it. Their diameter has been estimated at about 100 Li *viz. /* of the diameter of the Sun. That they do not appear bigger to us than eggs is the effect of their great distance (Chap. XX). They are made of the same substances as the Sun and the Moon and the various things, and not of stone like the meteors. They emit a strong light. The Five Planets:—Venus, Jupiter, Mercury, Mars, and Saturn consist of the essence of the Five Elements:—water, fire, wood, metal, and earth. The fact that the Five Planets are in Chinese named after the Five Elements:—The Water Star (Mercury), the Fire Star (Mars), etc. must have led *Wang Ch ung* to the belief that they are actually formed of these elements. The language must also be held responsible for another error into which *Wang Ch ung* has fallen. He seems to believe that the stars and constellations are really what their Chinese names express *e. g.,* that there are hundreds of officials. and two famous charioteers in Heaven, who by emitting their fluid, shape the fate of men, (p. 138) and that the 28 *Solar Mansions* are actually celestial postal stations (Chap. XIX). It is possible however that the intimations of *Wang Ch'iung* to this effect are not to be taken literally, and that he only makes use of the usual terminology without attaching to them the meaning which his words would seem to imply. We are sometimes at a loss to know, whether *Wang Ch'ung* speaks his mind or not, for his words are often only rhetorical and dialectical devices to meet the objections of his opponents.

Wang Ch'ung's ideas on *Meteors* and *Shooting Stars* are chiefly derived from some classical texts. He comes to the conclusion that such falling stars are not real stars, nor stones, but rain-like phenomena resembling the falling of stars (Chap. XX). *Bain* is not produced by Heaven, and, properly speaking, does not fall down from it. It is the moisture of earth, which rises as mist and clouds, and then falls down again. The clouds and the fog condense, and in summer become *Bain* and *Dew*, in winter *Snow* and *Frost (eod.)*. There are some signs showing that it is going to rain. Some insects become excited. Crickets and ants leave their abodes, and earthworms come forth. The chords of guitars become loose, and chronic diseases more virulent. The fluid of rain has this effect (p. 109).

The same holds good for *Wind*. Birds foresee a coming storm, and, when it is going to blow, become agitated. But *Wang Ch'ung* goes farther and adopts the extravagant view that wind has a strange influence on perverted minds, such as robbers and thieves, prompting them to do their deeds, and that by its direction it influences the market-prices. From its direction moreover, all sorts of calamities can be foreseen such as droughts, inundations, epidemics, and war (p. Ill). There is a special science for it, still practised to-day by the Imperial Observatory at *Peking*. *Heat* and *Cold* correspond to fire and water, to the regions, and to the seasons. Near

the fire it is hot, near the water, cool. The *Yang* fluid is the source of heat, the *Yin* fluid that of cold. The South is the seat of the *Yang*, the North of the *Yin*. In summer the *Yang* fluid predominates, in winter the *Yin*. The temperature can never be changed for man's sake, nor does Heaven express its feelings by it. When it is cold, Heaven is not cool, nor is it genial and cheerful, when it is warm (Chap. XXI).

When the *Yin* and the *Yang* fluids come into collision, we have *Thunder* and *Lightning* (p. 126). The fire of the sun colliding with the water of the clouds causes an explosion, which is the Urn-Heng. 8 thunder. Lightning is the shooting forth of the exploding air (Chap. XXII, XXIX). *Wang Ch'ung* alleges 5 arguments to prove that lightning must be fire (Chap. XXII). He ridicules the idea that thunder is Heaven's angry voice, and that with its thunderbolt it destroys the guilty. "When lightning strikes, he says, it hits a tree, damages a house, and perhaps kills a man. But not unfrequently a thunder-clap is without effect, causing no damage, and destroying no human life. Does Heaven in such a case indulge in useless anger?" And why did it not strike a fiend like the Empress *Lii Hon*, but often kills sheep and other innocent animals? *(eod.)* *Lucretius* asks the same question:—

"Quod si Juppiter atque alii fulgentia divi terrifico quatiunt sonitu caelestia templa et jaciunt ignem quo qoiquest cumque voluptas, cur quibus incautum scelus aversabile cumquest non faciuut icti flammas ut fulguris halent pectore perfixo, documen mortalibus acre, et potius nulla sibi turpi conscius in re volvitur in tlammis innoxius inque peditur turbine caelesti subito correptus et igni' cur etiam loca sola petunt frustraque laborant?" *(Lucr.* VI, 380-389).

The poet states that tempests are brought about by the conflict of the cold air of winter with the hot air of summer. It is a battle of fire on the one, and of wind and moisture on the other side. Lightning is fire *eod.* 355-375). Thunder is produced by the concussion of the clouds chased by the wind *(eod.* 94seq.).

c) Ethics.

In the *Lun-he'ng*, ethical problems take up but a small space. Probably *Wang Ch ung* has treated them more in detail in his lost work, the *Chi-su-chieh-yi* "Censures on Morals." In the *Lun-Mng* they are touched upon more incidentally.

Men are all endowed with the same heavenly fluid, which becomes their vital force and their mind. There is no fundamental difference in their organisation. But the quantity of the fluids varies, whence the difference of their characters. "The fluid men are endowed with, says *Wang Ch'ung*, is either copious or deficient, and their characters correspondingly good or bad" (Chap. XXXI). *Epicurus* explains the difference of human characters by the different mixture of the four substances constituting the soul.

The vital fluid embraces the Five Elements of Chinese natural philosophy: Water, fire, wood, metal, and earth, which form the Five Organs of the body: the heart, the liver, the stomach, the lungs, and the kidneys. These inner parts are the seats of the Five Virtues:— benevolence, justice, propriety, knowledge, and truth (p. 105). The Five Virtues are regarded as the elements of human character and intelligence. Thus the quantity of the original fluid has a direct influence upon the character of the person. A small dose produces but a small heart, a small liver, etc. and these organs being small the moral and mental qualities of the owner can be but small, insufficient, bad. The copiousness of the fluid has the opposite result.

The Five Organs are the substrata of the "Five Virtues." Any injury of the former affects the latter. When those organs become diseased, the intellect loses its brightness, and morality declines, and, when these substrata of the mind and its virtues are completely destroyed by death, the mind ceases likewise (p. 195).

Being virtually contained in the vital or heavenly fluid, the Five Virtues must come from Heaven and be heavenly virtues (Chap. XLIII). Heaven is unconscious and inactive, therefore it cannot practise virtue in a human way, but the results of the spontaneous movement of the heavenly fluid are in accordance with virtue. It would not be difficult to qualify the working of nature as benevolent, just, and proper, which has been done by all religions, although unconscious benevolence and unconscious justice are queer notions, but how about unconscious knowledge and unconscious truth, the last of the Five Virtues? *Wang Ch'ung* finds a way out of this *impasse:*—" The heart of high Heaven, he says, is in the bosom of the Sages," an idea expressed already in the *Liki* (Cf. *Legge's* transl. Vol. I, p. 382). Heaven feels and thinks with their hearts (p. 128 seq.). Heaven has no heart of its own, but the heart of the Sages as well as of men in general are its hearts, for they have been produced by the heavenly fluid. This fluid, originally a shapeless and diffuse mass, cannot think or feel by itself. To become conscious it requires an organism. In so far it can be said that by consulting one's own heart, one learns to know the will of Heaven, that "Heaven acts through man" and that "when it reprimands, it is-done through the mouths of Sages" *(eod.)*. *Wang Ch'ung* does not enter upon a discussion on what the moral law really is, and why it is binding. He simply takes the Five Virtues in the acceptation given them by the Confucianists. But he ventilates another question, which has been taken up by almost all the moralists from *Mencius* downward, that of the original goodness or badness of human nature. *Wang Chung* acquaints us with the different views on this subject. The two extremes are represented by *Mencius*, who advocates the original goodness, and by *Hsiln Tse*, who insists upon its badness. There are many compromises between these two contrasting theories. *Wang Ch'ung* himself takes a middle course, declaring that human natural disposition is sometimes good, and sometimes bad, just as some people are by nature very intelligent, while others are feeble-minded (Chap. XXXII).

Original nature may be changed by external influences. Good people may become bad, and bad ones may reform and turn good. Such results can be brought about by intercourse with good or bad persons. With a view to reforming the wicked the State makes use of public instruction and criminal law (Chap. XXXI). *Wang Ch'ung* adopts the classification of *Confucius,* who distinguishes average people and such above and below the average (Analects VI, 19). "The character of average people," he says, "is the work of habit. Made familiar with good, they turn out good, accustomed to evil, they become wicked. Only with extremely good, or extremely bad characters habit is of no avail." These are the people above and below the average. Their characters are so inveterate, that laws and instructions are powerless against them. They remain what they are, good or bad (Chap. XXXII).

The cultivation of virtue is better than the adoration of spirits, who cannot help us (Chap. XLIV). Yet it would be a mistake to believe that virtue procures happiness. Felicity and misfortune depend on fate and chance, and cannot be attracted by virtue or crime (Chap. XXXVIII). On the whole *Wang Ch'ung* does not think much of virtue and wisdom at all. He has amalgamated the Confucian Ethics with his system as far as possible, but the Taoist ideas suit him much better and break through here and there. The Taoists urge that virtue and wisdom are a decline from man's original goodness. Originally people lived in a state of quietude and happy ignorance. "Virtuous actions were out of the question, and the people were dull and beclouded. Knowledge and wisdom did not yet make their appearance" (p. 100). They followed their natural propensities, acted spontaneously, and were happy. Such was the conduct of the model emperors of antiquity, *Huang Ti, Yao,* and *Shun*. They lived in a state of quietude and indifference, did not work, and the empire was governed by itself (p. 98). They merely imitated Heaven, who's principle is spontaneity and inaction. Now-a-days this high standard can only be attained by the wisest and best men. "A man with the highest, purest, and fullest virtue has been endowed with a large quantity of the heavenly fluid, therefore he can follow the example of Heaven, and be spontaneous and inactive like it" *(loc. cit.)*. He need not trouble about virtue, or act on purpose, for he is naturally virtuous, and all his spontaneous deeds are excellent. The majority of people, however, cannot reach this height. Having received but a small quota of the heavenly fluid, they cannot follow its example, and become active. They practise the routine virtues, which for the superior man, who naturally agrees with them, are of little importance.

d) Critique. *Wang Ch'ung* not only criticises the common ideas, superstitions, and more or less scientific theories current at his time, but he also gives his judgment upon the principal scholars, whose tenets he either adopts or controverts, and it is not without interest to learn, how he values well known philosophers and historians. a) *Philosophers.*

Of all philosophers by far the most frequently cited is *Confucius*. In *Wang Ch'ung's* estimation he is the Sage of China. He calls him the "Nestor in wisdom and virtue, and the most eminent of all philosophers" (Chap. XXXII). *Wang Ch'ung* seems to believe that he has won his cause, whenever he can quote *Confucius* as his authority, and that with a dictum of the Sage he can confound all his adversaries. In quoting *Confucius* he uses great liberty, interpreting his utterances so as to tally with his own views. But this veneration does not prevent him from criticising even *Confucius*. He thinks it necessary to vindicate himself from the charge of impiety and immorality, intimating that even Sages and Worthies are not infallible and may err sometimes (Chap. XXXIII). He might have done anything else, but this offence the Literati will never condone. His attacks on *Confucius* are very harmless and not even very clever. He does not impugn the Confucian system, which on the contrary he upholds, though he departs from it much farther than he himself knows. His method consists in hunting up contradictions and repugnancies in the Analects. He not seldom constructs a contradiction, where there is none at all, by putting much more into the words of *Confucius* than they contain. He forgets that in freely talking with friends or pupils—and the Analects are nothing else than such conversations—one does not weigh every word. Besides the peculiar circumstances and the form of mind of the speaker must be taken into consideration, which *Wang Ch'ung* often neglects. In short, the essay on *Confucius* is in no way a master-piece of criticism and not worth the fuss made about it.

Mencius, the second Sage, is also very often mentioned. *Wang Ch'ung* holds him in high esteem, but treats his work in the same way as the Analects. The objections raised keep more or less on the surface, and do not affect the substance of his doctrine.

The highest praise is bestowed on *Yang Ihiung,* another famous Confueiauist of the *Han* epoch. *Wang Ch'ung* compares the historian *Sse Ala. Ch'it-n* with the Yellow River and *Yang Hsiung* with the Han (Chap. XXXVII). He rose like a star (p. 81), and his chief work, the *T ai-hsi-lan-ching* was a creation (p. 88).

Like *Huai Nan Tse, Wang Ch'ung* very often mentions *Mi Ti* conjointly with *Confucius* as the two great Sages of antiquity. At that time the fame of *Confucius* had not yet eclipsed the philosopher of mutual love. Though appreciating him, *Wang Ch'ung* rejects his system as unpractical, maintaining that its many contradictions have prevented its spreading (Chap. XXXVII). The Mehists believe in ghosts and spirits and adore them, imploring their help. At the same time they neglect the funerals and the dead, and they deny the existence of fate.

When *Lao Tse* is referred to, he is usually introduced together with *Huang 77,* who like *Lao Tse* is looked upon as the father of Taoism. They are both called truly wise (p. 98). The Taoist school established the principle of spontaneity and inaction. The philosophy of *Wang Ch'ung* is to a great extent based on their doctrines without, however, becoming Taoistic, for he leaves out the quintessence of their system, *Tao,* nor will he have anything of their transcen-

dentalism, mysticism or other extravagancies.

Wang Ch'ung is well acquainted with the Taoist writer *Huai Nan Tse,* from whose work he freely culls, oftener than he mentions him. He refutes the legend that *Huai Nan Tse* by his alchimistical studies obtained immortality, and with his entire household, including his dogs and poultry ascended to Heaven, submitting that he either was beheaded for some political intrigues or committed suicide (Chap. XXVIII).

Against *Han Fei Tse,* who wrote on the theory of government and legislation, and whose writings are strongly tainted with T aoism, *Wang Ch'ung* bhows a pronounced antipathy. He most vehemently attacks him for having declared the scholars and literati to be useless grubs in the State. *Han Fei Tse* was of opinion that rewards and punishineuts were sufficient to keep up order. *Wang Chung* objects that in his system virtue has no place. *Han Fei Tse* despises divination, which *Wang Chung* defends. *Han Fei Tse* was much appreciated by the Emperor *Ch in ShiJi Huang Ti,* a great admirer of bis works, which, however, did not hinder the tyrant from condemning him to death for some political reason. He ꞵ-ʂꞷꞷ ρ 134,180

It is passing strange that the great Taoist philosophers *Lieh Tse* and *Ch'uang Tse* are not once named. Were they so little read at *Wang Ch'ung's* time, that he did not know them? Some of his stories are told in *Lieh Tse* likewise with nearly the same words, but it does not follow, that they must be quoted from *Lieh Tse,* for such narrations are often found in several authors, one copying from the other without acknowledging his source.

A scholar, of whom *Wang Ch'ung* speaks very often is *Tung Chung Shu,* a very prolific writer of the 2nd cent. B.C. He was said by many to have completed the doctrine of *Confucius,* while others held that he had perverted it. *Wang Ch'ung* thinks that both views are wrong (Chap. XXXVII). *Tung Chung Shu* devoted his labours to the *Ch un-ch iu,* but he also wrote on the magical arts (p. 84) and on Taoism. *Wang Ch'ung*

says that his arguments on Taoist doctrines are very queer, but that his ideas on morals and on government are excellent. In human nature *Tung Chung Shu* distinguishes between natural disposition aud feeling. The former, he says, is the outcome of the *Yang* principle and therefore good, the feelings are produced by t he *Yin* and are therefore bad (Chap. XXXII). *Tung Chung Shu* seems to have been the inventor of a special rain-sacrifice. The figure of a dragon was put up to attract the rain. *Wang Chung* stands up for it with great fervour aud attempts to prove its efficacy (p. 55, N. 47).

Of *Tsou Yen* many miracles were already related at *Wang Ch'ung's* time. He rejects them as fictions. *I'sou Yen's* writings were brilliant, he says, but too vague and diffuse (Chap. XXXVII). With his above mentioned theory of the Nine Continents *Wang Ch'ung* does not agree.

The sophist *Kung Sun Lung* as well as *Kuan Tse* and *Shang Yang,* who both have philosophised on the State, are rather severely dealt with (Chap. XXXVII). On the other hand *Wang Ch'ung* is very lavish in his praise of the writers of the *Han* time viz. *Liu llsiang, Lu Chia,* author of the *Hsin-gil,* a work on government, *Huan Chun Shan,* author of the *Hsin-lun,* and *Huan K uan,* who wrote the *Yen-tieh-lun,* a work on finance and other State questions. Besides *Wang Ch'ung* gives the names of a number of his contemporaries to whom he predicts immortality, but he has been a bad prophet, for save one they are all forgotten now.

0) Historians.

It was a great controversy during the *Han* epoch, which commentary to the *Chun-ch'iu* was the best. The *Tso-chuan* had not yet secured the position, it holds now; many scholars gave the preference to the works of *Kung Yang* or *Ku Liang. Wang Ch'ung* avers that *Tso Ch iu Ming's Tso-chuan* surpasses all the others, and that having lived nearer to *Confucius'* time than the other commentators, *Tso Ch'iu Ming* has had more facilities to ascertain the views of the Sage and to give them in their purest form.

Wang Ch ung confirms that the *Kuo-yil* is also the work of *7so ch'iu Ming* (Chap. XXXVII). Many of *Wang Ch ung's* stories aud myths are taken from the *Tso-chuan.*

Of the *Lil-shih-ch'un-ch iu* of *LO Pu Wei,* an important work. for antique lore, *Wang Chung* says that it contains too much of the marvellous.

To illustrate his theories *Wang Ch'ung* often lays the *Shi-chi* under contribution. Of its author, *Sse Ma Ch'ien,* he speaks with great deference, and regards him as the greatest writer of the *Han* period. What he reproaches him with, is that *Sse Ma Ch'ien* too often leaves us in the dark as to his own opinion on a question, stating only the bare facts, or giving two different versions of the same event without deciding, which is the correct one *(loc. cit.).* *Pan Ku, Wang Ch'ung's* contemporary and the son of his teacher *Pan Pino,* is lauded for his good verses and memorials *loc. cit.).* He is the one contemporary of our philosopher, who really has become immortal by his great work, the *Han-shu.* At *Wang Chung's* time it had not yet appeared, and so is never referred to. It was completed and published after *Pan Ku's* death by his sister *Pan Chao.*

That he possesses some abilities in the field of literary and historical critique himself, *Wang Chvng* shows in his remarks on the origin and history of the Classics. He tells us, how they were composed, how discovered after the Burning of the Books, how handed down, and how divided into books and chapters (Chap. XXXVI). In spite of his profound veneration for the classical literature he does not hesitate to censure those passages, which do not find his approval, or to expose the exaggerations and fables With which they teem (p. 51, N. 27). In like manner he is indefatigable in detecting Taoist fictions and inventions and in reducing them to their true measure, for it does not satisfy him to demonstrate their impossibility; he desires to find out, how they originated (p. 50, N. 24). He combats the legends which have found their way into the historical literature, although they are less frequent than in the Taoist works (p. 50, N. 25-26). The entire *Lun-Mng* is a big battle agains these errors. His discussions would seem sometimes a little lengthy, and the subject not to require such an amount of arguments, for we would prove the same with a few words, or not discuss it at all, the proposition being for us self-evident. We must however bear in mind, that what for us now is self-evident and indisputable, was not so for the Chinese, for whom *Wang Ch ung* wrote his book, and that to shake them in their deep-seated persuasions a huge apparatus of logic was necessary. Even then probably the majority held fast to their preconceptions. The triumphant march of logic is checked, as soon as sentiment and prejudice comes in.

Historically *Wang Ch ung* takes another point of view than his contemporaries, who for the most part took little interest in their own time, and let their fancies wander back to the golden age of remote antiquity. *Wang Chung* is more modern than most Chinese of the present day. He was of opinion that the *Han* dynasty was as good, even better than the famous old dynasties (p. 56, N. 56). Five essays bear upon this thesis. His reasoning is very lame however, for instead of speaking of the government, he only treats of the auspicious portents proving the excellence of the ruling sovereigns.

e) Religion and Folklore.

The religion of the Chinese at the *Han* time was a cult of nature combined with ancestor worship. They regarded certain parts of nature and certain natural phenomena as spirits or as animated by spirits, and tried to propitiate them and the ghosts of their ancestors by prayers and sacrifices. Convinced that these spirits and ghosts could help them, or do them harm, as they chose, they contrived to win their good graces, praying for happiness, imploring them to avert evil, and showing their gratitude for received benefits by their offerings.

The chief deities worshipped during the *Chou* period were:— *Heaven* and its parts:—the *Sun,* the *Moon,* and the *Stars.* Among the latter the *Fire Planets* take the first place, but the *28 Solar Mansions* and other constellations, such as the *Dipper* and the *Stars of Longevity* were likewise adored.

Earth and its parts, *Mountains* and *Rivers,* the *Soil,* and the *Grain* growing on it, and some of its phenomena:— *Earth-quakes, Water* (Inundations), and *Droughts.*

Meteorological phenomena:—*Wind* and *Rain, Heat* and *Cold, Thunder* and *Lightning.*

The *Four Seasons* and the *Four Quarters.*

The Five Parts of the House:—The *Gate,* the *Door,* the *Wall,* the *Hearth,* and the *Court.*

Deified Heaven was often looked upon as an emperor, the Emperor on High or the Supreme Ruler, and so were the Planets, called the Blue, Red, Yellow, White, and Black Emperors. The other stars and constellations were their officials. All these deities have, as a rule, no distinct personality, and still quite clearly show the traces of their origin. The "Prince of the Wind," the " Master of Rain,"' the "Thunderer," the "Door God," and the "Spirit of the Hearth" or "Kitchen God" were perhaps more than the others apprehended as personal gods.

The Spirits of the *SoiJ* and *Grain* were at the outset probably not different from the other spirits animating nature, but according to very old traditions two persons:—*Kou Lung* and *Ch i* have after their deaths been deified and raised to the rank of tutelary genii of the land and grain. These apotheoses of men after their death became more frequent in later ages. Under the *Ch in* dynasty *Ch'ih Yu,* a legendary personage renownded for his military exploits, was worshipped as *War God.* The three sons of the mythical emperor *Chuan Hsi i* after their death became *Water Spirits* and *Spirits of Epidemics,* and a woman, who had died in childbed, and whose ghost had appeared to somebody after her decease, was made *Princess of Demons* under the *Han* dynasty.

Here we have ancestral worship. Every family used to revere the ghosts of its deceased ancestors, but only in such exceptional cases as those quoted above did these ghosts later on become national gods.

The cult of the afore-mentioned deities was continued during the *Han* epoch, and with some few alterations has gone on up to the present day. It is the State religion of China, sanctioned by Government, and practised by the Son of Heaven and his highest officials. Buddhism and Taoism are only tolerated. Confucianism is no religion, but the official moral system, which completely agrees with the cult of nature.

The *sacrifices* to the spirits of nature were in ancient times performed by the Emperor, the Feudal Princes, and the officials, acting as high-priests for their people. The people used to sacrifice only to their own ancestors and to the Spirits of the Door or the Hearth. The oblations were burnt-offerings of animals, and libations of wine. There was no clergy to mediate between the gods and the people. These rules were less strictly observed during the *Han* epoch, when occasionally priests sacrificed in the place of the Emperor, and even priestesses were allowed to make offerings in their temples. In out-of-the-way places, where no officials were near, the people could themselves worship the gods, whose service else was incumbent upon the magistrates (cf. Chap. XLI, XLII and *Shwhi* chap. 27-28).

Wang Chung asserts that most of these sacrifices are superfluous, because the deities thus honoured are merely parts of others, to which offerings are made likewise. The Sun, the Moon, and the Stars are parts of Heaven. They must participate in the oblations offered to Heaven, why then give them special sacrifices to boot? With Mountains and Rivers, the Soil and Grain, which are the constituent parts of Earth, it is the same. Would any reasonable person, irrespective of his usual meals, specially feed his limbs? (Chap. XLI.)

Moreover, spirits and ghosts cannot enjoy the sacrifices, for there are none, at least not personal beings, as people seem to imagine (Chap. XLIV). If they were air, they could not eat nor smell,

and if they had a body, it would be so enormous, that men could never satisfy their appetite. How should they feed the Earth or even a Mountain or a River? (*eod.* and Chap. XLI.) Being formed of the shapeless fluid, ghosts and spirits can neither feel nor act, consequently they cannot do anything for man nor against him. Ergo by sacrifices he does not obtain his end, divine protection (Chap. XLII). Therefore sacrifices can be nothing more than symbolical acts, showing the gratitude and the affection of the sacrificer. He is thankful for all the kindness he has received from Heaven and Earth, and from his parents and forefathers (*eod.*). Sacrifices are manifestations of the piety of him, who offers them, but-their omission cannot have any evil conseipuence.

Exorcism is the correlate of prayers and sacrifices. The ancient Chinese used to practise it particularly with the Spirit of Sickness, whom they expelled. *Wang Ch'ung* thinks it as useless as sacrifices, for, says he, provided the spirits are mist and vapours, they cannot do any harm, should they really exist, however, then they would indubitably not allow themselves to be driven off. They would not only offer resistance, but also resent the affront, and take their revenge upon the exorcist (Chap. XLIV).

Primitive Chinese religion has not produced a mythology worth speaking of, but a variety of superstitions have clustered around it. Some of them *Wang Ch'ung* brings to our notice. The principle aim of Chinese religion is to obtain happiness and to remove evil. But is does not suffice to worship the spirits, one must also avoid such actions, as might bring down misfortune. In the popular belief there is a certain mystic connection, a sort of harmony between fate and human activity, though one does not see how. When the Yamen officials are very bad, the number of tigers increases so much, that plenty of people are devoured by them. The rapacity of the underlings is believed to cause grubs and insects to eat grain (p. 55, N. 48-49). It is dangerous to extend a building to the west, one must not see women who recently have given birth to a child, and

children born in the first or the fifth months should not be brought up, for they will be the cause of their parents death (p. 59, N. 08). Exceptional precautions must be taken in building a new house (p. 60, N.74).

For most actions in every-day-life the time chosen is of the utmost importance. An unlucky time spoils everything. The Chinese at the *Han* epoch had not only their *dies fasti* and *nefasti,* but propitious and unpropitious years, months, days, and hours. Special books gave the necessary information. For some actions certain lucky days had to be chosen, for others certain unlucky ones had to be avoided. Special days were assigned for the commencing of a new-building or for funerals. Bathing on certain days, women were sure to become lovely, on others they would become illfavoured. Moving one's residence one should avoid a collision with the Spirit of the North, *T'ai Sui* (p. 59, N. 70, 72, 73). People neglecting these rules would fall in with malignant spirits, or meet with evil influences. These ideas have come down to our time, and are still cherished by the majority of the Chinese. The calendar published every year by the Board of Astronomy serves them as a guide, noting that which may be safely done on each day, and that which may not. *Wang Ch'ung* has done his best to eradicate these superstitions, showing their unreasonableness and futility, as we see with little success, so deeply are they still rooted in the Chinese mind after nearly two thousand years.

4.' Table of Contents of the Lun-heng. Book I.

1. Chap. I. *Feng-yil* #§

This chapter treats of the relation between officers and their sovereign. To be appreciated and successful an official must find the right prince, who understands him and puts him in the right place. One must not make the successful responsible for their success, or the unsuccessful for their failure, because not their talents, but time and circumstances are decisive.

The difficulties and annoyances which people have to endure come from abroad, and are not the result of their own works. Therefore they must not be blamed. Fear and good conduct have no influenceonjiiwfwne or misfortune. "Fortune is what we obtain wifhout any effort of our own, and misfortune what happens to us without our co-operation. " The chief annoyances of officials at the court and in the provinces are slanderous reports of envious persons. Three kinds of calumnies are distinguished. The wise do not feel troubled about this, and lead the life which most suits them.

3. Chap. III. *Ming-lu* Destiny and Fortune).

Destiny predetermines the length of man's life, and whether he shall be rich and honourable, or poor and mean. There is no correspondence between human virtue and fate. The wicked and the unintelligent are very often happy, whereas men endowed with the highest faculties and the noblest character perish in misery, as is shown by various examples from history. The knowing, therefore, do not hunt after happiness, but leave everything to Heaven, suffering with equanimity what cannot be avoided, and placidly awaiting their turn. The opinions of several philosophers holding similar views are given.

4. Chap. IV. *Ch'i-shou* f (Long Life and Vital Fluid).

There are two kinds of fate, the one determining the events of life, the other its length. The length of life depends on the *Note:*—The chapters marked with an asterisk have been translated. quantity of the vital fluid received at birth. Accordingly the body waxes strong or weak, and a strong body lives longer than a feeble one. The normal length ot human lite should be a hundred years. The Classics attest that the wise emperors of the Golden Age:—*Yao, Shun, Win Wang, Wu Wang,* and others all lived over hundred years.

Book II.

5. Chap. I. *Hsing-ou* fH (On Chance and Luck).

Happiness and misfortune are not the outcome of man's good or bad actions, but chance and luck. Some have good luck, others bad. Good and bad fortune are not distributed in a just way, according to worth, but are mere chance. This is true of man as well as of other beings. Even Sages are often visited with misfortune.

6. Chap. II. *Ming-yi* (What is meant by Destiny?).

The school of *Mi Ti* denies the existence of Destiny. *Wang Ch'ung* follows the authority of *Confucius*. There are various kinds of destinies. The length of human life is regulated by the fluid of Heaven, their wealth and honour by the effluence of the stars, with which men are imbued at their birth. *Wang Ch'ung* rejects the distinction of natural, concomitant, and adverse fate, but admits contingencies, chances, and incidents, which may either agree with the original fate and luck, or not. The fate of a State is always stronger than that of individuals.

7. Chap. III. *Wu-hsing* (Unfounded Assertions).

At birth man receives the vital fluid from Heaven. This fluid determines the length of his life. There are no means to prolong its duration, as the Taoists pretend. Some examples from history are shown to be untrustworthy. At death everything ends. The vital force disperses, and the body is dissolved.

8. Chap. IV. *Shuai-Jising* ' (The Forming of Characters).

There are naturally good, and there are naturally bad characters, but this difference between the qualities of low and superior men is not fundamental. The original fluid permeating all is the same. It contains the germs of the Five Virtues. Those who are endowed with copious fluids, become vrttuous, those whose fluid is deficient, wicked. But by external influences, human nature can turn from good into bad, and the reverse. Bad people can be improved, and become good by instruction and good example. Therefore the State cannot dispense with instructions and laws.

9. Chap. V. *Chi-yen* . (Auspicious Portents).

Auspicious portents appear, when somebody is destined to something grand by fate, especially, when a new dynasty rises. These manifestations of fate appear either in the person's body, or as lucky signs in nature, or under the form of a halo or a glare. A great variety of instances from ancient times down to the *Han* dynasty are adduced in proof. Book III.

10. Chap. I. *Ou-hui %-*
Fate acts spontaneously. There are no other alien forces at work besides fate. Nobody is able to do anything against it. Human activity is of no consequence.

11. Chap. II. *Ku-hsiang* (On Anthroposcopy).

The heavenly fate becomes visible in the body, and can be foreseen by anthroposcopy. The Classics contain examples. The physiognomists draw their conclusions from the osseous structure and from the lines of the skin. The character can also be seen from the features.

12. Chap. III. *Ch'u-ping ffjm.* (Heaven's Original Gift).

Destiny comes down upon man already in his embryonic state, not later on during his life. It becomes mind internally and body externally. This law governs all organisms. Heaven never invests virtuous emperors, because it is pleased with them, for this would be in opposition to its principle of spontaneity and inaction. Utterances of the Classics that Heaven was pleased and looked round, etc. are to be taken in a figurative sense. Heaven has no human body and no human qualities. Lucky omens are not sent by Heaven, but appear by chance.

13. Chap. IV. *Pen-hsing jfr* (On Original Nature).

The different theories of Chinese moralists on human nature are discussed. *Shih Tse* holds that human nature is partly good, partly bad, *Mendus* that it is originally good, but can be corrupted, *Sun Tse* that it is originally bad, *Kao Tse* that it is neither good nor bad, and that it all depends on instruction and development, *Lu Chia* that it is predisposed for virtue. *Tung Chung Shu* and *Liu Hsiang* distinguish between natural disposition and natural feelings. *Wang Chung* holds that nature is sometimes good and sometimes bad, but essentially alike, being the fluid of Heaven, and adopts the Confucian distinction of average people, people above, and people below the average. The latter alone can be changed by habit.

14. Chap. V. *Wu-shih* (The Nature of Things).

Heaven and Earth do not create man and the other things on earth intentionally. They all grow of themselves. Had Heaven produced all creatures on purpose, it would have taught them mutual love; whereas now one destroys the other. Some have explained this struggle for existence by the hypothesis that all creatures are filled with the fluid of the Five Elements, which fight together and overcome one another. *Wang Ch'ung* controverts this view and the symbolism connected therewith.

15. Chap. VI. *Chi-kuai* (Miracles). *Wang Cliung* proves by analogies that the supernatural births reported of several old legendary rulers, who are said to have been procreated by dragons or a special fluid of Heaven, are impossible. The Spirit of Heaven would not consort with a woman, for only beings of the same species pair. Saints and Sages are born like other people from their parents.

Book IV.

16. Chap. I. *Shu-hsil* fjyjjjif

The chapter contains a refutation of a series of wrong statements in ancient books. The assertion that *Shun* and *Yi l* died in the South is shown to be erroneous. *Wang Ch'ung* explodes the idea that the "Bore" at *Hang-chou* is caused by the angry spirit of *Wu Tse Hsii,* who was thrown into the *Ch'ien-t'ang River,* and remarks that the tide follows the phases of the moon. (Bk. IV, p. 5v.) 17. Chap. II. *Pien-hsil Wang Ch'ung* points out that many reports in ancient literature concerning extraordinary phenomena, not in harmony with the laws of nature, are fictitious and unreliable, *e. g.* the story that touched by the virtue of Duke *Ching* of *Sung,* the planet Mars shifted its place, that Heaven rewarded the Duke with 21 extra years, or that the great Diviner of *Ch'i* caused an earthquake.

Book V.

18. Chap. I. *Yi-hsii $.* The impossibility of some miracles and supernatural events is demonstrated, which have been handed down in ancient works,

and are universally believed by the people and the literati, *e. g.* the birth of *Pao Sse* from the saliva of dragons. 19. Chap. II. *Kan-hsii* Jg£jf*Wang Ch ung* contests that nature can be moved by man and deviate from its course. Various old legends are critically tested: — the alleged appearence of ten suns in *Yao's* time, the report that the sun went back in his course, the wonders which happened during the captivity of *Tsou Yen* and *Tan,* Prince of *Yen.*

The tenor of the last four chapters all treating of unfounded assertions or figments "*hsil*" is very similar.

Book VI.

20. Chap. I. *Fu-ksii* jjjg),Jf (Wrong Notions about Happiness).

Happiness is not given by Heaven as a reward for good actions, as the general belief is. The *Mihist* theory that the spirits protect and help the virtuous is controverted by facts. *Wang Ch ung* shows how several eases, adduced as instances of how Heaven recompensed the virtuous are illusive, and that fate is capricious and unjust.

21. Chap. II. *Huo-/lsii* (WrongNotions on Unhappiness).

The common belief that Heaven and Earth and the spirits punish the wicked and visit them with misfortune, is erroneous, as shown by examples of virtuous men, who were unlucky, and of wicked, who flourished. All this is the result of chance and luck, fate and time.

Lun-Heng. M 22. Chap. III. *Lung-Jisi'i* j (On Dragons).

The dragon is not a spirit, but has a body and lives in pools. It is not fetched by Heaven during a thunderstorm, as people believe. The different views about its shape are given:—It is represented as a snake with a horse's head, as a flying creature, as a reptile that can be mounted, and like earthworms and ants. In ancient times dragons were reared and eaten. The dragon rides on the clouds during the tempest, there being a certain sympathy between the dragon and clouds. It can expand and contract its body, and make itself invisible.

23. Chap. IV. *Lei-hail* ffjg (On Thunder and Lightning).

Thunder is not the expression of Heav-

en's anger. As a spirit it could not give a sound, nor could it kill a man with its breath. It does not laugh either. Very often the innocent are struck by lightning, and monsters like the Empress *Lii Hou* are spared. The pictorial representations of thunder as united drums, or as the thnnderer *Lei Kung,* are misleading. Thunder is fire or hot air, the solar fluid *Yang* exploding in its conflict with the *Yin* fluid, lightning being the shooting forth of the air. Five arguments are given, why thunder must be fire.

Book VII.

24. Chap. I. *Tao-hsii* g (Taoist Untruths).

Man dies and can become immortal. The Taoist stories of *Huang Ti* and *Huai Nan Tse's* ascension to heaven, of the flying genius met by *Lu Ao,* and of *Hsiang Man Tse's* travel to the moon are inventions. The magicians do not possess the powers ascribed to them. The Taoist theory of prolonging life by quietism and dispassionateness, by regulating one's breath, and using medicines is untenable.

25. Chap. II. *Yil-tseng* Hff" (Exaggerations). *Wang Ch'ung* points out a number of historical exaggerations *e. g.* that the *embonpoint* of *Chwh* and *Chou* was over a foot, that *Chou* had a wine-lake, from which 3,000 persons sucked like cattle, that *Win Wang* could drink 3,000 bumpers of wine, and *Confucius* 100 gallons, and some mis-statements concerning the simplicity of *Yao* and *Shun,* and the cruelty of *Shih Huang Ti,* and tries to reduce them to the proper limits.

Book VIII.

26. Chap. I. *Ju-tseng* ff (Exaggerations of the Literati). *Wang Ch ung* goes on to criticise some old traditions:—on the abolition of punishments under *Yao* and *Shun,* on the wonderful shooting of *Yang Yu Chi* and *Hskmg Ch'ii Tse,* on the skill of *Lu Pan,* on *Ching K o's* attempt upon *Shih Huang Ti's* life, on the miracles connected with the Nine Tripods of the *Chou* dynasty, etc. 27. Chap. H. *Yi-tsing* g.

People are fond of the marvellous and of exaggerations, in witness whereof passages are quoted from the *Shuking,* the *Shiking,* the *Yiking,* the *Lun-yil,* and the *Ch'un-ch'iu.*

Book IX.

28. Chap. I. *We"n K'ung ffl* (Criticisms on *Confucius*).

The Confucianists do not dare to criticise the Sages, although the words of the Sages are not always true and often contradictory. It is also, because they do not understand the difficult passages, and only repeat what the commentators have said. *Wang Ch'ung* vindicates the right to criticise even *Confucius.* Such criticisms are neither immoral nor irrational. They help to bring out the meaning, and lead to greater clearness. *Wang Ch'ung* then takes up a number of passages from the Analects for discussion, in which he discovers contradictions or other flaws, but does not criticise the system of *Confucius* or his theories in general.

Book X.

29. Chap. I. *Fei Han* (Strictures on *Han Fei Tse*). *Han Fei Tse* solely relies on rewards and punishments to govern a State. In his system there is no room for the cultivation of virtue. He despises the literati as useless, and thinks the world to be so depraved and mean, that nothing but penal law can keep it in check. *Wang Ch'ung* shows by some examples taken from *Han Fei Tse's* work that this theory is wrong. Men of letters are as useful to the State as agriculturists, warriors, and officials, for they cultivate virtue, preserve the true principles, and benefit the State by the good example they set to the other classes. 30. Chap. II. *T'se Meng* jjjlJjjJi (Censures on *Mencius*). *Wang Ch'ung* singles out such utterances of *Menckis,* in which according to his view his reasoning is defective, or which are conflicting with other dicta of the philosopher.

Book XI.

31. Chap. I. *T'an-t'ien %%%* (On Heaven).

The old legend of the collapse of Heaven, which was repaired by *Nil Wa,* when *Kung Kung* had knocked with his head against the "Pillar of Heaven." is controverted, as is *Tsou Yen's* theory of the existence of Nine Continents. Heaven is not merely air, but has a body, and the earth is a square measuring 100,000 Li

in either direction.

32. Chap. n. *Shuo-jih* fft; 0 (On the Sun).

A variety of astronomical questions are touched. *Wang Ch'ung* opposes the view that the sun disappeares in darkness during the night, that the length or shortness of the days is caused by the *Yin* and the *Yang,* that the sun rises from *Fu-sang* and sets in *Hsi-liu,* that at *Yao's* time ten suns appeared, that there is a raven in the sun, and a hare and a toad in the moon. Heaven is not high in the south and depressed in the north, nor like a reclining umbrella, nor does it enter into or revolve in the earth. Heaven is level like earth, and the world lying in the south-east. The sun at noon is nearer than in the morning or in the evening. *Wang Ch'ung* further speaks on the rotation of the sky, the sun, and the moon, on the substance of the sun and the moon, on their shape, the cause of the eclipses, meteors, and meteorological phenomena.

33. Chap. HI. *Ta-ning*

On the cunning and artful.

Book XII.

34. Chap. I. *Ch'tng-t'sai*

The difference between scholars and officials is pointed out. *Wang Ch'ung* stands up for the former, and places them higher than the officials, because they are of greater importance to the State. The people however think more of the officials.

35. Chap. II. *Liang-chih* Iji p.

The same subject as treated in the preceding chapter.

36. Chap. in. *Hsieh-tuan* f£g

Men of letters as well as officials have their shortcomings. The former are interested in antiquity only, and neglect the present, the *Ch'in* and *Han* time. They only know the Classics, but even many questions concerning the age and the origin of the Classics they cannot answer. The officials know their business, but often cannot say, why they do a thing, since they do not possess the necessary historical knowledge.

Book XIII. 37. Chap. I. *Hsiao-li*

The chapter treats of the faculties of the scholars and the officials, and of their energy and perseverance displayed

in different departments.

38. Chap. II. *Pieh-t'ung* £Jjj§.

There is the same difference between the learned and the uncultivated as between the rich and the poor. Learning is a power and more important than wealth.

39. Chap. III. *Ch'ao-chi ffij.*

There are various degrees of learning. Some remarks are made on the works of several scholars, *e.g.* the philosopher *Yang Tse Yiln* and the two historians *Pan.*

Book XIV.

40. Chap. I. *Chuang-liu* . Scholars do not strive for office. As for practical success they are outrivalled by the officials, who are men of business. 41. Chap. II. *Han-wen* (On Heat and Cold). *Wang Ch ung* contests the assertion of the phenomenalists that there is a correspondence between heat and cold and the joy and anger of the sovereign. He points out that the South is the seat of heat, and the North of cold. Moreover the temperature depends on the four seasons and the 24 time-periods. 42. Chap. III. *Ch'ien-kao* fjfj-(On Reprimands).

The *mvants* hold that Heaven reprimands a sovereign whose administration is bad, visiting him with calamities. First he causes extraordinary events. If the sovereign does not change then, he sends down misfortunes upon his people, and at last he punishes his own person. Heaven is represented like a prince governing his people. These heavenly punishments would be at variance with Heaven's virtue, which consists in spontaneity and inaction. Heaven does not act itself, it acts through man, and speaks through the mouths of the Sages, in whose hearts is ingrafted its virtue. The utterances of the Classics ascribing human qualities to Heaven are only intended to give more weight to those teachings, and to frighten the wicked and the unintelligent.

Book XV.

43. Chap. I. *Pien-tung $$3* (Phenomenal Changes).

Heaven influences things, but is not affected by them. All creatures being filled with the heavenly fluid, Heaven is the master, and not the servant. The *Yang* and the *Yin* move things, but are not moved. The deeds and the prayers of a tiny creature like man cannot impress the mighty fluid of Heaven, and the sobs of thousands of people cannot touch it. Heaven is too far, and its fluid shapeless without beginning or end. It never sets the laws of nature aside for man's sake.

44. Chap. II. *Chao-chih* (This chapter has been lost.) 45. Chap. III. *Ming-yu*

The rain sacrifice, which during the *Ch'un-ch'iu* period was performed at times of drought, forms the subject of this essay. People use to pray for rain and happiness, as they implore the spirits to avert sickness and other evils. Some believe that rain is caused by the stars, others that it depends on the government of a State, others again that it comes from the mountains. The last opinion is shared by *Wang Chung.* 46. Chap. IV. *Shun-ku*

The chapter treats of the religious ceremonies performed to avert inuudatious, in which the beating of drums is very important.

Book XVI.

47. Chap. I. *Luan-lung* jfLf

As a means to attract the rain by the sympathetic action of similar fluids *Tung Chung Shu* had put up a clay dragon. *Wang Ch ung* attempts to demonstrate the efficacy of this procedure by 15 arguments and 4 analogies.

48. Chap. II. *Tsao-hu* jg. *Wang Ch ung* controverts the popular belief that, when men are devoured by tigers, it is the wickedness of secretaries and minor officials which causes these disasters.

49. Chap. III. *Shang-ch'ung* j

The common belief that the eating of the grain by insects is a consequence of the covetousness of the yamen underlings is shown to be futile.

50. Chap. IV. *Chiang-jut* § jffij (Arguments on Ominous Creatures).

Wang Chung denies that the literati would be able to recognise a phoenix or a unicorn, should they appear, nor would they know a sage either. The phoenix and the unicorn are regarded as holy animals and as lucky auguries. The old traditions about their appearance at various times and their shape, which are very conflicting, are discussed. *Wang Chung* holds that these animals do not only appear at the time of universal peace, that as ominous creatures they are born of a propitious fluid, and do not belong to a certain species, but may grow from dissimilar parents of a common species of animals. Book XVII.

51. Chap. I. *Chih-jui* jfjftj-

The discussion on the phoenix and the unicorn is continued. *Wang Chung* impugns the opinion that these animals are not born in China, but come from abroad, when there is a wise emperor. They grow in China, even, when there is no sage.

52. Chap. II. *Shih-yiny jfa.*

This chapter treats of the various lucky omens of the Golden Age:—the purple boletus, the wine springs, the sweet dew, the *Clang* star, the monthly plant, the phoenix, the unicorn, and of some other fabulous animals.

53. Chap. III. *Chih-ch'i*

The praise of antiquity, its high virtue and happiness is unfounded. There is nothing but fate. Human activity is powerless.

Book XVIII.

54. Chap. I. *Tse-jan* $C (Spontaneity). Heaven emits its generating fluid spontaneously, not on purpose. It has no desires, no knowledge, and does not act. These qualities require organs:—a mouth, eyes, hands, etc., which it does not possess. Its body must be either like that of Earth, or air. Heaven's fluid is placid, desireless, and unbusied. This spontaneity is a Taoist theory, but they did not sufficiently substantiate it. Only Sages resembling Heaven can be quite spontaneous and inactive, others must act, and can be instructed. Originally men lived in a happy state of ignorance. Customs, laws, in short culture is already a decline of virtue.

55. Chap. II. *Kan-lei J$ffi.*

Natural calamities and unlucky events are not the upshot of human guilt, as a thunderstorm is not a manifestation of Heaven's anger.

56. Chap. III. *Ch'i-shUi* (The Equality of the Ages).

People of old were not better, nor stronger, taller or longer lived than at present. Heaven and Earth have remained the same, and their creatures likewise. There is a periodical alternation of prosperity and decline in all the ages. The present time is not inferior to antiquity, but the literati extol the past and disparage the present. Even sages like *Confucius* would not find favour with them, if they happened to live now. And yet the *Han* dynasty is quite equal to the famous old dynasties.

Book XIX.

57. Chap. I. *Hsiian Han* jf Vjl

The scholars hold that in olden days there has been a Golden Age, which is passed and does not come back owing to the badness of the times. *Wang Ch ung* stands up for his own time, the *Han* epoch. He enumerates the lucky portents observed under the *Han* emperors, and refers to the great achievements of the *Han* dynasty in the way of colonising and civilising savage countries.

.58. Chap. II. *Hui-kuo 'c.* *Wang Chung* gives to the *Han* dynasty the preference over all the others, and again discourses on the lucky auguries marking its reign.

59. Chap. ffl. *Yen-fu ffffitffi.*

The discovery of gold under the *Han* dynasty, and of purple boletus, the sweet-dew-fall in several districts, and the arrival of dragons and phoenixes are put forward as so many proofs of the excellence of the *Han* dynasty.

Book XX.

60. Chap. I. *Hsu-sung* J(4$-

This chapter is a variation of the two preceding.

61. Chap. II. *Yi-wen*

The subject of this treatise is purely literary. It discusses the discovery of the Classics in the house of *Confucius,* the Burning of the Books under *Ch in Shih Huang Ti,* and the literature of the *Han* epoch, of which several authors are mentioned.

62. Chap. III. *Lun-sse* f§ % (On Death).

Man is a creature. Since other creatures do not become ghosts after death, man cannot become a ghost either. If all the millions that have lived, became spirits, there would not be sufficient room for all the spirits in the world. The dead never give any sign of there existence, therefore they cannot exist any more. The vital fluid forming the soul disperses at death, how could it become a ghost. A spirit is diffuse and formless. Before its birth the soul forms part of the primogenial fluid, which is unconscious. When at death it reverts thereto, it becomes unconscious again. Tbe soul requires the body to become conscious and to act. If sleep causes unconsciousness, and if a disease disorganises the mind, death must do the same in a still higher degree.

Book XXI.

63. Chap. I. *Sse-wei* (False Reports about the Dead).

A number of ghost stories are quoted from the *Tso-chum* and other ancient works, where discontented spirits are reported to have taken their revenge upon, and killed their enemies. *Wang Ch ung* either rejects these stories as inventions, or tries to explain them in a natural way.

Book XXII.

64. Chap. I. *Chi-yao* (Spook Stories).

Several spook and ghost stories recorded in the *Shi-chi* and the *Tso-chuan* are analysed. *Wang-Ch'ang* explains them in accordance with his theory on the spontaneity of Heaven, and on the nature of apparitions and portents.

65. Chap. II. *Ting-hm* ffTJ, (All about Ghosts). *Wang Chung* sets forth the different opinions on the nature of ghosts, propounded at his time. Some hold that ghosts are visions of sick people, or the fluid of sickness. Others regard them as the stellar fluid, or as the essence of old creatures, or as the spirits of cyclical signs. After an excursion on the demous, devils, and goblins mentioned in ancient books, *Wang Ch ung* gives his own views, according to which ghosts are apparitions and phantoms foreboding evil, which have assumed human form, but are only semblances and disembodied. They consist of the solar fluid, the *Yang,* are therefore red, burning, and to a certain extent poisonous. Book XXIH.

66. Chap. I. *Yen-tu* ff (On Poison).

Animal and vegetable poison is the hot air of the sun. All beings filled with the solar fluid contain some poison. Snakes, scorpions, and some plants have plenty of it. Ghosts, which consist of the pure solar fluid, are burning poison, which eventually kills. There is poison in some diseases, in a sun-stroke for instance and in lumbago. *Wang Ch ung* discovers real poison in speech, in beauty, and in several tastes, which only metaphorically might be called poisonous, and mixes up the subject still more by improper symbolism.

67. Chap. II. *Po-tsang*

This chapter is directed against the extravagance in funerals, on the score that the dead have no benefit from it.

68. Chap. III. *Sse-wei*

There is a popular belief that four things are dangerous and bring misfortune *viz.* to enlarge a house at the west side, to allow a banished man to ascend a tumulus, the intercourse with women, during the first month after they have given birth to a child, and the rearing of children born in the 1st and the 5th months, who will cause the deaths of their parents. *Wang Ch ung* combats these superstitions.

69. Chap. IV. *Lan-shih Wang Ch'ung* discourses on the common belief that in building one must pay attention to an unpropitious time, which may be warded off by amulets. He further speaks of the spirits of the year, the months, etc. Book XXIV.

70. Chap. I. *Chi-jil* $ 0.

Some more superstitions concerning unlucky years, months, and days, which must be shunned to avoid misfortunes, are investigated. For many actions the election of a proper time is deemed to be of great importance, *e. g.* for a funeral, or for commencing a building. Bathing on certain days, women become beautiful; bathing on others makes their hair turn white. On the day of *T sang Hsieh's* death, who invented writing, one must not study calligraphy, and on the day of the downfall of the *Yin* and *Hsia* dynasties one does not make music.

71. Chap. II. *Pu-skih jfe* (On Divination). People often neglect virtue and only rely on divination. They imagine that by means of tortoise shells and mil-foil they can interrogate Heaven and Earth about the future, and that they reply by the signs of the shells and the straws. *Wang Ch ung* shows that such an opinion is erroneous, but, whereas *Han Fei Tse* condemns divination altogether, he upholds this science. In his idea visions, signs, and omens are true by all means, only they are very often misunderstood or misinterpreted by the diviners. The lucky will meet with good omens, which, however, are not the response of Heaven, but happen by chance. 72. Chap. III. *PiensuiffijL* (Criticisms on Noxious Influences).

Most people are under the delusion that by disregarding an unpropitious time *viz.* years, months, aud days of dread, they will have to suffer from noxious influences, falling in with evil spirits, which work disaster. This is an error, as shown by experience, but horoscopists and seers are silent on all cases contradicting their theory. A vast literature has sprung up on this subject, and the princes dare not take any important step in lite, any more than their people, without reference to it.

73. Chap. IV. *Nan-sui IjUjjtfijfcWang Ch'ung* impugns the view that by moving one's residence one may come into collision with the Spirit of the North Point, *Nan Sui,* which would be disastrous. Book XXV.

74. Chap. I. *Ch'i-shu* fgj-

The chapter treats of the precautions which used to be taken in building houses, special attention being paid to the family name, the number of the house, the situation, etc.

75. Chap. II. *Chieh-ch'u* (On Exorcism). By exorcism malignant spirits are expelled after having been feasted. Exorcism and conjurations are of no use, for either would the ghosts not yield to the force employed against them, and resent the affront, or, if they are like mist and clouds, their expulsion would be useless. In ancieut times, sickness was expelled in this way. The propitiation of the Spirit of Earth, after having dug up the ground, is also useless, for Earth does not hear man nor understand his speech. All depends upon man, not on ghosts.

76. Chap. III. *Sse-yi* fliHH (Sacrifices to the Departed).

Sacrifices are merely manifestations of the feelings of love and gratitude, which the living cherish towards ghosts and spirits. The latter cannot enjoy the sacrifices, which are presented to them, because having no body, they are devoid of knowledge and cannot eat or drink. If Heaven and Earth could eat or drink, they would require such enormous quantities of food, that man could never appease their hunger. *Wang Ch'ung* treats of the nature of ghosts, and refers to the sacrifices to Heaven and Earth, to the House, to the Gods of Wind, Rain, and Thunder, to the Sun, the Moon, and the Stars, and to the Ancestors.

77. Chap. IV. *Chi-yi* ff; (Sacrifices).

The various old sacrifices are described, those to Heaven and Earth, to the Mountains and Rivers, to the Spirits of the Land and Grain, to the Six Superior Powers, to the Seasons, Heat and Cold, Water and Drought, the Rain Sacrifice, those to the Four Cardinal Points, to the Sun, the Moon, and the Stars, the Five Genii of the House, and to the Ancestors. All these sacrifices saving the last were State sacrifices and reserved for the emperor, the feudal princes, and their officials. They are thank-offerings for kindness received. There are no spirits present to enjov them, nor can they bestow happiness on the sacrificers, or visit with misfortune those who neglect them. Therefore sacrifices are a beautiful custom, but of no great consequence.

Book XXVI.

78. Chap. I. *Shih-chih* fp.

Saints and Sages are credited with an extraordinary knowledge. They need not learn or study, for they are cognisant of everything intuitively, and know the past as well as the future. This is a fallacy. There are no supernatural faculties, and even those of the Sages follow the natural laws.

79. Chap. II. *Ckih-shih* $ *Confucius* was not prescient and not a prophet, as has been asserted. 16 examples are given, all showing his inability to foreknow the future.

Book XXVII. 80. Chap. I. *Ting-hsien*

The nature of the Worthies is defined.

Examples are adduced of what they are not. No exceptional talents are required, but a certain amount of intelligence and honesty. Worthies belong to the same class as Saints or Sages, but are somewhat inferior.

i

Book XXVm.

81. Chap. I. *Cheng-shuo* jJifft; (Statements Corrected).

This chapter contains critical remarks on the composition and the history of the *Shuking*, the *Shiking*, the *Ch'un-ch'iu*, the *Yiking*, the *Liki*, and the *Analects*. The meaning of the dynastic names of *T ang, Yd*, the *Hsia, Yin*, and *Climi* dynasties is explained, and some hints as to how the Canons are to be interpreted are added.

82. Chap. II. *Shu-chie/i*

The chapter deals with learning and erudition, with literary composition, and with the various kinds of men of letters.

Book XXIX.

83. Chap. I. *An-shu* (Critical Remarks on Various Books).

Wang Ch ung criticises the famous authors of his time and their works, beginning with some writers of the *Chou* epoch. He finds fault with *Mi Ti*, the sophist *Kung Sun Lung*, and the speculative philosopher *Tsou Yen*, and commends *Tso Ch'iu Ming*, the author of the *Tso-chuan* and the *Kuo-gil*. He speaks with great respect of the historians *Sse Ma Ctiien* and *Pan Am*, the philosopher *Yang Tse Yiln*, and *Liu Hsiang*, and in the highest terms of *Lu Chia*, who published the *Ch'un-cli iu-fan-lu*, and of IJuan *Chiln Shan* and *Huan K nan*, the authors of the *Hsin-lun* and the *Yen-t'ieh-lun*. 84. Chap. II. *Tui-tso* $-f£ (Replies in Self-Defence). *Wang Ch ung* gives the reasons, why he wrote his principal works, the *Lun-heng* and the *Cheng-wu*, a treatise on government. In the *Lun-heng* he wishes to explain common errors, to point out the exaggerations and inventions in literature, and thus deliver mankind of its prejudices. The *Lun-heng* weighs the words and holds up a halance for truth and falsehood. *Wang Ch ung* shows the advantage which might be derived from dif-

ferent chapters, and meets the objections which his opponents would perhaps raise.

Book XXX.

85. Chap. I. *Tse-chi* g (Autobiography). *Wang Chung* is a native of *Shang-yil-h. tien* in *Chelating*. His family originally lived in *Chihli*. He was born in A.d. 27, and already as a boy was very fond of study. In his official career he was not very successful. The highest post which he held about A.d. 86 was that of a sub-prefect. The equanimity of a philosopher helped him over many disappointments. His ideal was to possess an extensive knowledge, a keen intellect, and a noble mind. Resides his chief work the *Lun-hing*, he wrote 12 chapters on common morals in a plain and easy style, and a treatise "*Macrobiotics* ' in A.d. 91. He defends the style, the voluminousness, and the contents of the *Lun-heng* against the attacks directed against it.

Lun-Heng.

Selected Essays of the Philosopher Wang Ch'ung.

CHAPTER I.

Autobiography *(Tse-chi)*.

Wang Chung is a native of *Shang-yil-hsien* in *K'uei-chi2*. His style is *Chung Jin*. His family hails from *Ywtn-ch ' ing* in the *Wei* circuit. One of his clan, *Sun-yi*, served his whole life as a soldier, and distinguished himself so much, that he was appointed warden of the southern part of *Kuei-chi*. but, when one year a disturbance broke out, which disorganised the State, he continued to reside there, and became a farmer and cultivator of mulberry-trees.

His great grand-father was very bold and violent, and, when in a passion, cared for nobody. In a year of dearth he behaved like a ruffian, and wounded and killed people. Those whom he had wronged, and who were waiting for an opportunity to wreak their vengeance, were very numerous. As in *Kuei-chi* revolts were of constant occurrence, and there was danger tbat his enemies would seize upon him, the grand-father *Fan* removed his family and his household from *K'uei-chi*, and settled in *Ch'ien-t'ang-hsim*, where he lived as a merchant. He had two sons, the elder was called *Ming,* the younger *Sung. Sung* is the father of *Wang Ch ung.*

The grand-father had a violent temper, which in his sons, *Meng* and *Sung,* became so intense, that many people in *Ch'im-t'ang* had to suffer from their vehemence. At last they became involved again in a feud with *Ting Po* and other influential families, in consequence of which they emigrated with their families to *Shang-tlu.*

In the third year of *Chien-wu,"* *Wang Ch ung* was born. When playing with his companions, he disliked all frivolous games. His comrades would entrap birds, catch cicadas, play for money, and gambol on stilts. *Wang Chung* alone declined to take part in their games to the great amazement of his father.

In *Shao-hsing-fu (Chekiang).* Under the *Han* dynasty *K'uei-chi* comprises *Chekiang,* the South of *Anhui,* and the North of *Fukien.* In *Ta-ming-fu (Chili).* A circuit comprising parts of *Chili* and *Honan.* In the *Hang-chou* prefecture of t *hekiang.* 27 A.d.

At the age of six, he received his first instruction, and learned to behave with politeness, honesty, benevolence, obedience, propriety, and reverence. He was grave, earnest, and very quiet, and had the will of a great man. His father never flogged him, his mother never gave him a harsh word, and the neighbours never scolded him. When he was eight years old, he went to school. There were over one hundred small boys in this school. As a punishment for faults committed they used to be stripped, or were whipped for bad writing. *Wang Ch'ung* made daily progress, and never committed any offence.

When he could write sentences, his teacher explained to him the *Analects* and the *Shuking,* of which he daily read a thousand characters. When he knew the Classics, and his virtue had thus been developed, he left his teacher, and devoted his private studies to writing and composing so, that every one was astonished, and the extent of his reading widened day by day. But he did not make bad use of his talents, and though he possessed great dialectical skill, he

was not fond of disputations. Unless he found the proper audience, he did not speak the whole day. His speech was quaint and not like that of others, but those who listened to him to the end, agreed with him. Such were also the productions of his pen, and so were his conduct, and his behaviour towards his superiors.

In a district he rose to the rank of a secretary, and held the same office in the department of a military governor. In a prefecture he was one of the five chief secretaries, and in a department he was appointed assistant-magistrate. He did not strive for fame, and did not regulate his conduct in accordance with his personal profits. He always spoke of people's merits and seldom of their faults. Those who had not yet got on in their career, were specially recommended by him, and he exposed only the faults of those who had secured a position. When he thought anything wrong, he did not praise it, and when a fault was not done away with, he did not again condemn the man. He could pardon the great faults of a man, and also pitied his minor mistakes. His desire was to be unimpeachable himself, but he did not wish to shine. He endeavoured to base his claims on recognition upon his actions, and was ashamed to presume upon his talents.

A prefecture or a circuit—of which there were 36 during the *Han* epoch—was devided into 5 regions:—the centre and four quarters. Each region was superintended by a chief secretary of the prefect, who had the jurisdiction over his region. Luo-Heog. 6

In public meetings he did not speak, unless he was asked, and in the presence of princes and generals he only replied, when he was addressed. In the country he attempted to follow the example of *ChG Po Yd,* and in the court he wished to imitate *Shih Tse Yii.*

When insulted, he did not white-wash himself, and, when in his career he was not promoted, he did not feel grieved. Although he was poor and had not an acre to dwell upon, his mind was freer than that of kings and dukes, and though he had no emoluments counted by pecks

and piculs, he felt, as if he had ten thousand *chung* to live upon. Obtaining an appointment, he was not overjoyed, and losing it, he did not feel distressed. lie enjoyed a tranquil happiness, but his desires did not run riot, and though hc was living in a state of poverty, his energy was not broken. The study of ancient literature was his debauchery, and strange stories his relish. In the current books and common sayings he found much, in which he could not aquiesce. A recluse in his solitary retirement, he tried to find truth and falsehood.

Wang Ch ung had a pure and sterling character. He made friends wherever he went, but did not contract these friendships carelessly. The position of his friends might be ever so low, and in years they might be ever so young, provided only that they rose above common-place mediocrity, he would seek their friendship. He had a great admiration for superior men, and liked to associate with distinguished people, but would not lightly become intimate with men of common gifts. In case these latter slandered him for a slight fault or any insignificant mistake, he would not clear himself of these accusations, nor did he bear any grudge against them. A disciple of *Confucing,* whom the master esteemed very much. *Shih Tse Yii —Shih Yii,* a high officer in *Wei.* When Duke *Ling* of *Wei* (533-492) did not employ *Chii Po Yii, Shih Tse Yii* remonstrated with the duke, but in vain. Soon afterwards he fell sick. Feeling his end coming, he told his son to place his corpse under the window, without performing the usual funeral rites, because he did not deserve them, not having been able to convince the duke of what was right. When the duke paid his condolence, the son informed him of what his father had said. The duke repented, and then appointed *Chii Po Yii.* When *Confucius* heard of this, he exclaimed:—" How upright was *Shih Tse Yii,* who still as a corpse admonished his sovereign." *Chii Po Yii* was of a different turn of mind. *Confucms* said of him that, when bad government prevailed, he could roll his principles up, and keep them in his breast. *(Analects* XV, G.)

One chung = 4 pecks.

Some one might ask, why a man of re-
markahle gifts and extraordinary literary talent should not defend himself
against false incriminations. *Yang Shing*
and others were foul-mouthed and
glibtongued; hut *Tsou Yang* vindicated
himself and came out of jail again.
When a man's conduct is perfect, people should not attempt to find flaws in
it, and when somebody exerts himself to
come to the front, they should not keep
him down.

I reply that none but the pure remark
dust, and none but the exalted perceive
dangers. Only those living in abundance, feel restraints, and those in opulence know what is want. The scholars
at present talk too much of themselves,
therefore they are slandered by others,
which is their due. Desirous to get on,
they show themselves, and resenting neglect, they assert themselves. Being free
of these desires and resentments, I keep
quiet.

The slanders of *Yang Shing* were
probably prompted by somebody, and
when *Tsou Yang* was delivered, some
one saved him. *Confucius* spoke of destiny and *Mencius* of heaven. Luck and
mishap, quietude and danger do not depend on man. The ancients knew this,
therefore they ascribed these things to
destiny and attributed them to time.
Placid, tranquil, and equanimous, they
did not complain of injustice. When
happiness came, they did not imagine
that they themselves had brought it
about, and when misfortune befell
them, they did not consider it their own
doing. When they were successful, their
joy was not immoderate, and when they
suffered reverses, their courage did not
fail them. They did not hate need, and
therefore crave for plenty, nor did they
brave dangers to win peace. Their wisdom they did not sell for wages, and
they did not decline honours to become
famous. Not being bent on success, they
did not try to show off, and not resenting reverses, they did not complain of
others. Tranquillity and excitement
were the same to them, life and death
equal, luck and mishap identical, and
victory and defeat one. Meeting even

ten *Yang Shengs,* they would have said
that it mattered not; they left everything
to heaven, and therefore they did not wish to
shine.

Wang Ch'ung was of a cheerful and
easy-going disposition, and did not
strive for wealth and honour. When his
superiors took notice of him, and promoted him above the heads of others,
Tsou Yang lived under the reign of
Ching Ti (156-141 B.c.). At the court of
King *Hsiao* of *Liang* he was denounced
by *Yang Sheng* and others, and thrown
into prison, but by a memorial, which
from his confinement he sent to the
king, he obtained his release, and was
re-instated into all his honours. 5« he
did not cling to hiss high post, and,
when they ignored, denounced, and degraded him, he did not pine at his low
rank. When in the district magistrate's
office, he had no ambition and no repugnance.

Some one might object that to act like
this is easy enough, but that the difficulty lies with the heart. Meeting with con-
genial friends, scholars do not care for
the place, but whose example can they
follow, when they have dirty and dis-
tasteful business to do?

There is no better paragon than *Confucius,* I should say. *Confucius* as an
official had no aversions. In charge of
the public fields and as keeper of the
granaries he was not low-spirited, and
when he was superintendent of works
and minister, his face was not beaming
with joy. *Shun* tilled the land on the *Li-
shan,* as though he should continue to
do so for ever, and when he had received the empire from *Yao,* he behaved, as if he had obtained it later on
as a matter of course. We must be sorry
that our virtue is not quite perfect, but
not regret our humble rank, and we may
be abashed, if our name is not without
blemish, but should not feel chagrined,
because we do not advance in our career. Marble may be kept in the same
box with tiles, and moon-stones in the
same bag with pebbles. Being both of
precious stuff, they are not injured by
being mixed with other things in the
world. For him who knows what is
good, good things shine even in base

places, whereas to those who cannot
make these distinctions, they look common even in a prominent place. As long
as the deeds of people in low and high
spheres can be measured, and as the
virtues of men in humble positions, and
of noble rank can be compared, it is all
right.

The world courts those who have
been successful, and disdains those who
have failed. It hails the victor, and
spurns the defeated. As long as *Wang
Ch'ung* was rising, and holding rank and
office, all the people swarmed around
him like ants, but, when he had lost his
position and was living in poverty, his
former friends abandoned him. He pondered over the heartlessness of the
world and in his leisure he wrote twelve
chapters "Censures on Common Morals
", hoping that the reading of these books
would rouse the public conscience. For
this purpose he expressly wrote It is not
certain where this Mount *Li* was situated. Various places are assigned to it.

Chi su chieh gi. it in an easy, popular
style. Should anybody condemu it as
shallow, I would reply that if the style of
the Sacred Institutions be employed for
the Lesser Odes, or if an elegant speech
be addressed to rustics, they would not
understand anything, and therefore not
agree. Thus *Su Ch in* spoke very ele-
gantly in *Chao,* but *Li Tui* was not enchanted at all. *Shang Yang* spoke in
Ch'in, as if he had addressed au emper-
or, but Duke *Hsiao* did not follow his
advice. If no attention be paid to the in-
dividuality and inclinations of the hearers, one may exhaust the eloquence of
Yao and *Shun,* it would be like giving
an ox wine to drink and feeding a horse
on preserved meat. A refined, rhetorical, and scientific style is fit for the upper classes of society, but out of place
for smallminded people. It happens very
seldom, that those who must hear something *nolens volens,* take it to heart.

When *Confucius* had lost a horse in the
country, the countrypeople locked it up,
and did not return it. *Tse Kung* spoke
to them in well turned sentences, but
only made them angry, but when the
groom addressed them in a familar, joc-
ular tone, they relented.

To use high-flown expressions at all costs instead of the plain and simple language of the people is like mixing an elixir, as the spirits use, to cure a cold or a cough, and to put on a fur-coat of sable or fox to fetch firewood or vegetables. As regards propriety, a thing is often out of place, and many an action is often better left undone. To give a decision, and understand a grievance, one must not be a *Kao Yao J* and to cook sunflower-seed and onions, no *Yi Ti* or *Yi Ya* is required. In a side-alley one does not play the music of *Shun* and *Wu,* and to the Village Mother one does not sacrifice a whole ox. What is unnecessary, is also inadequate.

Parts of the *Shu-king.* The minor odes of the *Shi-king.* A politician of the 4th cent. B.c. (Cf. Chap. XXXVII.)
4 Vid. p. 171, Note 2.
Duke *Hsiao* of *Ch'in,* 361-337 B.c. This adventure is related by *Hani Nan Tse* (quoted in the *Pei-wen-gun-fu)* likewise, who adds that the horse of *Confucius* was retained by the peasants, because it had eaten their corn. A minister of *Shun.* "*Yi Ti,* the inventor of wine, who presented the first cup to *Great Yii.* *Yi Ya,* the famous cook of Duke *Huan* of *Ch'i,* 7th cent. B.c. (Cf. *Mencius,* Bk. VI, Pt. I, chap. 7, *Legge* Vol. II, p. 281.) The matron-saint of a village.
To carve a fowl with a butcher's knife, to reap sun-flowers with a *Shu* spear, to cut chop-sticks with an iron halberd, and to pour a glassful into a basin or a tureen would be incongruous, and few would recommend it. What is the principle of debating? To illustrate deep thoughts by simple ones. And how do we prove that we possess knowledge'. ' By illustrating difficult points by easy ones. Sages and worthies use to weigh, what suits the different talents. Hence the difference of style, which may be difficult or easy.

Since *Wang Ch ung* deplored the popular feeling, he wrote his Censures on Public Morals, and also lamenting the vain efforts of the emperor's government, which was endeavouring to govern the people, but could not find the right w ay, nor understand what was required, and mournful and disheartened

did not see its course, he wrote the book on government. Furthermore disgusted with the many deceitful books and popular literature devoid of veracity and truthfulness, he composed the Disquisitions *(Lun-heng).*

The worthies and sages are dead, and their great doctrine has split up. Many new roads have been struck out, on which many people have stumbled. Every one must have his own school. Intelligent men have seen this, but were unable to find the right way. Old traditions have been transmitted, either written down, or spread by hearsay. Since they were dating from over a hundred years backwards and growing older from day to day, people have regarded them as antique lore and therefore near the truth, and this belief became so rooted in their minds, that they themselves were incapable of eradicating it again.

For this reason the Disquisitions have been written to show the truth. They are in a lively style and full of controversy. Every specious and futile argument has been tested, semblance and falsehood have been rejected, and only what is real and solid has been preserved. Loose manners have been suppressed, and the customs of *Fu Hsi's* time revived. *Wang Ch ung's* writings are lucid and easy to understand. There are those who pretend that the words of a good debater must be profound, and the compositions of an able writer obscure. The An old State in *Anhni. Ching-wn.* The Golden Age. style of the classic, literature and the sayings of worthies and sages are grand and majestic, beautiful and refined, and difficult to grasp at first. Those who study their whole life, learn to understand them with the necessary explanations. The. genius of the lirst thinkers being so wonderful, their expressions cannot be the same as those of ordinary people. Gems, they say, are concealed in stones, and pearls in fish-maws. Only jewel-lapidaries and pearl-experts can find them. These precious things cannot be seen, because they are hidden, and thus truisms must be profound and deep, and hard to grasp.
The "Censures on Morals" are intended to rouse people, therefore the meaning

is perspicuous and the style quite plain. But why must the *Lung-heng* be like this too? Is the talent of the author so shallow, that it was absolutely impossible to hide anything? Why is the style so perspicuous, and quite a different principle followed than in the classical literature?

My reply is as follows. A gem is concealed in a stone and a pearl in a fish-maw, and therefore they are covered and in the dark. But, when the colour of the gem beams from the heart of the stone, and the lustre of the pearl breaks through the fish-maw, are they still hidden? They are like my thoughts, before they have been fixed in books. Enshrined in my bosom, they are like gems or pearls in their concealment, shining forth, brilliant as the splendour of the heavenly bodies, and clear as the distinct lines of the surface of the earth.

Lest things should remain doubtful and obscure to us, we can describe them all by names, and, provided that the names are clear, all the things become defined. The *Lun-hing* discusses these questions impartially.

In speaking, it is essential to use clear words, and in writing, to employ plain signs. The style of eminent scholars is refined, but their words can always be understood, and their meaning always be caught. Their readers are suddenly enlightened like blind men who recover their sight, or stirred up like deaf men who suddenly learn to hear. When a child who has been blind for three years, unexpectedly sees his parents, he would not, at once, know them on perceiving them, why then should he give utterance to his joy?

Let a huge tree stand by the roadside, and a long ditch run along a bank, then the locality is well defined, and everybody knows it. Now, should the tree not be huge any more and disappear, and the ditch not be long and be hidden, and the place be shown to people, even *Yao* and *Shun* would be perplexed.

The human features are divided into more than seventy different classes. The flesh of the cheeks being pure and white, the five colours can be clearly discerned, and the slightest sorrow, pleasure, and other emotions, all find expression in the features. A physiognomist will not once be mistaken in ten cases. But if the face be blackened and begrimed, or covered with a layer of dirt so, that the features are hidden, then physiognomists will give wrong answers nine times out of ten.

The style is formed of words. It may be shallow, perspicuous, and distinct, or deep, abstruse, elegant, and polished. Who shall distinguish it?

We speak to express our thoughts, and from fear, that our words might be lost, we commit them to writing. Writing having the same purpose as speaking, wherefore should it conceal the meaning?

A judge must hate wrong. Now, would a magistrate, who while deciding a doubtful case gives a confuse and unintelligent verdict, be a better official than another, who clearly distinguishes every point, and can easily be understood?

In oral discussions, one makes clear distinctions out of regards for the audience, and in written disputatious one elucidates one's meaning to be understood. In historical works, a clear and intelligible style is most appreciated, and of profound productions, full of beautiful thoughts, but hard to read, there are only pieces of irregular verse and dithyrambs. As for the classical and semiclassical works and the words of the worthies and sages, the ancient and modern languages are different, and speech varies in the different parts of the empire. At the time, when these men spoke, they did not wish that their words should be difficult to understand, or that their meaning should be hidden. If later ages did not understand them, this is owing to the remoteness of time. Therefore one may speak of the difference of language, but not of genius or shallowness of style. If the reading offers great difficulties, the works may be considered as not very cleverly written, but this should not be reputed a great wisdom.

Ch'in Shiit Huang Ti reading *Han Fei Tse's* work exclaimed with a sigh! "Alas! that I am alone, and have not got this man! " They were contemporaries, he could understand his words and According to the *Shi-chi* chap. 63 p. llv (Biography of *Han Fei Tse)* the emperor said:— " Alas! If I could see this man, I would be willing to live and die with him!" reflect upon what he said. If the book had been so profound and exquisite, that he wanted a teacher to comprehend it, he would have flung it to the ground, and it was no use sighing.

An author wishes his work to be intelligible, but difficult to write, and he does not care, if it be hard to grasp, but easy to write. In lectures one aims at perspicuity, that the hearers can follow, and does not affect obscurity and ambiguity to baffle the readers. *Meneius* knew an intelligent man by the sparkling of his eyes. One learns to know what a text is worth by its lucidity.

The book of *Wang Ch'ung* is of another type than the usual writings. The following objection might be raised against it: —

In literature it is of importauce to conform to the public feeling, and not to be in opposition to received ideas. Then not one out of a hundred readers will find anything to blame, and not one out of a thousand hearers will take exception. Therefore *Kuan Tse* said that, where somebody is speaking in a house, the audience must fill the whole house, and, when he speaks in a hall, the entire hall should be full. Now *Wang Ch'ung's* arguments are not in accordance with public opinion. Consequently his words controvert all common ideas, and do not tally with the general views.

I reply that in arguing, the essential thing is truth, not elegance, that the facts should at all events be correct, and that co?isensus is not the highest aim. Investigating a question, one discusses the *pros* and *cous*, how would it be possible not to deviate from old ideas and perhaps offend the ears of the common hearer? When the general feeling is wrong, it cannot be followed. One denounces and discards that which is false, and keeps and establishes that which is true. If we were to go by majority, and conform to the public feeling, we could only follow the good old rules and precedents, and recite them over and over again, but how could there be any discussion?

Han Fei Tse was sent as envoy from his native State *Han)* to t *'Win Shih Huang Ti,* who first appreciated him very much and wished to appoint him to some high post. By the intrigues of *Li Sse,* however, he was induced to imprison him, and to condemn him to death. The emperor afterwards repented, and cancelled the death warrant, but is was too late, for meanwhile *Han Fei Tse* had taken poison. (Cf. p. 170.) Cf. Chap. XXXII. The philosopher *Kuan Chung.*

When *Confucius* was attending the court and sitting next-to Duke *Ai* of *Lu,* the duke favoured him with a peach and millet. *Confucius* first ate the millet and then the peach. This, we must admit, was the right order of eating the two courses. The courtiers, however, all covered their mouth and laughed. They had, for a long time, been used to another custom. Now I, in fact, resemble *Confucius* eating the two dishes in the order described above. Ordinary people take exception like the courtiers laughing in their sleeves.

Beautiful festive songs were considered as too melancholic, in *Clung* and pantomimes, at great celebrations, found no favour in *Chao.*

The five Leading Princes' declined to cast a look upon the Canons of *Yao* and *Shun,* and *Chi* and *Ming* would not read the works of *Confucius* and *Mi Ti.* Plans for securing the peace in times of danger are scoffed at in side-alleys, and schemes of reform ridiculed by common people. If there were an exquisite dish, vulgar people would not taste it, though *Yi Ti* and *Yi Ya* might eat it with the greatest relish, and if there were a precious jade-stone, ordinary people would throw it away, whereas *Pien Ho'* would hoard it up as a. treasure. Who would be right, who wrong, and who could be trusted? Propriety and common usage are always in opposition, when has it not been so? When Duke *Win* of *Lu* infringed the rule of-sacrifices, five men resisted him.

Great scholars will never give up researches of the above mentioned kind, and common people will always dislike them. And so will the *savants* enjoy and appreciate books, which bewilder the masses, and which the narrow-minded will flee.

Wang Ch ung's book cannot be free from imperfection. Some say that in speaking he does not choose the words, nor in writing, the phrases. Compositions must be tastefully written, and discussions Li *Cheng* licentious music, but not the serious songs of the Book of Odes were appreciated. The five leaders of the empire, the most powerful princes during the 7th cent. B.c. to wit:—Duke *Huan* of *Ch'i,* Duke *Wen of Chin,* Duke *Hidang* of *Sung,* Duke *Chuang* of *Ch'u,* and Duke *Mu* of *Ch'in.* They were more bent on conquest than interested in the moral laws expounded in the Canons of *Yao* and *Shun* in the Shu-king. The chiefs of two noble families in *Lu,* contemporaries of *Confucius.*
Vid. p. 6l).
Cf. p. 89. Duke *Wen* placed the tablet of his deceased father above that of his uncle in the ancestral temple. The latter, Duke *Min,* was a younger brother of Duke *Hsi,* but he preceded in reign. For more details vid. *Tso-chuan,* Duke *Win* 2nd year. ingeniously conducted. When such words strike the ear, they cause a pleasant feeling in the heart, anil when the eye falls on writing, the hand does not lay the book aside again. Such disputations are always listened to, and excellent compositions always appreciated. Now, since this new hook chiefly consists of comparisons and strictures on the depravity of the age, and does not praise what is good, it does not please the reader. The tunes played by the music-master *K uang* were always full of feeling, and the delicacies prepared by *Yi li* and *Yi Ya* were never tasteless. When a clever man writes a book, it is without a flaw. *Lil Shih'* and *Hum Nan* made an advertisement on the market gates, and the readers did not find fault with one word in their books. Now the *Lun-heng* does not possess the beauties of these two books. It is long enough, but open to objections in many respects.

In reply I beg to state that he who cherishes veracity does not trouble much about beauty, and that regulating the conduct, he does not polish his words. Luxuriant grass has often abundance of blossoms, and mighty forests have many dry branches. The purport of words is to clearly show the nature of things, how can they be polished and above all censure? Saving a man from fire or out of water, we do not care, whether we do it in a beautiful style or not, and, when we debate on a question, our words must not necessarily be ingenious. Plunging into a lake to seize turtles, we have no time to think, whether we place our feet right, and catching dragons in deep water, we have no time to care for the position of our hands.

In spite of bad style and faulty terms the meaning may be excellent and far reaching sometimes, and sweet words and beautiful expressions give often a very poor sense. When a thousand *chung* of grain are cleansed, more than half are husks, and examining a hundred thousand cash, one finds that the broken coins exceed ten thousand. Fine soups are often insipid, and the best jewels have their flaws. A slip-shod production may possess great beauties, and a great artist do very second-rate work. Every discussion has its weak points, and in the ahlest production some deficiencies can be detected.
The music-master of the Duke of *Chin* (cf. Chap. XVII).
Lii Pu Wei, the author of the *Lii Shih ch'un-ch'iu.*
It is related of *Lii Pu Wei* that he placed a copy of his work in the market place and offered a reward of a thousand *chin* to any one who could alter one character in it. The same is not known of *Hum* JVan *Tse.*
Golden words come from noble houses, and foul productions from poor families, they think.— *Huai Nan Tse* and LiX *Shih* did not encounter any difficulties, because they were descendants of rich houses and of high rank. Since they were noble, they could well advertise on the market place, and being so wealthy, they could easily make the alternate promise of a thousand *chin.*

Their readers were intimidated and in awe, and would never have ventured to criticise one character, even if it had been quite out of place.

When *Wang Ch'ung's* book was completed, it was compared by some with the works of the ancients, and found to be quite different from the writings of previous authors. Some hold that the book may be said to be written partly in a slovenly style. Sometimes it is terse, at others diffuse, sometimes concise, sometimes prolix. When a problem is being discussed or a question investigated, the author is too summary or too loquacious, half sweet, half sour. The Classics he does not resemble, with the semi-classics he does not agree, nor does he harmonize with either *Yang* CK ing *Tse Chang* or *Yang Tse Yiln.* Since he is unlike the ancient authors, how can he be considered a good writer, or his book be reputed an able production?

I answer that, if anybody puts on an alien appearance forcibly to be like somebody else, his own shape is lost, and if he changes his style to resemble others, he loses his peculiar character. The sons of a hundred persons have not the same parents. Being all born in different families, they cannot be similar. Each one distinguishes himself by his peculiar gifts. If writings could only then be considered good, when they are conform to a certain standard, this would be like substituting one workman for another aud declaring his work to be a master-piece, provided that in hewing he did not cut his own hand.

AH literary men have their own specialties. The one polishes his phrases to produce an elegant composition, the other combats all errors to establish the truth. Their ultimate aims are the same, and the words follow of themselves. Thus the deeds of the Five Emperors were not different, and there was no conflict between the actions of the Three Rulers. Beautiful looks are not Both were princes. Vid. p. 88. the same, but their aspect is always pleasing to the eye: sentimental airs are not identical, but their music is always gratifying to the ear. Wines have different flavours, but they all inebriate, the tastes of various cereals vary, but they all appease our hunger. If conformity to old standard be required of a literary production, then we would be entitled to expect that *Shun* also should have eyebrows with eight colours and *Yü* eyes with double pupils. *Wang Ch'ung's* book is very voluminous. Some say that in writing the chief thing is to be brief and clear, and that in sneaking one must be short and plain. The words of a good debater are succinct, but to the point, the style of a good writer is concise, but perspicuous. Now *Wang Ch'ung's* new work contains more than ten thousand sentences. For a reader it is impossible to work through such an enormous mass, and there are so many chapters, that they cannot all be transmitted. The author of so much had stuff may well be called a fool. Short sentences are easy to enunciate, whereas a bulky work presents great difficulties. Gems are few, stones many; that which occurs in great number, is not precious. Dragons are rare, fish numerous: that which is of rare occurence, is justly deemed divine. I admit that there is such a saying. Concise language is not long, but beautiful language must not be concise. If they are useful to the world, a hundred chapters do no harm, while one paragraph, if useless, may be superfluous. If there are several things, all useful, the longer rank before the shorter. Who is richer, he who has piled up a thousand *chin*, or he who possesses a hundred'.'

Longer works are preferable to shorter ones, and a small amount of wealth is better than poverty. Most people have not a single book. I possess a hundred chapters: others have not one character, I have more than ten thousand sentences. Who is the cleverer?

Now they do not say that my words are wrong, but that they are too many: they do not say that the world does not like good things, but that it cannot take them all in. The reason why my book canuot be so concise is that for building many houses a small ground would not be sufficient, and that for the registration of a large populace few registers would be inadequate. At present, the errors are so many, that the words necessary to point out the truth, show what is right, and controvert what is false, cannot well be brief and succinct.

Han Fei Tse's work is like the branch of a tree. The chapters are joined together by tens, and the sentences count by ten thousands. For a large body the dress cannot be narrow, and if there be many subjects, the text must not be too summary. A great variety of subjects requires abundance of words. In a large extent of water, there are many fish, in an emperor's capital, there is plenty of grain, and on the market of a metropolis, there is a throng of people.

My book may be voluminous, but the subjects treated are manifold. *T'ai Kung Wang* in ancient times and recently *Tung Chung Shu* produced books containing more than a hundred chapters. My book also contains more than a hundred chapters. Those who contend that they are too many, only mean to say that the author is of low origin, and that the readers cannot but take exception to it.

When we compare a river, whose waters overflow the banks, with others, which is the biggest? And, when the cocoons of a certain species of worms are especially heavy and big, which worms yield most silk?

Wang Ch'ung was not lucky in his official career, and only wrote books and this autobiography. Some one might find fault with him, arguing thus:

"The important thing is always that a man of great talent should make a good career. "When he finds employment, and his words are listened to, he can distinguish himself by his work, and thus rise to high honour. Now, you are living in misery, and your career has been spoiled. You had no opportunity of trying your talents in practice, or using your strength in the fulfilment of official duties. Therefore you only committed your speculations to writing and made your notes. What use are your beautiful words to yourself, and what aim are you pursuing with your extensive writings?"

Nobody was ever more talented than *Confucius*, and yet his talents were not appreciated. He was expelled, and a tree felled over him. He had to hasten the washing of his rice and was *T'ai Kung Wang* is the full appellative of *Wen Wang's* minister, usually called *T'ai Kung*, on whom cf. Chap. XXXIX.

Cf. p. 39 and Chap. XXXVII. When forced to leave *Ch'i*. (Vid. *Menciim* Bk. V, Pt. II, chap. I, 4, *Legge* Vol. II, p. 247.) surrounded. His traces were obliterated, he was tormented by hunger between *Ch'in* and *T'sai*. and his disciples looked starved. Now, my talents do not come near those of *Confucius,* but my hardships do not equal his. Am I to be despised therefore?

Besides the successful are not always clever, or the distressed, simpletons. The lucky win, and the unlucky lose. With a liberal fate and good fortune, even a vulgar person becomes noble and genteel, with a niggardly fate and bad fortune, the most remarkable man remains wretched and miserable. If talents and virtue were to be measured by success, then the great lords invested with the domain of a town, and living on the soil, would all be wise men.

Confucius and *Mi 77* were noble of themselves, but their rank was low. If, therefore, people are living in pure spheres, but do black deeds, or if they have a yearly income of a thousand *chung* to live upon, but not a single accomplishment, we can only smile. Provided that our virtue be high and our name untarnished, then our office may be low and our income meagre, it is not the fault of our talents, and we should not feel oppressed by it.

Scholars would like to share the hut with *Hsien,'* but not to be put on a level with *T'se,* they would gladly wander about with *Po Yi'* but decline to associate with robber *Chi*. Great scholars have other ambitions than their people. Therefore their fame is not that of the world. Their bodies decay like grass and trees, but their glory shines as long as the sun and the moon send their rays. Their condition may be as poor as that of *Confucius,* provided only that their writings rank with those of *Yang Ihiung*. That is my ideal. Outward success, but a limited knowledge, a high post, but little virtue: that is the ambition of others; I would consider it a bondage.

If somebody has the luck to be heard with his advice, and lives in honour and well being, all this is gone after a hundred years like other things. Ilis name does not come down to the next generation, and not a word from his band is left in any document. He has had stores full of emoluments perhaps, in the Cf. Chap. XL.

-Hsien = Yuan Sse, a disciple of Confucius, noted for his contempt of wordly advantages. Made governor of a town, he declined his official allowance (AnalecfaVl, .',) t'huang T,tc makes him live in a mud hut. He contrasts him with T 'se, another follower of Confucius, who came driving up to his door in a fine chariot and in a white robe lined with purple. T'se = Tnan Mu Ts'e or Tse Kung, a disciple of Confucius, who became a high official, and very wealthy (vid. Chap. XXXI and XXXIII). He was a swell, just the reverse of llnen. realms of literature and virtue he leaves no riches. That is not what I prize. Vast virtue of the highest excellence, abundance of extensive knowledge, a pencil dripping with characters like rain, and an overflowing spring of words, rich talents, a wonderful erudition, generous deeds, and a noble mind, with such qualities a man's body may belong to one generation, his name will be transmitted for a thousand years. That seems extraordinary and desirable to me. Wang Ch'ung is from a simple family, in which he stands quite alone. A caviller might say:—

"Your ancestors have not left you a treasure of pure virtue, nor a collection of literary works. You may yourself write the most brilliant essays, you have no basis to stand upon, and therefore no claim to our admiration."

"When a force bursts upon us quite suddenly, not by degrees, we call it a phenomenon. When a creature is born from quite dissimilar parents, we call it a wonder. When something quite unusual appears all at once, it is regarded as a supernatural appearance, and when something different from anything else quite abruptly comes forth, it is termed a miracle."

"Who are your ancestors? Their names have not been recorded in former times. You did not spring from a learned family, whose members have already walked the path of literature, and you write disquisitions of several thousand or ten thousand sentences. This must be considered a supernatural phenomenon. How could we appreciate such writings, or think them able productions?"

I beg to reply that a bird without a pedigree is a phoenix, an animal without a family, a unicorn, a man without an ancestry, a sage, and a thing without a peer, a jewel. And so it is with men of great talents, who are browbeaten and viewed with disfavour by their age. Scholars of worth appear single, and precious things grow solitary. How could literature be inherited? If a man could learn to become a sage, then the water of the Feng river would have a source, and auspicious grain an old stem.

The Chinese are in awe of, but do not like wonders, miracles, monsters, in short all that is against the regular course of nature. So they are prejudiced against Wang Ch'ung, because he is a homo novus. Not being a descendant from a literary or a noble family, he should not attempt to rise above the average of his fellow-citizens. The source of the Feng, an affluent of the Wei in Shensi is well known. I presume that for "Feng river" yC ought to read " Wine Spring" jS The phonetic element for Feng and Li "Wine" is very similar, and the Wine Springs are often mentioned as auspicious omens in connection with phoenixes, unicorns, and auspicious grain.

When a remarkable scholar appears and puts forward his noble doctrines, he does not fall under the general rule, and his capacity cannot be measured by the bushel. Therefore events which seldom happen are recorded on tablets and books, and rare things engraved on bronze vases. The Five Emperors did not rise in one generation, and Yi Yin and T'ai Kung Wang2 did not issue from one family. There was a distance of thousand Li between them, and one lived several hundred years after the other. When scholars of note quietly develop their marvellous faculties, they do not become famous as descendants of noble lines.

The calf of a black cow may be brown, this does not affect the nature of the animal. The ancestors of a scholar may be coarse, provided that he himself is pure, it has no influence upon his character. K'un was wicked, and Yil a sage, Sou was perverse, and Shun divine. Po Niu was visited with a horrible disease, and Chung Kung was clean and strong. Yen Lu was vulgar and mean, and Yen IIui outvied all his companions. Confucius and Mi Ti had stupid ancestors, and they themselves were sages. The Yang family had not been successful, when Yang Tse YOn rose like a star, and the house of Huan had been tolerably well off, until Ibum Chiin Shan took his brilliant flight. A man must have been imbued with more than the ordinary dose of the original fluid to become an able writer.

—

In the third year of Yuan-ho, Wang Ch ung emigrated to Tanyang, Chiu-chiang, and Lu-chiang in the province of Yang-chou, and was appointed sub-prefect. His abilities were small, and his office Minister of T'ang, the founder of the Shang dynasty.

Cf. p. 78. Yu's father. Ku Sou, Shun's father. A disciple of Confuciax, who suffered from leprosy (cf. Chap. XXXIII). Another disciple of Confucius, a relation of Po Niu, both belonging to the Jan clan. Yen Hut's father. Cf. p. 39 and Chap. XXXVII. 86a.d. Under the Han a circuit comprising parts of Kiangsu and Anhui. A circuit in Anhui. Another circuit in Anhui. A very large province under the Han dynasty, comprising nearly the whole territory of the modern provinces of Kiang.su, Anhui, Kiang-i, Fukien, and Chekiang.

Lun-Heng. 6 was important. His chief duties were in connection with official correspondence. All plans of writing anything he had given up for many years. In the second year of Chang-Iio, his business in the province ceased. He lived at home, and gradually advanced in age, till he reached about seventy years. Then he gave up his official carriage, and his official career was definitely closed. He could not help it. I He had many annoyances, and his body felt the infirmities of age. His hair grew white, his teeth fell out, he became older from day to day, and his comrades dispersed. He had nothing to rely upon, was too poor to nurse himself, and had no joy left. But time went slowly on, the *kthig* and *hsing* years2 came to an end, but though he was afraid that his death was near at hand, he was still full of silly ideas. Then he wrote a boob on *Macrobiotics3* in sixteen chapters.

To keep himself alive, he cherished the vital fluid. As a stimulant for the appetite he used wine. Closing eyes and ears against external influences, he spared his energy as a means of selfprotection. Using medicines he kept up his forces, and by following this method he hoped to prolong his days. For a while he did not age, but when it was too late, there was no return.

This book was left as a guide to posterity. But the duration of human life is limited. Men like animals live for a while and die. We can only remember the years gone by, who can order them to stand still? We must go down to the yellow sources, and become earth and ashes. From *Huang Ti* and *T ang* down to the *Ch in* and *Han* many have been guided by the holy doctrine and have found the truth by their genius, just like a scales and bright like a mirror, yet young and old they have lived and died, of old and now all have been included. Life cannot be prolonged, alas!

88a.d. The cyclical years *krng-yin:* 90 A.d. and *hsing-mao:* 91 A.d.

Yang hsmg shu.

CHAPTER H.

Replies in Self-Defense *(Tui-tso).*

Some one might put the following question: The worthies and sages were not born for nothing; decidedly their minds were required. How is it that from *Confucius* and *Mi Ti* down to *Hsiln Tse* and *Mencius* they all acted as teachers and left their works to posterity?

Our reply is that the sages wrote the Classics, and the worthies composed their records. They rectified the depraved customs, and enjoined upon the people to revert to truth and sincerity. The thirteen thousand chapters of the Six Departments of literature increased the good and diminished the evil, sometimes restricting, sometimes expanding, and urging on the stragglers, with a view to leading them back from their by-paths into the right way.

Confucius wrote the *Ch'un-ch in* in consequence of the depravity of the people of *Chou.* He, therefore, established the smallest merit, and blamed the slightest wrong; he removed every disorder, and re-established propriety. The ways of men as well as those of the sovereign were well ordered by him. To check extravagant and mean practices one must take every precaution, and use every means. When a dyke breaks, and no measures are taken, there will be a disastrous inundation. When a net opens, and is not shut again, the animals caught in it are lost. Had the ways of *Chou* not degenerated, the people would not have been uncultured, and had the people not been uncultured, the *Ch'un-ch'iu* would not have been written.

If the doctrines of *Yang Chu* and *Mi Ti* had not perverted the traditions, the records of *Mencius* would not have been published. Had the *Han* State not been small and weak, and its system of government corrupt, *Han Fei Tse's* book would not have appeared. Had *Kao Tsu* not contested that the conquerors of The philosopher *Hmn Tse: Sun Ch'ing,* cf. Chap. XXXII. Vid. Chap. XXXVII and the Catalogue of Literature, *Han-shu* chap. 30. The philosophers of egoism and altruism, both combated by *Menciu.* The philosopher *Han Fei Te* was the son of a Duke of the *Han* State in *Shawn.* empires had not alighted from their horses nor changed their martial habits, *Lu Chin* would not have written his memorials. If the truth had not been lost everywhere, and scientific researches not been in a state of great confusion, the discussions of *Huan Tan* would not have come forth.

Ergo, when worthies and sages write something, they do not do so for nothing, but have their good reasons. Thus their writings are by no means purposeless, but conducive to reforms, and their reforms to re-establish the right principles.

Accordingly the *Han* created the censorate to review books and examine their contents. *Tung Chung Shu* wrote a book on magical arts, in which he spoke much about calamitous events as being caused by the faults of the government. When the book was complete, and the text revised, it was presented to the Imperial Court of the *Han. Chu Fu Yen* from jealousy slandered the book in a memorial to the throne. The emperor handed *Tung Chung Shu* over to the tribunal, and the judges declared that he was very stupid, and deserved to die, but the emperor pardoned him. *Hsiao Wu Ti* did not punish *Tung Chung Shu* for his remarks on calamities, on the contrary, he honoured him. How much more would he have done so for *Tung Chung Shu's* inoffensive utterances, for his researches into the nature of the fundamental principles and his collection of old and true sayings?

As long as a wise man holds an official position in this world, he is perfectly loyal to his sovereign, and propagates his reforms to enlighten the government. When he has retired, he still teaches and criticises to rouse the simple-minded who have gone astray. They cannot find their way back to the right path, their principles are shallow, and their doings wrong. Unless we scholars hurry to their rescue, they come to perdition, and do not awake from their slumber. This has prompted me to write the *hun-hing.* An allusion to an event in the life of *Lu* CMa, narrated in his biography, *Shi-chi* chap. 97 p. 7. When *Lu Chia* had returned from his successful mission to the King of *Yueh,* whom he induced to acknowledge the suzerainty of the *Han, Kao Tsu* conferred a high rank upon him. Subsequently, when relating his adventures, *Lu Chia* would always refer to poetry and history. The emperor displeased with these utterances, told him that he had won his laurels on horseback, why must he make such a fuss about literature. Then *Lu Chia* showed him, how former conquerors had lost the empire again, if they had not consolidated their power by the arts of peace. This conversation with the emperor lead to the composition of a series of memorials, in which *La Chia* developed his ideas about government. This collection of memorials received the title " New Words ", *Hsin-gii,* cf. Chap. XXXVII. ; In a great many books reality has no place left: falsehood and immorality triumph over truth aud virtue. Therefore, unless such lies be censured, specious arguments cannot be suppressed, and, as long as they spread, truth does not reign. For this reason the *Lun-hing* weighs the words, whether they be light or heavy, and holds up a balance for truth and falsehood. It does not trouble about polishing the phrases and embellishing the style, or consider this of great importance.

It has its *raison d'etre* in the innate human weakness. Consequently it criticises the common people most vigorously. By nature these people are very prone to strange words and to the use of falsehoods. Why? Because simple truisms do not appeal to the imagination, whereas elegant inventions puzzle the hearers, and impress their minds. Therefore, men of genius, who are fond of discussions, will magnify and exaggerate the truth, and use flowery language. Masters of style, they simply invent things, and tell stories, which never happened. Their hearers believe in them, and are never tired of repeating them. Their readers take these stories for facts, and one transmits them to the other in an unbroken chain so, that at last the words are engraved on bamboo and silk. Being repeated over and over again, these stories impose even upon the wise. May be that even His Majesty honours such a man as a teacher, and spreads his forgeries, and that magistrates and wearers of red girdle pendants all read these inventions.

He who knows how to discriminate between truth and falsehood, must feel a pang at it; why should he not speak? *Mencius* was grieved that the discussions of *Yang Chu* and *Me Ti* did great harm to the cause of Confucianism, therefore he used plain and straightforward language to recommend what was

right, and to reject what was wrong. People fancied that he was a controversialist, but *Mencius* replied, "How should I be a controversialist? I cannot do otherwise."

Now I also cannot do otherwise. Lies and folly appear in the garb of truth, veracity and sincerity are superseded by imposture. People are in a state of apathy, right and wrong are not determined, purple and vermilion confounded, and tiles mixed up with jade-stones. As regards my feelings, how could my heart endure such a state? The lackey in *Wei* riding the outer horse Princes and nobles.

Mencius Bk. III, Pt. II, chap. IX, 1. Vermilion is regarded as a primary colour, and much liked, purple as secondary, and not much esteemed. transgressed his functions, crying out for the carriage. His sympathy carried him away, for he was apprehending a danger for his prince. Critics commiserate the world, and feel sorry for its deceptions, a sentiment similar to that of the outrider in *Wei* A sorrowful mind and a melancholy spirit disturb the tranquil fluid in our breast, which tells upon our years, shortens our span, and is not beneficial to our life. It is a greater misfortune than that suffered by *Yen Hui,* and against the rules of *Huang Ti* and *Lao Tse,* and nothing which men like to do. But there was no help, therefore I wrote the *Lun-heng.* Its style is indifferent, but the meaning all right, the diction bad, but the feeling good. The *Cheng-wu'''* treats of the system of government; all the chapters of the *Lung-lwng* may be read by ordinary people, for it is like writings of other scholars.

As for the Nine Inventions and the Three Exaggerations, and the essays on Death and on Ghosts, the world has long been led astray by the errors exposed therein, and people did not become aware of it.

When a ruler goes wrong, representations must be addressed to the highest place, when the citizens are blindfold, one speaks to them. If this be of effect, their leader will learn also. 1 fervently desire to rouse the misguided minds, and to teach them, how to tell the full

from the hollow. As soon as the difference of reality and emptiness is fully understood, specious arguments will be discarded, and then the progress made in true and real knowledge will daily increase.

Some say that the sages create, whereas the worthies relate, and that, if worthies create, it is wrong. The *Lunheng* and the *Ching-utu* are creations, they think. These works are neither creations nor relations. The Five Classics can be regarded as creations. The History of the Grand Annalist, the Introduction of *Liu Tse Ching,* and the Records of *Pan Shu Pi* may be called Cf. p. 154. The favourite disciple of *Couf'ucim,* who died very young, cf. Chap. XXXIII. Another of *Wang Ch'ung's* works, which has been lost.

4 *Ltm-heng* N. 16-24, N. 25-27, N. 62 and 65 (cf. p. 48 seq. and p. 57 seq.). The *Shi-chi.*

The *Hsin-fmi. Pan sau P'i* — *Pan Piao,* the father of the historian *Pan Ku.* He also was devoted to the study of history, and intended to continue the *Shi-chi,* which was finally done by his sou. relations, and the *"New Reflections"* of *lh-tan Clitin Shun* and the *"Ci-itiecd Reflections "* of *Tsou Po Chi,* discussions. Now the *Luniting* and the *Chfotg-wu* are like the two Reflections of *Lhtan Chilli Shan* and *Tsou Po Chi,* and not what they call creations.

To produce something new that did not exist in the past, as *T'sang Hsieh* invented writing and *I lsi Chung,* chariots, is creating. The *Yi-king* says of *Fu Hsi* that he created the eight diagrams. They did not exist before, and *Fu Hsi* made them,6 hence the term creating is used. *Wen Wang* evolved these eight pictures, and brought their number up to sixty-four, which is called amplifying. To say that the composition of the *Lun-hing* is similar to that of the sixty-four figures is not correct either. In regard to the sixty-four diagrams, these figures were increased by au amplification of their forms, and their number was thus augmented. Now in the *Lun-hing* the current literature is taken up with the object of defining right and wrong and distinguishing between truth and falsehood. It is not an original production of something that did not exist previously. The Confucianists take the sayings of former teachers and criticise them, as clerks subject the decisions of the lord chief-justice to a new examination. If the term creating be applied to the *Lun-hing,* would the same word be used of the Confucianists and the clerks?

In their reports to the throne and their memorials the memorialists use to propose useful measures. There is always the desire to help the government. Now the creators of classical works are like those memorialists. Their words proceed from the innermost heart, and it is their hand which reduces them to writing. Both cases are identical. In regard to those who address the emperor one speaks of memorialising, whereas for those records another word has been adopted *viz.* writing.

During the first years of *Chien-cUu,* there was a great dearth in *Chung-chou.* The people from *Yin-chuan* and *Ju-nan* had to Cf. Chap. XXXVII.

Chien-lun. Cf. Chap. XXXVII. A mythical personage. Another legendary person, who is said to have been a descendant of *Huang Ti* and director of chariots under *Yii.* Vid. Chap. XXXVI, where *Wang Ch'ung* maintains that *Fu Hsi* did not make the diagrams, but received them in a supernatural way. The first year of the emperor *Chang Ti: 76* A.d. An old name for *Honan.*

A circuit in *Anhvi.*

A place in *Honan.* leave their homes, and were scattered in all directions. His Holy Majesty felt very much distressed, and many edicts were issued. The writer of the *Lun-hing* presented a report to the prefect, urging that all dissipations and extravagancies should be prohibited in order to provide for the time of need. His suggestions were not accepted however. He went home and entitled the draft of his report "Provisions for Times of Want."

When the grain is used for the destillation of wine, robbery is rampant, and as long as there is much drunkeness, robberies never cease. In a memorial sent to the prefect the writer proposed that the use of spirits should be interdicted,

and afterwards gave to this report the name " Prohibition of Spirits." From this it may be seen that the writing of the classical authors is like that of memorialists. Those reports are regarded as independent creations presented to the emperor. Reports and memorials to the throne are always creations.

In the *Ch'ing* of *Chin,* the *T ao-um* of *Ch'u,'* and the *Ch unth iu* of *Lu* persons and things are all different. As regards the diagrams *ch'ien* and *k'un* of the *Yiking,* the *guan* of the *Cli un-ch iu* and the mystical principle of *Yang Tse Yiin,* they use diverse terms for divination and time periods. From this we may infer that the *Lun-heng* and the *Ching-wu* have the same aim as the memorials of *T'ang Lin* and the essays of *Ku Yung.*

The *Han* time is very rich in literary talents, and the number of essays is especially large. *Yang Ch eng Tse Chang* produced the *Ydeit-ching* and *Yang Tse Y&n* the *T ai-hsiiau-ching.* These two books were current in the court and read in the side-halls. The impression they caused was enormous, they were not relations but creations, and people doubted, whether the ingenious authors were not sages. The court found nothing to blame in them. Now, fancy the *Lunhing* with its minute discussions and thorough arguments, intended to explain the common errors and elucidate the right and wrong principles so, that future generations can clearly see the difference between truth and falsehood! Lest all this be lost, I have committed it to the writing tablets: remarks on chapters and passages of the classics of our ancestors, and on queer sayings of former A report for the emperor, which *Wang Ch'ung,* not being of sufficiently high rank, could not present directly.

The official chronicles of these two States. (Of. Chap. XXXVI.) 8 A term employed for the first year of a sovereign, also denoting the original fluid of nature. 4 The "Classic of Music." masters. I offer critical remarks and reject many common traditions. The delusion caused by such traditions and the spread of so many lying books give endless pain to the knowing. *Confucius* said:— "When a man is touched by poetry, he

cannot remain silent. When I am moved, I cannot keep quiet, but must speak."

Jade is being confounded with stones. People cannot distinguish it, as for instance the inspector of works in *Ch'u* took jade for a stone, and suddenly ordered *Pien Ho* to have his foot cut off. Right is being turned into wrong, and falsehood into truth. How is it possible not to speak of it?

As the common traditions are full of exaggerations, so the common books teem with falsehoods. *Tsou Yen e. g.* pretends that our world is one continent, and that beyond the four seas there are still nine other continents like our world. *Huai Nan Tse.* says in his book that, when *Kung Kung,* fighting for the throne with *Oman Hsil,* was not victorious, he ran against Mount *Pu-chou* in his wrath so, that he caused the "Pillar of Heaven" to break, and the confines of the earth to be smashed. In *Yao's* time ten suns appeared simultaneously. *Yao* shot an arrow at nine of them. During the battle fought by the Duke of *Lu-gang* the sun went down. Swinging his spear he beckoned to the sun, when he came back. There are a great many books and records of a similar nature in the world. Truth and reality are drowned in a flood of inventions and fabrications. Can we remain silent, when our heart swells to overflowing, and the pencil trembles in our hand?

Discussing a question we must examine into it with our mind, and demonstrate it by facts, and, if there be any inventions, proofs must be given. As the history of the Grand. Annalist testifies, *Hsu Yu* did not hide, nor did *Tan,* the crown-prince of *Yen,* cause the sun to revert to the meridian. Nobody can read these passages without applauding.

Cf. p. 113.

China.

Cf. Chap. XIX.

Vid. Chap. XIX.

Cf. Chap. XX.

A city in *Honan.* We learn from the *Lnn-hi'ng* V, 6v. *(Kan-ktii)* that this battle was foiight by Duke *Hsiang* of *Ln* against *Han.* This prince reigned from 572 to 541. *Huai San Tie* VI, lv., how-

ever, from whom this passage is quoted, speaks of the Duke of *Ln-gang* and the commentary remarks that this was a grandson of King *Ping* of *Cit'u* (52(S-515), called *Lu-ganj Wen Te* in the *Kuogii*.
'A legendary hermit of *l ao's* time. (Cf. Chap. XXXV.)

I composed the *Cheng-ten* for the purpose of showing to the incumbents of the prefectures and the district magistrates, what is of paramount importance in the administration, and with a view to induce all people to reform and gratefully acknowledge the kindness of the government. The nine chapters of the *Lun-hing* on Inventions and the three chapters on Exaggerations are intended to impress upon people that they must strive for truthfulness, and the chapters on Death and Ghosts shall induce them to give their dead a simple burial.

Confucius avoided all pomp, but people were very extravagant in burying the dead and decorating the coffin. *Liu Tse Cheng* was in favour of simple funerals, but people would put costly things into the graves, and spare no money. *Kuang Wu ft* regarded straw carriages and reed horses as sufficiently good objects for the sacrificial worship of the dead. Why do the common books and traditions not mention this? The belief in the talk on death has defiled them.

Now I have written the essays on Death and on the False Reports about the Dead to show that the deceased have no consciousness, and cannot become ghosts, hopiug that, as soon as my readers have grasped this, they will restrain the extravagance of the burials, and become more economical. Such would be the advantage derived from the *Lun-heng*. Provided that my words have this effect, what would it matter, if my work were a creation?

The writing of *Ts'ang Hsieh* is universally used to record things, the carriages of *Hsi Chung* for locomotion, the clothes of *Po Yil* as a protection against heat and cold, and the tiled houses of *ChieU* to keep off wind and rain. If, irrespective of their usefulness or obnoxiousness, suxh things be solely found fault with for being innovations, then men like *Tsang Hsieh* would have to be condemned, and the fifteen dynasties at the beginning of history all be blameworthy. Provided that a thing be useful, there is no harm, even if it should be an innovation, and if there be no harm, what can be amiss?

In ancient times great public entertainments were given by imperial order with the object of seeing the customs and learning Cf. pp. 57 and 58.
Lun-hiing N. 62 and 63. The tyrant *Chieh* is reported to have built the first brick houses *(Tiwang-shi-ch!).* The ten dynasties of the fabulous age of Chinese history together with the Five Emperors and their houses, whom Chinese fancy has credited with the invention of all the fundamental institutions of civilisation, such as house building, dress making, writing, etc the feelings of the people. Then the Odes originated among the people. The holy emperors might have said, "Ye, people, how dare you produce such novel things?," and have thrown them into prison, and destroyed their Odes. This was not done, and the Odes were thus handed down. Now the *Lun-hing* and the *Chengtvu* are like the Odes. I trust that they will not be condemned, before they have been perused. This is the origin of the *Lun-heng*. The reason why people so often take exception to new productions is that they often contain so many unfounded assertions and disparaging remarks on others. The *Lun-heng* aims at truth and dislikes all wild speculations. The chapters entitled: — *CKi-shih, Hsilan Han, Hui kuo,* and *Yen-fu* are full of praise and well-deserved applause, and not disparaging at all. Such a creation might well escape reproach.
The Odes of the *Shi-king.*
"Equality of the ages."
» Contained in Books XVIII and XIX, N. 56-59.
Wang Ch'ung eulogises the emperors of his own time, and places them on a level with the model sovereigns of antiquity.
CHAPTER HI.
Spontaneity *(Tse-jan).*
By the fusion of the fluids of Heaven and Earth all things of the world are produced spontaneously, just as by the mixture of the fluids of husband and wife children are born spontaneously. Among the things thus produced, creatures with blood in their veins are sensitive of hunger and cold. Seeing that grain can be eaten, they use it as food, and discovering that silk and hemp can be worn, they take it as raiment. Some people are of opinion that Heaven produces grain for the purpose of feeding mankind, and silk and hemp to cloth them. That would be tantamount to making Heaven the fanner of man or his mulberry girl, it would not be in accordance with spontaneity, therefore this opinion is very questionable and unacceptable.

Reasoning on Taoist principles we find that Heaven emits its fluid everywhere. Among the many things of this world grain dispels hunger, and silk and hemp protect from cold. For that reason man eats grain, and wears silk and hemp. That Heaven does not produce grain, silk, and hemp purposely, in order to feed and cloth mankind, follows from the fact that by calamitous changes it does not intend to reprove man. Things are produced spontaneously, and man wears and eats them; the fluid changes spontaneously, and man is frightened by it, for the usual theory is disheartening. Where would be spontaneity, if the heavenly signs were intentional, and where inaction?

Why must we assume that Heaven acts spontaneously? Because it has neither mouth nor eyes. Activity is connected with the mouth and the eyes: the mouth wishes to eat, and the eyes to see. These desires within manifest themselves without. That the mouth and the eyes are craving for something, which is considered an advantage, is due to those desires. Now, provided that the mouth and the eye do not affect things, there is nothing which they might long for, why should there be activity then?
Who feeds the silkworms. -Inaction does not mean motionlessuess, but spontaneous action without any aim or purpose. It is more or less mechanical, and not inspired by a conscious spirit.
How do we know that Heaven possesses neither mouth nor eyes? From Earth.

The body of the Earth is formed of earth, and earth has neither mouth nor eyes. Heaven and Earth are like husband and wife. Since the body of the Earth is not provided with a mouth or eyes, we know that Heaven has no mouth or eyes neither. Supposing that Heaven has a body, then it must be like that of the Earth, and should it be air only, this air would be like clouds and fog. How can a cloudy or nebular substance have a mouth or an eye?

Some one might argue that every movement is originally inaction. There is desire provoking the movement, and, as soon as there is motion, there is action. The movements of Heaven are similar to those of man, how could they be inactive? I reply that, when Heaven moves, it emits its fluid. Its body moves, the fluid comes forth, and things are produced. When man moves his fluid, his body moves, his fluid then comes forth, and a child is produced. Man emitting his fluid does not intend to beget a child, yet the fluid being emitted, the, child is born of itself. When Heaven is moving, it does not desire to produce things thereby, but things are produced of their own accord. That is spontaneity. Letting out its fluid it does not desire to create things, but things are created of themselves. That is inaction.

But how is the fluid of Heaven, which we credit with spontaneity and inaction? It is placid, tranquil, desireless, inactive, and unbusied. *Lao Tse* acquired long life by it. He obtained it from Heaven. If Heaven did not possess this fluid, how could *Lao Tse* have obtained this nature? For it does not happen that the disciples alone speak of something, which their master never mentioned.

Perhaps this nature appeared again in Duke *Huon,* who was wont to say, "Let *Kuan Chung* know." His attendants replied, "is it so easy to rule, if *Kuan Chung* is always the first and second word?" The duke rejoined, "Before I had secured the services of *Kuan Chung,* I was in the greatest difficulties, now, after I have got him, I find everything easy." When Duke *Huan* had taken *Kuan Chung* into his service, he left

the affairs to him, entrusted him with the administration, and did not trouble any more about it. Should high Heaven, which in its exalted virtue confers the government upon an emperor, reprove man, its virtue would be inferior to that of

Duke *Huan,* and the conduct of a feudatory prince surpass that of great Heaven.

Somebody might object that Duke *Huan* knew *Kuan Chung* to be a wise man, and therefore appointed him, and that but for *Kuan Chung* he would also have given vent to his displeasure. Meeting with men like *Y.ao* and *Shun* Heaven would certainly not have reprimanded people either.

I beg to reply, that, if Heaven can reprimand, it might as well purposely appoint a wise prince, select a genius like *Yno* and *Shun,* confer the imperial dignity upon him, and leave the affairs of the empire to him without taking further notice of them. Now it is different. Heaven creates very inferior princes, who have no principles, and neglect virtue, and therefore has to reprove them every now and then. Would it not be afraid of the trouble?

Ts ao Tsan, a minister of the *Han,* was given to wine, songs, and music, and did not care about government. When his son remonstrated with him, he gave him two hundred blows with the bamboo. At that period there was no insurrection in the empire. In *Huai-yang* people coined counterfeit money, and the officials were powerless to check the abuse. *Chi Yen* was prefect then. He did not destroy a single furnace, or punish a single individual. Quite indifferent, he was comfortably reclining on his couch, and the conditions of *Huai-yang* became well ordered again. *Tsao Tsan* behaved himself, as though he were not a minister, and *Chi Yen* administered his prefecture, as if nobody were living in it. Albeit yet the empire of the *Han* had no troubles, and in *Huai-yang* the punishments could be discontinued. So perfect was the virtue of *Tsao Tsan,* and so imposing *Chi Yen's* dignity. The majesty of Heaven and its virtue are quite something else than those of *Tsao Tsan* and

Chi Yen, but to affirm that Heaven entrusts an emperor with the government, and then reproves him, would amount to nothing less than that Heaven's virtue is not as exalted as that of *Tsao Tsan,* and its majesty not as imposing as that of *Chi Yen.* One of the counsellors and supporters of *Han Kao Tsu,* died 100 B. C. On his *laisser /aire* policy vid. his biography in the *Shi-chi* chap. 54. A State in *Honan.* A minister of the emperor ꮩꮩu 77, like *T'mo T'san* a follower of the doctrine of inaction inculcated by *Lao Te,* His policy of governing consisted in letting things alone.

When *Chft Po Yil* was governing *Wei,* *Tse Kung* asked him through somebody, how he governed *Wei.* The reply was, "I govern it by not governing."—Government by not governing is inaction as a principle.

Some opponent might say that as a sequel of universal peace a plan came forth from the *Yellow River,* and a scroll from the Lo. Without drawing no plan can be made, and without action nothing is completed. The fact that Heaven and Earth produced the plan and the scroll shows that they are active, they think.—When *Chang Liang* was walking on the banks of the river *Sse,* he met the "Yellow Stone Genius," who gave him the "minister's book." Heaven was supporting the *Han* and destroying the *Ch'in,* therefore he ordered a spiritual stone to change into a ghost. That a book was handed to somebody is again considered a proof of activity.

I am of opinion that all this was spontaneous, for how could Heaven take a brush and ink, and draw the plan, or write the scroll? The principle of Heaven is spontaneity, consequently the plan and the book must have been produced of themselves.' *Tang Shu Yil* of *Chin* and *Ch'hg Chi Yo* of *Lm* had a character in their hands, when they were born, therefore one was called *Yil,* the other *Yo.* When *Ch ung Tse* of *Sung* was born, the characters *"Duchess of Lu"* were written on her palm. These letters must have been written, while the three persons were still in their mother's womb. If we say that Heaven wrote them,.while they were in their mother's womb, did

Heaven perhaps send a spirit with a style, a brush, and ink to engrave and write the characters A disciple of *Confitcius,* cf. Chap. XXXIII. The Taoists also claim him as one of theirs. *Chuang Tse,* chap. XXV, 33, informs ns that "when *Chi i Po Yd* reached his sixtieth year, he changed his opinions. What he had previously regarded as right, he now came to regard as wrong," i. e. from a Confucianist he became a Taoist, and as such upheld the principle of quietism.

Vid. Chap. XXII. *Huang Shih,* cf. Chap. XXX. From this mysterious book *Chang Liang* is believed to have derived his plans consolidating the power of the *Han* dynasty. *T ang Shu,* the younger prince of *T'ang,* was a son of King Wu *Wang* and younger brother of King *Ch'cng* (1115-1078). He became the founder of the princely house of *Chin.* Cf. *Shi-chi* chap. 39 p. Iv where the character of his palm is likewise referred to. *Ch'eng Chi* was a younger son of Duke *Huan* of *Lu* (711-693). We read in the *Shi-chi* chap. 33 p. 13v the story of his having been born with the character *Yo* in his hand. A daughter of Duke Wu of *Sung* (765-747 B.c.) who became married to Duke *Hui* of *Lu.* Cf. Chap. XXJJ. on their bodies? The spontaneity of these processes seems dubious, and is difficult to understand. Externally there seemed to be activity, but as a matter of fact, there was spontaneity internally. Thus the Grand Annalist recording the story of the yellow stone, has his doubts, but cannot find the truth. Viscount *Chien* of *C/iao* had a dream that he was ascending to heaven. There he saw a lad by the side of the Ruler of Heaven. When he went out subsequently, he perceived a young man in the street, who was the one whom he had seen previously in his dream by the side of the Ruler of Heaven. This must be regarded as a lucky augury the future flourishing of the *Chao* State, as the transmission of of the book by the "yellow stone" was a sign of the rise of the *Han* dynasty. That the supernatural fluid becomes a ghost, and that the ghost is shaped like a man, is spontaneous, and not the work of anybody. When plants

and trees grow, their flowers and leaves are onion green and have crooked and broken veins like ornaments If Heaven is credited with having written the above mentioned characters, does it make these flowers and leaves also? In the State of *Sung* a man carved a mulberry-leaf of wood, and it took him three years to complete it. *Confucius* said "If the Earth required three years to complete one leaf, few plants would have leaves." According to this dictum of *Confucius* the leaves of plants grow spontaneously, and for that reason they can grow simultaneously. If Heaven made them, their growth would be as much delayed as the carving of the mulberry-leaf by the man of the *Sung* State.

Let us look at the hair and feathers of animals and birds, and their various colours. Can they all have been made? If so, animals and birds would never be quite finished. In spring we see the plants growing, and in autumn we see them full-grown. Can Heaven and Earth have done this, or do things grow spontaneously? If we may say that Heaven and Earth have done it, they must have used hands for the purpose. Do Heaven and Earth possess many thousand or many ten thousand hands to produce thousands and ten thousands of things at the same time? In his remarks added to the biography of *Chang Liang (Shi-chi* chap. 55 p. 13) *Ste Ma Ch'ien* says that many scholars deny the existence of ghosts, but that the story of the yellow stone is very strange. Cf. Chap. XVII. We find this same story in *Lieh Tse* VIII, 2 and in *Ihiai Kan T«e* XX, 2, but both authors ascribe the words put in the mouth of *Confuciax* here *to Lieh Tse. Hnai Kan Tse* makes the mulberry-leaf to be made of ivory, *Lieh Tse,* of jade. The things between Heaven and Earth are like a child in his mother's womb. After ten months pregnancy the mother gives birth to the child. Are his nose, his mouth, his ears, his hair, his eyes, his skin with down, the arteries, the fat, the bones, the joints, the uails, and the teeth grown of themselves in the womb, or has the mother made them?

Why is a dummy never called a man?

Because it has a nose, a mouth, ears, and eyes, but not a spontaneous nature. *Wu ft* was very fond of his consort *Wang.* When she had died, he pondered, whether he could not see her figure again. The Taoists made an artificial figure of the lady. When it was ready, it passed through the palace gate. *Wu ft* greatly alarmed rose to meet her, but, all of a sudden, she was not seen any more. Since it was not a real, spontaneous being, but a semblance, artificially made by jugglers, it became diffuse at first sight, dispersed, and vanished. Everything that has been made does not last long, like the image of the empress, which appeared only for a short while.

The Taoist school argues on spontaneity, but it does not know how to substantiate its cause by evidence. Therefore their theory of spontaneity has not yet found credence. However, in spite of spontaneity there may be activity for a while in support of it. Ploughing, tilling, weeding, and sowing in Spring are human actions. But as soon as the grain has entered the soil, it begins growing by day and night. Man can do nothing for it, or if he does, he spoils the thing.

A man of *Sung* was sorry that his sprouts were not high enough, therefore he pulled them out, but, on the following day, they were dry, and died. He who wishes to do what is spontaneous, is on a par with this man of *Sung.*

The following question may be raised:—" Man is born from Heaven and Earth. Since Heaven and Earth are inactive, man who has received the fluid of Heaven, ought to be inactive likewise, wherefore does he act nevertheless?"

For the following reason. A man with the highest, purest, and fullest virtue has been endowed with a large quantity of the heavenly fluid, therefore he can follow the example of Heaven, and be spontaneous and inactive like it. He who has received but a small quota of the ffuid, does not live in accordance with righteousness and virtue, and does not resemble Heaven and Earth. The apparition of the lady was evoked by the court magician *Shao Wtng* in 121

B.c. (Cf. *Shi-cM* chap. 28 p. 23.)
Luu-Heng. 7

Hence he is called unlike, which means that he does not resemble Heaven and Earth. Not resembling Heaven and Earth he cannot be accounted a wise man or a sage. Therefore he is active.

Heaven and Earth are the furnace, and the creating is the melting process. How can all be wise, since the fluid of which they are formed is not the same? *Huang* and *Lao* were truly wise. *Huang* is *Huang Ti,* and *Lao* is *Lao Tse. Huang* and *Lao's* conduct was such, that their bodies were in a state of quietude and indifference. Their government consisted in inaction. They took care of their persons, and behaved with reverence, hence *Yin* and *Yang* were in harmony. They did not long for action, and things were produced of themselves; they did not think of creating anything, and thiugs were completed spontaneously.

The *Yi-king* says that *Huang Ti, Yao,* and *Shun* let their robes fall, and the empire was governed. That they let their. robes fall means that their robes fell down, and that they folded their arms, doing nothing. *Confucius* said, "Grand indeed was *Yao* as a sovereign! Heaven alone is great, and *Yao* alone emulated it!" and, "How imposing was the way in which *Shun* and *Yii* swayed the empire, but did not much care for it." The Duke of *Chou* makes the remark that the supreme ruler enjoyed his ease. By the supreme ruler *Shun* and *Yi l* are meant. *Shun* and *Yii* took over the peaceful government, which thev continued, appointing wise men and men of talent. They respected themselves, and did no work themselves, and the empire was governed. *Shun* and *Yii* received the peaceful government from *Yao. Yao* imitated Heaven; he did not do meritorious deeds or strive for a name, and reforms, for which nothing was done, were completed of themselves. Hence it was said, "Excellent indeed," but the people did not find the right name for it. Those aged 50 years were beating clods of earth together on their land, but they did not understand *Yao's* virtue, because the reforms were spontaneous.

The *Yi-king* says, "The great man

equals Heaven and Earth in virtue." *Huang Ti, Yao,* and *Shun* were such great men. Their *Yi-king, Chi-ts'e* II *(Legge's* t-ransl. p. 383).
Analects VIII, 19.
Analects VUL 18.
4 *Shu-king, To-shih,* Pt.V, Bk. XIV, 5 *(Legge* Vol. IH, Pt. II, p. 455).
All other commentators take the "supreme ruler" as a synonym for God, and I think that they are right, and that *Wang Ch'vng's* interpretation is forced for the purpose of supporting his theory. Cf. p. 128. virtue was on a level with that of Heaven and Earth, therefore x they knew inaction. The principle of Heaven is inaction. Accordingly in spring it does not do the germinating, in summer the growing, in autumn the ripening, or in winter the hiding of the seeds. When the *Yang* fluid comes forth spontaneously, plants will germinate and grow of themselves, and, when the *Yin* fluid rises, they ripen and disappear of their own accord.

When we irrigate garden land with water drawn from wells or drained from ponds, plants germinate and grow also, but, when showers of rain come down, the stalks, leaves, and roots are all abundantly soaked. Natural moisture is much more copious than artificial irrigation from wells and ponds. Thus inactive action brings the greatest results. Bv not seeking it, merit is acquired, and by not affecting it, fame is obtained. Rainshowers, merit, and fame are something great, yet Heaven and Earth do not work for them. When the fluid harmonises, rain gathers spontaneously.

The literati in speaking of the relation of husband and wife establish similarities with Heaven and Earth. For husband and wife they find similarities with Heaven and Earth, but in so far as they are unable to make use of the relation of husband and wife, when discussing the nature of Heaven and Earth, they show a regrettable lack of acumen.

Heaven expands above, and Earth below. When the fluid from below rises, and the fluid on high descends, all things are created in the middle. While they are growing, it is not necessary that Heaven should still care for them, just

as the father does not know the embryo, after it is in the mother's womb. Things grow spontaneously, and the child is formed of itself. Heaven and Earth, and father and mother can take no further cognisance of it. But after birth, the way of man is instruction and teaching, the way of Heaven, inaction and yielding to nature. Therefore Heaven allows the fish to swim in the rivers, and the wild beasts to roam in the mountains, following their natural propensities. It does not drive the fish up the hills, or the wild beasts into the water. Why? Because that would be an outrage upon their nature, and a complete disregard of what suits them. The people resemble fish and beasts. High virtue governs them as easily, as one fries small fish, and as Heaven and Earth would act.

Shang Yang changed the la"vs of *Ch'in* wishing to acquire extraordinary merit. He did not hear the advice of *Chao Liang,* consequently he incurred the horrible penalty of being torn asunder by carts. If the virtue be poor, and the desires many, prince and minister hate one another. The Taoists possess real virtue:—the inferiors agree with the superiors, and the superiors are at peace with their inferiors. Being genuinely ignorant, they do nothing, and there is no reason, why they should be reproved. This is what they call a well balanced government. Prince and minister forget one another in governing, the fish forget each other in the water, and so do the beasts in the forests, and men in life. That is Heaven. *Confucius* said to *Yen Yuan,* "When I deferred to you, I did not think of it, and when you deferred to me, you likewise did not think of it. " Although *Confucius* was like a prince, and *Yen Yuan* like a minister, he could not make up his mind to reprimand *Yen Yuan,* how much less would *Lao Tse* have been able to do so, if we consider him as a prince and *Win Tse* as his minister? *Lao Tse* and *Win Tse* were like Heaven and Earth.

Generous wine tastes sweet. When those who drink it, become drunk, they do not know each other. Bad wine is sour and bitter. Hosts and guests knit the brows. Now, reprimands are a proof of the badness of one's principles. To say that Heaven reprimands would be like pretending that Heaven's excellence is inferior to that of generous wine.

Ceremonies originate from a want of loyalty and good faith, and are the beginning of confusion. On that score people find fault with one another, which leads to reproof. At the time of the Three Rulers people were sitting down self-satisfied, and walking about at perfect ease. Sometimes they took themselves for horses, and sometimes for oxen. Virtuous actions were out of the question, and the people were dull and beclouded. Knowledge and wisdom did not yet make their appearance. Originally, there happened no calamities or catastrophes either, or, if they did, they were not denoted as reprimands. Why? Because at that time people were feeble-minded, and did not restrain or reproach one another.

"The fish forget each other in the rivers and lakes," says *Hum Kan T«e* II, 4r. Both were in a state of blissful forgetfulness and purposelessness. The passage is quoted from *liuai Kan Tse* XI, 5r. A Taoist philosopher, disciple of *Lao Txe*. Reprimands tell against the system by which they are required, perfect virtue pervading the universe necessitates no recriminations, for all are filled with it as with generous wine. This argument is quite Taoist.

Later generations have gradually declined:—superiors and inferiors recriminate, and calamitous events continually happen. Hence the hypothesis of reprimands has been developed. The Heaven of today is the Heaven of old, and it is not the case that the Heaven of old was benign, whereas now Heaven is harsh. The hypothesis of reprimands has been put forward at present, as a surmise made by men from their own feelings.

Declarations and oaths do not reach up to the Five Emperors, agreements and covenants to the Three Rulers, and the giving of hostages to the Five Princes. The more people's virtue declined, the more faith began to fail them. In their guile and treachery they broke treaties, and were deaf to admonitions. Treaties and admonitions being of no avail, they reproached one another, and if no change was brought about by these reproaches, they took up arms, and fought, till one was exterminated. Consequently reprimands point to a state of decay and disorder. Therefore it appears very dubious that Heaven should make reprimands.

Those who believe in reprimands, refer to human ways as a proof. Among men a sovereign reprimands his minister, and high Heaven reprimands the sovereign. It does so by means of calamitous events, they say. However, among men it also happens that the minister remonstrates with his sovereign. When Heaven reprimands an emperor by visiting him with calamities, and the latter wishes at that time to remonstrate with high Heaven, how can he do it? If they say that Heaven's virtue is so perfect, that man cannot remonstrate with it, then Heaven possessed of such virtue, ought likewise to keep quiet, and ought not to reprimand, When the sovereign of *Wan Shih* did wrong, the latter did not say a word, but at table he did not eat, which showed his perfection. An excellent man can remain silent, and august Heaven with his sublime virtue should reprimand? Heaven does not act, therefore it does not speak. The disasters, which so frequently occur, are the work of the spontaneous fluid.

Heaven and Earth cannot act, nor do they possess any knowledge. When there is a cold in the stomach, it aches. This is not caused by man, but the spontaneous working of the fluid. The space between Heaven and Earth is like that between the back and the stomach. The five leading feudal princes during the later *Chou* epoch, to wit:—Duke *Huan* of *Ch'i* D.b.c. 643, Duke *Wen* of *Chin* D.b.c. 628, Duke *Hsiang of Sung* D.b.c. 637, King *Chuang* of *Ch'u* D.b.c. 591, and Duke *Mu* of *Ch'in* D.b.c. 621. And it is likewise filled with the spontaneous fluid.

If Heaven is regarded as the author of every calamity, are all abnormities, great and small, complicated and simple, caused by Heaven also? A cow may give birth to a horse, and on a cherrytree a plum may grow. Does, according to the theory under discussion, the spirit of Heaven enter the belly of the cow to create the horse, or stick a plum upon a cherry-tree?

Lao said, "The Master said," " Having no official employment, I acquired many arts," and he said, "When I was young, my condition was low, and therefore I acquired my ability in many things, but they were mean matters." What is low in people, such as ability and skilfulness, is not practised by the great ones. How could Heaven, which is so majestic and sublime, choose to bring about catastrophes with a view to reprimanding people?

Moreover, auspicious and inauspicious events are like the flushed colour appearing on the face. Man cannot produce it, the colour comes out of itself. Heaven and Earth are like the human body, the transformation of their fluid, like the flushed colour. How can Heaven and Earth cause the sudden change of their fluid, since man cannot produce the flushed colour? The change of the ffuid is spontaneous, it appears of itself, as the colour comes out of itself. The soothsayers rely on this, when they foretell the future.

Heat and cold, reprimands, phenomenal changes, and attraction, all these four errors have already been treated. Reprimands are more contrary to the ways of Heaven than anything else, therefore I have discussed them twice, explaining where the difficulties in the way of the two antagonistic views lie. The one is in accordance with human affairs, but does not fall in with Taoism, the other agrees with Taoism, but is not in harmony with human affairs. But though opposed to the belief of the ('onfucianists, it corresponds to the ideas of *Huang Ti* and *Lao Tse. Ch'in Chang*, styled *Tse K'ai*, a disciple of *Confucius. Analects* IX, fi.

In the preceding chapters of the *Lun-hcng.* CHAPTER IV.

The Nature of Things *(Wu-shih)*.

The literati declare that Heaven and Earth produce man on purpose. This assertion is preposterous, for, when Heaven and Earth mix up their fluids, man is born as a matter of course unintentionally. In just the same manner a child is produced spontaneously, when the essences of husband and wife are harmoniously blended. At the time of such an intercourse, the cquple does not intend to beget a child. Their passionate love being roused, they unite, and out of this union a child is born. From the fact that husband and wife do not purposely beget a child one may infer that Heaven and Earth do not produce man on purpose either.

However, man is produced by Heaven and Earth just as fish in a pond, or lice on man. They grow in response to a peculiar force, each species reproducing itself. This holds good for all the things which come into being between Heaven and Earth.

It is said in books that Heaven and Earth do not create man on purpose, but that man is produced unintentionally, as a matter of course. If anybody holds this view, how can he admit that Heaven and Earth are the furnace, all things created, the copper, the *Yin* and the *Yang,* the fire, and all the transformations, the working? If the potter and the founder use fire in order to melt the copper, and to burn their ware, their doings are dictated by a certain purpose. Now, they own that Heaven and Earth create man without a purpose, that, under given circumstances, he grows spontaneously. Can it be said of the potter and founder, that they too make their ware purposeless, and that it grows naturally, and of its own accord?

If a comparison is not to the point, it cannot be called an analogy, and if words do not express the truth, the statement cannot be considered correct. It may be urged that the purport of the above simile is but to show that the heavenly fluid, with which man is imbued, is not quite uniform, as the moulds into which the liquid copper runs, and the fire applied in burning earthenware, may be different, and that it is not said that Heaven and Earth create man in the same way as potters and founders do their business.

Whenever human affairs are referred to, to explain human nature, they must be taken as a whole, which cannot be divided into different parts. When the eye tries to have a look at its own head, the head will turn, and when the hand grasps at the foot, the foot will move. Eye and head belong to the same organism, hand and foot to the same body.

The potter and founder having first prepared the clay for the vessel, require a mould to form it, which is a designed act. Burning coal in order to have a fire, they regulate the furnace or stove, which is done on purpose also. Yet not all the molten copper gets a proper shape, and the burned vessels do not invariably turn out well, for their completion is not a designed act.

Since Heaven and Earth cannot create man on purpose, the creation of all the other things and beings cannot be intentional either. The fluids of Heaven and Earth mixing, things grow naturally and spontaneously.

Tilling, weeding the ground, and sowing are designed acts, but whether the seed grows up, and ripens, or not, depends on chance, and spontaneous action. How do we know? If Heaven had produced its creatures on purpose, it ought to have taught them to love each other, and not to prey upon and destroy one another. One might object that such is the nature of the Five Elements, that when Heaven creates all things, it imbues them with the fluids of the Five Elements, and that these fight together, and destroy one another. But then Heaven ought to have filled its creatures with the fluid of one element only, and taught them mutual love, not permitting the fluids of the five elements to resort to strife and mutual destruction.

People will rejoin, that wishing to use things, one must cause them to fight and destroy each other, because thereby only can they be made into what they are intended to be. Therefore they The meaning is that, if the creation of man by Heaven and Earth be compared to the melting of copper or the burning of earthenware, these latter processes must be taken in their entirety like a body or an organism. Touching one member, one affects the whole organism. One cannot single out some constituent parts of the process, such as the moulding or the firing. Then "purpose" is comprised in the image, which thereby becomes distorted.

The completion of a work done by man on purpose, depends on conditions and circumstances over which he has not always control. Man acts with a purpose, but the forces of nature which he sets in motion, and which bring about the final result, have no purpose. The Five Elements of Chinese natural philosophy:— metal, wood, water, fire, and earth. say, Heaven uses the fluids of the Five Elements in producing all things, and man uses all these things in performing his many works. If one thing does not subdue the other, they cannot be employed together, and, without mutual struggle and annihilation, they cannot be made use of. If the metal does not hurt the wood, the wood cannot be used, and if the fire does not melt the metal, the metal cannot be made into a tool. Thus the injury done by one thing to the other turns out to be a benefit after all. If all the living creatures overpower, bite, and devour one another, it is the fluids of the Five Elements also that compel them to do so.

Ergo we are to understand that all created things must injure one another, if they are to be useful. Now tigers, wolves, serpents, snakes, wasps, and scorpions attack and hurt man. Did then Heaven design man to be made use of by those animals?

Furthermore, because the human body harbours the fluids of the Five Elements, man practises the Five Virtues, which are the outcome of the Five Elements. As long as he has the Five Organs in his bosom, those fluids are in order. If, according to this view, animals prey upon and destroy one another, because of their being endued with the fluids of the Five Elements, the human body with the Five Organs in its breast ought to be a victim of internecine. strife, and the heart of a man living a righteous life be lacerated by discord. But what proves us that there is really an antagonism of the Five Elements, and that therefore animals oppress each other?

The sign *Yin* corresponds to wood, its proper animal is the tiger. *Hsii* corresponds to earth, its animal is the dog. *Ch'ou* and *Wei* correspond to earth likewise, *Ch'ou* having as animal the ox, and *Wei* having the sheep. Wood overcomes earth, therefore the dog, the ox, and the sheep are overpowered by the tiger. *Hai* goes with water, its animal being the boar. *Sse* goes with fire, and has the serpent as animal. *Tse* means also water, its animal being the rat. *Wu* also corresponds to fire, its animal is the horse. Water overcomes fire, therefore the boar devours the serpent. Fire is quenched by water, therefore, when the horse eats the excrements of rats, its belly swells up. In the ancient, so called natural philosophy of the Chinese, a cyclical character, such as *H&ii, Ch'ou, Wei,* etc., and a certain animal are supposed to correspond to each of the five elements. From the relations between the elements one has drawn conclusions concerning their attributes. The greatest Chinese scholars have indulged in these plays, and mistaken them for natural science.

To wit the horse is hurt by the rat, because fire, the element of the horse, is quenched by water, which corresponds to the rat.

However, going more thoroughly into the question, we are confronted with the fact that not unfrequeutly it does not appear that animals overpower one another, which they ought, after this theory. *Wu* is connected with the horse, *Tse* with the rat, *Yu* with the cock, and *Mao* with the hare. Water is stronger than fire, why does the rat not drive away the horse? Metal is stronger than wood, why does the cock not eat the hare? *Hot* means the boar, *Wei* the sheep, and *Ch'ou* the ox. Earth overcomes water, wherefore do the ox and the sheep not kill the boar. *Sse* corresponds to the serpent, *Shen* to the monkey. Fire destroys metal, how is it that the serpent does not eat the monkey? The monkey is afraid of the rat, and the dog bites the monkey. The rat goes with water, and the monkey with metal. Water not being stronger than metal, why does the mon-

key fear the rat? *Hsi i* is allied to earth, *Shin* to the monkey. Earth not forcing metal, for what reason is the monkey frightened by the dog?

The East is represented by wood, its constellation is the Blue Dragon, the West by metal, its constellation is the White Tiger. The South corresponds to fire, and has as constellation the Scarlet Bird, the North is connected with water, its constellation is the Black Tortoise. Heaven by emitting the essence of these four stars produces the bodies of these four animals on earth. Of all the animals they are the first, and they are imbued with the fluids of the Five Elements in the highest degree. Now, when the dragon and the tiger meet, they do not fight, and the scarlet bird and the tortoise do each other no harm. Starting from these four famous animals, and from t hose belonging to the twelve horary characters, we find that all the other animals endued with the Five Elements, can much less be prompted to strife and discord by their natural organisation.

As all created things struggle and fight together, the animals subdue one another. When they try to tear their enemies to pieces, The points of the compass, the stars, hours, days, months, and years, colours, grains, etc. have all heen incorporated into the afore-mentioned scheme, based on the interaction of the elements.

These Four Constellations are the Four Quadrants into which the Twentyeight Stellar Mansions are divided. (Cf. *Mayers*-Manual, Pt. II, N. 91 and 313.) Those four constellations arc stars, but not animals, though they bear the names of animals. How then could Heaven produce animals from their essence? The Twelve Horary Characters are the Twelve Branches or Twelve Cyclical Signs applied to the twelve double hours of the day. They as well as their corresponding animals have been enumerated above, though not in their regular sequence. The Twelve Animals are:—Rat, ox, tiger, hare, dragon, serpent, horse, sheep, monkey, cock, dog, boar. (Vid. *Giles,* Diet. p. 1383.) and devour them, all depends on the sharpness ot their teeth, the strength of their

muscles and sinews, the agility of their movements, and their courage.

If with men on earth the power is not equally divided, or their strength equally balanced, they vanquish and subjugate one another as a matter of course, using their strength to subdue, and their swords to despatch their foes. Man strikes with his sword just as the beasts butt, bite, and scratch with their horns, teeth, and claws. A strong arm, pointed horns, a truculent courage, and long teeth win the victory. Pusillanimity, short claws, cowardice, and blunted spurs bring about defeat.

Men are audacious or faint-hearted. That is the reason why they win or lose their battles. The victors are therefore not necessarily endowed with the fluid of metal, or the vanquished with the essence of wood. *Confucius* afraid of *Yang Hu2* took himself off, covered with perspiration. *Yang Hus* colour was not necessarily white, and *Confucius* was not blue-faced. Because the falcon pounces upon pigeons and sparrows, and because the hawk-owl kills, and devours wild geese, it does not follow that the falcon and the hawk-owl are born in the south, or that pigeons, sparrows, and wild geese inhabit the west. It is but bodily strength and courage that lead to victory.

In the mansion there will always be people disputing, and in the cottage, litigating. In a law-suit there must be right and wrong, in a discussion truth and error. He who is in error, and in the wrong, loses, whereas he who tells the truth, and is right, wins.

It may happen, however, that in arguing, the glib-tongued, whose speech (lows with flippant rapidity, win, and that the ineloquent, who falter and stammer in their speech, are beaten. The tongue plays the same roll in debates as swords and halberds in battles. Sharp swords, long halberds, strong and quick hands and feet secure the victory. Blunt swords, short spears, and slow hands and feet cause the defeat.

Metal is stronger than wood, as we were told above. *Yang Ha* was the principal minister of the *t hi* family, one of the three leading families in the *Lu* State,

Confucias' country. *Yang Hu* being an usurper, scheming to arrogate the whole authority of the *La* State to himself, *Confucius* refused to see him. (Cf. *Analects* XVII, 1.) White overcomes blue. Because the south is supposed to be stronger than the west.

Whether one creature vanquishes the other, depends on its bodily strength, or its prowess, or its dexterity. If a small being is courageous, and possesses a quick tongue and nimble feet, a small animal may overpower a big one, and a big one without bodily strength and destitute of powerful horns or wings, may succumb to a small antagonist despite its bigness. The magpie eats the skin of the hedgehog, and the shrike swallows the snake, for the hedgehog and the snake are not very nimble. Gnats and mosquitoes are not as strong as the ox or the horse, yet these latter are tormented by gnats and mosquitoes, which are a very audacious lot.

The horns of a stag are strong enough to pierce a dog, and a monkey might well catch a rat with its hands, but the stag is brought to bay by the dog, and the monkey driven away by a rat, for they do not know how to make use of their horns and claws. Thus an ox, ten years old, is lead by a herdsboy, and an elephant, eight cubits high, obeys the hook of a young Annamese mahout, all for want of skill. With cleverness a small creature gets the better of a big one, but without it the weak succumbs to the strong.

CHAPTER V.

Phenomenal Changes *(Pien t'ung)*.

Arguing on calamitous events I have already expressed my doubts as to Heaven reprimanding man by misfortunes. They say, moreover, that the sovereign, as it were, moves Heaven by tiis government, and that Heaven moves the fluid in response. Beating a drum and striking a bell with a hammer would be an analogous process. The drum represents Heaven, the hammer the government, and the sound of the drum or the bell is like Heaven's response. When man acts below, the heavenly fluid survenes, and accompanies his actions. I confess that I doubt this also.

Heaven can move things, but how can things move Heaven? Men and things depend upon Heaven, and Heaven is the master of men and things. Thus one says that, when *Wang Liang* whips the horses, the carriage and the steeds rush over the plain. It is not said that, when the carriage and the steeds chase over the plain, *Wang Liang* subsequently whips the horses The heavenly fluid changes above, and men and things respond to it below. Consequently, when Heaven is about to rain, the *shang-yang3* begins to dance, and attracts the rain. The *"shang-yang"* is a creature which knows the rain. As soon as Heaven is about to rain, it bends its single leg, and commences to dance.

When Heaven is going to rain, the mole-crickets and ants leave their abodes, the earth-worms come forth, the chords of guitars become loose, and chronic diseases more violent. This shows, how Heaven moves things. When Heaven is about to blow, the creatures living in nests become restless, and, when it is going to rain, the insects staying in holes become excited. The fluid of wind and rain has such an effect upon those creatures. Man takes the same position between Heaven and Earth as fleas and bugs between the upper and lower garments, or crickets and ants in crevices. Can fleas and bugs, crickets and ants, in so far as they In chap. VI, which in the *bun-heng* precedes chap. V.

A famous charioteer (cf. p. 138). A one-legged bird said to portend rain. are either rebellious or peaceful, wild or quiet, bring about a change of the fluid in the crevices? Fleas and bugs, mole-crickets and ants cannot do this. To pretend that man is able to do so, shows a misconception of the nature of the fluid of things.

When the wind comes, the boughs of the trees shake, but these boughs cannot produce the wind. In the same manner at the end of summer the field crickets chirrup, and the cicadas cry. They are affected by the *Yin* fluid. When the thunder rolls, the pheasants become frightened, and, when the insects awake from their state of torpidity, the snakes

come forth. This is the rising of the *Yang* fluid. When it is near mid-night, the cranes scream, and when at dawn the sun is about to rise, the cocks crow. Although these be not phenomenal changes, they show at least, how the heavenly fluid moves things, and how those respond to the heavenly fluid. One may say that heat and cold influence the sovereign in such a way, that he emits a fluid by which he rewards or punishes, but are we warranted in saving that rewards and punishments affect high Heaven so, that it causes heat or cold to respond to the government?

In regard to the Six Passions the expositors of the wind theory maintain that, when the wind blows, robbers and thieves set to work under its influence, but the nature of robbers and thieves cannot move Heaven to send the wind. When the wind blows, it has a strange influence on perverted minds so, that robbers and thieves do their deeds. How can we prove that? Robbers and thieves seeing something, take it away, and beholding an enemy, kill him. This is an off-hand business, and the work of a moment, and not premeditated day and night. When the heavenly afflatus passes, the time of greedy scoundrels and stealthy thieves has come.

Those who predict dearness and cheapness from the wind, hold that a wind blowing over residences of kings and ministers brings dearness, whereas a wind coming from the dwellings of prisoners, or of the dead, brings cheapness. Dearness and cheapness refer to the amount of pecks and bushels to be got. When the wind arrives, the buyers of grain raise or lower the prices, such is the wonderful influence exercised by the heavenly fluid on men and things. Thus the price of grain rises, or falls, becomes dear, or cheap.

Cheerfulness, anger, grief, joy, love, and hatred. It is more common to speak of Seven Passions. They are the same as those given above, but joy is replaced by fear, and desire is added.

In the book on the Celestial Governors it is stated that the wind blowing from the four quarters is determined on the morning of New Year's Day-When the wind blows from the south, there will be droughts: when it blows from the north, inundations. Coming from the east, it forebodes epidemics, and coming from the west, war. The Great Annalist is right in saying that water, dryness, war, and diseases are predetermined from the wind, for luck and mishap of men and things depend on Heaven.

It is spring that animates things, and winter that causes them to die. Spring vivifies, winter kills. Should Heaven for any reason wish spring to kill, and winter to vivify, things would not die or live at all, why? Because the life of things is governed by the *Yang* principle, and their death depends on the *Yin2*

By blowing air upon a person one cannot make him cold, nor can one make him warm by breathing upon him. But if a person who has thus been blown or breathed upon, comes into winter or summer, he will have the unpleasant sensation of chill or heat. The cold and hot fluids depend on heaven and earth. and are governed by the *Yin* and the *Yang*. How could human affairs and government have any influence upon them?

Moreover, Heaven is the root, and man the apex. Climbing up a tree, we wonder that the branches cannot move the trunk, but, if the trunk is cut down, all the twigs wither. Human affairs resemble the branches of a tree, that which gives warmth is like the root and the trunk.

For those creatures which are born from Heaven and filled with its fluid Heaven is the master in the same manner as the ear, the eye, the hand, and the foot are ruled by the heart. When the heart has that intention, the ear and the eye hear and see, and the hand and the foot move and act. To maintain that Heaven responds to man would be like saying that the heart is under the command of the ear and the eye, the hand and the foot.

Streamers hanging down from flags arc attached to the flagstaff. The flagstaff moving eastward, those streamers follow, and float westward. If they say that heat and cold follow rewards and punishments, then the heav-

enly fluid must be like those streamers. *Shi-chi* chap. 27 p. 34v. The "Celestial Governors" are the sun, the moon, and the planets. The passage referred to here speaks of 8 winds, however, and their attributes are different from those given by *Wang Ch'ung*. Heaven could not puqiosely act against the laws of nature, by which the vegetation grows in spring, and fades in winter.
The fact that the "Hook" star (Mercury) is amidst the "House" constellation forebodes an earth-quake. The Great Diviner of *Ch'i* was cognisant of this, and told Duke *Ching* that he could shake the earth, which Duke *Ching* believed. To say that a sovereign can cause heat and cold is like Duke *Ching's* trusting in the ability of the Great Diviner to shake the earth. Man cannot move the earth, nor can he move Heaven. Heat and cold are heavenly fluids. Heaven is very high, man very small. With a small rod one cannot strike a bell, and with a f1re-fly one cannot heat a cauldron. Why'.' Because a bell is large, and a rod short, a cauldron big, and a fire-fly small. If a tiny creature, seven feet high. would attempt to influence the mighty fluid of great Heaven, it is evident that it would not have the slightest effect.

When it has been predetermined that a great general is about to enter a territory, he will be angry, in case the air is cold, and pleased, if it be warm. Now. joy and anger are called forth by actions. Previous to his entering the territory, they are not yet manifest, and do not come forward, before the conduct of the people and the officials has been inquired into. But the hot or the cold fluids have been there previously. If joy and anger evoked heat and cold, those fluids ought to appear later than joy and anger. Therefore only the hot and the cold fluids evoke the sovereign's pleasure or wrath.

Some will say 'Not so; the greatest sincerity is required. In one's actions one must be most sincere, as *Tsou Yen* was, who implored Heaven, when frost began to fall, or the wife of *Ch'i Liang"* who by her tears caused the city wall to collapse. How? The heavenly fluid can-

not be moved'.''

The greatest sincerity is shown in the likes and dislikes of the heart. When fruits are hanging before a man's face, no more than one foot away from his mouth, he may desire to eat them, and his breath may touch them, yet he does not obtain them Cf. p. 127 and *SM-chi* chap. 27 p. 27v.
546-488 B.c.
We learn from *Huai Kan Tse* XII, 22 quoted in *Lun-heng* IV, 13 *(Pien-hsii)* that) *en Tse* told the Great Diviner that the earth-quake would take place, because the "Hook" star was between the constellations of the "House" and the "Heart,'whereupon the Qrcat Diviner confessed to the Duke that the earth would shake, but that it would not be his doing (cf. p. 127).
/. e. man. The ancient Chinese foot was much smaller than the one now in use. Cf. chap. XXI. ' On officer of the *Ch'i* State, who was slain in a battle against the *Chii* State (cf. *Mencius* Book VI, P. II chap. 6). thereby. But, when he takes them in his hand, and conveys them to his mouth, then he can eat them. Even small fruits which can easily be moved in a basket, and are not far from the mouth, cannot be procured merely by a desire, be it ever so strong. How about Heaven then, which is so high and distant from us, and whose fluid forms the shapeless empyrean without beginning or end?
During the dog-days, people stand against the wind, and in the depth of winter, they sit turned towards the sun. In summer, they are anxious to obtain coolness, and in winter, they would like to have warmth. These wishes are most sincere. When their desires reach their climax, they will perhaps stand against the wind, and simultaneously fan themselves, or turned towards the sun-shine, light a fire in a stove. Yet Heaven will never change its fluid for summer or winter's sake. Heat and cold have their fixed periods, which are never transmuted for man's sake. With an earnest desire one does not obtain it, how should it be brought about by rewards and punishments, when the thoughts are not longing for heat or cold at all?

The sighs of ten thousand people cannot move Heaven, how should it be possible that the sobs of *Tsou Yen* alone could cause the frost to fall? Could the predicament of *Tsou Yen* be compared to that of *Ch'i l Yuan*? Was his unjust imprisonment like jumping into the river? Were the lamentations of the *Li-sao* and the *Ch ut'se* nothing more than a sigh?—When *Ch'ii Yuan* died, there fell no frost in the State of *Ch'u*.

This happened during the reign of the Kings *Huai* and *Hsiang*? At the time of the Kings *Li* and *ll'a*, *Pien Ho* presented them with a jade-stone, and had his two feet cut off". Offering his stone he wept, till his tears ran dry, when he went on weeping blood. Can the sincerity of *Taou Yen* bear a comparison with *Pien Ho's* sufferings, or his unjust arrest with the amputation of the feet? Can the sighs towards heaven be put on a parallel with tears of blood? Sighs are surely not like tears, nor *Tsou Yen's* imprisonment The "Elegies of *Ch'u*" comprising the *Li-sao* and some other poems of *Ch'u Yuan* and his contemporaries, all plaintive pieces referring to *Ch'ii l turn's* disgrace.

King *Huai* of *Ch'u* 327-294, King *Ch'mg Hsiang* 294-261. *Ch'u Yuan* committed suicide in 294 B.c. King Wu reigned from 739-688. His predecessor is called *Hsiung Hsiin* (756-739) in the *Shi-chi*, not *Li. Pien Ho* was taken for an impostor, and first sentenced to have his left foot cut off. When he presented the stone, a second time, his right foot was cut off. At last the genuineness of the jade-stone was discovered.

Lu1-11ciig. 8 like the cutting of the feet. Considering their grievances *Tsou Yen* is not *PienHo's* equal. Yet at that time no frost was seen in the *Ch'u* country.

Li Sse and *Vhao Kao* caused the death of the crown-prince *Fu Su* by their calumnies. *Ming T wn* and *Ming Ao* were involved in his fall. At that time they all gave vent to their pain, which was like sighing. Their misfortune culminated in death, and was not limited to unjust banishment. Albeit yet no cold air was produced, where they died. *Ch'in* buried alive 400,000 soldiers of *Chao* below *Ch'ang p' ing*, where they

were all thrown into pits at the same time. Their wails and cries then were more than sighs. Even if their sincerity was less than that of *Tsou Yen*, yet the sufferings of 400,000 people must have been commensurate to the pain of one wise man, and the cries they uttered, while falling into the pits, must have been worse than the moans of one fettered prisoner.

In spite of this no hoar-frost was seen falling down below *Ctiang-p ing*,-when the above related event took place.

We read in the *"Fu-hsing"* chapter:— '"The people maltreated universally complained that they had not failed against the Killer of Heaven." This means that *Ch'ih Yu's* subjects suffering under his vexations universally complained that they had not sinned against high Heaven. Since the complaints of a whole populace could not cause a fall of frost, the story about *Tsou Yen* is most likely ficticious also.

In the south it is extremely hot:—the sand burns, stones crumble into dust, and father and son bathe in the same water. In the north it is bitterly cold:—water turns into ice, the earth cracks, and father and son huddle together in the same den. *Yen* is situated in the north. *Tsou Yen* was there in the 5th month of *Chou*, which corresponds to the 3d month of the corrected year. Cf. p. 171. A eunuch, who together with *Li Sse* caused the death of *Fu Su*, eldest sou of *Ch'in Shih Huang Ti*, and under *Hu Hai* usurped all power. In 20V B. c. he was assassinated by order of 7e 1 ing, son of *Fu Su*. Cf.p. 167. The grand father of *Ming T'ien*, also a general of *Shih Huang Ti*.

Cf. p. 136 and p. 166.

The chapter on Punishments in the *Shu-king*, now entitled *Lu-hMng*.

'*Shu-king, Lu-hMng*, Pt. V, Bk. XXVII, 4 (*Legge*, Vol. lll, Pt. *U*, p. 502).

The *Chou* epoch. The *Chou* calendar began with the 11th month, the *Ch'in* calendar with the 10th. In 104 B.c. *Han Wu Ti* corrected the calendar, and made the year commence with the 1st month, so the *Chou* were "2 months ahead with their months.

In the central provinces frost, and snow-

falls are of frequent occurrence during the first and the second months. In the northern region, where it is very cold, frost may fall even during the third month, and that would not be an extraordinary phenomenon. Perhaps it was still cold in the north in the third month, and frost happened to fall, when by chance *Tsou Yen* gave vent to his feelings, which just coincided with the frost.

It has been recorded that in *Yen* there was the " *Cold Valley"* where the five graius did not grow.. *Tsou Yen* blew the flute, and the "Cold Valley" became warm. Consequently *Tsou Yen* was able to make the air warm, and also to make it cold. How do we know that *Tsou Yen* did not communicate his grievances to his contemporaries, and instead manifested his sincerity through the heavenly fluid? Did he secretly blow the flute in the valley of *Yen*, and make the air of the prison cold, imploring Heaven for that purpose? For otherwise, why did the frost fall?

Fan Sui calumniated by *Hsi i Chia* was most disgracefully treated by *Wei Chi*, had his back broken, and his ribs doubled up. *Chang Yi* while travelling in *Ch'u*, was arrested by the prime minister of *Ch'u*, and beaten, until the blood ran out. The way in which these two gentlemen were maltreated has been narrated by the Great Annalist. The imprisonment of *Tsou Yen* resembles the adventures of *Fan Sui* and *Chang Yi*. Why does *Sse Ma Chien* omit to mention this? Since it is not mentioned in *Tsou Yen's* biography that during his imprisonment he caused the frost to fall, it must be an invention, and a random statement like the story of Prince *Tan*, who is believed to have ordered the sun to return to the A native of *Wei* of humble origin, who first served under *Hsii Chin*, and accompanied him on a mission to the court of King *Hiiiang of Ch i* (696-683). This prince appreciating *Fan Sui* for his great dialectical skill, sent him some presents. *Hsu Chia* presuming that *Fan Sui* had betrayed some State secrets of *Wei*, denounced his servant to the premier of *Wei*, *Wei Ch i*, who had him beaten almost to death. *Fan Sui* was then wrapped in a mat, and thrown into a privy, where the drunken guests urinated upon him. Still he managed to escape, and later on became minister in *Ch'in.* Also a native of the *Wei* State from a poor family, who played a very important political role in *Ch'in* and *Wei.* In his youth, he was suspected in *Ch'u* of having stolen a valuable gem, and severely beaten. Died 310 B.C. *Shi-chi* chap. 79 and 70. Prince *Tan* of *Yen* was detained as a hostage in the *('h'in* State. Its sovereign promised with an oath to set him free, when the sun returned to the meridian, and Heaven rained grain, when the crows got white heads, and the horses, horns, and when the wooden elephants, decorating the kitchen door, got legs of flesh. Heaven meridian, and Heaven to rain grain. Thus we may assume that the story about the frost falling down upon *Tsou Yen* imploring Heaven is untrue, and that the report of the wife of *Ch'i Liang* causing the city wall to collapse is false.

When *Tun-mao2* rebelled, the Viscount *Hsiang* of *Chan* led an army against it to invest it. When his soldiers had arrived at the foot of the city wall, more than one hundred feet of this wall of *Tun-mao* crumbled down. Viscount *Hsiang* thereupon sheathed his sword, and went back. If the wife of *Ch'i Liang* caused the collapse of the city wall by her tears, was there anybody crying among *Hsiang 7'se's* men? When *Ch in* was about to be extinguished, a city gate collapsed inside, and when the house of *Ho Kuang* was going to ruin, a wall of the palace was demolished of itself. Who was weeping in the *Ch in* palace, or crying in the house of *Ho Kuang?* The collapse of the gate, and the demolition of the wall were signs of the catastrophe awaiting *Ch in* and *Ho.*

Perhaps at the time, when the *Ch'i* State was about to be subverted, the wife of *Ch'i Liang* happened to cry at the foot of the wall, just as *Tsou Yen* chanced to cry to Heaven, when it was still very cold in the *Yen* State. There was a correspondence of events and a concordance of time. Eye-witnesses and people who heard about it, most likely were of this opinion. Moreover, provid-

ed that the city wall was old, and the house-wall, rotten, there must have been a collapse, and a destruction. If the tears of one woman could make 50 feet of the wall tumble down, the wall must have been such, that one might have pushed a beam of 30 feet into it with one finger.

During the Spring and Autumn period several mountains were transformed in an extraordinary way. Mountains and walls belong to the saae class. If tears subvert a city wall, can they demolish a mountain also? If somebody in white mourning like a woman helped the Prince, and brought about these wonders, when *Tan* was released, or, as others say, he made his escape in 230 B.c. The story is narrated in *Lun-heng* V, 7 *(Kan-hsu).* The same is said of *Hsin Yuan Ping (Shi-chi* chap. 28 p. 19v).

A city in *Honan.* 456-424 B.C. A faithful servant of the Emperor *Han Wu Ti,* who appointed him Regent for his minor son, *Chao Ti.* He died in 68 B.C. His family was mixed up in a palace intrigue aiming at the deposition of the reigning emperor, which was discovered, when all the members of his family were exterminated. Instead of *Ch'i yjcjl,* an old feudal State in *Honan,* we ought probably to read, the name of the *Ch'i* State in *Shantung,* of which *Ch'i Liang* was a native. cries so, that his tears flow like rivers, people generally believe that a city wall can collapse through these tears, and regard it as quite the proper thing. But *Ch'i Liang* died during the campaign, and did not return. His wife went to meet him. The Prince of *Lu* offered his condolence on the road, which his wife did not accept. When the coffin had arrived in her house, the Prince of *Ln* coudoled with her again. She did not say a word, and cried at the foot of the wall. As a matter of fact, her husband had died in the campaign, therefore he was not in the wall, and, if his wife cried turned towards the city wall, this was not the right place. In short, it is again an unfounded assertion that the wife of *Chi Liang* caused the city wall to tumble down by her tears. On this principle of sympathetic actions a white halo encir-

cled the sun, when *Ching K'o* stabbed the king of *Ch in,* and *Venus* eclipsed the *Pleiades,* when the scholar from *Wei* drew up the stratagem of *Chang-ping* for *Ch in.* This again is an absurdity. When *Yu Tse* was planning the murder of Viscount *Hsiang,* and was lying under a bridge, *Hsiang Tse's* heart throbbed, as he approached the bridge. *Kw1n Kao* intended to murder *Kao Tsu,* and had concealed a man in the wall. When *Kao Tsu* arrived at *Po-jen,* his heart also beat high. Those two individuals being about to stab the two princes, the hearts of the latter palpitated. If we reason in a proper way, we cannot admit that the princes were affected by the souls of the two assassius, and should we do so in the case of the king of *Ch in?* When *Ching K'o* was preparing to stab him, the king's heart was not moved, but a white halo encircled We learn from the *Tao-chuan,* Duke *Hsiang* 23rd year (550 B.c.) *(Legge,* Classics Vol. V, Pt. II, p. 504) and from the *Liki, T 'an Kung* Pt. III, 1 *(Legge,* Sacred Books Vol. XXVII, p. 188) that, when the bier of *Ch'i Liung* was brought home to *Ch i, the Marquis of Ch'i, Chuang,* sent an officer to present his condolences, but the widow declined them, because the road was not the proper place to accept condolences. The Marquis then sent them to her house. The *"Prince of Lu"* of our text is probably a misprint, for why should the prince of *Lu* condole in *Ch'i?* The *Lieh-nu-chuan* relates that (*'h i Liang's* wife cried seven days over her husband's corpse under the city wall, until it collapsed, and then died by jumping into a river. Cf. chap. XXXIX and XL. Cf. p. 114. lu *Jang,* a native of the *Chin* State, who made an unsuccessful attempt on the life of Viscount *Hsiang* of *Chao,* who had killed his master, Earl *Chih.* Vid. chap. XXIX. A minister of *Chao.* A place in the prefecture of *Shun-te'-fu (Chili).* This attempt on the life of *Han Kao Tsu* in 199 B.c. was frustrated. the sun. This celestial phenomenon of a white halo encircling the sun happened of its own accord, and it was not the mind of *Clung K'o* which produced it. *Mercury* hetween the constellations of the *House* and the *Heart* denotes an impending earth-quake. When an earthquake is going to take place, *Mercury* corresponds to the *House* and the *Heart*. The offuscation of the *Pleiades* hy *Venus* is like the position of *Mercury* between the *House* and the *Heart*. Therefore the assertion that the design of *Ch'ang-p tug*, devised by the scholar from *Wei*, caused *Veuu s* to eclipse the *Pleiades,* is very doubtful.

When *Jupiter* injured the *Bird* and the *TaiJ* stars, *Chou* and *Ch'u* were visited with disasters, and when a feather-like fluid appeared, *Sung, Wei, Chin,* and *Cheng* suffered misfortunes. At that time, *Chou* and *Ch u* had not done any wrong, nor had *Sung. Wei, Chen,* or *Cheng* committed any wickedness. However, *Jupiter* first occupied the place of the Tail star, and the fluid of misfortune, for a while, descended from heaven, whereupon *Chou* and *Ch a* had their disasters, and *Sung, Wei, Chen,* and *Cheng* suffered likewise at the same time. *Jupiter* caused injury to *Chou* and *Ch'u,* as the heavenly fluid did to the four States. Who knows but that the white halo encircling the sun, caused the attempt on the life of the king of *Ch in,* and that *Venus* eclipsing the *Clehuies,* brought about the stratagem of *Ch ang-p ing?* The star *('or Hydro,* mentioned in the *Shu-king* (cf. *Leyye* Vol. Ill, Pt. 1, p. *W.)* The *"Tail"* is a constellation consisting of nine stars in the tail of Scorpio, the tith of the 28 Solar Mansions.

CHAPTER VI.

On Reprimands *(CItien-kao).*

Iu regard to extraordinary calamities they say that, when of old a sovereign in his administration departed from the right way, Heaven reprimanded him by visiting him with calamities. Those calamities are manifold. Heat and cold are put forward as proof. When a prince punishes at a wrong time, it becomes cold, and when he grants rewards, but not at the right moment, it becomes warm. The Spirit of Heaven reprimands a sovereign in the same manner, as a sovereign shows his displeasure to his subjects. Therefore King *Yen* of *Ch'u* said, "Heaven does not send down mis-

fortunes. Has Heaven forgotten me?" Those calamities are a reproof, therefore King *Yen* thought of them with fear.

I say that this seems very doubtful to me. The calamities of a State are like the misfortunes of an individual. If they say that Heaven reprimands a sovereign through calamities, does it also reprove an individual through bis misfortunes? Since the individual is known to us, we may make use of the human body for comparison. A sickness of the body is like a calamity from Heaven. When the circulation of the blood is not in order, a man contracts a disease, and when the wind and the air do not agree, the year develops calamities. Provided that Heaven blames the administration of a State by calamities, does it blame an individual by his sickness?

By fermenting wine in jars, and cooking meat in cauldrons, one wishes to make their tastes palatable. Sometimes they are too salty, bitter, sour, or insipid, and not to our taste, just as a spoonful of medicine does not taste well. The calamities of Heaven are like the bad taste of cooked meat or fermented wine. If calamities are believed to be expressive of Heaven's displeasure, we ought to see such manifestations also in case of a mistake in cooking or fermenting. One measures big things by small ones, and learns to know Heaven, if one understands analogies.

Were King *Yen's* knowledge like that of *Vonfucius,* his utterance could be believed, but as a leading prince during a time of decay, he did not possess more ability than the pheno1uenalists, and his words are not to be trusted. Hence my doubts.

Heaven's principle, spontaneity, consists in inaction. If it did reprimand people, that would be action, and not spontaneous. The school of *Uuang Ti* and *Lao Tse* arguing on Heaven's principle have found the truth.

If Heaven could really reprimand the sovereign, it should change the fluid to call his attention. In case the prince punished at the wrong time, the fluid of punishment would be cold, and Heaven ought to make it warm, and should the prince reward unseasonably, the fluid of

reward would be warm, and it would be incumbent upon Heaven to make it cold. A transmutation of the fluid in case of the perversion of government would call the attention of the sovereign to his fault. Now Heaven lets the cold and the heat' go on, and again causes cold and heat with a view to reprove the sovereign, and to induce him to change.

The illustrious prince *Tan Fu* thinking that he might elevate the later king *Chi,* on purpose changed his name 'of *Chi* into *Li,* which is synonymous with ' ='heir.' *T ai Po* took the hint, and went to collect medicines in *Wu* and *Yileh* in order to get out of King *Chi's* way. Had the illustrious prince not changed the name of *Chi,* and again styled him *Li,* how could the eldest son have taken the hint, and got himself out of the way'. ' Now, if rewards and punishments are not given in the proper way, and Heaven wishes a change of administration, it ought to use a different fluid, just as the illustrious prince changed the name of *Chi.* Instead of that it again produces the same fluid to show its displeasure to the sovereign, but, when will the latter become aware of it, and see the mistake he has made in rewarding and punishing?

When a guitar-player makes a mistake in tightening the cords and placing the bridges, *"kung"* and *"shang"* change their tunes. When the music-master hears it, he changes the strings, and shifts the bridges. Heaven sees mistakes in rewarding and punishing, as the music-master takes notice of the wrong handling of the cords and bridges. If Heaven did not change the fluid to rouse the Who explain natural phenomena by transcendent causes.

The grandfather of *Wen Wang,* the founder of the *Chou* dynasty.

» Cf.p. 131.

The first and the second of the five ancient notes of the Chinese gamut. sovereign, on the contrary, still increased it, and made the wrong worse, it would be unprincipled, and blindly commit the same mistake as the sovereign, which cannot be. *Chou* had banquets lasting the whole night; *Wen Wang* said every morning and evening, "Pour out this wine in libation." *Ch'i* was very extravagant in sacrifices: *Yen Tse3* offered a sucking pig in the temple, which did not fill the dish.4 Such disapprobation was necessary to bring about a change.

When sons and younger brothers are impudent, their fathers and older brothers instruct them in politeness. When officials behave rudely, their elders teach them good manners. *K'ang Shu* and *Po Ch'in"* disregarded the duties of sons and younger brothers. They called upon *Chou Kung*, prostrated themselves, and rose in a haughty manner. Thrice they called, and thrice they were bambooed. They went to see *Shang Tse. Shang Tse* bade them look at the pine and the Rottlera. Both looked at the pine and the Rottlera. Their hearts were moved, they caught the meaning, and understood the rules of etiquette to be observed between father and son. *Chou Kung* might have followed the two princes in their haughtiness, and *Shang Tse* might have imitated their arrogance, but it was necessary to resort to blows and parables to make them see the difference, and awaken their conscience by this strange procedure. The wrong government of a sovereign is like the bad behaviour of the two princes. If Heaven did not make any announcement about the style of government in order to rouse the conscience, just as the two princes were roused, when looking at the pine and Rottlera, but on the contrary made the mistake in rewarding and punishing his own by requiting the sovereign with heat and cold, Heaven's fault would not be less than that of the sovereign.

It cannot be the intention of high Heaven that people's conscience should not be roused, and that one fluid should be exactly like the other. It would not love its subjects, nor reprimand them in this way. All things which can destroy one another, must *Shutting* Part V, Bk. X, 2 *Legge*, Vol. lll, Pt II, p. 390) cf. chap. XXXIX.

The *Ch'i* State in *Shantung. Yen l ing*, an official of *Ch'i*, noted for his thrifty habits, died 493 B.C. So small was the offering. A younger brother of *Chou Kung*, the first Duke of *Wei*. A son of *Chou Kung* and his successor in the

Dukedom of *Lu*. A minister of *Wu Wang*. The lofty pine and the low Rottlera tree are emblems of father and son. have a different nature, whereas those which further and complete each other, are of the same fluid. *Li* below and *Tui*-above are called transformation. which is equivalent to change.. Fire and metal are different fluids, therefore they can change one another. If they were both fire, or both metal, how could they complete each other? *Ch il Yiktn* was sick of the stench and filth of *Chu*, therefore he composed the stanzas on perfumes and purity. The fisherman remonstrated with him for not following the common habits, thereupon he spoke the words on bathing. Whenever a man feels unclean, some will advise him to put on fragrant flowers, others to carry a pig. Both advices aim at removing stench and filth. Which is right, and which wrong? At all events, there must be a change, but no increase by any means. If heat and cold are produced as a protest against rewarding or punishing, could they be changed thereby then? *Hsi Men /'ao* used to tighten his leather belt to soothe himself, and *Tung An Yil* would loosen the strings of his girdle to stimulate himself. These two wise men knew that the belt and the girdle will help us to change countenance, consequently they made use of them for the purpose of repressing their bodily weakness, which was very intelligent indeed. If in case of bad government of a sovereign high Heaven did not reprimand him with another fluid, that he might change, on the contrary, followed his error, emitting the same fluid, Heaven's wisdom would be inferior to that of the two men. King *Chuang* of *Chu3* had a passion for hunting, therefore Lady *Fan* did not eat any game, or poultry. Duke *Mu* of *Chin* was very fond of voluptious music, for this reason the Princess of *Hua Yang* declined to listen to the tunes of *Ch'eng* and Win'. The The 3rd diagram.

The 58th diagram. In the terminology of the *Yi-king*. Filth in a metaphorical sense. The first advice of course. Bad odour can be removed by its contrary, perfumes, but not by more stench. A worthy of the 5th century B.C. *(Giles,*

Biogr. Diet. N. 678). Another famous character of old *(Giles, Biogr. Diet.* N. 2088). *Giles* gives another version of the peculiarities of the two gentlemen regarding their belts. Cf. chap. XXXI. 612-589 B.C. 658-619. The music of these two States was considered licentious, and most objectionable. two ladies found fault with the two princes. They opposed their wishes, and did not agree to what they did. Heaven, on the other hand, shows its disapproval of the sovereign's rewarding and punishing by letting him act as he pleases, and still increasing the Iluid. Thus the virtue of high Heaven would not be equal to that of the two wise ladies.

To remonstrate means to reject by words. To keep the good, and reject the bad must certainly be regarded as a mistake. King *Mu* of *Chou* relied on punishments. In the Chapter on Punishments 11e says that violence is requited with force. Force and violence are both bad. To requite evil with evil is the most serious misrule. Now, in criminal law not to give mercy, when it should be given, is wicked. Heaven, however, adds wrong to wrong to correspond to it. Thus Heaven would act like King *Mu*.

With goodness one combats badness, and with badness good people are frightened. This is the way to admonish people, and to induce them to do good. *Shun* exhorted *Yii* saying:—"Be not as overbearing as *Tan Chu*."-*Chou Kung* called King *Cheng* and said to him, ''Be not like King *Chou* of *Yin*." 'Not' is preventive. *Tan Chu* and *Chou* of *Yin* were the greatest scoundrels, therefore the word 'not' was used to prevent them (from following their example); *Shun* and *Chou Kung* said "Be not like," who would say "Be like?" The Sages discriminated between the positive and the negative, would they have reproved the wrong doing by doing wrong themselves, or would they by continuing the faults of others have even increased the evil? Heaven and man obey the same law, and great men equal Heaven in virtue. Sages and worthies reform bad people by goodness. If Heaven added wrong to evil, would that be a manifestation of the same law, or show the similarity of virtue?

The emperor *Hsiao Wu* took a great interest in immortals. *Sse Ma Hsiang Ju* presented to him a poem on the Great Man, by which the emperor became so excited, that he felt like flying up to the clouds. The emperor *Hsiao Ch eng* was very fond of building In the *Shu-king, Lu-hsing* Pt. V, Bk. XXVII, 5 *(Legge* Vol. lll, Pt. II, p. 593) King *Mu* uses these words with reference to *Huang Ti,* who in this manner repressed the lawlessness of the *Miao-tse. Shu-king, Yih-chi* Pt. II, Bk. IV, 1.

Shu-king, Wu-yi Pt. V, Bk. XV, 13 *(Legge* Vol. lll, Pt. II, p. 471). *Hsiao Wu — Han Wu Ti,* 140-86 B.c. A distinguished scholar and poet. The emperor *Han Wu Ti* was infatuated with alchemy, and the magical arts taught by the Taoists. "*Hsiao Ch eng = Han Ch eng Ti,* 32-6 B.C. big palaces. *Yang Tse Yiin* offered him a hymn on the *Kan-ch'San* palace, which he extolled as something supernatural, as if he were saying that human force could not achieve such a work, and that spirits must have lent their aid. *Hsiao Ch'ing,* without knowing it, was induced thereby to go on building. If *Sse Ma Hsiang Ju* in his poem spoke of immortals, he had no proof for it, and, if *Yang Tse Ydn* wrote a panegyric on extravagance, he did the emperor a bad service. How could *Hsiao Wu* have the feeling of flying, and how could *Hsiao Ch'ing* be under a delusion without knowing it? If Heaven does not use auother fluid to reprimand the sovereign, on the contrary meets his wishes, and responds to him with evil, he acts like the two scholars, who imposed upon the two emperors by their poetry so, that their conscience was not roused. *Tou Ying* and *Kuan Fu* were so disgusted with the wickedness of the time, that every day they mutually pulled a string to fasten their hearts. Their disgust was such, that they would, on no account, have yielded to their desires. *T at Fo* taught the *Wu5* to wear a cap and a girdle, how would he have followed their customs, and been naked, as they were? Thus the *Wu* learnt propriety and rightheousness, and it was *T'aiPo* who

changed their customs. *Su Wu* went to live among the *Hsiungnu,* but he never buttoned his coat on the left side. *Chao T o* lived among the southern *Yileh.* He would sit down, spreading out his legs, and wear his hair in a tuft upon a frame. At the court of the *Han, Su Wu* was praised, and *Chao T n* blamed, because he had taken to the uncivilised fashions of the *Yileh,* abandoning the cap and the girdle. *Lu Chia* spoke to him about the costume of the Chinese, and their polished The philosopher *Yang Hsiung,* a philosopher of note of the Confucian school, 53 B.C.-18 A.d. A celebrated palace near *Hsi-an-Ju* ((*'h'ang-an*) originally founded by *('hin Shih Huang Ti.* Two high officers of the 2nd cent. B. C. Cf. chap. XVIII.

Cf. p. 131.

Aborigines in modern *Kiangsu.* In 100 B.C. *Su Wu* was sent as envoy to the *Hsiungnu,* who kept him prisoner for about nineteen years. Though the *Hsiungnu* made every endeavour to win him over to their cause, he never threw off his allegiance to the *Han,* wherefore he is praised as a paragon of loyalty. Only a barbarian would button his coat on the left side, a Chinaman will button it on the right. A famous general of the 2nd cent. B.C., who subjugated the southern barbarians, and subsequently became their king. (Cf. chap. XXXL) Aborigines in *Canton* province. Cf. chap. XXXI. manners, and held up their morality to him. *Chao To* felt remorse, and turned his heart hack to his native land. Had *Lu Chia* again used the dress of the *Yiieh,* and their harbarian language, and followed their wild customs, how could he have caused *Chao T o* to feel remorse, to reform, and to adopt again the rules of *Han.* A divergence of government, and culture necessitates the use of different language, and different arguments. If a bad government be not transformed, it goes on as before.

In case that a sovereign be reprimanded for a mistake, but that his bad government be not changed, and his wrong continued, why is the advice given him as a reproof not heeded?—When *K1uin Shu Hsien* and *T sai Shu Tu* were revolting, *Chou Kung* remonstrated with

them several times. Did he tell them that they should revolt, when he admonished them?

It is human law to like good, and hate evil, to do good as reward, and to inflict evil as punishment. The law of Heaven must be the same. Now. if rewards and punishments be not meted out in the proper way, there is evil. Should the fluid of evil respond to it, the principle of hating the evil would not be preserved.

The *Han* improved the punishments for the hiding of criminals. and fixed penalties for the assistance given to accomplices to make their escape. They were indignant that the criminals found helpers, and that bands were organised. By restraining the prisoners, when they were taken before the magistrates, and separating them from bad characters, keeping them in different places, the law concerning the hiding of criminals, and the absconding of the accomplices might have been dispensed with.

Ti Ya knew how to give the right flavour to what he was cooking. When it was too sour, he poured water in, and, when it was tasteless, he added salt. Water and fire mixing and transforming one another, the food became neither too salty, nor too tasteless. Now, if in case of improper rewarding or punishing the Two brothers of *Chou Kupg* and of *Wu Wang,* who attempted to deprive their nephew *Ch'eng Wang* of the throne, but their rebellion was put down by *Chou Kung.* A new law was enacted in the 4th year of the Emperor *Hsilan Ti* (70 A.d.), by which descendants concealing their ascendants, and wives hiding their husbands guilty of a crime, were to be acquitted, whereas ascendants and husbands doing the same for their sons and wives, had to suffer capital punishment. Descendants were no doubt under a moral obligation to help their ascendants under any circumstances, but the same moral law did not exist for ascendants towards their sons. (Cf. *Ch'ien Han-shu* chap. 8 p. 11.) fault is not made good by another fluid, cold being still added to cold, and heat to heat, this would be like finding a food too sour, and adding salt, or thinking it too insipid, and pouring water in. Hence, are there not serious doubts about the alleged reprimands of Heaven, or must we believe in them?

When by burning fuel one heats a cauldron, the water in it boils, if the fire is strong, but it remains cool, if the fire is weak. Government is like the fire, heat and cold like boiling and coolness. Speaking of the government of a sovereign, we may say that he does not keep the right medium in rewarding and punishing, but in case the *Yin* and the *Yang* are in disorder, and the fluids not in harmony, are we justified in saying that Heaven produces heat or cold for the sovereign's sake with the object of reproving him?

The *savants* also maintain that, when the administration of a sovereign is bad. Heaven sends extraordinary events. If he does not change, Heaven visits his people with misfortunes, and if he does not reform even then, it visits his own person. That is to say:—first extraordinary events, afterwards calamities, first exhortations, then punishments. I doubt this likewise. If one plants something in summer, it withers, and does not grow, and if one reaps corn in autumn, it lies about and cannot be harvested. Administration and instruction may be compared to planting and reaping. We may say that in governing the right time has been missed, but can we pretend that, in case of disasters caused by fluids or other things, Heaven has sent extraordinary events to reprimand the sovereign, and that, because the latter did not reform, Heaven sent down misfortune upon him in order to slay him? These opinions of the literati are those of illiterate people.

In mid-summer the *Yang* fluid is broiling hot. The *Yin* fluid rushes against it, and there is a hissing, shooting forth, and crashing. When a human being is hit by it, and killed, they hold that Heaven has punished him for his hidden sins. To a superficial observer this may seem quite likely, but in reality it is not so. First they pretend that calamitous events serve to reprimand, and punish a sovereign, and then again they say that a man killed by a thunderstroke is punished for his bidden crimes,—a wrong statement, and an untenable assertion!

Some say that *Ku Tse Ytln* in a memorial to the emperor explained that extraordinary phenomena were visible signs of Heaven's Which begins in November.

reprimands, which would be repeated, unless a change took place. He was prepared to await that time in fetters. Subsequently they were repeated in fact. Wherefore were they repeated, provided that they were not meant as reprimands? For these reasons the words of *Ku Tse Yiiti* were later on used as an incentive to reforms.

My reply is that in case of extraordinary phenomena the *Yin* and the *Yang* can be determined beforehand. The fluids of all things, of course, have their beginning and their end. Walking upon frost,. one knows that hard ice will necessarily follow. That is Heaven's law. *Ku Tse Yi-in* possessed this subtle knowledge, and was aware of what subsequently was bound to happen. Therefore lle borrowed the theory of the phenominalists to corroborate his own view. Thus he was resolved to await the time in fetters. Just like *Yen Tse* of *Chi*,-who saw the 'Hook' star between the constellations of the.House' and the 'Heart'. he knew that there would be an earth-quake. Had *Ku TseYi'm* seen the'Hook' star, he would again have said that through this star Heaven expressed its displeasure, and that, unless the government was changed, an earth-quake would happen. *Ku Tse Yiln* was looking out for the time to come as *Tse Wei* did, who fell down on the steps of the throne to await that the planet Mars should shift its position, an event which was sure to take place. Hence the theory of reprimands was believed. If we admit it, would it be contrary to justice, or injure high Heaven's virtue? Spontaneity and inaction would be humanised thereby, therefore we cannot listen to it.

By crediting Heaven with, the power of reprimanding, one extols its wisdom in investigating the truth. However, this wisdom would conflict with Heaven's excellence. "How do we know that any one is deaf?—If he hears distinctly.— How do we know that he is blind?— If he sees clearly. — How do we know that he is mad? —If he talks properly. " Proper talking, and clear and distinct hearing; and seeing is what the Taoist school calls madness, In 34 *B.C. Ku Tse Yiin = Kn Yung* attributed an eclipse and an earth-quake to the excessive favour shown by the emperor to the ladies of his seraglio. He wrote many memorials against the abuses of the palace. Cf. p. 121. The planet Mercury. The stars Beta, Delta, Pi, and Nun, in the head of Scorpio. The stars Antares, Sigma, and Tau, in the heart of Scorpio. Cf. p. 158. A Taoist rhyme, quoted from the *Lu-shih-ch'un-ch'hi*. See also *Iluai JXan Tse* XVII, lv:—"He who hears the sounding sound is deaf, but he who hears the soundless sound is quick at hearing.'' blindness, and deafness. Now to speak of Heaven's reprimanding would therefore be tantamount to calling it mad, blind, and deaf.

The *Yi-king* says that the great man equals Heaven and Earth in virtue. Therefore *T at Po* holds that Heaven does not speak, but that its law is ingrafted in the hearts of the wise. Consequently, the virtue of the great man is the virtue of Heaven, and the words of the wise are the words of Heaven. When the great man reproves, and the wise rebuke, it is Heaven which reprimands, and yet people see its reprimands in calamitous events, which I cannot believe.

In the text of the Six Classics and in the discourses of the Sages every now and then Heaven is referred to, because they intend to reform the lawless, and to frighten the ignorant. They wish to make it understood that what they say is not only their private opinion, but that it is Heaven's thought also. They speak of Heaven, as if they were dealing with a human heart, for it is not the blue empyrean which they have in view. The phenomenalists hearing the unfounded assertion that the calamitous events of Heaven always happen at a fixed time, have therefrom derived the theory of reprimands.

The past affords us a key for the present. Heaven acts through man "*(S/um)* received *(Yao's)* abdication from the

Accomplished Ancestor." It is not said that he received the abdication from Heaven. From *Yao's* heart we learn to know Heaven's sentiments. *Yao* made an appointment, and Heaven did the same, and all the officials, and subjects became inclined towards *Shun. Shun* appointed *Yil,* and *Yil* transmitted the sway to *Chi.* In all these cases we learn from the human heart, what Heaven's feelings were like. As regards the "affectionate looks" of the *Shi-king* and the "mighty anger" in the *Hung-fan,* the human body serves to exemplify Heaven's feelings.

The Taoists despise the natural organs:—the eye, the ear, the mouth, and pretend to see with a spiritual eye, to hear with a spiritual ear, etc. *Yi-king,* 1st diagram *(Ch'ien).* The son of *Tan-fu* (cf. p. 120). We now speak of the Five Classics:—*Yi-king, Shu-king, Shi-king, Liki,* and *Ch'un-ch'ht.* During the Han period the "Book of Music"' was added, ranking as the fifth Classic before the *Ch'un-ch'iu. Shu-king, Shun-tien* Pt. H, Bk. I, 2 *(Legge,* Vol. III, Pt. I, p. 32) According to the commentators this passage means that *Shun* received the empire from *Yno* before the hrine of the latter's ancestor, who thus might be regarded as the donor. Vid. p. 134. We read in the *Shu-king, Hung-fan* Pt. V, Bk. IV, 3 *(Legge,* Vol. III, Pt. II, p. 323) "A' *'un* dammed up the inundating waters, and thereby threw into disorder the arrangement of the five elements. God was thereby roused to anger."

When King *W6n* and King *Wn* had died. King *Ch'ing* was still an infant, and the institutions of the *Chou* dynasty were not yet completed. The duke of *Chou* acted as lord protector, but there was no special instruction from Heaven. The duke of *Chou* asked his own heart, and conformed to the intentions of Heaven.

The heart of high Heaven is in the bosom of the Sages. When Heaven reprimands, it is done through the mouths of the Sages. Yet people do not believe the words of the Sages. They trust in the fluid of calamitous events, and strive to make out Heaven's meaning therefrom. Why go so far? But, should there be no sages during a generation, where are

their words to come from?— Wise men, whose talents are almost up to the mark, rank closely after the Sages.

CHAPTER VII.

Heaven's Original Gift *(Ch'u-ping).*

A man predestinated at his birth for wealth and honour, is imbued with the spontaneous fluid from the beginning. After he has been brought up, and grown to manhood, his lucky fate manifests itself.

Wen Wang received a scarlet bird, *Wu Wang,* a white fish and a red crow. The scholars are of opinion that with the bird Heaven's decree was transmitted to *Win Wang,* which in the case of *Wu Wang* was done by the fish and the crow. Thus *Win Wang* and *Wu Wang* would have received their fate from Heaven, which used the bird, the fish, and the crow to pass it on to them. Heaven used a scarlet bird to invest *Win Wang,* but *Win Wang* did not receive the mandate of Heaven. Then Heaven took a fish and a crow, and enfeoffed *Wu Wang.* This would imply that primarily the two received no fate from above, and that it was not before they purified themselves, and did good, and the news thereof reached Heaven, that Heaven endowed them with imperial honours. The bird, the fish, and the crow would then be heavenly messengers carrying the investiture, which emperors must have received to have the power over life and death. However, a thorough investigation shows us that fate has nothing to do with these cases.

Fate is what comes over people at the beginning, when they are created. They then receive their mind as well as their fate. Mind and fate come together and at the same time. The mind does not precede, or fate follow. How can this be made clear?

Citi served under *Yao* as territorial official, became superintendant of agriculture, and therefrom received the title of *Lard of Agriculture (Hon Chi).* His great-grandson Duke *Liu* lived at *T ai,* but later on moved to *Pin* His great-great-grandson *Tan Fu,* the Cf. *Shi-chi,* chap. 4 p. 8 *Chavannes, Mem. Hist.* Vol. I, p. 216 Note 1, and p. 226). *Win Wang* did not attain the imperial dignity,

which subsequently devolved upon his son, *Wu Wang.* The ancestor of the *t'hou* dynasty. *T"ai* and *Pm* were both situated in *Shensi.*

"*Old Puke*" had three sons:—*lai Po, Chung Yung* and *Chi Li.* The son of *Chi Li* was *('h ang,* the later *Win Wang.* When he was still in his swaddling clothes, there appeared portents indicative of his holiness. Therefore *Tan Fa* said:—"It is through *Chang* that my family will hecome illustrious." When *T ai Po* heard of it, he retired to *Wu,* tattooed himself, and cut his hair in order to make room for *Chi Li. Win Wang* is believed to have met with his fate at that period. Yet Heaven's fate is already at work, when man comes into being. *Tan Fu,* the Old Duke, found it out very soon, but it was already there, before *Win Wang* was even conceived by his mother. The fate which emperors acquire becomes their mind internally and their body externally. To the body belong the features and the osseous structure, which man gets at his birth.

Officials with a yearly income of more than a hundred piculs, but of a lower rank than princes and counts, such as *lang-chiang,3 ia-fu,* and *yuan-shih,* or provincial offlcials like intendants and prelects, in short, all salaried functionaries have obtained a fate predestinating them for wealth and honour, which after their birth is apparent in their faces. *Hsu Fu* and *Ku Pit Tse Ching* perceived these signs. Officials rise in office, some to the ranks of lords and ministers. They are predestinated to grandeur and a very exalted position. An emperor possesses the highest dignity, and his rank is the most exalted. At his birth, he is endowed with a glorious fate, and his body shows peculiar signs of nobility at that time. The "Old Duke" was well aware of this, when he beheld the remarkable four nipples," lor these four nipples were the marks of a Sage. *Wen Wang* received the heavenly decree making him a sage, when he was still in his mother's womb, or did the four nipples grow only, after he had become a man, and practised virtue?

The *Shi-chi* chap. 4 p. 4 relates that *T'ai Po* as well as *('h'ung Yung,* whom the

Shi-chi styles 1 *ii Ch'ung*, retired to the barbarians out of regard for their younger brother *Chi Li*. The kingdom of *Wu*, the modern province of *Kiangm*, at that time still inhabited by aborigines, hence the tattooing. Chamberlains of the Palace Guard. These offices are mentioned by *Menciw* Bk. V, Pt. II, chap. 2, who informs us that a chief minister had four times as much income as a *ta-fu*, and a *tu-fu* twice as much as a *guan-shih*. *Legge* translates "great officer" and "scholar of the first class," which does not say much. I would like to say "Director of a Department" and "First Clerk." Two renowned physiognomists, cf. chap. XXIV.
A peculiarity of *Wm Wang*, cf. chap. XXIV..

,

As regards the four nipples, we know also that lambs have them already as embryos. Dame *Liu* sleeping by a big lake dreamt that she met with a genius, and thereupon gave birth to *Kao-Tsu*. At that time, he had already obtained his fate: When *Kuang Wu'* was born in the *Chi-yang* palace, a brilliant light shone in the room at midnight, though there was no fire. One of the soldiers *Su Yung* said to the secretary *Ch'ung Lan:*—"This is a lucky thing," and nothing more. At that time *Knang Wu* had already got his destiny. The assertion that *Win Wang* and *Wu Wang* received Heaven's decree together with the scarlet bird, the fish, and the crow is, therefore, erroneous. Heaven's order once being issued, an emperor arises, and there is no further need for another decree.

Favoured with a fate conferring the highest distinctions upon them, emperors are born as a matter of course, as will be seen from the following: —Old men of wealthy families hoard up thousands of *chin*. They come into the world with the physiognomies of rich men. They work, and produce, and amass wealth, until, in their old age, they have become rich old folks. Emperors are the old men in possession of the empire. Their fate is inherent to their bodies, precisely as with birds the distinction between cocks and hens exists already

in the egg-shell. When the eggs are hatched, cocks and hens creep out. After days and months their bones wax stronger, and at last the cocks pair with the hens quite of their own accord. They are not taught to do so, after they have grown up so, that they would dare to pair only then. This is a spontaneous act, after their constitution has been strengthened. Now emperors are the cocks in the empire. They are destined to become emperors. This, their destiny comes down upon them, when they are still in an embryonic state in the same manner, as the future grandees get their peculiar physiognomies, which they possess at their birth, and as the cocks are formed in the egg.

This is not only true of men and birds, but of all organisms. Plants and trees grow from seeds. They pierce the earth as sprouts, by their further growth stem and leaves are formed. Their length and coarseness are developed from the seeds. Emperors are the acme of greatness. The stalk of the "vermilion grass" is like a needle, the sapling of the "purple boletus" like a bean. Both See p. 177.
The first emperor of the Later *Han* Dynasty, 25—58 A.d.
» Cf.p. 180.
Old coins. plants are auspicious. There is something auspicious about emperors also, who come into existence, endowed with the heavenly fluid.
Some people believe that emperors have received Heaven's decree, when they are born, but that Heaven invests them again, when they assume the supreme power, just as lords, ministers, and the lower grades await the imperial brevet, before they dare to take charge of their post, and that the scarlet bird, the fish, and the crow were emblems of the investiture by august Heaven. That would mean that human affairs are ordered and regulated by Heaven's interference, whereas spontaneity and inaction are the principles of Heaven. To enfeoff *Win Wang* by means of a scarlet bird, and *Wn Wang* through a white fish, would be on purpose.
Kuan Chung divided gain with *Pao Situ* and apportioned more to himself. *Pao*

Shu did not give it him, and he did not ask for it. That is, they knew each other, one regarded the other as his own self, and had no scruples about takiug anything for himself. A Sage takes the empire, as *Kuan Chung* the property. Amongst friends their is no question about giving or taking. August Heaven is spontaneous. If it really issued orders, then its principle would be purpose, whereas friendship is spontaneous.
When *Han Kao Tm* slew the big snake, who prompted him to do so? Did an order from Heaven arrive first, which encouraged him to do the deed'.' It was an outburst of his valour, a spontaneous impulse. The slaying of the big snake, the destruction of *Ch'in*, and the killing of *Ilsiang Yii*, all amount to the same. That the two Chou emperors *Win Wang* and *Wu Wang* received Heaven's decree, and defeated the *Yin* dynasty, must be understood in the *Kuan Chung* and *Pao Shu Ya* lived in the 6th cent. *h.c.* They were intimate friends, and are the Chinese Damon and Pythias.
The *Shi-chi* chap. 62 p. lv, Biography of *Kuan Chung*, states that *Kuan Chung* cheated his friend. He there admits himself that in doing business with *Pao Shu Ya*, he took more than his share of the gain, but that he did it, because he was very poor, and not out of greed. *Kuan Chung* took more than his share not on purpose, out of greed, but unintentionally. The empire falls to the share of the Sage, he takes it as a matter of course, but does not long for it. His actions are like those of intimate friends:-natural, unpremeditated, and spontaneous. This incident is told more fully on p. 178. The imperial house of *Chin*, which was dethroned by *I fan Kao Tm. Huang Yii* committed suicide, when defeated by *Han Kao Tm.* same sense. If *Kao Tsu* took the reins of government without a special order, it cannot be true that *Win Wang* and *Wu Wang* alone were invested through a bird and a fish.
The objection may be raised that in the "Announcement to *KangShn*" it is stated that:—"God heard of it, and was pleased, and Heaven gave *Win Wang* a great charge." If such a decree were impossible, how could the Annals and

Classics speak of a great command given by Heaven to *Win Wang?*—The expression great command does not signify that Heaven issued orders to *Win Wang.* Whatever a Sage does, he fulfills the commands of Heaven, He agrees with Heaven, as if he had done what Heaven bade him. In the *Shu-king K ang Shu* is just admonished and exhorted to do good, therefore it is mentioned that Heaven above heard of *Wiit Wang's* good deeds, and thereupon gave him a great charge.

The *Shi-king* says:—" (God) sent his kind regards round to the west, and then gave an abode." This is the same idea. Heaven has no head and no face, how could.it look about. Man can look around. Human qualities have been ascribed to Heaven. It is easy to see that. T hus one speaks of looking about. Heaven's command given to *Win Wang* and his looking are very much the same. In reality Heaven gives no orders, which can be proved in this way:—

"The perfect man resembles Heaven and Earth in virtue, sun and moon in brightness, the four seasons in regularity, and ghosts and spirits with regard to lucky and unlucky omens. When he acts first, Heaven does not disagree with him, and, when he follows Heaven, he conforms to his periods."

If in order to act there would always be a decree of Heaven required, how could there be actions preceding that of Heaven, and others following it. Since the Sage acts, without waiting for Heaven's decree, just on the impulse of his heart, sometimes he takes the initiative, sometimes he follows Heaven, which means that he is always in harmony with Heaven's periods. Hence it is said that Heaven does not disagree, and that the Sage conforms to Heaven.

The *Analects* say: — "Great is *Yao* as a sovereign! Heaven is great, and *Yao* corresponded to him." Emperors correspond to 1 *Shu-king* Pt. V, Book IX, 4. *Shi-king* Pt.IU, Book I, Ode VII, 1. Quotation from the *Yi-king, Ch'ien* Hexagram (N. 1). The commentator says that the Sage and Heaven are always in accordance, no matter who acts first, because they both follow the same princi-ples. *Analect s* VIII, 12.

Heaven, that is. to say, they are not in opposition to, and obey Heaven. Bringing the spontaneous nature into harmony with Heaven, that is the meaning of the great command given to *Win Wang.* *Win Wang* had his own ideas, and acted by himself. He was not driven on by Heaven, nor was the scarlet bird commissioned to tell him that he should be emperor, whereupon he dared to assume the imperial sway. *Win Wang's* scarlet bird and *Wu Wang's* white fish were not messengers bringing the assurance of Heaven's glorious help.

Whatever a lucky man begins, turns to his advantage. He finds adherents without seeking them, and auspicious objects without taking any trouble to get them. A latent sympathy pervades all things. If he be induced to come forth, and to hear and look, and he then sees something very propitious, it is mere spontaneity. When *Win Wang* was going to stand up as emperor, the scarlet bird happened to appear. The fish jumped up, and the bird came flying, and *Wu Wang* chanced to perceive them. It was not Heaven which sent the birds and the white fish. The lucky objects were moving about, and the Sages met them. Of the white fish which jumped into the Emperor's boat, *Wang Yang* said that it was a chance. At the time, when *Liu K un,* president of the Banqueting Office, was still governor of *Hung-nung* a tiger crossed the Yellow River. The emperor *Kuang Wu Ti* said that it was nothing but a curious coincidence, and a spontaneous act, and that nobody had sent the tiger. What *Wang Yang* called a chance and *Kuang Wu Ti* a coincidence, were all, so to speak, instances of spontaneity.

Shi-chi chap. 4 p. 8. A famous teacher and in later years a minister, of the 1st cent. A.d. A native of *Hunan,* died 57 B. c. *triles,* Biogr. Diet. N. 1323. A city in *Honan.* CHAPTER VIII.

What is meant by Destiny? *(Ming-yi.)* The Mehists hold that man's death is not predestinated, whereas the Confucianists are of opinion that it is. The believers in Destiny rely on the authority of *Tse Hsia* who says, "Life and death

depend on Destiny, wealth and honour come from Heaven." Those who deny the existence of Destiny refer to the city of *Li-yang.* which sunk into a lake in one night, and to *Po-Ch'i,* a general of *Ch in,* who buried alive the troops of *Chao* after their submission below *Ch'ang-p'ing,*5 altogether 400000 men, who all died at the same time." When in the *Ch'un-ch'iu* period armies were defeated, sometimes, they say, the grass was hidden by thousands of dead bodies. In time of famine, all the roads are full of starving people. During epidemic caused by malarial exhalations, thousands of families are extinguished. If there really should be Destiny, how is it, they ask, that in *Ch in* all were involved in the same catastrophe?

The believers in Destiny will reply, "When the vastness of the earth, and the great number of its inhabitants is taken into account, it is not to be wondered at that the people at *Li-yang* and *Chang-ping* should equally be doomed to die. Those whose destiny it was to be drowned, assembled at *Li-yang,* and those who were to be crushed to death, came together at *Ch ang-p ing* for that purpose."—

When *Han Kao Tsu* began his career, a fortune-teller, who entered the territory of *F6ng* and *P ei,* found many persons who were made counts afterwards. But not all the old and young people, men and women bore the mark of nobility. As a rule exceptional The followers of *Me Ti.* A disciple of *Confucius. Analects* XII, 5.

A city in *Anlmi.*

A city in *Shansi.*

This massacre took place in 260 H.c. (Cf. *Mayers Reader's Manual* N. 544.) '722-481 B.c.

The founder of the former *Han* dynasty, a native of *P ei* in *Kiangsu. Ffrnj* was another region in the neighbourhood. persons are met with occasionally only. Yet at *Li-gnng* men and women were all drowned, and at *Ch ang p ing* the aged and the young were buried to the last. Among tens of thousands there were certainly many who had still a long life before them, and ought not to have died. But such as happen to live in a time of decay, when war breaks out everywhere, cannot terminate their long lives. The span allotted to men is long or short, and their age flourishing or effete. Sickness, disasters, and misfortunes are signs of decay. The States of *Sung, Wei, Ch'en,* and *Ch'eng* were all visited with fire on the same day. Among the people of the four kingdoms were certainly not a few whose prosperity was still at its height, and who ought not to have been destroyed. Nevertheless they all had to suffer from the conflagration, being involved in their country's doom, for the destiny of a State is stronger than that of individuals.

The destiny regulating man's life-time is more powerful than the one presiding over his prosperity. Man shows by his appearance, whether he will die old or young, and there are signs indicating, whether he will be rich or poor, high-placed or base. All this is to be seen from his body. Length and shortness of life are gifts of Heaven. Whether the structure of the bones be good or bad, is visible in the body. If a man's life must be cut off in its prime, he cannot live long, although he be endowed with extraordinary qualities, and if it be decreed that he shall be poor and miserable, the very best character is of no. avail to him.—When *Hsiang Yil* was going to die, he turned to his followers, and said, I am vanquished, but by fate, not by force of arms." This is true, for in warfare *Hsiang Yil* was superior to *Km Tsu.* The latter's rise was due to Heaven's decree only.

The destiny of the State is connected with the stars. Just as their constellations are propitious or unpropitious, the State is happy or unhappy. As the stars revolve and wander, men rise and fall. Human prosperity and distress are like the abundance and the scarcity of a year. Destiny is flourishing or declining; things are either expensive or cheap. Within the space of one year, they are sometimes expensive, and at others cheap, as during This great fire, which on the same day broke out in the capitals of the four States, is recorded in the *Chun-ch'iu* Book X, 18 (Duke *Cit'no)* as happening in 529 B.c. It is

believed to have been foreshadowed by a comet, which appeared in winter of the preceding year.—These four States were comprised in *flonan,* except *Sung* which occupied the northern part of modern *Kiangm.* The rival of *Hun Kuo Tsu,* before the latter ascended the throne.

a long life prosperity and distress alternate. The prices of things do not depend on the abundance or scarcity of the year, nor is human prosperity the outcome of ability or ignorance.

How is it that *Tse Hsia* says, "Life and death depend on Destiny, wealth and honour come from Heaven" instead of saying, "Life and death come from Heaven, wealth and honour depend on Destiny '.'" — For life and death there are no heavenly signs, they depend on the constitution. When a man has got a strong constitution, his vital force is exuberant, and his body strong. In case of bodily strength life's destiny is long: the long-lived do not die young. Conversely, he who has got a weak constitution possesses but a feeble vital force, and a delicate bodily frame. Delicacy is the cause of the shortness of life's destiny; the short-lived die early. Consequently, if we say that there is a destiny, destiny means constitution.

As regards the transmission of wealth and honour, it is like the vital force, *viz.* an effluence emanating from the stars. Their hosts are on heaven, which has their signs. Being born under a star pointing at wealth and honour, man obtains wealth and honour, whereas under a heavenly sign implying poverty and misery, he will become poor and miserable. Thus wealth and honour' come from Heaven, but how is this brought about? Heaven has its hundreds of offlcials and multitudes of stars. Just as Heaven emits its fluid, the stars send forth their effluence, which keeps amidst the heavenly fluid, lmbibing this fluid, men are born, and live, as long as they keep it. If they obtain a fine one, they become men of rank, if a common one, common people. Their position may be higher or lower, and their wealth bigger or smaller, according as the stars distributing all this, rank higher

or lower, are larger or smaller.—Heaven has many hundred officials and multitudes of stars, and so we have on earth the essence of tens of thousands of people, of the Five Emperors and the Three Rulers. Heaven has his *Wang Liang* and *Tsao Fu,* men have them also. He who is endued with their essence, becomes skilled in charioteering.

It is said that three different kinds of destiny can be distinguished, the *natural,* the *concomitant,* and the *adverse* one. One *Wang (h'ung* puts a construction upon the words of *Tse Hsia,* of which he probably never thought. *Tse Hsia* used Destiny and Heaven as synonyms, as we do.-Namely the stars. The first legendary rulers of Chinese history. Two famous charioteers of old, the latter the driver of the eight celebrated steeds of Ring *Mu* of *Chou.* speaks of natural destiny, if somebody's luck is the simple consequence of his original organisation. His constitution being well ordered, and his bones good, he needs not toil in order to obtain happiness, since his luck comes of itself. This is meant by natural destiny. Concomitant destiny conies into play, when a man becomes happy only by dint of hard work, but is pursued by misfortune, as soon as he yields to his propensities, and gives rein to his desires. This is to be understood by concomitant destiny. As for adverse destiny, a man may. contrary to his expectations, reap bad fruits from all his good deeds; he will rush into misfortune and misery, which will strike him from afar. Therefore, one can speak of adverse destiny.

Every mortal receives his own destiny: already at the time of his conception, he obtains a lucky or an unlucky chance. Man's nature does not correspond to his destiny: his disposition may be good, but his destiny unlucky, or his disposition bad, and his fate lucky. Good and bad actions are the result of natural disposition, happiness and misfortune, good and bad luck are destiny. Good deeds may lead to mishap, then the disposition is good, but destiny cruel, and likewise misdeeds may result in happiness, in that case man's nature is wicked, but fate smiling. Nature is good or bad of its own accord, and so is fate lucky or unlucky. A favourite of fate, though not doing well, is not, of necessity, deprived of happiness for that reason, whereas an ill-fated man does not get rid of his misfortune, though trying his best.

Mendus said:—"To strive for a thing, one must have wisdom, but whether he attains it, depends upon destiny." With a good disposition one can struggle for it and, if fate be favourable, obtain it; should, however, fate be averse, one may with a good nature strive for it, but never get it.

Bad deeds are followed by misfortune. Yet the robbers *Chi* and *Chuang Ch'uio* were scourges to the whole empire. With some thousands of other bandits, whom they had collected, they assaulted and robbed people of their property, and cut them to pieces. As outlaws they were unequalled. They ought to have been disgraced: far from it, they flnished their lives as old men. In the face of this, how can the idea of a concomitant destiny be upheld?

Men with an adverse destiny do well in their hearts, but meet with disasters abroad. How is it that men like *Yen Yuan* and *Mencim,* Book VII, Pt. I, chap. 3.

Two famous robbers of antiquity, especially the former, to whom a chapter is devoted in *Chuang l'e.* The same as *Yen Hui,* the favourite disciple of *Confucius. Po Niu* came to disgrace? They were both virtuous, and should have been rewarded by a concomitant destiny with bliss and happiness. Wherefore did they meet with misfortune? *Yen Yuan,* confined to his study, killed himself by his great talents, *Po Niu,* while living quite alone, caught a horrible disease. *Ch'i l P ing* and *Wu Yuan* were the most loyal ministers of their sovereigns, and scrupulously fulfilled their duties as servants to the king. In spite of this, the corpse of *Ch'il P ing* was left unburied in *Ch'u,* and in *Wu Yuan'x* body was cooked. For their good works they should have obtained the happiness of concomitant destiny, but they fell in with the misfortune of adverse fate. How is such a thing possible?

Concomitant destiny excludes adverse destiny, and adverse destiny, a concomitant one. On what basis can the scholastic distinction of three kinds of destiny then be established? Moreover, fate is already visible from the structure of bones at the time of birth, now, if it be said to follow the actions, it comes afterwards, and is not yet there from the beginning. Wealth and honour, poverty and misery are determined at the first moment of receptibility of the human being, they do not arrive only in company with his actions, after the individual has grown up.

A man with a natural fate will die at the age of a hundred years, another with a concomitant fate at the age of fifty, but he whose fate is adverse, meets with distress from the moment he receives vitality; as people say, he is confronted with ill-luck already as an embryo. He may have been born during a thunderstorm and, when he is grown up, die young.

These are what they call the three destinies, there are also distinguished three kinds of natures: *natural, concomitant,* and *adverse.* Naturally man is endowed with the five virtues, concomitant nature corresponds to that of father and mother, and adverse nature is caused by meeting some unpropitious object. Thus a pregnant He worked too hard, and died at the age of thirty-two. His hair had turned quite white already. (Cf. *Legge, Analects,* Prolegomena p. 113.) -*Ch'ii Yuan* or *Ch'u P'ing,* a faithful counsellor of Prince *Hu m* of *Ch'u* in the 4th century B.c., committed suicide by drowning himself, because his admonitions were disregarded. The dragon-boat festival is celebrated in commemoration thereof. *Wu Yuan* or *Wu Yi-in,* a minister of the last king of Wu circa 520 B.c. was sentenced to perish by his own hand. His body was afterwards sewn into a leather wine-sack, and cast into the river near Soochow, where he has been deified as the spirit of the water like *Ch'u P'ing.* This is the common tradition. (Cf. *Magers Manual* N. 879 and *Giles, Biogr. Diet.* N. 2358. According to *Wang Ch'ung* the body of *Wu Yuan* was cooked.) The term nature is used in the sense of spiritual nature, dis-

position, as well as for constitution, i. *e.* physical qualities.

woman eating a hare will bear a hare-lipped son. In the *Yileh-ling* it is stated that, in the same month the thunder is about to utter its voice, and that those who are not careful of their behaviour, will bring forth crippled children, and have great calamities.

They become dumb or deaf, lame or blind. The embryo having been affected by external influences, the child's character will be violent and rebellious. *Yang She Shih Wo's* voice, after his birth, sounded like that of a wolf. When he grew older, he showed a wicked disposition: he met with misfortune, and died. He got this character already, when still in his mother's womb. The like holds good for *Tan Chn* and *Shang Chiln.* Character and destiny are there from the beginning. Therefore the *Li* points out a method to instruct embryos. As long as the child is in the uterus, the mother must not sit down, if the mat be not properly placed, nor eat anything not cut in the proper manner. Her eyes must see but the proper colours, and her ears hear but the proper sounds. When the child grows up, it must be given intelligent teachers and good instructors, who will make it familiar with the relations of sovereign and subject, father and sou, for at that period its virtue or depravity will become manifest. If at the moment, when the ehild receives the vitalising fluid, the mother does not take care to keep her heart free from wild fancies and fears of wickedness, her child, when grown up, will not be good, but fierce and refractory, and look ugly and wicked. A heavenly maiden explained to *Huang Ti* that to have five wives not only entails bodily injury on father and mother, but also most seriously affects the characters of sons and daughters.

Men have their destiny and luck, contingencies and chance. By destiny they are wealthy and poor, exalted and base: their luck is thriving or declining, flourishing or fading. Those whose destiny it is to be rich and honoured, meet with a thriving luck; they enjoy perpetual tranquillity, and are never in jeopardy. On

The *Yueh-ling* is the Book HI, N. 6 of the *Li-Ki,* the *Book of Rites.* The "same month" referred to in the passage, quoted from the *Yueh-ling,* is the second month of spring. *Wang Ch'ung* seems to have had in view the final paragraph as well, which says that, if in the last month of winter the spring ceremonies were observed, the embryos would suffer many disasters. (Cf. *Legge, Li Ki,* Book IV, p. 260 and 310 Sacred Books of the East, Vol. XXVII.) A native of Chin, 6th cent. B.c. The unworthy son of the emperor *Yao* 2357 B.c. The degenerated son of the emperor *Shun* 2255 B.c.

Cf. *Ta-tai-li* chap. 3, p. 6v *(Han Wei tsung shu).*

The first emperor, a mythical personage.

the other hand do such as are doomed to poverty and misery, fall in with a declining luck: they are the victims of ill-fortune; always in trouhle. they know no pleasure.

A *contingencg* is some extraordinary change, such, for instance, as were experienced by *CKing T'ang,* when he was kept a prisoner in *Hsia-tai* and by *Win Wang,* when detained at *Yu-U.* For sages, with all their perfections, to be thrown into jail, this certainly can be called an extraordinary contingency. But however great the change may be, in the case of a favourable destiny and a thriving luck it does no harm. This it what they call a contingent mishap. That which befell *Yen Tse* must be regarded as a great one. Let us suppose that a weapon be pointed at a man's breast, that the bright blade be already touching his neck, that he rush forward to certain death, or that he oppose himself to the points of swords and halberds, let such a man be saved just at the moment, when he expects to die, then his destiny is so good, and his luck so flourishing, that the misfortune he encounters cannot injure him. At *Li-yang* and *Chang ping,* where the catastrophe took place, were certainly people with a propitious fate and a thriving luck, who were all crushed to death in the same night. The disaster they met with was so paramount, that their good fate

and thriving luck could not ward it off. This may be compared to the antagonism between water and fire. If the water is stronger, it quells the fire, and if the fire is stronger, it overcomes the water. To find employment, a man must get hold of an employer. In spite of a propitious fate and thriving luck nobody will be able to show what he is capable of, unless he comes into contact with a master who takes an interest in him.

The word *chance* conveys the idea of good and evil derived from accidents. A culprit, who succeeds in making his escape, has The founder of the *Shang* dynasty, who was imprisoned by the last emperors of the *Hsia.* The ancestor of the house of *Citou.* He was incarcerated at *Yu-U* by the last emperor of the *Shang* dynasty.

Under *Yen Tse* -p *Yen Ying* , a celebrated statesman of the Dukes of *Ch'i,* is usually understood. Since *Yen Ying* was very successful in his career, no misfortune whatever being recorded of him, I would suggest to alter *-f'* into HH-, abbreviated for jpj e *Yen Hui,* the name of the ill-fated disciple of *Confucius,* whose misfortune, his untimely death, is mentioned above p. 26 and elsewhere. See above p. 136. In addition to good luck, according to our author, he who seeks employment requires a contingency, he must find some one who appreciates him. good fortune, whereas it is bad fortune, if an innocent man be arrested. He who after a short incarceration obtains his release, has a propitious destiny and thriving luck so, that the misfortune of an untimely end cannot affect him.

Now for the meaning of *incident,* which will be illustrated by the service offered to a sovereign. Provided that somebody serve the sovereign in the proper way, that the latter appreciate his words, and afterwards employ him, this is a lucky incident. Conversely, if the prince disprove of the man's ways so, that he dismisses him, and sends him away, this is an unlucky incident. Should a man after a short period of disgrace still get an appointment through the recommandation of a higher official, he owes it to his good destiny and thriving luck, which

do not allow that the harm caused by an unlucky incident keeps on for long.

Contingencies and chance either tally with destiny and luck or disagree with them. To hit on good chances, and thus reach the goal, or to meet with bad ones, and be ruined, is tallying with destiny and luck. To fall off in mid-career, without completing what is to come, good being suddenly turned into evil, this is contrary to fate and luck. In tins world men's dispositions and destinies are auspicious or unfavourable, their happiness and misfortune flourish or decline. All depends on contingencies. According to the chances they have, they either live or die. But those who accomplish all their good or bad deeds, and obtain all their heart's desires, are few.

CHAPTER IX.

On Destiny and Fortune *(Ming-lu).*

Man's success as well as his troubles depend upon destiny. It determines his life and his death, and the length of his span, and it likewise provides for his rank and his wealth. From the princes and dukes downwards to the commoners, and from the sages and worthies down to the illiterate people, all those who have a head and eyes, and blood in their veins, each and every one possess their own destiny. If any one is to become poor and miserable, he will be involved in misfortunes and disasters, even though he passes through wealth and honour, whereas he for wdiom wealth and honour are in store, meets with happiness and bliss even in the midst of penury and misery. Therefore, whoever is predestinated for great things, rises by himself from his humble position, while another whose fate is misery, falls down from his high sphere.

Thus it seems, as if the gods lent their help to the wealthy and the great folks, and as if the mishap of the poor and low class people were the work of the demons. When future grandees study with others, they alone reach the goal, and after having taken office, they alone are promoted from among their colleagues. What the future rich men strive for with other competitors, they alone obtain, and what they do conjointly, they alone complete. With poor and low people it is just the reverse. They fail in their studies, fail to be promoted, and fail to complete what they have begun. They make themselves guilty, suffer punishment, fall sick, die, and perish. The loss of wealth and honour means poverty and meanness.

Consequently, there is no guarantee whatever that men of high endowments and excellent conduct will in any case attain to wealth and honour, and we must not imagine that others whose knowledge is very limited, and whose virtue is but small, are therefore doomed to poverty and misery. Sometimes, men of great

Passing the examinations, which is mere luck.

talents and excellent conduct have a bad fate, which cripples them, and keeps them down, and people with scanty knowledge and small virtue may have such a propitious fate, that they soar up and take a brilliant flight.

Wisdom and dullness, pure and mean conduct under given circumstances are character and natural gifts: high and low rank in the official career, and wealth and poverty in business depend on destiny and time. Destiny is not amenable to coercion, or time to compulsion. The knowing, therefore, leave every thing to Heaven, placid, serene, and equanimous even in case their poverty or misery should be changed into wealth and honour.

When in digging a creek or cutting firewood a special energy be shown, or great strength be displayed, then by dint of digging the creek will be deepened, and by dint of hewing much wood will be cut down. Even people without a fate would thus obtain their ends, how then would poverty and meanness, disasters and dangers come in? Perhaps heavy showers might interfere with the completion of the creek, or the wood-cutter might fall in with a tiger, before he had gathered much wood. The low rank of an official and the unprofitableness of a business are like the showers interrupting the digging of a creek, and like the tiger met by the wood-cutter.

Perhaps able men find no occasion to use their talents, and the wise cannot practise their wisdom, or they use their talents, but have no success, and practise their principles, but do not accomplish what they had in view. Though being as gifted and as wise as *Confucius*, it may happen that they never come to the front. The world seeing their high moral standard will ask, "How is it that these sort of worthies and wise men do not become exalted?," and admiring their deep thoughts, they will say, "Why do men of such a wonderful intellect not become rich?"

Rank and wealth depend upon fate, happiness and fortune are not connected with wisdom and intelligence. Therefore it is said that wealth cannot be acquired by calculations,. nor rank be secured by talents. Profound philosophy does not procure riches, and the highest accomplishments do not win an official post. Those who carry silver in their bosoms and wear pendants of red jewels, are not necessarily a *Chi* or a *Hsieh* in talent, and those who amass gold or heap up precious stones, must not be a *Chu* of The god of cereals (cf. p. 130). The wise minister of *Shun* (cf. chap. XXXIX).

Lun-Heng.

T ao in wisdom. Not seldom simpletons areinpossession ofathousand *chin,* and blockheads are made governors of a city. Officers may show the same ability in their administration, their different rank is the result of their fate, and in doing business people may display the same knowledge, their different wealth is the outcome of their fortune. It is fortune which determines wealth and poverty, through knowledge one does neither thrive nor perish, and it is destiny that fixes one's high or low position, through talents one does not advance or fail in one's career.

King *Ch'eng's2* ability did not equal that of the Duke of *Chan.* and Duke *Huan's3* intelligence fell short of that of *Kuan Cliung.* Nevertheless *Ch big* and *H1um* were endowed with the most glorious fate, whereas the Duke of *Chou* and *Kuan Cltung'* received inferior appointments. In ancient times, princes very seldom did not learn from their ministers. Possessing an extensive knowledge the latter would, as a rule, act as their fathers and instructors. In spite of this unsufficiency, the princes would take the place of sovereigns, and their ministers with all their accomplishments had to serve as their menials. That shows that rank depends upon destiny, and not on intelligence, and that wealth is good fortune, and has nothing to do with mental faculties.

Most people discussing these questions fancy that men of genius ought to be made generals and ministers, and that less gifted persons should become peasants and traders. Observing that scholars of great abilities are not called to office, they are surprised, and reproach them with incompetency for practical business, and likewise they wonder at other scholars, who have a turn of mind for the practical (but do not get on), and imagine that they must be too weak in theory. As a matter of fact, they are not aware that, though a person may be most admirable either in theory or in practice, it is merely destiny that governs his official status and his emoluments. When clever men undertake something at a lucky and propitious time, and happiness survenes, then people will call them clever, whereas, when they witness a decline, and the arrival of misfortune, they regard them as stupid. They do not know a lucky and inauspicious fate, or a thriving and declining fortune.

This was the name assumed by the famous minister of the *Yiieh* State *Fan Li,* when, having retired from public life, he lived incognito in *Ch'i.* Under this name he amassed a large fortune so, that *T'ao Chu Kung* has become a synonym for a "millionaire." (Cf. *Giles, Bibl. Diet.* N. 540.) King *Ch'eni/* of the *Choxi* dynasty (cf. chap. XL). *lluan,* duke of *Chti* (cf. p. 171i). *Po Kuei* and *Tse Kung* made a fortune by the transport of wares, and had heaps of gold and jewels. People spoke of their excellent methods and their great learning. *Chu Fu Yen* was despised and slighted in *Chi,* which would have none of him. He went to the imperial palace, and presented a memorial, whereupon he was employed by the *Han,* and rose in office as high as a minister of State. *Hsu Yileh* of *Chao* also sent up a memorial, when he was together with *Yen Chang.* His Majesty was pleased with his words, and appointed him secretary of a board. People praise the talents of *Chu Fu Yen* and the skill of *H,ii Yileh,* but they are mistaken. When literati are able to comment upon one classic, in which they have become well versed in the capital, as lucidly as *Huang ChiJt Kuei* and as thoroughly as *Chao Tse Tu,* who passed the flrst and the second examinations at the first trial, and immediately were promoted to the rank of a secretary of a ministry and of an academician, people believe that they have obtained this by their profound knowledge of the classics and their genius, which is wrong.

In the case of able speakers such as *Fan Sui,* who in *Ch in* was ennobled as a Marquis of *Ying,* and of *T sai Tse"* who after he had spoken to *Fan Sui,* was appointed alien minister, they pretend that these happy results were brought about by the excellence of *Fan Sui* and *T sai Tse,* but that is erroneous. All the above-mentioned persons were predestinated for opulence and nobility, and it was just the proper time for these lucky events to happen.

Confucius said, "Life and death depend on Destiny, wealth and honour come from Heaven." Duke *P ing* of *Lu* wished to see *Mencius,* but his minion *Tsang T sang* slandered *Mencius,* and dissuaded him. *Mencius* said, "It is Heaven." *Confucius,* a sage, A keen business man, who flourished under the Marquis *Wen* of *Wei* in the 5th cent. B.c. A disciple of *Confucius,* who became very rich. *Chu Fu Yen* lived in the 2nd cent. B.c. He was an enemy of *Tung Chung Shu* tcf. p. 84). Who could explain a book, and solve knotty questions in the presence of the sovereign. Cf. p. 115. Cf. chap. XXIV. Because *T'sai Tse* was not a native of *Ch'in,* but of *Yen.* King *Ch'ao* of *Ch'in* (305—250 B.c.) made him his minister on the recommendation of *Fan Sui.* Cf. p. 136.. See chap. XXXIV. and *Mencius,* a "worthy, exhorting people to conform to the right principles, did not confound truth and untruth. Since they spoke of destiny, it is evident that

there is a destiny. *Huai Nan Tse* says in his work, "Benevolence and meanness depend upon time, not on conduct, and profit and loss are brought ahout by fate, not by knowledge." And *Chia Yi* states, "With Heaven one cannot fix a time, and with *Tuo* one cannot lay plans. Early and late are predetermined by destiny. How could the time be known?" When *Kao Tsu* fought against *Ch ing Pu,*-he was hit by a stray arrow. His illness being very serious, the Empress *Lil Hon* consulted an able physician. This doctor said that the disease could be cured, but *Kao Tsu* abused him saying, "I. a simple citizen, have with my sword of three feet conquered the world. Was that not Heaven's decree? Destiny depends on Heaven. Even a *PU'n Ch'ioh* would he no use." When *Han Hsin* spoke with the emperor on military things, he said to *Kao Tsu,* "The heavenly appointment, of which Your Majesty speaks, cannot be won by skill or force. " *Yung Tse Yiln* teaches that to meet with what one desires, or not to meet with it, is fate, and the *Grand Annalist* asserts that wealth and honour do not exclude poverty and meanness, and that the latter do not exclude wealth and honour. That means that opulence and nobility may turn into indigence and humbleness, and that indigence and humbleness may be changed into opulence and nobility. Rich and noble persons do not desire poverty and misery, but poverty and misery may come of themselves, and poor and humble fellows may not strive for wealth and honour, yet wealth and honour fall to their sort spontaneously.

When in spring or summer people die in prison, and when in autumn and winter they wear an air of prosperity, this is not the result of their works. The sun rises in the morning, and sets in the evening, not because people wish it, for the principle of Heaven is spontaneity. The King of 7at arrived from *Tai,* and A scholar of the 2nd cent., who wrote the *Hsin-shu* and some poetry. The king of *Huai-nan,* who had revolted. A celebrated physician. The passage is quoted from the *Shi-chi,* chap. 8 *(Chavannes, Mhn. Hist.* Vol. II, p. 400).

One of the Three Heroes who helped *Han Kao Tsu* to win the throne. Cf. p. 124. According to Chinese customs executions of criminals take place in autumn. The fifth son of the emperor *Kao Tsu.* The empress *Lii hou* wished to leave the empire to one of the *Lii* princes, her own kinsmen. became the Emperor *Win Ti. Cl10u Yn Fu,* an illegitimate son, was made Marquis of *Tiao.* At first, the King of *Tea* was not heirapparent, and *Chou Ya Fu* was not the legitimate son, but they encountered the proper time, and fell in with the right moment, which led to their elevation.

In case a person predestinated for poverty, acquires wealth by his exertions and his energy, he dies, when he has made a fortune, and should another doomed to humility win honours by his talents and abilities, he will be dismissed, when he has made himself a position. They win wealth and honour by their energy and their genius, but are unable to keep in possession of fate and hick, just as a vessel holds but a certain quantity, and as a hand lifts but a certain weight. If a vessel holds just one pint, then one pint exactly fills it, but, as soon as there is more than one pint, it flows over. Provided that a hand can just lift one *chiin,* then it balances one *chiln,* but, when one *chiin* is exceeded, he who lifts it up, tumbles and falls.

Former generations knew the truth, therefore they ascribed every thing to destiny, and such is destiny indeed. Those who trust in destiny, can live in retirement and await their time. They need not exhaust their vitality, or harass their bodies, hunting after it—for it is like pearls and jewels, concealed in lakes and mountains. Heaven's fate is difficult to know. People are unable to find it out. Although their fate be propitious, they have no confidence in it, and therefore seek it. If they understood it, they would be aware that, though fleeing wealth and shunning honour, at length they cannot get rid of it.

Thus they presume that force overcomes poverty, and that diligence vanquishes misfortune. They exert themselves, and do their utmost to acquire wealth, and they cultivate their faculties, and purify their conduct to win honour. But neglecting the proper time, and acting in a wrong way, they will never obtain the wealth and honour they crave for. Even though they admit the existence of fate, they imagine that it must be sought.

He who is convinced that fate cannot be sought, maintains that it must come of its own accord. One obtains it of itself without any alien assistance, it is completed without any work, and it arrives spontaneously without any cooperation on the part of the recipient. The nerves and sinews of those who are to be 179-157 B.c. Chief minister of *Han Wm Ti* (cf. chap. XXIV).

30 catties.

rich, become strong of themselves, and those who are to have rank and titles, get a fine intellect spontaneously, just as in a thousand *A* horse the head, the eyes, the feet, and the hoofs all suit together.

That fate, if sought, cannot be obtained, does not mean that it can be won, if not affected. Men of great knowledge need not seek honour, for it comes of its own accord, and the active and energetic need not seek wealth, for it falls to them spontaneously. The happiness of wealth and honour cannot be attracted by any efforts, nor can the unhappines of poverty and humbleness be simply avoided. Consequently, the fate of wealth and honour is obtained without any effort. Those who believe in fate will say they know that luck requires no seeking. When the heavenly fate is particularly lucky, it is obtained spontaneously without an effort, whereas, when it is unpropitious, all endeavours are of no help against it.

As creatures are born not because they have wished it, so men become exalted without having struggled for it. Human character is such, that some people are good of themselves without instruction, and that others never become good in spite of instruction. The heavenly nature is like fate. King *Yi* of *Yfoh* escaped into the mountains, earnestly desiring not to become king, and w ishing to find a substitute. But the people of *Ytieh* smoked his den so, that at last he could not escape, and ascend-

ed the throne by force. By Heaven's fate it had to be so. Though fleeing and running away from it, he could not avoid it at last. Thus he spontaneously obtained the honour which he had not sought.

A swift horse supposed to make a thousand Li in one day. He was assassinated by his younger brother in 376 B.C. *(CAavarmes, Min. Hist.* Vol. IV, p. 433, Note 5). CHAPTER X.

On Chance and Luck *(Hsing-ou).*

In their doings men may be clever or stupid, but with regard to the happiness or unhappiness, which fall to their share, they are either lucky or unlucky. Their works are good or evil, but, whether they meet with rewards or punishment, depends on their good or bad fortune. If several people suffer an armed attack at the same time, those who find a hiding place, are not wounded, and if some persons are overtaken by frost on the same day, those who obtain shelter, suffer no injury. It does not follow that the wounded or injured are wicked, or that those who found a hiding place or a shelter, are meritorious. To find a refuge or shelter is good luck, to be wounded or injured is bad luck. There are many who would be pleased to give proofs of their loyalty, but out of these some are rewarded, some punished: many would fain benefit their country, but only some are trusted by their sovereign, the others he suspects. Those whom he rewards and confides in, are not necessarily trustworthy, nor are those whom he punishes and mistrusts, of necessity traitors. Reward and trust is good fortune, punishment and suspicion, bad.

From among the seventy odd pupils of *Confucius, Yen Hui* died in early youth. *Confucius* said, "Unluckily his span was short, therefore he died." If a short life he spoken of as unlucky, then longevity must be a matter of luck, and a short life, something unlucky. He who walks in the footsteps of sages and worthies, and expounds the doctrines of kindness and justice, ought to enjoy bliss and happiness. However, *Po Niu* fell sick, and did not fare much better than *Yen Hui:* they were both unlucky.

Mole-crickets and ants creep on the

ground. If man lifts his foot, and walks on them, the crickets and ants crushed by his feet die at once, whereas those which are untouched continue alive and unhurt. Wild grass is consumed by fire kindled by the friction of cart-wheels. People are fond of the grass which remained unburnt, and commonly call it "lucky grass." Nevertheless, that an insect has not been trodden upon, or some grass not been reached by Another disciple of *Confucius.* On his sickness cf. *Analects* VI, 8 and p. 105. the fire, is not yet a proof of their excellence. The movement of the feet, and the spread of the fire are merely accidental.

The same reasoning holds good for the breaking out of ulcers. When the free circulation of humours is stopped, they coagulate, and form a boil: as it begins to run, it becomes a sore:—the blood comes out, and matter is discharged. Are those pores, where the ulcer breaks through, better than others? No, only the working of the good constitution has been checked in some places.

When the spider has woven its web, some of the flying insects pass it unharmed, others are caught; when the hunter has spread his nets, some of the beasts stirred up come to bay, the others escape. In the fishing nets thrown into rivers and lakes many fish are pulled out, others get away. It happens that robbers and the like, guilty of the worst crimes, are never found out, whereas people who have committed a small offence to be atoned for by a fine only, are immediately discovered. Thus, general calamities affect people differently. Such as are unlucky die of the shock, and the lives of the fortunate are spared. Unlucky means not favoured by circumstances. *Confucius* said:—" Plan's life must be upright. A life without it is based on good fortune only." Accordingly, those who on a smooth road meet with accidents, have bad luck.

Should anybody standing at the foot of a high wall be crushed by its fall, or, while walking on a river bank full of crevices, be buried by the earth's collapsing under his feet, such a one would simply have met with an accident, that is to say would have been unlucky.

The city gate of the capital of *Lu* was in a state of decay since a long time, and about to tumble down. When *Confucius* passed it, he hurried up, and quickened his pace. His attendants said to him:— " It has been like this ever so long." *Confucius* replied saying, "Its having so long remained so is just what displeases me." *Confucius* was precautious in the extreme; had the gate fallen down, just when he passed it, one might speak of him as unlucky. *Confucius* said, "Superior men may have no luck, but there are none who have luck. Low people often have luck, and there are none quite devoid of luck,'" and further:—" The superior man keeps *Analects* VI, 17. The meaning is that the successes of superior men are due to their own excellence, not to mere chance, but that they are often visited with misfortune. With common people it is different. Their happiness is never their own work, but luck, which often favours them. in safe places, thus awaiting his destiny, the ordinary man courts dangers, relying on favourable circumstances." Impostors like *Hung Ju,* and *Chieh Jn,* though possessed of no virtue or ability, were nevertheless admired for their beauty; unworthy of love, they found favour, and unfit to associate with, they were chosen as companions. According to right and reason this ought not to be. Therefore, the Grand Annalist devotes a chapter to them. Bad characters who in a similar way, though perverting all moral principles, are honoured, and held in high esteem, are by a common name called adventurers.

If a man devoid of virtue receives favours, it amounts to the same, as if another without any fault of his own meets with misfortune. All creatures originally endowed with vitality become partly men, partly beasts, or birds. Of human beings, men though they be one and all, some are honoured, others despised, some are rich, others poor. The rich man may hoard up heaps of gold, whereas a poor fellow is compelled to beg for his food. A nobleman will perhaps rise to the rank of a marquis, whilst the low born sinks into a state of slavery. It is

not, because Heaven has given them different qualities.

Man's natural disposition may be kind or mean; yet even if the conduct of some persons be equally honest and virtuous, happiness and misfortune are not equally divided among them, and although they practise benevolence and justice in the same way, success and failure are not the same. *Win* of *Chin* sought to acquire knowledge and virtue, and *Yen* of *Hsil* acted with benevolence and justice; the former was rewarded, the latter utterly ruined. A man of *Lu* having avenged his father, remained quietly where he was, and did not flee. The pursuers let him off. *Niu Ch'ileh* was abducted by robbers; he endured it fearlessly and with equanimity, but the robbers killed him. Now, knowledge and virtue are about the same as benevolence and justice, and not running away as much as fearlessness, nevertheless Duke *Win* and the man of *Lu* were happy, and King *Yen* and Aim *Chileh,* unhappy, the *Chung-gung* (Doctrine of the Mean) chap. XV. Two minions of the emperors *Han Kao Tm* (206—194 u.r.) and *Hui Ti* (194-187). *Slu-chi* chap. 125. An old State in modern *Slmnsi,* where the Marquis *Wen* reigned from 779-744 B.c. The name of a State, whose lords were viscounts, in modern *Anhui,* An old feudal State in *Shantung.* Higher titles used to be given to those feudal princes than they were entitled to. one had good luck, the others bad. The Duke of *Han, Chao,* while drunk fell asleep, and would have caught cold but for the master of caps, who covered him with a cloak. When the duke became aware of it, he made inquiries, and learnt that the master of caps had shown him this mark of his affection, yet he punished him for having transgressed his proper duties. A lackey in *Wei* perceiving that the charioteer was driving wrong, shouted from behind towards the chariot with a view to preserving it from danger, but was not called to account. The lackey when shouting towards the chariot, and the master of the caps when spreading the cloak, had the same intentions. The one

was afraid that his master might catch cold, the other that his prince would be hi danger. Both followed the impulses of goodness and kindheartedness, but the man in *Han* was punished, the other in *Wei,* considered a faithful servant. The lackey had good fortune, the master of the caps not.

The same principle applies to things as well as to man. Bamboos several tenths of feet in height, and trees measuring some yards in circumference are cut down by artisans for use. Some are worked into tools, and carried here and there, others are not taken as material, and neglected. The artisans are not biased in favour of some, or prejudiced against others, but knives and adzes cut down the wood, as it were, by chance.

Grain, when steamed, becomes food; out of cooked grain wine is distilled. Distilled wine has different flavours, it may be sweet or bitter. Cooked food tastes differently, being either hard or soft. The cook and the distiller while at work have not different intentions, but the movements of hands and fingers are subject to chance. Well done food is kept in different baskets, and sweet wine is filled in various vessels. Supposing an insect drops into such a vessel, then the wine is spilled, and not drunk; should a mouse contaminate a basket, the food is thrown away, and not eaten.

The various plants are all good for something. Those which happen to be plucked by a physician, become medicine, others are left in the dried-up ravines, and burnt as fuel. So with metals: — some are wrought into swords and halberds, some into spears and hoes; so with wood:—some is shaped into the beams of a palace, some into the pillars of a bridge. The same with fire:—it may have to light a candle, or to burn dry grass; the same with earth:— some builds up halls and mansions, some serves as plaster for porches, and with water, which may be used for cleansing tripods and cauldrons as well as for washing filthy things.

All things, whether good or bad, are used by man. If one can be sorry for those things, which in this respect have no luck and no chance, living creatures are still much more to be pitied.

Shun was a sage, and ought to have obtained perfect peace and happiness in life. But he had a blockhead for a father and a silly mother, and his brother was arrogant and brutal. They disliked him, the faultless, and punished him, although he did no wrong. His was extremely bad luck. Confucius was inferior to Shun. He never owned a foot of land in his life, but restlessly wandered about, seeking employment. His traces were obliterated, and his food cut off. In spite of their being sages these two personages were visited with bad luck and bad chance. Shun still happened to take over the empire, which Yao resigned to him, but Confucius died in Cliueh-li. If even with the qualities of a sage one has no luck, we cannot be surprised to find much bad luck and misfortune among ordinary men. Chuang Tse XIV, 25v. (T'ien-giin) informs us that the traces of Confucius were obliterated in Wei. Confucius spent there many years of his life, but without gaining any influence on its prince, and therefore left no trace. When Confucius was travelling from the Ch'en State to T'sai, his provisions became exhausted, and Confuciax with his followers had to suffer hunger. Analects XV, 1. Chen and T'sai were situated in south-eastern Honan. CHAPTER XI.

Wrong Notions about Happiness (Fu-Jisii).

People universally believe that he who does good, meets with happiness, and that the evil-doers are visited with misfortune. That Heaven sends down happiness or misfortune in response to man's doings. That the rewards graciously given by the sovereigns to the virtuous, are visible, whereas the requital of Heaven and Earth is not always apparent. There is nobody, high or low, clever or imbecile, who would disagree with this view. Only because people see such deeds recorded in books, and witness that sometimes the good really become happy, they come to believe this, and take it as self-evident. Sometimes also sages and wise men, with a view to inducing people to do good, do not hesitate to assert that it must be so, thus showing that virtue gets its reward. Or those who hold this view, have themselves experienced that felicity arrived at a certain juncture. A thorough investigation, however, will convince us that happiness is not given by Heaven as a favour.

King Hui of Ch'u, when eating salad, found a leech upon his plate, and forthwith swallowed it. He thereupon felt a pain in his stomach, and could eat nothing. On his premier asking him, how he had got this disease, he replied:—" Eating salad, I found a leech. I thought that, if I scolded those responsible for it, but did not punish them, I would disregard the law, and not keep up my dignity. Therefore, I could not allow my subjects to get wind of the matter. Had I, on the other hand, reproved and chastised the defaulters, strict law would have required the death of all the cooks and butlers. To that I could not make up my mind. Fearing, lest my attendants should perceive the leech, I promptly swallowed it."

The premier rose from his seat, bowed twice, and congratulated the king, saying, "I have been told that Heaven is impartial, and that virtue alone is of any avail. You have benevolence and virtue, for which Heaven will reward you. Your sickness will do you no great harm."

The same evening, when the king withdrew, the leech came out, and an ailment of the heart and stomach of which he had been suffering for a long while, was cured at the same time. Could not this be considered an evidence of Heaven's partiality for virtue?—No. This is idle talk.

If King Hui swallowed the leech, he was far from being what a sovereign should be, and for unbecoming deeds Heaven does not give marks of its favour. King Hui could not bear to reproach the guilty with the leech for fear, lest his cooks and butlers should all have to suffer death according to law. A ruler of a State can mete out rewards and punishments at pleasure, and pardoning is a prerogative of his. Had King Hui reprimanded all for the leech found in his salad, the cooks and butlers would have had to submit to law, but afterwards the king was at liberty not to allow that the lives of men were taken merely for a culinary offence. Thus to forgive, and to remit the penalty, would have been an act of great mercy. If the cooks had received their punishment, but were not put to death, they would have completely changed for the future. The king condoning a small offence, and sparing the lives of the poor devils, would have felt all right, and not been sick. But he did nothing of that sort. He ate perforce something obnoxious to his health. Allowing his butlers to remain ignorant of their fault, he lost his royal dignity, because he did not repress their bad conduct. This was objectionable in the first place.

If cooks and butlers in preparing a dish do not make it sweet or sour enough, or if an atom of dust no bigger than a louse, hardly perceptible or visible to the eye, falls into the salad, if in such a case a sovereign in fixing a penalty takes into consideration the mind of the offender, and therefore abstains from divulging his fault, one may well speak of clemency. Now, a leech is an inch or more long and '/io of i broad. In a salad a one-eyed man must see it. The servants of the king showed an utter want of respect, taking no care to cleanse the salad. Theirs was a most serious offence. For King Hui not to reprimand them was a second mistake.

In a salad there must be no leech. If so, one does not eat it, but throws it to the ground. Provided one is anxious, lest the attendants should discover it, he may hide it in his bosom. Thus the leech can escape observation. Why must one eat it coute-quecoA/e? If something uneatable is by inadvertence in a salad so, that it can be concealed, to eat it by force is a third mistake.

If Heaven had rewarded an unbecoming act, an unworthy person would have been the recipient of Heaven's grace. The inability to reprove for the sake of a leech is, in the eyes of the world, something very excellent. Now, there is many an excellent man, whose deeds are similar to the swallowing of a leech.

If for swallowing a leech Heaven grants liberation from sickness, excellent men must always be without ailiugs. The virtue of this kind of men is, however, small only and not to be compared with the perfect character of the true sages and their guileless demeanour. There are many sages who would push their kindness of heart so far as to put up with human faults. Yet the Emperor *Wu Wang* was of a weak health, and *Confucius* seriously ill. Why has Heaven been so inconsistent in the distribution of its favour?

It may be that after King *Hui* had swallowed the leech, it came out again in a natural way of itself. Whenever anybody eats a living thing, it will inevitably die. The stomach is hot inside. When the leech is gulped down, it does not die instantaneously, but owing to the high temperature of the stomach it begins to move. Hence the pain in the stomach. After a short while, the leech dies, and the pain in the stomach ceases also.

It is in the nature of leeches to suck blood. King *Hut's* heart and bowel complaint was probably nothing but a constipation of blood. Therefore this constipation was cured along with the death of the blood-sucking animal, just as a men suffering from the skin disease known as "rat" can be cured by eating a cat, because it is natural to cats to eat rats. The various things overcome one another. Remedies and antidotes are given on the same principal. Therefore it cannot be a matter for surprise that by eating a leech a disease should be removed. Living things, when eaten, will die. Dead, they invariably come out in a natural way. Consequently, the re-appearance of the leech cannot be an act of special grace.

The premier seeing the kindheartedness of King *Hut* and knowing that the leech after entering the stomach must come forth again, when dead, therefore bowed twice, and congratulated the king upon his not being injured by his disease. He thereby showed his power of forethought, and pleased his sovereign. His utterance.is in the same style as that of *Tse Wei,* who said that a star

Astrologer at the court of Duke *Vhing* of *Sung* (515—451 B.o.) who venerated him like a god.
would shift its place, and ot" the "Great Diviner,"-who asserted that the earth was going to move.

A family in *Sung* had for three generations never swerved from the path of virtue. %Vithout any apparent reason a black cow belonging to this family dropped a white calf. *Confucius* was asked, and said that it was a lucky omen, and that the calf ought to be sacrificed to the spirits, which was done accordingly. After one year, the father of the family became blind without a reason. The cow then produced a white calf a second time. The father sent his son to ask *Confucius,* who replied that it was a propitious portent, and that the animal must be immolated, which was done again. After a year, the son lost his eye-sight, nobody knew why. Subsequently, *Cli u* attacked *Sung,* and besieged its capital. At that time the besieged were in such a distress, that they exchanged their sons, and ate them, breaking their bones, which they used as firewood. It was but for their blindness that father and son were not called upon to mount guard on the city wall. When the enemy's army raised the siege, father and son could see again. This is believed to be a proof of how the spirits requited great deserts, but it is idle talk: —

If father and son of that family in *Sung* did so much good, that the spirits rewarded them, why must they first make them blind, and afterwards restore their sight? Could they not protect them, if they had not been blind and always seeing? Being unable to help men, if not blind, the spirits would also be powerless to protect the blind.

Had the two commanders of *Sung* and *Chu* made such a furious onslaught, that the weapons were blunted, the dead bodies covered with blood, the warriors captivated, or killed never to come back, then blindness might have afforded an excuse for not going to the front, and that might have been construed as a divine protection. But before the armies of *Sung* and *Ch'u* came to blows, *Hun*

Yuan and *Tse Fan* made a covenant, and went back. The two forces returned home unscathed, and the blades of the swords, and the points of the arrows were not blunted by use. The duty The planet Mars (cf. p. 127).
The "Great Diviner" of *Ch'i,* on whom vid. p. 112. This fact is mentioned in the *Shi-chi* chap. 38, p. 14v. The siege took place from.",!).,—504 n.c. The whole story seems to be a quotation from *Lieit Tie* VIII, 6v. or from *Hunt Kan Tse* XVIII, 6 who narrate it with almost the same words. *Hua Yuan* was the general of *Sung, Tse Fun* that of *Ch'u.* Both armies being equally exhausted by famine, the siege was raised. of mounting the city wall did not entail death, consequently the two good men could not have obtained the divine protection, while this duty was being performed. In case they had not been blind at that time, they would not have died either. The blind and the not blind all got off. What benefit did those good men derive then from their blindness, for which the spirits were responsible?

Were the families of the blind alone well off, when the State of *Snug* was short of provisions? All had to exchange their sons with the families which mounted guard on the wall, and they split their bones. If in such straits such good people alone were still blind and unable to see, the spirits in giving their aid have failed to discriminate justly between the good and the wicked.

Father and son had probably been blinded by exposure to cold wind, a mere chance. When the siege was over, they owed their cure to chance also. The world knowing that they had done good works, that they had offered two white calves in sacrifice, that during the war between *Swig* and *Ch'u* they alone had not mounted the wall, and that after the siege they regained their sight, thought this to be the recompense of virtue, and the protection granted by the spirits.

When the minister of *Ch'u, Sun Shu Ao* was a boy, he beheld a two-headed snake, which he killed and buried. He then went home, and cried before his mother. She asked him, what was the matter. He replied:—"I have heard say that he who sees a two-headed snake must die. Now, when I went out, 1 saw a two-headed snake. I am afraid that I must leave you and die, hence my tears. " Upon his mother inquiring, where the snake was now, he rejoined:—"For fear lest others should see it later, 1 have killed it outright, and buried it."

The mother said:—"I have heard that Heaven will recompense hidden virtue. You are certainly not going to die, for Heaven must reward you." And, in fact, *Sun Shu Ao* did not die, but, later on, became prime minister of *Ch'u*. For interring one snake he received two favours. This makes it clear that Heaven rewards good actions.

According to *Lieh Tse* and *Hum Ann Tse* the two blind men were, in fact, saved from death by their blindness. *Lieh Tse he. cit.* adds that over half of the defenders of the city wall were killed, and *Huai Nan Tse* says that all except the two blind men were massacred by the besiegers. *Wang Ch'ung* follows the *Shi-chi* in his narrative of the salvation of the city. 6th cent. B.c.

No, it is idle talk. That he who sees a two-headed snake, must die, is a common superstition, and that Heaven gives happiness as a reward for hidden virtue, a common prejudice. *Sun Shu Ao,* convinced of the superstition, buried the snake, and his mother, addicted to the prejudice, firmly relied on the heavenly retaliation. This would amount to nothing else than that life and death were not depending on fate, but on the death of a snake.

T'ien Win of *Ch'i,* Prince of *Ming Ch'ang,* was born on the 5th day of the 5th moon. His father *T'ien Ying* expostulated with his mother saying, why do you rear him? She replied:—"Why do you not wish to rear a fifth month child?" *T'ten Ying* said: — "A fifth month sou will become as high as a door, and kill both his father and mother." She rejoined:—" Does the human fate depend on Heaven or on doors? If on Heaven, you have nothing to complain of, if on a door, he must become as high as a door. Who ever attained to that?"

Later on, *T'ien Wen* grew as high as a

door, but *T'ien Ying* did not die. Thus the apprehension to rear a child in the fifth month proved unfounded. The disgust at the sight of a twoheaded snake is like the repugnance to rear a child of the fifth month. Since the father of such a child did not die, it follows that a two-headed snake cannot bring misfortune either.

From this point of view, he who sees a two-headed snake, does not die, as a matter of course, but not on account of having buried a snake. If for interring one snake one receives two favours, how many must one obtain for ten snakes? *Sun Shu Ao* by burying a snake, lest other persons should look at it, showed an excellent character. The works of excellent men do not merely consist in burying snakes. *Sun Shu Ao* may have accomplished many other meritorious acts, before he buried the snake. Endowed with a good nature by Heaven, people do good under all circumstances. Such well deserving persons ought to see propitious things, instead of that he unexpectedly falls in with a snake that kills man. Was perhaps *Sun Shu Ao* a wicked man, before he beheld the snake, and did Heaven intend to kill him, but condoned his guilt, and spared his life upon seeing him burying the snake?

Died 279 B.c. Tins day is still now regarded as very unlucky in many respects, although it be the Great Summer Festival or the Dragon Boat Festival. On the reasons cf. *Oe Groot, Les Fetes annuelles) Kmoni.* Vol. I, p. 320. A quotation from the *Sfu-chi*, chap. 75, p. 2v,

Lun-Henf. 11

A stone is hard from the time of its formation, a fragrant flower has its perfume from the time, when it came out. If it be said that *Sun Shu Ao's* virtue became manifest, when he buried the snake, then he would not have received it from Heaven at his birth.

The Confueianist *Tung Wu Hsin* and the Mehist *Ch'an Tse* met, and spoke about *Tuo. Chan Tse* extolled the Mehist theory of the help of the spirits, and as an instance adduced duke *Mu .of Ch'in.* His excellent qualities were so brilliant

that God granted him an age of ninety years. *Ch'an Tse* gets into trouble with *Yao* and *Shun,* who were not favoured with a long life, and *Chieh* and *Chou,* who did not die young. *Yao, Shun, Chieh,* and *Chou* belong to remote antiquity, but in modern times likewise duke *Mu* of *Ch'in* and duke *Win* of Gviitt are difficult to account for.

The posthumous name expresses man's actions. What he has done during his life-time, appears in his posthumous title. *Mu* is an expression for error and disorder," *Win* means virtue and goodness. Did Heaven reward error and disorder with long years, and take the life of him who practised virtue and benevolence?

The reign of Duke *Mu* did not surpass that of Duke *Win* of Chin, and the latter's posthumous title was better than that of Duke *Mu.* But Heaven did not extend *Win* of *Chin's* life, he only granted longer years to Duke *Mu.* Thus the retribution A scholar of the *Han* time.
-Demons and spirits who reward the virtuous, and punish the perverse, play an important part in the doctrine of *Me Ti.* (Cf. *Falier, Micrus,* Elberfeld 1877, p. 91.) The parallel passage in chap. XXVII speaks of nineteen extra years, with which the Duke was rewarded. 658-619 B.c. 634-626 B.c. The *Mu* in the Duke of *Ch'in's* name = "Jjj does not mean:- error and disorder, it signifies: —majestic, grand, admirable. But this *Mu* is often replaced by the character which has the bad meaning given by *Wang Ch'ung.* I pre sume that in the original text of the *Lmn-lu'mg* the latter character was used, whereas we now read the other. In the parallel passage chap. XXVII jp. *J£* is actually written, and so it is in the *Shi-chi* chap. 5, p. 9v. et seq. The *Shi-chi* knows nothing of such a miracle. Duke *Mu* was a great warrior as was Duke *Wen,* but the latter's rule is described by *Sse Ma Ch'ien* as very enlightened and beneficial. (Cf. on Duke *Mu: -Chavannes, Man. Historique.* Vol. 1I, p. 25-4.", and on Duke *Wen.* Vol. IV, p. 291-308.) of Heaven would appear as capricious and perverse as Duke *Mn* himself was.

Under heaven the good men are few,

and the bad ones many. The good follow right principles, the bad infringe Heaven's commands. Yet the lives of bad men are not short therefore, nor the years of the good ones prolonged. How is it that Heaven does not arrange that the virtuous always enjoy a life of a hundred years, and that the wicked die young, or through their guilt?

CHAPTER XII.

Wrong Notions on Unhappiness *(Huo-hsil).*

Since what the world calls happiness and divine grace is believed to be the outcome of moral conduct, it is also a common belief that the victims of misfortune and disgrace are thus visited because of their wickedness. Those sunk in sin, and steeped in iniquity Heaven and Earth punish, and the spirits retaliate upon them. These penalties, whether heavy or light, will be enforced, and the retributions of the spirits reach far and near.

Tse Hsia is related to have lost his sight, while mourning for his son. *Tsing Tse* by way of condolence wept. *Tse Hsia* thereupon exclaimed "0 Heaven, 1 was not guilty!" *Tseng Tse* grew excited, and said "In what way are you innocent, *Shang?* " I served our master with you betw een the *Citu* and the *Sse,* but you retired to the region above the West River, where you lived, until you grew old. You misled the people of the West River into the belief that you were equal to the master. That was your first fault. When mourning for your parents, you did nothing extraordinary, that people would talk about. That was your second fault. But in your grief over your son, you lost your eye-sight. That was your third fault. How dare you say that you are not guilty?" *Tse Hsia,* threw away his staff, went down, on his knees and said, "I have failed, I have failed! I have left human society, and also led a solitary life for ever so long."6

Thus *Tse llsia* having lost his sight, *Tsing Tse* reproved him for his faults. *Tse Hsia* threw away his stick, and bowed to *Tseng Tse's* words. Because, as they say, Heaven really punishes the guilty, therefore evidently his eyes lost their sight. Having thus humbly A disciple

of *Confumts.* One of the most famous disciples of *Confucius,* whose name has been connected with the authorship of the Great Learning.

Pu Shang was the name of *Tse Hsia. Tse Hsia* is his style. A small river in the province of *Shantung,* flowing into the *Sse.*

Presumably the western course of the Yellow River.

Quoted from the *Li-ki, T an Kung 1* (cf. *Legge's* translation, *Sacred Books* of the East Vol. XXVII, p. 135). acknowledged his guilt, he is reported to have regained his sight by degrees. Everybody says so, nevertheless a thorough investigation will show us that this belief is illusory.

Loss of sight is like loss of hearing.' Loss of sight is blindness, and loss of hearing, deafness. lie who suffers from deafness, is not believed to have faults, therefore it would be erroneous to speak of guilt, if a man becomes blind. Now the diseases of the ear and the eye are similar to those of the heart and the stomach. In case the ear and the eye lose their faculties, one speaks of guilt perhaps, but can any fault be inferred, when the heart or the stomach are sick?

Po Niu was ill. *Confucius* grasped his hand through the window saying "It will kill him, such is his fate! Such a man to get such a disease!" Originally *Confucius* spoke of *Po Niu's* bad luck, and therefore pitied him. Had *Po Niu's* guilt been the cause of his sickness, then Heaven would have punished him for his wickedness, and he would have been on a level with *Tse Hsia.* In that case *Confucius* ought to have exposed his guilt, as *Tseng Tse* did with *Tse Hsia.* But instead he spoke of fate. Fate is no fault.

Heaven inflicts its punishments on man, as a sovereign does on his subjects. If a man thus chastised, submits to the punishment, the ruler will often pardon him. *Tse Hsia* admitted his guilt, humiliated himself, and repented. Therefore Heaven in its extreme kindness ought to have cured his blindness, or, if *Tse Hsids* loss of sight was not a retribution from Heaven, *Tse Hsia* cannot have been thrice guilty.

Is not leprosy much worse than blindness? If he who lost his sight, had three faults, was then the leper ten times guilty?

Yen Yuan died young and *Tse Lu* came to a premature end, being chopped into minced meat. Thus to be butchered is the most horrid disaster. Judging from *Tse Hsia s* blindness, both *Yen Yuan* and *Tse Lu* must have been guilty of a hundred crimes. From this it becomes evident that the statement of *Tsing Tse* was preposterous. Quotation of *Analects* VI, 8. -*Po Niu,* who was suffering from leprosy. The favourite disciple of *Confiunus,* whose name was *Yen Hui.* The *Tso-chuan,* Book XII *Duke Ai* 15th year, relates that *Tse Lu* was killed in a. revolution in *Wei,* struck with spears, no mention being made of his having been hacked to pieces (cf. *Legge, Ch'un Ch'ht* Pt. II, p. 842). This is related, however, in the *Li-ki, T'an-kung 1* (*Legge Sacred Books* Vol. XXVII, p. 123) and by *Hum Nan Tse* VII, 13v. *Tse Hsia* lost his sight, while bewailing his son. The feelings tor one's children are common to mankind, whereas thankfulness to one's parents is sometimes forced. When *Tse Hsia* was mourning for his father and mother, people did not notice it, but, when bewailing his son, he lost his sight. This shows that his devotion to his parents was rather weak, but that he passionately loved his son. Consequently he shed innumerable tears. Thus ceaselessly weeping, he exposed himself to the wind, and became blind. *Tseng Tse* following the common prejudice invented three faults for *Tse Hsia.* The latter likewise stuck to the popular belief. Because he had lost his sight, he humbly acknowledged his guilt. Neither *Tseng Tse* nor *Tse Hsia* could get rid of these popular ideas. Therefore in arguing, they did not rank very high among *Confucius* followers.

King *Ihiang* of *Chin* sent a sword to *Po Chi,* who thereupon was going to commit suicide, falling on the sword. "How have 1 offended Heaven?," quoth he. After a long while he rejoined:—"At all events 1 must die. At the battle of *Ch'angliing* the army of *Chao,* several hundred thousand men, surrendered, but

I deceived them, and caused them to be buried alive. Therefore 1 deserve to die. " Afterwards he made away with himself. *Po Ch'i* was well aware of his former crime, and acquiesced in the punishment consequent upon it. He knew, how he himself had failed, but not, why the soldiers of *Chao* were buried alive. If Heaven really had punished the guilty, what offence against Heaven had the soldiers of *Chao* committed, who surrendered? Had they been wounded and killed on the battle-field by the random blows of weapons, many out of the four hundred thousand would certainly have survived. Why were these also buried in spite of their goodness and innocence? Those soldiers being unable to obtain Heaven's protection through their virtue, why did *Po Ch'i* alone suffer the condign punishment for his crime from Heaven? We see from this that *Po Ch'i* was mistaken in what he said.

King *Chao Hsiang* of *Chin* :i05-249 B. o. -A famous general of the *Chin* State who by treachery annihilated the army of *Chao* Vid. p. 136. In *HhunM*. Po ('h i had fallen into disfavour with his liege upon refusing to lead another campaign against *t.%io*.

The *Ch in* emperor *Erh Shiit Huang Ti* sent an envoy to *Ming T ien,* and commanded him to commit suicide. *Ming T ien* heaving a deep sigh said "How have I failed against Heaven? I die innocent." After a long while, he slowly began, "Yet I am guilty, therefore I am doomed to die. When I was constructing the Great Wall connecting *Liio-tnng* with *Lin-t'ao* ten thousand *Li* in a straight line, I could not avoid cutting the veins of the earth. That was my guilt." Upon this he swallowed a drug, and expired.

The Grand Annalist *Sse Ma Cit'ien* finds fault with him. "When the *Cli in* dynasty, he said, had exterminated the feudal princes, and peace was not yet restored to the empire, nor the wounds healed, *Ming T'ien,* a famous general at that time, did not care to strongly remonstrate with the emperor, or help people in their distress, feeding the old, befriending the orphans, or bringing about a general concord. He flattered those in power, and instigated them to great exploits. That was the fault of men of his type, who well deserved to be put to death. Why did he make the veins of the earth responsible? "8

If what *Ming T'ien* said was wrong, the strictures of the Grand Annalist are not to the point either. How so? *Ming Tien* being guilty of having cut the veins of the earth, deserved death for this great crime. How did the earth, which nourishes all beings, wrong man? *Ming T'ien,* who cut its veins, knew very well that by doing so he had committed a crime, but he did not know, why by lacerating the veins of the earth he had made himself guilty. Therefore it is of no consequence, whether *Ming T wn* thus impeached himself, or not. The Grand Annalist blames *Meng T ien* for not having strongly protested, when he was a famous general, 209-207 B.c. -A general of *Erh Shiit Huang Tts* father, *Ch'in Shih Hunng Ti,* who fought successfully against the *Hshtng-nu,* and constructed the Great Wall as a rampart of defence against their incursions.

The Manchurian province of *Ftmgt'ien*. A city in *Kanm* at the western extremity of the Great Wall. Quoted from the *Shi-chi* chap. 88, p. 5. ' Remarks of *Sse Ma Ch'ien* to *Shi-chi* chap. 88, p. 5v. The earth is here treated like an animated being, and its wounding by digging out ditches for the earth-works requisite for the Great Wall, and by piercing mountains, is considered a crime. But provided that *Meng T'ien* suffered the punishment of his guilt, then another difficulty arises. Why did Heaven allow Earth to be thus maltreated, why did it punish innocent Earth? *Wang Ch'nng's* solution is very simple. Heaven neither rewards nor punishes. Its working is spontaneous, unpremeditated, and purposeless. *Meng 'I ten's* death is nothing but an unfelicitous accident. that therefore he met with this disaster, for those that do not speak, when they ought to remonstrate, will have to suffer a violent death. *Sse Ma Ch'ien* himself had to suffer for *Li Ling* in the warm room. According to the Grand Annalist's own view the misfortune suffered tells against a person. Consequently capital punishment takes place by Heaven's decree. If *Sse Ma Ch'ien* censures *Meng T ien* for not having strongly remonstrated with his sovereign, wherefore he incurred his disaster, then there must have been something wrong about himself likewise, since he was put into the warm room. If he was not wrong, then his criticisms on *Ming T ien* are not just.

In his memoir on *Po Yi* the Grand Annalist, giving examples of good and bad actions says, "Out of his seventy disciples *Confucius* only recommended *Yen Yuan* for his ardent love of learning. Yet *Yen Yuan* was often destitute. He lived on bran, of which he could not even eat his fill, and suddenly died in his prime. Does Heaven reward good men thus?"

"Robber CM assassinated innocent people day after day. and ate their flesh. I3y his savageness and imposing haughtiness he attracted several thousand followers, with whom he scourged the empire. Yet he attained a very great age after all. Why was he so specially favoured?" *Yen Yuan* ought not to have died so prematurely, and robber *Che* should not have been kept alive so long. Not to wonder at *Yen Yuans* premature death, but to say that *Meng Tien* deserved to die, is inconsistent.

The *Han* general *Li Kuang3* said in a conversation which he had with the diviner *Wang She,* "Ever since the *Han* have fought the *Hdung-nu,* I was there. But several tens of officers of a lower For Iiis intercession in favour of the defeated general *Li Ling* the emperor W n *Ti* condemned *Sse Ma Ch'ien* to castration, which penalty was inflicted upon him in a warm room serving for that purpose. (Cf. *Chavannes, Mem. Historique* Vol. I. p. XL.) *Shi-chi* chap. 61, p. 3v. *Po Yi* (12th cent. B.C.) and his elder brother *Shu Ch i* were sons of the Prince of *Kn-chu* in modern *Chili*. Their father wished to make the younger brother *Shu Chi* his heir, but he refused to deprive his elder brother of his birthright, who, on his part, would not ascend the throne against his father's will. Both left their country to wander about in the mountains, where at last they died of cold and hunger. They are regarded as models of virtue.

Died 125 B.c. The *Han* dynasty. The Former *Han* dynasty reigned from 206 B.c.-25 A.d. the Later *Han* dynasty from 25 220 A.d. A Turkish tribe. rank than commander of a city gate, with scarcely moderate abilities, have won laurels in the campaigns against the *Hu* and marquisates withal. I do not yield the palm to these nobles, but how is it that I have not even acquired a square foot of land as a reward of my services, and much less been enfeoffed with a city? Are my looks not those of a marquis'.' Surely it is my fate." *Wang Slt i* asked him to think, whether there was anything which always gave him pangs of conscience. *Li Kuang* replied, "When I was magistrate of *Lung-lm?* the *Chiang3* continuously rebelled. I induced over eight hundred to submission, and, by a stratagem, had them all killed on the same day. This is the only thing for which I feel sorry upto now." *Wang She* rejoined:—"There can be no greater crime than to murder those that have surrendered. That is the reason, why you, general, did not get a marquisate." *Li Kuang* agreed with him, and others, who heard of it, believed this view to be true. Now, not to become a marquis is like not becoming an emperor. Must he who is not made a marquis, have anything to rue, and he who does not become emperor, have committed any wrong? *Confucius* was not made an emperor, but nobody will say of him that he had done any wrong, whereas, because *Li Kuang* did not become a marquis, *Wang Shi* said that he had something to repent of. But his reasoning is wrong.

Those who go into these questions, mostly hold that, whether a man will be invested with a marquisate or not, is predestinated by Heaven, and that marks of Heaven's fate appear in his body. When the great general *Wei Ch'ing* was in the *Chien-chang* palace, a deported criminal with an iron collar predicted his fate to the effect that he was so distinguished, that he would even be made a marquis. Later on, he in fact became a marquis over ten thousand families, owing to his great ser-

vices. Before *Wei Ch'ing* had performed his great achievements, the deported criminal saw those signs pointing to his future rank. Consequently, to be raised to the rank of a marquis depends on fate, and man cannot attain to it by his works. What the criminal said turned out true, as shown by the result, whereas *Wang Shi's* assertion is untenable and without proof. Very often people are perverse and selfish without A general term for non-Chinese tribes in the north. District in *Kama*. Tribes in the West of China. A quotation from *Shi-chi* chap. 109. p. ti, the biography of General *L A* favourite and a general of *Han u Ti,* died 106 B.c. becoming unhappy by it, and others who always follow the path of virtue, may lose their happiness. *Wang Shi's* opinion is of the same kind as the self-reproach of *Po Chi,* and the self-impeachment of *Ming T ten.*

In this flurried, bustling world it constantly happens that people rob and murder each other in their greed for wealth. Two merchants having travelled together in the same cart or the same boat a thousand Li, one kills the other, when they arrive at a faroff place, and takes away all his property. The dead body is left on the spot, uncared for, and the bones bleech in the sun unburied. In the water, the corpse is eaten up by fish and turtles, on laud, ants and vermin feed upon it. The lazy fellows won't exert their strength in agriculture, but resort to commerce, and even that reluctantly, in order to amass grain and goods. When then in a year of scarcity they have not enough to still the hunger of their bellies, they knock down their fellow-citizens like beasts, cut them to pieces, and eat their flesh. No difference is made between good and bad men, they are all equally devoured. It is not generally known, and the officials do not hear of it. In communities of over a thousand men up to ten thousand only one man of a hundred remains alive, and nine out often die. This is the height of lawlessness and atrocity, yet all the murderers walk publicly about, become wealthy men, and lead a gay and pleasant life, without Heaven punishing them for their utter want of sympathy and

benevolence.

They kill one another, when they meet on the roads, not because they are so poor, that they cannot undertake anything, but only because they are passing through hard times, they feed on human flesh, thus bringing endless misery on their fellow-creatures, and compassing their premature deaths. How is it possible that they can make their guilt public, openly showing to the whole world the indelible proofs thereof? *Wang She's* opinion can certainly not be right.

The historians tell us that *Li Ss?,* envious that *Han Fei Tse* equalled him in talent, had him assassinated in jail in *Ch'in,* but A Chinese does not take exception to the incongruity of the equation:— $100 : 1 = 10 : 1$. The meaning is plain:—a small percentage of survivors, and a great many dying. Prime Minister of *Ch'in Shih Hvang Ti* and a great scholar. He studied together with *Hun Fei Tie* under the philosopher *Hmln Tic.* A Taoist philosopher, son of a duke of the *Han* State. By his intrigues *Li Sse* had induced the king of *Chin* to imprison *Han Fei Tse.* Me then sent him poison, with which *Han Fei Tie* committed suicide. Vid. *Slu-chi* chap. t33, p. 11 v., Biography of *Han Fei Tse.* that, afterwards, he was torn to pieces by carts, furthermore that *Shang Yang,* under pretence of his old friendship, captured *Ang,* prince of *Wei,* but that, subsequently, he had to suffer death. They wish to imply that those men had to endure these misfortunes as a punishment for their having destroyed a wise man, or broken an old friendship. For what cause had *llan Fei Tse* given, to be incarcerated by *Li Sse,* or what fault had prince *Ang* committed, to be taken prisoner by *Shang Yang?* How did the murder of a scholar, who died in prison, and the breaking of an old friendship resulting in the arrest of the prince, bring about the violent death of the culprit, torn to pieces by carts, or the decapitation? If *Han Fei Tse* or prince *Ang* were wicked, and Heaven had placed retribution in the hands of *Li Sse* and *Shang Yang,* then the latter would have acted by Heaven's order, and be deserving of his reward, not of misfortune. Were

Han Fei Tse and prince *Ang* blameless, and not punished by Heaven, then *Li Sse* and *Shang Yang* ought not to have imprisoned and captured them.

It will be argued that *Han Fei Tse* and Prince *Ang* had concealed their crimes, and hidden their faults so, that nobody heard about them, but Heaven alone knew, and therefore they suffered death and mishap. The guilt of men consists, either in outrages on the wise, or in attacks on the well-minded. If they commit outrages on the wise, what wrong have the victims of these outrages done? And if they attack the well-minded, what fault have the people thus attacked committed?

When misery or prosperity, fortune or mishap are falling to man's share with greater intensity, it is fate, when less so, it is *Li Se* fell a victim to the intrigues of the powerful eunuch *Chao Kao*. The *Shi-chi* chap. 87, p. 2('v., Biography of *Li Sse*, relates that he was cut asunder at the waist on the market place. At all events he was executed ix an atrocious way. The tearing to pieces by carts driven in opposite directions is a punishment several times mentioned in the *Ch'un-clihi*. *Shang Ynng* is ww *Yang*, Prince of *Shnng*, died B.C. In the service of the *Chin* State he defeated an army of Wei, commanded by Prince *Ang*, whom he treacherously seized, and assassinated at a meeting, to which he had invited him as an old friend. According to the *Shi-chi*, chap. 08, p. 9, Biography of Prince *Shang*, he lost his life in battle against his former master, and his corpse was torn to pieces by carts like *Li Sse* The culprit being bound to the carts, which then wen; driven in different directions.

Why docs Heaven punish the innocent through the guilty? If *Han Fei Tiie* and *Ang* had sinned in secret, Heaven would have been unjust towards those they had wronged, and so on. time. *T ni Kung* was in great distress, when he happened to be enfeoffed with a territory by the *Chou* king *Win Wang*. *Ning Ch'i* was living in obscurity and difficulties, when Duke *Huan* of *Ch'i* gave him an appointment. It cannot be said that these two men, when they were poor and mis-

erable, bad done wrong, but had reformed, when they obtained their investment or appointment. Calamity and prosperity have their time, and good or bad luck depend on fate. *T ni Kung* and *Ning Ch'i* were worthies, but they may have had their faults. Sages, however, possess perfect virtue. Nevertheless *Shun* was several times almost done to death by the foul play of his father and brother. When he met with *Yao*, the latter yielded the throne to him, and raised him to the imperial dignity. It is evident that, when *Shun* had to endure these insidious attacks, he was not-to blame, and that he did not behave well, when he was made emperor. First, his time had not yet come, afterwards, his fate was fulfilled, and his time came.

When princes and ministers in olden days were first distressed, and afterwards crowned with success, it was not, because they had at first been bad, and Heaven sent them calamities, or that subsequently they suddenly improved, and then were helped and protected by the spirits. The actions and doings of one individual from his youth to his death bear the same character from first to last. Yet one succeeds, the other fails, one gets on, the other falls off, one is penniless, the other well-to-do, one thriving, the other ruined. All this is the result of chance and luck, and the upshot of fate and time.

A high officer, who had gone into exile to avoid the tyrannous rule of *Chou Hsin* 1122 B.c., and subsequently joined *Wen Wang*. *King Ch'i* lived in the 7th cent. B.c. Cf. p. 173. CHAPTER XIII. Auspicious Portents (CM-yen).

Whenever men are predestined for something grand by Heaven, auspicious portents are seen on Earth. When such appear on Earth, Heaven's destiny is at work. There are different kinds of omens, either do they appear in the men themselves or they are lucky signs, or take the form of a sort of halo.

Huang Ti is reported to have been an embryo for 20 months, before he was born. After birth his intelligence was marvellous. Weak as he was, he could already speak. When he was full-grown, he took the lead of all the feudal princes,

who submitted to his sway. He taught the bears to fight, and thus defeated *Yen Ti*, who was completely routed. His nature was different from that of other people, therefore he remained for ten months longer in his mother's womb. Being predestined to become emperor, he taught the creatures, and they were subservient to him. *Yao's* body was like the sun, when closely inspected, viewed at a distance, he appeared like a cloud. When the great flood rose up to the, sky, and snakes and dragons did mischief. *Yuo* employed *Yil* for the regulation of the water and the expulsion of the snakes and dragons. The water, when regulated, flowed eastward, and snakes and dragons absconded. His bones were abnormal, thence the extraordinary events. As he was endowed with a wonderful intellect, portents appeared in things. Since by fate he was to become noble, he ascended the imperial throne as a marquis of *T ang*.

Previous to his meeting with *Yao*. *Shun* was living unmarried in a nasty, out-of-the-way place. *Ku Sou* together with *Hsiang* attempted to kill him. They bade him complete the building of a granary, and kindled a fire underneath. They directed him to dig a well, and then they threw earth down from above. *Shun* contrived to get out of the granary unharmed by the fire, and to make his escape from the well by one side, unhurt by the The harsh and unfeeling father of the virtuous *Shun*.

Shuns wicked brother.

earth. When *Yao* heard of this, he summoned him, and gave him an office on trial. *Shun* filled his post with great credit, and no disorder occurred. He would enter a solitary, big forest without being pounced upon by tigers and wolves, or being bitten by vipers or snakes. In the midst of thunderstorm and a gushing rain-shower he did not go astray. Men bent upon his assassination, could do him no harm, and wild birds and reptiles with venomous stings were unable to wound him. Suddenly he attained imperial sway, and mounted the throne of the son of heaven.

Prior to *Hou Chi's* time, his mother walked upon the footstep of a giant.

Others say that she put on *Ti Ku's* clothes, or that she rested in *Ti Kn's* place. At all events, she became *enceinte* with a child, which she cast away in a narrow alley, regarding it as an ill omen. But oxen and horses did not dare to tread upon it. She placed it on ice, but the birds covered it with their wings. From all these auspicious signs converging on the baby's body, the mother learned, what wonderful qualities it possessed. Therefore, she brought it up. When *llnu Chi* had attained to manhood, he assisted *Yao,* and rose to the rank of a minister of war.

The *Wusun* Prince bearing the surname of *K'un Mo* had his father slain by the *Hsiung-nu,* and was himself thrown into the desert, still alive. The birds fed him on flesh, which they carried in their beaks. The *Shan Yii* was amazed at this, which appeared to him supernatural. Ho took care of the boy, and, when he had grown strong, he gave him a military post. After he had won many laurels, the *Shan Yil* put the people formerly obeying his father again under *Km Mo's* command, and directed him always to guard the Western City. Cf. *Menchis* Book V, Pt. I, chap. II *(Legge* p. 222-223) and *Shi-chi* chap. I, p. 23.

Vid. *Shu-king* Pt. II, Book I, chap. II. A mythical personage, the "Lord of the Grain," said to have been Director of Husbandry under *Yao* and *Shun.* The word mother, required by the context, must be supplemented in the original. A legendary emperor prior to *Yao, Hou Chi's* father, after one tradition. A *Kirghis* tribe settled in the N. E. of *Ferghana* in the 2nd cent. B.o. *(Shield* chap. 123, p. 4). The powerful Turkish tribes, which were China's northern neighbours during the *Han* time, perhaps the *Huns.* Long wars were waged between the Chinese and the *Hsiung-nu.* The title of the chieftain of the *Hsiung-nu.* This passage is taken almost literally from the *Shi-chi* chap. 123, p. ftv. The *Shi-chi* still adds that *K an Mo* was suckled by a she-wolf. *Hou Chi* was not to be cast away, therefore the oxen and horses did not kick him, and the hirds covered and protected him with their plumage. *K un Mo* was not doomed to

die, therefore the birds came with flesh in their beaks to feed him.

A servant girl of the king of *T o-li* of the northern *Yi* was with child. The king wanted to kill her. The girl said by way of apology:—''A vapour, big as an egg, descended from heaven, and made me *enceinte."* Afterwards, she was delivered of a child, which she threw away into a pig-stye. The pigs sniffed at it, but it did not perish. Then it was removed again to the horse stable, in order that the horses should kill it. but the horses also only sniffed at it, and it did not die. The king thereupon imagined that the child would become a sovereign, and therefore ordered the mother to take it back, and had it nursed by his slaves. The boy received the name of *Tung Ming.* He was employed as a shepherd for cattle and horses. As he was an excellent archer, the king got afraid, that he might deprive him of his kingdom, and therefore wished to kill him. *Tung Ming* went southward to the *Yen-hu* river, where with his bow he shot fish and turtles in the water. They formed a floating bridge, enabling *Tung Ming* to cross. Then the fish and turtles separated again so, that the troops pursuing him could not follow. Subsequently he became king of *Fu-gii.* Among the northern *Yi* there is a kingdom of *Fu-gii.*

When *Tung Ming's* mother first became pregnant, she perceived a vapour descending from heaven, and. when she threw the newly born away, pigs and horses sniffed at him. After he had grown up, the king desired to kill him, but the fish and turtles, which he had shot, formed a floating bridge. According to heaven's fate he was not to die, therefore he was saved from pigs and horses. As he was predestinated to become king of *Fu-gii,* the fish and turtles formed a bridge to help him.

When *Yi Yin* was about to-be born, his mother dreamt that she saw a man, who said to her: "Water flows from the mortar. Forthwith travel eastward." The mother took note of this, and, on the next morning, found out that really water came out from A State in northern *Corea, Ma-tuan-lin* chap. 324, p. 14v., where our passage is quoted.

Barbarous, non Chinese tribes in the east. In *Liaotung.* The chief minister of *T ang,* the founder of the *Shang* dynasty 17GG n.c. Many legends are current about his origin. In ancient times holes in the earth were used as mortars. the mortar. She went 10 Li eastward. When she looked back to her native place, all was under water. *Yi Yin's* destiny was not to be drowned, consequently his mother had a dream, and went away.

The same principle holds good for the city of *Li-yang.* Those whose fate was like that of *Yi Yin,* were certainly roused beforehand, and removed to another place before the catastrophe.

When Duke *Hsiang* of *Ch'i* got into trouble, Duke *Llnan,* the crown-prince, had to fight for his throne with *Tse Chiu. toum Chung* assisted *Te Chiu, Pao Shu* stood by Duke *Hunn. Kuan Chung* in a combat against duke *I nan,* shot at him with arrows, and hit him on the buckle of his belt. Man is generally 7 feet high, the belt clasps the waist, and the buckle attached to the belt covers only a spot less than an inch wide. Its smallness makes it difficult to be hit. Moreover, the pointed edge is curbed ou its polished surface. All the arrows hitting the buckle are deflected. Yet *Kuan Chung* just hit the buckle in the middle. The arrow struck against it, and then fell down without deviating into the flesh on either side. Duke *Huan's* fate was wealth and honour, and a god helped him, so that the arrow hitting his buckle did not hurt him.

King *Kung* of *Ch u* had five sons:— *Tse Chan, TseYii, Tse Kan, Tse Hsi,* and *Ch'i Chi,* who all were much liked by him. But having no son from his first wife, whom he might make his successor, he sacrificed to the mountains and rivers, and invoked the decision of the gods. Together with his second wife *Pa* he buried a jade badge in the ancestral hall, and bade his five sons to enter after having feasted, and make obeisance. The later king *K ang* stepped over it, *Tse Yii* reached it with his elbow, *Tse Kan* and *Tse Hsi* both remained far from it. *Ch i Chi.* was carried in as a baby. With each prostration he pressed on the top of the jade badge. When King *Kung* died,

Tse Chao became King *K'ang,* but his son lost the kingdom. *Tse Yil* became King *Ling,* but was Namely the underground water.

Cf. p. 136.

In 086 B.c. Duke *Hsinng* was assassinated by his nephew Wti *Chih Ch'unch'iu* III, 8). *Tse Chiu* was a brother of Duke *Huan. Kuun Chung* and *Pao Shu Ya* were bosom-friends. At the recommandation of *Pao Shu Ya, Kuan Chung,* later on, entered into the service of Duke *Hunn,* whom he had first opposed.

The ancient Chinese foot was much smaller than ours.

589-558 B.C.

'558-543 B.c.

539-527 B.c.

himself assassinated. *Tse Kan* reigned but ten odd days. *Tse Hsi* did not come into power, and even was afraid of being beheaded. All were exterminated and left no progeny. *Ch i Cĩi i* mounted the throne later, and continued the sacrifices of the house of *Ch'u,* for such had been the presage.

The duration of the reigns of these princes corresponded to the distance they kept from the jade badge, when prostrating themselves. The piece of jade was in the earth, while the five sous, unaware of it, entered one by one, and bowed nearer or farther off. When they pressed down the top of the jade ornament, they were, so to speak, induced by their spirits to kneel down.

T u An hu of *Chin* out of hatred destroyed the sons of *Chao* 7«««(. After the death of *Chao So,* his wife had a posthumous child. When *T'u An Ku* heard of it, he sought it in the Palace. The mother put it into her pantaloons, and swore the following oath:—"The whole *Chao* family will be lost, if the child cries, it will not be so, if it does not utter a sound." While being searched for, it did not cry at all. Then its escape could be effected, and its life be saved. *Ch'ing Ying Ch i* carried it away, and concealed it on a mountain. During Duke *Ching* time, *Han Chileh* mentioned it to the duke, who together with *Han Chileh* raised the orphan of *Chao* to his former rank, so that he could continue the sacri-

ficial rites of his family under the name of *Win Tte.* The orphan of *Chao* did not utter a sound, as though its mouth had been closed. Thus the elevation of *Win Tse* was predetermined by fate.

The mother of *Han Kao Tu,*-dame *Liu,* reposed on the banks of a large lake. In a dream, she met with a spirit. At that time there was a tempest with thunder and lightning. In the darkness a dragon appeared on high. The son, of which she was delivered, had an excellent character, but was very fond of wine. He would buy wine on credit from Mrs. *Wang* and mother *Wu.* When he was drunk, he stopped, and lay down to sleep. Mrs. *Wang* and mother *Wu* then always saw some miraculous signs about him. Whenever he re The *Shi-chi* chap. 40, p. 14 tells this story with nearly the same words, and has taken it from the *Tso-chuan,* Duke *Ch'ao* 13th year. Vid. *Le/ye, Chinese t fassics* Vol.V, p. (150, 1st col. and *Chavannes, M'm. Historiques* Vol. IV, p. 3t57.

A minister of the State of *Chin* 597 B.c. Also a minister of *Chin* and rival of *T'u An Ku.* Likewise slain by *T'u An Ku.* . . *Chao So'a* widow, being a daughter of the ducal house of *Chin,* had sought refuge in the palace. ' A faithful adherent of *Chao So.*

598-579 B.c.

mained to drink wine, the price of the wine then sold was many times as much as usual.

Later on he walked into the lake, and cut a big snake into pieces with his hand. An old woman filled the roads with her wails, crying that the Red Emperor had killed her son. This miracle being very striking was much talked about. *Ch'in Shih Huang Ti* used to say that in the south-east there was the spirit of a son of heaven. Therefore he travelled eastward in order to suppress it. This was *Kao Tsu's* spirit. Together with *Li l Hon* he concealed himself amidst the marshes in the *Mang* and *T ang* Mountains. When *Lii Hou* with other people went in search for him, they always saw a vapour rising in a straight line above him, and thus discovered where he was.

Later on *Kao Tsu* agreed with *Hsiang Yil* that whoever first entered the gates

of *Ch'in,* should be king. *Kao Tsu* arrived first, which was deeply resented by *Hsiang Yil. Fan T sing* said:— "I pray to look at his vapours. They all take the shape of a dragon, and have five colours:—they are those of the son of heaven. He must be despatched forthwith."

When *Kao Tsu* went to thank *Hsiang Yil,* the latter and *Ya Fu* hatched a plot to kill him. At their instigation *Hsiang Chuang* performed a dance with a drawn sword. *Hsiang Po,* who knew their intentions, began to dance together with *Hsiang Chuang,* and no sooner was the sword raised over *Kao Tsu's* head, than *Hsiang Po* covered him with his own body so, that the sword did not fall, and the murderous plot was not carried out. At one time, *Kao Tsu* was rescued by *Chang Liang* and *Fan K uai,* and after all got off unhurt. Thereupon he swayed the whole empire.

When his mother conceived him, the spirit of a dragon made its appearance. When he grew up, peculiar clouds were seen about the wine shop. During the night, he killed a snake, and the snake's old mother lamented, and cried. *Ch'in ShiJt Huang Ti* and *Lii Hou* saw an aureole above him. *Hsiang Yii* planned his assassination, but *Hsiang Po* protected him, and the scheme fell through.

Cf. the detailed account given in Chap. XVII. -The *Mang* Mountains were situated in *Hunan,* the *T ang* Mountains in *Kanm.* These myths about the first emperor of the *llan* dynasty are related in almost the same words in the *Shi-chi* chap. 8, p. lv. The famous counsellor of *Kao Tsu's* rival, *Hsiang Yii.*

The title of *Fan T'seng.*

The story is told more in detail in the *Shi-chi* chap. 7, p. 14v. Partisans of *Kao Tsu,* whose success is to a great extent due to then-efforts. He found such helpmates as *Chang Liang* and *Fan K'uai.* For there being signs pointing to his future wealth and honour, all things obeyed him, and men lent him their help and support.

A younger brother of the Empress Dowager *Ton,* of the name of *Kuang Kuo,* was, at the age of 4 or 5 years, robbed from his poor family, and sold, bis people not knowing his whereabouts. More tban ten times he was sold again to other families, till he came to I-llang. There he went on the hills for his master to make charcoal:— When it grew cold at night, over a hundred people lay down under the coal. The coal collapsed, and all were crushed to death, save Kuang Kuo, who managed to escape. He then divined himself, and ascertained that, after a certain number of days, be would be made a marquis. He left bis home, and betook bimself to Chang-an3 There be learned that the Empress Ton bad lately settled her family at Kuan-chin in Ch ing-ho. He reported himself to the emperor. Tbe Empress Dowager prevailed upon Ching Ti to grant him an audience. Wbat he replied to the questions about bis origin proved true, and the emperor made him rich presents. At the accession of Win Ti, Kuang Kuo was created a marquis of Chung Wu. Wben the coal heaps came down, more than a hundred people were killed, only Kuang Kuo escaped. Being preserved by fate for wealth and bonour, be did not only keep alive, but was made a marquis to boot.

Yii Tse Ta, a native of Tung Kuan in Ch en-liu" came into the world at night. His mother beheld something like a skein of silk over him, which went up to heaven. She asked other people's advice about it. All were agreed that it was an auspicious fluid foreboding honour, which reached up to hea ven. Yii Tse Ta, when-grown up, became an official, and was promoted to the rank of Minister of Education. Kuang Win Po from /' u-fan in Ho-tung was likewise born about midnight. At that time some one called his father's name The wife of the emperor Wen Ti, 179-156 B.C., and the mother of Ching Ti, 156-140. A district in Ho-nanfu, The capital under the former Han dynasty. Ch'ing-ho, a State in Honan, the present prefecture of K'ui-feng-fu, of which Kuan-chin formed a district. Probably a misprint for Wu Ti; for Wu Ti, not Wen Ti succeeded Ching Ti. ' In K'ai-feng-fu (Honim). The 7"ui-p'mg-yii-lan quoting this passage writes T'ung Wen Po. Nothing more is to be learned about this person from the cy-

clopedias. The modem P'u-chou in Shanm. Literally: — the country east of the tYellow) River. from without doors. The father went out, and replied, but nobody was to be ween, only a big wooden stick was planted next to the door. He understood well that it was different from common ones. The father took the stick into his house, and showed it to somebody, who prognosticated the future from it, saying:—"A lucky omen, indeed. When Kuang Wen Po is grown up, he will study, and in his official 'career be appointed prefect of Kuang-han. " Kuang Wen Po was to be wealthy and honoured, therefore his father was presented with the stick. The diviner, as it were, implied that the stick represented the strength of the child.

On the day Chia-tse in the twelfth moon of the first year Chien-ping,3 when the Emperor Kuang Wu Ti saw the light in the second hall of the seraglio in the rear of the Chi-gang palace, his father was magistrate of Chi-gang During the night this room was lighted of itself without there being any fire. His father summoned the secretary Chung Lan, and despatched him to consult a fortune-teller. For that purpose Chung Lan, accompanied by the groom Su Yung, went to Wang Ch ang Sun's place. Wang Ch ang Sun said to the two:—"That is a lucky thing, I cannot say more." That same year a blade of grain grew among house-leek and wallpepper. It had three roots, one stalk, and nine ears, and was by one to two feet higher than a common one, it being an auspicious blade.

At the beginning of Yuan Ti's' reign a phenix alighted on the Chi-gang kung. Hence there exists still to-day in the Chi-gang palace a phenix cottage. Yuan Ti together with Li Fu and others travelled into the region of Ch'ai. On the road they fell in with insurgents, and greatly alarmed, fled to the old cottage of Chi-gang. When they arrived, they beheld a red glare like fire just south from the road leading to the old cottage. A stream of light went up to heaven, and after a moment was gone.

An ancient name of the region about Ch'eng-tu and T'ung-ch'uan in Sse-chuan. The first number of the sexage-

nary cycle. 6 2 B.c. This palace, once used by the Emperor Han Wu Ti as a travelling lodge, had been closed. Kuang Wu Ti's father finding his yamen too wet to live in, had moved into the old palace, and installed himself in the halls at the back. The modem T'sao-chou-fu in Shantung. Cf. T'ai-p'ing-gii-lan (Kuang Wu Ti) where the Tung-kuan llan-chi is quoted. Hun luau Ti 48-32 B.c. The Tung-kuan llan-chi relates that the phenix came down at the birth of Kuang Wu Ti, 6 B.c. An old name of T ai-an-hsien in Shantung.

At Wang Mnng's time, the Lord Marshal Su Po A could distinguish the currents of air. When, on an embassy, he passed through the suburb of ChHang-ling, he found the air very brisk and fresh. Kuang Wu It came to Ho-pin where he had an interview with Su Po A. He put to him the question: "How did you know that a lucky wind was blowing, minister, when you passed Ch'uang-ling?"—"Only because I saw the air brisk and fresh" was Su Po A's reply.

Ergo, when by Heaven's decree a new man is to rise, and a wise emperor to come forth, the manifestations of the original fluid before and after can clearly be made out. But, when there is only a succession of power, and-a continuation of former institutions, insomuch as the latter serve as a basis, then the manifestations of the heavenly fluid are not worth mentioning. When there is a complete revolution, and a new dragon rises, he starts from very small beginnings, and passes first through all sorts of calamities, as in the case of Han Kao Tsu and Kuang Wu Ti. Were they not ushered in with wonderful signs from heaven, men, and spirits, and great splendour?

A city in llonan. Under the Han a district "north of the Yellow River," corresponding to the modem P ing-lu-hsien in Sltansi. In case of a great political revolution. In case of regular succession, the son following the father.

Both founders of new dynasties.

CHAPTER XIV.

On Divination (Pu-shih).

The world believes in divination with shells and weeds. The first class of diviners question Heaven, they say; the second. Earth. Milfoil has something spiritual, tortoises are divine, and omens and signs respond, when asked. Therefore they disregard the advice of their friends, and take to divination, they neglect what is right and wrong, and trust solely to lucky and unlucky portents. In their belief, Heaven and Earth really make their wishes known, and weeds and tortoises verily possess spiritual powers.

As a matter of fact, diviners do not ask Heaven and Earth, nor have weeds or tortoises spiritual qualities. That they have, and that Heaven and Earth are being interrogated, is an idea of common scholars. How can we prove that'. Tse Lu asked Confucius saying, " A pig's shoulder and a sheep s leg can serve as omens, and from creepers, rushes, straws, and duckweed we can foreknow destiny. What need is there then for milfoil and tortoises?"

'That is not correct,' said Confucius, 'for their names are essential. The milfoil's name means old, and the tortoise's, aged.1 In order to elucidate doubtful things, one must ask the old and the aged.'

According to this reply, milfoil is not spiritual, and the tortoise is not divine. From the fact that importance is attached to their names, it does not follow that they really possess such qualities. Since they do not possess those qualities, we know that they are not gifted with supernatural powers, and, as they do not possess these, it is plain that Heaven and Earth cannot be asked through their medium.

Moreover, where are the mouths and the ears of Heaven and Earth, that they may be questioned? Heaven obeys the same laws A gratuitous etymology, of which the Chinese are very fond. Shih — milfoil and ku?i -tortoise have nothing whatever to do with ch'i = old and kin-&L — aged.
as man. To form a conception of Heaven, we must start from human affairs. When we ask anybody, we caunot learn his opinion, unless we see him ourselves before us, and personally address him. If we wish to ask Heaven, Heaven

is high, and its ears are far away from us. Provided that Heaven has no ears, it is incorporeal, and being incorporeal, it is air. How could air like clouds and fog speak to us?

By milfoil they ask the Earth. Earth has a body like man, hut, as its ears are not near us, it cannot hear us, and not hearing us, its mouth does not speak to us. In fine, if they speak of questioning Heaven, Heaven being air cannot send omens, and, if they address themselves to Earth, the ears of Earth are far, and cannot hear us. What reliable proofs are there for the assertion that Heaven and Earth speak to man.

We are living between Heaven and Earth, as lice do on the human body. If those lice, desirous of learning man's opinion, were emitting sounds near his ear, he would not hear them. Why'.' Because there is such an enormous difference of size, that their utterances would remain inaudible. Now, let us suppose that a pigmy like a man puts questions to Heaven and Earth, which are so immense; how could they understand his words, and how become acquainted with his wishes?

Some maintain that man carries the fluid of Heaven and Earth in his bosom. This fluid in the body is the mind, I daresay. When man is going to divine by weeds and shells, he puts questions to the milfoil and the tortoise. The replies which he heats with his ears, his mind regards like its own thoughts. From the depth of the bosom and the stomach the mind hears the explanation. Thus, when the tortoise is cut to pieces and the divining stalks grasped, omens and signs appear. Man thinks with his mind, but when in his thoughts he cannot arrive at a decision, he consults the milfoil and the tortoise. In case their omens and si,j-ns harmonize with the thoughts, the mind may be said to have been a good adviser.

Yet it happens that the heart regards something as leasable, but the omens and signs are inauspicious, or these are felicitous, but the heart considers them as unlucky. Now. the thoughts are one's own spirit, and that which causes the omens and signs is also one's spirit. In

the bosom, the spirit of a body becomes the mental power, and outside the bosom, omens and signs. It is, as
'From Chuang Tse chap. 26, p. 4v. it appears that for divining purposes the tortoise shell used to be cut into 72 pieces or divining slips.
if a man enters a house, and sits down, or goes out through the door. The walking and sitting makes no difference in his ideas, and entering or issuing does not change his feelings. Provided that
O D DO the mind produces omens and signs, they would not be opposed to man's thoughts.

Heaven and Earth have a body, therefore they can move. In so far as they can move, they are like living beings, and being alive, they resemble man. To ask a living man, we must use a living person, then we can be sure of a reply. Should we employ a dead man for this purpose, we would certainly not obtain an answer. Now, Heaven and Earth are both alive, and milfoil and tortoises are dead. How could we elicit a reply by asking the living through the dead? The shell of a dried tortoise and the stalk of a withered weed are supposed to question living Heaven and Earth! Ergo the common assertion that Heaven and Earth respond is quite erroneous.

If milfoil and tortoises be like tablets, omens and signs would represent the written characters thereon, and resemble the instructions emanating from a prince. But where would be the mouths and the ears of Heaven and Earth, that such instructions might be possible? "How can Heaven speak?" said Confucius. "The four seasons roll on, and the various things are produced."

Heaven does not speak, nor does it hear what men say. Heaven's nature is said to be spontaneity and non-interference. Now, if people question Heaven and Earth, and they respond, this response would require that interference be coupled with spontaneity.

According to the text of the i-king, the art of grasping the straws consists in sorting them into two parcels to resemble Heaven and Earth, in grasping them by fours in imitation of the four seasons, and in returning the superfluous straws as an emblem of an intercalary month. These resemblances are marked with the object of forming the necessary number of diagrams, and not a word is said about Heaven and Earth conjointly replying to man. It is usual among men to answer, when asked, and not to reply, unless there be any question. Should anybody knock at other people's door without any reason, not wishing anything, or make a useless discourse in their presence, without asking their opinion, the master of the house would laugh, but not reply, or he would become angry, and not give an answer. Now, let a diviner per f`orate a tortoise shell in sheer play, or sort the milfoil for nothing, and thus mock Heaven and Earth, he would obtain omens and signs all the same. Would Heaven and Earth then reply indiscriminately? Or let a man revile Heaven, while divining by shells, or beat the Earth, while drawing the lots, which is the height of impiety, he would obtain omens and signs nevertheless. If omens and signs are the spirit of Heaven and Earth, why do they not extinguish the fire of the diviner, burn his hand, shake his fingers, disturb his signs, strike his body with painful diseases, and cause his blood to freeze and to boil, instead of still showing him omens and sending signs'.' Do Heaven and Earth not fear the bother, and not disdain to take this trouble? Looking at the problem from this point of view it becomes plain to us that the diviners do not ask Heaven and Earth, and that omens and signs are not the replies of the latter.

Besides, those who divine are sure to be either lucky or unlucky. Some are of opinion that good and bad luck correspond to the good and the bad actions of mankind. Thus bliss and felicity would accompany goodness, and calamitous changes follow in the rear of badness. Good or bad government is the result of goodness or badness, but I doubt that Heaven and Earth purposely reply, when questioned by diviners. When a lucky man cuts up a tortoise, he finds auspicious omens, whereas an unlucky one, grasping the milfoil, obtains contrary signs. This will be shown by the following examples.

Chou was the worst of rulers: during his reign there was an abundance of calamitous events. Seventy times the tortoise was consulted, and the replies were always unlucky. Therefore *Tsu Yi* said, "Excellent men anil the great tortoise dare not know anything about happiness. The worthy are not called to office, and the large tortoise does not give good omens. A catastrophe is impending."

When King *Wu* of *Chou* received the heavenly appointment, aud *Kao Tm* ascended the dragon throne. Heaven and men conjointly lent them their aid, and there were great numbers of wonders and miracles. The sons of *Fbig* and *P'ei* divined by shells, and Which he uses in burning the tortoise shell.

The minister of *Chou*. Cf. *Shu-king, Hm po k'an Li* and *Sfu-cfu* chap. 3 ((*'havannes, Mem. Hisi* Vol. I, p. 204). The countrymen of *Kao Tm*, who was born in *Feng*, in the sub-prefecture of P'« in *Kiangsu*, they likewise received propitious replies. The omens which a lucky man attracts by his personality are invariably good, whereas those brought about by the doings of an unlucky person are always bad.

When *Shih T ai* of *Wei* died, he had no rightful heir, but six illegitimate sons. They divined, who would be the successor, and made out that bathing and the wearing of gems would afford an omen. Five of the sons took a bath, and adorned themselves with precious stones, but *Shih Chi Tse* said, "Who, being in mourning for a parent, can bathe and wear gems?" Hence he did not bathe, nor wear any gems. It was he who hit the omen. The men of *Wei* divining confided in the wisdom of the tortoise, but it did not possess any wisdom, the wise one was *ShiJt Chi Tse* himself. He governed his State well, and what he said was excellent, hence the felicitous auguries. Had no recourse been taken to divination at that time, and the people alone be consulted, they would nevertheless have declared in his favour. Why'.' Because the heart and its feelings are nothing else than luck and mishap. If this be true, it disposes of the truth of divination. While the shells are being cut in pieces, and the straws sorted, omens and signs take place spontaneously, and while they appear, happiness and misfortune happen of their own accord, and the lucky as well as the unlucky fall in with them by chance.

The lucky meet with good omens, whereas the unlucky encounter bad signs. Thus wherever the lucky pass, things are pleasant to them, and wherever they look, they behold felicitous objects. Yet those pleasant things and felicitous objects are not special auguries for the lucky. In a similar manner the unlucky encounter all sorts of hardships on their way. These good and bad things are not the response of Heaven, it is by chance that they fall to the lot of the good and the bad. The lucky and unlucky omens obtained by cutting the tortoise and drawing the milfoil are like the happiness and the unhappiness which we experience. This much we gather from the following instances.

When King *Wu* of *Chou* was downspirited, the Duke of *Choh* consulted three tortoises, and said that he would *meet* with The *Li-ki* writes *Shih T'ai t hung*.
-From his concubines.

A feudal lord in *Wei*, mentioned in the *Tso-chunn*, Duke *Chuang* 12th year (681 B.C.), as influencing the policy of his native State.

So far the story is culled from the *Li-ki, T an Kung 11 (Legge, Sucred Books* Vol. XXVII, p. 181). success. When the minister of *Lu, Ch1ang* »S/w, had got a son, *Ma Shu*, he drew the lots with the help of the *Yi-king* and *encountered* the 36th diagram, which hecame the 15th. In regard to the divination with shells the term to *meet* is used, and the expression to *encounter* is applied to the drawing of straws. Thus, as a matter of fact, the replies were obtained by mere chance, and were not the outcome of goodness or badness.

The good *meet* with happiness, and the wicked *encounter* misfortune. The law of Heaven is spontaneity, it does nothing for the sake of man. The happiness attending the government of a ruler must be judged by the same principle.

When a prince chances to be virtuous, it just so happens that there is peace and joy, and that many wonderful and auspicious things appear. Contrariwise, when there happens to be a degenerate ruler, all this is reversed.

There are many people discoursing on divination, but very few who understand its real meaning. Some hold that divination must not be practised by itself, but that circumstances are to be taken into account. The tortoise being cut, and the milfoil grasped, omens and signs appear. Seeing unusual signs, the diviners resort to their imagination: auspicious omens they explain as disastrous, and unlucky signs as auspicious. If in such a case luck and mishap do not become manifest, people say that divination is not to be trusted.

When King *Wu* of *Chou* destroyed *Chou,* the interpreters put a bad construction upon the omens, and spoke of a great calamity. *T'ai Kung* flung the stalks away, and trampled upon the tortoise saying, "How can dried bones and dead herbs know fate?"

In case the omens and signs obtained by divination do not correspond to happiness and misfortune, there must have been a The Duke of *Chou* had built three altars to his three ancestors, whom he consulted on the fate of his sick brother *Wu Wang.* He probably had one tortoise for each altar. (Cf. *Shi-chi* chap. 33, p. lv. and p. 205.) *Shu Hun Chuang Shu* or *Shu Sun Te Chen.* When he died in 603 B.C., he received the posthumous name *Chuang.* The same as *Shu Sun Mu Tsc* mentioned in Chap. XVII. His clan name was *Shu Sun, Mu* being his posthumous title.
The diagram *Ming-i.* The diagram *Ch'ien. Wang Ch ung* here (juotes a passage from the *Tsochuan,* Duke *Ch'ao* 5th year *(Legge* Vol. V, Pt. II, p. ti04) where the expression "encountered" § i used. 6 mistake. When the soothsayers are unable to ascertain fate, it is thrown into confusion, and owing to this confusion *T ai Kung* disparaged divination.
Divination by shells and stalks bears a resemblance to the administration of a wise emperor, and the omens of divination are like the auspicious portents dur-

ing the reign of such an emperor. These portents are unusual, and the omens are extraordinary and marvellous. It is for this reason that the diviners fall into error, and it is the unusual which blindfolds the emperor's advisers to such a degree, that in their blindness they declare a peaceful government to be mismanaged, and in their error call bad what is auspicious. Lucky omens a lucky man can fall in with, and, when during a reign auspicious portents are met with, jt is a manifestation of the virtue of a wise ruler. When the King of *Choh* destroyed *Chou,* he encountered the omens of a bird and a fish, why did his diviners regard these as unlucky omens? Had King *Wu's* elevation not been predestinated, he ought not to have met with portents, when going out. Provided that it was *Wu Wang's* fate to rise, the diviners should not have thought it inauspicious. Thus, since the divination for King *Wu* could not be unlucky, but was declared to be so, this interpretation was erroneous.

When *Lu* was going to attack *Yueh,* the diviners by milfoil gave their verdict to the effect that the tripod had broken its leg. *Tse Kung* explained this as evil. Why? Because the tripod had its leg broken, and for moving on one uses the legs. Consequently he considered it unlucky. *Con/ucius,* on the other hand, explained it as lucky, saying, "The people of *Yueh* are living on the water; to reach them one requires boats, not legs." Therefore he called it lucky-*Lu* invaded *Yueh,* and in fact defeated it.
Tse Kung explained the breaking of the leg of the tripod as evil, just as the interpretation of the diviners of *Chou* was adverse. But in spite of this adverse comment there was certainly luck, and in accordance with the right explanation of the broken leg *Yueh* could be invaded. In *Chou* there were many persons who could give a straightforward interpretation like 7«; *Kung,* but very few gifted with the same subtle reasoning power as *Confucius.* Consequently, upon viewing an unusual omen, they were unable to catch the meaning.
Because *Wu Wang* had no fault, when the divining took place, and neverthe-

less got a bad omen, people think that divination must not be practised by itself, and is but of little service in government. But it serves to show that there are spiritual powers, and that a plan is not merely the production of somebody's brain.

Writers and chroniclers have collected all sorts of events, as *Han Fei Tse* for instance, who in his chapter on the embellishment of false doctrines examines the proofs of those manifestations. There he depreciates divination by shells, stigmatises that by weeds, and condemns the common belief in their usefulness. As a matter of fact, divination can be made use of, yet it happens that the diviners are mistaken in their interpretations. In the chapter *Hungfan* we read concerning the investigation of doubts that, as regards exceptional portents explained by divination, the son of heaven must be asked, but that sometimes the ministers and officials are also able to offer a solution. Owing to this inability to give a correct. explanation, omens and signs often do not prove true, hence the distrust in the usefulness of divination.

Duke *Win* of *Chin* was at war with the viscount of *Ch'u.* He dreamt that he was wrestling with King *Ch eng* who gained the upper hand, and sucked his brains. This was interpreted as inauspicious, but *Chin Ftui* said, "It is lucky. Your Highness could look up to heaven, while *Ch'u* was bending down under the weight of his guilt. Sucking your brains means softening and craving for mercy."" The battle was fought, and *Chin* was in fact victorious, as *Chin Fan* had prognosticated.

The interpretation of dreams is like the explanation of the signs of the tortoise. The oneirocrities of *Chin* did not see the purport of the visions, as the diviners of *Chou* did not understand the nature of the omens of the tortoise-shell. Visions are perfectly true, and omens perfectly correct, but human knowledge is unsufficieut, and the reasoning therefore not to the point.

There is still another report, according to which King *Wu,* when attacking *Chou,* consulted the tortoise, but the tortoise was deformed. The diviners regarded this as very unpropitious, but *T'ai* Those in power win the people over to their views by showing that the omens are favourable, and that the spirits causing them give their approval. Chapter XIX of *Han Fei Tse's* work.

Cf. *Shu-king, Hung-fan,* Pt. V, Bk. IV, 20 (*Legge* Vol. III, Pt. II, p. 334). The viscount of *Ch'u,* who styled himself king. The *Tso-chuan* calls him *Tse Fan.* ' Quotation from the *Tso-chuan,* Duke *fls i* 28th year (631 B.C.). I surmise from the context that the character must denote some deformity of the tortoise. *Knng-lu* says in the appendix that the meaning is unknown. *Kung* said, "The deformation of the tortoise means bad luck for sacrifices, but victory in war. " King *Wu* followed his advice, and at length destroyed *Chou.* If this bc really so, this story is like the utterances of *Confucius* on the diagrams, and *Chin Fan's* interpretation of the dream. Omens and signs are true by any means, if good and bad fortunes do not happen as predicted, it is the fault of the diviners who do not understand their business. CHAPTER XV.

On Death (*Lun-sse*).

People say that the dead become ghosts, are conscious, and can hurt men. Let us examine this by comparing men with other beings: —

The dead do not become ghosts, have no consciousness, and cannot injure others. How do we know this? We know it from other beings. Man is a being, and other creatures are likewise beings. When a creature dies, it does not become a ghost, for what reason then must man alone become a ghost, when he expires? In this world you can separate man from other creatures, but not on the ground that he becomes a ghost. The faculty to become a ghost cannot be a distinctive mark. If, on the other hand, there is no difference between man and other creatures, we have no reason either to suppose that man may become a ghost.

Man lives by the vital fluid. When he dies, this vital fluid is exhausted. It resides in the arteries. At death the pulse stops, and the vital fluid ceases to work:

then the body decays, and turns into earth and clay. By what could it become a ghost?

Without ears or eyes men have no perceptions. In this respect the deaf and the blind resemble plants and trees. But are men, whose vital fluid is gone, merely as if they had no eyes, or no ears? No. their decay means complete dissolution.

That which is diffuse and invisible, is called a ghost, or a spirit. When people perceive the shape of a ghost or a spirit, it cannot be the vital fluid of a dead man, because ghost and spirit are only designations for something diffuse and invisible. When a man dies, his spirit ascends to heaven, and his bones return to the earth, therefore they are called *Kwei* (ghost) which means " to return." A spirit *(Shin)* is something diffuse and shapeless.

Some say that ghost and spirit are names of activity and passivity. The passive principle opposes things and returns, hence its name *Kuei* (ghost). The active principle fosters and produces things, and therefore is called *Sheu* (spirit), which means "to extend." This is re-iterated without end. When it finishes, it begins again.

Man lives by the spiritual fluid. When he dies, he again returns this spiritual fluid. Activity and passivity are spoken of as spirit and ghost. When man dies, one speaks likewise of his spirit and his ghost.

The fluid becomes man, just as water turns into ice. The water crystallises to ice, and the fluid coagulates, and forms man. The ice melting becomes water, and man dying becomes spirit again. It is called spirit, just as molten ice resumes the name water. When we have a man before us, we use another name. Hence there are no proofs for the assertion that the dead possess knowledge, or that they can take a form, and injure people.

When men see ghosts, they appear like living men. Just from the fact that they have the shape of living men we can infer that they cannot be the essence of the dead, as will be seen from the following: —

Fill a bag with rice, and a sack with millet. The rice in the bag is like the millet in the sack. Full, they look strong, stand upright, and can be seen. Looking at them from afar, people know that they are a bag of rice, and a sack of millet, because their forms correspond to their contents, and thus become perceptible. If the bag has a hole, the rice runs out, and if the sack is damaged, the millet is spilt. Then the bag and the sack collapse, and arc no more visible, when looked at from afar.

Man's vital fluid resides in the body, as the millet and the rice do in the bag and the sack. At death the body decays, and the vital fluid disperses, just as the millet and the rice escape from the pierced or damaged bag, or sack. When the millet or the rice are gone, the bag and the sack do not take a form again. How then could there be a visible body again, after the vital fluid has been scattered and lost?

When animals die, their flesh decomposes, but their skin and their hair still remain, and can be worked into a fur, which appears still to have the shape of an animal. Therefore dog thieves will don dog skins. People then do not discover them, because disguised in a dog's fur-skin, they do not rouse any suspicion.

Now, when a man dies, his skin and hair are destroyed. Provided that his vital force did still exist, how could the spirit again enter the same body, and become visible? The dead cannot borrow the body of a living man to re-appear, neither can the living borrow the soul of the dead to disappear.

The Six Animals can only be transformed into a human shape as long as their bodies and their vital fluid are still unimpaired. When they die, their bodies putrefy, and even, if they possess the courage and the audacity of a tiger or a rhinoceros, they can no more be metamorphosed. *Niu Ai,* duke of *Lu* during an illness could be transformed into a tiger, because he was not yet dead. It happens that a living body is transformed into another living body, but not that a dead body is changed into a living one.

From the time, when heaven and earth were set in order, and the reign of the "Human Emperors" downward people died at their allotted time. Of those, who expired in their middle age, or quite young, millions and millions might be counted. The number of the persons actually living would be less than that of those who died. If we suppose that after death a man becomes a ghost, there would be a ghost on every road, and at every step. Should men appear as ghosts after death, then tens of thousands of ghosts ought to be seen. They would fill the halls, throng the courts, and block the streets and alleys, instead of the one or two which are occasionally met with.

When a man has died on a battlefield, they say that his blood becomes a will-o'-the-wisp. The blood is the vital force of the living. The will-o'-the-wisp seen by people, while walking at night, has no human form, it is desultory and concentrated like a light. Though being the blood of a dead man, it does not resemble a human shape in form, how then could a man, whose vital force is gone, still appear with a human body?

If the ghosts seen all looked like dead men, there might be some doubt left that the dead become ghosts, and sometimes even assume human form. The Six Domestic Animals are:— the horse, the ox, the goat, the pig, the dog, and the fowl. Cf. Chap. XXVII. A series of mythical rulers of remotest antiquity. I.un. I Ii'n-. 13

Sick people see ghosts, and say that So-and-So has come to them. At that time So-and-So was not yet dead, hut the fluid perceived resembled him. If the dead become ghosts, how is it that sick people see the bodies of the living?

The nature of heaven and earth is such, that a new fire can be lighted, but an extinguished fire cannot be set ablaze again. A new man can be born, but a dead one cannot be resurrected. If burnt-out ashes could be kindled again into a blazing fire, I would be very much of opinion that the dead might take a bodily form again. Since, however, an extinguished fire cannot burn again, we are led to the conclusion that the dead cannot become ghosts.

Ghosts are considered to be the vital spirits of the dead. If this were really the case, people seeing ghosts ought to see their bodies naked only, but not wearing dresses, or covered with garments, because garments have no vital spirits. When men die, their clothes become decomposed together with their bodies, how could they be put on again?

The vital spirits have their original seat in the blood fluid, and this fluid always adheres to the body. If notwithstanding the decay of the body the vital spirits were still extant, they might become ghosts. Now garments are made of silk stuffs and other fabrics. During man's life-time his blood fluid does not permeate them, nor have they any blood of their own. When the body is destroyed, they share its fate, how could they of themselves reassume the shape of garments. Consequently, if ghosts are seen which bear a resemblance to dresses, they must also be like bodies, and if they are, we know that they cannot be the vital spirits of the dead.

Since the d,ead cannot become ghosts, they cannot have any consciousness either. We infer this from the fact that before their birth men have no consciousness. Before they are born, they form part of the primogenial fluid, and when they die, they revert to it. This primogenial fluid is vague and diffuse, and the human fluid, a part of it. Anterior to his birth, man is devoid of consciousness, and at his death he returns to this original state of unconsciousness, for how should he be conscious?

Man is intelligent and sagacious, because he has in himself the fluid of the Five Virtues, which is in him, because the Five Organs are in his body. As long as the five parts are uninjured, man is bright and clever, but, when they become diseased, his intellect is dimmed and confused, which is tantamount to stupidity and dullness.

After death the five inward parts putrefy, and. when they do so, the five virtues lose their substratum. That which harbours intelligence is destroyed, and that which is called intelligence disappears. The body requires the fluid for its maintenance, and the fluid, the body to become conscious. There is no fire in the world burning quite of itself, how could there be an essence without a body, but conscious of itself?

Man's death is like sleep, and sleep comes next to a trance, which resembles death. If a man does not wake up again from a trance, he dies. If he awakes, he returns from death, as though he had been asleep. Thus sleep, a trance, and death are essentially the same. A sleeper cannot know what he did, when he was awake, as a dead man is unaware of his doings during his life-time. People may talk or do anything by the side of a sleeping man, he does not know, and so the dead man has no consciousness of the good or bad actions performed in front of his coffin. When a man is asleep, his vital fluid is still there, and his body intact, and yet he is unconscious. How much more must this be the case with a dead man, whose vital spirit is scattered and gone, and whose body is in a state of decay?

When a man has been beaten and hurt by another, he goes to the magistrate, and makes his complaint, because he can talk to people, and is conscious. But, when a person is slain by somebody, the murderer is unknown, his family perhaps not knowing even the place, where his corpse is lying. If under such circumstances the murdered man was conscious, he would assuredly be filled with the greatest wrath against his murderer. He ought to be able to speak into the magistrate's ear, and give him the name of the miscreant, and, if he were able to go home, and speak to his people, he would inform them, where the body was. But all that he cannot do. That shows that he has no consciousness.

'The Five Virtues are:—Benevolence, Justice, Propriety, Knowledge, and Truth; the Five Organs:—the Heart, the Liver, the Stomach, the Lungs, and the Kidneys.
No dictionary gives this meaning for t'ien , which usually means "to exterminate, to cut off, to cease." But it cannot be anything else here. The Chinese of to-day will likewise call a faint "death,''

or 'small death,'' *haao-sse* J *jfc*

Now-a-days, living persons in a trance will sometimes as mediums speak for those who have died, and diviners, striking black chords, will call down the dead, whose souls then will talk through the diviner's mouth. All that is brag and wild talk. If it be not mere gossip, then we have a manifestation of the vital fluid of some being.

Some say that the spirit cannot speak. If it cannot speak, it cannot have any knowledge either. Knowledge requires a force, just as speech does.

Anterior to man's death, his mental faculties and vital spirit are all in order. When he falls sick, he becomes giddy, and his vital spirit is affected. Death is the climax of sickness. If even during a sickness, which is only a small beginning of death, a man feels confused and giddy, how will it be, when the climax is reached'.' When the vital spirit is seriously affected, it loses its consciousness, and when it is scattered altogether?

Human death is like the extinction of fire. When a fire is extinguished, its light does not shine any more, and when man dies, his intellect does not perceive any more. The nature of both is the same. If people nevertheless pretend that the dead have knowledge, they are mistaken. What is the difference between a sick man about to die and a light about to go out? When a light is extinguished, its radiation is dispersed, and only the candle remains. When man has died, his" vital force is gone, and the body alone remains. To assert that a person after death is still conscious is like saying that an extinguished light shines again.

During the chilly winter months the cold air prevails, and' water turns into ice. At the approach of spring, the air becomes warm, and the ice melts to water. Man is born in the universe, as ice is produced, so to say. The *Yang* and the *Yin* fluids crystallise, and produce man. When his years are completed, and his span of life comes to its end, he dies, and reverts to those fluids. As spring water cannot freeze again, so the soul of a dead man cannot become a body

again.

Let us suppose that a jealous husband and a jealous wife are living together. The debauchery and the disreputable conduct of one party is the cause of constant outbursts of anger, fighting, and quarrelling. Now, if the husband dies, the wife will marry again, and if the wife dies, the husband will do the same. If the other knew of it, he would undoubtedly fly into a rage. But husband and wife, when dead, keep perfectly quiet, and give no sound. The other may marry again, they take no heed, and it has no evil consequences. That proves that they are unconscious.

Confucius buried his mother at *Fang*. Subsequently such heavy rain fell, that the tomb at *Fang* collapsed. When *Confucius* heard of it, he wept bitterly and said:—The ancients did not repair graves." Therefore he did not repair it. Provided the dead are conscious, they ought to be angry with those who do not keep their tombs in repair. Knowing this, *Confucius* would have repaired the grave to please the departed soul, but he did not do so. His intelligence as a Sage was of the highest order, but he knew that spirits are unconscious.

When dried bones are lying about in lonely places, it may happen that some mournful cries are heard there. If such a wail is heard at night-time, people believe that it is the voice of a dead man. but they are wrong. When a living man talks, he breathes. I lis breath is kept in his mouth and his throat. He moves his tongue, opens and shuts his mouth, and thus produces words. It is like playing a flute. When the flute is broken, the air escapes, and does not keep inside, and the hands have nothing to touch. Consequently no sound is produced. The tubes of the flute correspond to the human mouth and throat. The hands touch the holes in the tubes in the same manner, as man moves his tongue. When he is dead, his mouth and throat decay, and the tongue moves no more. How should words be articulated then? If, while dried bones are lying about, wails and laments are heard, they come from men, for bones cannot produce them.

Others imagine that it is the autumn

(which produces these sounds). This statement is not much different from the other that ghosts cry at night. If the autumn air causes these extraordinary moans and wails, it must have some substratum. Because this has happened near the bones of a dead man, people have presumed that these bones are still conscious, and utter these mournful cries in the wilderness. There are thousands and thousands of skeletons bleaching in the grass and in the swamps, therefore we ought to be haunted by their laments at every step.

It is possible to make somebody speak, who usually does not speak, but impossible that somebody who speaks, should be induced to speak again after death. Even he who spoke before, cannot be caused to speak again. Similarly, when a plant comes

'A place in *Lu (Shantung)*. A quotation abridged from the *Li-ki, Tan Kung*. Cf. *Legge, Li-ki* Vol. I, p. 123. Modern commentators explain the passage quite differently. The dictum of *Confuciax* would mean that the ancients did not repair tombs, because they built them so well, that they could not collapse. *Wang Chung's* interpretation is more natural. forth, its fluid is green, which is, as it were, given it. When the same plant dies, the green colour disappears, or is taken away. Endowed with the fluid, the plant is green, deprived of it, it loses the green colour. After the latter is gone, it cannot be added again, nor can the plant grow green again of its own accord. Sound and colour correspond to one another, and are both derived from Heaven. The brilliant green colour is like a lugubrious cry. The colour of a faded plant cannot become green again, it would, therefore, be a mistake to assume that a dead man's cry could still be produced of itself.

Man is able to talk, because he possesses vital energy. As long as he can eat and drink, the vital energy is well fed. but no sooner do eating and drinking cease, than the energy is destroyed. After this destruction there are no more sounds possible. When the person is worn out, and cannot eat any more, the mouth cannot speak any further. Death is exhaustion in the highest degree, howcould man still speak then?

There are those who say that the dead smell the sacrificed meat, and eat the air, and that they are thus enabled to speak. The vital force of the dead is that of the living. Let a living being neither eat nor drink, and only inhale the smell of offerings, and feed upon air, and he will die of starvation after no more than three days.

Another opinion is that the vital force of the dead is more powerful than that of the living, and that for this reason it can smell the air, and produce sounds.

The vital force of the living is in their body, that of the dead, out of it. lu what do the dead and the living differ, and what difference does it make that the vital fluid is within the body, or outside of it? Take water, and fill it into a big jug. When the jug breaks, the water flows to the earth, but can the water on the floor be different from that in the jug? The water on the floor is not different from that in the jug, then why should the vital force outside the body be different from that within?

Since a man, when dead, does not become a ghost, has no knowledge, and cannot speak, he cannot hurt others either for the following reason. In his anger, a man uses breath, but in order to injure others, he requires strength. To make use of it, his sinews and bones must he strong, then he can hurt others. An angry man may breathe heavily so near to others, that his breath shoots forth against their faces, but though he possess the valour of *Meng Pen,* it does them no harm. However, when he stretches out his hand, and strikes, or lifts the foot and kicks, he breaks whatever he hits. The bones of the dead decay, the strength of his muscles is lost, and he does not lift hand or foot. Although the vital fluid be still existant, it is, as if it were, only breathing, and nothing else follows. How then should it do barm to anybody?

Men and other creatures hurt others by means of knives, which they grasp with their hands and arms, and with their strong and sharp nails or teeth. Now, when a man is dead, his bands and arms waste away, and cannot lift a blade any more, and nails and teeth fall out, and cannot bite any more. How should they do harm to others then?

When a child is just born, bis hands and feet are quite complete, yet the hands cannot grasp, and the feet cannot kick. The fluid has just concreted, but has no strength. Hence it is evident that the vital fluid possesses no strength. The fluid forms the body. As long as the body is still feeble and weak, it cannot do harm to any one, and how much less still, when through death the fluid becomes lost, and the vital spirit is dissolved. Something feeble and weak is uncapable of injuring people, and one asserts that cold bones can do it? Is the fluid of the dead not lost? How should it injure anybody?

Before a ben's egg is hatched, there is a formless mass in the egg-shell, which, on leaking out, looks like water. After a good hen has covered the egg, the body of the chicken is formed, and when it has been completed, the young bird can pick the shell, and kick. Human death resembles the time of the formless mass. How could a formless fluid hurt anybody?

A man becomes bold and fierce, so that he can assault others, by eating and drinking. Eating and drinking his fill, he grows stout and strong, bold and fierce, and can do barm to others. While a man is sick, he can neither eat nor drink, and his body becomes worn out and weak. When this weariness and languor reach the highest degree, death ensues. During that time of sickness and languor his enemy may stand by his side, be cannot revile him, and a thief may take his things away, he has no means to prevent him, all on account of his debility and lassitude. Death is the debility and languor in the extreme, how then could a man after death still injure any one? If chickens or dogs, which somebody keeps, are stolen, he will, at all events, wax angry, though he be timid, and not very strong, and his anger may be so violent, that he tries conclusions with the robber, and is slain by him. During the time of great anarchy people will use one another as food. Now, provided that the spirit was conscious, it ought to be able to destroy its enemies. A human body is worth more than a chicken or a dog. and one's own death is of greater consequence than a robbery. The fact that a man is excited over a chicken or a dog, but has no bad feeling against the individual who devoured him, shows that he has not the power to hurt any one.

Prior to its casting off its cxuvi;e, a cicada is a chrysalis. When it casts them oft", it leaves the pupa state, and is transformed into a cicada. The vital spirit of a dead man leaving the body may be compared to the cicada emerging from the chrysalis. As cicada it cannot hurt the chrysalides. Since it cannot do so, why should the vital spirit of a dead man hurt living bodies?

The real nature of dreams is very doubtful. Some say that, while people are dreaming, their vital spirits remain in their bodies, and produce lucky or unlucky visions. Others hold that the vital spirit communicates with men and other creatures. Now, if it really remains in the body, the vital spirit of the dead must do the same. If. however, the spirit mixes with men, people may dream that they have killed somebody. Having killed somebody, they are perhaps themselves murdered by somebody else. But if, on the following day, they look at the body of that person, or examine their own, they will find no trace whatever of a wound inflicted by a sword. Dreams are caused by the vital spirit, and this spirit is identical with the vital spirit of the dead. The vital spirit of dreams cannot injure people, therefore the spirit of the dead cannot do so either.

When the fire burns, the caldron boils, and when the boiling stops, the steam ceases. All depends on the fire. When the vital spirit is incensed, it can do harm, not being angry, it cannot injure people. The fire blazing in the stove, the kettle bubbles, and the steam rises. When the vital force is enraged in the bosom, there is an innervation of strength, and the body is hot. Now, when a man is about to die, his body is cold and chilly. The cold and chilliness increase, until at last he expires. At the time

Those who used its body as food.
His spirit.
of death, the vital spirit is not irritated, and after the death of the body it is like the hot water taken from the caldron, how should it hurt people?

Things have a certain relation to man. When a man becomes insane, and one knows the proper thing, his malady may be cured by applying this thing as a remedy. As long as a thing is alive, its vital spirit adheres to its body, and consequently can change its form, and enter into close connection with man. After it has died, its body rots, and the vital spirit is dispersed. In default of a substratum it cannot undergo any more changes. The human vital spirit is like that of things. While they are alive, their spirit may become sick, when they die, it evaporates and disappears. Men are like things in this respect, when they die, their vital spirit also becomes extinguished, how could it still do any mischief?

Should anybody object by saying that men are much more precious than things, and that their vital spirit is different, we can reply that, as a matter of fact, things can be metamorphosed, but man cannot, and that so far his vital spirit is on the contrary inferior to that of things, whose essence surpasses that of man.

Water and fire drown and burn. All that can injure man must be a substance belonging to one of the five elements. Metal hurts man, wood beats him, earth crushes him, water drowns him, and fire burns him. Is the vital spirit of the dead a substance like the five elements? Does it injure people, or is it not a" substance?—It cannot injure people. Not being a' substance, it must be a fluid. Of the fluids which injure man that of the sun is the most virulent. Does the fluid of a man, when he dies, become virulent? Can it injure people or not?—It cannot injure people.

Thus we hold that the dead do not become ghosts, are not. conscious, and cannot hurt people. Consequently, it is evident that the ghosts, which are seen, are not the vital force of dead men, and

that, when men have been hurt, it cannot have been done through this vital force.

CHAPTER XVI.

False Reports about the Dead (Sse-wei).
King *Htflan* of the *Cîlou* dynasty is reported to have killed his minister, the Earlof *Tu*, who was innocent. When King *Hsilan* was going to hunt in his park, the Earl of *Tu* rose on the roadside with a red bow in his left hand. IIe shot an arrow at the king, who expired under the cover of his own how-case.—Duke *Chim* of Chao put his minister *Chuang Tse Yi* to death, although he was innocent. When Duke *Chien* was about to pass through the *Huan* gate, *Chuang Tse Yi* appeared on the road, a red cudgel in his left hand, with which he struck the duke, that he died under his carriage. This is considered as proving that two dead persons became ghosts, and as showing that ghosts are conscious, and can hurt people, and that there is no help against it.

1 say that man is created as one of the ten thousand creatures. When these creatures die, they do not become ghosts, why then must man alone become a ghost after death? If it be owing to his superiority that man can become a ghost, then all the dead ought to be transformed into ghosts, wherefore then did the Earl of *Tu* and *Chuang Tse Yi* alone become ghosts'.' If those who have innocently suffered can become ghosts, there have been a great many ministers thus wronged. Men like *Pi Kan* and *Tse HsQ* did not become ghosts. Now, the Earl of *Tu* and *Chuang Tse Yi* were immoral. Full of spite and hate, they assassinated their sovereigns, out of revenge. There is no crime worse than the assassination of one's sovereign. Those who were deemed worthy to become ghosts, would again have to be executed. Therefore the Earl of *Tu* and *Chuang Tse Yi* would certainly not have dared to commit such a crime. 827-781 B.c. The story is given a little more in detail in the *Chou Ch'un-ch'ru*, which adds that the king broke his spine (cf. (*Imvannes, Mem. Hist.* Vol. I, p. 278, Note 2) and also by *Me Ti* chap. 8, p. 2. In the *Lun-heng* Bk. IV, p. ri *(Shu-hsu)* he is called Viscount *Chien*

of *Chao,* the same who is mentioned in chap. XVII. On their fates cf. p. 140 and chap. XXXLX.

When one man injures another, he does not wish him to live, and hates to see his person. Therefore he does away with him. Then not only the family of the murdered man goes to the magistrate, and lodges a complaint against their enemy, but the victim also must hate to see him. Life and death are different spheres, and men and ghosts live in different places. If, therefore, the Earl of *Tu* and *Chuang Tse Yi* were grieved at King *Hsiian* and Duke *Chien,* they should not have killed them, for then they would also have become ghosts, and again have been together with them.

Princes have great power, and the.ir officers, guards, and underlings are very numerous. Had the two ministers killed the two princes, their deaths would have been avenged. Therefore no intelligent man would have made such a scheme, or committed such an act in his wrath. If the two ministers were spirits, they must have been aware that the deaths of the two princes would be avenged upon them, and, if they were not aware of it, then they were not spirits either, and not being spirits, how could they have injured anybody? In the world many things seem real, which are not, and there are many falsehoods, which are taken for truths. Thus the stories of the Karl of *Tu* and *Chuang Tse Yi* have been handed down.

Duke *Hui* of *Chin* removed the crown-prince *Shen Sheng* from his grave, and had him re-interred. When in autumn his charioteer *Hn Tu* went to *Hsia-kuo?* he met the crown-prince there. The crownprince stepped upon his carriage, and spoke to him saying, "/ *Wu* is a brute. I have asked God. He will give *Chin* over to *Ch'in,* and *Ch'in* will offer sacrifice to me."—*Hu Tu* replied, "I have been told that spirits enjoy only the offerings of their own kindred, and that people do not sacrifice but to their own clan. Would the sacrifice to Your Highness not be terminated then? Besides the people of *Chin* are not responsible. Their punishment would be unjust, and there would be the cessation of the sacrifice. Your Highness should take this into consideration."—The crown-prince said, "Well, I will pray again. Seven days hence, there will be a wizard west of the New City, through whom you shall have an interview with me." After *llu Tu* had agreed to it, he vanished. At the fixed time, *Hu Tu* went to the hut of a wizard on the west A brother of the Duke, who had been driven into death by court intrigues. The "Lower Capital" of *Ohin i. e. ('h'u-vu* in modern *Ping-yang-fu (Shansi).* The personal name of Duke *Hui.* side of the New City, and had a second interview with *Shin Sheng. Shen Sheng* told him. "God has promised to punish the guilty one. He will slay him in *Han."*—Four years later Duke *Hui* fought with Duke *Mu* of *Ch'in* in the *Han* territory.-and was taken prisoner by Duke *Mu,* exactly as had been predicted. What else was this than the work of a spirit'.'

This story bears a great resemblance to those of the Earl of *Tu* and *Chuang Tse Yi.* How can we show that? The removal of a grave is a private grievance. God is a public spirit. Would a public spirit take heed of a complaint addressed to him on a private grievance? God is said to have promised to give *Chin* over to *Ch in. I hi Tu* thought that this could not be. *Shen Shing* following //« *Tu's* words, was quite right, and therefore God's promise to *Shin Sheng* was wrong. It is evident that a spirit which as God would be inferior to *Ilu Tu,* cannot be God.

Furthermore, a subject dares not implore a sovereign to consider his private affairs. A sovereign has such an exalted position in comparison with a humble subject, that the latter does not venture to trouble him with things that do not concern him. And was the distance between *Shen Sheng* and God not still greater than between a subject and his sovereign? He would not have vented his anger against Duke *Hui* for having removed his grave in the august presence of God.

Li Chi caused the death of *Shen Shing* by her slander, and Duke *Hui* removed his corpse from his grave. The removal of a corpse is less wicked than a murder,

and the guilt of Duke *Hui* less than that of *Li Chi.* If *Shin Shing* prayed for the punishment of Duke *Hui,* and not for the death of *Li Chi,* then he resented the removal of his grave, but was not grieved at his own death.

By the advice of *Li Sse, Ch'in Shih Huang Ti* burned the books of poetry and history, and subsequently buried the scholars alive. The grievances of the literati against him were not of a less serious character than those of *She n Shing,* and the misery of being buried alive, much more pitiful than the removal of a corpse. Yet the dead scholars of *Ch'in* did not implore God, nor appear in the shapes of ghosts, and those *savants* did not conjointly accuse *Ch'in Shih Huang Ti* of viciousness, and *Li Sse* of depravity.

Quotation from the *Tso-chuan,* Duke *Hsi* 10th year (649 B.c, *Legge, Classic* Vol. V, Pt. I, p. 157). In *Shan&i.* A wife of Duke *Htiien* of *Chin,* who, in order to secure the throne for her own son, removed the heir-apparent, *Shen Sheng.*

When King *Wu* of the *Chou* dynasty was sick and low-spirited, the Duke of *Chou* asked for Heaven's commands. He erected three altars with one platform for sacrifices, and with the jade sceptre and the baton in his hands, addressed *T at Wang, Wang Chi* and *Win Wang.* The annalist composed the prayer. In his address he said." I am benevolent like my ancestors, have many talents and abilities, and can serve the spirits. The great-grandson so-andso has not as many talents or abilities as *Tan,* and cannot serve the spirits."—By spirits the three princes are meant. The dead are unconscious, and cannot become spirits, they say. However, the Duke of *Chou* was a sage; the words of a sage are true, and he finds out the reality of things that seem dark. Such being the case, the three princes must have been spirits.

1 ask, can men really become spirits or not? Provided, they can, then one must know the opinions of the three princes, and. not solely inquire, whether they were ghosts. The Duke of *Chou* asked for Heaven's commands, and the annalist composed the prayer. When the

prayer was completed, and the address finished, the Duke of *Chou* did not know, whether the three princes gave their assent, and how. Upon this he consulted three tortoises. All three bearing lucky signs, he was pleased. He was able to know that the three princes were conscious and spirits, but not, whether they assented or not. To find out the truth, he was obliged to still consult the three tortoises. Yet in order to determine in an unmistakable way, whether they were spirits or not, it should have been possible to interrogate them. The question, whether the dead had knowledge or not, depended on the other, whether they could give their approval or not. If the Duke of *Chou* could know that the three princes did not grant his request, then the statement that they were ghosts is reliable, but if he could not, then his statement that the three princes were ghosts, would not have any more weight than one made by ordinary people. His knowledge would not reach further than that of the generality, and be inadequate to show us the real state of the dead.

Moreover, by what means did the Duke of *Chou* obtain Heaven's commands, by his perfect sincerity, or by the correctness of his address'.' If it was by his perfect sincerity, then his prayer was said with sincerity, and he did not care, whether his address to The spirits of the father, the grandfather, and the great-grandfather of King *Wu* and his younger brother *Tan,* Duke of *Chmi.* Quoted in an abridged form from *Shu-king, Chin-t'eng,* Pt. V, Bk. VI, 1 seij. *(Legge* Vol. HI, Pt. II, p. 351 sei).).

attract the splrits was correct or not. *Tung Chung Shu's* method ot' praying for rain consisted in putting up a dragon, made ot" earth, with a view to affecting the fluid. An earth dragon was not a real dragon, and could not attract rain. While making use of it, *Tung Chung Shu* showed perfect sincerity, and did not mind, whether the dragon was genuine or ficticious. The Duke of *Chan's* prayer for Heaven's commands was like *Tung Chung Shu's* prayer for rain. The three princes were not ghosts, as a heap of earth was not a dragon. *Ihi-*

in Yen of *Chin* invaded *Ch i.* hut had to return, hefore the campaign came to a close, for he was taken ill with ulcers, and a sore broke out on his head. When he reached the *Cho-ytmg* territory, his eyes protruded from their sockets, and when his death ensued, he went on staring, and his mouth could not receive anything. *Fan Hsiian Tse* washed him, and said by way of consolation, "To serve under Your Lordship was decidedly better than under *Wu,"* but he still continued staring. *Fan Hsiian Tse* observing that he did not close his eyes, fancied that he was vexed with his son *Wu,* for vexation with one's own son is a very common human grievance. Therefore, he spoke of *Wu* to comfort him, but this was not the cause of his resentment, for he went on staring. *Luan Hnili Tse* rematked, "Is it perhaps, because he did not complete his designs in *Ch'i?",* and he again comforted him by saying. "Your Lordship died an untimely death. The things which you did not bring to a close in *Ch'i,* are as vast as the Yellow River." Upon this, he closed his eyes, and received the gem into his mouth. It was the incompleteness of his invasion of *Ch'i* which *Hsiin Yen* regretted. *Luan Huai Tse* found it out, therefore the dead man closed his eyes, and received the gem into his mouth. *Fan Hsiian Tse* missed it, therefore his eyes remained wide open, aud his mouth was locked.

I say that *Hsiin Yen's* death by sickness was very painful, so that his eyes protruded. When his eyes came out, he firmly closed his mouth, and therefore could not receive anything in it. Immediately after death the fluid was still strong, and the eyes protruded owing to the pain caused by the disease. *Fan Hsiian Tse* soothed him too soon, therefore the eyes did not close, and the mouth not open. A short while afterwards, the fluid was weakened.

An officer of the *Chin* State. As was customary. Thus far the story, with some additions and omissions, has been culled from the *Tso-clman,* Duke *Hsiariy* 19th year (55.'i B.C.). Consequently, when *Luan Hum Tse* comforted him, his eyes closed, and his mouth received the gem. This was a sequence of *H,iin Yen's* sickness, and the soul of the deceased did not manifest his resentment in his mouth and his eyes.

All people have something; to regret, when they die. A generous character regrets that he could not accomplish all the good works he intended, a scholar that his researches had still so many *lacune,* a husbandman that he did not reap the grain he had sown, a merchant that he did not make a fortune, au official that he did not obtain the highest posts, and a brave that his attainments were not yet perfect. Every one on earth who has desires, has something to regret. If in every case regrets be considered the cause of the non-closing of the eyes, then all the dead on earth could not shut their eyes.

The souls of the dead are dissolved, and cannot hear any more what men say. This inability to hear what others say is called death. If after their separation from the body they became ghosts, and kept near to men, their connection with the body would already have been severed, and, though people addressed them, it would be impossible for them to again enter the body, and close the eyes, or open the mouth. If they could enter the body, and through tin; corpse express their dissatisfaction, then the inevitable consequence would be that they must have been preserved together with the body. Ordinary people hold that the spirits of the dead can, so to speak, re-animate the bodies, and show themselves so, that corpses would be like living men, which is a great mistake.

King *Ch eng* of *Ch'u* set aside the heir-apparent *Shang Chen,* and wished to put Prince *Chih* in his place. When *Shang Chen* heard of it, he surrounded the king with the palace guards, and made him prisoner. The king desired to eat bear's paws, before he was put to death, but *Shang Chen* did not grant this request, and the king died by strangulation. *Shang Chen* gave him the posthumous title *Ling,* but the king did not shut his eyes. Then he called him *Cheng,* and he closed his eyes. This circumstance that he closed his eyes on being called *Ching,* but not on being called *Ling,* proves that King *Ch eng* had consciousness. The posthumous title *Ling* displeased him, therefore he did not shut his eyes. When it was altered into *Ching,* his hurt feelings were mollified, whereupon he closed his eyes. His spirit heard people consult, and saw them change the title. This gave him such satisfaction, that he closed his eyes. They were not sick, and nobody soothed him. The eyes opened, and closed of their own accord; if that was not spiritual, what else was it?

I am of opinion that this story is like that of *Hsten Yen.* Although the eyes were not sick, they did not remain open for nothing. When King *Ching* died by strangulation, his vital fluid was still strong, and, when his lite was suddenly cut ofl", his eyes still opened. Owing to this the epithet *Ling* was given him. After a short while, the fluid relaxed, and the eyes were just going to close, when simultaneously his title was changed into *(ii eng.* It was by chance that the staring and the shutting of the eyes coincided with the selection of *Ling* as a posthumous title. The people of that time, noticing that the king shut his eyes as if in response to the title *Ching,* believed that it was the soul of King *Ching.* If he was really conscious, he ought never to have closed his eyes, for the murder committed by the heir-apparent upon his person was a heinous crime, whereas the selection of the word *Ling* as a posthumous title was only a small fault. He did not resent the great crime, but took offence at the small fault. That does not make the existence of a spirit probable, and would not seem a reliable utterance of his feelings. Of improper posthumous titles we have not only *Ling* but also *L».* In the annals many princes bearing the epithets *Ling* and *Li* are mentioned. They did not all keep their eyes open, before their bodies were shrouded. Did the dead princes of the various ages not resent the name, and was it King *Ch eng* alone wl1o took umbrage? How is it that there were so many of the name of *Ling,* and so few who did not close their eyes?

Po Yu of *Ching* was greedy and perverse, and his desires were many. *Tse Hs i* wished to rank before every one else. Both, of course, could not get on together. *Tse Hsi* assaulted *Po Yu,* who took to flight. *Sse Tai* led his countrymen against him, and defeated him. *Po Yu* died. Nine years later the people of *Ching* took *Ling* pit might mean:—animated, alive, a spirit, but it has many other significations besides, as: — intelligent, ingenious, clever, which might well be used as a posthumous title. This would mean: —the completer, the perfect one. *Li Ji=ji* is in fact not a proper honorary epithet, its sense being: —oppressive, cruel, malicious, ugly, terrible. According to the *Tsu-chuan* in 542 B.C. alarm owing to *Po Yu.* They said that *Po Yu* was coming. Consequently, they all ran away, not knowing where to go. In the following year, some people saw *Po Yu* in their dreams walking about in armour, and saying, "On the day *jin-tse,* I will slay *Sse Tai,* and next year on *jen-gin,* I will slay *Kung Sun Tnan.* "—When the *jin-tse* day arrived, *Sse Iai* died, and the fright of the citizens still increased. Afterwards, when the *jen-gin* day came, *Kung Sun Tuan* died also, and the citizens felt still more alarmed. *7ie Chan* promoted his descendant to soothe him, and he kept quiet ever since. *Po Yu* appeared in dreams, and said, "On the *jfoi-tee* day I will slay *Sse Tai,* and on *jin-gin* I will kill *Kung Sun Tuan."* When the *jen-tse* day came, *Sse Tai* died, and when the *jin-gin* day arrived, *Kung Sun Tuan* breathed his last. When subsequently *Tse Ch'an* betook himself to *Clan, Ching Tse of Chao* questioned him saying, "Could *Po Yu* still become a ghost?"—*Tse Ch'an* rejoined, "He could. When man is born, that which is first created, is called animal soul, and, when the animal soul has been formed, its *gang* becomes the mind. In case the substance and the elements are abundantly used, the soul and the mind grow very strong, and therefore show great energy, until they become spirits. Even the soul and the mind of an ordinary man, or an ordinary woman, who have met with a violent death, can attach themselves to men, as evil spirits, and fancy *Po Yu,* a descen-

dant of a former sovereign of mine, Duke *Mu,* the grandson of *Tse Liang,* and the son of *Tse Erh,* who was governor of a small territory, the third of his family who held this post! Although *Ch'ing* is not a rich country, and, as a saying of *Ch'ing* is, a small and unimportant State, yet three successive generations have ruled over it. The stuff *Po Yu* was made of was copious and rich, and his family great and powerful. Is it not natural that having met with a violent death, he should be able to become a ghost?" *Po Yu* killed both *Sse Tai* and *Kung Sun Tuan,* and did not miss the appointed time. That shows that he was really a spirit. When *Tse Ch'an* had raised his descendant, he kept quiet. *Tse Ch'an* understood the doings of ghosts, and therefore knew that they really existed. Since they are real, and not an illusion, *Tse Ch'an* answered the question addressed to him unhesitatingly. *Tse Ch'an* was a wise man who understood the nature of things. If *Po Yu* after *Tae Ch'an* is the style of the celebrated statesman *Kun Sun Ch'iao* of *Ch'eng* 581-521 B.c.

» Duke *Mu* of *Ch'eng* 626-604 B.c.
Quotation from the *Tso-chnan,* Duke *Ch'ao* 7th year (534 B.c.) *(Legge* Vol. V, Pfc II, p. 61$).
Lun-H'-ng. 14 death possessed no knowledge, how could he kill *Sse Tai* and *Kung Sun Tuan?* And if he could not become a ghost, why had *Tse Ch'an* not the slightest doubt about it?

My answer is, as follows. The man who lived at enmity with *Po Yu* was *Tse Hsi.* He attacked *Po Yu,* who fled. *Sse Tai* led his countrymen against *Po Yu,* and defeated him. *Knng Sun Tuan* merely followed *Sse Tai,* but did not settle his own dispute. His wrong was much smaller. *Po Yu* killed *Sse Tai,* but did not wreak his vengeance upon *Tse Hsi.* Since *Kung Sun Tuan* died along with *&e Tai,* though his guilt was not worth speaking of, the soul of *Po Yu* was not conscious. Taking his revenge as a ghost, he did not make any distinction between a grave and a small offence, as he ought to have done.

Furthermore, *Tse Ch'an* asserted that he who dies a violent death can become

a ghost. What does a violent death mean? Does it mean that according to fate *Po Yu* ought not yet to have died, when he was killed? Or does it mean that *Po Yu* was guileless, but hardly dealt with? If the idea is that he was slain, before the time of his death had arrived, there are many others who likewise died before their appointed time, and if it signifies that *Po Yu* was not guilty, but the victim of an outrage, then *Po Yu* was not alone outraged. If murdered men can become ghosts, *Pi Kan* and *Tse Ihii* did not.

During the "Spring and Autumn" period thirty-six sovereigns in all were assassinated. Theirs were violent deaths *par excellence.* Their sway extended over entire States, the fine substance of which they were formed must have been very abundant, and they succeeded one another as lords of the soil, not only through three generations. The dignity of a reigning prince is not on a level with that of a governor. Their ancestors, who were first enfeoffed, were certainly the equals of *Tse Liang,* the son of Duke *Mu.* Since the sovereigns of States who suffered death at the hands of their treacherous subjects, were of the highest nobility, their souls as ghosts would have been more enlightened than *Po Yu,* who in taking his revenge and killing his enemies went so far as to destroy *Sse Tai* and *Kung Sun Tumi.* The thirty-six princes did not become ghosts, nor did their thirty-six subjects feel their vengeance. If the spirit of *Po Yu* possessed knowledge, because he was a reckless character, the world has never seen more desperate men than *Chieh* and *Chou,* yet, when *Chieh* and *Chou* were put to death, their souls did not become ghosts.

Tse Ch'an's reasoning is *a posteriori.* Noticing that *Po Yu* met with a violent death, he held that all people dying an unnatural death can become ghosts. Had *Po Yu* become a ghost without having met with a violent death, he would have maintained that all people can become ghosts, unless they have died an unnatural death. What difference was there between *Tse Hsi* and *Po Yu,* while both were living in *Ch'eng?* Why should his death be otherwise than that of *Po Yu?* Both were killed by their contrymen for their lawlessness. *Po Yu* could become a ghost, and *Tse Hsi* could not. The argument on the violent death would suit in the case of *Po Yu,* but be inadmissible in that of *Tse Hsi.* The story of *Po Yu* is like the tale of the Earl of *Tu.* The tale of the Earl of 7« being unreliable, that of *Po Yu* cannot be regarded as true either. Duke *Huan* of *Ch in* invaded *Chin,* and encamped himself at *Fu-shih.* The Marquis of *Chin* had gathered his troops in *Chi,* to seize the land of the *Ti,* and restore the Marquis of *Li.* When he came back from this expedition, *Wei K'o* defeated the army of *Chin* at *Fu-shih,* and made *Tu Hui* prisoner. *Tu Hut* was the strongest man in *Ch'in.* Previously *Wei Wu Tse* had a favourite concubine, but no son by her. When he fell sick, he bade *Wei K'o* to give his concubine to somebody in marriage. Afterwards, when his case became more serious, he ordered *Wei K'o* again to bury the concubine with him, but, when *Wei Wu Tse's* death ensued, *Wei K'o* did not bury her. Some people found fault with him, but *Wei K'o* replied, "During his delirium the mind of my father was deranged, therefore I followed the orders he gave, when he was in his senses." At the battle of *Fu-shih, Wei K'o* perceived an old man plaiting grass with a view to ensnaring *Tu Hui,* who stumbled, and fell down, and thus was caught. In the night he beheld the old man in his dreams, who said to him, "1 am the father of the woman which you have given away. You have obeyed your father's orders of the time, when he was still in his right mind, therefore I have paid you my debt of gratitude."

The father of the favourite knew the virtue of *Wei K'o,* therefore he appeared in the shape of a ghost, plaited grass, and helped

'603-575 B.c. Near *Hsi-an-fu* in *Shengi.* In the *Ping-yang* prefecture *(Shami).* Aboriginal, non-Chinese tribes.

The *Ti* had dethroned him, and conquered his territory.

Wei TTo's father.

Quolalion from the *Tso-chuan,* Duke

lhiiun 15th year (593 B.C.). him to win the battle. This clearly proves the enlightenment and the knowledge of the spirit.

I say that, provided that the father of the woman did know the virtue of *Wei K'o,* and appeared as a ghost to help him in battle, he should have been able to reward those whom he liked during his life-time, and to destroy whom he hated, while alive. Human intercourse is amicable or otherwise. Kindness and unfriendliness must be requited, just as gratitude was to be shown for the sake of the woman. Now, the old man was unable to requite the kindness he had received, while alive, and only could show his gratitude for the goodness which he received after death. That is no proof of knowledge, or of the ability to become a ghost.

When *Chang Liang* walked on the banks of the river *Sse,* an old man presented him with a book. *Kuang Wu Ti 2* was sorely pressed in *Ho-pei* when an old man gave his advice. One's fate being grand, and the time lucky, one must meet with felicitous aud pleasant auguries. *Wei K'o* was to take *Tu Hui* prisoner, and to distinguish himself in battle, consequently the phantom of an old man appeared plaiting grass, where the hosts were passing.

Wahg Chi was buried at the foot of Mount *Hua.* The *Litan* river having undermined his tumulus, the front part of his coffin became visible. *Win Wang* said, "How pleasing! Our old lord certainly wishes to see his officers and people once more, therefore he caused the *Luan* to bring his coffin to light." Upon this, he held a court, and all the people could view him for three days. Then he had him buried again.— *Win Wang* was a sage, who knew the true nature of things and principles. Seeing that *Wang Chi's* coffin was visible, he knew that his spirit was desirous of seeing the people, therefore he took him out, and showed him.

I fancy that all the kings and emperors who from ancient times were entombed in the earth after their deaths, must be counted by thousands. They did not desire to see their people again, wherefore

should *Wang Chi* alone have done so? On the banks of the *Yellow River* and the *Sse,* many tombs have been built, and the coffins which by an inundation and a land-slip have been uncovered are Cf. p. 95.

» 25-57 A.d, In *Shansi.* The father of *Wen Wang.* innumerable. Did all those persons wish to see their people again? The undermining of the foot of Mount *Ku* by the *Luan* is like the inundations and the ruptures caused by the waters of the *Yellow River* and the *Sse. Win Wang* perceiving the front part of the coffin exposed, commiserated the old lord, and felt sorry for him, and imagined that he wished to come out again. This is the natural sentiment of a devoted and filial son, and a natural feeling for the other's well-being. As the wise man and the sage he was, he felt deeply touched, and did not take the time to reason and analyse his feelings. He treated a dead man, as though he were living, and therefore gave him a new tomb. The masses believe in the words of wise men and sages, hence they fancy that *Wang Chi* wished to see his people.

Duke *Ching* of *Ch i* was going to invade *Sung.* When his troops passed Mount *T'ai,* the duke saw two old gentlemen in his dream, who stood there in a fit of passion. The duke told *Yen Tse,* who replied, "They are *Tang* and *Yi Yin,* former worthies of *Sung."*—The duke was incredulous, and thought that they were the spirits of Mount *T'ai. Yen Tse* said, "Your Highness disbelieves me, allow me to describe the appearance of *T'ang* and *Yi Yin. T ang* is pale and tall, and has a beard on the chin, which is pointed above, and full below. He keeps himself straight, and talks with a loud voice."—The duke said, " Yes, so he is." *Yen Tse* continued, "*Yi Yin* is dark and short, and has dishevelled hair and whiskers, which are full above and pointed below. He has a stooping gait, and talks low."—The duke said, "Yes, so he is, but what is to be done now?"— *Yen Tse* replied, *"T'ang, T'ai Chia, Wu Ting,* and *Tsu Yi* were excellent rulers of the empire. It is not right that they should have no offspring left. Now there remains only *Sung,* which Your Highness is going to invade. Therefore *T'ang* and *Yi Yin* are enraged, and ask you to dismiss your army, and keep peace with *Sung."*—The duke did not take heed, and invaded *Sung* 546-488 B.c. The Great Diviner of *Ch'i* tcf. p. 112) and reputed author of the *Yen Tse ch'un-ch'iu.* The founder of the *Shang* dynasty, 1766-1753 B.c.

Tang's prime minister.

All four were sovereigns of the *Shang* dynasty. *T'ai Chia* reigned from 1753-1720, *Wu Ting* 1324-1265, and *Tm Yi* 1525 1506 B.c. The dukes of *Sung* derived their descent from the sovereigns of the *Shang* dynasty.

Quoted from *Yen* 7VV *Ch'un-ch'iu (T'ai-p'ing-yii-lari)* with some variations. after all, when his army was in fact beaten.— *T'ang* and *Yi Yin* possessed knowledge, and resented the attack of Duke *Ching* upon *Sung,* therefore they appeared to him in his dreams enraged, for the purpose of checking him, but Duke *Ching* did not stop, and his army met with a reverse.

They say that previously Duke *Ching* had already seen a comet in his dreams. At the time in question, the comet did not appear, which was unlucky. It may be so, but all this were dreams. Duke *Ching* saw a comet, but it was not a real comet, and he dreamt of *T'ang* and *Yi Yin,* but they were not real. Perhaps they were inauspicious visions accompanying the defeat of his army. *Yen Tse* believed in the dream, and said that the figures were those of *T ang* and *Yi Yin.* Duke *Ching* accepted *Yen Tse's* explanation as true. When the *Ch'in* united the empire, they destroyed the descendants of *Yi Yin.* From that time up to the present the sacrifices to *T'ang* and *Yi Yin* have been discontinued, why did they not resent it?

Tse Ch'an of *Clting* was sent on a complimentary mission to *Chin.* The marquis of *Chin* was sick. *Han Hsilan Tse* went to meet the guest, and privately said to him, "My prince is laid up three months already. Although we all have run about to sacrifice to the hills and streams, his sickness increases instead of improving. Now he has dreamt of a yellow bear passing through the door of his bedchamber. What devil can that be?"—*Tse Ch'an* replied, "Since the prince is so enlightened, and your administration so grand, why should there be a malignant spirit? Of yore *Yao* banished *Kun* for perpetuity to Mount *Yii.* His spirit became a yellow bear, which entered into the deep holes of the *Yii,* It eventually became an object of veneration to the *Ilsia,* and the Three Dynasties sacrificed to it. The marquis of *Chin* is an allied prince, has he perhaps not sacrificed to it?"—*Han Hsilan Tse* performed the sacrifice of the *Hsia,* and the marquis of *Chin* felt a relief. The yellow bear was Vid. p. 209. His name was *P'ing* (556-530 B.c.). Prime minister of *Chin.* The father of the Emperor *Yii.*

South of *1-chou* in *Shantung.*

The *Hsia* dynasty. *Hsia, Shang,* and *Chou.*

'Allied to the reigning house of *Chou.* Quoted from the *Tso-chuan,* Duke *Ch'ao* 7th year (534 B.c.) *Legge* Vol. V, Pt. II, p. 617).

the spirit of *Kun.* The marquis of *Chin* had not sacrificed to it, therefore it passed through the door of his bedroom. When *Chin* knew it, and performed the sacrifice, the disease was interrupted. Does that not show that the dead are conscious?

That *Kun* was left to die on Mount *Yii* every one knows, but wherefrom should people learn that his spirit became a yellow bear, and entered the depths of the *Yii?* If it was like Duke *Niu At* of *Lu,* who during a disease was transformed into a tiger, it could have been verified at the time of death. Now *Kun* died far away on Mount *Yii,* nobody was with him, where did the news come from then'.' Moreover, it is expressly stated that his spirit became a bear, which implies that he died. That after death his spirit became a yellow bear, men had no means to ascertain.

People call a dead man a ghost. A ghost is like a living man in form, and does not look otherwise than a man, and yet it is not the spirit of the deceased. How much less a bear, which has no human form, and does not resemble man! If really the spirit of *Kun* after death was transformed into a yellow bear, then the spirit of a dead bear might also eventually become a man. How could anybody dreaming of it know but that it was the spirit of a dead animal? Those who believe that the bear was the spirit of *Kun* will also imagine that the ghosts which appear are the vital force of the dead. There is no proof that it is the vital force of human beings, and we cannot own that a yellow bear was the spirit of *Kun.*

Furthermore, dreams are visions. When good or bad luck are impending, the mind shapes these visions. Thus the sight of a bear will also admit of an interpretation. Now, in case that the spirit of *Kun* really became a yellow bear after death, must the yellow bear which appeared in the dream at all events have been the spirit of *Kun?* The feudal princes were wont to sacrifice to the mountains and streams. Should the marquis of *Chin* have viewed mountains and streams in his dreams, would it not have been, because he had offered sacrifice to them, that those mountains and streams appeared to him?

When people are sick, they often see their deceased ancestors arriving and standing by their side; are we again to suppose that these deceased ancestors show themselves for the purpose of asking Cf. Chap. XXVII.

Like other dreams. The visions have mostly a symbolical meaning, and must not be semblances of real beings. They would be evoked by his remembrance, but not be real. for food? What we see in our dreams is, moreover, being interpreted as having some other meaning, and is not real anyhow. How can we prove that? When in a dream we have perceived a living man, this man, seen in our dream, does not meet us on the following day. Since the man seen in the dream, does not meet us, we know that the yellow bear of *Kun* did not pass through the bedroom door, as a matter of fact, and, since it did not, *Kun* did not ask for food either. *Kun* not having asked for food, the disease of the marquis of *Chin* was not a misfortune caused by his neglect of the *Hsia* sacrifice, and since it was not a calamity brought about by the non-observance of this ceremony, the relief of the marquis of *Chin* was not a lucky event caused by the performance of the sacrifice. There having been no real luck, it is evident that there was no consciousness on the part of *Kun*.

This is like the case of *Lin An,* Prince of *Huai-nan,* who died charged with high-treason, and is nevertheless commonly reported to have ascended to heaven as an immortal. Whether *Tse Chan* also had heard such a false rumour, we cannot make out now. By chance the force of the sickness of the marquis of *Chin* was just going to be broken of itself, when *Tse Ch'an* happened to explain the appearance of the yellow bear. Thus the statement that the yellow bear was the spirit of *Kun* found credence.

The Emperor *Kao Huang Ti* intended to make *Ju Yi,* Prince of *Chao,* his successor, because he was like him. The Empress *Lil Hou* was furious, and afterwards poisoned the prince of *Chao.* When, later on, *Li i Hou* went out, she beheld a grey dog, which bit her under her left arm. She thought it strange, and by divination found out that it had been *Ju Yi,* prince of *Chao,* who had haunted her. She then began to suffer from the wound under her arm, which did not heal, and died. People believe that the spirit of *Ju Yi* transformed itself into a grey dog to take his revenge.

I say that, when a valiant warrior fighting, flushed with anger, succumbs, sword in hand, and being hurt, sinks to the ground, and The Taoist philosopher *Huai* ɪvan *Tse.* Vid. chap. XXVIII. With regard to the metamorphose of *Kun.*

Han Kao Tsu, 206-194 B.c.

Cf. chap. XVIII. breathes his last, he sees with his eyes the adversary, who has hit him, yet, after death, his spirit is incapable of taking its vengeance. When *Lil Hou* poisoned *Ju Yi,* she did not step forward personally, but had instructed some one to administer the poison. First the prince was not aware of his being poisoned, and then in his anger did not know, who the murderer was. How then could he become a demon, and avenge himself upon *Lti Jɪou?*

If the dead possessed knowledge, no-body had more reason to hate *La Hou* than the Emperor *Kao Tsu.* He loved *Ju Yi,* whom the empress killed. The soul of *Kao Tsu* ought to have been like a peal of thunder in his wrath, and not have waited one day, before he called *Lti Hou* to account. Why was the spirit of *Kao Tsu* not like that of *Ju Yi,* and why did he dislike *Ju Yi* after his death, and acquiesce in the murder of the empress?

When the report of a quarrel which the prime minister *T'ien Fin,* Marquis of *Wu-an,* had had with the former generalissimo *Kuan Fu* over a glass of wine reached the emperor, *Kuan Fu* was imprisoned. *Tou Ying* attempted to rescue him, but could not save him, and the consequence was that *Kuan Fu* brought down capital punishment upon himself, and that *Tou Ying* had to suffer death likewise. Subsequently, *T'ien Fin* contracted a very painful disease, during which he cried, "Yes, yes," and asked the by-standers to look. They beheld *Kuan Fu* and *Tou Ying* sitting by his side. *T'ien Fin's* sickness did not release, until he died.

I reply that he was not the only man who killed another. Other murderers have not seen their victims, when they fell sick afterwards, whereas *T'ien Fin* beheld the two men whose deaths he had brought about. *T ien Fen* alone did so, because he felt their anger, and in his delirium had hallucinations. Or maybe he perceived some other ghost, and the necromancer having heard of his former dispute with *Kuan Fu* and *Ton Ying,* and of his wish to Uncle of the Emperor *Han Wu Ti.* District in *Honan.* Commander-in-chief under the Emperor *Ching Ti,* 156-140 B.C., who was supplanted by *T'ien Fen.* We learn from the *Ch'ien Han-shu,* chap. 52, p. 12, Biography of *Kuan Fu,* that *T'ien Fen* felt pain all over the body, as if he were flogged, and cried for mercy. The emperor sent his visionist to look at him, who reported that the ghosts of *Kuan Fu* and *Tmt Ying* were holding him, and beating him to death.

learn the real name of the spirit, and seeing him crying, "Yes, yes," at random, gave the answer that *Kuan Fu* and *Tou*

Ying were sitting near him.

The governor of *Huai-yang, Yin Ch'i,* was a very cruel and oppressive magistrate. When he had passed away, the people whom he had wronged intended to burn his body, but it disappeared, and reverted to its grave. He was conscious, therefore the people were going to burn him, and he was a spirit, therefore he could disappear.

I presume that the vanished spirit of *Yin Ch'i* has his analogies. During the *Ch'in* epoch three mountains disappeared. and about the end of the *Chou* dynasty the Nine Tripods were engulphed. Provided that things which can disappear are spirits, then the three mountains and the Nine Tripods must have had consciousness. Perhaps the then magistrate, apprised of the design of the angry populace, stealthily removed the corpse, and pretended that it had disappeared, and for fear, lest the outraged people should vent their wrath upon himself, declared that it had done so of its own accord. All persons who can disappear must have their feet to walk upon. Now, the circulation of the blood of the deceased had been interrupted, and his feet could not move any more. How should he have managed his flight?

In *Wu, Wu Tse Hsii* was cooked, and in *Han, f'eng Yiieh* was pickled. Burning and pickling is the same torture. *Wu Tse Hsii* and *P eng Yueh* were equally brave. They could not escape the cooking, or avoid the pickling, and *Yin Ch'i* alone is said to have been able to return to his tomb. That is an untruth and an unfounded assertion.

Doomed *Wang Mang* removed the empress *Fu Hou,* the wife of the emperor *Yuan Ti,* from her tomb. He desecrated her coffin, and took from it boxes with jewels and seals. Afterwards he con The present *C'h'en-chosi* in *Honan.*

Cf. chap. XX.

Cf. chap. XL.

Cf. p. 140.

P'i'ng Yiieh, King of *Liang,* was executed by order of *Han Kao Tsu* in 196 B.C. , when he had revolted against the emperor. All his relations to the third degree were put to death along with him.

Vid. *Shi-chi* chap. 8, p. 33v. An epithet often given to *Chin Shih Huang Ti* and *Wang Mang,* both eijually detested by the literati. 48-32 B.c. veyed the corpse to *Ting-t'ao,* where he had it buried again after the fashion of common people. When the coffin was taken out, a stench rose to heaven. The governor of *Logang* on approaching the coffin smelled it, and dropped down dead. *Wang Mang* likewise disinterred the empress *Ting Hon,* wife to the emperor *Kung Wang'* in *Tingt'ao,* but fire issued from her crypt, and burned several hundred officials and scholars to death. The re-interment was done in a low style, and the dead were robbed of their valuables. These two insults induced them to cause the stench, and send the fire to destroy the offenders.

I say that the stench rose to heaven, because many eatable things had been placed into the grave. It is not passing strange that men could not stand the mephetic vapours, when the smell of the putrid matter came forth in abundance, but it is strange that flames should have flashed from the crypt. At all events, it was not the spirit of the empress *Ting Hon,* for the following reason. Must he who breaks open, and despoils graves not be much more hated than he who merely changes the tombs? Yet, during a yeax of scarcity, those who dig up tombs for the purpose of appropriating the garments of the dead must be counted by thousands. Provided that the departed know, when others strip them of their clothes, and leave their bodies naked, they cannot hinder it at that time, and, later on, have no means to take their revenge.

But these are people of small account, not worth mentioning. *Chin Shiit Huang Ti* was buried near the *Li-slian.* At the close of *Erh Shih Huang Ti's* reign the robbers of the empire dug up his grave, and he could not send forth either stench or fire, nor kill a single man! He had been the Son of Heaven, and could not become a spirit. How then should *FuHou* and *Ting Hou,* two women, have been able to do miracles? They are believed to have become spirits, but not in the same way, and to have

shown their powers in different places. People saw flames, and smelled bad odour. Consequently the assertion that both became spirits is erroneous.

In *Ts'ao-chou-fu (Shantung).* 946-934 B.c. Near *Hsi-an-fu,* where the tumulus of the mighty emperor is still visible. 209-206 B.c. CHAPTER XVII.

Spook Stories *(Chi-yao).*

Duke *Ling* of *Wei* was proceeding to *Chin.* When he had arrived on the banks of the river *Pu,'* he heard at night-time a new tune played on the guitar, which pleased him so well, that he ordered somebody to ask his attendants about it. They all reported that they had heard nothing. Then he called for the musicmaster *Chilan,* and told him saying, "There was some one playing a new melody, I gave orders to ask my followers about it, but they all stated that they had not heard anything. It is, as if a ghost made the music for me. Pray, listen to it and write it down for me. " The music-master *Chilan* acquiesced, sat quietly down, played the guitar, and wrote down the tune. On the following morning he reported that he had got it, but still required some practice. He therefore asked for one night more to practise. Duke *Ling* granted this request. *Chilan* practised one more night, and on the next morning he had mastered it. They then went on to *Chin.*

Duke *P'ing* of *Chin* feasted him on the *Shi Yi* terrace. When they were flushed with wine, Duke *Ling* rose and said, "I have a new tune, which I would like to have played for Your Highness to hear." The duke consented, and he called upon the musicmaster *Chilan* to sit down next to the music-master *K'uang,* to take the lute, and strike it, but, ere *Chilan* had finished, *K'uang* grasped the instrument, and stopped him saying, "This is a song 1 533-499 B.c.

On the border of the provinces *Chili* and *Shantung.* 556-530 B.c. Mil- '- chap. 24, p. 39 v. calls it the "*Shi-hui* terrace," g. which was situated on the *Fen* river in *Shansi.* of a doomed State. You must not proceed." Duke *P'ing* inquired, "Where does it come from?"—The music-master *K'uang* replied, "It is a li-

centious melody composed by the music-master *Yen,* who made this voluptuous music for *Chou. Wu Wang* executed *Chou,* hanging his head on a white banner. *Yen* fled to the east, and, when he had reached the river *Pu,* he drowned himself. Therefore to hear this tune one must be on the banks of the *Pu.* If formerly any one heard it, his State was wiped out. It must not be continued."—Duke *P'ing* said, "I am very partial to music. Let him go on." *Chilan* then finished his tune.

Duke *P'ing* said, "What do they call this air? "—The musicmaster replied, "It is what they call G major." "Is not G major most plaintive?", asked the duke.—"It does not come up to C major," replied *K'uang.*—" Could I not hear C major? ", inquired the duke.—The music-master rejoined, "You cannot. Of old, only princes possessed of virtue and justice were allowed to hear C major. Now the virtue of Your Highness is small. You could not stand the hearing of it."—The duke retorted, "I am very partial to music, and I would like to hear it." *K'uang* could not help taking up the lute and thrumming it. When he played the first part, two times eight black cranes came from the south, and alighted on the top of the, exterior gate. When he played again, they formed themselves into rows, and, when he played the third part, they began crowing, stretching their necks and dancing, flapping their wings. The notes F and G were struck with the greatest precision, and their sound rose to heaven. Duke *P'ing* was enraptured, and all the guests were enchanted. The duke lifted the goblet, and rose to drink the health of the music-master *K'uang.* Then he sat down again, and asked, "Is there no more plaintive music than that in C major?" *K'uang* replied, "It falls short of A major."—" Could I not hear it? ", said the duke.—The music-master replied, "You cannot. Of yore, *Huang Ti* assembled the ghosts and spirits on the Western Mount *T'ai.* He rode in an ivory carriage, to which were yoked Cf. *Shi-chi* chap. 4, p. 11 and Chap. XXXVIII.

I am not quite certain, whether *G, C,* and *A maior* are a correct rendering of

Chinese ch'ing (clear) shang, chih and chio jfjlj jJ (-Ii l the Alihnoires concernant les Chinois Vol. VI, p. 115 these notes are identified with sol, ut, and la. At any rate ch'ing (clear) and its correlate cito (obscure) would be ap propriate terms to designate sharp and flat notes. —The parallel passage of the Shi-chi omits to specify the airs, as is done here. The sacred Mount T'ai is in the East, in Shantung, not in the West. six black dragons. The Pi-fang bird came along with it, and Ch'ih Yu was in front. The Spirit of the Wind came forward sweeping the ground, and the Spirit of Rain moistened the road. Tigers and wolves were in front, and ghosts and spirits in the rear, reptiles and snakes crawling on the ground, and white clouds covering the empyrean. A great assembly of ghosts and spirits! And then he began to play in A major. Your virtue, Sire, is small and would not suffice to hear it. If you did, I am afraid, it would be your ruin."

Duke Ping rejoined, "I am an old man and very fond of music. I would like to hear it."—The music-master K'uang could not but play it. When he had struck the first notes, clouds rose from the north-west, and when he played again, a storm broke loose, followed by torrents of rain. The tents were rent to pieces, the plates and dishes smashed, and the tiles of the verandah hurled down. The guests fled in all directions, and Duke P ing was so frightened, that he fell down under the porches. The Chin State was then visited with a drought. For three years the soil was scorched up. The duke's body began to suffer pain and to languish thereafter.

What does that mean? Since the State of Duke Ling of Wei was not going to ruin, whereas Duke P ing of Chin fell sick, and his State suffered from a drought, it was not spook. The music-master K'uang had said that the States of those who had heard this tune before, were destroyed. Now the two States had both heard it before.

How do we know that the new tune was not played by the music-master Yen?-When Yen had jumped into the Pu, his body decomposed in the water, and

his vital essence dissolved in the mud. How could he still touch the lute? Ch'ii Yuan flung himself into the river. He was as able a writer as Yen was a player of the guitar. If Yen could strike the lute again, then Ch'ii Yuan would Some say that it is the spirit of wood. It is described as a bird with one wing, always carrying fire in its mouth, and portending fire in the house where it appears. According to the Shan-hai-king it would be a bird like a crane, but with one leg, a green plumage adorned with red, and a white beak.

A legendary person said by some to have been a minister of Huang Ti. Cf. Chap. XXXV. All the details about the assembly of ghosts are omitted in the Shi-citi. The same story, illustrative of the magical force of music, is told in a parallel passage of the Shi-chi, chap. 24, on music, p. 39 seq. Since the text of the Lun-heng is fuller, 1 presume that Wang Ch'ung did not quote the Shi-chi, but had an older source, probably the same, from which the Shi-chi has copied. have been able to write again. When Yang Tse Yun lamented Ch'il Yuan's death, wherefore did he not show his gratitude? While alive, Ch il Yuan was a very active writer, but he could not thank Yang Tse Yiin, because, when dead, he became mud and earth. His hand being rotten, he could not use it again to write. Since Ch'i l Yuan could not use his rotten hand to write, Yen could not thrum the guitar with his tainted thumb either. When Confucius was buried opposite to the Sse river, the Sse flowed backwards. They say that it was the spirit of Confucius which caused the Sse to flow backwards. Confucius was very fond of teaching, just as Yen liked to play the lute. Provided that the music-master Yen could strike the lute on the banks of the Pu, why could not Confucius teach in the vicinity of the Sse?

Viscount Chi en of Chao was sick, and for five days did not know anybody. His high officers were alarmed, and then called Pien Chio2 He entered, inquired into the nature of the malady, and then went out again. Tung An Yil3 asked him, and Pien Ch'io replied, "His blood circulation is all right, but it is

strange. Formerly Duke Mu of Ch'in has been in such a state. After seven days he awoke, and, when he had recovered consciousness, he spoke to Kung Sun Chih and Tse Yii saying, 'I have been in God's abode. I was very happy, and I stayed away so long, because I was lucky enough to acquire some knowledge. God told me that the Chin State would be in convulsions for five generations and have no repose, and that the next powerful prince would die, before he was old. Owing to the son of this monarch no distinction between men and women would be made in my country.' Kung Sun Chih wrote it all down, and kept the paper in a trunk. Then ensued the revolution under Duke Hsien of 67(H), the domination of Duke Win, the victory of Duke Hsiang3 over the army of Ch in

'516-457 B.c. Pien Ch io is the honorary appellative of Ch'm Yiieh Jen, a celebrated physician who travelled from State to State.

A minister of Viscount Chien. 4 658-620 B.c. Officers of Ch'm. 8 675-651 B. c.

'634-627 B.c. 626-620 B.c. at Yao, and his weakness towards his woman-folk on his march home. The sickness of your prince is identical with this. Within three days it will cease, and then the patient will have something to say."

When two days and a half had elapsed, Viscount Chien became conscious again, and said to his high officers, "I have been with God, and was very happy. With the spirits I roamed about heaven, and enjoyed the highest bliss. The music and the dances there were different from the music of the three dynasties, and the sound went to heart. There was a brown bear preparing to seize me. God bade me shoot it; I hit the animal, and it died. Then a spotted bear attacked me; I hit it also, and it died. God was very much pleased, and presented me with tw o caskets of the same contents. I then beheld a lad by God's side. God entrusted to me a 7P dog and said, 'When your son has grown up, give it to him.' God told me further. 'The Chin State is going to be destroyed; after ten generations it will have disappeared. Some one of the family name of *Ying* will inflict a crushing defeat on the people of *Citou* west of *Fan-kuei,* but he will not keep the country all the same. Now I think of the merits of *Shun,* therefore I will marry his descendant *Ming Yao* to your grandson of the tenth generation.'"' *Tung An Yil* committed all these words to writing and kept the document. He informed Viscount *Chien* of what *Pien Ch'io* had A defile in *Honan.* On the battle of *Yao* which took place in 62G u.c. cf. *Tso-chuan* Duke *Hsi,* o3d year. The weakness of Duke *Hsiang* consisted in releasing his prisoners at the request of his mother, a princess of *Ch'in,* which was deeply resented by his officers. *Vid.* Chap. XL.

Northern barbarians. A *Ti* dog was probably a huge Mongolian dog, resembling a St. Bernard, much bigger than the common Chinese dog. We ought to read "seven generations" as the *Shi-chi* does. The characters for seven and ten can be easily confounded. *Chien s* sickness took place in 500 B.c. under the reign of Duke *Ting* of *Chin.* From Duke *Ting* to the end of the *Chin* State, which in 375 broke up into the three marquisates of Wei, *Chno,* and *Han,* there are only seven rulers, *Ting* included. Viscount *Chien* was a vassal of Duke *Ting* and ancestor of the later marquises and kings of *Chao. l ing* was the family name of the viscounts of *Chao.* This does not mean the people of the royal domain of *Chou,* but the people of *Wei (Hunan),* whose princes were descended from a side branch of the royal house, their ancestor being *K'ang Shu,* a younger brother of the Emperor *Wu Wang.* After the extinction of *Chin,* the Marquis *Cheng* of *Chao* conquered seventy-three towns from *Wei.* It should be "of the seventh generation," lor King *Wu Ling,* who was married to *Meng Yao,* was a descendant of Viscount *Clu-en* in the seventh degree. said. *Chien Tse* then made *Pien Ch'io* a graut of forty thousand mou of land.

When, one day, Viscount *Chien* went out, a man stood in his way. Though warned *off,* he did not go. The retinue were going to arrest him, when the man on the road said, "I wish to have an audience with His Lordship." The attendants informed *Chien Tse,* who called the man crying, "How delightful! I saw you in my rambles."—" Send your attendants away," said the man on the road, "I would like to speak to you." When *Chien Tse* had dismissed his men, the man on the road continued, "Some time ago, when Your Lordship was sick, I was standing by God."— "That is true," said Viscount *Chien,* "What did I do, when you saw me? "—" God bade Your Lordship," replied the man on the road, "to shoot the brown and the spotted bears, which both were killed."—" What does that mean," asked *Chien Tse.* —" The *Chin* State," replied the man, "will be in extremities, and Your Lordship will take the lead. God ordered you to destroy the two ministers, for the brown and the spotted bears were their forefathers."—" What does it mean," inquired the Viscount, " that God gave me two caskets both having the same contents? "—The man on the road said, "Your Lordship's son will conquer two kingdoms in the *Ti* country, which will be named after him."—"I perceived a lad near God, said *Chien Tse,* and God entrusted to me a 75 dog saying, 'When your son has grown up, give it to him.' Would my son be pleased to have such a dog? "—" That lad, rejoined the man, "is your son, and the *Ti* dog is the ancestor of *Tax.* Your Lordship's son will get possession of *Tai.* Among your descendants there will be a change of government, they will wear Mongolian dress, and two States will be added to that of the *Ti.* " *Chien Tse* asked the man's name and proposed to employ him in an offlcial capacity, but the man on the road declined saying, "I am but a rustic and have delivered God's message." Then he disappeared.

What does this mean? It was all spook, they say. The explanation of the things seen in God's presence, as given by the man on the road was the correct interpretation, and the man on the road himself an apparition.

Tai and Chih.

' So far the story has been quoted from the *Shi-chi,* chap. 43, p. 7 seq. Lun-

Heng. 16

Later on, the tw o ministers of *Chin, Fan Win Tse* and *Chung Hang Chao Tse* mutinied. Viscount *Chien* attacked and routed them, and both fled to *Ch'i.*

At that time *Chien Tse* had his sons examined physiognomically by A« *Pit Tse Ch'ing.* None of them had any auspicious signs, but, when the physiognomist arrived at *Wu Hsii,* his son by his *Ti* wife, he declared him to be noble. *Chien Tse* conversed with him, and discovered that he was very intelligent. *Chien Tse* then called all his sons and said to them, "I have hidden a precious charm on Mount *Ch'ang.* He who first finds it, will be rewarded." All the sons ascended the mountain, but did not find anything. When *Wu Hsii* returned, he said that he had found the charm. Viscount *Chien* asked, how. "On Mount *Ch'ang*" replied *Wu Hsii,* one is near *Tai3* which might be acquired."—*Chien Tse* thought him to be very clever, therefore he deposed the heir-apparent, and put *Wu Hsii* in his place. When *Chien Tse* died, *Wu Hsii* became his successor under the name of Viscount *Hsiang.*

After Viscount *Hsiang* had come to power, he instigated somebody to assassinate the king of *Tai,* aud annexed his territory, and likewise he seized the territory of the *Chih* family. Later on, he married a *Jung* from *K'ung-t'ung."* Ten generations after *Chien Tse"* came King *Wu Ling3 Wu Clung* introduced to him his mother of the name of *Ying* and his daughter *Ming Yao.* Subsequently King *Wu Ling* seized *Chung shan* and annexed the *Hu* territory. In his nineteenth year King *Wu Ling* assumed the *Hu* dress, and his subjects adopted the *Hu* customs. Everything happened as predicted, Comp. p. 307.

Another name for Mount *Heng* in *Ta-iung-fu* in *North Shansi.*

A *Ti* State occupying the confines of *JS'orth Shansi* and *Mongolia.* Cf. *Shi-chi,* chap. 43, p. 11 v.

An earldom in the south of the *Chin* State. Name of a mountain in *Kansu* and of an aboriginal tribe *(Jtmg)* settled there. It must be "seven generations." *Wu Ling's* reign lasted from 325-29!) B. c. In the *Shi-chi,* chap. 43, p. 19. *Wu*

Ching is called *Wu Kuang.* He was a descendant of *Shun.* The passage seems to be corrupt. The *Shi-chi* says " *Wu Kuang* through his wife introduced (to the king) his beautiful daughter *Ying Mf. ng Yao.* " First a palace girl, *Meng Yao,* some years later, was raised to the rank of a queen. See on this passage *Chavannes Mem. Hit.* Vol. V, p. 68 Note 7. Originally a part of *Chin,* in the modern *Ting-chou* of Chili province. These *Hu* tribes were settled in the northern provinces:—*Chili, Shan-si, Shensi,* and *Kansu.* and nothing was wrong. The supernatural lucky signs manifested by portents all proved true; so they say.

All these things are not true. The lucky and unlucky omens happening one after the other were like manifestations of Heaven, but how do we know that, as a matter of fact, Heaven did not send any message? Because the man on the road was by God's side, for only spirits of the highest degree can keep near the Ruler of Heaven. Those who forward God's commands are the heavenly envoys. The envoys of human princes are provided with horses and carriages, and it would not be dignified for an envoy of the Ruler of Heaven to stand alone on the road. Of heavenly officials there are one hundred and twenty, who do not differ from those of the kings of the earth. The kings of the earth have plenty of officials and attendants, who have received their power after the model of the heavenly officials. Since the officials of Heaven and Earth are alike, their envoys must resemble each other also, and, there being such a similarity, it is impossible that one man should have been so dissimilar.

How do we know that God, whom *Chien Tse* saw, was not the real God? We know it from the interpretation of dreams. Towers, belvederes, hills, and mountains are images for an official post. When a man dreams of ascending a tower or a belvedere, or of mounting a hill or a mountain, he will get an office. In reality a tower, a belvedere, a hill, or a mountain are not an official post. Hence we know that God, whom Viscount *Chien* saw in his dream, was not the Ruler of Heaven. When an offi-

cial dreams of a prince, this prince does not appear at all, nor does he give presents to the official. Therefore the interpretation of dreams teaches us that God who gave *Chien Tse* two caskets and a *Ti* dog, was not the Supreme Ruler. Since it was not the Ruler of Heaven, the heaven over which *Chien Tse* roamed with the other ghosts, as he says, was not heaven.

Shu Sun Mu Tse of *Lu* dreamed that heaven fell down upon him. If this had really been the case, heaven would have dropped upon the earth, and approaching the earth, it would not have reached *Shu Sun Mu Tse* owing to the resistance offered by towers and terraces. Had it reached him, then towers and terraces ought to have been demolished first. Towers and terraces were not de The stars, considered as the officials of God, the Ruler of Heaven, and as divinities. A nobleman of the *Iai* State of the 6th cent. B.C. This dream is narrated in the *Tso-clman,* Duke *Ch'ao* 4th year (537 B.c.). molished, therefore heaven did not descend upon the earth. Since it did not descend upon the earth, it could not reach him, and, since it did not reach him, that which fell down upon him was not heaven, but an effigy of heaven. As the heaven which fell down upon *Shu Sun Mu Tse* in his dream was not the real heaven, so the heaven through which *Chien Tse* had been roving was not heaven.

Some one might object that we also have direct dreams, insomuch as we dream of so-and-so, and on the next day see him or, as we dream of a gentleman, whom we see on the following day. I admit that we can have direct dreams, but these direct dreams are semblances, and only these semblances are direct, which will become evident from the following fact. Having a direct dream, we dream of so-and-so, or of any gentleman, and, on the following day, see Mr. So-and-so, or the gentleman in question. That is direct. But, when we ask so-and-so or that gentleman, they will reply that they have not appeared to us in our dreams. Since they did not appear, the persons we saw in our dreams were merely their likenesses. Since so-

and-so and the said gentleman were likenesses, we know that God, as perceived by *Chien Tse,* was solely a semblance of God.

The oneirocritics say that, when a man dreams, his soul goes out. Accordingly, when he sees God in a dream, the soul ascends to heaven. Ascending to heaven is like going up a mountain. When we dream of ascending a mountain, our feet climb up the mountain, and our hand uses a stick; then we rise. To mount up to heaven there are no steps, how should we rise then? The distance from heaven to us amounts to upwards of ten thousand *li.* A man on a journey uses to travel one hundred *li* daily. As long as the soul is united to the body, it cannot move very rapidly, how much less, when it walks alone! Had the soul moved with the same speed as the body, *Chien Tse* would have required several years for his ascension to heaven and his return. Now, he awoke after seven days, and became conscious again. How could the time be so short?

The soul is the vital fluid: the movement of the vital fluid is like that of clouds and fog, and cannot be very quick. Even if the soul moved like a flying bird, it would not be very rapid. Sometimes people dream that they are flying; the Hying is done by the soul, but it could not be quicker than the flight of a bird. That fluid of heaven and earth which possesses the greatest speed is the storm, yet a storm does not blow a whole day. Provided that the soul were flying like the storm, its speed would not last longer than one day, and it would be unable to reach heaven.

When a mau dreams that he ascends to heaven, it is during the short span, while he lies down. At his awakening, he is perhaps still in heaven, and not yet descended, as a person, dreaming of having arrived at Loyang, still finds himself in Loyang, when roused. How can the flight of the soul be deemed quick? Rapidity is not in its nature, consequently the ascension to heaven was not real. Not being real, it must have been a supernatural omen. The man on the road, perceived by Viscount *Chien* in his sickness by God's side and subsequently met on the road, speaking like a man, was the same with the one whom he had seen near God. Therefore the explanation that a dream during the sleep is a state of obscuration, which can be interpreted, when the sleeper awakes to light again, is quite correct.

When Viscount *Hsiang* of *Chao* had been appointed, the Earl of *Cfrih* became more and more arrogant. He asked land of *Han* and *Wei*, which *Han* and *Wei* gave him. Then he made the same demand to *Chao*, but *Chao* refused. This roused his anger to such a degree, that with troops of *Han* and *Wei* he assaulted *Hsiang Tse* of *Chao*. Viscount *Hsiang* alarmed fled to *Chin-gang,* and sought shelter there. *Yuan Kuo* followed him. When he had arrived at the post-town of *T'o-p'ing,* he beheld three men, who from the belt upwards were visible, but invisible from the belt downwards. They handed two joints of bamboo, still unopened, to *Yuan Kuo* saying. "Forward this for us to *Wu Hsil* of *Chm."* Upon this he told *Hsiang Tse. Hsiang Tse* first having fasted three days, personally cut open the bamboo, which contained a red letter reading as follows:—" *Wu Hsil* of *Chao* We are the *Huo-t'ai* Mountain, the Marquis of *Yang,* and the Son of Heaven. On the *ping-hsii* day of the third moon, we will cause you to destroy *Chili,* and, provided that you sacrifice to us in a hundred cities, we will also give the . Id 456 B.c. (cf. above p. 226).

I. e. the viscounts of *Han* and *Wei,* who together with those of *Chao* had usurped the power in *Chin.* Near *T ai-guan-fu* in Shansi. The *Shi-chi* calls this place *Wang-tw,* which was situated in *Chiang-chou (Shansi).* The personal name of Viscount *Hsiang* (cf. p. 226). A mountain in *Yung-an-hsicn (Shansi) Ho-tung* circuit. The reading of the *Shi-chi:*—" Marquis of *Shan-gang* (name of city) and Envoy of Heaven ' seems preferable. territory of the *Lin Hn* to you."—*Hsiang Tse* made obeisance again, and accepted the commands of the spirits.

What does that mean? This was an augury of *Hsiang Tse's* future victory. The three States were beleaguering *Chin-*

yang for over a year. They diverted the *Fen* and flooded the town, so that only three blocks of the city wall were not submerged. Viscount *Hsiang* frightened sent his minister *Chang Ming T'an* to open secret negotiations with *Han* and *Wei.* They made an agreement with him, and on the *ping-hsil* day of the third month they completely annihilated *Chih,* and divided his country among them.—Therefore the fluid of the supernatural portent was shaped like a man, and called itself the spirit of the *Huo-t'ai* Mountain, as the apparitions in the *Hsia* palace had the form of dragons, and called themselves Princes of Pao. *Chien Tse's* omen had human shape, and pretended to be an envoy of God.

How do we know that it was not the spirit of the *Huo-t'ai* Mountain? Because a high mountain is a formation of the earth just as bones and joints are of the human body. How can bones and joints be spiritual? If the high mountain had a spirit, it should be shaped like a high mountain. What people call ghosts is the essence of the departed, in appearance they are formed like living men. Now the high mountain was broad and long, and not at all like a man, but its spirit did not differ from a man. Such being the case, the ghost resembled a man, and since it was like a man, it must have been the fluid of a supernatural portent.

In the 36th year of the reign of *Ch'in Shih Huang It* Mars offuscated the constellation of the Heart, and a star fell down. When it reached the earth, it became a stone, on which were engraved the following words:—" *Ch in Shih Huang Ti* will die, and his land will be divided." A subdivision of the *Hu* tribes, probably Mongols. A tributary of the *Huang-ho.* One "pan" block is said to measure 8 feet. The *Shi-chi,* chap. 43, p. 13, writes:. j. So far the narration has been culled with some omissions and alterations from the *Shi-chi,* chap. 43, p. 12 v. seq. When the *Hsia* dynasty had begun to decline, two divine dragons made their appearance in the imperial palace, and said that they were two princes of *Pun.* Cf. *Shi-chi,* chap. 4, p. 25 *(Chavannes, Mem.* Vol. I,

p. 281) which quotes the *Kuo-gii.* '6 211 B.c.

When *Ch'in 'Shih Huang Ti* heard of it, he ordered a censor to interrogate the people one by one, but nobody would confess. Whereupon the emperor bad all the people living near the stone arrested and put to death. The weird stone he then caused to be destroyed by fire.

When his ambassador, coming from *Tung-kuan,* had passed *Hua-gin* at night-time, and come into the open country, a man with a jade badge in his hands happened to block his passage. "Transmit this to the prince of the *Hao Lake* for me," said the man, and went on saying, "This year the dragon ancestor will die."

The ambassador was just going to ask him for particulars, when the man disappeared, leaving his badge. This the ambassador took, and apprized the emperor of everything. *Chin Shih Huang Ti* kept silent for a long while, then he exclaimed, "The spirit of the mountain knows only the affairs of one year. The dragon ancestor, of whom he speaks, must be a forefather, however." He then gave orders to the imperial household to examine the badge. They ascertained that it was a badge which had been thrown into the *Yangtze,* while it was crossed in the 28th year of the emperor's reign. The next year, the 37th of his reign, he had a dream that he was fighting with the spirit of the ocean, which was shaped like a man.

What does this mean? All these were auguries of *Ch'in Shih Huang Tis* impending death. Having dreamt that he was trying conclusions with the spirit of the ocean, he entered into the sea in high dudgeon, waiting for the spirit, and shot at a huge fish. From *Lang-geh6* to the *Lao* and *Ch eng* Mountains he did not perceive any, but having arrived at the *Chefoo* Mountain, he again came A place at the bend of the Yellow River in *Sitensi.* A town half-way between *Tung-kuan* and *Hsi-an-fu.* The *Hao* Lake was near *Hsi-an-Jii,* the capital of *Ch'in Shih Huang Ti,* who is meant by the prince of the lake.

219 B.c. The foregoing are extracts from the *Shi-chi,* chap. 6, p. 24 v. seq.

On the south coast of *Shantung.*
'*Jf J$L* LU - *yung-ch'mg 1 ffc* Jj (be. cit. p. 28). The *Lao xhan* and the *Ch'eng shan* are two high mountain ranges in *Chi-mo (Kiaocitou)* reaching to the sea. The *Tu-shih fang gu chi gao*, chap. 36 rejects the reading *Yung-ch'atg*. The mountains must have been on the sea-shore, north of *Lang-gch* and south of *Chefoo,* for this was the way taken by the emperor, as results from *Lunhmg* Bk. IV, 9 *(Shu-tmi)* and Bk. XXVI, 1 *(Shih-chih).*

"The *I 'hefoo* Promontory, forming the harbour of the treaty-port *Chefoo.* in view of enormous fishes, of which he killed one by a shot with his arrow. Hence he proceeded along the sea-shore as far as *P ingyuan2* ford, where he was taken ill. When he had reached *Shach'iu,* he collapsed and breathed his last.

At the time of the falling star, Mars provoked the unlucky augury, therefore the people dwelling near the stone cut characters into it, as though they had done so purposely. The inscription was to the effect that *Chin Shih Huang Ti* was going to die or to he killed. The queer sayings of children, of which we hear sometimes, are likewise not of their own invention, but they have been inspired by some force. All such supernatural apparitions are either ghosts shaped like men, or men behaving like ghosts. The principle is the same in both cases.

Ch'ung Erh, prince of *Chin,* having lost his country, had nothing to eat on his journey. He asked some labourers on the field for food, but they gave him a clod of earth, The prince became angry, but *Chiu Fan* said to him, "This is very auspicious. Heaven grants you earth and land." Subsequently the prince reconquered his country, and was re-instated upon his soil, as *Chiu Fan'* had predicted. *T'ien Tan* of *Ch'i,* defending the city of *Chi-mo,* wished to deceive the army of *Yen,* therefore he said that the Spirit of Heaven had come down to help him. A man stepped forward and declared that he could act as the Spirit. *T'ien Tan* then went and still made obeisance before him. And, in fact, the rumour that

a spirit had come down, spread among the soldiers of *Yen.* They believed in the spirit, and, when still further they had viewed the oxen shining in five colours, they became so alarmed by this belief, that the army According to the *Shi-chi* the emperor shot those big fishes with a *repenting cross-bow (lien-nu)* tjl, (on which cf. my article on the Chinese Cross-bow in *Yerhandlungen der Berliner Gesellschaft fur Anthropologie* 1896, p. 272). In the *Chi-nan-fu* prefecture, *Shantung.* In *Shun-te-fu (Chili).* As though under a spell or a charm, which is the supernatural. Later Duke *Wen* of *Chin,* 634 (527 B.C. Banished from *Chin,* he lived for many years in other States. This happened in *Wei,* whose prince had treated him discourteously. Cf. *Tso-chuan,* Duke *Hsi* 23d year, where the incident is told, though with other words. Called *Tse Fan* in the *Tso-chuan.* An official of *Ch'i,* who delivered his country from the invading army of *Yen,* in the 3rd cent. B.c. City in *Shantung,* near *Kiao-chou.* was discomfited, and the soldiers routed. *T'ien Tan* gained the victory, and could recover the lost territory. In these apparitions there were men resembling ghosts.

When the ambassador passed *Hua-yin,* an individual, with a jade badge in his hands, blocked his passage, and went away, leaving him the badge. This was a ghost in human shape. The jade badge had been thrown into the *Yangise* for the purpose of praying for happiness. Now, the badge was returned, which showed that the offer was not accepted, and that happiness could not be obtained.

The badge was like that which formerly had been submerged, but it was not really the same for the following reason. When a ghost appears in human shape, it is not a genuine man. If people, after having seen a ghost looking like a living man, thoroughly question other living men, they will find out that none of them have come to see them Consequently a supernatural force has appeared to them in human form. Since this force has merely taken human shape, the things carried by the apparition cannot be real things either.

By the dragon ancestor, which was to

die, *Ch'in Shih Huang* 77 was designated. Ancestors are the root of mankind, and a dragon is an image of a sovereign If there be a resemblance between man and other creatures, a disaster concerning one part likewise affects the other.

In the year of *Ch'in Shih Huang 7V's* death the Emperor *Han Kao Tsu* was a village-elder in *Sse-shang.* As such he had to escort convicts to the *Li* Mountain, but most of them escaped on the road. *Kao Tsu* then allowed those he had still in his power to run away, which they did never to return. *Kao Tsu,* who was under the influence of liquor, was continuing his journey through *T'ien Tan* used.1 similar stratagem as Hannibal. During the night he fantastically dressed 1000 oxen, tied sharp blades to the horns and greased rushes to their tails, and lighting these rushes let them loose against the enemy, who were taken by surprise and completely beaten by the men of *Yen* following in the rear. Vid. the biography of *T'ien Tan* in the *Shi-chi,* chap. 82, p. 3.

Therefore the death of the dragon implies the end of the emperor. P-, P-- writes *Sse-shui* jfjjlj *yj,* which was a district in the present *Yen-chou-fu (Shantung).* A mountain near *Ch'in Shih Huang Ti's* mausoleum in *Shansi,* which was built by convicts. a marsh at night, and had ordered a man to keep in front. This man came back and reported that there was a big snake in front, obstructing the way, and besought him to go back.

"What does a valiant warrior l'ear?," asked *Kao Tsu* inebriated, and he went forward, drew his sword, and with one stroke cut the snake in two. The path was free then. After he had proceeded still several miles, his intoxication caused him to fall asleep.

When *Kao Tsu's* companions arrived at the place, where the snake was lying, they found there an old woman crying over it in the silence of night. They asked her, wherefore she cried. "A man has killed my son," replied the old woman.—" How was your son killed?," asked the men.—" My son," said the woman, "the son of the White Emperor, was transformed into a snake to keep watch on the path. Now the son of the Red Emperor has slain him. therefore I cry."—The men thought that the old woman was telling spook stories, and were going to give her a flogging, when the old woman suddenly disappeared.

What does this signify? It was a felicitous omen of *Kao Tsu's* rising to power. The old woman suddenly vanished. Since she became invisible, she cannot have been a human being, and not being human, she must have been a spectre. Since the old dame was not human, it is plain that the slain serpent was not a snake. The old woman spoke of it as the son of the Wbite Emperor, but why did he become a snake, and block the road at night? She asserted that the serpent was the son of the White Emperor and *Kao Tsu* that of the Red Emperor. Thus the son of the White Emperor would have become a snake, and the son of the Red Emperor, a man, whereas the Five Planetary Emperors are all heavenly spirits. In one case the son would have grown a serpent, in the other, a man. Men and snakes are different creatures, whereas the Emperors all belong to the same class of beings. The human state of those sons would not be conformable to the laws of heaven.

And further, if the snake was the son of the White Emperor, was the old woman the White Empress perhaps? An empress must have her suite in front and behind, and an imperial prince, a large The story is quoted from the *Shi-chi,* chap. 8, p. 5. It is meant as a prophecy of the overthrow of the *C/'in* dynasty hy that of *Hun.* The *Chin* used metal, to which the white colour corresponded, as the symbol of their power, whereas the *Him* relied on fire, which has a red colour. According to Chinese symbolism fire overcomes metal, ergo the *Ch'in* were doomed to be overpowered hy the *Han.* The Five Planets which from ancient times were worshipped as deities. The Red Emperor is Mais, the White Emperor Venus. retinue of officials. Now, the snake died on the pathway, and an old woman cried on the road! This makes it evident that her statement about the son of the White Emperor was not true. Not being a real

prince, it was a semblance, and being a semblance, it was an apparition. Consequently, everything seen was not genuine, and not being genuine, it was a fluid. The serpent slain by *Kao Tsu* was not a serpent.

When Duke *Li* of *Ch'eng* was on the point of entering into his dukedom, a snake in the city was fighting with one outside the city,"' but they were not genuine snakes. It was a supernatural force marking Duke *Li's* entrance into *Ch'eng* under the form of contending snakes. The fighting serpents of the *(Xing* State were not snakes, hence we infer that the two dragons in the *lluia* palace were merely images of dragons likewise. Such being the case, we are convinced that the dragons, which were fighting during *Tse Ch'an* of *Cheng's* time, have not been dragons.

The ways of Heaven are hard to understand. There are apparitions, when things are all right, and there are also some, when things go wrong. *Chang Liang,* Marquis of *Liu,* dealt a blow at *Ch'in Shih Huang Ti* with a club, but by mistake hit one of the chariots of his retinue. *Ch in Shih Huang Ti,* infuriated, gave orders to search for *Chang Liang* everywhere, but he changed his name and concealed himself in *Hsiapei,* where he had always leisure to stroll about at pleasure. Up the river *Ssa,* there was an old man in coarse clothes, who came to *Chang Liang's* place. He had just lost one shoe down the river, therefore he said to *Chang Liang,* "Go down, and fetch me my shoe, my boy."—*Chang Liang* grew angry, and was going to give him a 699-694 B.c. Duke *Li* had been forced to quit his country. Cf. *Tso-chuan,* Duke *Chuang* 14th year. The snake inside the city was killed. *Vid.* above p. 230. The *Tso-chuan,* Duke *Ch'ao* 19th year (522 B.c.) relates:—"There were great floods in *Ch'eng;* and some dragons fought in the pool *of Wei,* outside the *Shi* gate. The people asked leave to sacrifice to them; but *Tse Ch an* refused it, saying, 'If we are fighting, the dragons do not look at us; when dragons are fighting, why should we look at them?'" *(Legge* Vol.V, P. II, p. 675). *Chang Liang* had

engaged a bravo to deal the blow with an iron club or mallet weighing 120 pounds. In the moder n *P"ei-chou* of *Kiangsu* province. Instead of *S'se* jftrt(the *Shi-chi* writes:—"i" *jp,* the "bridge. " beating, but noticing, how strong the old man looked, he repressed his feelings, and went down to fetch the shoe, which he offered him on his knees. The old man slipped it on his foot, and went away laughing. *Chang Liang* felt greatly excited.

When the old man had gone to about a Li's distance, he returned. "You can be taught, my boy," he said, "Five days hence, at sunrise, meet me here." *Chang Liang* bewildered, knelt down and assented. After five days, at sunrise *Chang Liang* went, but the old gentleman had already arrived before him. "Why must you come later, when you have an appointment with an old man?," asked he angrily. "Five days after my departure, very early, we will meet again."—After five days *Chang Liang* went again at cockcrow, but again the old man had arrived before, and repeated his angry question, wherefore he had arrived later. "Five days after I have left," said he, "come again very early. "—On the fifth day *Chang Liang* went before midnight, and after a short while the old gentleman arrived. "So you are right," said he, very pleased.

He then produced a pamphlet, which he gave him saying, "Read it, and you will become preceptor to an emperor. After thirteen years you will see me. A yellow stone at the foot of Mount *Kucliing* in *Ch'i-pei* that is I." Whereupon he went away, saying nothing further, and was not seen again. At dawn *Chang Liang* looked at the book. It was *"T'ai Kung's* Strategy." *Chang Liang* amazed, studied it very thoroughly.

What was this? An augury of *Kao Tsu's* elevation by *Chang Liang's* assistance. *Chang Liang* lived ten years at *Hsia-pei* as a knight and a hero. When *Ch'en Shi* and his confederates, rose in revolt, and the Governor of *P'ei* visited *Hsia-pei, Cliang Liang* joined them. Subsequently, he was made a general and ennobled with the title Marquis of *Liu.* Thirteen years later, when with *Kao*

Tsu he crossed the *Ch'i-pei* territory, he found a yellow stone at the foot of Mount *Ku-ch'eng.* He took it, stored it away, and worshipped it, and, when he died, it was buried with him.

In *Tung-o* district *(Shantung).* The helpmate of *Wen Wang,* who had been invested with the marquisate of *Ch'i* in *Shantung* (cf. p. 172). The story is quoted from *Chang Liang's* Biography in the *Shi-chi,* chap. 55, p. 1 v., but somewhat abridged. A simple soldier who in 209 B.C. brought about an insurrection against *Erh Shih Hunng Ti,* and assumed the title of a king of *Ch'u. Liu Pang = Kao Tsu,* at that time still governor of *P'ei* in *Kiangsu.*

This yellow stone was a supernatural transformation conveying an omen. The metamorphoses of heaven and earth are most ingenious, for is it not wonderful to make an old man take the form of a yellow stone, and a yellow stone the form of an old man?

Some one might ask, whether the yellow stone was really an old man, and the old man really a yellow stone. A yellow stone cannot become an old man, nor an old man a yellow stone. The appearance of a supernatural portent made it look so.

During the time of Duke *P'ing* of *Chin* a stone spoke in *Wei*yfl. The duke asked the music-master *K'uang,* why the stone had spoken. *"A.* stone cannot speak," was the reply. "Perhaps it was possessed by a spirit, otherwise the people have heard wrong."

A stone cannot utter human speech, and so it cannot take human shape. The speaking of the stone is not different from the falling down of the stone in *Tung-chiln* in *Ch'in Shih Huang Ti's* time, which was engraved by the people. Engraving gives an inscription, and talking, speech. Script and speech fall under the same law. The people engraved the inscription, and a force made the speech. The nature of the people and the force is the same. A stone cannot engrave itself, nor can it talk, and not being able to talk, it cannot become a man either. *"T'ai Kung's* Strategy" was formed by the force. How do we know that it was not real? Because the old

man was not a man, whence we infer that the book was not *T ai Kung's* Strategy either. Since the force could take the likeness of a living man, it could liken itself to *T'ai Kung's* Strategy too.

The question may be raised, how a force could write characters, having neither knife nor pencil.—When *Chung Tse,* wife to Duke *Rut* of *Lu,* was born, she had on her palm the words:—"Future princess of *Lu." T'ang Shu Yii* of *Chin* bore on his hand the character *Yii,* and *Ch'ing Chi Yo* of *Lu* the character *Yo"* These three inscriptions have been written by a spontaneous nature, and thus the force had composed the old man's book of itself. The spontaneous nature and the self-producing force must be classed together with the self-speaking queer sayings of children. When children utter such strange things, they do not know, where they got them 556-531 B.c. A city in modern *T'ai-yuan-fu (Shansi). Tm-chuan,* Duke *Ch'ao* 8th year *(Legge* Vol. V, Pt. II, p. 622).
Circuit comprising the northern part of *Honan,* north of *K'ai-feng-fu.* See above p. 230. Cf. p. 95. from, their mouths speak of themselves. The self-speaking mouths and the self-produced writing are the active agents so to say. This argument may serve as a cue for the better understanding of other events. *T'at Kung* angling caught a big fish, and, when he cut it open, there was a letter in it reading, *"LiX Shang* will be invested with *Chi."* At *Wu Wang's* time, one caught a white fish, marked under its throat with the words, "Give it to *Fa. "* There was truth in all this. In fine, the "Plan of the Yellow River" and the " Scroll of the *Lo"* indicated the rise and fall, the progress and the decline, and the opportunities of emperors and kings. There certainly have been such writings. They were apparitions caused by a supernatural force and lucky or unlucky omens. The surname of *T'ai Kung, Wen Wang's* associate, who later on hecame prince of *Ch'i.* The personal name of *Wu Waiig.* Cf. p. 295. CHAPTER XVIII. All about Ghosts *(Ting-kuei).*
The ghosts that are in the world are not the vital spirits of the dead, they are

evoked by intense thinking and meditating. Where do they originate?—With sick people. When people are sick, they are inclined to melancholy and easily frightened. In this state of mind they see ghosts appear. People who are not sick, are not apprehensive. Thus, when sick people lying on their pillows are haunted with fears, ghosts appear. Their fears set them pondering, and when they do so, their eyes have visions. How can we prove this?
Po Lo was learning to distinguish horses: everything he saw, when sight-seeing, took the form of horses. A cook in *Sung* was learning to dissect an ox. For three years he did not perceive a living ox, those he saw were all dead ones. These two men strained their mental powers to the utmost. By dint of thinking and pondering they came to have strange visions. Sick men seeing ghosts are like *Po Lo* seeing horses or the cook seeing oxen. What *Po Lo* and the cook saw, were not real horses or oxen. Hence we know that the visions of the sick are not real ghosts either.
When sick people have a severe attack, and feel much pain in their bodies, they believe that ghosts with bamboos and sticks beat them, and have the impression that ghosts with hammers, locks, and cords are standing by their side, watching. These are empty visions caused by pain and fear. When they first feel ill, they become alarmedand see ghosts coming. When their disease grows more violent, that they fear to die, they see the ghosts incensed, and, when they feel pain, they have the idea that the ghosts are beating them. It is nothing but the effect of too much pondering, but there is no reality.

When the vital fluid is thinking or meditating, it flows into the eyes, the mouth, or the ears. When it flows into the eyes, the A somewhat legendary character, mentioned by *Chuang Tse* chap. 9, p. 1.
For more details on this famous cook or butcher see *Chuang Tse* chap. 3, p. 1. We might translate mental fluid, for here the mental functions of the vital fluid are referred to, which is the bearer of hfe as well as the originator of mind,

animu.1 and *anima.* eyes see shapes, when it flows into the ears, the ears hear sounds, and, when it flows into the mouth, the mouth speaks something. At day-time ghosts appear, at night, during sleep, they are heard in dreams. If a person sleeping quite alone in a lonely house is nervous, he will see ghosts in his dreams, and, if anybody puts his hands on him, he will scream. What we see, while awake, or hear, while asleep, is all the work of our spirit, of fears and thoughts, which amounts to the same.

There is an opinion that, when people see ghosts, their vision and their sleep are disturbed. If during the day their vigour is worn out, and their vital force exhausted, they desire to sleep at night. While they are asleep, their vision is distorted, hence their spirit perceives the images of men and things. When a person is sick, his vigour is worn out, and his vital force exhausted likewise. Although his eyes may not be asleep, their seeing power is still more disturbed than if they were. Consequently they also behold the shapes of men and things.

The sick see things, as if they were asleep. If they were not like dreaming, they ought to know, when they see something, whether they are awake, or dreaming. Since they are unable to distinguish, whether, what they see, are ghosts or men, it is evident that their vital force is exhausted, and their vigour worn out. The following will corroborate this.

Madmen see ghosts. They are mentally deranged, speak to themselves, and keep away from sane people, all owing to the severe form of their disease, and the disturbance of their vital force. When people are sick, and about to die, they are very much like madmen. All the three states:—sleep, sickness, and insanity are accompanied by a decay of the vital force and a disturbance of vision. Hence 'all those people have visions of men and things.

Others say that ghosts are apparitions of the fluid of sickness. This fluid being stirred up strikes against other people, and by doing so becomes a ghost. It imitates the human shape, and becomes

visible. Thus, when the fluid of very sick persons is in a state of excitement, it appears in human form, and the sick see it in this form. In case they fall sick in mountains and forests, the ghosts they see will be the essence of those mountains and forests, and. if their sickness breaks out in *Yiieh,* they will behold people of that country sitting by their side. Accordingly, ghosts like that of *Kuan Fu* and *Tou Ying* were apparitions of that particular time.

The fluid of this world is purest in heaven. The heavenly signs present certain forms above, and their fluid descends, and produces things. When the fluid is harmonious in itself, it produces and develops things, when it is not, it does injury. First it takes a form in heaven, then it descends, and becomes corporeal on earth. Hence, when ghosts appear, they are made of this stellar fluid. The bodies of the stars form men, beasts, and birds. Consequently sick people see the shapes of men, beasts, and birds.

Some maintain that ghosts are the essence of old creatures. When creatures grow old, their essence forms a human being, but there are also those, which by their nature can be transformed, before they are old, and then take a human shape. If the fluid a man is endowed with, is the same as the essence of another creature, there will be some relation between him and this creature, and, when it becomes sick, and its vital fluid begins to decline, it falls in with that person as a ghost. How can we prove that?

Those creatures which people usually have to do with, appear to them as ghosts, for what difference is there between the ghosts seen by sick people and those sick creatures? If people see ghosts resembling a dead man in his grave, who is coming to meet and call them, it is one of the domestic auimals in their houses. If they see other ghosts, unknown to them previously, those ghosts are caused by other people's animals *e. g.* those in the open fields.

According to another opinion ghosts originally live in men, and, when they cease to be men, they are transformed

and disappear. The organisation of the universe is such, that these transformations take place indeed, but the votaries of Taoism cannot discuss this subject. See p. 217.

The stars. The constellations. This seems to refer to the animals connected with the twelve cyclical signs (cf. p. 106). A man born under one of these signs is supposed to have been imbued with the same essence as the corresponding animal has. Their views are too phantastic, as can be seen from their works.

Luii " Hcng. 16

That which assaults men, is sickness. Sick people are doomed to die, but the deceased do not give up all intercourse with men. This will become clearer from the following:

The *Liki* tells us that *Chuan Hsu* had three sons living who, when they died, became the ghosts of epidemics. One living in the water of the *Yangtse,* became the *Ghost of Fever,* the second in the *Jo* was a *Water Spirit,* the third, dwelling in the corners of palaces and houses, and in damp store-rooms, would frighten children. Anterior to *Chuan Hxil's* time there have been more sons living, consequently there must have been hundreds of spirits like those of *Chuan lhii's* time. All spirits and ghosts possess a body, and there is a method to make them stand upright. Those who meet with people have all lived in good men, and acquired their fluid, hence in their appearance they are like good men. That which can injure the good is the fluctuating *Yang* and *Yin* fluid, as a fluid like that of the clouds and vapours it could not do so.

Another idea is that ghosts are the spirits of the first and second cyclical signs.' These spirits are a peculiar fluid of heaven. In their shapes they appear like human beings. When a man is sick, and about to die, the spirit of the first and second day makes its appearance. Provided that somebody falls sick on the first or second day, he will perhaps see the spirit of the seventh or eighth, when he dies. Why? Because the ghost of the first and second day is the messenger of the seventh and eighth, therefore the person is taken ill on the first and second, and when his end is near, and the ghost that destroys him appears, it is the spirit of the seventh and eighth. This is evident from the fact that for a malady, that broke out on the first or second day, the crisis which decides on life and death, sets in on the seventh or the eighth.

Critics do not accept this view as correct. However, the ways of Heaven are difficult to understand, and ghosts and spirits abscond and hide. Therefore I have noted all the different opinions, that my contemporaries may judge for themselves.
A legendary ruler of the 20th cent. B.c. According to the "Water Classic'' a river in the south-east of China. This passage is not to be found in our *Liki*, According to the *Pei-in'ngiin-fu* it is contained in the *Sou-shen-chi* (4th cent. A. d.). The signs *chia* and *gi*.
Some say that ghosts are creatures in no way different from men. There are spiritual beings in the world, usually staying beyond the frontiers, but from time to time coming to China, and mixing with men. These are malignant and wicked spirits, hence they appear to men, who are sick, and going to die. As a being created in this world man is like a beast or a bird. When demons are created, they also resemble men, or are like beasts or birds. Thus, unhappy families see corpses flying about, or crawling demons, or beings like men. All three are ghosts, they may be styled ghosts or demons, goblins or devils. They really exist, as long as they are, and are not empty, formless beings. How do we know?

Commonly people who will be visited with misfortune see a ray of light descending on their homes, or they perceive something having the shape of a bird flitting several times into their hall, but on looking carefully, they discover that it is not like a bird, or an animal. Creatures having a body can eat; by eating they acquire activity, and, if they give signs of activity, their body must be real.
Tso Ch'iu Ming says in his *Ch'uu-ch' iu:*—"They were banished into the four

frontier States to repulse the goblins and devils," and the *Shan-hai-king* reports that in the North there is the Kingdom of the Ghosts.'' They say that goblins are dragon-like creatures. Devils arc also related to dragons, therefore they must resemble dragons. Moreover, a kingdom is defined as a congregation of men and other creatures.
The *Shun-hai-king* also relates that in the midst of the Green Ocean there is the *Tu So* Mountaiu, on which grows an enormous peach-tree. Its girth measures 3,000 Li. Between its boughs to the north-east there is the so-called door of the ghosts, where the ten thousand ghosts pass in and out. On the tree there are two spirits, one called *Shin Shu*, the other *Yil Lil*, who have the superintendence over all the ghosts. They bind the wicked ones, who have wrought evil, with reeds, and feed the tigers with them.

Subsequently *Huang Ti* worshipped for the purpose of expelling the ghosts for ever. He erected a huge human figure of peachwood and painted *Shin Shu* and *Yil Lil* along with tigers and cords In his commentary to the *Ch un-eA in*, the *Tso-ch'uan*. Four wicked princes were cast out by *Shun* into the four distant regions, which were believed to be inhabited by devils. *Tso-ch'uan*, Duke *Wen* 18th year *(Legge, CUuncs* Vol.V, Pt. I, p. 283).
Cf. *Shan-hai-lcing* XII, 1. of reeds hanging down on the house-doors, and thus frightened them away.
Malignant devils have bodies, therefore they can be caught hold of, and thrown as food to tigers. Being eatable creatures, they cannot be unsubstantial or unreal. Yet these creatures have a different nature from that of man. Sometimes they are visible, sometimes hidden. In this respect they do not diner from dragons, which are not always visible either.

Some people hold that anterior to a man's fortune or misfortune lucky or unlucky apparitions become visible, and that, when a man is approaching his death, a great many miracles appear to him. Ghosts belong to these miracles. When apparitions and miracles come

forth, they take human form, or they imitate the human voice to respond. Once moved, they do not give up human shape.

Between heaven and earth there are many wonders, in words, in sound, and in writing. Either does the miraculous fluid assume a human shape, or a man has it in himself, and performs the miracles. The ghosts, which appear, are all apparitions in human shape. Men doing wonders with the fluid in them are sorcerers. Real sorcerers have no basis for what they say, and yet their lucky or unlucky prophecies fall from their Hps spontaneously like the quaint sayings of boys. The mouth of boys utters those quaint sayings spontaneously, and the idea of their oration comes to wizards spontaneously. The mouth speaks of itself, and the idea comes of itself. Thus the assumption of human form by the miracles, and their sounds are spontaneous, and their words come forth of their own accord. It is the same thing in both cases.

They say that during the time of *Chou*, ghosts cried at night out-side the city, and that when *T'sang Hsieh* invented the art of writing, ghosts wept at night likewise. If the fluid can imitate human sounds, and weep, it can also imitate the human shape, and appear in such a form, that by men it is looked upon as a ghost.
According to the *Feng-su-t'ung* of the 2nd cent. A.d. this story is narrated in the *Huang Ti shu*, the Book of *Huang Ti*. On New-year's Eve the pictures of *Shen Shu* and *Yu Lii* are still at present pasted on the doorways as a talisman against evil spirits. A legendary personage.
A ghost that appears is an evil omen to somebody. When in this world fortune or misfortune approach, they are always accompanied by portents. These come slowly, not suddenly, and not in great numbers. According to the laws of nature, when a man is going to die, an unlucky phantom comes forth also, and, when a State is going to perish, an evil portent becomes visible. Conversely, when somebody is going to prosper, there are lucky omens, and, when

a State is going to flourish, there are signs indicating this prosperity beforehand. Good and bad omens or portents are the same thing after all.

Now, however, the general belief is that ghosts are not a kind of portents, but spirits, which can hurt people. One does not understand the nature of portents, nor pay attention to the transformations undergone by the fluid of creatures. When a State is near its ruin, and a phantom appears, it is not this phantom which ruins the State. When a man is near his end, and a ghost comes forward, the ghost does not cause his death. Weapons destroy the State, and diseases kill man, as the following example will show:

When Duke *llsiang* of *Chi* was going to be killed by robbers, he travelled in *Kn-fin,* and subsequently hunted in *Pei-ch'iu,* where he beheld a big hog. His followers said:—" Prince *P'ing Shing*!" The duke got angry, and said, "*P'eng Sheng* dares to show himself?" Then he pulled his bow, and shot the hog, which rose like a man, and howled. The duke became so panic-stricken, that he fell down in his carriage, hurt his foot, and lost one shoe. Afterwards he was assassinated by robbers.

Those who killed duke *Hsiang* were robbers, the big hog which appeared on the road previous, was a portent indicating duke *Hsiang's* impending death. People called it *P eng Shing,* because it resembled him. Everybody knows that duke *Ilsiang* was not killed by the hog. Therefore it would also be a great error to assert that ghosts can kill men.

The fluid of the universe which forms phantoms foreboding evil is the solar fluid. Phantoms are the same as poison. That part of the fluid which injures man, is called poison, that which is being transformed, a phantom. People say that the quaint ditties Two places in the *Ch'i* State, in *Shantung.* Prince *P'i'ng Slu'ng* was a half-brother of Duke *Hsiang* of *Ch'i,* who employed him to murder his brother-in-law, the duke of *Lu.* The people of *Ch'i* put *P'eng Sheng* to death. Cf. *Txo-ch'uan,* Duke *Huan* 18th year (693 B.c.).

Quoted from the *Tso-ch'uan,* Duke *Chi-ang* 8th year, corresponding to 685 B. c. of boys are due to the influence of the Glimmering-Star upon men. There is ttuth in these words. The Glimmering Star is the Fire Star (the planet Mars). Fire has a poisonous glare. Therefore, when Mars reigns in the sky during the night, it means a disaster and defeat for a State.

The fluid of fire flickers up and down, and so phantoms are at one time visible, at another not. A dragon is an animal resorting from the *Yang* principle, therefore it can always change. A ghost is the *Yang* fluid, therefore it now appears, and then absconds. The *Yang* fluid is red, hence the ghosts seen by people have all a uniform crimson colour. Flying demons are *Yang,* which is fire. Consequently flying demons shine like fire. Fire is hot and burning, hence the branches and leaves of trees, on which those demons alight, wither and die.

In the *Hung-fan* of the *Shnking* the second of the five elements is called fire, and the second of the five businesses speech. Speech and fire are the same essence, therefore the ditties of boys and ballads are weird sayings. The words come forth, and a composition is completed. Thus there are always writings full of the supernatural. They say that boys are of the *Yang* fluid, hence the weird sayings come from small boys. Boys and sorcerers have the *Yang* fluid in them, therefore at the great rain sacrifice in smn= mer boys must dance, and sorcerers are exposed to the..sun. According to the rites of this sacrifice the *Yin* principle, which has separated, is united with the *Yang* principle.

In the same manner at an eclipse of the sun, when the *Yin* predominates, an attack is made on the *Yin* of the land. As during an eclipse, while the *Yin* reigns supreme, everything belonging to the *Yin* fluid is being assaulted, so at the time of a drought, when the *Yang* is in the ascendant, the indignation is directed against all allies of the *Yang.* Sorcerers belong to this class. Therefore, *Shaking, Hung-fan* Pt. V, Bk. IV, 5 and 6 *(Legge* Vol. III, Pt. II, p. 325 and 326). All weird things are manifestations of the *Vang,* the solar fluid, which is fiery.

The *Yang* principle is male. The Chinese believe that popular songs and sayings foretelling future events, of which they have collections, are supernatural inspirations or revelations. Hence they bring them into connection with ghosts or supernatural beings. *Wang Chung* falls back on the *Yang* principle as the origin of those quaint ditties. "The J in fluid is the rain.

'The sun is eclipsed by the moon, which belongs to the *Yin* fluid.

when Duke *Hsi* of *Lu* was visited with a drought, he had resolved to burn all the sorcerers. The sorcerers being imbued with the *Yang* fluid, there are for this reason a great many sorcerers in the *Yang* region (the South). The sorcerers are related to ghosts, accordingly sorcerers have something diabolical.

These sorcerers bear a certain resemblance to the boys singing those quaint ditties. The real sorcerers know how to determine luck and misfortune. Being able to do that, they are the messengers of fate.

Thus the phantom of *She n Shing* appeared in a sorcerer. Since they are filled with the *Yang* fluid, phantoms can appear in sorcerers. As *Shin Shing* appeared as a phantom, we may infer that the Marquis of 7u, *Chuang Tse Yi"* and the malignant ghost were likewise phantoms.

As the discontented spirit of the Marquis of *Tu* was a phantom, the bow and arrows used by him were the poison of this phantom. The phantoms assuming human shape, their poison must have resembled human weapons. The ghosts and their poison being of the same colour, the bow and arrows of the Marquis of *Tu* were all red. The poison was like a weapon used by man, therefore, when it hit a man, he died, when it hit him but slightly, he faded away, but did not die at once. His incurable disease was the effect of the poison.

Phantoms either emit their poison, but do not show themselves, or they show themselves, but do not emit any poison, or they produce sounds, which, however, do not form any words, or they make known their thoughts, but do not know their sounds. *Shin Shing* showed himself and pronounced words, the Marquis of 659-620 B.c. The South is the land of the sun, the *Yang* principle. The foregoing futile speculations are based on the gratuitous analogies, in which Chinese natural philosophers, starting from the *Yi-king,* indulge. Heir-apparent to Duke *Hsien* of the *('hin* State, by whom he was put to death in 654 B.c. We learn from the *Tso-ch'uan,* 10th year of Duke //.«', that in 640 the ghost of the murdered prince appeared to an officer of *Chm,* and spoke to him. He told him that in seven days he would have a new interview with him through a wizard, and that he would take his revenge on Duke *Hui* of *Chin.* Cf. p. 203. The Earl of 7'u had been unjustly put to death by King *Hsuan* of the *Chou* dynasty, 826 780 B.c. Accoiding to a legend the ghost of the murdered man appeared to the king while hunting. He was dressed in red, and carried a red bow and red arrows. One of these arrows he shot through the king's heart, who died on the spot. Cf. *Chavannes. Mem. Hist.* Vol. I, p. 278 Note 2. *Vid.* also p. 202. See p. 202. ". By which *Yeh Ku* of *Sung* was killed. Cf. chap. XLL *Tu* became visible, and sent forth his poison. Queer songs, the ditties of boys, and the words on stones are thoughts uttered. The music of the harp on the *P'u* River and the wails of the ghosts in the suburb of *Chou* were sounds produced. At the appearance of ill omens, either mishap is impending, and the omens appear in advance, or misfortune comes, and is accompanied by those omens. In that case omens and poison are both at work. When omens appear beforehand, they cannot be poisonous. *Shin Shing* was an omen seen before, the discontented ghosts of the Marquis of *Tu* and *Chuang Tse I* were phantoms appearing simultaneously with misfortune.

When King *Hs'uan* of *Chou,* Duke *Chim* of *Yen* and *Yeh Am* of *Sung* were going to die, ill omens appeared, and the poison hit them. When Duke *Hui* of *Chin* was to be captured, but not yet to die, merely a phantom made its appearance, but no poison shot forth. The appearance of the Earl of *Tu, Chuang Tse I,* and the discontented spirit howev-

er, were ill omens, announcing the impending deaths of King *HsOan* of *Chou, Chien* of *Yen,* and *Yeh* Am. *Shin Shing* coming forward was an omen indicative of the captivity of Duke *Hui* of *Chin.* By *Po Yu* appearing in people's dream the deceases of *Sse Tai* and *Kung Sun Tuan* were foreshadowed. The knitting of grass by the old man was an auspicious portent for the victory of *Wei K'o,* and for the capture of *Tu Hui* at that time. The grey dog, by which the Empress *Lil Hou* was bitten, was the shape of a phantom showing that her death was near. When The thoughts of ghosts, uttered through the mouth of boys, singing queer songs, or mysteriously written on stones. » Cf. p. 220. See above p. 244.

Duke *Chien* of *Yen,* 503-491 B.c. I, p. 382 speaks of Duke *Chien* of *Chao* and *Lun-heng* Bk. IV, p. 5 of Viscount *Chien* of *Chao.* See chap. XLI. Duke *Hui* of *Chin,* 649-635 B.c. In 644 the duke was taken prisoner by *Ch'in.* 'Cf. p. 208. *Wei K'o* was a commander of the forces of *Chin* in the 6th cent, B.c., with which he worsted those of the *Ch'in* State, and took their strongest man, *Tu Hui,* prisoner. He was supported during the battle by an old man twisting the grass in such a way as to impede the movements of his enemies. This old man was the spirit of the father of a concubine of *Wei K'o's* father, whom he had saved from death. Out of gratitude for the kindness shown to his daughter the spirit thus contributed to his victory and to the capture of *Tu Hui.* Cf. p. 211. *Vid. Sfu-chi* chap. 9, p. 8 v. The Empress *iAi Hou* was bitten by a grey dog, which suddenly vanished. The diviners declared it to have been the phantom of *Ju I,* Prince of *Chao,* whom *Lii Hou* had assassinated. *Lu Hou* died of the bite. the Marquis of *Wu-an* was near his end, the portents had the mien of *Tou Ying* and *Kuan Fu?* In short, what we call lucky or unlucky omens, ghosts and spirits, are all produced by the solar fluid. The solar fluid is identical with the heavenly fluid. As Heaven can create the body of man, it can also imitate his appearance. That by which man is born are the *Yang* and the *Yin* fluids, the *Yin* fluid produces his

bones and flesh, the *Yang* fluid, the vital spirit. While man is alive, the *Yang* and *Yin* fluids are in order. Hence bones and flesh are strong, and the-vital force is full of vigour. Through this vital force he has knowledge, and with his bones and flesh he displays strength. The vital spirit can speak, the body continues strong and robust. While bones and flesh, and the vital spirit are entwined and linked together, they arc always visible, and do not perish.

When the solar fluid is powerful, but devoid of the *Yin,* it can merely produce a semblance, but no body. Being nothing but the vital fluid without bones or flesh, it is vague and diffuse, and when it appears, it is soon extinguished again. *T'ien Fen,* Marquis of *Wu-an,* a minister of the Emperor *Han Wu Ti* had in 140 B.c. caused the death of his predecessor and rival *Tou Ying.* The ghost of the latter appeared to him, when he was about to die. The general *Kuan Fu's* death was likewise the work of *T'ien Fen.* Cf. p. 217. CHAPTER XIX.

On Heaven *(Tan-fien)-*

In the books of the Literati we find the statement that *Knng Kung2* struggled with *Chuan Hsii* for the empire, and that out of anger that he was defeated, he knocked against the *Pu Chou* Mountain, thereby causing the break-down of the "Pillar of Heaven" and the *delabrement* of the confines of the earth. But *Sil Wa* melted multicoloured stones, and therewith plastered up the blue sky, and cut off the legs of a sea-turtle, which she erected at the four extremities of the universe. However, heaven was not complete in the north-west, therefore sun and moon moved," and there was a piece of the earth missing in the southeast, hence all the rivers (lowed to the ocean. This is a very old tradition, believed by most people. Well educated persons will think it strange, hut they have nothing to say against it, or if they have, they are unable to settle the question. They may also he afraid, lest the thing should be really true, and therefore dare not discuss it seriously. According to the laws of nature and from a human point of view, it is all idle talk.

If a man fighting with another for the

empire, out of anger that he did not win, knocked against the *Pu Chou* Mountain, and caused the pillar of heaven to break, and the confines of the earth to be smashed, if his strength was like that, he would have no opponent on earth. With such a force he could engage three armies, and the soldiers would be to him like ants, and their weapons like blades of grass. Why should he, resenting his defeat, strike against Mount *Pu Chou?*

There is nothing harder and heavier than a mountain. The strength of ten thousand men pushing would not be able to move In *Hvai A'nn Tse.* Cf. p. 89.

-A legendary being of prehistoric times. A mythical emperor.

The *Pu t'hnn* Mountain forms part of the *K'un-lun,* which latter is also called "Pillar of Heaven" *(T'ien-chu). .'* The sister of the mythical emperor *Fa fJsi.* To wit from east to west.

'The ocean is in the east of China.

Cf. *Lieh Tip* V, 5v.; where this old tradition is told with almost the same words. even a small mountain, and Mount *Pu Chou* must have been a big one. If it was really the "Pillar of Heaven," it would be a difficult thins: to break it. If it was not. then it cannot be admitted that by knocking against the *Pu Chmi* Mountain the "Pillar of Heaven" was broken. — *Chuan Hsil* in his fight against *Kung Kung* might have mustered all the soldiers on earth and all the multitudes peopling the land within the seas, he would not have been a match for him. How should *Rung Kung* not have been victorious?

Moreover, is heaven air or a body? If it be air, it cannot be different from clouds and mist. Then there could be no pillar which might be broken. Since Am *Wa* repaired it with stones, it must be a body. If it be so in fact, then it is something like gems and stones. The substance of stones is heavy, a single pillar would not be a sufficient support for a thousand Li. Not even the peaks of the Five Mountains could prop heaven as pillars.

When Mount *Pu Chou* was struck, did it support heaven? The mountain was broken by *Kung Kung.* At that time

heaveu ought to have fallen down. How could it be raised again, once collapsed, and how could the four poles be erected with cut off legs of a sea-turtle? Some one might sav that a sea-turtle was a monster of olden times with immense legs, and that its legs therefore could be erected as the four poles.

Now *Pu Cliou* is a mountain, a sea-turtle an animal. Originally a mountain was serving as pillar of heaven. *Kung Kung* broke it, and it was replaced by the legs of an animal. Bones become putrified, how could they long stand upright? If the legs of a sea-turtle could support heaven, the body of the turtle must have been of such enormous dimensions, that it would not have had room enough between heaven and earth. How could *Nil Wa* have killed it, though she was a saint? If she was able to do it, how did she manage it? Provided that the legs could be used as the pillars of heaven, their skin must have been as hard as stone and iron; swords as well as halberds would have been ineffective against it, nor could a sharp arrow, shot from a strong cross-bow, have pierced it.

We see that at present heaven is very high and far distant from the earth. The heaven of to-day is the same with that of antiquity. When *Kung Kung* damaged it. heaven did not fall down upon the earth. Am *Wa* was human: a man may be very tall, he never will reach up to heaven. When *Nil Wa* was repairing it, on The Five Sacred Mountains of China:—*Tai-shan* in *Shantung, Heng-shan* in *Hunan, Hua-shan* in *Shrnsi, Heng-shan* in *Chili,* and *Sung-xhan* in *Honan.* .what steps (lid she climb up, and on what did she stand, while doing her work? Was the heaven of olden days perhaps like the roof of a hall, and not far distant from men, so that *Kung Kung* could destroy, and *Nil Wa* repair it? If this was actually so, there would have been many *Nil Wa's.* Of people living prior to *Nil Wa* the *Human Emperors* were the oldest. Was at the time of the Human Emperors heaven like a canopy?

The commentators of the *Yiking* say that previous to the separation of the

primogenial vapours there was a chaotic and uniform mass, and the books of the Literati speak of a wild medley, and of air not yet separated. When it came to be separated, the pure elements formed heaven, and the impure ones earth. According to the expositors of the *Yiking* and the writings of the Literati the bodies of heaven and earth, when they first became separated, were still small, and they were not far distant from each other, so much so, that heaven might well have reclined on the *Pu Chou* Mountain, and that *Kung Kung* could smash, and *Nil Wa* repair it.

All beings filled with air grow. Heaven and earth contain air, which develops spontaneously. A great many years have elapsed since their first beginning. Hence it is impossible to calculate the distance between heaven and earth now, whether it be wide or narrow, far or near. What the scholars write about it may so far be correct, the statement, however, that *Kung Kung* knocked against Mount *Pu Chou,* broke the "Pillar of Heaven," and smashed the borders of the earth, that with liquified multi-coloured stones the blue sky was repaired, and that the legs of a sea-turtle were cut off, and set up as the four poles, is all the same untenable. Even though a mountain might be moved, *Kung K1mg's* force would not suffice to break it. Were at the time, when heaven and earth first separated, the mountains small and men great? How else could they have knocked against a mountain, and broken it?

The repairing of heaven by means of five kinds of stones may at least be discussed. These stones might have worked like mineral drugs curing a disease. But the cutting off of the legs of a seaturtle and putting them up at the four poles, cannot be mentioned in earnest. It is a long time since *Nil Wa.* Do the four poles look like the legs of a turtle?

These are still believed to have been preceded by a dynasty of sovereigns of Heaven, and of sovereigns of Earth, all fabulous beings. Supposing heaven to be a spirit or a human-like living being. In *Tsou Yen's* book there is a notice to the effect, that there are nine divisions of the Empire *viz.* the nine divisions forming the tributary land of *Yil.* The Nine Circuits of *Yd* are so to speak but one continent. If in the " *Tribute of* Yft" Nine Circuits are mentioned, they are the present Nine Circuits of the Empire. They are situated in the south-east of the earth and bear the name of *Ch'ihhsien* or *Shen-chou* (China). But there are eight continents besides. Each continent is hemmed in by the Four Seas, which are called *Paihai.* Beyond the Nine Continents there is still the Great Ocean.—

This statement is extraordinary and bewildering to the hearers, but they are unable to make out, whether it be correct or not. Thus it is being handed down by books, which are read, or repeated by word of mouth. Reality and fiction are equally transmitted to posterity, and the world does not distinguish between truth and untruth. People become perplexed, and a discussion is very difficult.

Tsou Yens knowledge did not surpass that of *Yil.* When *Yil* controlled the deluge, *Yi* acted as his assistant. While *Yil* was regulating the water, *Yi* noted all things. He explored the expanse of heaven, and penetrated to the farthest limits of the earth. He distinguished what was beyond the Four Seas, and thoroughly investigated the region within the Four Mountains. In the thirty five States he enumerated all the beasts and birds, plants, trees, minerals, stones, waters, and earths, but he did not say that there are still nine continents besides. *Liu An,* prince of *Huai Nan* invited scientists like *Wu Pei* and *Tso Wu.* His palaces were full of such men, who wrote books on the Taoist doctrine. In the chapter where he treats of the things of the world and the shape of the earth," he speaks of A scholar of the 4th cent. B.c. who wrote on cosmogony and geography. See p. 19. The well known chapter of the *Shuking.* Literally the "Red Region," The "Divine Circuit," jjjjjj j«i.

Minor Seas, *ffiffifr.*
8 *Ying-hai,* Cf. p. 330. The Four Seas supposed to surround the habitable land i. *e.* China. The Four Sacred Mountains:—*Tai-shan, Heng-shan, Hua-shan* and *Hfng shun* in the East, South, West, and North of ancient China. The *Sung-shan* in the Centre is omitted. See above p. 251. The Taoist philosopher *Huni Nan Tae* cf. p. S35. Chap. IV of *Huai JXan Tse'* work. prodigies and the wonders of foreign lands, he also talks of the peculiarities of the thirty-five countries, but does not mention the existence of Nine Continents. *Tsou Yen* did not travel as far as *Yii* and *Yi* on earth, and his experience was not greater than that of either *Wu Pei* or *Tso Wu.* His talents were not those of a sage, and he did not learn things by a special revelation from heaven. How then could he make such statements? Examined by the light of *Yds* "Mountain Book " and of *Huai Nan's* chapter on the shape of the earth, his words are utterly wrong.

The Grand Annalist says:—"In the 'Chronicle ofYu' it is said that the Yellow River has its fountain-head in the *K'un-lun,* which is three thousand and five hundred Li high. There where sun and moon hide in the *K'un-lun,* it is full of splendour. On the mountain there is the Jade Spring and the Flower Lake. Now, after *Chang Ch'ien* went as envoy to *Bactria,* he traced the springs of the Yellow River, hut did he see what the Chronicle relates about the *K'un-lun?* In what it says about the nine divisions, mountains, and rivers the *Shnking* may be near the truth, of the wonderful things to be found in *Yii's* Chronicle and the ' Mountain Book.' I dare not express myself."

"1 dare not express myself" means that there is no truth in them. Every one has heard about the height of the *K'un-lun,* the Jade Spring, and the Flower Lake, but, when *Chang Ch'ien* went there personally, he found that these things did not exist. In the Tribute of *Yil*" mountains, rivers, and wonderful things, precious metals and stones occurring in the Nine Circuits are all enumerated, but there is no reference to the Jade Spring or the Flower Lake on the *K'un-lun.* In the opinion of the Grand Annalist the reports of the "Mountain Book" and the "Chronicle of *Yii*" are inventions.

The.' Mountain Book" = *Slum-king* forms the first five chapters of the "Mountain and Sea Classic" r= *Shan-hai-king,* which tradition ascribes to *Yii* and his minister Fi, but it is probably not earlier than the 4th or the 3d cent. B.C. = *Shi-chi* chap. 123, p. 19 v. This book is now lost. The *Shi-clu* has 2,500 Li. 5E yf and yjj. The *Shi-chi* writes:— "the Sweet Wine Spring and the Jasper Lake": and iftj',. *Chang Ch'ien* started on his famous expedition in 122 B.c. These subjects are treated in the chapter entitled the "Tribute of *Yii.*"' The *Shi-chi* writes:—The *Shan-hai-king.*
In all things which arc difficult to know, it is not easy to find out the truth.

The pole is the centre of heaven. At present the world lies south from the pole of *Yii,* therefore the heavenly pole must be in the north, heaven must be high there, and more people living in that region. According: to the "Tribute of *Yii*" the east is washed by the ocean, and the west covered with "flying sand. " These must be the extreme limits of heaven and earth.

When the sun pricks, his diameter measures a thousand hi. Now, if the sun is observed at his rise from *Yin* and *Chili hsien* in *jCuei-chi* on the eastern sea-shore, his diameter appears to be no more than two feet, which proves that the sun is still very far. Consequently there must be more land eastward. This being the case, the assertion about the pole being in the north and about the extension of heaven and earth is not made at random. In this way the statements of *Tsou Yen* cannot be controverted, and what the "Chronicle of *Yii*" says on mountains and seas, and *Hum Nan Tse's* lucubrations on the shape of the earth appear unreliable.

Tsou Yen holds that at present the "land under heaven" lies in the south-east of the earth, and is called *Ch'ih hsien* or *Shen chou.* Now, the heavenly pole is the centre of heaven. If at present the "land under heaven" were situated in the south-east of the earth, the pole ought to appear in the north-west. Since in fact it is straight north, the world at present lies south of the pole. In regard to the pole the world cannot lie in the south-east, hence *Tsou Yen's* statement to this effect is wrong.

If it were in the south-east, it would be near to the sun's rising place, and the light of the rising sun ought to appear bigger. Now, whether looked at from the Eastern Sea or from the Gobi, the size of the sun remains the same. Although the points of observation be ten thousand Li distant, it makes no difference in the size of the sun. That shows that at present the world occupies but a small part of the expanse of the earth.

Chih = must be a misprint, for such a character is not to be found in the dictionaries. We ought to read *Mou* = p. I'm and *Mou* were two districts of the *JCuei-chi* circuit comprising *Chekiang* and parts of *Anhvi* and *Fukien* under the *Han* dynasty. *Yin* was in the south-east of *Mou,* both situated in the present *Ningpo* prefecture. (Cf. *Kanghi'x* Diet.) *Tsou Yen's* assertion. *1. e.* the habitable land or China. *Loyang* is the centre of the Nine Circuits. Viewed from *Loyang* the north-pole appears direct north. The shore of the Eastern Sea is three thousand Li distant from *Loyang.* Seen from there the pole is likewise in the north. By analogy we may safely assume that viewed from the Gobi the pole will also appear in the north. The Eastern Sea and the Gobi are the eastern and western borders of the Nine Circuits, ten thousand Li distant from one another, nevertheless the pole appears always north. The earth must therefore be very small and occupying a narrow space, since one never gets away from the pole.

The principality of *Annam (Jili Nan* i. e. the South of the Sun) is ten thousand Li distant from *Loyang.* People who had emigrated there, and came back, when asked, have said that, when the sun culminates, his resting-place cannot be in *Annam.* If we go ten thousand Li further south, the sun there must reach his south-point. Then the south-point of the sun would be twenty thousand Li distant from *loyang.* Now, if we measure the distance of the way made by the sun from *Loyang,* it cannot be the same, as if we measure from the north-pole, because the pole is still very far from

Loyang. Let us suppose that we went thirty thousand Li north. Even then we would not arrive under the pole. But provided we did, then we could say that we had reached the place just beneath the north-pole. Since from there to the south-point there would be fifty thousand Li, there must be fifty thousand Li north of the pole likewise, and under these circumstances there would also be fifty thousand Li from the pole eastward and westward in either direction. One hundred thousand Li from north to south, and one hundred thousand Li from east to west multiplied would give a million square Li. *Tsou Yen* opines that between heaven and earth there are nine continents like China. At the *Chou* period the Nine Circuits measured five thousand Li from east to west, and from north to south also five thousand Li. Five times five gives twenty-five, one continent therefore would contain twenty-five thousand square Li, which would be the size of China. Twenty-five thousand Li multi *Loyang* is considered the centre of the world i. e. China.

Wang Ch'ung is a better theorist than arithmetician. The square of 100,000 is 10,000 millions, not 1 million. *Wang Ch'ung* supposes the earth to be an equilateral, rectangular square. The same mistake. The square of 5,000 is 25 millions. 25 million square Li, about 8 million square kilometer is approximately the area of the Eighteen Provinces or China Proper. plied by nine would give two hundred and twenty-five thousand square Li. *Tsou Yen's* figure may appear too high, but computation and a thorough investigation show us that, on the contrary, it is too low."

The Literati say that heaven is air, and therefore not far from man. Consequently it immediately knows, whether they are right or wrong, and whether they possess secret virtues or vices, and also responds to them. This is regarded as a proof of its vicinity. But, if we examine the question critically, we find that heaven's body is not air.

Men are created by heaven, why then grudge it a body? Heaven is not air, but has a body on high and far from men.

According to private traditions heaven is upwards of sixty-thousand Li distant from the earth. Some mathematicians reckon the entire circumference of heaven at 365 degrees. Thus the world all round is divided into degrees, and its height measures a certain number of Li. If heaven were really air, air like clouds and mist, how could then be so many Li or so many degrees? Besides we have the "twenty-eight constellations," which serve as resting-places to sun and moon, just as on earth the couriers lodge in postal stations. The postal stations on earth correspond to the solar mansions on heaven. Hence the statement found in books that heaven has a body is not baseless. To him who considers the question, as we have done, it becomes evident that heaven cannot be something diffuse and vague.

225,000 square Li (225 millions), which number is based on *Tsou Yen's* hypothesis that there are nine continents as largo as China. *Wang Ch'ung* has calculated a million square Li (10,000 millions). The area of our Earth measures about 510 million square kilometer, not 2,500 millions (= 10,000 million square Li) as results from *Wang Ch'ung's* calculation. *Huai* iVan *Tse* says 50,000 Li. Lun-Heng.

17 CHAPTER XX.

On the Sun *(Shuo-jih).*

The Literati say that the sun, when he becomes visible in the morning-, comes forth from darkness, and that, when he disappears in the evening, he re-enters darkness. The *Yin* fluid of darkness is obscure, they say, therefore the sun disappears in it, and becomes invisible.

In reality the sun neither leaves nor re-enters darkness, but how can we prove that?

Night is darkness; its fluid is also obscure. But if a fire is made during the night, its light is not extinguished by the night. The darkness of night is the darkness of the north. The setting sun, which rises in the morning, is the kindled fire. The light of a fire, kindled at night-time, is not extinguished, that shows that, when the sun sets in the evening, a fluid cannot be the cause of his disappearance.

Observing the sun-rise and the sun-set in winter, we remark that, in the morning, he rises in the south-east, and, in the evening, he sets in the south-west. The south-east and the south-west are not the region of the *Yin* or darkness. How then can it be said that the sun proceeds from and reverts to darkness? Furthermore, the stars notwithstanding their smallness remain visible, and the sun is extinguished in spite of his greatness? The reasoning of the scholars of to-day is thoughtless and shallow.

They again say that the shortness of the days in winter, and their length in summer are also brought about by the *Yin* and the *Yang*. In summer, the *Yang* fluid abounds, and the *Yin* fluid falls short. The *Yang* fluid shines with the same splendour as the sun. Consequently, when the sun comes forth, there is nothing to obscure him. In winter, the *Yin* fluid is dusky, and overshadows Night is here taken as something positive, something like a black veil, or dark air, not as the absence of light, which does not cause the disappearance of the sun, but is its consequence.

The dark fluid of night. According to Chinese symbolism the *Tin* principle of darkness corresponds to the north. the sun-light. Therefore, although the sun rises, he remains dark and invisible. Thus in winter the days are short. The *Yin* is paramount, and the *Yang* is scarce, just the reverse of what takes place in summer.

However, if we consider the question seriously, we will find that the *Yin* and the *Yang* are not responsible for the length or the shortness of the days. This is made evident by the northern stars. The *Yin* of the north is the *Yin* of the sun. The *Yin* of the north does not overshadow the sparkling of the stars, why then should the *Yin* in winter obfuscate the brightness of the sun? Hence those who speak about the *Yin* and the *Yang* miss the truth.

As a matter of fact, in summer the sun stands in Gemini, in winter in Aquila. Aquila is far from the pole, therefore the curve described by the sun is short. Gemini being near the pole, the solar curve is long then. In summer the sun

proceeds northwards as far as Gemini, in winter southwards as far as Aquila. Therefore the extreme solar points in winter and summer are called "winter" and "summer limit." Because in spring and autumn those extremes are not reached, one speaks of "vernal" and "autumnal division."

Some people hold that in summer, when the *Yang* fluid abounds, it is in the south, and that in consequence heaven rises and becomes high. In winter the *Yang* fluid decays, and heaven sinks down, and becomes depressed. When heaven is high, the course of the sun increases in length, and the days are lengthened; when heaven is low, the solar curve decreases, and the days are short.

Now, if owing to the exuberance of the solar *Yang* fluid, heaven rises in the south, and the course of the sun is lengthened, the same increase ought to take place in regard to the moon. In summer, when the days are long, the sun rises in the north-east, but the moon in the south-east. In winter, when the days are short, the sun rises in the south-east, whereas the moon rises in the north-east. If in summer heaven were raised in the south, sun and moon ought equally to rise in the north-east, and, if in winter heaven were lowered, sun and moon should both rise in the south-east. It results from this, that in summer heaven does Literally: *Tung-ching* Jt the "Eastern Well," and *Ch'ien-nu* J—, the "Herdsman." - ijs. The two solstices. The two equinoxes. not rise in the south, and that in winter it is not depressed. On the contrary, in summer, when the days are long, the stars from which the sun rises are in the north, and in winter, when the days are short, these stars are in the south.

The following question may be raised. In summer, in the fifth moon, when the days are long, the sun stands in Gemini, which are near the pole, therefore the course of the sun is long. Now, we see that in the fifth moon the sun rises in the sign *Yin* and sets in *Ifcil* The solar curve being so long and far from men, how is it that we see the sun rise in *Yin* and set in *HsG?* When the sun stands in

Gemini, he is very near to men. Gemini are near the pole, hence, when the pole turns round, they ought to remain always visible. Provided that Gemini are by the side of the pole, ought we not to have no night, but continuous day?

Some scholars assert that sun and moon have nine different courses, therefore, they say, the sun in his course is near or far, and day and night are long or short.—However, in the fifth month day-time makes up / and night-time /, and in the sixth month the day is / and the night /. From the sixth month to the eleventh month every month the day decreases by '/. That means that to the course of the sun every month '/i6 is added. In the lapse of a year the sun takes 16 different courses on heaven and not i) only.

Another idea is that heaven is high in the south and depressed in the north. When the sun rises into the higher region, he becomes visible, and when he sets into the lower one, he disappears. Heaven is believed to be like a reclining umbrella, which is shown by the fact that the pole, as seen from us, is in the north. The pole is the centre of the world. Since it is north from us, heaven must evidently resemble a reclining umbrella.

If to illustrate the shining of the sun the analogy of a reclining umbrella be used, heaven must really have the shape of an umbrella. The polar star in the north of the upper part would correspond to the top of the umbrella, the south in the lower part would be like the stick of the umbrella, but where would that be? An umbrella reclining on the earth cannot turn round, but raise it straight, and it rotates. Now, provided that heaven revolves, This cyclical sign denotes ENE/N on the compass and corresponds to Gemini.

HsH = WNW/N and Aquarius. Turning round with the pole. The sun turning round the pole in Gemini and never disappearing. its northern edge cannot touch the earth, for how could it revolve, if it knocked against the earth? We see from this that heaven cannot be shaped like a reclining umbrella, and that the sun rising or setting does not follow the elevation, and the depression of heaven.

Some people maintain that the northern edge of heaven sinks down into the earth, and that the sun following heaven enters into the earth. The earth being massive, obscures him, so that men cannot see him. But heaven and earth arc husband and wife. They unite in one body, heaven is in earth, and earth joined to heaven. Their fluids mix and produce things. The north is *Yin*. When both are coupled, and their fluids mingle, it is in the north therefore, but does heaven revolve in the earth? If not, the earth in the north would be depressed, and not even.

Let us suppose that heaven really is revolving in the earth. On digging up the earth ten feet deep we find springs. Does then heaven revolving in the earth plunge into the water, and then come out again? If the north were depressed and not level, the Nine Streams ought to flow north without ever filling it up. In reality heaven does not revolve in the earth, nor does the sun become obscured, because he follows heaven. Heaven is quite as level as earth, and the sun rises, and sets, being turned round along with heaven.

Heaven appears to us in the shape of a bowl turned upside down. Therefore the sun rising and setting looks like coining from and entering into the earth. When the sun rises, he is near, when he sets, he is far, and becomes invisible, hence the term setting or entering. When in his rotation the sun appears in the east, he is near, hence we say that he is rising or coming out. But what proof have we? If you attach a moonlight pearl to the bow over a cart, and turn the cart round, the pearl will also turn.

To men heaven and earth seem to unite at a distance of no more than ten Li. That is the effect of the distance, for they do not come together in fact. When we behold the sun setting, he does not set either, it is also the distance. At the time, when the sun sets in the west, the people living there will perhaps say that he is culminating, and looking from the point, where the sun is setting, eastward

to our world, heaven and earth may appear to The north is *Yin,* which is synonymous with female, here the female organ.

Viz. by heaven knocking against it in its rotation. The Nine Streams regulated by *Yii.* See *Mayers* Pt. II, No. 207. the beholder joined together. Our world is in the south, therefore the sun rises in the east, and disappears in the northern regions. If the sun rose in the north, he would set in the south, for everywhere, what is near seems to rise, and what is far, to set. In reality there is no setting, but it is the distance.

If standing on the shore of a big lake, you look out to its limits in the four directions, they are blended with heaven. As a matter of fact, they are not blended, but the distance gives this impression. Through distance the sun seems setting, and through distance the lake seems to be blended with heaven. It is the same in both eases. The lake is bordered by land, but we do not see it, for to the observer it looks, as if it were blended with heaven. The sun also looks like setting. All this is brought about by distance.

The height of Mount *T'ai* equals that of heaven, and is lost in the clouds, yet from a distance of one hundred Li the mountain docs not appear as big as a clod of earth. At a distance of one hundred Li Mount *T'ai* disappears, how much more the sun, whose distance from us is counted by ten thousands of Li! The example of the *T'ai-ahan* gives an explanation.

Let a man take a big torch, and walk at night on a level road, where there are no gaps. He will not have walked to a distance of one Li from us, before the light of the fire is gone out. It does not go out, it is the distance. In the same manner the sun revolving westward and disappearing does not set.

The following question may be asked:—Heaven is level as much as the earth. Now, looking up to heaven and regarding the movements of the sun and the moon, it seems as thou'rh heaven were high in the south and low in the north. How is that to be explained?

See above p. 255. On p. 263 *Wang*

Ch'ung says that our world lies in the south-east of the universe. The sun sets in the west and passes through the north, before he rises again in the east. To people living in the east of the universe e. below the farthest eastern limit reached by the sun in his course, the sun would appear to rise in the north, to culminate in the east, and to set in the south. The context requires that we should read J *blended* instead of *look oul* of the text. The light becomes invisible for those who look after him. The great distance makes the sun invisible. 'Because the sun and the moon, which are supposed. to be attached to heaven and revolving with it, rise on the southern hemisphere, and go down on the northern.

The answer is this:—Our actual world is lying in the southeast. Seen from below, heaven looks, as if it were elevated, and the courses of the sun and the moon are south of us. Now, our world lies beneath the courses of the sun and the moon, therefore it seems to us, as if in their motions they rose in the south, and descended in the north. How shall we account for that?

If heaven were elevated in the south, the southern stars should be elevated likewise. However, we see them going down. Is then heaven again depressed in the south? The celestial bodies which are near appear high, those which are distant, low. To people north of the pole it seems high, and the south they regard as low. The same holds good for the regions east and west of the pole. All regard as high, what is near, and as low, what is far from them.

He who from beneath the *Northern Passes* looks up, sees the polar constellation above him. The north of the *Hsiung-nu* is the border-land of the earth. Seen in the north, heaven still appears high in the north and low in the south, and sun and moon in their courses ascend heaven there also. For a man standing on Mount *T'ai* it is high, whereas ten Li from its loot it appears low. The height of heaven is like that of Mount *T'ai* as seen by men.

The four cplarters and the centre, which are level, are of the same height, if, therefore, heaven seems to be depressed at the four cardinal points, this must be an illusion caused by the distance. Heaven does not only seem depressed there, but joined to the earth.

Some *savants* hold that at sunrise and sunset, in the morning and in the evening, the sun is near, and that while in the zenith he is far away. Conversely, others maintain that the sun in the zenith is near, whereas at sunrise and sunset he is a long way off. Those who believe that the sun is near, when he rises or sets, and far off, when he culminates, have remarked the large size of the sun rising or setting, and his smallness at noon. We find that things are large, when they are near us, and small, when seen from a distance. Therefore the rising and setting sun is considered to be near, and the sun in the zenith to be far distant. Those who believe that at sunrise and sunset the sun is far off, and at noon near us. have on the other hand made the observation that at noon the sun is warm, and that he is cool, while rising or setting. When a fire comes near us. we feel hot. whereas, when it is at a distance, *I.e.* China.

"In Mongolia.

we feel cold. Hence the idea that the sun at noon is near, while he is at a distance, when he is rising or setting.

Both views are well-founded, and it has not yet been ascertained, which is right, and which is wrong. If we consider the question seriously, we arrive at the conclusion that the sun in the zenith is near, and at sunrise and sunset far off, as the following experiment will show. Place a pole upright in a room. The room is 30 feet high. The pole placed vertically under the roof-beam knocks against the latter above, and reaches to the bottom below. The beam then is 30 feet distant from the bottom. When the pole is inclined a little sidewards, its top diverges sidewards, and cannot touch the beam anymore, because the distance from the bottom is more than 30 feet.

When the sun is culminating, he just reaches the highest point on heaven, exactly like the pole standing upright so, that the distance from the bottom measures 30 feet. The sun rising or setting is

deflected to our right or left like the pole inclining to one side, whereby the distance from the bottom exceeds 30 feet. We learn from this that the sun in the zenith is near, and the rising or setting sun more distant.

Let again a man be seated in the central hall of a house, and another walk on its roof. When he has reached the centre of the house, he is just above the man seated, and the distance from the man on the roof to the man sitting in the house, is 30 feet. When he is at the eastern or the western corner of the roof, his distance from the man in the house is greater than 30 feet.

The sun in the zenith is like the man standing in the middle of the roof, *when* the sun is just rising or setting, he resembles the man at the eastern or western corner. The sun in the zenith is near us, therefore warm, at the time of his rising or setting, he is far, and consequently cool. However, when the sun stands in the zenith, he is small, whereas at sunrise and sunset he is large. That is because, when the sun is culminating, the brightness of daylight makes him appear small, and when the sun is rising or setting, daylight is fading, and he looks larger in consequence. In the same manner a fire looks small at daytime, but big at night. What is shown by fire, can be proved by the stars also. The stars This problem is already enunciated by *Lich Tse* V, 9 who makes two lads expose it to *Confucius*. They ask the Sage to decide between the two antagonistic views, but he is unable to give a satisfactory reply.

Wang Ch'ung seems to think that daylight is distinct from the light of the sun. are not visible during the day, because the brightness of the day eclipses them. At night there is no light, and the stars become visible. Now the sun and the moon are stars. When the sun approaches the horizon, and is about to set, his light fades, and he appears bigger.

The scholars argue that in the morning the sun rises from *Fu Sang,* and in the evening sets in *Hsi Liu, Fu Sang* is the eastern region, *Hsi Liu* the western desert, both are the confines of heaven and earth, and the places where the sun

and the moon use to rise and set.

I beg to put the following question:— Every year in the second and the eighth months the sun rises exactly in the east, and sets exactly in the west. We might say then that the sun rises in *Fu Sang,* and sets in *Hsi Liu.* But in summer, when the days are long, the sun rises in the north-east, and sets in the northwest. In winter, when the days are short, the sun rises in the south-east and sets in the south-west. In winter and summer rising and setting take place in four different corners. In which place exactly are *Fu Sang* and *Hsi Liu* situated then? The above statement, therefore, is true for spring and autumn, but not for winter and summer. Yet, after all, the sun does not rise in *Fu Sang* nor set in *Hsi Liu* for the reason that he revolves with heaven and is visible, when near, and invisible, when far off. While he is in *Fu Sang* or *Hsi Liu,* the people there, from their standpoint, will say that the sun is in the zenith. At other times it may appear from *Fu Sang* and *Hsi Liu,* as though the sun were rising or setting. When he is above people's heads, they call it noon, when he is on one side, they call it morning or evening! How can the sun unckr these circumstances rise in *Fu Sang,* and set in *Hsi Liu?*

The Literati again assert that heaven is revolving from right to left, and that the sun and the moon in their courses are not attached to heaven, but have each their own movement. It might be objected that, in case the suu and the moon had their proper movements, and were not attached to heaven, the sun would proceed one degree, and the moon thirteen. After their rise, both ought to go on and turn from west to east, how is it that nevertheless *Fu Sang* has been identified with *Sakhalin.*

Hsi Liu must be the *Mongolian Desert.* At the equinoxes. See above p. 258.

Vid.' above p. 259. From right to left, facing the polar star which remains motionless and round which heaven revolves from east to west (cf. p. 267). they commence to turn westward? They are attached to heaven, and follow its movements during the four seasons. Their movement may be compared to that of ants crawling on a rolling mill-stone. The movements of the sun and the moon are slow, whereas heaven moves very fast. Heaven carries the sun and the moon along with it, therefore they really move eastward, but are turned westward.

Perhaps the following question might be raised:—The sun. the moon, and heaven have their movement each, but the number of degrees which they traverse is not the same. To what can their velocity be compared, if referred to the things of this world?

I would reply that heaven makes one circumvolution every day. The sun moves on one degree cipial to 2,000 Li, of which he makes 1,000 during the day-time and 1,000 during the night. The unicorn also runs 1,000 Li during the day, therefore the speed of the sun is very much like the pace of the unicorn.

The moon moves on 13 degrees. 10 degrees being equal to 20,000 Li, and 3 degrees to 6.000, the distance, made by the moon in one day and one night is 26,000 Li, which is like the flight of a wild duck.

Since heaven turns round 305 degrees, the multiplication gives 730,000 Li. This movement is very fast, and there is nothing like it. It can be compared to the rotation of a potter's wheel or the speed of an arrow, shot from a cross-bow.

But although the rotation of heaven be so very fast, it appears to us slow, because heaven is so high, and far away, for distant objects in motion look motionless, and things shifting their place, stationary, as the following observation will show. If any body is on board a ship, sailing with the wind, in a river or on sea, her speed is fast, while she is near the shore, and slow, while she is far off. The ship's real speed remains the same, its quickness or slowness merely depending on the distance from which she is seen.

When we look up to heaven, its movement does not appear as quick as that of the unicorn. With the sun over it the unicorn hastens on, but when darkness falls, the sun is in front, why? Their own movement being from west

to cast, opposite to that of heaven. -The *Kilin,* by Europeans usually called unicorn, whose prototype seems to have been the girafTe. The giraffe gallops like the fastest horse. The swiftest horses are likewise said to make 1,000 Li a day.

Because the unicorn is near, whereas the sun is far. Distance conveys the impression of slowness, and proximity that of speed. If a journy extends over 00,000 Li. it is difficult to form an adequate idea of the real movement.

The Literati assert that the sun moves one degree, and heaven 365 during one day and one night, that heaven turns to the left, and the sun and the moon to the right, and that they *meet* heaven.

The following question may be asked:—The movements of the sun and the moon depend on heaven, they move, attached to heaven, not straight on. How shall we describe it? The *Yiking* says:—"The sun, the moon, and the stars rely on heaven. Fruits, grasses, and trees rely on earth." Helving means that they are attached. The movement attached to heaven is like that of men walking round on the earth. The simile is like that of the ants crawling on the rolling mill-stone.

There is the question:—How do we know that the sun does not detach himself from heaven, nor move straight on independently? If the sun could do so, he ought to turn eastward of himself, and not share heaven's movement to the west. The movement of the moon is the same as that of the sun, both being attached to heaven. This is proved by a comparison with the clouds.

The clouds are not attached to heaven, they always remain in their place. Provided the sun and the moon were not attached to heaven, we would expect them to keep their places likewise. From this it is evident that' the sun's movement is connected with that of heaven.

Another question arises:—The sun is fire. On earth fire does not move, why then does the sun move on heaven?

The fluid attached to heaven has motion, that attached to the earth has not. If fire be attached to the earth, the earth

does not move, consequently the fire does not move either.

Some one might object, how could water move, if the fluid attached to earth had no motion. The reply is that the water *Yiking,* 30th diagram (Li), *Legge'* transl. p. 237.—Our text slightly differs. It adds "and the stars,'' and writes "fruits" instead of " grains." flows eastward into the ocean, because the north-western region is high, and the south-eastern low. It is the nature of water to seek the low places, whereas fire will rise. If the earth were not high in the west, the water would not run eastward either.

We will have to meet another objection as to how men, being attached to the earth, can move, if the fluid attached to the earth is motionless.

Human actions and desires all have an aim. Since purpose is at the root of human nature, man works and strives.

The ancients were plain and simple-minded. Though on the frontier of a neighbouring country they heard the cocks crow and the dogs bark, they never had any intercourse with that country.

Somebody will ask perhaps, why the stars do not move, if the fluid attached to heaven is in motion. I reply that the stars are fixed in heaven. Heaven moves, and since they are turned round along with heaven, they move also.

An opponent might urge that human nature is based on purpose, and therefore acts, but how could heaven move, since its principle is absence of purpose?—Heaven's movement consists in the spontaneous emission of fluid. The fluid being emitted, things are produced of themselves, but the fluid is not emitted on purpose, in order to produce things. Without movement the fluid cannot be emitted, and unless the fluid be emitted, things cannot be created. It is different from the movement of man. The movements of the sun, the moon, and the five planets all consist in the emission of fluid.

The Literati hold that there is a three-legged raven in the sun, and a hare and a toad in the moon. However, the sun is the heavenly fire which does not differ from the fire on earth. In the fire on earth there are no living beings, how could there be a raven in the heavenly fire? There are no living creatures in the fire, when they enter it. they are burnt to death. How could a raven remain unscathed?

The moon is water. There are living beings in the water, but not hares or toads. When a hare or a toad remain long in the water, they inevitably die. The sun and the moon are attached to heaven just as shells and oysters swim in the deep, evidently Again the misleading symbolism. The moon represents the female principle, *Tin,* to which water corresponds, whence the naive deduction is made that the moon *is* water.

because they belong to the same fluid. Are perhaps that what we call a hare and a toad, shells or oysters?

And let us ask the Literati whether the raven, the hare, and the toad are living or dead. If they be dead, and remain for a long time in the sun and the moon, they must become charred, decay and putrefy. If they be alive, where are they at the time of a total eclipse of the sun or, when on the last day of a month the moon totally disappears?

The raven, the hare, and the toad must be the fluid of the sun and the moon, as the intestines of man, or the heart, and backbone of animals are the fluid of these creatures. It is still possible to examine the moon, but, when we look at the sun, our eyes are dazzled, and we cannot make out what fluid really pervades the sun, yet we should be able to distinguish an object in the sun, and call it a raven? In fact, we cannot see the entire body of a raven, and we should remark that it has three legs? This is certainly not true.

Moreover, we hear the Literati speak of many animals, why then is there only one raven in the sun, and one hare and a toad in the moon?

The savants maintain that the eclipse of the sun is caused by the moon. They have observed that the eclipses of the sun always fall on the last and the first day of a month. At that time the moon is united with the sun, therefore she must eclipse him, they think. Many eclipses

of the sun have occurred during the "Spring and Autumn" period. The Classic records that on the first day of such and such a moon the sun has been eclipsed, but it does not follow that the moon has any thing to do with these eclipses. If the chroniclers had known that the sun was eclipsed by the moon, why have they been silent on this point, and did not speak of the moon?

They say that, when an eclipse of the sun takes place, the *Yang* is weak and the *Yin* strong. When a man possesses great strength, he can subdue others in this world. Now, on the last day of a month, the light of the moon is extinguished, and, on the first day of the new moon, it is gone so to say, which is the highest degree of weakness. How could it vanquish the sun, for the eclipse of the sun is said to be caused by the moon? If, in an eclipse of the sun, the moon is believed to eclipse it, where is the moon? The eclipse is not caused by the moon, since the moon herself is destroyed. If we regard the sun from the same point of view as the moon, his light at an eclipse is destroyed of itself.

On an average, an eclipse of the sun occurs every 41 or 42 months, and an eclipse of the moon, every 180 days. These eclipses have their fixed time, and these changes do not always take place. When they happen, it is through the spontaneous action of the fluid. The last and the first day of a month recur very often, hut does the moon cause an eclipse then? The sun being in his full, the change is brought about by his shrinking together. Must we suppose something that consumes (eclipses) the sun? What consumes the mountains or the earth, when the mountains collapse and the earth shakes?

Some say that, when the sun is eclipsed, the moon covers him. The sun being above, the moon below, her shadow falls on the sun's body. When the sun and the moon are united, but the moon is above, and the sun below, the moon cannot cover the sun, whereas, when the sun is above, and the moon underneath him, she casts her shadow on him. The light of the moon then covers the light of the sun, hence the ex-

pression: — eclipse. The shadow of the moon is like that of the clouds which cover the sky in such a way that the sun and the moon are invisible.

Provided that both unite with their extremities, they must eclipse one another, and if both, when they come together, are joined like two pieces fitting one into the other, the sun must disappear as a matter of course. That the sun and the moon meet on the last and the first day of the month is a very common celestial phenomenon, but it is wrong to say that at an eclipse the moon covers the light of the sun for the following reason:—

In case that, when the sun and the moon unite, the moon covers the light of the sun, the edges of the two luminaries must fall together at the beginning of the eclipse, and they must change their places, when the sun comes out again. Now, let us suppose that the sun stands in the east, the moon in the west. The moon moves quickly eastward, wdiere she falls in with the sun. She covers the edge of the sun, and after a short time she passes the sun and proceeds eastward. The western edge of the sun has been covered first, its light must then come back. The eastern edge has not yet been overshadowed, it will be eclipsed next.

The Chinese expression is "to consume," "to eat'' or lf). In the popular belief the sun at an eclipse is being devoured by the "heavenly dog," an idea perhaps derived from India. In *Wanj Chung'x* time it must not yet have been current, for otherwise he would most likely not have omitted to mention and controvert it.

Thus we see that during an eclipse of the sun the light of the western edge is extinguished, and that, when the sun comes back, the light of the western edge returns. Then the moou goes on, and covers the eastern edge, while the western edge returns. Can we say then that the sun and the moon are joined together, and that one covers and overshadows the other?

The scholars assert that the shape of the sun and the moon is quite round. When they look up to them, they appear'shaped like a peck, or a round basket. Their shape is a regular circle, they are not like the fluid of a fire seen from afar, for a fluid is not round.—In reality the sun and the moon are not round, they only appear so through the distance, as will be seen from the following: —The sun is the essence of fire, the moon the essence of water. On earth fire and water are not round, why should they be round in heaven alone? The sun and the moon in heaven are like the Five Planets, and the Five Planets like the other stars. The stars are not round, only their radiance appears round, because they are so far from us. This will become evident from the following fact:—During the "Spring and Autumn" period stars fell down in the capital of *Sung*. When people went near to examine them, they found that they were stones, but not round. Since the stars are not round, we know that the sun, the moon, and the planets are not round either.

The scholars discoursing on the sun, and the mechanics hold that there is only one sun, whereas in the "*Tribute of Yil*" and in the *Shan-hai-king* it is stated that there are ten suns. Beyond the ocean in the east there is the " Hot Water Abyss," over which rises *Fusang*. The ten suns bathe in the water. There is a huge tree. Nine suns remain in its lower branches, while one sun stays on the upper branch. *Huai Aan Tse* also writes in his book about ten suns which were shining. During the time of *Yao* the ten suns came out together, and scorched everything, whereupon *Wang Ch'ung* here speaks of' a partial eclipse. That the shadow of the moon in most eases covers only" part of the sun cannot invalidate the right view, which *Wang Ch'ung* rejects on unsufficient grounds.
Ch'un-ch'iu, Duke *Hei* 16th year (*Leyge*, Classics Vol. V, I't. I, p. 170). *T'ang-ku. Slian-hai-king* chap. 9, p. I v. *Yao* shot at them. Hence they never were seen together anymore on the same day.
Commonly the "celestial stems" are called suns. From the first to the last stem there are ten suns. There are ten

suns, as there are five planets. Intelligent people and disputing scholars are at a loss, how to find out the truth, and do not wish to decide in favour of either opinion. Thus the two antagonistic statements are transmitted without criticism, and neither of the two opinions meets with general approval. Yet, if we examine the question thoroughly, there are not. ten suns.

The sun is like the moon. If there be ten suns, are there twelve moons? There are five planets, but the five elements:— metal, wood, water, fire, and earth all burn with a different light. Should there be ten suns, their fluids ought to be different. Now, we do not discover any difference in the light of the sun, and we find that his size is the same at different times. If there were really different fluids, the light would certainly be different. If, on the other hand, the fluid is identical, it must be united into one sun, and there cannot be ten.

We see that with a sun-glass fire is drawn from heaven, the sun being a big fire. Since on earth fire is one fluid, and the earth has not ten fires, how can heaven possess ten suns? Perhaps the so called ten suns are some other things, whose light and shape resembles that of the sun. They are staying in the "Hot Water Abyss," and always climb up *Fusang. Yii* and *Yi* saw them, and described them as ten suns.

Some people have measured the light of the sun, and calculated his size. They found the diameter to be 1,000 Li long. Provided that the rising suu is the sun on the *Fu-sang* tree, this tree must overhang 10,000 Li to cover the sun, for the diameter of one sun being 1,000 Li, ten suns will require 10,000 Li.

Heaven is more than 10,000 Li distant from us.

When we look up at the sun, his brilliancy is so dazzling, and his glare so bright, that it becomes unbearable. If the rising According to other accounts *Yao* ordered his minister *Yi*, a famous archer, to shoot at the suns, of which he destroyed nine.

The appearance of ten suns is mentioned in many ancient works:—in *Chuang Tse, the Li-suo,* the "*Bamboo*

Annals," the *Tso-chuan,* etc The ten cyclical signs. The five elements are considered to be the substances of the Five Planets, which have been named after them:—Metal Star (Venus), Wood Star (Jupiter), etc.
» Cf. p. 330.
sun was the sun from the *Fu-sang* tree, *Yil* and *Yi* would not have been able to recognise him as the sun. A look at one sun would have sufficed to dazzle the eyes, how much more so, if there were ten suns. When *Yil* and *Yi* saw the suns, they appeared to them like pecks and round baskets, therefore they called them suns. The fires looked like pecks and baskets, but an object seen at a distance of 60,000 Li appears different from one looked at and examined quite near. Consequently what *Yil* and *Yi* saw they took for suns, but were not suns.
Among the things of heaven and earth many resemble one another in substance, yet they are not the same in fact. Beyond the ocean in the south-west there is a pearl-tree. It has pearls, but they are not fish-pearls. The ten suns are like pearls of the pearl-tree. The pearls of the pearl-tree look like pearls, but are not real pearls. Thus the ten suns look like the sun, but are not real suns. *Huai Nan Tse* having read the *Shan-hai-king* wrongly asserted that for a Sage ten suns were lighted, and made the random statement that at *Yao's* time ten suns rose together.

The sun is fire, the "Hot Water Abyss" water. Water and fire annihilate one another. Therefore the ten suns bathing in the "Hot Water Abyss" should have been extinguished and destroyed. Fire burns trees, *Fu-sang* is a tree. When ten suns rested upon it, it ought to be parched and scorched up. However, in spite of the bath in *Tang-ku* the light did not become extinguished, and though the suns ascended *Fu-sang*, its boughs were not scorched or parched. The ten suns are like the sun which rises to-day, yet they cannot be tested by the five elements. Hence we infer that they were not real suns.

When *Yil* and *Yi* beheld ten suns, it cannot have been nighttime, but must have been day. When one sun rose, the other nine must have been left behind, how could they rise all ten together? It must have been like dawn before the sunrise.

Furthermore, heaven turns and passes through a certain number of degrees. If the various suns follow this movement, and turn Presumably a coral-tree in the Persian Sea is meant.

The Chinese imagine that pearls or the produce of fish, not of shells or oysters. If they were of the same stuff as our sun, *viz.* fire, they would have been extinguished in water, and have burned the wood of the *Fu-sang* tree. Since they did not do that, they cannot have been real suns like ours. The one sun in the upper branches of the *Fu-sang* tree must have risen prior to the nine others still lingering in the lower branches. As far as the nine suns are concerned, which were still below the horizon. Luu-Hrng. 18 round with heaven, how could tliey remain in the branches of *Fu-sang* or in the water of the "Hot Water Abyss?" In case they stay hack, they miss the movement, and differences in the movement would bring disharmony. If, therefore, the rising sun be different from the ten suns, they only resemble suns, but are not suns.

"During the 'Spring and Autumn' period on the *Jtsin mao* day, in the fourth month of summer, in the seventh year of Duke *Chuang* at midnight the common stare were invisible, and stars fell down like rain." *Kung Yang* in his commentary asks: — What does "like rain" mean? It is not rain. Then, why use this expression? "The uurevised *Ch'un-ch'iu*" says, "It rained stars, which previous to approaching to within a foot of the earth departed again." The Sage corrected this, and said, "The stars fell down like rain."

"The unrevised *Ch un-ch'iu*" refers to the time, when the *Ch unch'iu* was not yet revised. At that time the Chronicle of *Lu* had the following entry:—"The stars fell down like rain. The came near the earth at a distance of over a foot, and then departed again." The Sage is *Confucius*. *Confucius* revised it, and said "The stare fell like rain." His idea was that on the earth there are mountains,

hills, and high buildings, and he was afraid lest the statement about the stars coming near the earth at a distance of over a foot should not be true. Therefore he made an alteration, and said "like rain." Being like rain they came down from above the earth. The stars also fall down from heaven and depart again. On account of this similarity he says "like. " Although there was the notice that the stars came near the earth at a distance of over a foot, he merely said "like rain. " The expression "falling" which he uses refers to those stars. Though he assigned them their places, and fixed the text, he speaks of the falling stars in the same way as the Chronicle does-.

When from the plain we look up at Mount *T'ai*, and behold a crane on its summit, it appears to us as big as a crow, and a crow, like a sparrow. It is the height of Mount *T ea* and its distance which cause us to lose the true estimate of the size of things. Cf. *Chun-ch'iu (Legge,* Classics Vol. V, Pt. I, p. 70). The seventh year of Duke *Chuang* of *Lu* is 686 B.c. A quotation from *Kung Yang'x* commentary to the *Cliun-chiu.* Had the distance of those meteors not been more than one foot from the surface of the earth, they would inevitably have collided with the elevations of the earth, such as mountains, buildings, etc. Therefore *Confucius* omitted the remark of tike original text.

The distance of heaven from earth amounts to upwards of 60,000 Li, which is not only the height and the distance of the summit of Mount *T'ai*. The stars are fixed to heaven. When we examine them, we do not obtain a correct idea of their nature, for the conditions, under which we see them, are still more unfavourable than those, under which we look at the crane or the crow. By calculations we find that the size of the stars must be a hundred Li. Their brilliancy is so strong, that they shed light. If, nevertheless, they appear to us only as big as a phoenix egg, we have lost the true estimate by distance.

Let us suppose that the falling stars are in fact stars falling from heaven, then we would not he aide to recognise

them as stars, when they approach the earth, because during their fall their size is not the same as that which they have in heaven. Now, as long as we see the falling stars in heaven, they are stars, if they are not, they are made up of air. We see ghosts having the semblance of dead people. In reality it is but air condensed into those forms, not real dead people. Thus the falling stars are in reality not shaped like stars. *Confucius* correctly calls them falling, which means that they are not stars, and rightly characterises them as being like rain, i. *c.* they are not rain, both features being opposed to the real nature of stars.

The *Tso-chuan* remarks on the above quoted passage of the *Chun-chiu,* "On the *hsin-mao* day, in the fourth moon during tlfe night the common stars were not visible, because the night was bright. The stars fell like rain i. e. together with rain." This remark that the stars were invisible owing to the brightness of the night tallies with a passage in the *Yiking* to the effect that at midday the Dipper is visible. If during the day the Dipper is visible, it must be dark, not bright, and if during the night the stars were invisible, the night must have been bright and clear. The facts were different, but the idea is the same, and it is consistent with truth.

The *Tsochuan* says "together with rain," which is tantamount to "combined." On the *hsin-mao* day the night was bright, therefore the stars were invisible, but this brightness shows that there was no rain. The rain fluid is dark and obscure, how could there be brightness than? There being brightness, rain is impossible, how could the stars fall "together with rain?" Consequently the The meteors never measure a hundred Li.

-*l iking,* 55th diagram *(Feng), Legge's* transl. p. 330. A constellation. expression "together with rain" is wrong. Moreover, if it be said that the night was so bright, that the stars became invisible, how could the stars falling together with rain be seen?

"On the *wu-sh4n* day of the first month in the 16th year of Duke *Hsi* five stones fell down in *Sung."* The *Tso-chuan* remarks that they were stars. Since falling stones are called stars, those stars are believed to have become stones by falling. The stars falling in the *hsin-mao* night were stars, but in reality stones then. If the stars falling in the *hsin-mao* night were like those stones, the earth had high buildings, which must have been smashed. Although *Confucius* omitted to mention that the stars came near the earth as far as one foot, there certainly has been a certain distance from the earth, and the historigrapher of *Lu,* who saw the event with his own eyes, would not have said so at random.

According to the *Tso-chuan* the stars fell down together with rain. As rain collects on the earth, the stones must have done so likewise, but, since, when they touched the earth, they did not demolish the buildings, it is evident that they were not stars. Besides, on what does *Tso Chiu Ming* base his statement that the stones were stars? When the stones came down, their fall was very light, but why must they have fallen down from heaven?

During the *Chin* epoch three mountains disappeared. Partly they were not dispersed, but collapsed, where they stood, which must have caused a great noise. Perhaps at that time the mountain of the *I* 77 went off its base, and came down in *Sung.* When the people of *Sung* heard the stones fall, they called them stars, and when *Tso Ch iu Ming* had examined them, he also gave them this name.

The substance of the stars is identical with that of the various things and like that of the sun and the moon. The so-called Five Planets are the light of the substance of the five elements. The Five Planets and the other stars all have the same light, therefore I am afraid that we miss the truth, if we regard the fixed stars alone as stones. In reality the stars which fell during the *hsin-mao* night were like rain, but they were not stars, just as the ten suns in the " Hot Water Abyss" resembled the sun. but were not real suns.

The Literati also maintain that the expression that rain comes from heaven means that it positively falls down

"from heaven. How Quoted from the *Ch'un-ch'hi (Legge* Vol. V, Pt. I, p. 170). The event took place in 643 B.c. ever, a discussion on this subject leads us to the conclusion that rain comes from above the earth, but not down from heaven. Seeing the rain gathering from above, we simply say that it comes down from heaven. As a matter of fact, it comes from above the earth. But how can we demonstrate that the rain comes from the earth, and rises from the mountains? The Commentary to the *Ch un-ch'iu* says, "It breaks through the stones one to two inches thick, and gathers. That in one day's time it spreads over the whole Empire, is only the case with the *T'ai-shan"*2 — From the *T'ai-shan* it rains over the whole Empire, from small mountains over one State, the distance depends on the height. As regards the forthcoming of the rain from the mountains, some hold that the clouds carry the rain with them. When the clouds disperse, the water falls down, and is called rain. Thus the clouds are rain, and rain, clouds. When the water comes forth, it is transformed into clouds; they condense, and become rain, and, when they are compressed still more, coagulate into dew. When garments are moistened as with rain, it is not the effect of the clouds, but of the rain which they carry.

Some persons will refer to the *Shuking* which says, "When the moon follows the stars, there is wind and rain," and to the *Slnking,* where we read that "The moon approaches the Hyades, which will bring heavy showers of rain. " They all believe that according to these passages of the two Classics it is not heaven which is causing the rain. How is that?

When the rain comes from the mountains, the moon passes the stars, and approaches the Hyades. When she approaches the Hyades, it must rain. As long as it does not rain, the moon does not approach, and the mountains have no clouds. Heaven and earth, above and below, act in spontaneous harmony. When the moon approaches above, the mountains are heated below, and the fluid unites. The fortuitous connexion

between the various fluids and bodies is due to spontaneity. Clouds and fog show that there is rain. In summer it becomes dew, in winter frost. Warm it is rain, cold, snow. Rain, dew, and frost all proceed from earth, and do not descend from heaven.

Kung Tang's Commentary, Duke *Hsi* 31st year. The highest peak in *Shantung. Shaking, llung-fan,* Pt, V, Bk. IV, 38 *(Legge* Vol. Ill, Pt. II, p. 342). *Shiking* Pt. II, Bk. VIII, Ode 8 *(Legge* Vol. IV, Pt. II, p. 422). CHAPTER XXI.

On Heat and Cold *.(Han-wen).*

People reasoning on heat and cold assert that, when the sovereign is pleased, it is warm, and, when he is angry, it is cold. How is that?

Joy and anger originate in the bosom. Subsequently they find their way out, and once outside, are the causes of rewards and punishments, rewards and punishments being the manifestations of joy and anger. When heat and cold are sufficiently strong, things become withered, and men are injured, and that is done by heat and cold, which are said to be the representatives of joy and anger.

Within the course of a few days a sovereign is not always full of joy or anger, which sentiments having broken forth from the bosom, expand and appear as heat and cold outside, thus showing the feelings of the bosom. When the sovereign is pleased or angry, this fluid of his bosom is not changed into heat or cold. Why should the fluid in his bosom be different from the fluid within the territory of a country? The fluid of the bosom is not transformed through joy or anger, how then should heat and cold originate within the territory?

During the time of the *Six States,* and the *Ch'in* and *Han* epoch the feudal princes were subjugating one another, armour-clad warriors filling all the roads. The States were investing each other with the greatest animosity, and their leaders thought of nothing else than of vanquishing their enemies. A feeling of universal slaughter pervaded everything. Yet at that time it was not always cold in the Empire. The time of

Yii was one of universal peace. The government was good, the people contented, and the sovereign always pleased. In every house they were playing the guitar, singing, beating drums, and dancing. Yet at that time it was not constantly warm in the Empire. Is the feeling of joy and anger evoked by small things only, and does it not care for great ones? How is it so little in accordance with the deeds done?

Yen, Chao, Han, Wei, Ch'i and *Ch'u,* which in 332 B.c. made an offensive and defensive alliance to check the encroachments of the *Ch'in* State, but by and by the latter overpowered and absorbed them all.

Near the water it is cold, near the fire warm, the heat and the cold decrease in proportion to the distance, for the quantity of the fluid varies according to the distance. The seat of the fire is always in the south, that of the water in the north, therefore the northern region is cold, and the southern limit hot.

The fire in a stove, the water in a ditch, and the fluid in the human body are all governed by the same principle. When the sovereign is pleased or angry, this fluid of heat or cold ought to be especially strong in his private apartments, and much less so outside his territory. Now the temperature is the same without and within, consequently it cannot well be the result of the sovereign's joy or anger, and the assertions of our scholars to that effect are futile.

With an emperor a sudden change of the mental fluid takes place in the empire, with princes in their territory, with ministers and high officers in their department, and with common people in their house. Since even ordinary people are liable to such changes, their joy and their anger must also produce such fluids (as heat and cold). The father quarrels with the son, and husband and wife reprove one another. If there ought to be anger, but anger be turned into joy, or if faults be forgiven, and the wrong done hushed up, there would be cold and heat in the same house. This shows us that the sudden changes (of temperature) are not being caused by joy and anger.

Some one will say that there is attraction by affinity. If a man be pleased, he is kind and genial, and in his kindness gives rewards. The *Yang* principle is giving, and the *Yang* fluid is warm, therefore the warm fluid corresponds to it. If a man be angry, he is enraged and indignant, and in his rage puts people to death. The *Yin* principle is cold murder, and the *Yin* fluid is cold, therefore the cold fluid corresponds to it. "When the tiger howls, the wind blows from the valley, and when the dragon performs its antics, the brilliant clouds rise. " Their fluids being identical, and their species the same, they attract one another. Hence the saying that with the body one removes the shadow, and that with the dragon one attracts the rain. The rain responds to the dragon and comes, the shadow responds to the body and goes. The nature According to ancient natural philosophy. Consequently temperature cannot be the result of the feelings of the sovereign.

A quotation from *Hnai Xan* TV III, 2, with a slight variation of the text. Therefore during a drought clay figures of dragons are set up and worshipped to attract the rain. Cf. p. 55, No. 47. *Viz.* with the body. of heaven and earth is spontaneity. In autumn and winter punishments are meted out. Smaller misdemeanours are partly pardoned, but the capital punishments cause a bitter cold. The cold comes as an accompaniment of punishment, which shows that they attract one another.

If heat and cold be compared with wind and clouds, and joy and anger refer to the dragon and the tiger, a mutual attraction might be possible, provided that the fluids be the same and the categories similar. When the tiger howls, the wind rises from the valley, and when the dragon gambols, the clouds rise within a radius of one hundred Li, but in other valleys and other regions there is no wind nor clouds. Now, sudden changes of temperature take place everywhere, and at the same time. There may be executions within a territory of a hundred Li, but it is cold within a thousand Li, consequently this could not well be considered a proof of a connexion between the two events. *Ch'i* and *Lu* were conterminous, and gave rewards and punishments at the same time. Had *Ch'i* rewarded, while *Lu* punished, the effects would have been different also. Could then the *Ch'i* State have been warm, whereas it was cold at the same time in the *Lu* country?

In former times nobody was more cruel in punishing than *Ch'ih Yu* and the doomed prince of *Ch'm* The subjects of *Ch ih Yu* were most perverse and dissolute, and in doomed *Ch'in* red clad criminals were walking on the roads shoulder to shoulder, and yet at that time it was not always cold in the Empire. On the market of the emperor's capital oxen and sheep were slaughtered every day by hundreds. He who executes man as well as he who kills animals has a wicked heart. Albeit, the air on the market place of the capital cannot always be cold.

One might object that a man is far superior to animals, and that man alone provokes the fluid. However, does the one who puts to death provoke the fluid, or do those who are put to death, cause the change? In the first case, no matter, whether the one who inflicts the death penalty executes a man, or kills an animal, the mind is the same, and in the latter men and beasts are both creatures. They all belong to the ten thousand beings, and would not a hundred mean ones be worth as much as one precious one?

Some people will maintain that a sovereign alone can evoke the fluid, but not common people. If, to set the fluid in motion, Cf. p. 148 Note 7.

An attraction between joy and heat, anger and cold.

3 *Chin Shih Huang Ti.*

a sovereign is required, why does the world make so much of *Tsou Yen? Tsou Yen* was a commoner, and yet he could move the fluid quite alone, as everybody admits..

When one man is put to death, the air becomes cold, but, when a man is born, does the temperature become warm then? When a general amnesty is granted to the four quarters, and all punishments are remitted at the same time, the fluid of the month and the year does not become warm thereby.

In former years thousands of people have had their houses burnt, so that the flames and the smoke went up to heaven, and the Yellow River broke through its dykes, flooding a thousand Li, so that far and wide there was no bound to the prospect. Fire is identical with the hot fluid, and water with the cold one. At the time of the conflagration or the inundation of the Yellow River it has not been warm or cold. The setting in of heat and cold do not depend on government, I dare say, but eventually heat and cold may be simultaneous with rewards and punishments, and it is for this reason that the phenomenalists describe them as such.

Spring is warm, summer hot, autumn cool, and winter cold. These four seasons are spontaneous, and do not concern the sovereign. The four seasons are not caused by government, but they say that heat and cold correspond to it. At the beginning of the first month and subsequently at the "commencement of spring" all the punishments have been meted out, and the prisons remain empty. Yet one day it is cold, and one day warm. What manner of punishment is being inflicted, when it is cold, and what kind of rewards are given, when it is warm? We see from this that heat and cold correspond to the time periods of heaven and earth, and are not made by men.

When people are suffering from a cold or from fever, their actions have no influence upon these diseases. By exposure to the wind, or to bad air their body has become chilly or feverish. By changing their habits, or altering their style of life they do not When Tsou Yen, a scholar of the 4th cent. B.c., had been put into prison upon a trumped up charge, he looked up to heaven and wept. All of a sudden snow began to fall, although it was midsummer. See also p. 194.

A class of scholars, often mentioned in the L,m-heng, who seem to have devoted themselves to the study of natural phenomena and calamities, such as heat and cold, inundations, droughts, famines, etc. to which, however, they did not ascribe natural, but moral causes, misled by the pseudo-science of the Yiking and similar works. Of which the Chinese distinguish 24, beginning with li-ch'un "commencement of spring." They count from the days on which the sun enters the first and fifteenth degree of one of the zodiacal signs. get rid of their cold or their fever. Although the body is quite near, it cannot bring about a change and a cure. Now a city or a State is much more distant, how should it be possible to regulate their fluids?— When a man has caught cold, he drinks medicine, which soothes his pain, and when, being somewhat weak, he has got fever, he swallows pills, which make him perspire, and thus cure him.
In Yen there was the "Cold Valley" in which the five kinds of grain did not grow. Tsou Yen blew the flute, and the "Cold Valley" could be cultivated. The people of Yen sowed millet in it, and salled it " Millet Valley." If this be true that with playing the flute the cold fluid was dispelled, how could this calamity be averted by a change of government or action? Therefore, a cold and fever cannot be cured but with medicine, and the fluid of the "Millet Valley" cannot be transformed but with music.

When Yao was visited with the Great Flood, he ordered Yil to regulate it. Cold and heat are essentially the same as the Great Flood. Yao did not change his administration or conduct, being well aware that the Great Flood was not the result of government or conduct. Since the Flood was not brought about by government or conduct, we know that heat and cold cannot be caused by government either.

Some one might in disproof quote from the "Various Verifications" of the Himg-fan which says that "excitement is as a rule accompanied by cold, and cheerfulness by tepidity." Accompanied means: followed, tepidity: warmth, and "as a rule:" always. When the sovereign is excited, cold weather always follows, when he is cheerful, warm weather follows. Cold and heat correspond to excitement and cheerfulness, how can their connexion with the government be denied? Does the Classic say that excitement causes no cold, and cheerfulness no warmth?

The sovereign being excited or cheerful, cold or heat set in, but by chance and of their own accord. If they corresponded intentionally, it would be like the obtaining of omens by divining with shells, or like the finding of numbers by telling the fortune from straws. People pretend that heaven and earth respond to the questions addressed to them, but, as a matter of fact, it is nothing but chance. Heat and cold respond to excitement and cheerfulness, as omens and numbers are the response to the in They are all natural phenomena.
2 Shaking, thing-fan Pt.V, Bk. IV, 31 (Legge Vol. III, Pt. II, p. 340). quiries of the diviners. Externally they seem to respond, but actually it is hazard. How can we prove that?
The principle of heaven is spontaneity. Spontaneity means absence of purpose. When the two kinds of divination are applied, things may meet eventually, or happen by accident, and perhaps coincide with human affairs. The heavenly fluid is there already, therefore one may speak of a principle. Should it correspond to government, however, there would be no more spontaneity.
Clang has distributed the 64 symbols of the Yiking over one year. One symbol rules over 6 days and /. The symbols consist of Yin and Yang. The fluid rises and falls. When the Yang fluid rises, it becomes warm, and, when the Yin fluid rises, it becomes cold. According to this theory heat and cold depend on the symbols, but do not correspond to government. In accordance with the "wu-wang" symbol of the Yiking, inundations and droughts have fixed times. All the innumerable calamities and disasters are of the same kind.
I am afraid that the p'henomenalists have missed the truth for the following reason:—"The ideal man is endowed with the same virtue as heaven and earth. When man takes the lead, heaven does not disagree with him, and when he follows heaven, he respects heaven's time." The Hung-fan on the other hand says that "excitement is as a rule accompanied by cold, and cheerfulness by

tepidity." According to this passage of the *Hung-fan* the heavenly fluid follows man. The *Yiking* however only says that, when man takes the lead, heaven does not disagree with him. But why does it add that, when he follows heaven, he respects heaven's time? To follow means that heaven was already cold or hot before, and that man followed with bis rewards and punishments afterwards. This statement of men does not agree with the *Shuking*. That is my first doubt.

Ching determines heat and cold by the *Yin* and the *Yang* fluids ascending and descending, whereas the phenomenalists lay all the stress on punishments, joy and anger. The two schools walk different ways. That is my second doubt.

When people determine heat and cold, it may be cold to-day, and warm to-morrow, or at dawn there is plenty of hoarfrost, *Ching Fang,* a metaphysician of the 1st cent. B.c., who spent much labour on the elucidation of the *Yiking.* Marked by broken and unbroken lines. The 25th hexagram of the *Yiking.* Quotation from the *Yiking,* 1st diagram *(Ch'ien).* Cf. pp. 98 and 128. and in the evening resplendent light, or one morning is rainy, but warm, and another bright and cold. Now rain is *Yin,* and brightness *Yang,* and conversely cold is *Yin,* and warmth is *Yang.* A rainy day may clear up, and become cold, and a bright day become rainy, and warm. The categories do not correspond correctly. That is my third doubt.

These three doubts are not set at rest, and the principle of spontaneity is not upheld either.

CHAPTER XXII.

On Thunder and Lightning *(Lei-hsu).*

In midsummer thunder and lightning rapidly following each other, split trees, demolish houses, and occasionally kill men. Common people arc of opinion that, when the lightning strikes a tree, or demolishes a house, Heaven fetches a dragon, whereas, when a man is killed, they say that it is for his hidden faults. If in eating and drinking people use impure things, Heaven becomes angry, and strikes them dead. The deep rolling sound is the expression of Heaven's anger like the breathing and gasping of angry men. Every one, no matter whether intelligent or stupid, says so. But if we look into the matter, taking human nature as a basis, we find that all this is nonsense.

By a thunder-stroke one fluid is set in motion, and one sound produced. A tree is hit, and a dwelling damaged, and at the same time a man may be killed. When a man is slain, a tree may be struck, and a house damaged also. But they assert that, when a tree is struck, and a house damaged, Heaven fetches a dragon, whereas, when it kills a man, it punishes him for his hidden guilt. In that case something inauspicious would clash with the auspicious fetching of the dragon. That both things should happen at the same moment, and with the same sound, would not be proper.

It has been argued that the rolling is the sound of Heaven's growling. That would be appropriate for the punishment of the guilty, but out of place for fetching dragons. In meting out punishment, Heaven may be angry, but, when it fetches a dragon, what fault has it, that it should be irritated like that? Provided that the dragon be a spirit, then Heaven in fetching it, ought not to be angry. If, however, a dragon has faults, which are to be atoned for like those of man, Heaven would kill it, but why must it still fetch it? While destroying a man, Heaven may be in wrath, but, when it fetches a dragon, what wrong has the dragon done, that Heaven should be so enraged at it? Having smitten a man, Heaven does not fetch him. If under the same circumstances it The same force destroys the tree, the house, and the man.

The dragon is accounted a sacred animal.

does so with a dragon, what difference is there between human guilt and that of dragons? If both are put to death, where does a difference come in? We can no more accept the assertion that Heaven fetches dragons, than approve of the idea that the guilty meet with their dues for the following reasons:

When the thunder instantaneously follows upon the lightning, and a man falls to the ground dead, the rolling sound is close above his head, which brings about his death. But is the rolling really Heaven's anger? If so, in its wrath, it would kill a man by the angry breath of its mouth. But how can the angry breath of a mouth kill a man? Ou examining the body of a man, who has been struck by a thunderbolt, one discovers traces of burning. Provided that Heaven used its mouth in its anger, could its angry breath become fiery then?

Moreover, the mouth is connected with the body, and its movements must be the same as those of the body. When lightning strikes, the sound is on the earth, and, when the work of destruction is done, it is again in the sky. Now, the moment, when the sound is on the earth, the mouth must approach it, and the body do the same. But, if at a thunder-clap we look up to Heaven, we do not see it descending. Since we do not see it come down, the rolling sound cannot be the expression of Heaven's anger.

Heaven's anger cannot be different from that of man. When an angry person comes near anybody, his voice sounds loud, when he is for off, his voice seems low. Now, Heaven's voice is near, but its body far away. Therefore, anger is out of the question.

When the peals of thunder rapidly succeed one another, the sound may be in the East, the West, the North or the South. Provided that Heaven be angry and move its body, then, if its mouth is in an eastern, western, northern, or southern direction, looking up we ought to see Heaven in one of these directions likewise.

Some one might object that Heaven really was in one of these directions, but could not be seen by man owing to the obscurity, caused by the clouds and the rain. Yet over a distance of a thousand Li there are not the same winds, and within a hundred Li there is not the same tempest. As the *Yiking* has it:—"A hundred Li are frightened by the concussion."[1] The region where the thunderstorm is raging, is darkened by the thunder-clouds and the rain, but beyond

a hundred Li, where no rain is falling, one ought to *Yiking* Book V, *Chen* Hexagram (No. 51).
see Heaven moving eastward, westward, north-or southward. The mouth heing joined to Heaven, Heaven must follow it. Whenever the mouth moves, the entire Heaven must shift its place also, and it is not only where the tempest rages, that Heaven follows the movements of its mouth.

Aud who is it, whom we helieve to be angry? The Spirit of Heaven or the dark blue sky? If we say, the Spirit of Heaven, an angry spirit can give no sound, and, if we say, the dark blue sky, its body cannot become angry, for anger requires a mouth.

Heaven and Earth are like husband and wife, they are father and mother of mankind. Now, let a son have committed a fault, and his father in a fit of passion beat him to death, would not his mother weep for him? When Heaven in its wrath slays a man, Earth ought also to cry over him, but one only hears of Heaven's anger, and never of Earth's crying. If Earth cannot shed tears, Heaven cannot be angry either.

Furthermore, anger must have its counterpart in joy. Men have hidden faults, but they have also latent virtues. Hidden faults in a man call forth Heaven's anger, which prompts it to kill him, but in case of latent virtues Heaven ought also to requite him with good. If the rolling sound is regarded as an expression of Heaven's anger. Heaven, when pleased, ought to give a hearty laugh.

Men are pleased or angry, therefore the same is said of Heaven. We try to get a conception of Heaven by ascribing human qualities to it. The source of this knowledge of Heaven is man. If man would feel no anger, there is no reason either, why Heaven should. Since our knowledge of Heaven is derived from that of man, human nature in its entirety must be taken as basis. A man, when angry, breathes heavily, when pleased, he sings and laughs. We much less often hear of Heaven's joy, than of its anger, and much more seldom see it reward, than punish. Is Heaven always irritated

and never content? Does it mete out punishment pretty freely, but is rather sparing of its rewards? How does its anger and vindictiveness become manifest, whereas there are no instances of its joy and liberality?

When lightning strikes, it hits a tree, damages a house, and eventually kills a man. This is looked upon as Heaven's anger. But not unfrequently a thunderclap is without elleet, causing no damage, and destroying no human life. Does Heaven in such a case indulge in useless anger? A sovereign's joy and anger are not in vain. Being pleased or angry, he will certainly reward or punish. Useless anger without punishment would be unbecoming in Heaven.. Doing something unseeming, it would lose its dignity thereby. That is not Heaven's way.

The writers on government hold that cold and heat coincide with joy and anger. When the sovereign is pleased, ths weather is mild, when he is angry, it is cold. Then on the day of a thunderstorm the temperature ought to be cold.

Before *Han Kao Tsu* was boru. Dame *Liu* while sleeping on the banks of a big pond had intercourse with a spirit in her dream. At that time there was thunder and lightning, and a great darkness. Heaven was just then emitting its fluid, and ought to have been pleased, why was it irritated and thundering?

If striking and breaking is construed as a sign of Heaven's anger, and not striking or breaking as a sign of Heaven's joy, the rolling noise would not be appropriate in both cases. Man expresses joy and anger by different sounds, if Heaven used the same sound for two different purposes, there would be a fundamental difference between him and man. From what circumstance then could we infer Heaven's anger?

To give other persons impure things to eat is a small offence. For Heaven to chastise such small offenders in person with its own most precious body, would be derogatory to its majesty. Exalted persons do not punish personally, therefore does the emperor not execute the criminals with his own hand. Heaven is more exalted than the emperor. If it punished small misdemeanours itself,

its virtue would be inferior to that of the emperor.

Heaven's sentiments must be similar to man's feelings. When a prince punishes the wicked, he upon first hearing of their crime, becomes furious and condems them, but when it comes to taking their lives, he commiserates and pities them. Therefore the *Analects* say "When you have found out the truth, be grieved and pity them, and do not feel joy. " *Chou* was utterly depraved, yet, when *Wu Wang* was going to put him to death, he deplored and pitied him. Thus in the *Shuking* he says:—" I commanded the wild tribes, but I am sorry for you." A sovereign puts the bad to death. The mother of the emperor *Kao Tsu.* Cf. p. 177. Heaven as a spirit was just then engendering *Han Kao Tsu,* the Son of Heaven. In the case of joy as well as of anger. *Analects* XIX, 19. The criminal judge *Yang Fu* having consulted the philosopher *Tseng Tse* on the duties of his office, the latter advised him to pity the offenders, whose misdeeds were perhaps a consequence of bad administration. This passage is not to be found in our text of the *Shuking.* but with a feeling of commiseration, whereas Heaven in punishing misdemeanours, strikes people dead in its rage. Thus Heaven would be less merciful than man.

Rain is believed to be a fluid emitted by Heaven. Put forth by Heaven, it becomes moistened, and gives the rain. When the rain saturates everything, one speaks of timely showers. Unless he be in good humour, man does not show kindness, and unless it be pleased, Heaven does not pour down rain. If thunder be taken for an expression of Heaven's anger, then rain must be a sign of its joy. When there is thunder, it is always accompanied by rain. One must suppose, therefore, that Heaven is at the same time grumbling and laughing. A sovereign does not mete out rewards and punishments on the same day. Should Heaven's anger and joy coincide in time, Heaven and man would not be in harmony, and their ways of rewarding and punishing quite different. Moreover, anger and joy are both fitful.

To fly into a fit of passion out of disgust at man's conduct, to punish him for his offence, and, in doing so, to be guided by passion, would be unwortly of Heaven.

Regarding a thunderstorm in winter, people assert that the *Yang* fluid has lost its force. When it thunders in spring, they say, it comes out, but when there is a tempest in summer, instead of owning that then the fluid has its greatest force, they speak of Heaven's anger. Of course that is nothing but idle talk.

Man is a creature between Heaven and Earth. Other creatures are likewise creatures. What other creatures eat and drink, Heaven does not know, and it should be aware of what man eats and drinks? All beings are to Heaven like children. The kindness and love of father and mother to all their children are the same. Why then does Heaven watch the nobler and more intelligent being so closely, but takes no heed of the humbler and less gifted ones? Why does it pry into all that man does, but ignores other creatures?

Dogs and pigs eat human excrements, yet Heaven does not kill them for that. Provided that Heaven restricts only man on account of his superiority, then, if rats contaminate his drink or food, and man unwittingly eat it by mistake, Heaven does not destroy the rats. If Heaven can pardon the rats, it can do the same for man. Man may by mistake give others impure things to eat, and those unaware of it, may eat them. But they will never offer rotten things on purpose. Should they do so, the others would not take them.

The Empress *Lil Hou* cut off Lady *Ch'i's* hands, tore out her eyes, and placed her in a privy as a human swine. Then she called people, and showed them her victim. All felt sick at heart. When the emperor *Hui Ti* saw her, he fell sick, and did not rise again. *Lil Hou* acted on purpose, but Heaven did not punish her. If on the other hand Heaven strikes people dead for a mere inadvertence without mercy or regard for the faults, its government is tyrannical.

When men eat something impure, they do not discover it by the taste. If

they feel it, after having swallowed it, they call it a pollution of their bowels. When Lady *Ch'i* was put into the cesspool, her whole body was disgracefully soiled, which is nothing else than impurity, for the body does not differ from the bowels. To care for the intestines, but disregard the body, to resent impurity, but not to feel the afore-mentioned horrible disgrace, would not be like Heaven.

The news that anybody has eaten something unclean does not disturb people's minds, whereas all that saw Lady *Ch'i* felt sick at heart. Man being hurt, Heaven must feel pity too. Commiserating Lady *Ch'i*, it must hate *Lil Hou*. Notwithstanding, when *Lil Hou* died, she was not struck by a thunderbolt.

The Taoist *Liu Ch'un* made a fool of the king of *Ch'u, Ying,* and caused him to eat some dirty stuff. *Liu Ch'un* died later on, but it needed no lightning to make him die.

In the 6th month of summer of the year 79 A.d. *Chin Chuan* of *K'uei-chi* was killed by lightning. Of the sheep which he used for his daily meals, five died together with him. What hidden faults had these animals, that the lightning killed them?

Boatmen sometimes pollute a stream up-river, while other people drink its water down-river. Yet the boatmen do not die by lightning.

The Spirit of Heaven dwells in heaven just as a king in his residence. A king lives behind many gates, therefore the Spirit of The first wife of *Han Kao Tsu,* who usurped the imperial power, and reigned under her own name against all custom from 187-179 B.c. Her son, the Emperor *Hui Ti,* whose nominal reign lasted from 194-187 B.c., was nothing but a puppet in her hands. *Lii Hou* was a fiend in human shape, who had always some poison ready for her enemies. One of her first acts, after she came to power, was to wreak her vengeance on her rival, Lady *Ch'i,* a concubine of *Han Kao Tm,* who had attempted to have her own son made heir-apparent in place of *Hui Ti,* the son of *Lii Hon. Hui Ti,* a very kind-hearted, but weak sovereign did all

in his power to shield his half-brother from the wrath of his mother, who poisoned him all the same.

This story is abridged from the *Shi-chi* chap. 9, p. 3. A city in *Chekiang.*

Heaven must stay in some secluded place likewise. As the king has his palaces and halls, Heaven also has the *T'ai-tcei, Tse-kung, ILilanyuan* and *Winchang* mansions.

A king being far away from men does not know their occult crimes. How could the Spirit of Heaven in his four palaces see the secret misdeeds of men? If a king hears of the faults of his subjects, he learns it through others. If Heaven becomes cognizant of the crimes of men, it must have it from its angels. In case the spirits are Heaven's informants as to crimes, it must also entrust the spirits with retributive justice. Such being the case, the so-called auger of Heaven is not that of Heaven, but of the spirits.

A king inflicts capital punishment in autumn, Heaven kills in summer. Thus the king in meting out justice, does not observe the time of Heaven. As Heaven's anointed he should in executions also imitate the example of majestic Heaven. Heaven chooses summer for killing, whereas the king executes in autumn. Heaven and man are thus at variance, which would never do for Heaven's deputy.

Some people will argue that giving impure things to eat or drink is a great crime before Heaven, which in killing the culprit does not pay attention to time. Great crimes in the eyes of kings are high-treason, rebellion, and lawlessness, whereas Heaven considers the offering of unclean things to others as food or drink as a serious offence. The crimes condemned by Heaven are of different gravity. Were the light and the serious ones all equally dealt with, the king would have to imitate Heaven's government, and put to death every one, who had given others unclean things to eat or drink. When the holy emperors were ruling, they had not such a penalty. That would mean that the holy emperors were remiss, and had forgotten this punishment.

It may be said that the ghosts have power over what is secret, and that a king's sway extends over what is public only. Secret faults are wrapt in darkness and invisible to man, therefore spirits must be employed to watch over them. I reply, there being Names of constellations.

In China the regular executions take place in autumn. It destroys the guilty on the spot, and does not delay judgment until autumn. A *deduclio ad ahsurdum* from a Chinese point of view, for the holy emperors, *Yao, Shun,* and the like, were perfect, and could not have omitted to punish serious misdeeds. not only one secret fault, why are not all the offenders put to death? To fix upon one single offence would not be a just retribution for hidden sins.

Heaven vents its anger, before the sun returns, and an outburst of human ire takes less than the time one needs to turn round upon one's heels. However, secret crimes of men often become manifest in winter and not exclusively in summer. If he who misconducts himself in winter, is not struck by thunder forthwith, but must wait till summer, Heaven's wrath cannot be quicker than a revolution of the sun.

When painters represent the thunder, it is like so many joined drums, heaped together. They also paint a man having the semblance of an athlete and call him "the Thunderer" *(Lei Kung).* With his left hand they give him joined drums to pull, in his right hand he brandishes a hammer, as though he were going to strike. It means that the rolling sound of thunder is produced by the knocking together of the united drums, and that the sudden crashing noise is the blow of the hammer. When a man is killed, he is struck with the drums and the hammer at the same time.

People also believe in this, and nobody objects. But if we get at the bottom of it, we find that these pictures are pure fictions. Thunder is either a sound or a fluid. How can a sound or a fluid brandish a hammer, or rmll drums, and have the shape of joined drums? If the thunder can really swing or pull these things, it must be a creature. That which, when knocked together, produces sounds, can be either a drum or a bell. Should the rolling sound be produced by drums or bells? In that case, bells and drums could not hang free in the air, they would require a frame with vertical and cross-beams. Suspended between, they could be sounded. Now, the bells and drums have nothing to hang upon, and the feet of the Thunderer nothing to walk upon, how then should the thunder be produced?

Somebody might object that for this very reason there must be a spirit, for, if in order to produce thunder a frame were required, or a support for the feet, it would be quite human, and by no means spirit-like.

I hold that spirits are diffuse and incorporeal. Departing or coming in they need no aperture, nor have they any hold above or below. Therefore one calls them spirits. Now the Thunderer has a body, and for the thunder there are instruments, how can he be

This seems to be an old adage. deemed a spirit? If the Thunderer were incorporeal, his semblance could not be drawn, and, if he possesses a body, he does not deserve the name of a spirit.

People talk of the dragon spirit rising to heaven. But whoever thoroughly examines the question, discredits this idea. Men sometimes see the shape of a dragon, and owing to this circumstance they paint the shape of a dragon rising to heaven. The best proof that, as a fact, there is no spirit is, that it can be pictorially represented.

My opponents will argue: "Men also see apparitions of ghosts. Are they not spirits?" I say: "If men see ghosts sometimes, has anybody already seen the Thunderer? Ghosts are called spirits, but they walk about on earth like men. The Thunderer, however, does not rest his head in heaven, nor walk on earth with his feet. How can he, therefore, be a thunderer?"

All flying creatures have wings. Those who can fly without wings are styled genii. In representing the forms of genii men give them wings. Provided the Thunderer is like the genii, he ought to have wings equally. If, in case the Thunderer does not fly, the painters pretend that he can fly, they are wrong, and if he really could fly, but had no wings, it would be wrong likewise. Thus the pictures of the Thunderer's outward appearance, made by painters, are merely fancy work.

Those who argue about thunder aver that it is Heaven's angry snorting, whereas those who sketch it, contend that the Thunderer in his anger pulls the joined drums. If it is really as the critics say, the painters are wrong, and if they are right, the critics must be in error. The two classes are antagonistic. If both their views were taken as genuine, there would he no difference of right and wrong, and in default of that, no real right and wrong. Doubts would not be settled, and fallacies would triumph.

The *Liki* speaks of a goblet with the thunder carved upon it. One thunder rushes forth, the other reverts, one is coiled up, the other stretched forth. Their friction would give a sound. They look as if they were colliding, piled up in a grotesque and phantastic way. This form represents the thunder. When through friction the air breaks, there is a rolling sound, the sound of friction. Neither the *Liki* nor the *Chou-ti* contains such a passage, as far as I could make out. On the old sacrificial bronze vases, called *tsim* = goblets, clouds and thunders i. *e.* coiled up clouds were represented. The thunder ornament is the Chinese Meander. Specimens of these goblets can be seen in the *I'o-ku-fu-lu* chap. 7. A sudden crash is the sound of the shooting forth of the air. When this shooting air hits a man, he dies.

In fact thunder is nothing else than the exploding solar fluid. How do we know?—In the first month the *Yang* fluid begins to be roused, consequently we have the first thunder during the first moon. In the fifth month *Yang* is at its cynosure, therefore at that time thunder rapidly follows upon thunder. In autumn and winter *Yang* declines, therefore thunder ceases during these seasons. In the midst of summer the sun reigns supreme, but the *Yin* fluid endeavours to get the upperhand. In this dispute of the *Yang* and the *Yin* fluids it comes to frictions, and these frictions lead to explosions and shooting, which are destructive. A man struck by these forces is killed, a tree split, and a house demolished. A person under a tree or in a house may also by chance be hit and killed.

To test the justness of this statement take a basin full of water, and throw it on a fire, used for melting purposes. The vapour will explode with a puff like the sound of thunder. Should any one be too near, his body will be burned. Heaven and earth are like a great furnace, the *Yang* fluid is an immense fire, clouds and rain are huge masses of water. When they struggle, explode and shoot, the effects must be most violent, and a man hit and injured cannot but die.

When founders melt iron, they make a mould of earth, into which the liquid iron runs down. Else it bursts out, flows over, and spurts. Hitting a man's body, it burns his skin. The fiery *Yang* fluid is not only as hot as liquid iron, the exploding *Yin* fluid has not merely the wetness of earth and clay, und when the *Yang* fluid hits a man, it does not simply cause the pain of burning.

Thunder is fire. A man burned by this fluid must show traces of it. If those traces of burning look like written characters, people seeing them use to say that Heaven has written the man's guilt to make it known to the whole world. This is also unreasonable.

If Heaven destroys men with its thunder, after they have perpetrated their misdeeds, he ought to make their wickedness quite public, with a view to frightening for the future, and write the characters clearly, but not quite indistinctly, as it does. When the "Plan" came out of the Yellow River, and the "Scroll" emerged from The "Plan" appeared to the Emperor *Huang Ti* in the Yellow River. A big fish carried it on its back. *Huang Ti* received the Plan, which consisted of a combination of symbolical lines and diagrams like the *Pa-kua*. the *Lo*, Heaven and Earth produced them for men to read and take note of. The writing on people killed by thunder is also Heaven's work. Why is it so dif-

ficult to understand?

Let us assume that the human skin is not fit to be written upon. The wife of Duke *Hut* of *Lu*, *Ch'ung Tse* was daughter to Duke *Wu* of *Sung*. When she was born, she had a writing on her palm to the effect that she was to be duchess of *Lu*. The writing was distinct and intelligible. Therefore *Ch'ung Tse* was married to *Lu*. The thunder's handwriting not being clear, it cannot serve as a deterrent for the future. Ergo the burnt spots are not characters engraved by Heaven.

Sometimes people exaggerate things that really exist, sometimes they invent things that have no real basis at all. Imposed upon by fallacies, they indulge in fabricating wonders and miracles as the following arguments will prove:—

I. Thunder is fire. When a man dies struck by thunder, one discovers upon examining his body, if the head be hit, that the hair is singed, and if the body be struck, that the skin is charred. Coming near the body, one scents the smell of burning. 2. Taoist experimentalists hold that a stone heated by a thunder-clap, becomes red. If it be thrown into a well, the stone being burning hot, the well cool, an explosion ensues with a loud detonation like thunder. 3. When somebody takes cold, the cold fluid enters his stomach. The stomach being as a rule warm within, the warmth and the cold struggle together, and the exploding air gives a thunder-like sound. 4. In a thunder-storm brilliant lightnings appear every now and then like the glares of big fires. 5. When the lightning strikes, it often burns man's houses and buildings, or grass and trees.

Those who declare thunder to be fire have these five arguments, those who prentend that thunder is Heaven's anger, not a single one. Therefore this latter assertion is without any foundation.

However, it might be objected that there is a passage in the *Analects* to the effect that, when thunder followed thunder, and the storm raged, *Confucius* used to be deeply impressed. The *Liki* says, The "Scroll" was curried by a dragon-horse, which rose from the wa-

ters of the *Lo*, a tributary of the Yellow River, at *Fu Hat's* time. From the mystic signs on this "Scroll" the emperor is reported to have derived the Eight Diagrams and the first system of written characters, which took the place of the knotted cords, quipos, then in use.

767-721 B.c. 764-746 B.c. Quoted from *Analects* X, 16.

"when a strong wind blows, and the thunder-claps quickly follow each other, and rain falls in torrents, a superior man will be deeply moved. Though it be night, he will rise, don his clothes and cap, and sit up " in awe of Heaven's anger, fearing lest its punishment should reach him. If thunder were not the expression of Heaven's anger, nor its striking a punishment of the guilty, why should a good man be frightened by thunder, put on his official robe, and sit straight?

The Master means that the relation of Heaven to man is similar to that of father and son. The father being moved, the son canuot remain indifferent. Therefore, when Heaven is moved, man must be likewise. Being in harmony with Heaven, he proves that he does not act in opposition to it.

Man suddenly hearing a dog bark outside the house, will be startled, and with trembling limbs barken to find out, what it means. How much more so, when he hears Heaven assuming an extraordinary voice like the noise made by the quick rolling of heavy carts!

The remark in the *Analects* and the observation of the *Liki* both refer to the wise man. The wise man displays the utmost care in all his doings and knows that he has no guilt, just like sun and moon, which, when eclipsed, have not clandestinely given impure food to men. Examining his heart, he feels no fear, wherefore should he be afraid of thunder? If he is not afraid, his excitement can be no proof of Heaven's anger, because he fears nothing for himself. Should he really be afraid of thunder, even that would not suffice to prove the punishment of hidden crimes, for people struck by lightning are mostly quite innocent. The wise man apprehends that he might be hit by chance. Therefore he is anxious and alarmed. But this alarm of the wise man cannot be put forward to demonstrate that thunder is Heaven's anger. It shows, on the contrary, that thunder strikes at random. Because it hits at random, and does not punish the guilty, people are afraid. If thunder actually punished the guilty, the wicked ought to stand in awe, and the wise had no cause for apprehensions.

The king of *Sung* asked *Tang Yang* saying "I have killed a great number of people, yet all the officials are still quite fearless. What is the reason?" *T'ang Yang* replied:—" Those that Your Highness has punished were exclusively bad characters. If the bad are called to account, Quoted from the *Liki* Book VI *Tu-tsao (Legge,* Sacred Books Vol. XXVIII, p. 5).

Confucius in the passage quoted from the *Analects.* why should the good be frightened? If Your Highness wishes all the officials to be in awe, the best way is to make no distinction between good and bad, and chastise them all occasionally. Then all the officialdom will be afraid."

The king followed his advice, and all the functionaries became frightened, whereupon the king of *Sung* turned very angry. Owing to the indiscriminate punishments of the king of *Sung,* the whole people of *Sung* got greatly alarmed. Because thunder and lightning strike indiscriminately, a wise man becomes agitated. His alarm is like the great fright of the kingdom of *Sung.* Quoted from *Hmn Tee.* CHAPTER XXIII.

On Poison *(Yen-tu).*

Sometimes the following question is considered:—Between heaven and earth there are the ten thousand heings with their characteristic nature. In the animal kingdom we find adders and vipers, bees and scorpions, which are poisonous. When their bite or sting has hurt a human body, the sickness which they cause must be most carefully treated, for without timely help, the virus spreads through the whole body. In the vegetable kingdom we have croton oil beans and wild dolichos, which, when eaten, cause a stomach-ache, and in large doses kill a man. What manner of fluid have these created beings received from heaven? The ten thousand beings, when created, are endowed with the original fluid. Is there any poison in the original fluid?

Poison is the hot air of the sun; when it touches a man, he becomes empoisoned. If we eat something which causes us such a pain in the stomach, that we cannot endure it, that which proves so unendurable is called poison. The fiery air of the sun regularly produces poison. This air is hot. The people living in the land of the sun are impetuous. The mouths and tongues of these impetuous people become venomous. Thus the inhabitants of *Ch'u* and *Yileh* are impetuous and passionate. When they talk with others, and a drop of their saliva happens to fly against their interlocutors, the arteries of the latter begin to swell and ulcerate.

The *Sm1thirn Circuit* is a very hot region. When the people there curse a tree, it withers, and, when they spit upon a bird, it drops down. Wizards are all able to make people ill by their prayers as well as to avert their misfortunes. They hail from *Kiang-nan,* and are imbued with the hot fluid. Poison is the fluid of the sun, therefore it burns like fire, when somebody is aspersed by it. When people bitten by a viper cut out the flesh, as some *Hukuang* and *Chekiang. Hapei.* The country south of the *Yangtse,* now the provinces *Kiong-su, Kiangsi,* and *Anhui.* times they do, and put it on the ground, it burns and bubbles up, which shows that there is a hot fluid in it. At the four cardinal points are border-lands, but the south-eastern corner alone has broiling hot air, which always comes forth in Spring and Summer. In Spring and Summer the sun rises in the south-eastern corner, wbich is the proper sphere of the sun.

When the air of other things enters into our nose or eyes, they do not feel pain, but as soon as fire or smoke enter into our nose, it aches, and, when they enter into our eyes, they pain us. This is the burning of the hot air. Many substances can be dissolved, but it is only by burning fire that they are scorched.

Eating sweets is not injurious to man, but, when for instance he takes a little too much honey, he has symptoms of poisoning. Honey is a secretion of the bee, and the bee is an insect belonging to the *Yang* fluid.

If a man without having hurt himself against anything in his movements feels a sudden pain in his body, for which there is no apparent reason, and if those parts of his body which pain him show marks of flogging so to speak, he suffers from lumbago. This lumbago, they say, is caused by devils who are beating the person. Devils are supernatural apparitions produced by the sun. If the disease be less acute, one calls it sciatica, and uses honey and cinnabar to cure it Honey and cinnabar are substances belonging to the *Yang* fluid. This cure is homeopathic. As an antidote against a cold one uses cold, and against fever one uses heat. Since to cure sciatica they take honey and cinnabar, it shows us that sciatica is the effect of the *Yang* fluid and of the diffusion of a poison.

Poisonous air is floating between heaven and earth. When a man comes into touch with it, his face begins to swell, a disease which people call a su-ru-stroke.

Men who have seen ghosts, state that they have a red colour. The supernatural force of the sun must, of course, have this colour. Ghosts are burning poison; the man whom they assault, must die. Thus did Earl *Tu* shoot King *Hsuan* of *Chou* dead. The paraphernalia of these demons of death are like the fire of the sun. The bow as well as the arrow of *Tu Po* were both red. In the south they term poison "small fox." The apparition of Earl *Tu* had a bow in his hand, with which he shot. The solar fluid was kindled simultaneously, and, when it was thus intensified, it shot.

Therefore, when he hit the king, he seemed provided with bow and arrow.

When heat is pent up, and the temperature increased, the poison in the blood is stirred up. Therefore eating the liver of a race horse will cause a man's death, the fluid pent up in the liver having been chafed. During the dog-days, when a scorching heat prevails, people die by insolation; the extreme heat has been turned into poison. We perspire, while running, near a stove, in the sunshine at noon, and, when we are feverish. The four causes have been different, but they all engender perspiration. The heat is the same, and it has been equally pent up.

Fire is a phenomenon of the sun. All created beings of the world are filled with the solar fluid and after their creation contain some poison. Reptiles and insects possessing this poison in abundance become vipers and adders, bees and scorpions, plants become croton seeds and wild dolichos, fishes become porpoises and "*toshu*" fish. Consequently men eating a porpoise liver die, and the bite of a "*to-shu*" is venomous. Fishes and birds are related, therefore birds can fly, and fishes too; birds lay eggs, and fishes also. Vipers, adders, bees, and scorpions are all oviparous and have a similar nature.

Among mankind bad characters take the place of these creatures. Their mouths do mischief. The bad men of the world are imbued with a poisonous fluid. The poison of the wicked living in the land of the sun is still more virulent, hence the curses and the swearing of the people of southern *Yileh* produce such wonderful results.

A proverb says, "Many mouths melt metal." The mouth is fire. Fire is the second of the five elements, and speech the second of the five actions. There is an exact correspondence between speech and fire, therefore in speaking of the melting of metal one says that the mouth and the tongue melt it. They do not speak of pulling out wood and burning it, but expressly refer to the melting of metal. Metal is overcome by fire, fire and mouth belong to the same class.

Medicinal herbs do not grow in one place only. *T'ai Po* left his country and went to *Wu*. The melting of metal does not take *Kang-hi* quotes this passage, but does not say what kind of a fish the "*io-ehu*" jj J£ SjjjjJ is. It may be a variety of the *ska*, which seems to be a kind of sturgeon.

Cf. *Shuking (Hung-fan)* Pt. V, Bk. IV, 5-6. Another instance of Chinese symbolism, which they mistake for science.

Cf. p. 120. place in one foundry alone. People speak very much of *T'ang-chi* in *Ch'u.* The warm air on earth has its regions. One dreads to go into the southern sea, for the secretary falcon lives in the south, and he who drinks anything that has been in contact with it, must die. *Shin* appertains to the dragon and *sse* to the snake. *Shin* and *sse* are placed in the south-east. The dragon is poisonous, and the snake venomous, therefore vipers are provided with sharp teeth, and dragons with an indented crust. Wood engenders fire, and fire becomes poison. Hence the "Green Dragon" holds the "Fire Star" in its mouth.

Wild dolichos and croton seed both contain poison, therefore the dolichos grows in the south-east, and croton in the south-west. The frequence of poisonous things depends on the dryness and the humidity of the soil, and the strength of the poison is influenced by the locality, where they have grown. Snakes are like fish, therefore they grow in the grass and in marshes. Bees and scorpions resemble birds and are born in houses and on trees. In *Kiang-pei5* the land is dry; consequently bees and scorpions abound there. In *Kiang-nan* the soil is wet, hence it is a breeding place for great numbers of snakes.

Those creatures growing in high and dry places are like the male principle. The virile member hangs down, therefore bees and scorpions sting with their tails. The creatures living in low and wet places resemble the female principle. The female organ is soft and extensible, therefore snakes bite with their mouths. Poison is either concealed in the head or the tail, whence the bite or the sting becomes venomous, or under the epidermis so that the eating causes stomach-ache, or it lies hidden in the lips and the throat, so that the movement of the tongue does mischief. A place in *Honan* celebrated for its foundries. Vid. p. 377.

Chin ftjjij = secretary falcon has become a synonym for poison. The fifth and the sixth of the Twelve Branches (Duodenary Cycle of symbols). The "Green Dragon" is the quadrant or the

division of the 28 solar mansions occupying the east of the sky. The "Fire Star" is tho Planet *Mars. Mars* in the quadrant of the "Green Dragon" forebodes war i. *e.* poison; nothing but inane symbolism. (Cf. *Shi-chi* chap. 27, p. 6 v.) The country north of the *Yangtie,* now the northern parts of the provinces *Kiangsu* and *Anhui.* Which hang down likewise. Which are soft and extensible. —To such ineptitudes even the most elevated Chinese minds are led by their craze of symbolisation. The mischief done by the tongue in speaking, which is not only compared to, but identified with poison.

The various poisons are all grown from the same fluid, and however different their manifestations, internally they are the same. Hence, when a man dreams of fire, it is explained as altercation, and, when he sees snakes in his dreams, they also mean contention. Fire is an emblem of the mouth and the tongue; they appear in snakes likewise, which belong to the same class, have sprung from the same root, and are imbued with the same fluid. Thus fire is equivalent to speed, and speech to bad men. When bad men say strange things, it is at the instigation of their mouths and their tongues, and the utterances of mouth and tongue are provoked by the influence heaven has exercised upon the persons in question. Consequently the second of the five actions is called speech. "The objectionable manifestation of speech is presemptuous error, symbolized by constant sunshine." Presumptious error is extravagant and shining. In the same manner snakes are gaudily ornamented. All ornaments originate from the *Yang,* which produces them, as it were. Sunshine is followed by talk, which accounts for the weird songs so often heard.

The magical force engenders beauty, but the beautiful are very often vicious and depraved. The mother of *Shu Hu* was a beauty. *Shu Hsiang's* mother knew her, and would not allow her to go to the chamber of her husband. *Shu Hsiang* remonstrated. "In the depths of mountains and in vast marshes dragons and snakes really grow," said his mother. "She is beautiful, but I am afraid, lest she give birth to a dragon or a snake, which would bring mishap upon you. You are of a poor family. In the States great favours are sometimes given, but what can the recipient of such favours do, when he is being slandered by malicious people. How should I be jealous of her?"

She then allowed her to go to her husband's couch, and she begot a son, named *Shu Hu.* Owing to his beauty and hero-like strength *Shu Hu* became a favourite of *Luan Ihtai Tsef* however, *Shuking (Hang-fan)* Pt. V, Bk. IV, 34. Cf. p. 246 and above p. 300.

A half-brother of *Shu Hsiang.* His mother was a concubine of *Shu Hsiang's* father.

An officer of *Chin.* Being an exceptional woman by her beauty, she would give birth to an extraordinary son —a dragon, and it would be dangerous for an ordinary man like her son *Shu Hsiang* to be a blood relation of such an extraordinary person, since fate likes to strike the exalted. Quoted from the *Tso-chuan,* Duke *Hsiang,* 21st year (551 B. C.). when *Fan Hsilan Tse* expelled *Luan Huai Tie,* he killed *Shu Ilu,* and so brought misfortune upon *Shu Hsiang.*

The recesses of mountains and vast marshes are the places where dragons and snakes breed. *Shu Hus* mother was compared to them, for under her charms the poison lay hidden. She bore a son, *Shu* whose beauty consisted in his hero-like strength. This strength grew from his beauty, and the disaster came from his strength.

Fire has splendour, and wood has a pleasant appearance. Dragons and snakes correspond to the east. Wood contains the essence of fire, hence its beautiful colour and graceful appearance. The gall being joined to the liver, courage and strength are produced. The force of the fire is violent, hence the great courage; wood is hard and strong, hence the great strength. When there is any supernatural apparition produced, it is through beauty that it brings about misfortune, and through courage and strength that it injures like poison. All is owing to beauty.

Generous wine is a poison; one cannot drink much of it. The secretion of the bees becomes honey; one cannot eat much of it. A hero conquers an entire State, but it is better to keep aloof from him. Pretty women delight the eyes, but it is dangerous to keep them. Sophists are most interesting, but they can by no means be trusted. Nice tastes spoil the stomach, and pretty looks beguile the heart. Heroes cause disasters, and controversialists do great harm. These four classes are the poison of society, but the most virulent poison of all is that flowing from the mouths of the sophists.

When *Confucius* caught sight of *Yang Hu,* he retreated, and his perspiration trickled down, for *Yang Hu* was a glib-tongued man. The poison from a glib tongue makes a man sick. When a man has been poisoned, he dies alone, whereas a glib tongue ruins a whole State. Thus we read in the *Shiking:*—" Endless are the slanderous reports. They threw four States into confusion." Four States were thrown into confusion, how much more would be a single individual. Therefore a man does not fear a tiger, but dreads the calumniator's mouth, for his mouth contains the worst poison.

Two noblemen of *Chin,* cf. p. 206. A powerful, but unworthy officer in *La. Shikmg* Pt. II, Bk. VII, 5. Moder n commentators explain the expression JUJ jj as meaning "the four quarters of the empire." CHAPTER XXIV.

On Anthroposcopy *(Ku-hsiang).*

It is a common belief that fate is difficult to foresee. Far from it, it can easily be known, and by what means? By means of the body and its bones. As man derives his destiny from heaven, it becomes visible in his body. An inquiry into these manifestations leads to the knowledge of fate, just as from a look at measures one learns their capacity. By manifestations I understand the osseous configurations.

According to tradition *Huang Ti* had a dragon face, *Chuan Hsu* was marked with the character *Wu* on his brow, *Ti Ku* had a double tooth, *Yao's* eye-brows had eight colours, *Shuns* eyes double pupils, *Yii's* ears three orifices, *T'ang*

had double elbows, *Win Wang* four nipples, *Wu Wang's* spine was curbed backwards, *Chou Kung* was inclined to stoop forward, *Kao Yao* had a horse's mouth, *Confucius'* arms were turned backwards." These Twelve Sages either held the positions of emperors and kings, or they aided their sovereigns, being anxious for the welfare of the people. All the world knows this, and the scholars speak of it.

These reports being given in the Classics and Annals can be relied upon. The light literature, such as journals, letters, and memoirs which the Literati do not read, afford a great many more instances: *T'sang Hsieh* had four eyes and became one of *Huang Ti's* officials. *Chung Erh,* prince of *Chin,* had a double rib, aud became the foremost of all the feudal lords. *Su Ch'in* with a bone *Huang Ti, Chuan Hsu, Ti Ku, Yao, Shun,* and *Yii* are mythical or half legendary rulers of old China.

T'ang, Wen Wang, and *Wu Wang* are the founders of the *Shang* and *Chou* dynasties. *Tan,* Duke of *Chou,* a younger brother of Wu *Wang,* whom he helped to win the throne. A minister of *Shun.* Like the wings of a bird. *Ch'ung Erh* reigned as marquis of *Chin* from 634-626 B.c. A famous statesman who in 333 B.c. succeeded in forming a league of the Six States: *Yen, Chao, Han, Wei, Chi,* and *Ch'u* against *Ch'in.* on his nose obtained the premiership in all the Six Kingdoms. *Chang Yi* having a double rib was also made a minister in *Ch'in* and *Wei. Hsiang Yii,* who owing to his double pupils was regarded as a descendant of the Emperor *Shun,* shared the empire with *Kao Tsu. Ch'en P'ing,* a poor fellow who had not enough to eat and drink, had nevertheless a very fine appearance, which surprised every one so much, that they exclaimed: what on earth does *Chin Ping* eat to become such a portly man. *Han Hsin* was rescued from the axe of the executioner, when he caught the eye of the duke of *T'ing,* and was pardoned also on account of his extraordinary appearance. Fine looks and stateliness can be characteristics as well.4 *Kao Tsu* had a high nose, a dragon face, a fine beard and

72 black spots on his left leg. *Lil* from *Shan-fu* was skilled in prognosticating from looks. When he saw *Kao Tau's* carriage, he thought him very remarkable, and therefore gave him his own daughter, the later empress *Lil Hou,* to wife. Afterwards she gave birth to Prince *Hsiao Hui* and to the princess *Yuan* of *Lu. Kao Tsu* was first a headborough on the river *Sse.* Then he gave up his post, and took to farming, again living with *Lil Hou* and his two children on his farm, when an old man passed by, and asked for a drink. In return he divined *Lil Hou's* fate by her features saying: "Madam, you belong to the great folks of the empire." Called upon to foretell the fortune of her two children, he said in regard of *Hsiao Hui:* "The cause of your greatness, Madam, will be this son," and with respect to *Yuan* of *Lu:* "You are all noble." When the old man had left, *Kao Tsu* came home from abroad. Upon being informed by *Lil Hou* of what had taken place, he ran after the old man, and stopped him, wishing to hear his own fortune too. The old fellow rejoined: "Before, the lady and her children bore a resemblance to you in their looks, but A celebrated politician of the 4th century B.c., in early life a fellow-student of *Su Chin.* A partisan of the founder of the *Han* dynasty, *Kao Tsu,* one of the *Three Heroes,* who in early youth lived in great poverty and subsequently rose to the highest honours. Another adherent of *Han Kao Tsu,* also one of the Three Heroes, the third being *Chang Liang.* He was to be executed for treason, but was pardoned. As anomalous features. This passage occurs in the *Shi-chi* chap. 8, p. 2, which treats of *Han Kao Tu.* A place in *Shantung.* He succeeded his father *Kao Tsu* in 194 B.c. A river in *Shantung.*

Lun-Hcng. your mien is so grand, that words fail me to describe it." Afterwards the empire devolved upon *Kao Tsu,* as the old man had foretold.

If we draw a general principle from this, we find that members of the same family all show their nobility in their appearance. Belonging to the same caste and animated by a similar spirit, they must necessarily have some kindred traits in their mental and physical qualities. It however happens that two persons of different classes and incongruous minds meet together. A grandee, when marrying, gets a great lady for his wife, and a gentlewoman also finds a noble lord. If two individuals meet despite discrepancies of appearance, a sudden death ensues. In case they have not yet come into contact, one party is overtaken by death previously.

Wang Mang's aunt Lady *Cheng* was bespoken in marriage. When the moment came for her to go, the bridegroom suddenly died. The same thing happened a second time. Then she was given away to the Prince of *Chao,* but the Prince had not yet taken her, when he breathed his last. *Nan Kung Ta Yu* of *Ching-ho* met with Lady *Ching's* father, the Honourable *Chih,* with whom he was acquainted, and prognosticated her fate saying: "She is so exalted, that she will become the mother of the empire." At that time *Hsilan Ti* was emperor and *Yuan Ti* heir-apparent. Through the governor of the principality of *Wei, Chih* then gave her in marriage to the heir-apparent, who was very pleased with her, and became father to a sou of the name of *Chiin Shang.* At the death of *Hsilan Ti* the heir-apparent ascended the throne, Lady *Clmtg* was made empress, and *Chun Shang* heir-apparent. When *Yuan Ti* died, the heir-apparent assumed the reins of government and became the emperor *Cheng* 27, and Lady *Cheng* became empress-dowager and thus mother of the empire. Lady *Cheng* had something in her features indicative of her future imperial motherhood. The two men to whom she was betrothed first, and the Prince of *Chao* had no marks showing that they would be fathers of the empire, therefore the two died, before the marriage could take place, and the prince expired. The two *Jiantrs* and the Prince of *Chao* were not predestinated Tor imperial sway, and Lady *Cheng* was apparently no match for them. Cf. *Shi-chi loc. cit.* which slightly differs. A city in *Shantung; Play/air* No. 1642. 73-48 B.c.

48-32 B.c.

32-6 B.c.

The prime minister *Huang T'seKung,* who was originally a border warden in *Yang-hsia,* travelled with a soothsayer in the same carriage, when they perceived a woman seventeen or eighteen years old. The fortune-teller pointed to her and said:—"This woman will be raised to high honours, and become consort to a marquis." *Huang T' se Kung* stopped the carriage, and looked at her carefully. The fortune-teller said:—"If this woman will not become noble, my divination books are of no use." *Huang T se Kung* inquired about her, and learned that she was from the next village, a female belonging to the *Wu* family. Thereupon he married her, and afterwards really gained high honours, was given the post of a prime minister, and created a marquis. Since *Huang I" se Kung* won wealth and honour, his wife had to be on a par with him. Consequently, when they were brought together, they both became illustrious. Had *Huang T se Kung's* fate been mean, he would not have got that woman as a consort, and had they not tallied together as man and wife, they would have had the same misfortune as the two persons above mentioned and the Prince of *Chao.* If an entire family has a glorious destiny, then later on every thing turns to their honour and advantage, whereas in case of incongruity of osseous structure and physical shape they will be separated and die, and cannot enjoy great happiness long.

In noble families even servants and slaves as well as cattle and horses which they rear are not like the common ones. From the looks of the slaves one sees that they do not easily die. The cattle and horses often produce young. The seeds in the fields grow up luxuriantly, and quickly put forth ripe grains. In commerce those sort of people manage to get excellent merchandise, which sells without delay. Those who know fate, find out the great folks amidst low people, and discern the miserable among the magnates. Judging from the osseous structure and distinguishing the lines on the skin, they discover man's fate, which always confirms their predictions.

Viscount *Chien* of *Chao* bade *Ku Pu Tse Ch ing* tell the fortunes of his sons. He found none of them lucky, until he came to the son of the slave-girl *Choi, Wu Hsii,* whom he declared to be a peer. *Wu Hsi i* had an excellent character, and was stamped a *Huang T'se Kung* was prime minister of the emperor *Hsiian Ti,* died 51 B C. In *Honan.* A parallel passage occurs in the *Han-shu,* quoted in the *T'ai-p'ing yi-lan* 729 p. 4.

516-457 B.c. nobleman to boot. Later on Viscount *Chien* put the heir-apparent aside, and raised *Wu Hsil,* who afterwards became Viscount *Hsiang.*

A soothsayer said of *Ch'ing Pu* that he would be tortured, but then become prince, and he really was made a prince after having suffered punishment.

The father of *Wei C/ting, Clting Chi* had illicit intercourse with a maid of the princess *Yang Ilsin, Wei. Wei C/t ing* was born in the *Chien-chang* Palace. A convict read his destiny in his features and said "He is noble, and will be invested with the rank of a marquis." *Wei C/ting* replied:—" For a slave it is quite enough not to be whipped or reviled. How could he dream of a marquisate? " Afterwards *Wei C/ting* entered the army as an officer. Having distinguished himself in several battles, he rose in rank, and was promoted, till he was made generalissimo with the title of marquis of ten thousand families.

Before *Chou Ya Fu* became a marquis, *I Ml Fu* predicted his fortune saying:—"Within three years hence Your Honour will be a general and minister, and have the control of the empire. You will rank so high, that among your fellow officials there will not be your equal. But nine years later, you will die of starvation."— *Chou Ya Fu* replied laughing, "My elder brother already inherits the title.of marquis. When the father dies, the son succeeds to his title. Why do you hint at my becoming marquis? But should I really attain to this dignity, as you say, how can you pretend that I shall die of starvation? Explain this to me." *Hsu Fu* pointed to the perpendicular lines converging at the corner of his mouth, and said, "This

means death by starvation." — Three years passed. His brother, marquis *S/ting* of *Chiang* was punished for an offence. *Win* 77 was in favour of the marquis of *Chiang's* son. The wise councillors proposed *Chou Ya Fu,* who thereupon was created marquis of 457-425 B.c. Cf. p. 226 and *Shi-chi* chap. 43, p. 8 seq.

A military adventurer of the 2nd century B.c. His surname was originally *Ying Pa.* It was changed into the sobriquet *Ch'intj Pa* "Branded Pu ", after he had been branded in his early life. He made his escape, joined in the rebellions which led to the rise of the *Han* dynasty, and was rewarded with the title and the fief of a "Prince of *Kiukiang."* *Magers Reader's* Manual No. 926. Quotation from *Shi-chi* chap. 91, p. 1. Cf. p. 169. Quoted from the *Shi-chi* chap. Ill, p. Iv. Cf. *Giles* Biogr. Diet. No. 426, where the end of *Chou Ya Fu* is told a little differently. The capital of the *Chin* State in *Shansi,* the modern *Chiang-chou.*

» *Han Wen Ti* 179-156 B.c.

T'iao and succeeded the marquis of *Chiang.* During the six later years of *Win Ti's* reign the *Hsiung-nu* invaded the Chinese territory, and *Chou Ya Fu* became general. When *Ching TP* assumed the government, *Chou Ya Fu* was appointed prime minister. Later on he retired on account of sickness. His son bought from the imperial arsenal five hundred mail-coats, which he wanted for his father's funeral. The coolies employed at the job were irritated against him for not having received their money. Knowing that fiscal property had been clandestinely purchased, out of spite they denounced *Chou Ya Fn's* son to the throne. *Ching Ti* gave orders for trying and torturing *Chou Ya Fu,* who did not eat for five days, spat blood, and died. *Teng T'ung* took the fancy of *Win Ti,* who held him in higher esteem than a minister, presented him with enormous sums of money, and treated him almost as his equal. A fortune-teller predicted his destiny. The verdict was that he would become poor and miserable and die of starvation. When *Win Ti* died, and *Ching Ti* had mounted the throne, *Ting T ung* was punished for unlawful

coinage. On examination *Ching Ti* found *Teng T'ung* already dead. He stopped at the deceased man's house, but did not discover a single cash.

The prime minister *Han* when a youngster borrowed 50 cash from a fortune-teller, and together with him entered the Imperial Academy. The fortune-teller divined the successes of the scholars in the academy. Pointing at *I Kuan* he intimated that this youth would rise so high as to become a chief minister of state. *Han* sent the fortune-teller with his card to / *Kuan,* with whom he contracted the most intimate friendship. He exerted himself to the utmost in order to show his reverence. For the purpose of living together with / *Kuan* he moved his residence, and drew as near as possible. / *Kuan* was sick, *Han* nursed him like a servant. His kindness towards *1 Kuan* was greater than towards those of his own blood. Later on his name became famous all over the world. / *Kuan* obtained the post of a secretary of state. The local officials had to obey his orders. He recommended his friend to the throne for an Another ancient city in *Shansi* not far from *Chiang. Han Ching Ti* 156-140.

Quotation in a abridged form from *Shi-chi* chap. 57, p. 6 v. seq. *Teng T'ung* was a minion of the Emperor *Wen Ti.* Cf. *Teng T'ung's* biography in *Shi-cni* chap. 125, p. 2. *Han An ICuo,* 2nd cent. B.c. . Died 112 B.c. appointment at the court. *Han* subsequently was promoted to the post of a prime minister.

The convict, *Hsi l Fu* and the men who told the fortunes of *Ting T'ung* and / *Kuan* can be considered as soothsayers who knew fate. These sort of people examine the symptoms of the physical frame, and perceive wealth and honour, poverty and disgrace, just as we on seeing plates, know the use thereof. Fine vessels are used by the higher classes, coarse ones with the same certainty find their way to the poor. Sacrificial vases and tripods are not put up in outer buildings, and gourds are not to be found in the principal hall. That is a matter of course. That noble bones do not meet with the hardships of the poor, and that wretched features never share the joys of the grand, is on the same principle.

Vessels used as measures may contain a peck or a picul. Thus between the human ranks there is a difference of high and low. If vessels are filled over their size, their contents runs out, and is lost. If the limit of a rank is surpassed, the holder perishes. By making in our discussion of fate this comparison with a vessel, in order to ascertain the nature of anthroposcopy, we arrive at the conclusion that fate is lodged in the corporeal form.

But not only are wealth and honour, poverty and wretchedness visible in the body, pure and base conduct have also their phenomena. Pre-eminence and misery are the results of fate, pure and base conduct depend on character. As there is a method determining fate by the bones, there is also such a science doing the same for the character. But, whereas there are famous soothsayers, it is not known that a science determining the character by the features exists.

Fan Li left *Yileh.* From *Ch'i* he despatched a letter to the high officer *Cittmg* reading as follows:—" When the flying birds are all exterminated, the good bow is put away. When the cunning hare is dead, one cooks the greyhound. The king of *Yiieh* has a long neck and a mouth like a beak. One may share hardships, but not enjoy happiness with him. Why do you not leave him?" The officer *Chung* could not leave, but he pretended sickness, and did not go to court, whereupon the king sent him a sword, by which he died. A native of the *Yiieh* State, and minister of King *Kou Chien* of *Yiieh,* in modern *Chekiang,* 5th cent. B.c. An old State in *Shantung.* 3 Quoted from the *Shi-chi* chap. 41, p. 6 v. The last clause is abridged. *Wei Liao,* a native of *Ta-liang,* proposed to *Ch'in ShiJl Huang Ti* a scheme to conquer the empire. *Ch'in Shih Huang Ti* accepted his proposal and conferred upon him the highest distinctions, giving him the same dresses and the same food as he had himself. *Wei Liao* said, "The king of *Chin* has a high nose, long eyes, the chest of a vulture, the voice of a jackal, the look of a tiger, and the heart of a wolf. He knows no kindness. As

loug as he is hard up, he is condescending, but, when he has got what he wanted, he despises men. I am a simple citizen, yet he always treats me with great condescension. Should I really serve the king of *Ch'in,* he would gain his ends, and the whole world would be robbed. I can have no dealings with him." Thus he went away. *Fan Li* and *Wei Liao* correctly determined future events by observing the outward signs of character. Things really happened, as they "had foretold from the features. It is evident, therefore, that character and destiny are attached to the body.

The instances quoted in the popular literature are universally regarded as true. Besides there are a great many cases in olden and modern times not much heard of, which are all well founded. The spirit comes from heaven, the body grows on earth. By studying the body on earth one becomes cognizant of the fate in heaven, and gets the real truth.

Confucius is reported to have examined *T an T'ai Tse Yii,* and *T ang Chh* to have divined for *T sai Tse,* and that both of them were mistaken. Where did their error come from? The signs were hidden and too delicate. The examination may have for its object the interior or the exterior, the body or the voice. Looking at the outside, one perhaps misses the inside, and occupied with the body, one forgets the voice.

When *Confuckis* came to *Cheng,* he lost his disciples. He stood by himself near the east gate of *Ching.* Some man of *Ching* asked *Tse Kung* saying:—" There is a man near the east gate with a *Wei Liao* wrote a work on the art of war.

An ancient name of *K'ai-fe'ng-fu.* The first emperor of the *Ch'in* dynasty 221-209 B.c.

SAih Huang Tfs kingdom in *Shensi.*

Quoted in an abridged form from the *Shi-chi* chap. 6, p. 6 seq. "A disciple of *Confucius,* extremely ugly, but very talented. Cf. *Analects* VI, 12. A famous physiognomist 3rd cent. B.c. A native of *Yen,* who first studied physiognomy with *T ang Chii* and later on was appointed minister by King *(liao Hsiang* of *Ch'in* (305-249 B.C.). In *Honan.* A disciple of *Confucius.* head like that of

Yao, a neck like that of *Kao Yao,* and shoulders resembling those of *Tse Ch'an.* But from his waist downward he is by three inches shorter than *Yil.* He is worn out like a stray dog." *Tse Kung* informed *Confucius. Confucius* laughed heartily and said, "My'appearance, never mind, but like a stray dog! just so, just so."

In the matter of *Confucius'* appearance the man of *Cheng* was wrong. He was not clever, and his method was very superficial. *Confucius* made a mistake with *Tse Yil,* and *T'ang Chil* was in the wrong with *Tsai Tsi,* as the man of *Ching* in looking at *Confucius* did not apprehend his real appearance. Judging from his mien *Confucius* was deceived with *Tse Yd,* and going by words he was in error in regard of *Tsai Yil.* The appellation of *Kung Sun Cliiao,* a famous minister of the *Cheng* State in the 6th cent. B.c. A quotation from *Shi-chi* chap. 47, p. 12 v. Cf. *Legge, Analects, Prolegomena* p. 78.

One of the disciples of *Confucius,* whose character was not quite on a level with his fluency of speech, wherefore the Master said of him, "In choosing a man for his gift of speech, I have failed as regards *Tsai Yii."* CHAPTER XXV.

Long Life and Vital Fluid *(Chi-shou).*

The fate which every one receives is of two kinds, one determines those events which he must encounter, the other is the fate of strength and weakness, of long or short life. The events to be encountered are war, fire, crushing, and drowning, etc.; strength and long life, weakness and short life are connected with the copiousness and scarcity of the received fluid. War and fire, crushing and drowning can supervene, therefore there is not necessarily a period of invariable length for what has been received as fate.

If the limit of strength and long life be a hundred years,. then the fluid of those who do not reach a hundred years must be insufficient.

When the fluid is copious, the body becomes strong, and the body being strong, life lasts long. On the other hand, when the vital force is scanty, the body is weak, and with a weak body life is short. A short life is accompanied by much sickness. If the span be short, people die soon after they are born, and are annihilated, before they are fully developed. That is because their vital fluid is too little and too weak.

Those imbued with a copious and a strong fluid do not all at once end their lives. If people do not meet with any accidents, and, leading a quiet life, become exhausted and worn out, until they die for want of vitality, it is owing to the insufficiency of their vital fluid, which they have completely used up. Their fate is similar to that of those who expire soon after their birth and are cut off, before they have grown up. In all these cases the deficiency of the fluid is the reason, why those persons do not live a hundred years.

The fluid which fills men is either full and abundant—then they are strong and vigorous, or scanty and poor—then they are weak and feeble. Imbued with a full quantity, they are strong, What has been received as fate is the vital fluid or life. The length of life depends on the quality of this fluid, but it can be shortened by accidents, such as war, fire, etc. coining from abroad, before vitality is exhausted, and death would ensue under normal conditions.—The Chinese word used here,-pjj means "fate" as well as "life." and live long, filled with a small dose, they are weak, and lose their bodies.

When Heaven and Earth produce things, sometimes these things do not grow to their full growth, and when father and mother engender a child, sometimes its full development is checked. It happens that a plant bears a fruit, but that this fruit withers, dies, and drops, and it also happens that people have a son who is killed in his youth. Had this fruit not withered, it would also have completed one year, and had the son not been killed, he would likewise have lived a hundred years. The decay of the fruit and the death of the son are brought about by the weakness of their vital force. Although their forms be complete, their feeble fluid does not suffice to fill them.

When the cries of a new-born infant are shrill and piercing, it will live long, when they are whining and pitiful, it will die young. Why? Because, when the new-borns receive their fate of longevity or short life, the greater or smaller quantity of their fluid forms their nature.

When a mother nurses her child at longer intervals, it will be fit for life, whereas, when she nourishes it very frequently, it will die. Why? Because the nursing at intervals shows that the fluid is copious, and the child is strong. The frequent suckling proves the insufficiency of the vital fluid and the weakness of the baby.

A fondling is a son anterior to whom another son has already been brought up and died. They say that such a fondling cannot live, and call it a fondling. The idea is that, another son having already died, the mother is too anxious about the new one, and spoils his nature. The former son is dead, and the fondling is doomed, because he is nursed much too often. His fluid being too feeble, he cannot thrive. Though he may grow up, he is too easily affected liy external influences. He will always be the first to catch a disease, and his alone will prove incurable.

A fate of a hundred years is the proper one. Those who cannot complete a hundred years, though they have no proper fate, still have a fate. In the same manner the proper height of the human body is ten feet. Therefore a man is called chang-fu, and And thls nature becomes manifest by the way in which the new-borns cry. Strong babies have strong voices, weak ones give only a whine.

On the Chinese foot see p. 320 Note 1. Wang Ch'ung explains the term chang-fu 7 "young man " as originally meaning a man of ten feet = chang. chang-jen is an honorary designation for an old gentleman and an old lady. A man not measuring ten feet has not the proper height, but nevertheless he possesses a body. A body cannot be declared to be no body because of its falling short of ten feet. And so fate cannot be said to be no fate on account of its not coming up to a hundred years.

Heaven does not distribute long and short fates, of which every one would obtain either. We may say that man receives his fate in his fluid from Heaven, which is the same, whether he finishes it sooner or later. There is a saying to the effect that, if somebody aspires to royalty and does not succeed, this pretender can remain a leading prince. Leading princes are unsuccessful pretenders to royalty. A pretender should rise to royalty, as a long life ought to come up to a hundred years. Unable to become a king, he retires and continues a leading prince, and thus he who cannot attain to a hundred years resigns himself to a premature death.

A king and a pretender do the same, but are given different names, the one an honourable, the other a contemptible one. A long and a short life are caused, as it were, by the same fluid, but they are of different duration, either long or short. How do we know that he who does not live a hundred years, and dies an untimely death, possesses a fate of a hundred years all the same? Because his bodily frame is as big and as tall as that of others. A body that has lived a hundred years does not differ from another of fifty years. The bodies not being different, the vital fluids cannot differ either. Birds and animals have other bodies than man, hence the length of their lives must differ from the human.

How can we prove that human life, if it be long, lasts a hundred years? There are such cases in the world, and the Literati say that during the time of universal peace people used to be very tall, and live about a hundred years, which was the effect of the harmonious fluid. In the Canon of Yao, Yao says, "I have been seventy years on the throne." He wished to abdicate, and found Shun. S/iun was tried and had occupied the throne thirty years, when Yao retired owing to his old age. Eight years afterwards he expired. Ninety-eight years had elapsed until his decease. But he Ah. A husband thus addresses his father and mother-in-law. Quotation from the Shaking Pt. I, chap. Ill, 12 (Legge Vol. Ill, Pt. I, p. 25). The Shi-chi chap. 1, p. 20 (Chavannes, Mem. Hist. Vol. I, p.

69) writes twenty years.

In that case *Shun* cannot have reigned for him longer than 20 years, for 70 + 20 + 8 = 98. must already have lived, before he ascended the throne. Counting all these numbers together we arrive at an aggregate sum of over a hundred years.

It is further stated that *"Shun* was thirty years old, that he was tried thirty years, and that he was on the throne fifty years, when he went on high and died," which makes just one hundred years. *Win Wang* said to *Wu Wang,* "I am a hundred years, and you are ninety. I will give you three years of mine." *Wing Wang* was ninety-seven years old, when he died, and *Wu Wang* ninetythree, when he departed.

The Duke of *Chou* was a younger brother of *Wu Wang.* Between brothers there is generally no greater difference than ten years. After the death of *Wu Wang, Chou Kung* became regent. Seven years later he returned the government, and retired owing to old age. That would make about a hundred years. The Duke of *Shao* was an elder brother of the Duke of *Chou.* At the time of King *K'ang* he was still Senior Tutor, which would make more than a hundred years.

Sages are endued with the harmonious fluid, therefore the years of their destiny have the proper number. The harmonious fluid is conducive to a tranquil government. Therefore during the age of universal peace the number of tall and long-lived persons was particularly great. One hundred years is the proper number of years of a long human life, as autumn is the proper time for the fate of plants, since plants live until autumn, when they die.

Plants perishing before or after autumn are similar to men whose life either exceeds or falls short of a hundred years. The time before or after autumn corresponds to more or less than a hundred years. Some plants fade already after they have pierced the earth, as men may die soon after their birth. Other plants may pass the autumn without withering just like men whose years may eventually be from one hundred to three hundred.

Quotation from the *Shuking (Shun-tien)* Pt. II, Bk. I, chap. VI, 28 *(Leggt* Vol. lll, Pt. I, p. 51). The computation gives 110 not 100 years. We should read "he was tried twenty years" instead of thirty, the reading adopted in the *Shi-chi* and defended by several old commentators. Cf. *Legge's* notes to the passage and *Chavannes lac.* eit. p. 91 Note 2. Quoted from the *Liki, Wen Wang shih-tse (Legge, Sacred Books* Vol. XXVII, p. 344). The commentators are at a loss, how to explain that *Wen Wang* was only ten years older than his son, *Wu Wang,* and how he could give him some of his years. 1078-1053 B.c.

It is on record that *Lao Tse* lived over two hundred years. The Duke of *Shao* became one hundred and eighty years old. *Kao Tsung* reigued one hundred years, and King *Mu* of the *Cliou* dynasty likewise one hundred. Including the time before his ascension, there must have been upwards of one hundred and thirty-four years altogether.

Sse Ma Ch'ien mentions this report in his biography of *Lao Tse (Shi-chi,* chap. 63, p. 3). Some said that *Lao Tse* became over 160 years old, others that he lived over 200 years, prolonging his life by the practice of virtue. The *Shuking* Pt. V, Bk. XV, 5 *(Legge* Vol. HI, Pt. II, p. 467) expressly states that *Kao Tsung* — *Wu Ting* enjoyed the throne for fifty and nine years, not for a hundred. He reigned from 1324-1266 B.c. Thus the *Shuking (Lu-hsing)* Pt. V, Bk. XXVII, 1 *(Legge* Vol. HI, Pt. II, p. 588) as *Wang Ch'ung* and others understand the passage (On *Lgge's* different view cf. his notes). According to the *Shi-chi* King *Mu's* reign lasted but 55 years. It is usually reckoned from 1001-947 B.c.

CHAPTER XXVI.

Miracles (Chi-kuai).

The Literati pretend that Sages are not born from human sperm, but that they are endowed with a special essence from Heaven. The mother of *Yil* swallowed pearl-barley, and gave birth to *Yil,* whence the *Hsia* dynasty has its surname S$e. *Hsieh's* mother consumed a swallow's egg, and was delivered of *Hsieh* whence the *Yin* dynasty derived

its surname *Tse.* The mother of *Hou Chi* walked in the foot-steps of a giant," and bore *Hou Chi,* whence the *Chou* received their surname *Chi.* The *Shiking* says, "There was no rending and no tearing, thus *Hou Chi* was born."

They further state that *Yil* and *Hsieh* were born unnaturally, issuing from their mother's back, and that *Hou Chi* was born naturally. There was no rending and no tearing, the mother's body did not suffer, hence the expression:— no rending and nb tearing. The descendants of those born unnaturally die an unnatural death, while the descendants of those born naturally die naturally. Therefore *Chieh* and *Chou* were executed, and *Nan Wang* was deprived of his cities. These words seem to be self-consistent, therefore i-Air This legend is mentioned in the *Wu 1 iieh Ch'un-ch'iu,* the Chronicle of Wu and *Yiieh,* by *Chao Yeh* of the 1st cent. A.d. *m* Cf. Chap. XXXVII. The *Shiking* Pt. IV, Bk. Ill, Ode 3 only says that Heaven commissioned the swallow to descend and give birth to *Hsieh (Legge* Vol. IV, Pt. II, p. 63G). -Jp,, which also may signify an egg. J».

Chiang i uan, the mother of *Hou Chi* "trod on the toe-print made by God" says the *Shiking,* Pt. Ill, Bk. II, Ode 1 *(LeggeVol IV,* Pt.II, p. 415). $15. 'd *Hou Chi* are the ancestors of the Three Dynasties: — *Hsia, Yin,* and *Chou.* The *Shuo-wen* observes that because the mothers of these Sages were moved by Heaven, Son of Heaven became a term for a Holy Emperor. *SMking* Pt. ID, Bk. H, Ode I, 2. The last emperors of the *Hsia* and the *Yin* dynasties. The last reigning emperor of the house of *Chou* (314-256 B.C.), who in 256 had to surrender 36 cities to the King of *Chin* and in the same year died as a prisoner of *Ch'in.* people believe them, and since, in addition, evidence is given to establish their truth, they rely on these utterances.

The *Chan-shu* also relates of the mother of *Yao, Ching Tu,* that she conceived from a red dragon, when she went out into the country, and gave birth to *Yao.* From the chronicle of *Kao Tsh* we learn that dame *Liu* was reposing on the banks of a large lake. In her dream she met with a spirit. At that time there was a tempest with thunder and lightning and a great darkness. *T ai Kung* went near, and perceived a dragon above her. She became *enceinte* and was delivered of *Kao Tsu.* These instances of the supernatural action of spirits are not only narrated, but also written down, and all the *savants* of the day swear by them. A thorough investigation, however, will show their futility.

The statement of the *Shiking* that there was no rending and no tearing *viz.* that the mother's body was not much affected may be true, but the assertion that *Yil* and *Hsieh* issued from their mother's back is irrational. When cicadas are born, they break forth from the back of the larva;. Did Heaven in generating those sages follow the law of the larvje?

Hares conceive by licking the pubescence of plants. When the leveret is born, it issues from the mouth of the hare. Since the mother of *Yil* swallowing the barley and that of *Hsieh,* who consumed the swallow's egg, were like hares licking the pubescence, their sons ought likewise to have issued from their mouths, and not from their backs. Consequently the statement about the back is preposterous.

In the world many persons die a sanguinary death by the sword, and it is not necessary that their first ancestor should have had an unnatural birth. When the *Ch'in* lost the empire, *Yen Yileh* beheaded *Hu Hai,* and *Hsiang* Fw executed *Tse Ying.* Was the forefather of the *Chin, PoYi* born unnaturally? Ergo the thesis of natural and unnatural births based on the ancestors of the Three Dynasties is erroneous.

A book of prophecies wrongly ascribed to *Confucius. Shi-chi* chap. 8, p. 2. The father of *Kao Tm.* The son-in-law of the powerful eunuch *Chao Kao,* who contrived the death of the emperor. Cf. *Chavannes, Mem. Hit.* Vol. II, p. 213 seq. The Emperor *Erh Shih Huang Ti,* son of *Ch'in Shih Huang H,* 209-206 B. c. Cf. p. 178. A child which occupied the throne 65 days only.

'The forester of the Emperor *Shun.*

Moreover, pearl-barley is a plant, a swallow's egg a bird, and a giant's footprints are earth. These three things are bodies, but not a fluid, how could they procreate a man? With regard to Sages people suppose that they receive the essence of Heaven, which is an exceptionally fine fluid, wherefore their doings are so different from those of the masses. Now the progenitors of the Three Dynasties are born from a plant, a bird, and earth. Could these be regarded as very fine essences?

Since among the productions of Heaven and Earth man is the noblest, the others are common. Now, if the essence of those common things should be the sperm for the noblest creature, man, how could it be very fine?

Let us suppose that a pigeon or a sparrow emitted their fluid into a wild goose or a wild swan, it would never produce an egg. Why? Because a pigeon and a sparrow are too small, compared with a wild goose and a wild swan. Now, the body of a swallow measures but five inches, and the stalk of pearl-barley not more than several feet. How could the two women who swallowed the egg and the grain have begot a creature of seven feet?

Supposing that one melts the copper required for a tripod and pours it into the mould of a cash, it is plain that one could not produce a tripod. Now the giant is the Spirit of Heaven, therefore his foot-prints were so big. The man with the huge foot-prints is like the molten copper for a tripod, and *Chiang Yuan's* body like the mould of a cash. Should the giant emit his fluid into *Chiang Yuan.* her body would be much too small to receive the whole essence, and without this whole essence *Ilou Chi* could not have been born.

If *Yao* and *Kao Tsu* were really the sons of dragons, their nature as sons ought to have been similar to that of their dragon fathers. Dragons can ride on the clouds, and *Yao* and *Kao Tsu* should have done the same.

All plants growing from earth resemble their own species, but not earth, for they are not produced by earth, which merely nourishes and feeds them. A mother with child is like the earth feeding plants. The mothers of *Yao* and *Kao Tsu* received the emissions of the dragons, as earth receives the seeds of plants. Since growing plants are similar to their own species, the two emperors also should have been like dragons.

Man measures seven feet according to the measurement of the *Chou* epoch, when 1 foot was like 20 cm., and 7 feet = 1,40 m. The *Shiking loc. cit.* explicitly states that the foot-prints were made by God. The name of *Ilou Chi's* mother.

Of animals with blood males and females pair. When they come together and see one of their own kind, their lust is excited, they wish to satisfy it, and then are able to emit their fluid. Should a stallion see a cow, or a male sparrow a hen, they would not couple, because they belong to different species. Now, dragons and man are of a different species likewise. How then could a dragon be moved by a human being so as to impart its fluid?

Some say that, when the *Hsia* dynasty was near its downfall, two dragons fought together in the court, and spat their saliva on the ground. When the dragons had disappeared, their saliva was preserved in a casket, until King *Yu* of the *Cîiou* dynasty opened it. Then the saliva of the snakes changed into a black lizard, which slipped into the seraglio, where it had intercourse with a palace girl. The result was the birth of *Pao Sse.*

A black lizard belongs to another class than man, how could it become enamoured with a palace girl, and emit its fluid? The intercourse with the black lizard was vicious, therefore *Pao Sse* caused disasters, and overthrew the *Chou* dynasty. When different species recklessly mix together, their offspring becomes unprincipled and mischievous. Now, the mothers of *Yao* and *Kao Tsu* had illicit intercourse, why did the two emperors become wise and sage men, and were cpaite different from *Pao Sse?*

They say that Viscount *Chien* of *Chao* was sick and for five days did not know anybody. When he awoke, he said, "I have been to God's abode. There appeared a brown bear. God bade me shoot it; 1 hit the animal, and it died.

Then came a spotted bear; I hit it also, and it died. After the two bears had died, I asked a ghost on the road. The ghost said:—"The brown and the spotted bears are the forefathers of two ministers of *Chin.*"

Bears are animals, and as such of a different class from man. How should they become of the same class and the ancestors of the two ministers? The time, when the ancestors of the two ministers, the brown and the spotted bears, killed by Viscount *Chien,* were doomed to die, was one of luck for the Viscount *Chien.* He saw them as in a dream. They were empty semblances and must For details cf. *Shi-chi* chap. 4, p. 25 (*Chavannes, Mnn. Hist. Vol.l,* p. 281) which quotes a passage from the *Kuo-yu,* and *Lun-heng* Bk. V, p. lv. *(I-hou).* 781-771 B.c. The famous favourite of King *Yu,* who ruined the empire by her extravagance.

With two dragons. .' See p. 225, where this story is told in detail. Lun-Heug. 21 not have been real. Should they really have existed, then perhaps the two bears were first metamorphosed into human beings, before they engendered the two ministers.

Atm *Ai,* Duke of *Lu,* was changed into a tiger during a sickness. Man can be transformed into an animal, as animals can become men. Probably the black lizard, which entered the harem, was also first changed into a man.

Between heaven and earth it does not happen that creatures of a different species mix and couple. Should Heaven have the same law as man, their likes and dislikes would also be similar. Man does not like different species, therefore Heaven would not consort with such either. Although man is created by Heaven, he is like the lice which are produced on man. Man does not love those lice, for what reason then should Heaven desire to beget through man? Different classes have different natures, and their sentiments and desires do not agree. Heaven and Earth are husband and wife. Heaven emits its fluid into Earth and produces the various things. Man is born by propagation. If Sages are formed of a very fine essence, yet

they receive the fluid from their fathers, and are not endowed with a special essence from Heaven.

Should the recipients of a special essence become Sages, *Hsieh* and *Ilou Chi* are not Sages, and, if it be necessary that all Sages should Lave received a special fluid, the Twelve Sages did not all meet this requirement. What fluid did the mothers of *Huang 'It, Ti K'n, Chuan Hsil* and *Shun* receive, and what did the mothers.of *Whi Wang, Wu Wang, Chou Kung,* and *Confucius* swallow to become pregnant?

Perhaps the surnames of the Three Dynasties:—*Sse, Tse,* and *Chi* gave the impetus to the invention of those unfounded and marvellous stories, as the legend of *Huang Ti's* ascension to heaven originated from the local name of *Tiug-hu.* Not only are they irrational, but those names are also misinterpreted. When *T sang Hsieh* invented writing, he made the signs agree with the ideas. *Chiang Yuan* walked into the foot-prints of a giant. "Foot-print" *(chi-*jjjjjj) means a "basis" *(chi =* 5j£), therefore the surname should be "his" *(ch'i =* it) with "earth" =) below, but it is "woman" (nfl = with "chin" *(i =* jji) at its side. This Cf. p. 326.

Cf. p. 304. For this legend *vid.* p. 332. A minister of *Huang Ti,* cf. p. 244. is not the character *chi =* or *chi =* JjJj nor in accordance with the circumstances, whence their truth becomes very doubtful.

Judging by the surname *Chi* of the *Chou* of those of the *Hsia* and *Yin,* we arrive at the conclusion that *Tse* and *Sse* have nothing to do with a swallow's egg or pearl-barley-May be that the mothers of *Yd, Hsie/i,* and *Ilou Chi* were just going to conceive, when they happened to swallow a grain of pearl-barley and a swallow's egg, or walked upon the foot-prints of a giant. The world is fond of the marvellous, a propensity which has been the same in ancient and modern times. Unless they see wonders, people do not believe that a person possesses extraordinary faculties. Thus they explain surnames according to their preconceived ideas. The world puts implicit faith in these explanations, and they

are therefore regarded as true. Sages have repeatedly uttered their doubts, but they could not solve them, and the shallow discussions of the scholars of the day cannot discriminate between right and wrong.

The literati, who approve of all that is old, have put forward those arguments. The *Shiking* says that there was no rending and no tearing, which means to say that by *Ilou Chi's* birth the body of his mother was not much affected. From this the literati, perverting the right principles, have derived the story of the unnatural birth of *Yil* and *Hsieh.* The fecundation by the dragon and the dream of the meeting with the spirit are of the same nature. The mothers of *Yao* and *Kao Tsu* were just about to become *enceinte,* when they met with a thunderstorm and a dragon carrying clouds and rain along. People seeing these phenomena then told the stories.

A dream that one meets with a dragon is an augury of the birth of a wise son. Is a dream of a meeting with ghosts not like a dream of a *rendez-vous* with a spirit? How could it be real? When the mother had intercourse with the dragon in the wilds, and when the dragon appeared on high, *Yao* and *Kao Tsu* perchance received their destiny of wealth and honour, for a dragon is an auspicious animal, and to meet it appearing above is a lucky omen and a sign that fate has been received.

When the Emperor *Kuang Wu Ti* saw the light in the *Chigang* palace, a phoenix alighted on the ground, and an auspicious grain grew in one room. When Sages are born, and strange birds and auspicious things appear as portents, strange and auspicious The surname *Chi =* does not point to the footprints which *Chiang Yuan* is believed to have walked upon., Cf. p. 1«0.

things become visible indeed. If, however, we are to regard the children born then as the offspring of those things, should we consider the Emperor *Kuang Wu Ti* as the essence of the auspicious blade or the fluid of the phoenix? According to the chapters on the pedigree of the Emperors and the Genealogical Tables of the Three Dynasties *Yil* was the son of *Kun,* and *Hsieh* and *Hon Chi* were both sons of the Emperor *K'u,* their mothers being second wives of A «. *Yao* also was a son of the Emperor *K'u.* Why then must the wives of kings and emperors walk into the country? Although the ancient times are noted for their simplicity, yet there were already certain rules of propriety established. And why did these ladies bathe in the rivers? It follows that the assertion about the Sages receiving a special fluid from Heaven and their mothers becoming pregnant by swallowing something is a fallacy.

As a matter of fact Sages have their prototypes among their ancestors; being as virtuous as *Win Wang* and *Wu Wang,* they still find their peers. *Confucius,* playing the flute, knew that he was a descendant of the *Yin* and *Hsiang Yit,* having double pupils, was cognisant of his being a scion of *Shun.* The Five Emperors and Three Rulers had all *Huang Ti* as their ancestor. He was a Sage, who first received a grand destiny. Therefore all his descendants became emperors and rulers. At their births there were miracles of course, which, if they did not appear in things, became manifest in dreams.

Chap. 2-4 of the *Shi-chi.*
Chap. 13 of the *Shi-chi.*
As the mother of *Hsieh* did, when she swallowed the egg, cf. chap. XXXVII. We learn from *Lun-heng* Bk. XXIV, p. 3 that it was against the custom to make music on the anniversaries of the downfall of the *Ilia* and *Yin* dynasties, as one did not write on the death day of *T sang Hsieh,* the inventor of writing. I infer from this that the last emperors of the *Ilsia* and *Yin* dynasties were famous for their music, and that *Confucum* feeling in himself a talent for music imagined that he was a descendant of the I'm emperors. *Shun* had double pupils as well, *vUl.* p. 304. CHAPTER XXVII.
Unfounded Assertions *(Wu king).*
Men receive the vital fluid from heaven at their birth, and are all given a fate fixing the length of their lives, in accordance to which their bodies exist for a longer or shorter period. Just so vases are formed out of clay by the potter, and

plates from copper by the founder. As the shape of a vessel, once completed, cannot bo made smaller or bigger, thus the duration of the corporeal frame having been settled, cannot be shortened or prolonged. The said fluid forms the constitution, which determines fate and shapes the body. The fluid and the material body pervade each other. Life and death correspond to fixed periods. The body cannot be transformed, and likewise fate cannot be lengthened or shortened. We may elucidate the question as to the duration of human life by observing the potter and founder.

Some one might object saying, "True, if a potter uses his stuff to make a vase, this vase, after its completion, lasts, until it breaks, but cannot be formed anew. If, however, a founder casts a plate out of copper, although it be finished, it can be melted again, and be made into a cup or, if that is not possible, into a vessel. Although men, who owe their spirits to heaven, all have a destiny fixing their span, by which their bodies are regulated, they can, if they know the right way and an effective elixir, change their bodies and prolong their lives all the same."

I reply, "If a founder recasts a finished vessel, he must first liquefy it in fire, before he is able to enlarge or diminish, extend or shorten it. If a man desiring to protract his years, should wish to be like the copper vessel, there must be some sort of a furnace with coal, where the change and the transmutation of his body could take place. The body having been changed, the lifetime might also be extended. How could men, in order to change their bodies, undergo a smelting process like a copper vessel?"

The *Li Ki* states, "When the water pours down, one does not offer fish or turtles for food." Why? Because, when the *Li Ki* chap. 1, No. 1 *(Chu-li),* p. 20 v. *(Legge's* translation Vol.1, p. 84.) Various reasons have been assigned by the commentators for this rule. They say, rain water rushes down, snakes and reptiles are changed and become fish or turtles. Since they give up their original real nature and are transformed on-

ly for a while, the servants take care and dare not offer them to their masters for food. Would men desirous of having their bodies transmuted, be satisfied with a change like that of reptiles and snakes? Those reptiles which are liable to a change are worse off than those which do not change at all. Before they change, they are not eaten by men, but, when they have been transformed into fish and turtles, men eat them. Being eaten, their long lives are cut short, and that is not what people desire.

Years and months change, and the intrinsic fluid may transform one species into another. Frogs become quails, and sparrows turn into clams. Man longing for bodily transformation would like to resemble quails and crabs. These are in the same plight as fish and turtles. Man fishes for crabs and eats them, when he catches them. Although without a metamorphose of the body, life cannot be lengthened, this result cannot be aimed at.

Duke *Niu Ai* of *Lu* was laid up with a malady for seven days, when he was transformed into a tiger. *Kun* when banished to Mount *Yil-shan* turned into a moose. Do those who seek transformation desire to become a tiger like *Niu Ai,* or a moose like *Kun?* The life of a tiger or a moose is not longer than the human. In this world the human nature is the noblest of all, therefore the transmutation of a man into a bird or a beast cannot be desirable. It would be a great boon, if an old man could be transformed into a youth, or if at least the white hair could turn black again, the lost teeth grow once more, and the animal forces be strengthened, so that the person could jump about, devoid of all decrepitude. This would be grand indeed! Where would be the advantage of a transformation, if life were not prolonged thereby?

If a thing is transformed, its concomitant fluid, as it were, favours the change. Human work may produce new forms, it is not Heaven which transforms things in order to prolong their duration. No more can a transformation be brought about by eating divine herbs or wonderful drugs. A man constantly using cordials can in opposition to *Wang Ch'ung,* that during heavy rainfalls fish are so easily got as not to be valuable, or that then they are muddy and not fit for eating. This last reason seems the most plausible.

To become like a quail or a crab. Quoted from *Huai Nan Tse,* who adds that the tiger devoured his brother, when he opened the door. A legendary minister of *Yao* and father to Great *Yii.* thereby merely strengthen his constitution and add to his years. A sudden transmutation is not caused by. the real heavenly fluid or the true nature, with which men are endowed. Heaven and earth do not change, sun and moon are not transformed, and the stars do not disappear. Such is their real nature. As man has received part of their real fluid, his body cannot be transformed either: men do not sometimes become women, or women men. A high mound may be turned into a valley, or a deep ravine into a hill. But then the change keeps pace with human labour, it is a change by labour, not by inherent nature.

At the rise of the *Han* dynasty, an old man presented *Chang Liang* with a book, and then was transformed into a stone. Therefore the essence of a stone was a propitious omen for the rising *Han.* Similarly the essence of the Biver became a man who gave a jade-badge to the envoy of *Ch in,* which was an unlucky augury, indicating the downfall of *Ch in.*

The silkworm feeds on mulberry leaves, when it grows old, it sets to spinning, and becomes a cocoon, and the cocoon again is changed into a moth. The moth has two wings, and in its altered form widely differs from the silkworm. Grubs change into chrysalisses, and these turn into crickets. The crickets are born with two wings, and are not of the same type as grubs. A great many of all worms and insects alter their shapes and transform their bodies. Man alone is not metamorphosed, being the recipient of the real heavenly fluid. Born as a child, he grows into a man, and, when he is old, into greybeard. From birth to death there is no metamorphose, for such is his original nature. Creatures

which'by their nature are not transformed, cannot be induced to do so, whereas those which must pass through a metamorphose, cannot forego it. Now, the length of life of those transformed creatures does not compare favourably with that of non-transformed ones. Nothing would be said, if a man desirous of a metamorphose could thereby prolong his years, but if he only changes his body without increasing his years, he would be merely on a level with crickets. Why should he like this?

Dragons are reptiles which appear sometimes, and then again become invisible, and which sometimes are long and sometimes short. It is in their nature to undergo transformations, but not for good, An adherent of the founder of the *Han* dynasty. The Taoists have claimed him as one of their patriarchs and mystics. See p. 235. The *Yellow Itiver.* This event is told in detail on p. 233.

since after a short while, they relapse into their previous state. Ergo, every thing considered, we find that the human being, endowed with an unchangeable body, is not liable to metamorphoses, and that his years cannot be prolonged. *Kao Tsung* having witnessed the abnormal growth of a paper mulberry, is reported to have repented of his faults, changed the style of government, and enjoyed happiness for one hundred years. This is not correct. Of Duke *Ching* of *Sung* it is said that on his having uttered three excellent maxims, the planet *Mars* left out three solar mansions, and twenty one years were added to the duke's life, which is likewise unfounded. Duke *Mu* of *Ch in* is believed to have been rewarded by God with nineteen extra years on account of his conspicuous virtue, an untruth too. *Chih Sung*3 and *Wang Ch'iao,* they say, became genii by their love of *Tao,* and lived on without dying, also a falsehood.

Let us suppose that a man is born, gets a body, and is given the name A, then he always preserves this body called A through his whole life up to his death. Adherents of Tao are said to have become genii, but it never has happened that A was transformed into B: neither

can the body pass through a metamorphose, nor years be added. Wherefore? Because of the body, the vital force, and the constitution, which are from heaven. The body being Posthumous name of the *Slmng* emperor *Wu Ting,* 1324-1265 B.c. A paper mulberry tree grew in the court of the Emperor, which had two spans of circumference on the second day already. This was, of course, regarded as a portent. Cf. *Lun-hmg* Bk. V, p. 1 *(Yi Hsu)* where the legend is told in full.

According to the *Shutting* Pt. V, Bk. xv *(Legge* Vol. lll, Pt. II, p. 407) *Kao Tsung* reigned 59 years. 4 515-451 B.c. This story is told in full in *Lm-heng* Bk. IV, p. 9 v. which seems quoted from *Huai IS'an Te* XII, llv. The planet Mars being in the constellation of the "Heart," the astrologer *Tse ei* informed the Duke that Heaven was going to inflict a punishment upon him, advising him, however, to shift this misfortune on his prime minister, or on his people, or on the year. The prince thrice declined to allow others to suffer in his stead, giving his reasons for each refusal. These are the three good maxims of our text. *Tse Wei* then changed and congratulated the Duke, saying that Heaven had heard the three excellent sentiments uttered by him, that the same night it would cause Mars to pass through three solar mansions, and that it would add twenty-one years to his life, each mansion consisting of seven stars and each star representing one year. 658-619 B.c. *Shang Ti,* the supreme being, God. A magician of the time of *Shen Aung.* A prince of *Chin* 571 B.c., who became a Taoist and an immortal. He was seen riding through the air upon a white crane. *Mayer,* No. 801. spring, the vital force is summer. Man's lifetime is the outcome of his vitality. The body follows the vital force in its actions. If the vital force and the constitution are not the same, there must be a diversity in the bodies also. The life of an ox is half as long as that of a horse, and a horse lives half as long as man. Therefore, the outward forms of the ox and the horse must be different from the human. Having obtained the shape of an ox or a horse, one cannot but get their spans too. As oxen and horses do not change into men, their lifetime is also shorter than that of human beings.

Because of *Kao Tsung* and the like it is not stated that they underwent a transmutation, but simply that their lifetime was lengthened, people put faith in these reports. The force pulsating in the veins of the body is like rice hoarded up in a sack. The bulk of a picul sack also corresponds to a picul. If rice be taken away or more added, the sack appears smaller or bigger. The vital force determines the length of the human life. It is like the rice, and the body like the sack. In order to increase or diminish the lifetime, the body too must become bigger or thinner, it cannot remain the same. Should anybody think the human body to be quite different from a sack, and that the vital force cannot well be compared to rice, we may still take another illustration from a gourd. The juice of a gourd is like the human blood, its pulp like flesh. Now, let a man take away or add some juice but so that the gourd's form remains unaltered; he will be unable to perform this. It being impossible to man to diminish or to replenish the juice of the gourd, how can Heaven extend or curtail the human span? As the human life can neither be lengthened nor shortened, who could have done such a thing in the case of *Kao Tsung* and others, so that we might speak of an increase of years? The assertion that *Kao Tsung* and others were metamorphosed, and their years increased would after all be credible, but the statement advanced now that their years were prolonged, no mention being made of any transformation of their bodies, is past all belief for the following reason:

Man receives the vital force from Heaven. When it is complete, the body is informed. During life both work harmoniously together up to the last, death. Since the body cannot be transformed, the years cannot be increased either. As long as man The meaning is. as summer is preceded by spring, thus the body exists, before it is informed by the vital force.

lives, he can move, but when he dies, he collapses. At death the vital force vanishes, and the body is dissolved and decomposed. As a man, while in possession of life, cannot be metamorphosed, how should his years be prolonged?

What changes on the body from birth to old age is the hair and the skin. The youth's hair is black, the aged man's, white. Later on, it turns yellow. But tins change concerns the hair alone, not the body. A youngster has a white skin, an old man a dark one, which, later on, becomes blackish, as if covered with dust. Eespecting the yellow hair and the dusty skin the *Li-ki* says: "We will have yellow hair and wizened faces indefinitely." If the hair changes, people reach an old age and die late. Despite this, bones and flesh do not change; the limit of life being reached, death ensues.

From amongst the five elements earth alone admits of several transformations. Moistened with water, it can be shaped into a horse, and this again be altered into a human being, but be it noted that it must not yet have been put in a kiln and burned. If, after having been modelled as a utensil, it has already been hardened by burning in the kiln, a new transformation is out of the question. Now, man may be thought of as having been baked and moulded in the furnace of Heaven and Earth. How can he still undergo a change after his shape has been fixed?

In representing the bodies of genii one gives them a plumage, and their arms are changed into wings with which they poise in the clouds. This means an extension of their lifetime. They are believed not to die for a thousand years. These pictures are false, for there are not only false reports in the world, but also fancy pictures. However, man in reality does not belong to the class of crickets and moths. In the thirty-five kingdoms beyond the sea there live plumigerous and feathered tribes. Feathered relates to their pinions. These people are the produce of their soil, it cannot be said that their bodies were covered with plumage and feathers through the influence of *Tao. Yil* and *Yi* visited *Hsi Wang Mu*5 This verse does not occur in the *Liki,* but in the *Shiking*

Pt. IV, Bk. III, Ode II *(Legge, Classics* Vol. IV, Pt. II, p. 635):—" He (the ancestor) will bless us with the eyebrows of longevity.—We will have yellow hair and wizened faces indefinitely." Fore more details see the *Shan-hai-king.*
3 Great *Yil* 2205-2197.
A minister of *Tii.* A Taoist goddess. Cf. my article "*Mu Wang und die Konigin von Saba*" in the *Mitteilungen des Seminars fur Orientalische Sjrachen zu Berlin* Vol. VII, 1904. but she is not reported to have had a plumage or feathers. There are also immortals in foreign countries, but they are not described as having a plumage and feathers, and, conversely, the plumigerous and feathered tribes are not said to be immortal. As plumage and feathers are not ascribed to the immortals, these attributes cannot imply immortality. How then can it be inferred that the genii must live for ever, because they have wings?

CHAPTER XXVIII.

Taoist Untruths (*Tao-hsii).*

In the books of the Literati it is stated that *Huang Ti* exploited the copper mines of Mount *Shou,*-and out of the ore cast tripods at the foot of the *Ching* Mountain/' When the tripods were completed, a dragon with a long beard came down, and went to meet *Huang Ti. Huang Ti* mounted the dragon. His whole suite including the harem, over seventy persons in all, mounted together with him, whereupon the dragon ascended. The remaining smaller officials, who could not find a seat on the dragon, all got hold of the dragon's beard, which they pulled out. *Huang Ti's* bow fell down. The people gazed after him, until he disappeared in the sky. Then they hugged his bow, and the dragon's beard, and moaned. Therefore later ages named the place *Ting-hu* (Tripod Lake) and the bow of the emperor *Wu-hao* (Raven's Cry).

The Grand Annalist in his eulogy on the *Five Emperors* also says that having performed the hill-sacrifice *Huang Ti* disappeared as a genius, and that his followers paid their respect to his garments and cap, and afterwards buried them. I say that this is not true.

The following story is taken from the

Shi-chi, chap. 28, p. 28 v., where an official relates it to *Han* Wu *Ti.* Cf. *Chacannex, Mim. Hixt.* Vol. III, p. 488. In *Shansi* Province, near *P'u-chou-fu.* This mountain lies in *Shensi,* near *Ihi-an-fu.* The context requires lJl "Tripod beard," but we read 'J instead of j?H. A place, called j'/JJ ' Tripod lake" actually exists in *Honan* (Playfair Cities and Towns No. 732!1). This naiuo has perhaps been the origin of the legend, as *Wang Chung* suggests (cf. above p. 322). In ancient times only the phonetic part of a character was often written, and the radical left out. Thus j(jHi could stand for "beard" as well as for yj'ijj "lake." Our text has '(J *ft* the "beard." Some commentators hold that the name *Wu-hao yjj* — Raven's Cry refers to the lament of the people, others that it was the name of a tree well fit for the fabrication of bows. *Huang Ti. Chuan Hii, K'a, Yao,* and *Shun.* According to other writers the Five Emperors are:—*T'ai ffao, Yen Ti, Huang Ti, Sliao Hao,* and *Chuan Hsu.* '*Shi-chi* chap. 28, p. 3D v. When *Ch in Shih Huang Ti* had sacrificed on the tomb of *Huang Ti* upon Mount *Cluao,* he asked, how *Huang Ti* could be an immortal, and yet be buried there. Then somebody replied that *Huang Ti* had ascended t6 heaven as a genius, and that only his garments and cap were left and interred.

What does *Huang Ti* really mean? Is it an appellative or a posthumous title? Being a posthumous title it must be some praise bestowed upon him by his subjects, for this kind of title is a glorification of what the deceased has done during his life-time. *Huang Ti* was a votary of Zoo, and subsequently, as they say, rose to Heaven. If his subjects wanted to honour him, they ought not to have styled him *Huang,* but ought to have given him a title implying his ascension as an immortal.

According to the rules for honorary titles the pacification of the people would be called *Huang,* which means that he who is styled so kept the people at peace, but the word does not denote the acquisition of 7ao. Among the many emperors those given to arts and literature were called *Wen i. e.* Scholarly,

those fond of War *Wu i. e.* Warriors. Both designations had their real basis. They served to exhort others to do the like.

If at the time of *Huang Ti* posthumous titles were not yet given according to qualities, of what generation were those who first called him *Huang Ti? Huang TVs* own subjects must have known their prince, and later generations could trace his doings. Although our doubts about the existence of appellatives and posthumous titles at *Huang Jt's* time may not be set at rest, at all events it is evident that *Huang* cannot mean an Immortal who rose to Heaven.

A dragon does not rise to Heaven. If *Huang Ti* rode on a dragon, it is clear that he could not have ascended to Heaven either. When a dragon rises, clouds and rain appear simultaneously and carry it along. As soon as the clouds disperse, and the rain stops, the dragon comes down again, and re-enters its pond. Should *Huang Ti* really have ridden on a dragon, he would afterwards have been drowned with the dragon in the pond.

Huang Ti was interred in the *Chiao* Mountain, and still they say that his officials buried his garments and cap. If he actually went up to Heaven on a dragon, his garments and cap cannot have separated from his body, and if he became a genius after the hill sacrifice and vanished, he cannot have left his garments and cap The fundamental principle of Taoism. The Taoists have always claimed *Huang Ti* as one of theirs. Hence the legend of his ascension to heaven. This seems to me a fancy etymology. *Huang* is "yellow," but never means "to pacify." The "Yellow Emperor" was called yellow from the colour of the earth, over which he ruled. Thus the name is generally explained, whether correctly is doubtful. Some say that this mountain is situated in the province of *Kanmi,* others more eastward in the province of *Sheimi. Vid. Mii-chi* chap. 1, p. 8. behind either. Did *Huang 71* really become a genius, who could not die, but rose to Heaven, his officers and people must have seen it

with their own eyes. Having thus witnessed his ascension to Heaven, they decidedly knew that he did not die. Now, to bury the garments and cap of somebody, who did not die, would have been, as if he had died. Such a thing would not have been in accordance with the feelings of the officials, who were aware of the real state of affairs, and could distinguish between life and death.

It is on record that the seventy-two sovereigns who ascended Mount *T at,* had troubled and toiled, worrying themselves over the state of the empire. Subsequently their efforts were crowned with success, and things settled, so that universal peace reigned throughout the land. When there was universal peace, the whole empire enjoyed harmony and tranquillity. Then they ascended the *T ai-shan,* and performed the hill-sacrifices. Now, the pursuit of *Tao* and the struggle for immortality are different from the vexatious of official life and business. He whose thoughts all centre in *Tao,* forgets worldly affairs, because to trouble about them would injure his nature. They say that *Yao* looked dried up at1d *Shun* withered. Their hearts were sorrowful, and their bodies feeble and care-worn. If *Huang Ti* brought about universal peace, his appearance must have been similar to that of *Yao* and *Shun.* Since *Yao* and *Shun* did not attain to *Tao,* it cannot be true that *Huang Ti* rose to Heaven. If *Huang Ti* in his pursuit of *Tao* neglected all wordly affairs, his mind would have been equanimous, and his body fat and strong. Then he would have been quite different from *Yao* and *Shun,* and consequently his achievements could not have been the same. In that case the universe would not have enjoyed universal peace. Without the universal peace his sacrifice on the mountain would not have taken place.

The Five Emperors and Three Rulers were all remarkable for their wisdom and virtue, *Huang Ti* not more than the others. If all the sages became genii, *Huang Ti* would not be one alone, and if the sages did not become genii, why should *Huang Ti* alone be China's most sacred mountain in *Shantung.* Taoism inculcates contemplation and quietism, and abhors an active life.

Only he who possesses *Tao,* becomes immortal, and can ascend to heaven. If the model emperors *Yao* and *Shun* did not attain to *Tao,* why should *Huang Ti,* provided that he worked as hard as *Yao* and *Shun.* The hill-sacrifice, was not performed, unless the empire enjoyed peace, and peace could not be secured without hard work. Hard work precluded a Taoist life, and without *Tao, Huang Ti* could not ascend on high. a genius? People seeing that *Huang Ti* was very partial to magical arts, which are practised hy genii, surmised that he was a genius.

Moreover, on finding the name of " *Ting-hu*" "Tripod beard " they said that *Huang Ti* exploited tlie copper of Mount *Shou,* and cast it into tripods, and that a dragon with a floating beard came to meet him. This explanation would be on the same line with that of the *K'uei-chi* Mountain. The purport of the name of this mountain is said to be that the emperor *Yd* of the *Hsia* dynasty on a tour of inspection held a meeting () and a review () on this mountain, whence its name *K'uei-chi. Yil* went to *K'uei-cM* for the purpose of regulating the water courses, but not on a tour of inspection, just as *Huang Ti* was addicted to magic, but did not ascend to heaven. There was no such thing like a meeting or a review, as there was no casting of tripods, nor a dragon with a long beard. There is a village called *Shing-mu* " Vanquish mother." Does that mean that there was really a son who vanquished his mother? A city is called *Chao-ko* "Morning song." Are we to infer that the inhabitants of that city used to sing, when they rose in the morning?

The books of the Literati relate that the Prince of *Huai-nan* in his study of Taoism assembled all the Taoists of the empire, and humbled the grandeur of a princedom before the expositors of Taoist lore. Consequently, Taoist scholars flocked to *Huai-nan* and vied with each other in exhibiting strange tricks and all kinds of miracles. Then the prince attained to *Tao* and rose to heav-

en with his whole household. His domestic animals became genii too. His dogs barked up in the sky, and the cocks crowed in the clouds. That means that there was such plenty of the drug of immortality, that dogs and cocks could eat of it, and follow the prince to Heaven. All who have a fad for Taoism and would learn the art of immortality believe in this story, but it is not true.

Man is a creature. His rank may be ever so high, even princely or royal, his nature cannot be different from that of other creatures. There is no creature but dies. How could man become an im The text says "Tripod lake." Cf. above p. 332.

In the province of *Chekiang.* This etymology is given by *Ste Ma Ch'ien, Shi-chi* chap. 2, p. 26. *Liu An,* Prince of *Huai-nan,* commonly known as *Iluai A'an Tse,* a Taoist philosopher and alchymist of the 2nd cent, *B.c.* He was a prince of the imperinl family of the *Han* emperors. His principality was situated in *Anhtu.* . mortal? Birds having feathers and plumes can fly, but they cannot rise to Heaven. How should man without feathers and plumes be able to fly and rise? Were he feathered and winged, he would only be equal to birds, but he is not; how then should he ascend to heaven?

Creatures capable of flying and rising, are provided with feathers and wings, others fast at running, have hoofs and strong feet. Swift runners cannot fly, and flyers not run. Their bodies are differently organised according to the fluid they are endowed with. Now man is a swift runner by nature, therefore he does not grow feathers or plumes. From the time he is full-grown up till his old age he never gets them by any miracle. If amongst the believers in Taoism and the students of the art of immortality some became feathered and winged, they might eventually fly and rise after all.

In case the nature of creatures could be changed, it ought to be possible that metal, wood, water, and fire were also altered. Frogs can be changed into quails, and sparrows dive into the water and become clams. It is the upshot of

their spontaneous, original nature, and cannot be attained by the study of *Tao.* Lest the Taoists should be put on a level with the aforesaid animals, I say that, if men could have all the necessary feathers and plumage, they might ascend to heaven.

Now. the growth and development of creatures is not abrupt, and its changes are not violent, but gradually brought about. If the Taoists and students of immortality could first grow feathers and plumes several inches long, so that they could skim over the earth, and rise to the terraces of high buildings, one might believe that they can ascend to heaven. But they do not show that they are able to fly even a small distance. How can they suddenly acquire the faculty of flying such a long way through the study of their miraculous arts without any gradual progress? That such a great result might be really effected by means of feathers and wings cannot be ascertained.

The human hair and beard, and the different colours of things, when young and old, afford another cue. When a plant comes out, it has a green colour, when it ripens, it looks yellow. As long as man is young, his hair is black, when he grows old, it turns white.

The elements of which the bodies of all creatures are composed cannot be transformed, therefore those creatures cannot change their nature. These metamorphoses are mentioned in ancient works, and believed by the Chinese up to the present day. Cf. p. 32ti.

Yellow is the sign of maturity, white of old age. After a plant has become yellow, it may be watered and tended ever so much, it does not become green again. When the hair has turned white, no eating of drugs nor any care bestowed upon one's nature can make it black again. Black and green do not come back, how could age and decrepitude be laid aside?

Yellow and white are like the frying of raw meat, and the cooking of fresh fish. What has been fried, cannot be caused to become raw again, and what has been cooked, to become fresh. Fresh and raw correspond to young and strong, fried and cooked, to weak and old. Heaven in developing things can keep them vigorous up till autumn, but not further on till next spring. By swallowing drugs and nourishing one's nature one may get rid of sickness, but one cannot prolong one's life, and become an immortal. Immortals have a light body and strong vital energy, and yet they cannot rise to heaven. Light and strong though they be, they are not provided with feathers and wings, and therefore not able to ascend to heaven.

Heaven and earth are both bodies. As one cannot descend into the earth, one cannot ascend into heaven. Such being the case, where would be a road leading up to heaven? Man is not strong enough to enter and pass through heaven's body. If the gate of heaven is in the North-west, all people rising to heaven must pass by the *K'un-lun* Mountain. The State of *Hwai Nan Tse* being situated in the South-east of the earth, he must, if he really ascended to heaven, first have gone to *K'un-lun* with all his household, where he would have found an ascent. Provided the Prince of *Huainan* flew straight across the land to the north-western corner, flapping his wings, then he must have had feathers and wings. But since no mention is made of his passing by the *K un-lun*, nor of feathers and wings growing out of his body, the mere assertion of his ascension cannot be but wrong and untrue.

Liu An, prince *of Huai-nan,* lived contemporaneously with the emperor *Hsiao Wu Ti.* His father *Liu Chang* was banished to *Yentao* in *Shu* for some offence, but died on the road, when he arrived at *Yung-chou Liu An,* who succeeded him in his princedom, bore a grudge against the emperor for having caused his father's 140-86 B.c. The modern *Ya-choufu.* An old kingdom in *Ssechuan.* One of the Nine Provinces, into which *Yü* divided the Empire, comprising *Shensi* and *Kantu.*
Lan-Heng.
death in exile, and thought of making rebellion. He attracted all sorts of schemers, and intended great things. Men like *Wu Pei* filled his palaces, busy in writing books on the Taoist arts, and

publishing essays on the most miraculous subjects. They were bustling about and putting their heads together.
In the "*Memoir of the Eight Companions*" they wished to prove supernatural forces, as if they had attained to *Tao.* But they never reached it, and had no success. Then *Huai Nan Tse* plotted a rebellion together with *Wu Pei.* The scheme was discovered, and he committed suicide or, as some say, was done to death. Whether this be the case, or whether he committed suicide is about the same. But people finding his writings very deep, abstruse, and mysterious, and believing that the predictions of the "*Pa-hingchuan*" had been fulfilled, divulged the story that he had become a genius, and went up to heaven, which is not in accordance with truth.

It is chronicled in the books of the Literati that *Lu Ao,* when wandering near the "Northern Sea," passed the "Great North," and through the "Dark Gate" entered upon the Mongolean plateau. There he beheld an individual with deep eyes, a black nose and the neck of a wild goose. Lifting his shoulders, he soared up, and rapidly came down again, gamboling and disporting all the time against the wind. When he caught sight of *Lu Ao,* he suddenly took down his arms, and sought refuge under a rock. *Lu Ao* saw him there resting on the back of. a tortoise and eating an oyster.
Lu Ao accosted him saying, "Sir, I believe that, because I have given up what the world desires, separating from my kindred and leaving my home, in order to explore what is outside of the six cardinal points, you will condemn me. I began travelling in my youth. When I had grown up, I did not care for the ordinary The eight principal Taoist associates of *Huai Nan Tse,* one of which was *Wei Pa.* The following story is taken from *Huai Kan Tse.*
A traveller of the 3rd cent. B.c.
This expression can mean the *Gobi.*
The "Great North" and the "Dark Gate" are Taoist fancy names. It is interesting to note the name *Mongol here.* The last character is written "jij" now. The Mongols were already known to the Chinese

under their actual name in the second century B.C., when they were living in the north of China.
'To wit the four quarters, above and below.
duties of man, but managed to travel about. Of the four poles the "Greath North" is the only one which I have not yet seen. Now unexpectedly I find you here, Sir. Shall we not become friends?"

The stranger burst out laughing and said, "Why, you are a Chinaman. You ought not to come as far as this. Yet sun and moon are still shining here. There are all the stars, the four seasons alternate, and the *Yin* and the *Yang* are still at work. Compared to the "Nameless Region" this is only like a small hill. I travel south over the "Weary Waste," and halt north in the.'Hidden Village." I proceed west to the "Obscure Hamlet," and pass east through the "Place of Dimness." There is no earth beneath, and no heaven above. Listening one does not hear, and to the looker-on the objects flit away from sight. Beyond that region there is still shape. Where that ends, one advances ten million Li by making one step. I could not yet get there. You, Sir, reached only this place in your travels, but speak of exploring. Is not that an exaggeration? But, please, remain. I have to meet *Han Man* on the ninth heaven, and cannot stay longer. "—The stranger then raised his arms, gave his body a jerk, and off he went into the clouds.
Lu Ao stared after him, until he became invisible. His heart was full of endless joy, and at the same time he was grieved, as though he had lost somebody. "Compared with you, my master, said he, I am nothing more than an earthworm is to a wild goose. Crawling the whole day, I do not advance more than some feet, but myself consider it far. It is pitiable indeed."—

Such as *Lu Ao* held that dragons alone have no wings, and when they rise, ride on the clouds. Had *Lu Ao* said that the stranger had wings, his words might be credible. But he did not speak of wings, how could the other then ascend to the clouds?

Those creatures which with agility

rise into the clouds, do not take human food or human drink. The dragon's food is different from that of snakes, hence its movements are not the same as those of snakes. One hears that the Taoists drink an elixir made of gold and gems and eat the (lowers of the purple bole-tus. These extremely fine stuffs make their bodies light, so that they become spirits and genii. The stranger ate the flesh of an oyster. Such is the food of ordinary people, by no means fine, or rendering the This is probably the name of a genius.

According to the belief of the Taoists there are nine superposed stages or spheres of the heavens. body light. How could he then have given himself a jerk and ascended to heaven?

I have heard that those who feed on air do not take solid food, and that the latter do not eat air. The above mentioned stranger ate something substantial. Since he did not live on air, he could not be so light, that he might have risen on high.

May be that *Lu Ao* studying *Tao* and trying hard to become an immortal, travelled to the Northern Sea. Having left human society, and gone far away, he felt that he did not succeed in acquiring *Tao*. He was ashamed and afraid, lest his fellowcountrymen should criticize him. Knowing that things would certainly turn out so, that every body would reproach him, he invented the extravagant stories. He said that he met with a stranger. The meaniug of the whole story is that his efforts to become immortal were not successful, and that time had not yet come.

In the ease of *Liu An,* Prince of *Huai-nan,* who suffered death as a punishment of rebellion, all people heard of it, and at that time saw it, and yet the books of the Literati say that he obtained *Tao,* and disappeared as a genius, and that his cocks and dogs went up to heaven also. We cannot be surprised then that *Lu Ao,* who alone went to a far-off country, leaving no trace, should speak obscure and mysterious words. His case is similar to that of *Hsiang Man Tu* of *P'u-fan* in *Ho-tung? Hsiang Man Tu* was a follower of *Tao* and a student of spiritism.

He abandoned his family, and went away. When after three years absence he came back, his people asked him, what had happened to him. *Hsiang Man Tu* replied "I have no clear recollection of my departure, but I suddenly found myself as if lying down. Several genii appeared, who took me up to heaven, until we were at some few Li's distance from the moon. I saw that above and beneath the moon all was dark, so that I could not distinguish East and West. Where we stopped near the moon, it was bitter cold. I felt hungry, and wished to eat, when a genius gave me a cupful of morning-red to drink. After having taken one cup, one does not feel hunger for several months. I do not know, how many years or months I stayed there, nor what fault I committed, for suddenly I found myself asleep again, and brought down to this place."

The *Ho-tung* people gave him the surname of "Fallen Angel." But dealing thoroughly with the subject, we find that this story is impossible. If *Hsiang Man Tu* could rise to heaven, he must have become a genius. How could he return after three years' time? If a man leaves his kindred, and ascends to heaven, his vital fluid and his body must have undergone a change. Now, all creatures that have been metamorphosed, do not return to their previous state. When a chrysalis has changed into a cricket, and received its wings, it cannot be transmuted into a chrysalis again. All creatures that fly up, have wings. When they fly up, and come down again, their wings are still there as before. Had *Hsiang Man Tu's* body had wings, his tale might be reliable, but since it had not, his talk is futile and not more trustworthy than *Lu Ao's.*

Perhaps it was known at his time that *Hsiang Man Tu* was a fervent believer in *Tao,* who stealthily left his home, and wandered about in distant lands. At last, when he achieved nothing, and felt his strength exhausted, and his hope gone, he stealthily returned home, but being ashamed, if he had nothing to say, he told the story of his ascension to heaven, intimating thereby that Tao could be learned, and that there really were

genii, and that he himself was degraded for some fault, after having reached the goal, first rising to heaven, and then coming down again.

The books of the Literati contain the statement that the king of *Ch'i* being dangerously ill, a messenger was sent to *Sung* to fetch *Wen Chih.* When he arrived and saw the king's sickness he said to the heir-apparent: "The king's illness can certainly be cured, but when it has been, the king is sure to kill me."

The heir-apparent inquired what for, *Win Chih* replied, "Without anger the king's illness cannot be cured, but when the king gets angry, my death is certain. "

The heir-apparent bowed his head, and entreated him saying, "Should you cure the king's sickness, myself and my mother are going to forcibly restrain the king at the cost of our lives. The king will certainly please my mother. We are wishing that you, master, shall have no trouble." *Win Chih* gave his consent and said that he was prepared to die. The king with his eldest son fixed a time. Thrice the phy A famous doctor, who cannot have lived later than the 4th cent. B.C., for he is mentioned in *Lieh Te.* sician was expected, but did not come so, that the king of *Ch i* was already very angry. When he came at last, he did not put off his shoes, but walked upon the bed and tread upon the sheets. He asked the king about his sickness, but the king was so furious, that he did not speak with him. Then he said something which but aggravated the king's wrath. The king abused him, and rose up, and his disease was gone. He was so enraged and so little pleased, that he wished to boil *Win Chih* alive. The heir-apparent and the queen forthwith interfered, but could obtain nothing. *Wen Chih* was actually boiled alive in a cauldron: After three days' and three night's cooking, his appearance had not yet changed. *Win Chih* said, "If one really is anxious to kill me, why does one not put on the lid to intercept the *Yin* and the *Yang* fluids."

The king had the lid put on, whereupon *Win Chih* died. *Win Chih* was a Taoist, in water he was not drowned, and in fire he did not burn. Hence he could remain three days and three nights in the kettle without changing colour.

This is idle talk. *Win Chih* was boiled three days and nights without changing colour. If then only in consequence of the lid being put on he was choked and died, this proves that he was not in possession of Tao. All living and breathing creatures die, when deprived of air. When they are dead and boiled, they become soft. If living and breathing creatures are placed in vessels with a lid on, having all their fissures carefully filled, so that the air cannot circulate, and their breath cannot pass, they die instantaneously. Thrown into a kettle with boiling water, they are also cooked soft. Why? Because they all have the same kind of body, the same breath, are endowed by heaven with a similar nature, and all belong to one class. If *Win Chih* did not breathe, he would have been like a piece of metal or stone, and even in boiling water not be cooked soft. Now he was breathing, therefore, when cooked, he could not but die.

If *Win Chih* could speak, he must have given sounds, which require breathing. Breathing is closely connected with the vital force, which resides in bones and flesh. Beings of bones and flesh being cooked, die. To deny that is the first untruth.

Provided that *Win Chih* could be cooked without dying, he was a perfect Taoist, similar to metal or stone. To metal or stone it makes no difference, whether a lid be put on, or not. There A parallel passage of this story occurs in the *Li-shih-ch'un-ch'ni.*

s That is what the Taoists say of themselves.

fore, to say that *Win Chih* died, when the lid was put on, is a second untruth.

Put a man into cold water, which is not hot like boiling water, and he will die for want of breath after a short interval, his nose and mouth being shut out from the outer air. Submerged in cold water, a man cannot remain alive, how much less in bubbling, boiling water, in the midst of a violent fire? To say that *Win Chih* survived in the boiling water is a third uutruth.

When a man is submerged in water, so that his mouth is not visible outside, the sound of what he says is inaudible. When' *Win Chih* was cooked, his body was certainly submerged in the kettle, and his mouth invisible. Under those circumstances one could not hear, what he said. That *Win Chih* should have spoken is the fourth untruth.

Had a man who after three days' and three nights' cooking died, not changed colour, even ignorant people would have been amazed. If the king of *Ch i* was not surprised, the heir-apparent and his ministers should have noticed this wonderful fact. In their astonishment at *Win Chih* they would have prayed that he be taken out, granted high honours, and be venerated as a master, from whom one might learn more about Tao. Now three days and three nights are mentioned, but nothing is said about the officials asking for his release. That is the fifth untruth.

At that time it was perhaps known that *Win Chih* was actually cooked, and that his death was caused by it. People noticing that he was a Taoist, invented the story that he lived a subtle life, and did not die, just as *Huang Ti* really died, whereas the reports say that he rose to heaven, and as the prince of *Huai-nan* suffered the punishment of rebellion, whilst the books say that he entered a new life. There are those who like to spread false reports. Hence the story of *Win Chih* has been propagated until now.

There are no instances of any one having obtained Tao, but there have been very long-lived persons. People remarking that those persons, while studying Tao and the art of immortality, become over a hundred years old without dying, call them immortals, as the following example will show.

At the time of *Han Wu Ti* there lived a certain *Li Shao Chan,* who pretended that by sacrificing to the "Hearth" and abstaining from eating grain he could ward off' old age. He saw the emperor, who conferred high honours upon him. *Li Shao Chan* kept his age 140-85 B. c. and the place where he was born and had grown up secret, always saying that

he was seventy old, and could effect that things did not grow old. On his journeys he visited all the princes around, and was not married. On hearing that he could manage that things did not age, people presented him with much richer gifts than they would otherwise have done. He had always money, gold, dresses, and food in abundance. As people believed that he did not do any business, and was. yet richly provided with everything, and as nobody knew, what sort of a man he really was, there was a general competition in offering him services.

Li Shao Chiln knew some clever manoeuvres and some fine tricks, which did not fail to produce a wonderful effect. He used to feast with the Marquis of *Wu-an*. In the hall there was a man of over 90 years. *Li Shao Chiln* indicated to him the places which his grand-father frequented, when shooting. The old man knew them, having visited them as a child with his father. The whole audience was bewildered.

When *Li Shao Chiln* saw the emperor, the emperor had an old bronze vase, about which he asked him. *Li Shao Chiln* replied that in the 15th year-of the reign of Duke *Huan* of *Ch'i3* it was placed in the *Po-ch in* hall. The inscription was examined, and it was found out that it was indeed a vessel of Duke *Huan* of *Ch i*. The whole Court was startled, and thought that *Li Shao Chiln* was several hundred years old. After a long time he died of sickness.

Those who now-a-days are credited with the possession of *Tao* are men like *Li Shao Chiln*. He died amongst men. His body was seen, and one knew, therefore, that his nature had been longevous. Had he dwelt in mountain-forests or gone into deserts, leaving no trace behind him, he would have died a solitary death of sickness amidst high rocks. His corpse would have been food for tigers, wolves, and foxes, but the world would again have believed him to have disappeared as a real immortal.

The ordinary students of *Tao* have not *Li Shao Chiln's* age. Before reaching a hundred years they die like all the others. Yet uncultured and ignorant people still hold that they are separated from their bodies, and vanish, and that, as a matter of fact, they do not die.

A district in *Honan*. The name of the Marquis was *T'ien Fen*. The *Shih-chi* says the tenth year. Duke *Huan* of *Ch'i* reigned from 683-641 B.c. The 15th year of his reign was 669. This story of *Li Shao Chun* is quoted from the *Shi-chi* chap. 28, p. 21.

What is understood by separation from the body? Does it mean that the body dies, and the spirit disappears? Or that the body does not die, but drops its coil? If one says that the body dies, and the spirit is lost, there is no difference from death, and every one is a genius. And if one believes that the body does not die, but throws off its coil, one must admit that the bones and the flesh of all the deceased Taoists are intact and in no wise different from the corpses of ordinary mortals.

When the cricket leaves its chrysalis, the tortoise drops its shell, the snake its skin, and the stag its horns, in short, when the horned and skinned animals lose their outward cover, retaining only their flesh and bones, one might speak of the separation from the body. But even if the body of a dead Taoist were similar to a chrysalis, one could not use this expression, because, when the cricket leaves the chrysalis, it cannot be considered as a spirit with regard to the chrysalis. Now to call it a separation from the body, when there is not even a similarity with the chrysalis, would again be an unfounded assertion missing the truth.

The Grand Annalist was a contemporary of *Li Shao Chiln*. Although he was not amongst those who came near to *Li Shao Chun's* body, when he had expired, he was in a position to learn the truth. If he really did not die, but only parted with his body, the Grand Annalist ought to have put it on record, and would not have given the place of his death.

The reference to the youth of the nonagenarian in the court would prove *Li Shao Chiln s* age. Perhaps he was fourteen or fifteen years old, when the old man accompanied his grandfather as a boy. Why should *Li Shao Chiln* not know this, if he lived 200 years? *Wu Ti's* time is very far from Duke *Huan*, when the bronze vase was cast, and *Li Shao Chiln* cannot have seen it. Perhaps he heard once that in the palace there was an old vessel, or he examined the inscription beforehand to speak upon it, so that he was well-informed, when he saw it again. When our amateurs of today see an old sword or an antique crooked blade, they generally know where to place it. Does that imply that they saw, how it was wrought?

Why 200 years? *Li Shao Chun* would have known the nonagenarian's grandfather, if he was about ninety years old himself. The interval is upwards of 500 years. *Tung Fang So* is said to have also been possessed of *Tao*. His name was *Chin*, his style *Man Chien*, but he changed his names and for a time took office with the *Han* dynasty. Outwardly he was considered an official, but inwardly he passed to another existence. This is wrong too. *Tung Fang So* lived together with *Li Shao Chun* under the reign of *Wu* 7», and must have been known to the Grand Annalist. *Li Shao Chun* taught *Tao* and a method to keep off old age by means of sacrificing to the "Hearth." He determined the period of a tripod cast under Duke *Huan* of *Ch i*, and knew the places frequented, when hunting, by the grandfather of a nonagenarian, and yet he did not really attain to *Tao*. He was only a long-lived man, who died late. Moreover, *Tung Fang So* was not as successful as *Li Shao Chim ia* magical arts, wherefore then was he credited with the possession of *Tao*? Under *Wu Ti* there were the Taoists *Wen Ch'ing* and *Wu Li* and others of the same type, who went on sea in search of the genii and to find the physic of immortality. Because they evidently knew the Taoist arts, they were trusted by the Emperor. *Tung Fang So* undertook no mission on sea, nor did he do anything miraculous. If he had done, he would only have been a man like *Li Shao Chun* or on a level with *Win Ch'ing* and *Wu Li*. Nevertheless he had the chance to be credited with the possession of *Tao*. He again resembled *Li Shao Chun*, in-somuch as he made a secret of his birth place, and the courtiers did not know his origin. He exaggerated his age. People finding that he looked rather strong and young and was of phlegmatic temper, that he did not care much for his office, but was well versed in divination, guessing, and other interesting plays, called him therefore a man possessed of *Tao*.

There is a belief that by the doctrine of *Lao Tse* one can transcend into another existence. Through quietism and dispassionateness one nourishes the vital force, and cherishes the spirit. The length of life is based on the animal spirits. As long as they are unimpaired, life goes on, and there is no death. *Lao Tse* acted upon this principle. Having done so for over a hundred years, he passed into another existence, and became a true Taoist sage.

Who can be more quiet and have less desires than birds and animals? But birds and animals likewise age and die. However, we will not speak of birds and animals, the passions of which are similar to the human. But which are the passions of plants and shrubs, that they are born in spring, and die in autumn'. ' They are dispassionate, and their lives do not extend further than one year. Men are full of passions and desires, and yet they can become a hundred years old. Thus the dispassionate die prematurely, and the passionate live long. Hence *Lao Tse's* theory to prolong life and enter a new existence by means of quietism and absence of desires is wrong.

Lao Tse was like *Li Shao Chun*. He practised his theory of quietism, and his life happened to be long of itself. But people seeing this, and hearing of his quietism, thought that by his art he passed into another existence.

The idea prevails that those who abstain from eating grain, are men well versed in the art of *Tao*. They say e. g. that *Wang Tse Chiao* and the like, because they did not touch grain, and lived on different food than ordinary people, had not the same length of life as ordinary people, in so far as having passed a hundred years, they transcended into another state of being, and became immortals.

That is another mistake. Eating and drinking are natural impulses, with which we are endowed at birth. Hence the upper part of the body has a mouth and teeth, the inferior part orifices. With the mouth and teeth one chews and eats, the orifices are for the discharge. Keeping in accord with one's nature, one follows the law of heaven, going against it, one violates one's natural propensities, and neglects one's natural spirit before heaven. How can one obtain long life in this way?

If *Wang Tse Ch ian* had got no mouth, teeth, or orifices at birth, his nature would have been different from that of others. Even then one could hardly speak of long life. Now, the body is the same, only the deeds being different. To say that in this way one can transcend into another existence is not warranted by human nature.

For a man not to eat is like not clothing the body. Clothes keep the skin warm, and food fills the stomach. With a warm epidermis and a well-filled belly the animal spirits are bright and exalted. If one is hungry, and has nothing to eat, or feels cold, and has nothing to warm one's self, one may freeze or starve to death. How can frozen and starved people live longer than others?
A magician of the tith cent. B.C., son of King *Ling* of the *Chou* dynasty. He is reported to have been seen riding on a white crane through the air as an immortal.
Moreover, during his life man draws his vital force from food, just as plants and trees do from earth. Pull out the roots of a plant or a tree, and separate them from the soil, and the plant will wither, and soon die. Shut a man's mouth, so that he cannot eat, and he will starve, but not be long-lived.

The Taoists exalting each other's power assert that the " pure man" eats the fluid, that the fluid is his food. Wherefore the books say that the fluid-eaters live long, and do not die, that, although they do not feed on cereals, they become fat and strong by the fluid.

This too is erroneous. What kind of fluid is understood by fluid? If the fluid

of the *Yin* and the *Yang* be meant, this fluid cannot satiate people. They may inhale this fluid, so that it fills their belly and bowels, yet they cannot feel satiated. If the fluid inherent in medicine be meant, man may use and eat a case full of dry drugs, or swallow some ten pills. But the effects of medicine are very strong. They cause great pain in the chest, but cannot feed a man. The meaning must certainly be that the fluid-eaters breathe, inhaling and exhaling, emitting the old air and taking in the new. Of old, *P'eng Tsu* used to practise this. Nevertheless he could not live indefinitely, but died of sickness.

Many Taoists hold that by regulating one's breath one can nourish one's nature, pass into another state of being, and become immortal. Their idea is that, if the blood vessels in the body be not always in motion, expanding and contracting, an obstruction ensues. There being no free passage, constipation is the consequence, which causes sickness and death.

This is likewise without any foundation. Man's body is like that of plants and trees. Plants and trees growing on the summits of high mountains, where they are exposed to the squalls of wind, are moved day and night, but do they surpass those that are hidden in mountain valleys and sheltered from wind?
The Chinese *Methusaleh,* who is believed to have lived over 800 years, and to have been a great grandson of the legendary Emperor *Chuan Hsu* 2514 B.C.
When plants and trees, while growing, are violently shaken, they are injured, and pine away. Why then should man by drawing his breath and moving his body gain a long life and not die? The blood arteries traverse the body, as streams and rivers flow through the land. While thus flowing, the latter lose their limpidity, and become turbid. When the blood is moved, it becomes agitated also, which causes uneasiness. Uneasiness is like the hardships man has to endure without remedy. How can that be conducive to a long life?

The Taoists sometimes use medicines with a view to rendering their bodies more supple and their vital force

stronger, hoping thus to prolong their years and to enter a new existence.

This is a deception likewise. There are many examples that by the use of medicines the body grew more supple and the vital force stronger, but the world affords no instance of the prolongation of life and a new existence following.

The different physics cure all sorts of diseases. When they have been cured, the vital force is restored, and then the body becomes supple again. According to man's original nature his body is supple of itself, and his vital force lasts long of its own accord. But by exposure to wind and wetness he falls a victim to hundreds of diseases, whence his body becomes heavy and stiff, and his force is weakened. By taking an efficacious remedy he restores his body and the vital force. This force is not small at the outset, or the body heavy, and it is not by medicine that the force lasts long, or the body grows supple and light. When first received, they already possess those qualities spontaneously. Therefore, when by medicines the various diseases are dispelled, the body made supple, and the vital force prolonged, they merely return to their original state, but it is impossible to add to the number of years, let alone the transition into another existence.

Of all the beings with blood in their veins there are none but are born, and of those endowed with life there are none but die. From the fact that they were born, one knows that they must die. Heaven and Earth were not born, therefore they do not die. The *Yin* and the *Yang* were not born, therefore they do not die. Death is the correlate of birth, and birth the counterpart of death. That which has a beginning, must have an end, and that which has an end, must necessarily have had a begin Viz. received by man at his birth, when Heaven endows him with a body and the vital fluid.
ning. Only what is without beginning or end, lives for ever and never dies.
Human life is like water. Water frozen gives ice, and the vital force concentrated forms the human being. Ice lasts one

winter, then it melts, man lives a hundred years, than he dies. Bid a man not to die, can you bid ice not to melt? All those who study the art of immortality and trust that there are means, by which one does not die, must fail as sure, as one cannot cause ice never to melt.

This the Taoists say of their fundamental principle. "*Tao* is without beginning, without end," says *Chuang Tse* chap. 17, p. 13, and thus the Taoists which have become one with *Too,* are immortal. CHAPTER XXIX.

On Dragons *Lung-/isii).*

When in midsummer during a thunderstorm lightning strikes a tree or demolishes a house, it is a common saying that Heaven fetches the dragon, which is believed to hide in the tree, or to be concealed in the house. The lightning striking the tree, or demolishing the house, the dragon appears outside. On its appearance, it is seized upon by the thunder, and carried up to Heaven. The unintelligent and the learned, the virtuous and the wicked are all agreed upon this, but trying to get at the truth, we find that it is idle talk.

Why should Heaven fetch the dragon? Provided that the dragon be a spirit and Heaven's envoy, as a virtuous minister is the deputy of his sovereign, then it ought to report itself at a fixed time, and would not have to be fetched. If, on the other hand, the dragon sneaks away, and does not come back, it does not behave like a spirit, and would be of no use to Heaven.

According to the dragon's nature its real abode is Heaven. Being there it certainly must have offspring. There would be no reason, why it should be on earth again. If there are rising and descending dragons, the latter class might bear its offspring on earth, and Heaven fetch it, when grown up. People call a tempest an expression of Heaven's anger, but in fetching the scion of a dragon it cannot be angry.

Further the dragon generally lives in ponds, not in trees or houses. Whence do we know that? *Shu Hsiang's* mother said: "In the depths of mountains and in vast marshes dragons and snakes really grow." And in books we read, "Where

the mountains are highest, the rain clouds rise, and where the water is deepest, the different species of dragons are born." The annals A minister in *Chin,* 6th cent. B.c. Quoted from the *Tso-chunn,* Duke *Hsiang* 21st year *(Legge, Clanics* Vol. V, Pt. II, p. 491). The mother of *Shu Hsiang* spoke these words in a figurative sense, with reference to *Shu Ihiang'"* half-brother, and his beautiful mother, a concubine of her husband. Cf. p. 302.

A parallel passage, worded a little differently, occurs in *Hsiin Tse.* go on to say that, when *Yil* crossed the *YangUe,* a yellow dragon carried his boat on its back, and that, when *Ching Tse Fei* went over the *Huai,* two dragons swam round his ship. Near the Eastern Sea there lived *Lu Chiu Hsin,* a bold and strong man. When he once passed the Spirit Pool, he ordered his charioteer to give his horse to drink there, but when it drank, it sank down. *Lu Chiu Hsin* got angry, drew his sword, and went into the pool in pursuit of his horse. He then beheld two dragons just in the act of devouring his horse. Sword in hand, he slew the two dragons. Hence it is evident that the dragons called "¢Atao" and the others always live in the water of pools, and not on trees or in houses.

Living in deep water dragons belong to the same category as fish and reptiles. Why should fish and reptiles ascend to Heaven, and what could Heaven use the dragon for, if it fetched it up? If the Spirit of Heaven should ride on the dragon, a spirit is something diffuse and incorporeal. Entering and departing, it needs no aperture, neither would it require a dragon to ride upon. Should the genii mount the dragon, then Heaven would fetch it for their sake. But the genii are imbued with the fluid of Heaven, and their bodies are so light, that they can fly up like wild geese. Therefore, why should they ride upon dragons?

People in general say that *Huang Ti* ascended to Heaven on a dragon. This statement is as inane as the other, made now-adays, that Heaven fetches the dragon. If the dragon is said to rise to Heaven, it implies a dragon spirit, be-

cause only a spirit can soar on high, this being in fact a characteristic feature of spirits.

Among the creatures produced by Heaven and Earth man being the noblest, the dragon must be inferior. If the noblest are not spirits, can the inferior be so? Let us suppose that the nature of dragons be such, that some of them are spirits, the others not, and that the spirits rise to Heaven, while those that are not spirits, cannot: are turtles and snakes likewise partly spirits and partly not, and can the turtle spirits and the snake spirits ascend to Heaven?

Moreover, what essence is the dragon endowed with, that it should alone be a spirit? Heaven has the four constellations of the Blue Dragon, the White Tiger, the Scarlet Bird, and the Black This fact is recorded in the *Lii Shih ch'un-ch'iu* and in *Huai Nan Tse* VII, 8v. *Vid.* also *Inin-heng* Bk. V, p. 4 *(Yi-hsii).* The Yellow Sea, east of China. This story is narrated in the *Han-shih-wai-chuan* 150 B.c. and the *Po-wuchih,* where the hero is called *Tsai Chht Hsin* however. *m* Tortoise. Earth also has dragons, tigers, scarlet birds, and turtles. The essence of the four constellations pouring down, produces those four animals. The tiger, the scarlet bird, and the turtle not being spirits, wherefore should the dragon alone be a spirit?

Man ranks first among the naked creatures, as the dragon is the foremost of the scaly animals. Both take the first place among their kindred. If the dragon is believed to ascend to Heaven, does man rise to Heaven likewise? If under the above respect the dragon is on the same level with man, but alone credited with the faculty of ascending to Heaven, the dragon must be supposed to be a spirit.

The world also says that the sages being spirits, have the gift of prophecy, as they say that the dragon spirits are able to soar to Heaven. The divination of the sages thus being accounted for, it is but natural that the special talent of the dragon should be found in its power to rise to Heaven.

That which amidst Heaven and Earth

is vague and unsubstantial as the vapours of cold and heat, wind and rain, has the nature of a spirit. Now the dragon has a body, having a body, it moves about, moving about, it eats, and eating, it has the nature of other creatures. According to the organisation of Heaven and Earth whatever possesses a body, moves about, and eats, cannot be a spirit. How so?

The dragon has a body. One finds in books the statement, that out of the three hundred scaly animals the dragon is the first. Being the first of the scaly animals, how can it be without a body? Confucius said that the dragon fed in limpid places, and lived there, that the tortoise fed in limpid places, and lived in the mud, and that the fish fed in the mud, and lived in clear water. He did not attain to the dragon himself, but was neither equal to the fish, he was only to be compared to the tortoise, which takes the middle rank.

The Shan-hai-king relates that beyond the four seas there are men riding on dragon snakes. As a rule, dragons are pictorially represented with a horse's head and a snake's tail. Hence they must be hybrids between the horse and the snake.

Shin Tse' informs us that the flying dragons mount the clouds, and that the soaring serpents ramble through the fog. When the clouds disperse, and the rain ceases, they are like earthworms and ants. The "Mountain and Sea Classic," the oldest geographical work of the 4th or the 3rd cent. B.c. The Taoist philosopher Shen Tao of the 5th cent, B.c., of whose works only fragments are left.

I.un-Hing. 23 Han Fei Tse teaches that the dragon is a reptile, which obeys a call, and allowes itself to be patted and mounted. But under its throat it has a protruding scale over a foot long. If a man knocks against it, the dragon always kills him.

In short, the dragon is compared with earthworms and ants, and it is further said to be a reptile, which can be patted and mounted. It must therefore have something in common with snakes and horses.

It is reported that when Chou used

ivory chopsticks, Chi Tse burst into tears. He wept, commiserating his excesses. There being ivory chopsticks, there must have beeu jade cups also. These jade cups and ivory chopsticks were certainly used to hold and to seize dragon liver and unborn leopard. Dragon liver was eatable, but a dragon hard to be found. This being the case, the emperor would frown upon his subordinates. That would bring them into distress, therefore Chi Tse's sympathy.

If the dragon were a spirit, its body could not be killed, and its liver not be eaten. The livers and the unborn young of birds and animals are not the same. Dragon liver and unborn leopard being specially mentioned, man must have eaten them, and thereby learned to appreciate their excellent taste.

During the epoch of Spring and Autumn, a dragon appeared in the outskirts of Chiang.1 Viscount Hsien of Wei interrogated T'sai Me saying, "I heard say that of all creatures none is as intelligent as the dragon, which therefore cannot be caught alive. Is it true what they say about its cleverness?" The other replied, "Those that say so, really do not know. As a fact, the dragon is not intelligent. Of old, dragons were domesticated, therefore the empire had its families of Dragon Keeper (Huan Lung) and its Master of the Dragons (Yil Lung)." Cf. p. 170.

Chou Haia, the last emperor of the Shang dynasty. Ivory chopsticks are very common in China now, and no luxury. Viscount Chi, one of the foremost nobles under Chou Hsin, 12th cent. B.c. Dragon liver and unborn leopard would seem to have been considered great delicacies. The historical period comprised by the Chun-chin (Spring and Autumn) between 722 and 481 B.c. A principality in Shansi. A feudal lord under Duke Ch'ou of Chin in Shansi, 530-524 B.c. , whose successors became marquises, and at last kings of Wei. The grand historiographer. The family names Huan Lung and Yii Lung, i 1 which literally mean Dragon Keeper and Master of the Dragons, have probably given rise to this queer story.

Viscount Hsien observed that of these

two he had heard also, but did not know their origin, and why they were called so. Tsai Me said, "In olden time there was Shu Sung of Liao.-One of his distant descendants, Tung Fu was very fond of dragons. He could find out their tastes and likings, so as to be able to supply them with food and drink. Many dragons came to him, and were thus bred by him. With them he waited upon Shun, who bestowed upon him the family name of Tung, and the clan-name of Dragon Keeper (Huan Lung), and invested him with Tsung-cKuan. The Tsung-J family were his descendants. Thus dragons were reared at the time of the emperor Shun."

"During the Hsia time K'ung Chia was obedient to God, who presented him with a team of dragons from the Yellow River and the Han, there being a male and a female from each. K'ung Chia was at a loss how to feed them, for no member of the Huan Lung family was to be found. But among the remains of the T'ao T ang family, which had perished, was one Liu Lei, who had learned the art of rearing dragons from the Huan Lung family. With that he served K'ung Chia, and was able to give food and water to the dragons. The Hsia ruler was so pleased with him, that he conferred upon him the clan-name of Master of the Dragons (Yi l Lung). He took the place of the descendants of Shih Wei."

"When one female dragon died, he secretly had it chopped up, and offered the meat to the ruling emperor of the house of Hsia as food. The emperor had it cooked, and asked for more. Then Liu Lei became frightened, because he could not procure it, and emigrated to Lu-hsien." The Fan family were his descendants."—

Viscount Hsien asked, why there were no dragons to-day. 7V at Me replied, "Such animals have their officials, who know their treatment, and think of them day and night. When they suddenly lose their post, the dragons die. The cashiered functionaries do not feed them any more. As long as the competent officials do their duty, there are always animals coining to them, but, when The *Lan-Mng* calls the man *Shu Sung*. In the *Tso-chuan* his name is *Shu An*. A small State.

The emperor *K'ung Chia* 1879-1848 B. c. *T'ao T'ang* was the princedom of the emperor *Yao* in *Shansi,* whose descendants took their clan name therefrom. '-A noble who flourished under the *Shang* dynasty.

0 The modern *Lu-xhan-fmen* in *Honan*. they are neglected, they lie down listless, and their production is stopped."—Thus we may say that dragons can he reared and eaten. What can be eaten, is certainly not a spirit. When the proper officials are not at hand, nor men like *Tung Fu* and *Liu Lei*, the dragons abscond, and hide themselves, and appear but rarely. When they once come out, they also ride on the clouds, a course, man can never take, and are then regarded as spirits. As long as there are the proper officials, or the proper men, the dragon is like an ox. Why should they be spirits?

Taking into consideration what the *Shan-hai-king* says, the evidence of *Shin Tse* and *Han Fei Tse,* the usual pictorial representations, the despair of *Chi Tse,* and the information given by *Ts ai Mi,* we see that the dragon cannot be a spirit, nor rise to Heaven, and it is evident that Heaven does not fetch it with thunder and lightning.

The common belief that the dragon is a spirit, and rises to Heaven, is preposterous. But there is a reason for it. In light literature we meet with the statement that without a tree one foot high the dragon cannot ascend to Heaven. They speak of ascending to Heaven, and of a tree one foot high, implying that the dragon rises to Heaven from within the tree. The authors of this sort of literature are uncultured people. They have observed that at the same time, when the thunder rolls and the lightning flashes up, the dragon rises, ami when thunder and lightning strike a tree, the dragon happens to be close to the tree, just like thunder and lightning. When they are gone, the dragon rises on high likewise. Therefore they pretend that it ascends to Heaven from within the tree. As a matter of fact, the thunder and the

dragon are of the same kind, and mutually attract one another, when set in motion by the forces of nature.

The *Yik'mg* says that the clouds follow the dragon, and the wind the tiger. It is further stated that, when the tiger howls, the wind passes through the valley, and that the variegated clouds rise, when the dragon gambols. There is a certain manner of sympathy between the dragon and the clouds, and a mutual attraction between the tiger and the wind. Therefore, when *Tung* This conversation between Viscount *Hsien* and *T'sai Me* on the rearing of dragons in ancient times is literally culled from the *Tso-chuan,* Duke *Ch'ao* 29th year. Cf. *Legge, Ch'un-cUiu* Pt. II, p. 731. *Yikimj* Book I, *Ch'ien* hexagram (No. 1). See also p. 279 Note 2. *Chung Shu* offered the rain sacrifice, he put up an earthen dragon with a view to attract the rain.

When the summer is at its height, the sun reigns supreme, but the clouds and the rain oppose it. The sun is fire, clouds and rain being water. At the collision with water, fire explodes, and gives a sound, which is the thunder. Upon hearing the sound of thunder, the dragon rises, when it rises, the clouds appear, and when they are there, the dragon mounts them. The clouds and the rain are affected by the dragon, and the dragon also rides on the clouds to Heaven. Heaven stretches to the farthest distance, and the thunder is very high. Upon the clouds dispersing, the dragon alights again. Men seeing it riding on the clouds, believe it to ascend to Heaven, and beholding Heaven sending forth thunder and lightning, they imagine that Heaven fetches the dragon.

The scholars of to-day reading the *Yiking* and the historical records, all know that the dragon belongs to the same class as the clouds. They adhere to the common gossip without knowing, what it means. Besides they look upon the light literature as an authority. Thus they say that Heaven fetches the dragon.

Heaven does not do that, nor does the dragon rise to Heaven. When *Lu Chiu Hsin* slew the two serpents, he dragged them out with his hands by the tail, but

the moment they were out of the pool, a thunder-bolt fell. Serpents are a species similar to dragons. When serpents or dragons make their appearance, clouds and rain arrive, upon their arrival there is thunder and lightning. If Heaven really fetched the dragon for its own use, what benefit would it have from dead serpents?

Fish, though living in the water, yet follow the clouds and the rain flying, and riding on them ascend to Heaven. The dragon belongs to the class of fish, it rides on thunder and lightning in the same way as the fish fly. For following the clouds and the rain, fish are not considered to be spirits, the dragons alone are called spirits because of their riding on thunder and lightning. This common belief is contraiy to truth.

All the creatures in the world have their peculiar vehicles:— The water serpents ride on the fog, the dragons on the clouds, and birds on the wind. To call the dragon alone a spirit, because it is seen riding on the clouds, would not be in accordance with its real nature, and would only detract from its skill.

But the reason why the dragon is looked upon as a spirit, is because it can expand and contract its body, and make itself visible A scholar of the 2nd cent. B.c. See p. 39.

or invisible. Yet the expansion and contraction of the body and its visibility and invisibility do not constitute a spirit. *Yii Jang* swallowed charcoal and varnished his body, so that he got ulcers, and nobody recognised him. *Tse Kung2* burned off his beard, and took the semblance of a woman, so that nobody knew him. When the dragon transforms itself and absconds, men are also unable to perceive it, such is its skill in metamorphosing and hiding itself.

Much in the nature of creatures is spontaneous:—The rhinopithecus knows the past, magpies foresee the future, and parrots can talk. These three peculiarities may be compared to the transformations, which are in the nature of dragons. If by astuteness one could become a spirit, *Yil Jang* and *Tse Kung* would be spirits.

Confucius said, "The roving animals

can be ensnared, the Hying birds be shot with an arrow. As regards the dragon, I do not know, whether it can ride on the wind and the clouds, and thus rise on high. To-day I saw *Lao Tse*. Should he perhaps be like a dragon?"

Provided that the dragon rises, mounted on a cloud, and, when the cloud disperses, comes down again, then the class of creatures, to which it belongs, might be ascertained, and all about its celestial and terrestrial state known. Yet they say that *Confucius* did not know. A sage like *Confucius* ignored the nature of dragons. How much less can common people know, whose learning is deficient, who are biassed in favour of the marvellous, and whose minds are unable to decide, what is possible and what not. That they should call the dragon a spirit, which rises to Heaven can therefore be no matter for surprise.

A native of the *Chin* State, 5th and 6th cent. B.c. He twice made an attempt upon the life of Viscount *Hsiang* of *Chao* to avenge the death of his master, the Earl of *Chih,* whom *Hxiang* had slain. Both attempts failed. The second time he disguised himself in the way described here. A disciple of *Confucius*. A kind of monkey in western China. This probably means that monkeys have an excellent memory. Magpies are believed to know, whether the next year will be very stormy, for in that case they build their nests near the ground. Moreover, they announce future joy, hence their popular name "birds of joy." A quotation from the Biography of *Lao Tse* in the *Shi-chi* chap. 63, p. 2 v. CHAPTER XXX.

Arguments on Ominous Creatures *(Chi-ang-Jui).*

The scholars in their essays claim for themselves the faculty of knowing the phoenix and the unicorn, when they see them. They, of course, rely on the pictures of the phoenix and the unicorn. Besides there is a passage in the *Chun-chiu* concerning the capture of a unicorn to the effect that it was a sort of a deer with a horn. Hence a deer with a horn must be a unicorn. When they see a bird like a phoenix, they take it for a phoenix.

Huang Ti, Yao, Shun, and the sovereigns of the *Chou* dynasty, when it was flourishing, all caused the phoenix to make its appearance. Under the reign of *Hsiao Hsilan* 7i a phoenix alighted in the *Shang-lin* park, and afterwards also on a tree at the east-gate of the *Chang-lo* palace. It was five feet high, and had a beautiful variegated plumage. The unicorn caught by the people of *Chou* resembled a deer, and had a horn; the unicorn of *Wu Ti* was also like a deer with a horn. If there be a huge bird with a variegated plumage, or an animal shaped like a deer having one horn on its head, it is possible, they fancy, to determine, whether it be a phoenix or a unicorn, by referring to drawings and pictures, and to ancient and modern traditions.

Now the phoenix is the holy bird, and the unicorn the holy animal as the *Five Emperors,* the *Three Rulers, Kao Yao,* and *Confucius* are the holy ones among men. The Twelve Holy Men vary considerably in their appearance, can we then call a deer with a horn a unicorn, or a bird resembling a phoenix by this name? Between the hair and the colour of the holy birds and the holy animals there is as much difference as between the osseous structure of the twelve holy men.

The horn is like the character " wu" worn on the front. *Chuan Hsil* had this character on his brow, but *Yao* and *Shun* were not necessarily marked in the same way. If the unicorn caught in *Lu* The last paragraph of the *Ch'un-ch'iu,* Duke *Ai* 14th year, merely mentions the capture of a *tin.* That it was a deer with one horn is recorded in the " Family Sayings" of *Confucius.* See *Legge'* transl. Vol. II, p. 834, Note.

73-48 B.c. 3 Cf. p. 304. had a horn, it does not follow anyhow that the unicorns observed later on had all a horn. Should we be desirous to learn to know the unicorn of the present day by using the unicorn caught in *Lu* as a prototype, we may be sure to fail in our endeavour. The fur, the bones, and the horn vary. Notwithstanding their difference, there may be a certain resemblance, but that does not mean identity. *Shun* had double pupils, and *Wang Mang* also, Duke

Win of *Chin* had his ribs all in one piece, and *Chang Yi* likewise. If a resemblance be based on the osseous structure, the hair and the complexion, then *Wang Mang* was a *Shun,* and *Cliang* Yi a Uuke *Win* of *Chin. Yu Jo* in *Lu* bore a striking resemblance to *Confucius.* After the death of the latter, his disciples all made *Yu Jo* sit down and questioned him on some points of the doctrine, but *Yu Jo* could not answer. Why? Because there was only a likeness of his external appearance, whereas his mind was different. Thus, variegated birds and animals with one horn may sometimes look like a phoenix or a unicorn, but, as a matter of fact, they are not real ones. Tberefore it is a mistake to distinguish a phoenix or a unicorn by their shape, their hair, or their colour.

In this manner did *Yen Yuan* almost equal *Confucius,* but he was not like him, whereas *Yu Jo,* quite an ordinary type of man, looked like a sage. Consequently a real phoenix or a real unicorn may perhaps not look like it, in its outward shape and, on the other hand, quite common birds and animals resemble the real phoenix and unicorn by their hair and colour. How can they be distinguished? The literati who maintain that they are able to recognise a phoenix or a unicorn, when they see them, must also say of themselves that they know a holy man, when they perceive him.

Kao Yao had a horse mouth, and *Confucius'* arms were turned backwards. If, later on, their wisdom far exceeded that of other people, still they could not be called sages on account of the horse mouth or the concave forehead, for as the features of the Twelve Holy Men differed from those of former sages, they cannot be characteristic either for future sages. The configuration of the bones differs, as do their names and their physical frame; and they The usurper. A political adventurer, cf. p. 115. An enlightened sovereign, cf. p. 162. Disciple of *Confucius.* Cf. p. 304.

are born in different places. Therefore, how could a sage be known, provided that one were born again? *Huan Chiln Shan* said to *Yang Tse Yiln,* "If in future generations there should be again a man like the sages, people would be well aware that his talents surpassed theirs by far, but they would not be able to know, whether he really was a holy man or not." *Yang Tse Yiln* replied, "So it is, indeed."

It is difficult to know a sage. Even men like *Huan Chiln Shan* and *Yang Tse Yiln,* who could judge the excellence and the attainments of a sage, felt incompetent. The scholars of the age represent mediocrity. The knowledge of mediocrity consists in the combination of ordinary observations, but we can be sure that, on seeing a sage, they would not be in a position to recognise him as such. Being unable to recognise a sage, they could not know a phoenix or a unicorn either. Why must people at the present day, who are speaking of the phoenix and the unicorn, pretend that they have such a knowledge?

In former generations people used the words phoenix and unicorn merely upon hearing of the queerness of a bird or an animal. If those had a peculiar plumage or horn, and if they did not fly at random, or wildly roam about, struggling for their food with other birds or animals, they were called phoenix or unicorn. The knowledge which the men of to-day have of the sages is of very much the same kind. They have been told that sages are wonderful men. Therefore, when a man's body shows some peculiarity of the bones, and his wisdom is profound and extensive, they call him a sage. Those who really know what a sage means, do not give that name at first sight, and when they have heard a man for the first time. They first bow to him, hear his lectures, and receive his instruction, and afterwards learn to know him. This will become more clear from the following facts.

When *Tse Kung* had served *Confucius* one year, he thought himself to be superior to *Confucius,* after two years he thought himself to be his equal, but after three years he had learned that he could never come up to him. During the space of one and two years, he did not yet know that *Confucius* was a sage, and it was not until three years had elapsed,

that he became aware of it. If *Tse Kung* required three years to find this out, our scholars *Huan Tan — Huan Chun Shan* lived in the 1st cent. B.c. and A.d. He was a man of wide learning. Of his works the "*Hsm-lun*" "New Reflections" have been preserved.

The Confucian philosopher, cf. p. 391. must be in error, when they imagine they know a sage, for they are less gifted than *Tse Kong,* they see a sage, but do not study under him, nor have they three years intercourse with him, a sudden glance is all they rely upon.

In *Ln, Shao Ching Mao* was placed on a level with *Confucitis.* The school of *Confucius* was three times full, and three times empty. Only *Yen Yuan* did not leave him. *Yen Yuan* alone knew that *Confucius* was a sage. The other pupils abandoned *Confucius,* and returned to *Shao Ching Mao.* Not only did they not understand the sagehood of *Confucius,* but they did not even know *Shao Ching Mao.* The disciples were all imposed upon, so that *Tse Kung* asked *Confucius* saging, "*Shao Ching Mao* is a famous man in *Lu,* how can you know more about government than he?" *Confucius* replied, "*Tse Kung I* You had better leave this, for you are not up to it."

Only the intelligent can distinguish the artificial. Since a man like *Tse Kung* was unable to know a sage, it is nonsense, if our scholars claim to know a sage upon seeing him. From their inability to know a sage we may infer that they do not know a phoenix or a unicorn either.

Let us suppose that a phoenix has long and broad feathers, and that the body of a unicorn is high and big. Then the beholder would regard them as a big bird or a huge animal, but by what should he distinguish them? If their big size were to be taken as a criterion, then one ought to know a sage by his size also. During the "Spring and Autumn" Period there arrived a bird and remained, but it could not be considered a phoenix, and, when the tall *Ti* made their appearance, they could not be taken for sages either. The phoenix and the unicorn being like other birds or animals, what can people do to know

them?

Should these creatures not live in China and come across the desert, they would be like the "mainah," which is not a Chinese bird; nor would the phoenix and the unicorn be Chinese animals then. Why then do the Literati decry the "mainah," and applaud the phoenix and the unicorn, if none of them is of Chinese origin?

Shao Cheng Mao, a high officer of *Lu,* was later on executed by *Confucius* for high treason, when *Confucius* was assistant-minister *(Shi-chi* chap. 47, p. 9v.). Some say that *Shao-ching* is the official title and *Mao* the cognomen. *Shao-cheng* might mean a subdirector. or an assistant-judge. (Cf. *lluaiNan Tse* XIII, 22 comm.) See also *Chavannes, Mem. Hist.* Vol. V, p. 326, Note 7. Cf. Chap. XXXIX. Acridotheres cristatellus.

Some one may say that, when at the time of *Hsiao Hsilan Ti* a phoenix alighted in the *Shang-Un* park, flocks of birds crowded around it on the trees, thousands and ten thousands. They reverently followed the phoenix, because it surpassed all the other birds by its size as well as by the holiness of its spirit. Provided that a large bird around which, when it alights, all the multitudes of birds gather, is a phoenix, then we would know what a phoenix really is. Now the phoenix has the same character as the unicorn. If, when a phoenix appears, all the birds follow it, then all the animals ought to accompany the unicorn, when it shows itself, likewise. But in regard to the unicorn of the "Spring and Autumn" no mention is made of all the animals following it. *Hsilan Ti* and *Wu Ti* both got a unicorn, but nothing is said about animals accompanying it.

Should anybody be of opinion that the train of the unicorn disperses, when it is caught by man, whereas the phoenix is never caught, and that the birds following it become visible, when it is flying about, I refer to the *Shuking.* There we read that, when the nine parts of the imperial music were performed, the male and female phoenix came gambolling. The *Ta-chuan* speaks of a phoenix on the trees, but does not mention that flocks of birds were following it. Was the phoenix attracted by *Hsilan Ti* of another kind perhaps?

One might suggest that this is an omission on the part of the chronicler, that under *Yfl's* reign the phoenix was really accompanied by other birds, that the time of remote antiquity is so far-away, that the chroniclers might well have omitted to mention it, and that the text of the Classics cannot be a proof. Of course, it may happen that something has really taken place, which the historians have dropped, but, in the same way, it can be the case that something really never happened, and was invented by the historians. Therefore it is difficult to find out the truth from the text of the works of the Literati, and our attempts to know a phoenix from its following are in vain.

Moreover, there are cunning fellows among men, who succeed in winning followers, as there are wily birds, which assemble others around themselves. Was the phoenix of the time of *Yil* honest then, and that of *Hsilan Ti's* time a trickster? How is it possible that they were both endowed with the virtue of holy men, and that still their actions should be so dissimilar?

Via. p. 359. *Shutting, Yi-chi* Pt. n, Bk. IV, 9 *(Leggs* Vol. HI, Pt. I, p. 88).

-hl iM--This must be the name of an ancient work.

A bird may perhaps be a phoenix, although there are no birds following it, or it may not be a phoenix, notwithstanding the great number of birds flocking around it. The superior man leads a pure life. He preserves his integrity, and does not care to have many adherents. In his doings and dealings he has not many followers. A cunning intriguer, on the other hand, uses all his energy, and bustles about so much, that the scholars gather around him like clouds. The phoenix is like the superior man. If the number of followers were to decide, whether a bird is a phoenix or not. then a cunning impostor ought to be considered a superior man.

The more" refined a song is, the fewer are the persons who can sing to the tune, and the more disinterested one's

actions are, the fewer are one's sympathisers. The same holds good for birds and animals. To find out a phoenix by the number of its followers would be like calling a song a good one, because it can be sung by many.

The dragon belongs to a similar class of animals as the phoenix. Under the reign of *Hsilan Ti* a yellow dragon came out at *Hsin-fing2* but the snakes did not accompany it. The "spirit bird" and the *"luan"* take a prominent place among the common birds. Although their goodness and their holiness be not as developed as that of the phoenix, still they ought to have a suite of at least some ten birds.

Hsin Ling and *Ming Ch'ang3* entertained three thousand guests, and were called wise and superior men. The *Han* general *Wei Ch'ing* and the general *HoCliilPing3* had not a single guest in their houses, famous generals though they were. The Grand Annalist notes that robber *Chi,* in spite of all his misdeeds, bad several thousand partisans, whereas *Po Yi* and *Shu Ch i* lived in concealment on Mount *Shao-yang.*

The actions of birds and animals are like those of man. A man may win the crowd, but that is not sufficient to characterize him as a wise man. Thus the fact that other birds follow it, is not a sufficient testimony for a phoenix either.

Some say that the phoenix and the unicorn are omens of universal peace, and that at a time of universal peace one sees them i 73-48 B.c. A locality in *Shensi* province.

The princes of *Hsin Ling* and of *Meng Ch'ang,* cf. chap. XL. *Vid.* p. 308. A celebrated commander, who gained many brilliant victories over the *Hsiung-nu.* Died 117 B.c. 8 Cf. p. 168. arrive. However, they also appear, when there is not universal peace. By their quaint plumage and extraordinary bones they distinguish themselves from the ordinary birds and animals, and can be known. Provided that the phoenix and the unicorn usually arrive at a time of general peace, then the unicorn of the Spring and Autumn period must have disliked to appear during the reign of

Confucius. When the Emperor *Kuang Wu TV* was born in the *Chi-gang* palace, a phoenix came down. *Kuang Wu 'It's* birth fell in the time of *Ching Ti 2* and *Ai Ti,* by no means a time of universal peace, nevertheless the phoenix made its appearance. If it did so, because it knew *Kuang Wu Ti's* wisdom and virtue, then it was an omen of the birth of a holy emperor, but not a sign of universal peace. Lucky omens may correspond to universal peace or happen to mark a special birth. It is difficult to find out the real cause. Therefore it would not be proper to think of a period of universal peace only.

Some say that the phoenix and the unicorn are born as members of a certain species of animals, just as the tortoise and the dragon belong to a certain species. For this reason a tortoise will always beget a tortoise, and a dragon will always beget a dragon. In shape, colour, and size the offspring does not differ much from the progenitors. Why should it not be possible for us to know these animals, seeing the father and beholding the son and the grand-son?

For the following reason. Common creatures have their species, but ominous creatures have not; they are born by accident. Therefore they say that the tortoise and the dragon are endowed with virtue. How can people distinguish a spiritual tortoise or a divine dragon, when they perceive them?

At the time of King *Yuan* of *Sung* fishermen caught a spiritual tortoise in their nets, but they did not know that it was a spirit. The scholars of our days are like those fishermen. Since the fishermen did not know a spiritual tortoise, we may be sure that the people of to-day do not know a divine dragon either.

Sometimes a dragon is like a snake, and sometimes a snake resembles a dragon. *Han Fei Tse* remarks that a horse resembling a stag is worth one thousand *chin.* An excellent horse resembles a stag, and a spiritual dragon sometimes looks like a snake. If 25-58 A.d. 32-6 B.c. 6 B.c.-l a.d. 530-515 B.c. those creatures really belonged to a certain species, there would be no discrepancy in shape or colour.

During the time of *Wang Mang* there was an enormous bird, as big as a horse, with variegated plumage adorned with dragon like ornaments, which, together with several ten other birds, alighted in *Ch ir-hsien* in the State of *P ei*. The phoenix, which during the time of *Hslian Ti* sat down on the ground, was 5 feet high, which would correspond to the size of a horse afore-mentioned. Its plumage was multicoloured, which would be like the variegated colour with dragon ornaments, and the several tens of birds would be like the flocks of birds all alighting at the same time. If at *Hslian Ti s* time it was a phoenix in shape and colour, accompanied by all the other birds, how do we know that it was one? Provided it was, then the bird attracted by *Wang Mang* was a phoenix likewise. That being the case, it cannot have been an omen, since *Wang Mang* caused its appearance, and if it was not a phoenix, how is it that in shape and colour and, as regards the following, it was exactly like it?

All ominous things originate from a propitious fluid. Born in an ordinary species, they have their peculiar character, and therefore become omens. Thus the arrival of a phoenix is like the appearance of the "red crow." If the phoenix is said to belong to a species, is there a distinct species of " red crows" also?

As regards the auspicious grain, the wine springs, and the sweet dew, the auspicious grain grows amidst other grain, but it has its peculiar spikelets, wherefore it is called auspicious grain. The wine springs and the sweet dew flow forth sweet and nice. They come from sources and dew, but there is not a special kind of sweet dew in heaven, or a certain class of wine springs on earth. During the just reign of a wise ruler the sweet dew falls down, and the wine comes up.

The "felicitous plant" and the "vermilion grass" also grow, on earth along with other plants, but they do not always sprout from the same root. They come forth for a certain time, and after ten days or a month they wither and fall off. Hence they are 9 B.C-23 A.d.

In modern *Anhui*. A propitious bird which appeared to *Wu Wang*, cf. p. 130. The felicitous plant, "*ming chia*" , was found in the court-yard of the emperor *Yao*. With the waxing moon it grew one new leaf every day, with the waning moon one leaf dropped every day. considered as omens. The phoenix and the unicorn are omens as well. Why should they form a distinct species?

When there was perfect peace under the *Chou* dynasty, the people of *Yileh-ch ang* brought white pheasants as a present. These white pheasants were short-lived and of white colour, but there was not a special class of white pheasants. When the people of *Lu* caught a deer with one horn, and called it a unicorn, it descended perhaps from a deer, and there was no species of unicorns.

Accordingly the phoenix is perhaps also born from a snow goose or a magpie, but differing so much from the majority of birds by its quaint plumage and peculiar feathers, it is given the name phoenix. Wherefore must it belong to quite another class than the other birds? *YuJo2* said, "The position the unicorn takes among quadrupeds, the phoenix takes among flying birds, Mount *T'ai* among hills, and the Yellow River and the Ocean among water-courses.' Consequently the phoenix and the unicorn are to be classed together with birds and animals, only their shape and colour is exceptional. They cannot constitute a separate class. Belonging to the same category, they have their anomalies, by these anomalies they fall out of the common run, and owing to this irregularity the distinction becomes difficult. *Yao* begot *Tan Chu*, and *Shun, Shang Chun. Shang Chiln* and *Tan Chu* belonged to the same species as *Yao* and *Shun*, but in body and mind they were abnormal. *Kun* begot *Yil*, and *Ku Sou*, *Shun. Shun* and *Yil* were of the same class as *Kun* and *Ku Sou*, but differed from them in wisdom and virtue. If we try to sow the seed of auspicious grain, we cannot reap auspicious grain thereby, but we may frequently find millet with abnormal stalks or ears. People beholding *Shu Liang Ho* could not know that he was the father of *Confucius*, nor

could they see in *Po Yil* the son of *Confucius*. The father of *Chang T'ang* was 5 feet high, *Chang T ang* himself 8, and. his grand-son 6. The phoenix of *Hsiao Hsilmi Ti* measured 5 feet. The bird from which it was born perhaps measured but 2 feet, and the own offspring of the phoenix only 1 foot, for why should a species be quite stereotype? Since classes and species are not stereotype, *Tsing Hsi* had a son, *Tsing Shin* whose character was

'/llSs'rfl' " P XL we read *Yiieh-shang*, which were a people near the Annamese frontier. See above p. 360.

Chang T'ang lived at the beginning of the 1st cent. A.d. *Vid.* chap. XXXVIII. *Tseng Te*, the well known disciple of *Confucius*, cf. p. 104. unique, and *Yen Lu* was father to *Yen Hui*, who outshone every one in ancient and modern times. A thousand Li horse must not be the colt of a unicorn, and a bird may be benevolent and wise without being the fledgeling of a phoenix.

The brooks on the mountain tops are not connected with rivers and lakes, still they are full of fish. The generative power of the water has produced them independently. On the terraces of ruined palaces and crumbling halls grows grass, sent forth by the force of the soil of itself. The fish in the brooks and the grass on the terraces of the halls have no progenitors of their own species. In the same manner an omen corresponding to something happens spontaneously, there is not a special class for it in the world.

An omen corresponds in the same way, as a calamitous event supervenes. The omen corresponds to something good, a calamity to something bad. Good and bad are opposites, it is true, but the corresponding is the same. As a calamitous revolution does not belong to a class, au omen corresponding to something has no species. The fluids of the *Yin* and the *Yang* are the fluids of Heaven and Earth. Falling in with something good, they harmonize with it, and meeting something bad, they suddenly turn. Do Heaven and Earth in addition to the government which they exercise over good and evil still produce a harmonious and a suddenly changing fluid? By no means:—when an omen corresponds to something, it is not of a certain class or category, but it comes forth along with something good, and grows from the harmony of the fluids.

Sometimes during a peaceful administration and, while the fluids are in harmony, various creatures undergo a metamorphosis. "In spring *e.g.* the eagle changes into a pigeon, and in autumn the pigeon becomes an eagle. Snakes, mice, and the like are transformed into fish and turtles, frogs into quails, sparrows into clams. These creatures change in accordance with their fluids. Their existence cannot be denied. *Huang ShiJl2* became an old man, presented *Chang Liang* with a book, and then became a stone again. The Literati know this. Perhaps at the time of universal peace, when all the fluids are in harmony, a deer might be transmuted into a unicorn, and a snow-goose into a phoenix. In this way the nature of animals would be changed at times, but there would not be a stereotype species. *Pao Sse* was the daughter of a black lizard, and born from the saliva of two snakes. Two ministers of *Chin* were the progeny of a brown and a spotted bear. The stories about the eating of the swallow's egg/ and the pearl-barley, and the walking upon an enormous foot-print are likewise accepted by the people of to-day, why then shall the omens belong to a stereotype species'.' If we consider the ipiestion from the point of view that creatures have not a well-defined species, nor men a separate class, and that a body can be metamorphosized, then the phoenix and the unicorn are not born from an unchangeable species. But wherefore must they be alike then in shape and colour?

We read in the chapter on omens in the *Liki* that the male phoenix is called *"Feng"* and the female *"Huang"* and that the male sings "c/ii, *chi"* and the female "fem, *tsu."* In the *Slaking* we find the following verses: — "The oil tree is growing on yonder high hill, and the male and female phoenix is singing there in the morning sun-shine. Luxuriant and flourishing is the tree, *"yung,*

gung, chieh, chieh" sing the phoenixes. "—The chapter on omens as well as the *Shiking* describe the singing of the phoenix, the one as *chi, tsu tsu"* the other as *"gung, gung, chieh, chieh."*

These sounds differ. Provided that they are really like this, then the shape of the birds cannot be the same, and if it is, then there is a discrepancy between the *Shiking* and the *Liki.* Consequently the common traditions about the singing of the phoenix are suspicious.

Of the unicorn caught in *Lu* it is said that it was a deer with a horn, that means that its colour was like that of a deer. The colour of a deer is invariable, as the colour of birds is. At the time of *Wu Wang* a stream of light appeared in the form of a crow. Its colour is said to have been red. Red not being the colour of crows, it is expressly stated that the colour was red.

The favourite consort of the Emperor *Yu Wang,* 781-771 B.c. On this legend, sec p. 321. *Fan Wen Tse* and *Ch'ung Hang Chao Txe,* cf. p. 225. The mother of *Hsieh,* the ancestor of the 1 *'in* dynasty swallowed an egg dropped by a swallow, and thereupon conceived. Cf. p. 318. The mother of Great *Yu* is said to have conceived after having eaten pearl-barley. See p. 318. *Via",* p. 318. There is no chapter on omens, *"Jui-ming"* in the *Liki* now. A similar passage occurs in the *Han-sluh-irai-chuan (T'ai-p'ing-gii-lan)* 2nd cent. B.c. *Miking* Pt. HI, Bk. II, Ode VIII *(Legge* Vol. IV, Pt. II, p. 404). I.un-Heng. 24

If the unicorn resembled a deer, but had a different colour, it would certainly have been added that its colour was white or black. Now the colour was the usual one, therefore they merely say that it was a deer. A deer is hornless. Since the deer in question was different from the ordinary ones in this respect, it is said that it had a horn. In this manner the unicorn caught in *Lu* was shaped like a deer.

During the time of *Wu Ti* a hunting party in the west caught a white unicorn with one horn and five feet. The horn was then as in other cases, but the reference to the five feet shows that it had not the same number of legs. The uni-

corn found in *Lu* is described as a deer. The colour not being mentioned, it must have been a deer of no unusual colour. *Wu Ti* is reported to have got a white unicorn. White colour does not agree with a unicorn. The statement that a unicorn is a deer, means therefore that it is an ordinary one, whereas the allegation that it is a white unicorn, shows that its colour is unusual.

Under the reign of *Hsiao Hsiian Ti* the *Chiu-cMn2* sent as a tribute a unicorn shaped like a deer, but with two horns. It thus differed from the unicorn of *Hsiao Wu Ti,* to which one horn is ascribed. During the Spring and Autumn Period the unicorn was like a deer, that of the emperor *Hsiian Ti* is described as resembling a stag. A stag is double the size of a deer, and differently shaped. The unicorns which appeared under the reigns of those three emperors vary very much, as regards the colour of their hair, the horn, the feet, and the size of the body. If we infer the future from these instances, it is quite evident that the unicorns eventually appearing at the present time will not be like those of former generations. In this respect the unicorn is like the phoenix. The unicorns varied at different periods in shape and colour. If we were to start from the phoenix seen at the time of *Hsiian Ti,* measuring five feet and being multi-coloured, and to foretell the future from the past, it would be a mistake to maintain that a phoenix appearing later on must be like that one. There can be no doubt that phoenixes and unicorns, which will appear later on, will not resemble those observed formerly. How can the scholars assert that on seeing them they would know them?

When the people of *Lu* caught the unicorn, they dared not straightway call it a unicorn, but said that it was a horned deer.

China possesses several varieties of hornless deer.

A tribe in *Annam.*

At that time in fact they did not know it. *Wu Ti* called upon the censor *Chung Chan* to give his opinion about the unicorn. *Chung Chun* replied that it was a wild animal with joined horns, showing that the whole empire had grown from the some root. He did not at once style it a unicorn, but declared it to be a wild animal. *Cluing Chiln* had his doubts as well, and did not know it. The knowledge of the scholars of our age does not exceed that of the people of *Lu* or of *Chung Chiln*. Should they see a phoenix or a unicorn, they would certainly have the same doubts as the latter.

How is it possible to find out a phoenix and a unicorn among uncommon birds and animals? If shape and colour be taken as a criterion, they are not always alike. If there be a big train of birds and animals following them, this is not always a proof of their excellence. If their rarity be regarded as a characteristic, there is the "mainah" also, and if importance be attached to peculiarities, then sages as well as wise men have strange physical features. Both sages and wise men are abnormal, and there is no means to distinguish between them.

Taking wisdom and sageness as a starting point, we find that sage birds and sage animals do not possess more peculiarities than ordinary birds or common animals. The wisdom of sage or wise men may be quite extraordinary, whereas their bones show no anomaly. Thus sage and wise birds and animals can be endowed with benevolence, honesty, unselfishness, and purity, though there be nothing remarkable in their physical constitution. Sometimes there are rich and noble persons who have not the body of a sage, and the osseous structure of many points to wealth and honour, who do not prove to be sage or wise. Accordingly some birds are multicolour, and some animals have a horn, but are devoid of benevolence or sageness. How do we know then but that the phoenixes and unicorns, seen in olden days, were common birds or animals, and the magpies and deer seen at present are phoenixes and unicorns? The present holy age is the result of the reforms emanating from *Yao* and *Shun*, why should no benevolent or wise creatures be born?

It may happen that phoenixes and unicorns are mixed with snow-geese,

magpies, deer or stags, so that our people cannot distinguish them. When precious jade was hidden in a stone, the governor of the king of *Ch'u* did not know it, which distressed the owner so much, that he wept tears of blood. Perhaps now a-days the phoenixes and unicorns also hide their benevolent and wise heart under a common plumage and ordinary fur, and have neither a single horn nor five colours as a distinctive mark, so that our people know them no more, than the jade in the stone was known. How can we prove that? By a reference to the plants, which at the commencement of the *Yung-ping* period were always presenting omens. When the emperor *Hsiao Ming Ti* was manifesting his kindness, all sorts of omens happened at the same time. At the *Yuau-lio* and *Chang-ho* epochs, when *Hsiao Chang It's* virtue was shining, perfect harmony pervaded the world, and auspicious omens and strange things corresponded. Phoenixes and unicorns came forth one after the other, and were observed on many occasions, much more than at the time of the Five Emperors. This chapter was already completed, therefore I could not mention it then.

It might be objected that arguing on omens, I have declared that the phoenix and the unicorn are hard to know, and that the omens of our age cannot be distinguished, whether, therefore, the phoenixes and the unicorns attracted now by *Hsiao Chang Ti* could not be known?—I say that according to the "Records on the Five Birds" there are big birds in the four regions and the centre which, when they roam about, are accompanied by all the other birds. In size, and the colour of the plumage they resemble a phoenix, but are difficult to know indeed.

Since the omens of our age do not allow of distinction, how can we find them out? By the government of the empire. Unless the virtue of the reigning emperor equalled that of *Yii*, we would not perceive phoenixes and unicorns with our own eyes. The omens of *Yii* were undoubtedly genuine, and *Yao's* excellence is evident. Under *Hsiao Hsi-lan Ti* the world enjoyed a still more

universal peace than at the time of *Yao* and *Shun*, as far as ten Style of the reign of the Emperor *Ming Ti*, 58-7H A.d. Styles of the Emperor *Chang Ti*, 84-87 and 87-89.

This chapter must have been written prior to 84 A.d., So that the auspicious reign of the Emperor *Chang Ti* could not yet be referred to. The author made this addition later »'. *e*. alter 89, for it was not before this year that the emperor received his posthumous title *Ilmao Chang Ti*. By the Five Birds perhaps the Five Phoenixes " *Wu Feng,*" five different kinds of phnenixes, which differ by their colours, are meant. The "*Feng*" is red, the "*Yuan chu*'' yellow, the "*Luan*" blue, the "*Yii tsu*" purple, and the "Ah" white. Whereas "*Feng*" and "*Luan*" are still used as names for the phoenix, one understands by "*Yuan chu*" a kind of peacock or pheasant, by "*Yii-tsa*" a kind of duck, and by *Ku*" the snow-goose or swan.

thousand Li, people were anxious for reforms and progress, and the moral laws found an echo everywhere. Affected by this state of things, the benevolent birds and animals made their appearance, only the size, the colour of the hair, the feet and the wings of those auspicious creatures were not always the same. Taking the mode of government and the intelligence of the rulers as a criterion for the various omens, we find them all to be genuine. That means that they are hard to know, but easy to understand.

The sweet dew may also serve us as a key. The sweet dew is produced by the harmonious fluid, it has no cause in itself which could make it sweet; this can only be done by the intervention of the harmonious fluid. When the harmonious fluid appears, the sweet dew pours down, virtue permeates everything, and the various omens come forth together. From the *Yung-ping* down to the *Chang-ho* period the sweet dew has continually been falling. Hence we know that the omens are all true, and that phoenixes and unicorns are likewise all genuine.

CHAPTER XXXI.

The Forming of Characters (*Shuai-hs-*

ing).

Speaking of human nature one must distinguish good and bad characters. The good ones are so of themselves, the wicked can be instructed and urged on to do good. A sovereign or a father seeing that his subjects or sons have good characters, provides for them, exhorts them, and keeps them out of the reach of evil. If the latter come into contact with it, they assist and shield them, and try to win them back to the cause of virtue. It is by the transition of virtue into wickedness and of wickedness into virtue that the characters are formed.

The duke of *Shao* admonished King *Ching* saying:—" Now you for the first time carry out Heaven's decree. Oh! you are like a youth with whom all depends on his first years of life."

By youth is meant the age up to fifteen. If a youth's thoughts are directed towards virtue, he will be virtuous to the last, but if his propensities tend to badness, he will end badly.

The *Shiking* says "What can that admirable man be compared to?" The *Tso-chuan* answers, "He is like boiled silk; dyed with indigo, it becomes blue; coloured with vermilion, it turns crimson." A youth of fifteen is like silk, his gradual changes into good or bad resembling the dying of boiled silk with indigo and vermilion, which gives it a blue or a red colour. When these colours have once set, they cannot be altered again. It is for this reason that *Yang Tse* wept over the by-roads and *Mi Tse* over boiled *Shuking,* The Announcement of *Shao* V, Bk. XII, 18-19. *Wang Ch'ung* reads g£ "alas!" instead of pjl.

Shiking I, Bk. IV, Ode IX, 2 where we read now 'JqT "what can he give?" instead of fp. "what can he be compared to?" *Yang Chu,* the philosopher of egoism. The story referred to here is told in *Lieh Tse* VIII, lOv. A sheep had been lost on by-roads. When *Yang Chu* heard of it, he became thoughtful and changed countenance. No mention is made of his having wept. *Wang Ch'ung* seems to have quoted from *Huai J'an Tse* XVII, 25 v, who expressly mentions *Yang Tse's* weeping. *Me Ti,* the philosopher of altruism. We read in his works:—*Me*

Tse chap. 3, l). 4 (What colours) and in the *Lti-shih-ch'un-ch'iu* chap. 2, No. 4, p. 8 (Colouring) that *Mi Tse* witnessing the dying of silk said, *heaving a sigh,* "Dyed blue, it turns blue, and dyed yellow, it turns yellow"' and then he goes oil to explain, how silk. They were sorrowful, because men having gone astray from the right path cannot be transformed any more. Human nature turns from good into bad, and from bad into good only in this manner. Creepers growing amidst hemp, stand upright without support by themselves. White silk yarn placed amongst dark, becomes black without boiling. Creepers are not straight by nature, nor is the black colour an attribute of silk yarn. The hemp affording support, and the dark silk lending the colour, creepers and white silk become straight and black. Human nature bears a resemblance to creepers and silk yarn. In a *milieu* favourable to transformation or colouring, it turns good or bad. *Wa»g Liang* and *Tsao Fu* were famous as charioteers: — out of unruly and vicious animals they made good ones. Had they only been able to drive good horses, but incapable of breaking bad ones, they would have been nothing more than jockeys and ordinary equerries. Their horsemanship would not have been remarkable nor deserving of world-wide fame. Of *Wang Liang* the saying goes that, when he stepped into a chariot, the steeds knew no exhaustion.

Under the rule of *Yao* and *Shun* people were neither seditious nor ignorant. Tradition says that the people of *Yao* and *Shun* might have been invested with fiefs house by house, whereas those of *Chieh Kuei* were worthy of death door by door. The people followed the way prescribed by the three dynasties. That the people of the holy emperors were like this, those of the wicked emperors otherwise, was merely the result of the influence of their rulers, not of the people's original nature.

The covetous hearing of *Po Yi's* fame became disinterested, and the weak resolute. The news of *Liu Hsia Hui's* reputation made the niggardly generous and the mean liberal. If the spread of fame

alone could bring about such changes, what then must be the effect of personal intercourse and tuition?

The seventy disciples of the school of *Confucius* were each of them able to creditably fill the post of a minister of state. Conman also takes the colour of his environments, especially of those with whom he has intercourse, wherefore "colouring" is a very serious affair. Nothing is said about his having shed tears. « So excellent were they all.

The last emperor of the *Hsia* dynasty, the type of a tyrant. *Po Yi* and *Shu Ch'i,* two brothers famous for their disinterestedness in refusing.to ascend the throne of their father, lest the other should be deprived of it. *Magers* No. 543. An official of the State of *Lu* famous for honesty and upright character, often mentioned by *Conjuciux.* forming to the holy doctrines, they became accomplished scholars, and their knowledge and skill grew tenfold. This was the result of teaching; thus latent faculties were gradually developed. Before they joined *Confucius'* school, they sauntered about in the streets as quite ordinary and in no wise exceptional people. The most ungovernable of all was *Tse Lu,* who is generally reported to have been a common and unsteady individual. Before he became *Confucius'* pupil, he wore a feather hat and a pig skin belt. He was brutal and unmannerly. Whenever he heard some reading, he tossed up his feather hat, pulled his belt, and uttered such a yell, that he deafened the ears of the worthies and sages. Such was his wickedness. *Confucius* took him under his guidance. By degrees he polished and instructed him. The more he advanced in knowledge, the more he lost his fierceness, and his arrogance was broken. At last he was able to govern a state, and ranked in the four classes. This is a shining example of how a man's character was changed from bad into good.

Fertility and sterility are the original nature of the soil. If it be rich and moist, the nature is good, and the crops will be exuberant, whereas, if it be barren and stony, the nature is bad. However, human efforts:—deep ploughing, thorough tilling, and a copious use of manure may help the land, so that the harvest will become like that of the rich and well watered fields. Such is the case with the elevation of the land also. Fill up the low ground with earth, dug out by means of hoes and spades, and the low land will be on a level with the high one. If these works are still continued, not only will the low land be on a level, but even higher than the high land. The high ground will then become the low one. Let us suppose that the human natures are partly good, partly bad; as the land may be either high or low. By making use of the good effects of education goodness can be spread and generalized. Reformation being pushed on and instruction persevered in, people will change and become still better. Goodness will increase and reach a still higher standard than it had before, just as low ground, filled up with hoes and spades, rises higher than the originally elevated ground.

T se though not predestinated thereto, made a fortune. His capital increased without a decree from Heaven which would have The four classes, into which the ten principal followers of Confucius were divided. Cf. Analects XI, 2. A disciple of Confucim, whose full name was Tuan Mu T'se alias Tie Knng, possessed of great abilities. He became a high official. him rich. The accumulation of wealth is due to the cleverness of the rich men of the time in making a fortune. Through this ability of theirs they are themselves the authors of their growing wealth without a special decree from Heaven. Similarly, he who has a wicked nature changes his will and his doings, if he happens to be taught by a Sage, although he was not endowed with a good character by Heaven.

One speaks of good swords for which a thousand chin are paid, such as the Yil-ch'ang sword of T ang-ch'i and the Tai-a sword of IAmg-ch tian5 Their blade is originally nothing more than a common piece of iron from a mountain, By the forger's smelting and hammering they become sharp-edged. But notwithstanding this smelting and hammering the material of good swords is not different

from others. All depends on excellent workmanship and on the blade-smith's ability in working the iron. Take a sword worth only one chin from Tung-hsia, heat it again, and forge it, giving it sufficient fire, and smoothing and sharpening its edge, and it will be like a sword of a thousand chin. Iron and stones are made by Heaven, still being worked, they undergo a modification of their 'substance. Why then should man, whose nature is imbued with the five virtues, despair of the badness of his character, before he has been thoroughly worked upon by Worthies and Sages?

The skillful physicians that in olden days were held in high esteem, knew the sources where virulent diseases sprang from, and treated and cured them with acupuncture and medicines. Had they merely known the names of the complaints, but done nothing besides, looking quietly on, would there have been anything wonderful in them? Men who are not good have a disease of their nature. To expect them to change without proper treatment and instruction would be hopeless indeed.

The laws of Heaven can be applied in a right and in a wrong way. The right way is in harmony with Heaven, the wrong one owes its results to human astuteness, but cannot in its effects be The name of the ancient copper coins, which first were called "metal," not "gold," as may be seen from the works on coinage. This sword is said to have been fabricated by the famous blade-smith Ou Yeh in the kingdom of Yueh. A place in Honan. This sword is the work of Ou Yeh of Yiieh and Kan Chiang of Wu, both celebrated sword-cutlers, who wrought it for the King of Ch'u. A place most likely in Chekiang, called jJ J11 "Sword river" under the Sung dynasty. Playfair, Cities No. 4650. distinguished from the right one. This will be shown by the following. Among the "Tribute of Yti" are mentioned jade and white corals. These were the produce of earth and genuine precious stones and pearls. But the Taoists melt five kinds of stones, and make five-coloured gems out of them. Their lustre, if compared with real gems, does not differ. Pearls in fishes

and shells are as genuine as the jade-stones in the Tribute of Yii. Yet the Marquis of Sui made pearls from chemicals, which were as brilliant as genuine ones. This is the climax of Taoist learning and a triumph of their skill.

By means of a burning-glass one catches fire from heaven. Of five stones licpieficd on the Ping-wu5 day of the 5th moon an instrument is cast, which, when polished bright, held up against the sun, brings down fire too, in precisely the same manner as, when fire is caught in the proper way. Now, one goes even so far as to furbish the crooked blades of swords, till they shine, when, held up against the sun, they attract fire also. Crooked blades are not burning-glasses; that they can catch fire is the effect of rubbing. Now, provided the bad-natured men are of the same.kind as good-natured ones, then they can be influenced, and induced to do good. Should they be of a different kind, they can also be coerced in the same manner as the Taoists cast gems, Sui Hon made pearls, and people furbish the crooked blades of swords. Enlightened with learning and familiarized with virtue, they too begin by and by to practise benevolence and equity.

When Huang Ti fought with Yen It for the empire, he taught bears, leopards, and tigers to combat for him in the wilds of Fanchilan. After three battles he gained his end, and Yen Ti was routed.

Yao yielded the empire to Shun. Kun, one of his vassals, desired to become one of the three chief ministers, but Yao did The Tribute of Yu, Yii-kung, is also the name of a book of the Shutting. Cf. Shaking Pt. III, Book I (Legge, Classic/ Vol. III, Pt. I, p. 127). A principality in Ilupei. The time of this Marquis of Sui is unknown. His pearls are very famous in Chinese literature. According to one tradition the Marquis found a wounded snake, and cured it. Out of gratitude the snake presented him with a precious pearl, which shone at night. Wang Oh'ung makes the Marquis produce artificial pearls himself. A number of the sexagenary cycle used for the designation of years, months, and days. Yen Ti is usually identified with *Shihi Nung* and said to have been his predecessor, but we do not learn that he fought with *Huang Ti* for the empire. According to *Kang Hi*, *Kun* = j$would be the same as fi *Kun*, *Yao's* Minister of Works, who in vain endeavoured to drain the waters of the great flood. His son *Yu*, who subsequently became emperor, succeeded at last in regulating the water courses. Here we seem to have a different tradition. not listen to this request. Thereupon *K1m* became more infuriated than even ferocious animals are, and wished to rebel. The horns of animals, all in a line, served him as a rampart, and their lifted tails were his banners. They opposed and tackled their foe with the utmost determination and energy.—If birds and beasts, which are shaped otherwise than man, can nevertheless be caused to fight, how much more so man's own kindred'.' Proceeding on this line of argument we have no reason to doubt that (by music) the multitudinous animals were made to dance, the fish in the ponds to come out and listen, and the six kinds of horses to look up from their fodder.

The equalization of what varies in different categories as well as the differentiation of what is the same in similar classes, does not depend on the thing itself, but is man's doing.

It is by instruction that living beings are transformed. Among the Three *Miao* tribes some were honest, some disreputable. *Yao* and *Shun* made them all alike by conferring the boon of instruction upon them.

Suppose the men of *Ch'u* and *Yileh* to settle down in *Chuang* or *Yil*. Having passed there months and years, they would become pliant and yielding, and their customs changed. They say that the people of *Ch'i* are soft and supple, those of *Ch'in* unsteady and versatile, of *Chu* lively and passionate, of *Yen* dull and simple. Now let us suppose that people of the four States alternately went to live in *Chuang* and *Yil* for a certain time, the prolonged stay in a place remote from their country would undubitably bring about a change of their character.

A bad natured man's heart is like wood or stone, but even wood and stone can be used by men, why not what really is neither wood nor stone? We may hope that it will still be able Six kinds of horses were distinguished in the studs of the *Chou* emperors, according to their height. *Tcheou Li Chou Li),* trad, par *Mot,* Vol. II, p. 262.
There are many myths illustrative of the power of music. *IIu l'n*, . played the guitar, so that the fish came out to listen, and *Po Ya, jf'* played the lute in such an admirable way, that the horses forgot their fodder, and looked up to harken. *Han-shih-wai ch'uan,* quoted by the *P'ei-ivin-y'un* fu chap. % under The aborigines of China. They were settled in moder n *Hukuang* and *Chekiang.* An allusion to *Nenchi* Bk. IIJ, Pt. II, chap. 6, where the difference of the dialects of *Ch i* and *Chu* is pointed out. *Chuang* and *Yu* were two quarters in the capital of *Ch'i.* The *Ch'i* State was in northern *Shantung, Ch'in* in *Shenri,* and *Yen* in *Chili.* The characteristic of the inhabitants of these provinces is partly still true to-day. to understand the precepts of superior men. Only in the case of insanity, when a person sings and weeps in the streets, knowing neither east nor west, taking no heed of scorching heat or humidity, unaware of his own madness and unconscious of hunger and satiety, nature is deranged and upset, and there is no help. As such a man sees nothing before him, he is afraid of nothing.
Therefore the government does not abolish the officers of public instruction or dispense with criminal judges, wishing thereby to inculcate the observance of the moral laws. The schools guide people at first, the laws control and restrain them later on.

Even the will of a *Tan Chu* might be curbed; the proof is that the soldiers of a big army are kept in order by reproofs. Men and officers are held in check to such an extent, that they look at death as a return.
Ho Lu put his soldiers to the test by the "Five Lakes." They all cut their arms with swords, that the blood trickled down to the ground. *Kou Chmi* also

gave his men a trial in the hall of his inner palace. Those who jumped into the fire and perished, were innumerable. Human nature is not particularly fond of swords and fire, but the two rulers had such a power over their men, that they did not care for their lives. It is the effect of military discipline to make light of cuts and blood. *Ming PSn* was bold, but on hearing the order for the army he became afraid. In the same way the officers who were wont to draw their swords to fight out, whose merits were first, went through all the ceremonial, and prostrated themselves (before the emperor), when *Shu Sun Tung* had fixed the rites. Imperious and overbearing first, they became obedient and submissive. The power of instruction and the influence of virtue transform the character. One need not sorrow that a character is bad, but it is to be regretted, if it does not submit to the teachings of the sages. Such an individual owes his misfortune to himself.
Beans and wheat are different from rice and millet, yet their consumption satisfies the appetite. Are the natures of low and King of the *Wu* State, 514-496 B. c. Another name of the *T'ai-hu* lake in *Kiangsu,* which consisted of five lakes, or five connected sheets of water.
The ruler of the *Yueh* State, 496 q.c, who overthrew the kingdom of *Wu.* A hero of enormous strength in the *Chou* epoch. An official of great power under *Han Kao Tsu,* who subdued the arrogance and superciliousness of the princes and nobles by the ceremonial they were made to undergo at an audience before the new emperor. *Shi-chi* chap. 99, p. 7v. superior men then of a different kind? They resemble the Five Grains, all have their use. There is no fundamental difference between them, only their manifestations are unlike. The fluid men are endowed with, is either copious or deficient, and their character correspondingly good or bad. The wicked have received but a small dose of kindness, the irascible, plenty of temper. If kindness be unsufficient, people do wrong, and there is not much hope for an improvement. With plenty of temper, people become violent, and

have no sense of justice. Moreover, their feeling of sympathy is defective, joy and anger do not happen at the proper time, and they have baseless and irreasonable fears. Reckless men like that commit outrages, therefore they are considered bad.

Man has in his body the Five Qualities ' and the Five Organs. If he got too little of them, or if they are too small, his actions do not attain to goodness. Man himself is either accomplished or deficient, but accomplishment and deficiency do not mean a difference of organisation. Use leaven in big, or in small quantities, and the result will be similar. In rich as well as in poor wine there is the same leaven. Good men as well as bad ones are permeated by the same original fluid. According to its greater or smaller volumen the mind of the individual is bright or dull.

Hsi Min Pao would tighten his leathern belt, whenever he wanted to relax himself. *Tung An Yil* loosened his girdle strings, when he was going to rouse himself. Yet neither passion nor indolence is the right medium. However, he who wears a belt or a girdle on his body is properly dressed. When the question arises, how deficiencies can be made good by means of belts and strings, the names of *Hsi Min Pao* and *Tung An Yil* must be mentioned together. Hemp, millet, rice, wheat, and beans. The Five Cardinal Virtues:—benevolence, justice, propriety, knowledge, and truth. The heart, the liver, the stomach, the lungs, and the kidneys. Human character, to wit the Five Qualities, depends on the volumen of the original fluid, the vital force, which shapes the Five Organs. According as they are bigger or smaller, the nature of the individual is different. This idea finds expression in the Chinese language. A man with a big heart, jsi is generous and liberal, with a small heart, mean. The fluid of the stomach, Jpp is equivalent to anger. Cf. p. 122. In both cases the belt or girdle is the same indispensible part of a gentleman's toilet, but the use made of it, and the results achieved, are quite different. The same may be said of human nature.

Houses of poor, wretched people are not in a proper state. They have holes in the walls under the roof, to which others take objection. When rich and well-to-do people build houses, they have the walls made in a way, that they find there real shelter. The whole house is in good repair, and nobody could say anything against it.

In *Wei* the land was divided in lots of a hundred *mow,* in *Yeh* alone the lots measured two hundred *mow. Hsi Men Pao* irrigated his land with water from the *Chang* and made it so fertile, that it yielded one bushel per *mow.* Man's natural parts are like the fields of *Yeh,* tuition and education, like the water from the *Chang.* One must be sorry for him that cannot be transformed, but not for a man whose character it is difficult to govern.

In the streets of the city of *Logang* there was no water. It was therefore pulled up from the *Lo* by watermen. If it was streaming quickly day and night, it was their doing. From this point of view kindness and justice must increase manifold in him who comes into close contact with an excellent man. *Mencms* mother changed her domicile, for she had ascertained this truth.

Water amongst men is dirty and muddy, in the open country it is clear and limpid. It is all the same water, and it flows from the confines of heaven; its dirtiness and limpidity are the effects of its environments.

Chao T'o, king of the southern *Yiieh,* was originally an honourable man of the *Han* State, but he took to the habits of the southern barbarians, disregarded the imperial commands, dressed his hair in a tuft, and used to squat down. He was so fond of Human nature is like those houses. They are all houses, and serve the same purpose, but some are in good repair, others in a wretched state. An ancient State in North *Honan* and South *Cfiili.* The modern *Chang-te-fu.* A large tributary of the river *Wei* in *Honan,* near *Chang-te-fu.* A *Chung,* an ancient measure equal to 4 pecks = 1 bushel, as some say. According to others it would be as much as 34 pecks. The capital of the *Chou* dynasty in *Honan,* the modern *Honanfu.* Probably with pump-works.

The excellent man is like the river *Lo.* Streams of kindness and justice part from him. She changed her domicile for the purpose of saving her son from the bad influences of the neighbourhood. *Chao T'o* went to *Yiieh,* modern *Kuangtung,* as general of *Chin Shih Huang Ti,* and subsequently became king of the southern barbarians, whose customs he adopted. *Lu Chia* was sent to him by the first emperor of the *Han* dynasty to receive his declaration of allegiance. this, as if it had been his nature. *Lu Chia* spoke to him of the virtues of the *Han,* and impressed him with their holy power, so that he suddenly rose up, and felt remorse. He received the commands of his sovereign, and communicated them to the savages. Against his hair-dress and to his squatting he felt something like a natural repugnancy. First he acted in the aforesaid manner, afterwards thus. It shows what force instruction also has, and that nature is not the only factor. CHAPTER XXXII.

On Original Nature *(Pen-hsing).*

Natural feelings and natural disposition are the basis of human activity, and the source from which morals and music spring. Morals impede, and music checks the excesses of original nature. The natural disposition may be humble, modest, and yielding. The moral laws are enforced with a view to generalizing such praiseworthy qualities. The natural feelings may be good or bad, cheerful or angry, mournful or merry. Music is made in order to make every one behave respectfully. What morals and music aim at are the natural feelings and natural disposition.

The ancient literati and scholars who have written essays have all touched upon this question, but could not give a satisfactory answer. The philosopher *Shih Tse* of the *Chou* time held that human nature is partly good and partly bad, that, if the good nature in man be cultivated and regulated, his goodness increases, and if his bad nature be, his badness develops. Thus in the human heart there would be two conflicting principles, and good and evil depend on cultivation. Accordingly, *Shih Tse* composed a chapter on cultivation.

Fn Tse Chien, Ch'i Tiao K'ai, and *Kung Sun Ni Tse2* also discuss this subject in very much the same way as *Shih Tse,* all declaring that nature is partly good, partly bad. *Mencius* wrote a chapter on the goodness of nature, contending that all men are originally good, and that the bad ones are corrupted by the world. Men, he says, are created by heaven and earth; they are all provided with a good nature, but when they grow up and come into contact with the world, they run wild, His full name is *Shih She.* He was one of the seventy disciples of *Confuchis* and a writer. The Catalogue of the *Han-shu* chap. 80 mentions twenty-one chapters of his pen. *Faber* in his *Doctrines of Confucius* p. 29 states that the title of the lost work of *Shih She"* was "*yang-shu"* and that he is said to have been a disciple of *Ch'i Tiao K'ai,* whom vide.

"All disciples of *Confucius,* whose writings were still extant during the *Han* dynasty, but are now lost. According to *Liu Ilsin's* Catalogue *Fu Tse Chien* alias *Fu Pu Ch'i* wrote 16 chapters, *Ch'i Tiao Kui* 12, and *Kung Sun JSi Tse* 28. *MeruAus* Bk. VI, Pt. I. and are perverted, and their wickedness increases daily. According to *Mencius'* opinion, man, when young, would be invariably good. *Wei Tse* said, "I have formerly remarked, that as a child the prince *(Chou)* did not show off."

When *Chou* was a child, *Wei Tse* observed that he had no good character. Inclined to evil, he did not eclipse the common people, and when he had grown up, he caused endless revolutions. Therefore *Wei Tse's* remark.

When *Yang-Shi Shih-Wo* was born and Lady *Shu* saw him, and upon entering the hall heard him cry, she went back and said, "His voice is that of a wolf. He has a reckless character, destitute of all affection. But for him the *Yang Shi* family would not perish." Afterwards she declined to see him. When he had grown up, *Ch'i Sheng* made a rebellion, in which *Shih-Wo* took part. The people killed him, and the *Yang Shi* family was extinguished thereby. *Chou's* wickedness dated from his childhood, and *Shi-Wo's* rebellion

could be foretold from the new-born's whine. As a newborn child has not yet had any intercourse with the world, who could have brought ahout his perversion?

Tan Chu was born in *Yao's* palace, aud *Shang Chun* in *Shuns* hall. Under the reign of these two sovereigns, the people house by house were worthy of being entrusted with a fief. Those with whom the two might have mixed, were most excellent, and the persons forming the suit of the two emperors, were all most virtuous. Nevertheless, *Tan Chu* was haughty, and *Shang Chiln* brutal. Both lacked imperial decorum to such a degree, that they were set up as a warning to coming generations. *Mencius* judges men by the pupils of their eyes. If the heart be bright, says he, the pupils are clear, if it be dark, the pupils are dim. However, the clearness and dimness of the eyes reaches back to as far as man's birth. These differences are due to the different fluids received from heaven. The eyes are not clear during childhood, or dimmed, when man grows, and associates with other people. Nature at first is spontaneous, goodness and badness are The Viscount of *Wei,* a kinsman of prince *Chou i. e. Chou Hmn,* the last emperor of the *Shang* dynasty, who lost the throne through his wickedness and tyrany (1154-1122 B.c.). The *Yang She* family was very powerful in the *Chin* State. Lady *Shu* had married one *Yang She* and was thus related to *Yang-Sh Shih-Wo.* This took place in the *Chin* State in 513 B.c. *Mencius* Bk. IV, Pt, I, chap. XV.

Lun-Heng. 25 the outcome of different dispositions. What *Mencius* says about original nature is not true.

Yet something may have contributed to the idea of the goodness of nature. A man may be benevolent or just, it is the wonderful proficiency of his nature, as in his locomotion and movements he shows his extraordinary natural ability. But his colour, whether white or black, and his stature, whether long or short, remain unchanged until old age and final death. Such is his heavenly nature.

Everybody knows that water, earth, and other substances differ in their na-

tures, but people are not aware that good and evil are due to different natural dispositions. A one year old baby is not inclined to violent robbery. After it has grown up, its greed may gradually develop, and lead to ferocity and aggressiveness.

Kao Tse, a contemporary of *Mencius* denies the difference of goodness and badness in nature, comparing it to flowing water which led to the east, runs eastward, and to the west, westward. As water cannot be divided according to its eastern or western direction, a division of men into good and bad ones is untenable. Therefore *Kan Tse* asserts that human nature is similar to the nature of water. Such being the case, water may well be used as an illustration.

Nature is as metal is metal, and wood, wood. A good man has a natural bent towards goodness, and a wicked man to wickedness. Man is endowed by heaven with a spontaneous mind, and has received a uniform disposition/ Therefore portents appear at the time of birth, from which man's goodness and badness can be discovered.

People with whom no difference of good and bad exists, and who may be pushed one or the other way, are called average people. Being neither good nor bad, they require instruction in order to assume a certain type. Therefore *Confucias* says that with people above the average one can discourse on higher subjects, but that with those under the average one cannot do so. *Kao Tse's* comparison with channelled water applies only to average people, but does not concern extremely good or extremely bad persons.

The spiritual nature may be transformed, but not the physical one. Human nature is so wonderful, that even origtnally bad people may by much training become benevolent and just. *Mencius* seeing these wonderful results was misled into the belief that human nature was originally good. *Mencius* Bk. VI, Pt, I, chap. II. Either good or bad, not partly good and partly bad. *Analect s* II, 19.

According to *Confucius* people are nearly related to one another by character, but become very different by habit. The character of average people is the work of habit. Made familiar with good, they turn out good, accustomed to evil, they become wicked. Only with extremely good, or extremely bad characters habit is of no avail. Therefore *Confucius* holds that only highly cultured and grossly ignorant people cannot be changed. Their natures being either good or otherwise, the influence of sages, and the teaching of wise men is impotent to work a change. Since *Confucius,* the Nestor in wisdom and virtue, and the most eminent of all philosophers, asserts the unchangeability of highly cultured and grossly ignorant people, we may conclude that *Kao Tse's* sayings are not correct.

However, there is some foundation for *Kao Tse's* view. The *Shiking* says:— "What can that admirable man be compared to?" The *Tso-chuan* answers:—" He is like boiled silk; dyed with indigo it becomes blue, coloured with vermilion it turns crimson." Leading water eastward or westward is like dyeing silk blue or red. *Tan Chu* and *Shang Chun* were also imbued with *Yao* and *Shuns* doctrines, but *Tan Chu* remained haughty, and *Shang Chun* cruel. The extremely bad stuff they were made of did not take the blue or the red colour.

In opposition to *Mencius, Sun Ching* wrote a chapter on the wickedness of nature, supposing human nature to be wicked, and its goodness to be ficticious. Wickedness of nature means to say that men, when they are born, have all a bad nature, and ficticiousness that, after they have grown up, they are forcibly induced to do good. According to this view of *Sun Ching,* among men, even as children, there are no good ones.

Chi as a boy amused himself with planting trees. When *Confucius* could walk, he played with sacrificial vessels. When a stone is produced, it is hard, when a fragrant flower comes forth, it smells. All things imbued with a good fluid develop accordingly with their growth. He who amused himself with tree planting, *Analects* XVII, 2.
» *Analects* XVII, 3.

Storing I, Bk. IV, Ode IX, 2. *Vul.* above p. 374. One of the Ten Philosophers, whose work has come down to us. He lived in the 3rd cent. B.C. His original surname *Hsun* — hence *Hsiin Tse* — was changed into *Sun Jj'j* under the reign of the Emperor *Hs-iian Ti* of the *Han* dynasty, 73-48 B.C., whose personal name was *Hsun.* Cf. *Edkim, "Siiin King the Philosopher"* in *Journal of the Royal Asiatic Society, Shanghai* Vol. XXXIII, p. 46. became the minister of *T'ang,* and the boy who played with sacrificial vessels, the sage of *Chou.* Things with a fragrant or stony nature show their hardness and fragrance. *Sun Ching's* opinion is, therefore, incompatible with truth, yet his belief in the wickedness of nature is not quite without foundation:

A one year old baby has no yielding disposition. Seeing something to eat, it cries, and wants to eat it, and beholding a nice thing, it weeps, and wants to play with it. After it has grown up, its propensities are checked, and its wishes cut down, and it is compelled to do good.

Liu Tse Ching objects that in this case heaven would have no fluid. Where would the first good deed come from, if the *Yang* and the *Yin* principles and good and evil were not counterbalancing each other? *Lu Chia* says that, when heaven and earth create men, they predispose them in favour of propriety and justice, that man can see what for ho. has received life and act accordingly, which accordance is called virtue. *Lu Chia* thinks that the human mind is turned towards propriety and justice, and that man also can discover what for he has come into life. However, the right-minded do good of their own accord without waiting for this discovery, and the evil-minded disregard propriety and defy justice, although they see quite clearly in the matter. It is impossible that justice should win them to the good cause. Thus the covetous can speak very well on disinterestedness, and the rebels on good government, robber *Chi* condems theft and *Chuang Cltiao* stigmatises lawlessness. They have a clear conception of themselves, and know

how to talk on virtue, but owing to their vicious character they do not practise what they say, and the good cause derives no benefit from it. Therefore *Lu Chins* opinion cannot be considered the right one. *Tung Chung Shu* having read *Mendus* and *Sun Ching's* writings, composed himself an essay on natural feelings and natural dis *Viz.* of *Yao* who reigned at *T'ang,* in *Chih.* A famous author, more generally known by the name *Lht Hsiang,* 80-9 B.c., whose works we still possess. A politician and scholar of the 3rd and 2nd cent. B.c., author of the " New Words" jjjlf f, the same as mentioned above p. 383 as envoy to the king of the southern *Yiieh.* Cf. p. 139. Another outlaw. An author of the 2nd cent. B.c. who wrote the "Dew of the Spring and Autumn" which is still extant. position, in which he says:— Heaven's great principles are on one side the *Yin,* on the other the *Yang.* The great principles in man are on one side the natural feelings, on the other natural disposition. The disposition comes out of the *Yang,* the feelings out of the *Yin.* The *Yin* fluid is hase, the *Yang* fluid humane. Who believes in the goodness of nature sees the *Yang,* who speaks of its wickedness the *Yin.* That is, *Tung Chung Shu* means to say that *Mencius* saw only the *Yang,* and *Sun Ching* the *Yin.*

The opinions of the two philosophers may well thus be distinguished, but as regards human nature, such a distinction does not hold good. Goodness and badness are not divided in this way. Natural feelings and natural disposition are simultaneously produced by the *Yin* and the *Yang* combined, either more or less copiously. Precious stones growing in rocks are partly of a single colour, partly multicoloured, how can natural feelings or natural disposition growing in the *Yin* and *Yang* be either exclusively good? What *Tung Chung Shu* says is not correct.

Liu Tse Ching teaches that the natural disposition is formed at birth, that it is inherent to the body and does not come out, that on the other hand natural feelings arise from the contact with the world, and manifest themselves outwardly. That which manifests itself outwardly, he calls *Yang,* that which does not appear, he calls *Yin* Thus *Liu Tse CMng* submits that the natural disposition is inherent to the body, but does not come out, whereas the natural feelings unite with external things, and appear outwardly. Therefore he designates them as *Yang.* The natural disposition he designates as *Yin,* because it does not appear, and has no communication with the outer world. *Liu Tse Cheng's* identification of natural feelings with *Yang* and disposition with *Yin* leaves the origin of these qualities quite out of the question, insomuch as the *Yin* and the *Yang* are determined in an off-hand way by outward manifestation and non-appearance. If the *Yang* really depends on outward manifestation, then it may be said that natural disposition also comes into contact with external things. "In moments of haste, he cleaves to it, and in seasons of danger he cleaves to it. " The compassionate cannot endure the sight of suffering. This non-endurance is an effluence of benevolence. Hues mility and modesty are manifestations of natural disposition. These qualities have all their external objects. As compassion and mod A quotation from *Analects* IV, 5, where we read that the superior man always cleaves to benevolence esty manifest themselves outwardly, I am afraid that the assertion that natural disposition is something inside without any connection with external things, cannot be right. By taking into consideration merely outwardness and inwardness, *Yin* and *Yang,* without reference to the goodness and badness of nature, the truth cannot be known. As *Liu Tse Chfoig* has it, natural disposition would be *Yin,* and natural feelings *Yang,* but have men not good as well as bad passions?

From *Mencius* down to *Liu Tse Ching* the profoundest scholars and greatest thinkers have propounded a great many different views without, however, solving the problem of original nature in a satisfactory way. The arguments of the philosophers *ShiJi Tse, Knug Sun Ni Tse,* and others of the same class alone contain much truth. We may say that

it is easy to understand the subject, but the difficulty is to explain the principle. Style and diction may be ever so brilliant and ffowery, and the conceptions and arguments as sweet as honey, all that is no proof of their truth.

As a matter of fact, human natural disposition is sometimes good, and sometimes bad, just as human faculties can be of a high or of a low order. High ones cannot be low, nor low ones high. To say that human nature is neither good nor bad would be the same as to maintain that human faculties are neither high nor low. The original disposition which Heaven gives to men, and the destiny which it sends down, are essentially alike. By destiny men are honoured or despised, by nature good or bad. If one disputes the existence of goodness and badness in human nature, he might as well call in question that destiny makes men great or miserable.

The nature of the soil of the Nine Provinces is different in regard to goodness and badness. It is yellow, red, or black, of superior, average, or inferior quality. The water courses are not all alike. They are limpid or muddy, and run east, west, north or southward. Man is endowed with the nature of Heaven and Earth, and imbued with the spirit of the Five Qualities. He may Who maintain that human nature is partly good and partly bad.

The tex' has Tjt which looks like a name:—the Record of *Fi'ng Wen Mao.* The fact, however, that a philosopher of the name of *Feng Wen Mao* is unknown, and the symmetry of the context leads me to the conclusion that instead of we should read Kjjj. and translate, as I have done. In prehistoric times China was divided into nine provinces, hence the term the Nine Provinces has become a synonym of China. Cf. p. 381 Note 2. be benevolent or just, it is the wonderful proficiency of bis nature. In bis locomotion and movements be may be majestic or agile, it is his extraordinary natural ability. But his colour, whether white or black and bis stature, whether long or short, remain unchanged until old age and final death. Such is heavenly nature. I am decidedly of opinion that what

Mencius says on the goodness of human nature, refers to people above the average, that what *Sun Ching* says on its badness, refers to people under the average, and that, if *Yang Hsiung* teaches that in human nature goodness and badness are mixed together, he means average people. Bringing people back to the unchanging standard and leading them into the right way, one may teach them. But this teaching alone does not exhaust human nature.

The last sentences are repeated from p. 386. CHAPTER XXXIII.

Criticisms on Confucius *(Wen K'ung).*

The students of Confucianism of the present day like to swear *in verba magistri,* and to believe in antiquity. The words of the Worthies and Sages are to them infallible, and they do their best to explain and practise them, but they are unable to criticize them. When the Worthies and Sages take the pencil, and commit their thoughts to writing, though they meditate, and thoroughly discuss their subject, one cannot say that they always hit the truth, and much less can their occasional utterances all be true. But although they cannot be all true, the scholars of to-day do not know, howto impugn them, and, in case they are true, but so abstruse that they are difficult to understand, those people do not know how to interpret their meaning. The words of the Sages on various occasions are often contradictory, and their writings at different times very often mutually clash. That however is, what the scholars of our time do not understand.

One always hears the remark that the talents of the Seventy Disciples of the school of *Confucius* surpassed those of the savants of our days. This statement is erroneous. They imagine that *Confucius* acting as teacher, a Sage propounding the doctrine, must have imparted it to exceptionally gifted men, whence the idea that they were quite unique. The talents of the ancients are the talents of the moderns. What we call men of superior genius now-a-days, were regarded by the ancients as Sages and supernatural beings, hence the belief that the Seventy Sages could not appear in other generations.

If at present there could be a teacher like *Confucius,* the scholars of this age would all be like *Yen* and *Min,* and without *Confucius,* the Seventy Disciples would be only like the Literati of the present day. For though learning from *Confucius,* they could not thoroughly inquire. The words of the Sage they did not completely understand, his doctrines and principles they were unable to explain. Therefore they ought to have · asked to get a clearer conception, and not understanding thoroughly, they ought to have raised objections in order to come to a complete understanding.

The sentiments which *Kao Yao2* uttered before the Emperor *Shun* were shallow and superficial, and not to the point. *Yil* asked him to explain himself, when the shallow words became deeper, and the superficial hints more explicit, for criticisms animate the discussion, and bring out the meaning, and opposition leads to greater clearness. *Confucius* ridiculed the guitar-playing and singing of *Tse Yn* who, however, retorted by quoting what *Confucius* had said on a previous occasion. If we now take up the text of the *Analects,* we shall see that in the sayings of *Confucius* there is much like the strictures on the singing of *Tse Yn.* But there were few disciples able to raise a question like *Tse Yu.* In consequence the words of *Confucius* became stereotyped and inexplicable, because the Seventy could not make any objection, and the scholars of the present time are not in a position to judge of the truth of the doctrine. Their scientific methods do not arise from a lack of ability, but the difficulty consists in opposing the teacher, scrutinizing his doctrine, investigating its meaning, and bringing evidence to ascertain right and wrong. Criticism is not solely permitted *vis-a-vis* to sages, as long as they are alive. The commentators of the present day do not require the instruction of a sage, before they dare to speak.

If questions be asked on things which seem inexplicable, and *Confucius* be pressed hard, how can this be deemed a violation of the moral laws, and if those who really are able to hand down the holy teachings, impugn the words of *Confucius,* why must their undertaking be considered unreasonable? I trust that, as regards *Yen Hui* and *Min Tse Ch'ien,* two prominent disciples of *Confucius.* The minister of *Shun.* The discussions of the two wise men before *Shun* are to be found in the *Shaking. Kao Yao mo.* Cf. *Analecl* XVII, 4. those inquiries into the words of *Confucius* and those remarks on his unintelligible passages, men of genius of all ages, possessing the natural gift of answering questions and solving difficulties, will certainly appreciate the criticisms and investigations made in our time.

"*Ming I Tse* asked, what filial piety was. The Master said, 'To show no disregard. ' Soon after, as *Fan Cliih* was driving him, the Master told him saying, "*Meng Sun* asked me, what filial piety was, and I answered him, 'To show no disregard. '" *Fan Chih* said, 'What does that mean?' The Master replied, 'That parents, while alive, should be served according to propriety; that, when dead, they should be buried according to propriety; and that they should be sacrificed to according to propriety.' "

Now I ask, *Confucius* said that no disregard is to be shown viz. no disregard to propriety. But a good son also must anticipate his parents' thoughts, conform to their will, and *never disregard their wishes. Confucius* said "to show no disregard," but did not speak of disregard for propriety. Could *Ming I Tse,* hearing the words of *Confucius,* not imagine that he meant to say, "no disregard for (the parents) wishes?" When *Fan Chili* came, he asked, what it meant. Then *Confucius* said, "That parents while alive should be served according to propriety; that, when dead, they should be buried according to propriety; and that they should be sacrificed to according to propriety." Had *Fan Chih* not inquired, what the words "no disregard" meant, he would not have understood them.

Ming I Tse's talents did not surpass those of *Fan Chih,* therefore there is no record of his sayings or doings in the chapters of the *Analects.* Since *Fan Chih* could not catch the meaning, would *Ming I Tse* have done so? *Ming Wu Po* asked what filial piety was. The Master replied "If the only sorrow parents have, is that which they feel, when their children are sick." *Meng I Tse* was the chief of one of three powerful families in *Lu.*

A disciple of *Confuciax.*

/. e. *Meng I Tse.*

Analects II, 5.—The citations from the *Analects* are quoted from *Legge's* translation, but here and there modified so as to suit the text, for *Wang Ch'ung* often understands a passage quite differently from *Legge* and his authorities. *Analects* II, 6. *Ming Wu Po* used to cause his parents much sorrow, therefore *Confucius* spoke the afore-mentioned words. *Ming Wu Po* was a cause of sorrow to his parents, whereas *Ming I Tse* disregarded propriety. If in reproving this fault *Confucius* replied to *Ming Wu Po* " If the only sorrow parents have is that which they feel, when their children are sick," he ought to have told *Ming I Tse* that only in case of fire or inundation might propriety he neglected. *Chou Kung* says that small talents require thorough instructions, wdiereas for great ones a hint is sufficient. *Tse Yu* possessed great talents, yet with him *Confucius* went into details. The talents of *Ming I Tse* were comparatively small, but *Confucius* gave him a mere hint. Thus he did not fall in with *Chou Kung's* views. Reproving the shortcomings of *Ming I Tse,* he lost the right principle. How was it that none of his disciples took exception?

If he did not dare to speak too openly owing to the high position held by *Ming I Tse,* he likewise ought to have said to *Ming Wu Po* nothing more than 'not to cause sorrow (is filial piety),' for both were scions of the *Ming* family, and of equal dignity. There is no apparent reason, why he should have spoken to *Ming Wu Po* in clear terms and to *Ming I Tse* thus vaguely. Had *Confitchu* freely told *Ming I Tse* not to disregard propriety, what harm would there have been?

No other family was more powerful in *Lu* than the *Chi* family, yet *Confucius* blamed them for having eight rows of

pantomimes in their court, and objected to their performing a sacrifice on Mount Iai. He was not afraid of the evil consequences, which this lack of reserve in regard to the usurpation of territorial rights by the *Chi* family might have for him, but anticipated bad results from a straightforward answer given to *Ming I Tse?* Moreover, he was questioned about filial piety more than once, and he had always his charioteer at hand. When he spoke to *Ming I Tse,* he was not merely in a submissive mood, therefore he informed *Fan Chih.* Confucius said "Riches and honour are what men desire. If they cannot be obtained in the proper way, they should not be *Analects* III, 1.
Analects III, 6. This sacrifice was a privilege of the sovereign. So that he might have used him as his mouth-piece as in the case of *Meng I Tse.* He was not afraid of *Mfng I Tse. Analects* IV, 5. held. Poverty and meanness are what men dislike. If they cannot be obtained in the proper way, they should not be avoided."
The meaning is that men must acquire riches in a just and proper way, and not take them indiscriminately, that they must keep within their bounds, patiently endure poverty, and not recklessly throw it off. To say that riches and honour must not be held, unless they are obtained in the proper way, is all right, but wdiat is poverty and meanness not obtained in a proper way? Wealth and honour can, of course, be abandoned, but what is the result of giving up poverty and meanness? By giving up poverty and meanness one obtains wealth and honour. As long as one does not obtain wealth and honour, one does not get rid of poverty and meanness. If we say that, unless wealth and honour cau be obtained in a proper way, poverty and meanness should not be shunned, then that which is obtained is wealth and honour, not poverty and meanness. How can the word "obtaining" be used with reference to poverty and meanness? Therefore the passage ought to read as follows:
"Poverty and meanness are what people dislike. If they cannot be *avoided*

in the proper way, they should not be avoided."
Avoiding is the proper word, not obtaining. Obtaining is used of obtaining. Now there is avoiding, how can it be called obtaining? Only in regard to riches and honour we can speak of obtaining. How so? By obtaining riches and honour one avoids poverty and meanness. Then how can poverty and meanness be avoided in the proper way?—By purifying themselves and keeping in the proper way officials acquire rank and emoluments, wealth and honour, and by obtaining these they avoid poverty and meanness.
How are poverty and meanness avoided not in the proper way?—If anybody feels so vexed and annoyed with poverty and meanness, that he has recourse to brigandage and robbery for the purpose of amassing money and valuables, and usurps official emoluments, then he does not keep in the proper way.
Since the Seventy Disciples did not ask any question regarding the passage under discussion, the literati of to-day are likewise incapable of raising any objection.
If the meaning of this utterance is not explained, nor the words made clear, we would have to say that *Confucius* could not *Wang Chung* thus interprets the passage, which gives no sense. I should say that he misunderstood *Confucius,* for every difficulty is removed, if we take the words to mean what *Legge* translates: —" if *it* cannot be obtained" eir. "if it is not possible to act in the aforesaid manner" instead of " if *theg* cannot be obtained." speak properly. As long as the meaning continues unravelled, and the words unexplained, the admonition of *Confucius* remains uncomprehensible. Why did his disciples not ask, and people now say nothing?
"*Confucius* said of *Kung Yeh Chang* that he might be wived and that, although he was put in bonds, he was not guilty. Accordingly he gave him his daughter to wife."
I ask what was the idea of *Confucius,* when he gave a wife to *Kung Yeh Chang.* Did he think him fit to marry,

because he was thirty years old, or on account of his excellent conduct? If he had his thirty years in view, he should not have spoken of his being in fetters, and if he looked upon his conduct, there was no occasion either for mentioning his imprisonment. Why? Because all who joined the school of *Confucius* were well-behaved. Therefore they were called accomplished followers. If among these followers one or the other was unmarried, he might have been married, but it need not be mentioned. If among the disciples many unmarried ones existed and *Kung Yeh Cliang* was the most virtuous of them, and should therefore *Confucius* have given him a wife alone, then in praising him *Confucius* ought to have enumerated his deeds instead of speaking of his imprisonment. There are not a few persons in the world, who suffer violence without being guilty, but they are not perfect sages therefore. Of ordinary people who are wronged, there are a great many, not only one. If *Confucius* made an innocent man his son-in-law, he selected not a virtuous man, but one who had suffered injustice. The only praise *Confucius* had for *Kung Yeh Chang* was his innocence; of his doings or his qualities he said not a word. If in fact he was not virtuous, and *Confucius* made him his son-in-law, he did wrong, and if he was virtuous indeed, but *Confucius* in praising him did not mention it, he was wrong likewise. It was like his giving a wife to *Nan Yung,* of whom he said that 'if the country were well-governed, he would not be out of office, and if it were ill-governed, he would escape punishment and disgrace,' a praise which left nothing to be desired. *Analects* V, 1.
ConfluMm gave *Nan Yung* the daughter of his elder brother to wife. *Analects* V, 1. *Wang Ch'ung's* objections arc again far-fetched and groundless. The words of *Confucius* imply that *Kung Yeh Cliang's* character was so excellent and above suspicion, that *Confucius* would not doubt him, even if he were condemned by the world and treated like a criminal, and therefore he made him his son-in-law.
The Master said to *Tse Kung,* "Which of

you two, yourself or *Hui* is superior?" *Tse Kung* replied, "How dare I compare myself with *Hui*? If *Hui* hears one point, he knows therefrom ten others. If I hear one, I know but two." The Master said "Not equal to him. I and you together cannot compare with him."

Thus with a view to setting forth the excellence of *Yen Hui* this question was put to *Tse Kung*. This calls for the following remark:

That which *Confucius* propounded was propriety and modesty. *Tse Lu* would govern a State with propriety, but his words were not modest, therefore *Confucius* criticized him. Had *Tse Kung* really been superior to *Hui*, he would, on being asked by *Confucius*, have replied nevertheless that he was not equal to him, and had he been inferior in fact, he would likewise have owned to his inferiority. In the first case the answer would not have been wrong or a deception of the Master, for propriety and modesty require depreciatory and humble words.

What was the purport of this inquiry of *Confucius*? If he was aware that *Yen Hui* surpassed *Tse Kung*, he did not need to ask the latter, and if he really did not know, and therefore asked *Tse Kung*, he would not have learned it in this way either, for *Tse King* was bound to give a modest and humble reply. If *Confucius* merely wanted to eulogise *Hui* and praise his virtue, there were many other disciples not enjoyiug the same fame, why must he just ask *Tse Kung*?

The Master said, "Admirable indeed was the virtue of *Hui!* " and further, "I have talked with *Hui* for a whole day, and he has not made any objection, as if he were stupid" and, "Such was *Hui*, that for three months there would be nothing in his mind contrary to perfect virtue." In all these three chapters *Hui* is praised directly, but not at the cost of any other person, why then must *Tse Kung* in one chapter serve to him as a foil?

Somebody might think that *Confucius* wanted to snub *Tse Kung*. At that time the fame of *Tse Kung* was greater than that of *Yen Hui*. *Confucius* apprehensive, lest *Tse Kung* should become too

conceited and overbearing, wanted to humble him.

If his name ranked above that of *Hui*, it was a simple fact at that time, but not brought about by *Tse Kung's* endeavours to *Analects* V, 8.

Analects XI, 10. *Analects* VI, 9. *Analects* 11,9. *Analects* VI, 5. supersede his rival. How could the judgment of *Tse Kung* have affected the case? Even supposing that, in case *Yen Huts* talents were superior to his, he had submitted of his own accord, there was no necessity for any snubbing. If *Tse Kung* could not know it himself, he would, notwithstanding anything *Confucius* might have said, have been convinced that the latter only wanted to humble him, and in that case. questioning or no questioning would have neither humbled nor elated him. *Tsai Wo* being asleep during the day time, the Master said, "Rotten wood cannot be carved; a wall of dirty earth will not receive the trowel. But what is the use of my reproving *Tsai Wo!*"— For sleeping during the day *Tsai Wo* was reprimanded in this way.

Sleeping during day time is a small evil. Rotten wood and dirty earth are things in such a state of decay, that they cannot be repaired, and must be regarded as great evils. If a small evil is censured, as though it were a great one, the person in question would not submit to such a judgment. If *Tsai Wo's* character was as bad as rotten wood or dirty earth, he ought not to have been admitted to the school of *Confucius* nor rank in one of the four classes of disciples. In case his character was good however, *Confucius* dealt too harshly with him.

"If a man is not virtuous, and you carry your dislike of him to extremes, he will recalcitrate." The dislike shown by *Confucius* for *Tsai Wo* has been, so to say, too strong. Provided that common and ignorant people had committed some smaller punishable offence, and the judge condemned them to capital punishment, would they suirer the wrong, and complain of the injustice, or would they quietly submit, and consider themselves guilty? Had *Tsai Wo* been an ignorant man, his feelings would have been the same with those people guilty

of some ofTence; being a worthy, he must have understood a reproof of *Confucius,* and have reformed at the slightest remark. An open word was sufficient *Analects* V, 9. The four classes into which the ten principal disciples of *Confucius* were divided according to their special abilities:—virtue, eloquence, administrative talents, and literary acquirements. *Tsai Wo* belongs to the second class of the able speakers together with *Te Kung*. Cf. *Analects* XI, 2. *Analects* VIII, 10. to enlighten him, whereas an exaggeration would have missed its mark. At the first allusion he would already have reformed. That however did not depend on the strength of the language used, but on *Tsai Wo's* ability to change.

The scheme of the *"Ch'un Ch'iu"* is to point out any small goodness, and to censure small wrongs. But if *Confucius* praised small deserts in high terms, and censured trifling wrongs immoderately, would *Tsai Wo* having the scheme of the *Chun Ch'iu* in view agree with such criticism? If not, he would not accept it, and the words of *Confucius* would be lost.

The words of a Sage must tally with his writings. His words come from his mouth, and his writings are in his books, but both flow from the heart, and are the same in substance. When *Confucius* composed the *"Ch'un Ch'iu"* he did not censure small things, as if they were very important, but in reproving *Tsai Wo* he condemned a small offence in the same manner as an enormous crime. His words and his writings disagree. How should they convince a man?

The Master said, "At first my way with men was to hear their words, and to give them credit for their conduct. Now my way is to hear their words, and look at their conduct. It is from *Tsai Wo* that I have learnt to make this change." That is from the time, when *Tsai Wo* was asleep in the day time, he changed his method of studying men. But one may well ask, how can a man's sleeping during the day time spoil his character, and how can a" man of bad conduct become good by not sleeping day or night? Is it possible to learn anything about people's goodness or badness from their sleeping during the day time?

Amongst the disciples of *Confucius* in the four classes *Tsai Wo* took precedence over *Tse Kung*. If he was so lazy, that nothing could be made out of his character, how could he advance so far? If *Tsai Wo* reached such a degree of perfection notwithstanding his sleeping during the day, his talents must have been far superior to those of ordinary people. Supposing that he had not yet reached the goal, but was under the impression that he had done enough, he did not know better himself. That was a lack of knowledge, but his conduct was not bad. He only wanted some enlightenment, but to change the method of studying men for that reason was superfluous.

This is professedly the aim of the "('h'un-ch'iu" or "Spring and Autumn" Record, the only classical work, of which *Confucius* claims the authorship. *Analects* V, 9.

Let us assume that *Tsai Wo* was conscious of his deficiencies, but felt so exhausted, that he fell asleep during day time. That was a relaxation of his vital force. This exhaustion may increase to such a degree, that death ensues and not only sleep.

As regards the method of judging human character by taking into consideration the actions, the words are disregarded, and by laying all stress on words, the conduct is left out of consideration. Now although *Tsai Wo* was not very energetic in his actions, his words were well worth hearing. There is a class of men who speak very well, but whose deeds are not quite satisfactory. From the time that *Tsai Wo* slept during the day, *Confucius* began to hear the words, and look at the conduct, and only in case they both corresponded, called a man virtuous. That means to say, he wanted a perfect man, but how does that agree with his principle that perfection must not be expected from one man? *Tse Chang* asked saying, "The minister *Tse Wen* thrice took office, and manifested no joy in his countenance. Thrice he retired from office, and manifested no displeasure. He made it a point to

inform the new minister of the way in which he had conducted the government;—what do you say of him?" The Master replied, "He was loyal."—" Was he benevolent?"—"I do not know. How can he be pronounced benevolent? *Tse Wen* recommended *Tse Yil* of *Ciiu* as his successor. *Tse Yil* attacked *Sung* with a hundred warchariots, but was defeated and lost most of his men. If *Tse Win* was ignorant like that, how could he be considered benevolent?"—

My question is this. When *Tse Win* recommended *Tse Yd,* he did not know him, but wisdom has nothing to do with virtue. Ignorance does not preclude benevolent deeds. There are the five virtues:—benevolence, justice, propriety, intelligence, and truth, but these five are separate, and not necessarily combined. Thus there are intelligent men, benevolent men, there are the well-mannered, and the just. The truthful must not always be intelligent, or the intelligent, benevolent, the benevolent, well-mannered, or the wellmannered, just. *Tse Win's* intelligence was obfuscated by *Tse Yil, Tsai Wo* could no more be made responsible for his bodily weakness, than for his death.

Analects XIII, 15 and XVIII, 10. A minister of the *Ch'u* State. *Analects* V, 18. The following words of (*'onfucius* are omitted in our Analects. This battle took place in 632 B.C. It is described in the *Tso-chuan* Book V, 27 (Duke *Hsi* 27th year).

Lbd-Heng. 26 but how did his benevolence suffer therefrom? Consequently it is not right to say, "How can he be pronounced benevolent?"

Moreover loyal means generous, and generosity is benevolence. *Confucius* said, "By observing a man's faults it may be known that he is benevolent." *Tse Win* possessed true benevolence. If *Confucius* says that loyalty is not benevolence, he might as well assert that father and mother are not the two parents, or that husband and wife are not a pair.

The duke *Ai* asked which of the disciples loved to learn. *Confucius* replied to him, "There was *Yen Hui.* He did not vent his anger on others, nor did he twice commit the same fault. Alas!

his fate was short and he died; and now there is none. I have not yet heard of any one who loves to learn."—

What was really the cause of *Yen Hui's* death? It is, of course, attributed to his short fate, which would correspond to *Po Niu's* sickness. All living men have received their fate, which is complete, and must be clean. Now there being the evil disease of *Po Niu*, one says that he had no fate. Those who remain alive, must have been endowed with a long fate. If a person has obtained a short fate, we should likewise say that he has no fate. Provided that heaven's fate can be short or long, it also must be good or bad. Speaking of *Yen Hui's* short fate, one can speak likewise of *Po Niu's* bad fate. Saying that *Po Niu* had no fate, one must admit that *Yen Hui* had no fate either. One died, the other was diseased; *Confucius* pitied them both, and called it fate. The thing which is derived from heaven is the same, but it is not given the same name, for which I do not see any apparent reason. *Analects* IV, 7.

Duke *Ai* of *Lu,* 494-468 B.c. *Analects* VI, 2. *Analects* VI, 8. *Wang Ch'ung* understands by fate something material, not a decree. Cf. Chap. VII and VIII. Leprosy. Cf. p. 165. Fate is a pure substance pervading the body, which cannot excite a foul disease like leprosy. The entire polemic is against the expression "short fate" used by *Confucius,* who takes fate in the usual acceptation of decree, or appointment of heaven. *Wang Ch'ung* from his materialistic point of view argues, that fate is always complete and pure, and that I here can be no long or short one. The premature death of e« *Hui* and the disease of *Po Niu* are not fate at all.

Duke *Ai* asked *Confucius* who loved to learn. *Confucius* replied, "There was *Yen Hui* who loved to learn, but now there is none. He did not vent his anger on others nor commit the same fault twice."—Why did *Confucius* say so?

There are those who presume that *Confucius* wished to add a criticism on Duke *Ai's* character, and that therefore he spoke of the venting of anger and committing faults twice. Sticking to the duke's inquiry, he gave him this reply, thereby at the same time censuring the duke's short-comings, but without committing himself.

However *K'ang Tse* likewise asked about the love of learning, and *Confucius* in his answer also indicated *Yen Hui*. *K'ang Tse* had his faults as well, why did *Confucius* not answer so as to reprove *K'ang Tse* too? *K'ang Tse* was not a sage, his doings were not without fault. In fact *K'ang Tse* was distressed about the number of thieves. *Confucius* replied, "If you, sir, were not covetous, although you should reward them to do it, they would not steal." This shows that *K'ang Tse's* weak point was his covetousness. Why did not *Confucius* attack it?

Confucius having visited *Nan Tse*, *Tse Lu* was displeased, on which the Master said, "If I have done a wicked thing, may Heaven fall down on me, may Heaven fall down on me!" — *Nan Tse* was the wife of Duke *Ling* of *Wei* She had invited *Confucius*. *Tse Lu* was displeased and suspected *Confucius* of having had illicit intercourse with her. In order to exculpate himself *Confucius* said, "If I have done any thing disgraceful, may Heaven crush me." To prove his perfect sincerity he swore that he did not deceive *Tse Lu*.

I ask:—by thus exonerating himself, does *Confucius* really clear himself? If it had happened once that Heaven fell down, and killed people for having perpetrated any disgraceful act, *Confucius* might allude to, and swear by it. *Tse Lu* would most probably believe him then, and he would be whitewashed. Now, nobody has ever The head of the *Chi* family in *La*.

Analects XI, G
Analects XII, 18.
Analects VI, 26.

A most disreputable woman, guilty of incest with her half-brother, Prince *Chou* of *Sung*. The commentators take great pains to whitewash *Confucius*, who called upon this unworthy princess. What induced her to invite the Sage, and him to accept the invitation, is not known. Various conjectures have been put forward. been crushed by Heaven.

Would therefore *Tse Lu* believe in an oath to the effect that Heaven might fall down on him?

It happens sometimes that a man is killed by lightning, drowned by water, burned by fire, or crushed by the tumbling wall of a house. Had *Confucius* said "May the lighting strike me, the water drown me, the fire burn me, or a wall crush me," *Tse Lu* would undoubtedly have believed him, but instead of that he swore before *Tse Lu* by a disaster, which has never before happened. How could this dispel *Tse Lu's* doubts, and make him believe?

Sometimes people are crushed while asleep, before they awake. Can we say that Heaven crushed them? All those who are crushed in their sleep, before they awake, have not of necessity done some dishonest deed. Though not far advanced in philosophy, yet *Tse Lu* knew how to distinguish the truth of a thing. *Confucius* swearing by something unreal *Tse Lu* would assuredly not have got rid of his doubts.

Confucius asserted that life and death were fate, and that wealth and honour depended on Heaven. Accordingly human life can be long or short, which has nothing to do with human actions, goodness or badness. In fact *Yen Hui* died prematurely, and *Confucius* spoke of his short fate. Are we entitled to conclude therefrom that people whose fate is short and who die young, must have done something wrong?

Although *Tse Lu* was not yet very proficient in philosophy, yet from the words of *Confucius* he knew the real meaning of life ami death. *Confucius* swore that, if he had done anything dishonest. Heaven might crush him instead of telling *Tse Lu* that he was only under the rule of fate, for how could Heaven fall down upon him and kill him, before the appointed time of his death had come? Thus on taking his oath before *Tse Lu* that Heaven might crush him, he could not expect to find credence, and in that case the exculpation of *Confucius* would have been no exculpation.

The *Shu-king* says, "He not as arrogant as *Tan Chu*, who only liked to saunter idly about." Thus the Emperor

Shun admonished *Yil* not to treat an unworthy son like a son, and to pay attention to the commands of Heaven. He was alarmed, lest *Yil* should be partial to his son, therefore he adduced *Tan Chu* as an example calculated to deter him. But *Yil* replied:—"I had my marriage
Cf. p. 136.
Cf. p. 151.

» *Shu-king, Yi-chi*, Pt. II, Bk. IV, 1 (*Legge* Vol. III, Pt. I, p. 84).

Yao'x son. *Shu-king loc. cit.* on the *hsmg, Jen, kwei,* and *chia* days. When the cries and whines of my son were first heard, I did not treat him like my son." He related something that had happened, from the past forecasting the future, and deducting what could not be seen from that which was apparent. Thus he demonstrated that he would not venture to show partiality for an unworthy son. He did not say:—"May Hearten fall down on me," knowing very well that common people in swearing like to invoke Heaven.

When *Tse Lu* suspected the actions of *Confucius,* the latter did not refer to his conduct in the past to prove that he had done nothing reproachable, but said that Heaven might crush him. How does he differ from common people, who for the purpose of dispelling a doubt will solemnly protest by Heaven?

Confucius said:—" The phoenix does not come; the River sends forth no Plan:—it is all over with me!"

The Master felt distressed that he did not become emperor. As emperor he would have brought about perfect peace. At such a time the phoenix would have made its appearance, and the Plan would have emerged from the Yellow River. Now he did not obtain imperial authority, therefore there were no auspicious portents either, and *Confucius* felt sick at heart and distressed. Hence his words:—"It is all over with me!"

My question is:—Which after all are the necessary conditions preceding the appearance of the phoenix and the Plan of the River, which though fulfilled, did not bring about their arrival? If it be perfect peace, it may be urged that not all the emperors, under whose reign perfect peace prevailed, attracted the phoenix or the Plan of the River.

The Five Emperors and the Three Rulers all brought about perfect peace, but comparing their omens, we find that they had not all the phoenix as an indispensable attribute. During the time of perfect peace the phoenix'is not a necessary omen. That *Confucius*, a sage, should have longed so much for something that was not at all indispensable, and that he worried himself, is not right. *Analects* IX, 8. On the Plan of the Yellow River *vuL* p. 294 Note 1. In the case of *Confucius*. 4 Cf. p. 138. Somebody might object that *Conftwins* did not sorrow, because he was not appointed emperor, but that, when he felt so sad, there was no wise ruler, and that therefore he did not find employment. The phopnix and the Plan of the River are omens of a wise ruler. As long as they are absent, there is no wise ruler, and without a wise ruler *Confucius* had no chance of finding employment.

How are these auguries called forth? By appointing wise and able men the government is set right, and great success obtained. Then the omens appear. After they have made their appearance, there is no further need for a *Confucius*. Why has *Confucius* only the end in view? He does not think of the first steps, and solely sees the end, does not assist a king as minister, but speaks of those portents. The government not being in order, those things, of course, do not become visible.

To conclude from their arrival that there must be a wise ruler, would also be a mistake. 'The emperor *Hsiao Win Ti* deserved the name of a wise ruler, yet in his annals we find nothing about a phoenix or the Plan of the River. Had *Confucius* lived under *Ilsuto Wen Ti* he would likewise have complained:—"It is all over with me!"

The Master was expressing a wish to live among the Nine Wild Tribes of the east. Some one said, "They are brutish. How can you do such a thing?" The Master said, "If a superior man dwelt among them, what brutality would Hiere be?"' *Confucius* felt annoyed, because his doctrine did not find its way

into China. This loss of his hopes roused his anger, and made him wish to emigrate to the Wild Tribes. Some one remonstrated, asking, how he could do such a thing, since the savages were brutish and unmannerly. To which *Confucius* retorted by syying, "If a superior man dwelt among them, what brutality would there be?", which means to say that, if a superior man were The time when the lucky omens become visible. The steps to secure a wise government and perfect peace, which must have been successful, ere the phoenix and the Plan will come forward. Wishing to behold those auspicious portents, *Confucius* ought first to have instituted an excellent administration, as minister of the reigning sovereign. He sees the result, but overlooks the causes. The *Han* emperor whose reign lasted from 170-156 B.c. In the *Shi-chi*. -*AnakcU* X, 13. living among them and imparting his doctrine, there would be no more rudeness.

How did *Confucius* conceive the idea of going to the Nine Tribes?—Because his doctrine did not spread in China, he wished to go there. But if China was no field for it, how could it have spread among the savages? "The rude tribes of the east and north with their princes are still not equal to China without princes. " That shows that things which are easily managed in China are very difficult among the savages. Can then something which has failed, where everything is easy, be carried through, where everything is difficult?

Furthermore, *Confucius* said, "If a superior man dwelt among them, how came one to speak of brutality." Does that mean that the superior man keeps his culture for himself, or that he imparts it? Should he keep it closed up in his bosom, he might do that in China as well, and need not go to the savages for that purpose. If, however, he should instruct the savages in it, how could they be taught?

Yd visited the State of the Naked People. He was naked himself, while he stayed with them, and only when he left, he put on his clothes again. The habit of

wearing clothes did not take root among the wild tribes. *Yii* was unable to teach the Naked People to wear clothes, how could *Confucius* make superior men of the Nine Tribes? ,

Perhaps *Confucius,* as a matter of fact, did not wish to go to the wild tribes after all, but grieved that his doctrine was not accepted, he merely said so in angry mood. Or, when some one remonstrated, he knew pretty well that the wild tribes were barbarians, but nevertheless he said, "What brutality would there be?", insisting on having his own way and warding off the attack of his interlocutor. If he really did not want to go, but said so out of disgust, he did not tell the truth. "What the superior man requires, is just that in his words there may be nothing incorrect." If *Confucius* knew that the wild tribes were uncivilized, but at all costs insisted on being right, this was like the discussion of *Tse Lu* with *Confucius* about *Tse Kao*. *Tse Lu* got *Tse Kao* appointed governor of *Pi*. The Master said, "You are injuring a man's son." *Tse Lu* replied, "There *Analects* III, 5. *Analects* XIII, 3. The disciple *Kao Tse Kao*. A city in *Shantung*. are the spirits of the land and grain, and there are the people. Why must one read books, before he can be considered to have learned?" The Master said, "It is on this account that I hate your glib-tongued people." *Tse Lu* knew that one must not give an inconsiderate answer in order to have one's own way. *Confucius* was displeased with him, and compared him with those glib-tongued people. He likewise knew the impropriety of such replies, but he and *Tse Lu* gave both glib-tongued answers. *Confucius* said, "*Tse* did not receive Heaven's decree, but his goods are increased by him, and his calculations are generally correct."

What does he mean by saying that *Tse* did not receive Heaven's decree? One might suppose that he received the fate that he should become rich, and by his own method knew beforehand, what was going.to happen, and in his calculation did not miss the right moment.

Now, does wealth and honour depend on Heaven's appointment or on human knowledge? In the first case nobody could obtain them by his own knowledge or cleverness, if, on the other hand, men were the chief agents, why does *Confucius* say that life and death are fate, and wealth and honour depend on heaven?

If we admit that wealth can be acquired by knowing the proper way without receiving Heaven's decree, then honour also can be won through personal energy without fate. But in this world there is nobody who has won honour quite by himself without a heavenly order to that effect. Hence we learn that we cannot acquire wealth by ourselves, unless we have received Heaven's order.

Analects XI, 24. *Tse Kung.* We must translate here "receive," and not "acquiesce," as' *Legge* does, relying on the commentators. "Acquiesce" gives no sense here, as can be seen by comparing *Hutchinson's* translation, *China Review* Vol. VII, p. 109. Moreover, "receive" is in accordance with *Wang Ch'ung's* system. Throughout his work he speaks of "receiving the fate." *Hutchinson* has felt, that "receive" is the proper word here — *vid.* his note to p. 170 *loc. cit.*— but is overawed by *Legge* and the commentators. We must bear in mind that *Wang t hung* very frequently puts another construction on the words of the Sage than other commentators. *Analects* XI, 18. Cf. p. 136.

In fact *Confucius* did not acquire wealth and honour. He wandered about, hoping that his services would be required. Having exhausted all his wisdom in remonstrating with the princes and being at his wits' end, he went home, and fixed the text of the *Shiking* and the *Shuking.* His hopes were gone, and expectations he had none. He said that it was all over with him, for he was well aware that his destiny was not to be rich and honoured, and that all his travels could not supply this want. *Confucius* knew that he had not received the destiny of a man who will become exalted, and that searching for honour on his travels, he would never find it. Yet he

maintained that *T'se* was not destined to be rich, but acquired wealth by his astuteness. The words and the actions of *Confucius* disagree, one does not know why.

Some say that he wished to attack the faults of *Tse Kung,* who did not care much for the right doctrine or virtue, but only for the increase of his wealth. *Confucius* therefore reproved his fault, wishing to induce him to comply entirely, and to change his conduct. Combating *Tse Kung's* shortcomings he might say that he did not love the doctrine or virtue, but only his wealth, but why must he assert that he had not received the fate, which is in opposition to his former utterance that wealth and honour depend on Heaven?

When *Yen Yuan* died, the Master said:—"Alas! Heaven is destroying me! Heaven is destroying me!"

This means that, when a man is to rise, Heaven gives him a support, whereas, when his destruction is impending, he deprives him of his assistance. *Confucius* had four friends, by whom he hoped to rise, but *Yen Yuan* died prematurely. Therefore his exclamation:—"Heaven is destroying me!"

One may ask: — Did *Yen Yuan* die, because *Confucius* did not become an emperor, snatched away by Heaven, or did he die an untimely death of himself, his allotted span being so short?—If he died prematurely, because his appointed time was short, he was bound to die, and even if *Confucius* had become an emperor, he would not have remained alive.

Cf. above p. 405. *Analects* XI, 8. These four friends were: *Yen Yuan, Tse Kung, Tse Chang,* and *Tse Lu,* all his disciples. The support of a man is like a stick, on which a sick person is leaning. A sick man requires a stick to walk. Now, let the stick be shortened by cutting off a piece, can we say then that Heaven compelled the sick man not to walk any more'.' If he could rise still, could the short stick be lengthened again? *Yen Yuan s* short life is like the shortness of the stick.

Confucius said that Heaven was destroying him, because *Yen Yuan* was a

worthy. But worthies in life must not necessarily act as supporters of somebody, just as sages do not always receive Heaven's special appointment. Among the emperors there are many who are not sages, and their ministers are very often not worthies. Why? Because fate and externals are different from man's talents. On this principle it was by no means certain that *Yen Yuan,* had he been alive, would have become the supporter of *Confucius,* or that by his death he ruined *Confucius.* What proof had the latter then for his assertion that Heaven was destroying him?

What was Heaven's idea after all that it did not make *Confucius* emperor? Did it not appoint him, when he received his life and his fate, or was it going to appoint him, but repented afterwards? If originally he was not appointed, what harm could be done by *Yen Yuan's* death? If he was first chosen for the imperial dignity, and this scheme was abandoned later on, no externals came into question, and the decision rested solely with Heaven. And then which good acts of *Confucius* did Heaven see to make him emperor, and which bad ones did it hear subsequently, that it changed its mind, and did not invest him? The Spirit of Heaven must have erred in his deliberations and not have made the necessary investigations.

When *Confucius* went to *Wei,* the funeral rites of a former land-lord of his wen; just going on there. He stepped into the house and wept, and, when he came out, he ordered *Tse Kung* to unharnass one outside horse, and give it as a present. *Tse Kung* remarked:—"At the death of your disciple, you did not unharnass a horse, but do it now for an old land-lord. Is that not too much?" As a worthy, a degree of excellence next to sagehood, he would have assisted *Cvnfocius* in his brilliant career.

In externals *viz.* the osseous structure and the physignomy of an individual his fate becomes manifest. Cf. Chap. XXIV. But fate by no means corresponds to talents and virtue. *Confucius* replied, "When I just now went in, I wept, and overwhelmed with grief, went out, and cried. I cannot bear the idea that my tears should not be accompanied by something. Therefore, my son, do as I told you." *Confucius* unharnassed his horse, and gave it away for the old lodging-house keeper, because he could not bear the thought that his feelings should not be accompanied by some act of courtesy. Along with such feelings politeness must he shown. When his feelings are touched, a man is moved to kindness. Courtesy and emotion must correspond. A superior man at least will act in that way.

When *Yen Yuan* died, the Master bewailed him, and was deeply moved. His disciples said to him:—"Master, you are deeply moved." He replied:—" If I were not deeply moved at this man's demise, at whose should I be?"

Such deep emotion is the climax of grief. Bewailing *Yen Yuan* his emotion was different from that of all the other pupils. Grief is the greatest sorrow.— When *Yen Yuan* died, his coffin had no outer shell. *Yen Lu* begged the carriage of the Master to sell and get an outer shell for the coffin, but *Confucius* did not give it, because a high officer could not walk afoot. Mourning over the old lodging-house keeper, he unharnassed a horse to give it away as a present, because he did not like that his tears should not be accompanied by some gift. Bewailing *Yen Yuan* he was deeply moved, yet, when asked, he declined to give his carriage away, so that his emotion had no counterpart in his actions. What difference is there between tears and emotion, or between a horse and a carriage? In one case politeness and sentiment were in harmony, in the other kindness and right feeling did not correspond. We do not see clearly what *Confucius* ideas about politeness were.

Confucius said, "There was *Li;* when he died, he had a coffin, but no outer shell. I would not walk on foot to get a shell for him."—The love for *Li* must have been deeper than that for *Yen Yuan.* When *Li* died, he got no shell, because it was not becoming for a high officer to walk on foot. *Li* was the son of *Confucius, Yen Yuan* bore another surname. When the son died, he did not receive that present, how much less had a man

of another name a right to it? Quotation from the *Li-ki, T'an Kung I (Legge's traiwl.* Vol. I, p. 136). *Analects* XI, 9. The father of *Yen Yuan.*
Analectx XI, 7.
Loc. cit.
Then this would be a proof of the real kindness of *Confucius.* If he showed himself affectionate towards his old land-lord, whereas his kindness did not extend to his son, was it perhaps, because previously he was an inferior official, and afterwards a high officer? When he was an inferior official first, as such he could ride in a carriage with two horses, as a high officer he would drive with three. A high officer could not do without his carriage and walk on foot, but why did he not sell two horses to get a shell, and drive with the remaining one'.' When he was an official, he rode in a carriage with two horses, and parted with one for the sake of the old lodging-house keeper. Why did he not part with two now to show his kindness, only keeping one to avoid walking on foot?

Had he not given away one horse as a present for the old lodging-house keeper, he would not have transgressed any statute, but by burying his son with a coffin, but without a shell he committed an offence against propriety, and showed a disregard for custom. *Confucius* attached great importance to the present, which he was kind enough to make to the old man, and treated the funeral ceremonies for his son very lightly. Honour was shown to a stranger, but the rites were neglected in the case of his own son. Since *Confucius* did not sell his carriage to get a shell for *Li,* he cannot clear himself of the reproach of being an office-hunter, who was afraid of being without his carriage. And yet he has maintained himself that a superior man "will even sacrifice his life to preserve his virtue complete." Could it then be so difficult to give up one's dignity in order to preserve propriety?

Tse Kung asked about government. The Master said, "The requisites of government are that there be a sufficiency of food, a sufficiency of military equipment, and the confidence of the people

in their ruler." *Tse Kung* said, "If it cannot be helped, and one of these must be dispensed with, which of the three should be foregone first?" "The military equipment" said the Master. *Tse Kung* again asked, "If it cannot be helped," and one of the remaining two must be dispensed with, which of them should be foregone?" The Master answered: "Part with the food. From of old, death has been the lot of all men; but if the people have no faith in their rulers, there is no standing for the State."— Faith is the most important of all. *Analects* XV, 8. 2 *Analects* XII, 7.
Now, if a State has no food, so that the people must starve, they care no more for propriety and righteousness. Those being neglected, how can confidence still be maintained?

It has been said that, as long as the granaries are full, people observe the rules of propriety, and that, while they have sufficiency of clothing and food, they know what honour and shame is. Charity is the upshot of abundance, and mutual fighting the result of privation. Now, provided that there is nothing to live on, how could faith he preserved'.'

During the *Ch'un-ch'iu* period the contending States were famine-stricken. People changed their sons in order to eat them, and broke their bones for fuel to cook with. Starving and without food, they had no time to trouble about kindness or justice. The love between father and son is based on faith, yet in times of famine faith is thrown away, and the sons are used as food. How could *Confucius* tell *Tse Kung* that food might be foregone, but that faith ought to be preserved? If there is no faith, but food, though unsought, faith will grow, whereas, if there is no food, but faith, it cannot be upheld, though we may strive for it.

When the Master went to *Wei, Jan F«* acted as driver of his carriage. The Master observed, "How numerous are the people!" *Jan Yu* said:—"Since they are so numerous, what more could be done for them?"—" Enrich them," was the reply.—"And when they have been enriched, what more could be done?"— The Master said: "Teach them."—

Speaking with *Jan Yu, Confucius* placed wealth first and instruction after, but he told *Tse Kung* that food might be dispensed with, provided there was faith. What difference is there between food and wealth, faith and instruction? Both scholars received different answers. The object prized most was not the same in both cases. The opinions of *Confucius* about political economy cannot have been very well settled.

Chu Po Yil sent a messenger to *Confucius,* who questioned him what his master was doing. The messenger replied, "My master is anxious to make his faults few, but cannot succeed." Cf. p. 159. A disciple of *Confucius.*

5 *Analects* XIII, 9.

A disciple of *Confucius* in *Wei,* with whom he lodged. After *Confucius'* return to *Lu,* he sent the messenger to make friendly inquiries.

He then went out, and *Confucius* said, "This messenger! This messenger!"

This is a reproach. Those discussing the Analects hold that *Confucius* reproves him for his humility on behalf of another. *Confucius* inquired of the messenger what his master was doing, he asked about his business, not about his conduct. The messenger ought to have replied to this question of *Confucius:*— "My master does such and such a thing," or, "is occupied with such and such a government affair," instead of saying:—"My master is anxious to make his faults few, but cannot succeed. " How do we know but that in his reply he missed the point of the question, and that it was to this that *Confucius* took exception? What did *Confucius* really reproach the messenger for'.' Because he spoke humbly on another's behalf, or because in his reply he missed the point?

The blame referred to something definite, but *Confucius* did not make clear his fault merely saying:—"This messenger! This messenger!" In later ages people began to have their doubts as to wherein the messenger had failed. *Han Fei Tse* says:—"If the style be too terse, it will prove a cause of dispute for the disciples." How concise is *Confucius'* remark:—"This messenger!"

Some say that the idea of the "Spring and Autumn " was to keep a respectful silence on the faults of worthies, that *Chil Po Yii* was such a worthy, and that therefore the same practice was observed with regard to his messenger.

If one wants to know a person one must look at his friends, and to know a prince one must observe his messengers. *Chil Po Yii* was not a worthy, therefore his messenger had his faults. The idea of the "Spring and Autumn" was to cover the faults of worthies, but also to censure smaller misdemeanours. Now, if no reproach was made, but silence kept, where would the censuring of minor offences come in? If *Confucius* was anxious to keep silence on *Chil Po Yii,* he ought to have kept quiet, but since he said with much pathos:—"This messenger! This messenger!", all his contemporaries must have understood the blame. How could such utterances serve the purpose of a respectful silence.

Analects XIV, 26. This may have been the view of the old commentators at *Wang Chung's* time. *Chu //«',* on the contrary, holds that the reply of the messenger was admirable, and that the laconic utterance of *Confucius* contains a praise, not a reproach. See p. 400 Note 1.

Of. above p. 400.

Pi Hsi inviting him to visit him, the Master was inclined to go, *Tse Lu* was displeased, and said:—" Master, formerly I have heard you say, 'When a man in his own person is guilty of doing evil, a superior man will not associate with him.' Pi Hsi* is in rebellion, holding possession of *Chung-mao;* if you go to him, what shall be said?"—The Master said, "So it is. But is it not said that, if a thing be really hard, it may be ground without being made thin? Is it not said that, if a thing be really white, it may be steeped in a dark fluid without being made black?—Am I a bitter gourd? How could I be hung up and not eat?" *Tse Lu* quoted a former remark of *Confucius* to refute him. Formerly *Confucius* had spoken those words with the object of inducing his pupils t6 act accordingly. *Tse Lu* quoted it to censure

Confucius. He was well aware of it, but did not say that his former words were a joke meaning nothing, which could be disregarded. He admitted that he had spoken those words, and that they must be carried out, but "is it not said," he continued "that, if a thing be really hard, it may be ground without being made thin, or if it be white, that it may be steeped in a dark fluid without being made black?" Could he invalidate. *Tse Lu's* objections with these words? "When a man in his own person is guilty of doing evil, a superior man will not associate with him." To invalidate this objection *Pi Hsi* ought not yet to have committed any evil, so that one might still associate with him. However *Confucius* said that what was hard, might be ground without becoming thin, and what was white, might be steeped in a dark fluid without turning black. According to this argument those whose conduct was, so to speak, perfectly hard or perfectly white, might consort with *Pi Hsi,* but why not those superior men, whose ways are soft and easily tainted by wickedness? *Confucius* would not drink the water from the "Robber Spring," and *Tseng Tse* declined to enter into a village called "Mother's Defeat. " They avoided the evil, and kept aloof from pollution, out of respect for the moral laws and out of shame at the disgraceful names. "Robber Spring" and "Mother's Defeat" were nothing but empty names, but nevertheless were shunned by *Confucius* and *Tsing Tse. Pi Hsi* had done some real wrong, yet A high officer in the service of the *Chao* family in the *Chin* State, who took possession of *Chung-mao,* a city in *Honan,* in the *Chang-ie* prefecture, for himself. *Analects* XVII, 7. Cf. *Muai Nan Tie* XVI, 13 who adds that *Mf Ti,* who condemned music, would not enter into a city named "Morning Song." *Confucius* intended visiting him. That he did not like the " Robber Spring" was correct, but that he wished to open up relations with *Pi llst* was wrong.

"Riches and honours acquired by unrighteousness are to me as a floating cloud." If *Confucius,* who said so, had taken the wrong way, and lived on the salary paid him by a rebel, his words about floating clouds would have been futile.

Perhaps he wanted to propagate his doctrine for a time only. If that was his aim, he could meet the objections of *Tse Lu* by speaking of the propagation of his doctrine, but not by speaking of food. There might be allowed some time for the propagation of his doctrine, but there would be none for his outlook for food.

In the words:—"Am I a bitter gourd? How could I be hung up, and not eat" *Confucius* compares himself to a gourd, saying that being in office a man must live on his salary. "I am no gourd that might be hung up, and would require no food." This is a rebuff to *Tse Lu,* but this rejoinder of *Confucius* does not dispose of *Tse Lu's* objection, for in criticising the master *Tse Lu* does not assert that he ought not to take office. But he should choose a proper State to live in. By the above comparison *Confucius* showed that his only wish was to comfortably eat his bread. How undignified is such an utterance! Why must he compare himself with an official who wants to eat? A gentleman must not speak like that.

It would make little difference, whether one speaks of being hung up like a gourd without eating, or of being hung up out of employ. In reply to *Tse Lu* he might have retorted "Am I a gourd to be hung up, and out of employ?" Now speaking of food *Confucius* admits that he sought office not for the sake of his doctrine, but merely to find food. In taking office the motive of men is their thirst for money, but giving it a moral aspect they say that they do it to propagate their principles. Likewise in marrying the motive is lust, but morally speaking it is to serve the parents. If an official bluntly speaks of his food, would a bridegroom also own to his sensuality?

The utterance of *Confucius* explains his feelings. The meaning is unmistakable, and not obscured by a well sounding moral name. It is very common, and unworthy of a superior man. The Literati

'*Analects* VII, 15.

Legge and some commentators take the words jflj in a passive sense "How could I be hung up and not be eaten?" ». e. "not be employed." say that *Confucius* travelled about to find employment, but did not succeed, and regretted that his doctrine did not spread. Methinks they misunderstand *Confucius'* character. *Kung Shan Fu.Tao,* when he was holding ft', and in an attitude of rebellion, invited the Master to visit him, who was rather inclined to go. *Tse Lu* said:—"Indeed you cannot go! Why must you think of going to see *Kung Shanl*" The Master said, "Can it be without some reason that he has invited me? If any one employ me, may 1 not make an eastern *Chou?"3*—Making an eastern *Chou* means that he intended putting forth his doctrine. *Kung Shan Fu Jao* and *Pi Ilst* were both in rebellion. With the former he hoped to introduce his doctrine, whereas from the latter he expected food. So his utterances are wavering, and his actions are consequently inconsistent. Should this perhaps have been the reason of his migrations and his inability to find employment? "*Yang Huo* wanted to see *Confucius,* but he did not see him." He offered him a post, but *Confucius* would not have it. That was disinterested indeed! When *Kung Shan Fu Jao* and *Pi Hst* invited him, he was inclined to go. That was very base! *Kung Shan Fu Jao* and *Yang Huo* both rebelled, and kept *Chi Huan Tse* prisoner. They were equal in their wickedness, and both invited *Confucius* in the same polite way. However *Confucius* responded to *Kung Shan Fu Jao's* call and did not see *Yang Huo.* Was *Kung Shan Fu Jao* still a fit person to associate with, and *Yang Huo* not? *Tse Lu* remonstrated against *Kung Shan Fu Jao's* invitation. *Confucius* ought to have removed this objection by showing that he was as good at least as *Pi Hsi,* and that his character was not so very bad. A city in *Shantung. Kung Shan Fu Jao* and *Yang Huo* combined were holding their liege, Prince *Huan* of *Chi,* imprisoned, and trying to arrogate the supreme power of the State of *Im. Analects* XVII, 5. The eastern *Chou* dy-

nasty 770-255 owes its name to its capital *Lo-yi,* where it had removed from *Ilao-ching* in the West *(Shensi).* The commencement of the Eastern *Chou,* prior to the civil wars, was felicitous. *AnaUcts* XVII, 1. CHAPTER XXXIV. Censures on Mencius *(T'se Ming).* When *Mencius* went to see King *Hui* of *Liang,* the king said, "You have not counted it far to come here, a distance of a thousand Li, Sir. By what could you profit my kingdom? "—*Mencius* replied, "I have nothing but benevolence and justice. Why must Your Majesty speak of profit?"

Now, there are two kinds of profit, the one consisting in wealth, the other in quiet happiness. King *Hui* asked, how he could profit his kingdom. How did *Mencius* know that he did not want the profit of quiet happiness, and straightway take exception to the profit by wealth?

The *Yiking* says, "It will be advantageous to meet with the great man." "It will be advantageous to cross the great stream."—" Chien represents what is great and originating, pene-/l trating, *advantageous,* correct and firm." And the *S/iuking* re- marks that the black-haired people still esteem profit.' They all have the profit of quiet happiness in view. By practising bene— volence and justice, one may obtain this profit.

Mencius did not say that he inquired of King *Hui,* what he meant by profiting his kingdom. Had King *Hui* said:—" The profit of wealth," *Mencius* might have given him the proper answer. But though he did not know the purport of King *Hut's* question, *Mencius* at once replied about *the* profit of wealth. Had King *Hui* really inquired about it, *Mencius* adduced nothing in support of his view. If, on the other hand, he had asked about the profit of quiet happiness, and *Mencius* in his reply had spoken about the *Mencius* I, Pt. I, 1. For the quotations from *Mencius* I adopt *Legge's* renderings, as far as possible. This interview took place in 335 B.c. *Liang* was the capital of the Win State, the modern *K'ai-fing-fu. Yiking* Bk. I, I, 2.

Yiking Bk. I, V, 1.

Yiking Bk. I, I, 1. *Legge's translation*

(Sacred Books of the East Vol. XVI), p. 57 and 67.

« Shaking Pt. V, Bk. XXX, 6.

profit of wealth, he would have failed to give the prince the proper answer, and would not have acted in the proper way.

The king of Chi asked Shi Tse saying, "I wish to give Mencius a house, somewhere in the middle of the kingdom, and to support his disciples with an allowance of 10,000 chung, that all the officers and the people may have such an example to reverence and imitate. Had you not better tell him this for me? "— Shi Tse conveyed this message to Mencius through Ch en Tse. Mencius said, "How should Shi Tse know that this cannot be? Suppose that I wanted to be rich, having formerly declined 100,000 chung, would my now accepting 10,000 be the conduct of one desiring riches?"

In declining 100,000 chung Mencius was wrongly disinterested, for wealth and honour is what man desires. Only he does not stick to them, if he cannot obtain them in the proper way. Therefore in the matter of rank and salary an honest man sometimes declines, and sometimes not, but why should he reject a present, which he ought to have taken, on the plea that he does not covet wealth or honour?

Ch en Chin asked Mencius saying, "When you were in Ch'i, the king sent you a present of 100 yi of the double metal, and you refused to accept it. When you were in Sung, 70 yi were sent to you, which you accepted; and when you were in Hsieh, 50 yi were sent, which you likewise accepted. If your declining to accept the gift in the first case was right, your accepting it in the latter cases was wrong. If your accepting it in the latter cases was right, your declining to do so in the first case was wrong. You must accept, Master, one of these alternatives."—Mencius said, "I did right in all the cases. When I was in Sung, I was about to take a long journey. Travellers must be provided with what is necessary for their expenses. The prince's message was, 'A present to defray travelling expenses.' Why should I have declined the gift? When I was in Hsieh, I was apprehen-

sive of my safety, and taking measures for my protection. The message was 'I have An officer of Ch'i. A chung is an ancient measure. As to its capacity opinions differ. 100 000 chung of rice was the customary allowance of a minister in a feudal State. A disciple of Mencius, his full name being Ch'en Chin. See below. Mencius II, Pt. II, 10. See above p. 395. The same as Ch'en Tse.

'One yi was about 24 taels.

Double silver "worth twice as much as the ordinary" (Legge). A small principality in the south of Shantung. heard that you are taking measures to protect yourself, and send this to help you in procuring arms. Why should I have declined the gift? But when 1 was in Chi, I had no occasion for money. To send a man a gift, when he has no occasion for it, is to bribe him. How is it possible that an honest man should be taken with a bribe?"

Whether money offered as a gift can be accepted or not, always depends on some reason. We are not covetous, if we accept it, nor are we not covetous, if we do not accept it. There are certain rules, why money can be taken, and why not, and there are likewise certain principles on which a house can be accepted or not. Now, Mencius does not say that he does not deserve it, and that it would not be right for him as a non-official to take the house, but he replies that he is not craving for wealth, and adduces the 100,000 cltung which he had declined on a former occasion to draw a conclusion in regard to the subsequent 10,000 chung. Formerly he ought to have accepted the 100,000, how could he decline them?

P'ing King asked Mencius saying, "Is it not an extravagant procedure to go from one prince to another, and live upon them, followed by several tens of carriages, and attended by several hundred men? "—Mencius replied, "If there be not a proper ground for taking it, a single bamboo-cup of rice may not be received from a man. If there be such a proper ground, then Shuns receiving the empire from Yao is not to be considered excessive."

How can the receiving of the empire from Yao be put on a level with the acceptance of 100,000 chung Shun did not decline the empire, because there was a proper ground. Now Mencius does not contend that for receiving 100,000 chung there is no proper cause, but he says that he is not greedy of wealth and honour. That is not the right modesty, and it could not be an example for others.

Shin T ung, on his own impulse, asked Mencius, saying, "May Yen be smitten?" Mencius replied, "It may. Tse K'uei9 had Mencius II, Pt. H, 3. P'eng Keng was a disciple of Mencius. Mencius III, Pt. II, 4.

Mencius II, Pt. II, 8.

A high officer of Ch'i. Tse ICuei, King of Yen, a silly man, had ceded his throne to his minister Tse Chih, hoping that the latter would decline the offer, but he unexpectedly accepted, and Tse K'uei lost his throne. During the troubles caused in Yen by Tse ICueis son seeking to recover the kingdom, the Ch'i State made an unsuccessful attempt to conquer Yen. Shcn T'ung had asked Mencius' advice about an invasion of Yen. no right to give Yen to another man, and Tse Chih had no right to receive Yen from Tse K'uei. Suppose there were an officer here, with whom you, Sir, were pleased, and that, without informing the king, you were privately to give to him your salary and rank; and suppose that this officer, also without the king's orders, were privately to receive them from you:—would such a transaction he allowable'.' And where is the difference between the case of Yen and this?"

The people of Ch'i smote Yen. Some one asked of Mencius, "Is it really the case that you advised Ch'i to smite Yen? "—He replied, "No. Shin T'ung asked me, whether Yen might be smitten, and I answered him, 'It may.' They accordingly went and smote it. If he had asked me, 'Who may smite it? ', I would have answered him, 'He who is the minister of Heaven may smite it.' Suppose the case of a murderer, and that one asks me, 'May this man be put to death?' I will answer him, He may.' If he ask me, 'Who may put him to death?' I will answer him, 'The chief criminal judge may put him to death.' But now with one *Yen* to smite another *Yen*—how should I have advised this? "

One might ask whether *Mencius* did not really advise the king to smite *Yen*. When *Shen T ung* inquired, whether *Yen* could be siriitten, he had his own designs, and wished to smite it himself. Knowing that he would be very pleased with the reply, *Mencius* ought to have answered that, although *Yen* could be smitten, it could not be done but by the minister of Heaven. Then *Shin T ung's* plans would have collapsed, and his intention of smiting *Yen* been given up. If *Mencius* was not aware of these designs, and straightway made a reply, he did not pay attention to what he said, and did not understand words.

Kung Sun Chou inquired of *Mencius*, "I venture to ask wherein you, Master, excel?" *Mencius* replied, "I understand words."—The other pursued, "And what do you mean by saying that you understand words?" *Mencius* said, "When words are one-sided, I know how the mind of the speaker is clouded over; when they arc extravagant, I know how the" mind is fallen and sunk; when they are depraved, I know how the mind has departed from principle, and when they are evasive, I know how the mind A man entrusted by Heaven with the execution of its designs. The one *Yen* is *Ch'i*, which was not better than *Yen,* and therefore not fit to punish *Yen* as Heaven's delegate. *Mencius* H, Pt. I, 2.

A disciple of *Mencius*.

is at its wits' end. These evils growing in the mind, do injury to government, and, displayed in the government, are hurtful to the conduct of affairs. Should a Sage again arise, he would undoubtedly follow my words." *Menchis* understood words and also knew, how a warning as to the catastrophe which *Shen T'ung* was bringing about, would after all have been to his benefit. From the nature of the question he must have known the desire implied in the words of *Hhin T ung*. Knowing his aims, he must have had an idea of the disaster, in which the thing was doomed to end. *Mencius* said, "It would be for the hap-

piness of the people of the whole empire. 1 hope that the king will change. I am daily hoping for this."

Was the king whom *Mencius* left, the same on whom he did not wait at court formerly? Why did he think so little of him first, and make so much of him afterwards? Had it not been the former king, he would not have abandoned him. If he quitted him later on, the second king must have been worse than the first. When he left the king, and stopped three days in *Chau,* it was a less drastic measure than his not going to court, and staying with *Ching Ch'ou* Why was his behaviour not identical in the two instances? Why did he not treat the king in the same manner in both cases?

When *Mencius* was in *Lm,* Duke *P ing* of *Lu* was about to pay him a call, but his favourite *Tsang Tsang* slandered *Mencius,* and stopped him. *Yo Cheng Te* told *Menchis* about it, who said,' "A man's advancement is effected, it may be, by others, and the stopping him, may be, from the efforts of others. But to advance a man or to stop his advance is really beyond the power of men. My not meeting with the prince of *Lu* is from Heaven." i *Mencius* II, Pt. II, 12.

The King of *Ch'i* wished *Mencius* to call on him at court, informing him, that he intended waiting upon *Mencius* himself, but had got a cold, and could not go out. *Mencius* knew this to be a pretence, and therefore declined to go to court on the pretence that he was unwell likewise. Cf. *Mencius* II, Pt. II, 2. The king and the philosopher were both too jealous of their dignity to get along well. A small place in *Ch'i,* where *Mencius* halted, expecting to be called back. An officer of *Ch'i,* with whom *Mencius* stayed, while the king was waiting for him, at the former occasion. A disciple of *Mencius. Mencius* I, Pt. II, 16.

First he did not find favour with the prince of *Lu* and afterwards with that of *Ch i.* There was no difference. But in the first instance he held Heaven alone accountable, in the second, the king. There is no stability in his reasoning. When the king of *Ch'i* disdained his services, and he did not advance, some fellow like *Tsang Tsang* must have slan-

dered him. That was likewise stopping or keeping back, but in both cases it was Heaven's decree that he should not find employment, and beyond the power of men. Why then did he still linger three days, when he left, and not go straight on? Provided it was the fate of Heaven that he should not meet with the king of *Ch'i,* who would not listen to his words, could Heaven have changed this fate within the space of three days, and bring about the interview'.' In *Lu* he gave all the credit to Heaven, abandoned his schemes, and lost all hope. In *Ch'i* he counted solely on the king, and was full of hopes. Thus the missing of one interview would have been merely the result of insinuations of men.

Some one may hold that Heaven's fate could not yet be settled first, and that for this reason *Mencius* hoped that within three days.the king would call him back. This may be so, supposing that fate requires three days. But would, upon such a supposition, the fact that the king of *Ch'i* first allowed him to leave not be due to fate'. If it was fate, and the limit three days, then Uuke *Ping* of *Lu* might as well after three days time have rejected *Tsang Tsang's* proposal, and followed the advice of *Yo Ching Tse,* and have called on *Mencius.* Wherefore was *Mencius* so hasty in attributing every thing to Heaven'.' Had the duke paid *Mencius* a visit within three days, how would the latter have justified his former utterance'.'

'When *Mencius* left *Ch'i,* Chung Yilquestioned him on the way, saying, "Master, you look like one who carries an air of dissatisfaction in your countenance. But formerly I heard you say, 'The superior man does not murmur against Heaven, nor bear a grudge against men.'" *Mencius* said, "That was one time, and this is another. It is a rule that a true Imperial sovereign should arise in the course of five hundred years, and that during that time there should be some one illustrious in his generation. From the commencement of the *Chou* dynasty till now, more than 700 years have elapsed. Judging numerically, the date is passed. Examining the time, we might i *Mencius* H, Pt. II, 13.

A follower of *Mencius*.

expect the rise of such individuals in it. But Heaven does not yet wish that the empire should enjoy tranquillity and good order. If it wished this, who is there besides me to bring it about? How should I be otherwise than dissatisfied?"—

What proof is there for the assertion of *Mencius* that in the course of five hundred years a true emperor should arise':' *Ti K'u* was such a sovereign, and *Yao* also ruled over the empire as a true sovereign. *Yao* transmitted the empire to *Shun,* who was likewise a true emperor. He transmitted the empire to *Yil,* who reigned in the same style. These four Sages were true Imperial sovereigns, but they followed one another quite closely. From *Yil* to *T'ang* there is an interval of a thousand years and from *T'ang* to *Chou* also. *Win Wang* commenced the reign, and at his death handed it over to *Wu Wang.* When *Wu Wang* expired, *Ch'eng Wang* and *Chou Kung* together ruled over the empire. From the beginning of the *Chou* dynasty to the time of *Mencius* 700 years again had elapsed, but no true emperor had arisen. In which period do we find then that in the course of five hundred years a true sovereign arises';' Who has made this statement that there will be a true emperor every five hundred years':1 *Mencius* says something which has no foundation and no proof, and is based on some wild hypothesis. Not having found favour with the king, he left *Ch i,* aud wore a dissatisfied look. That does not show his wisdom, and places him on a level with ordinary scholars.

Five hundred years is considered the period in which Heaven produces a Sage. Moreover, *Mencius* says that Heaveu did not yet wish that the empire should enjoy tranquillity and good order. Ilis idea is that, when Heaven is willing to bless the empire with tranquillity and good order, it must produce a wise emperor in the course of five hundred years. According to what *Mencius* says, Heaven produces a Sage on purpose. But are five hundred years *Wang Chung* omits *Ti Chih,* who followed his father *Ti K'u.* Owing to his

dissolute life, he was dethroned, and his brother *Yao* was elected in his place.

Those are rather round numbers. According to the common chronology *Yii* reigned from 2205-2197, *T'ang,* the founder of *theShang* dynasty from 1766-1753, and the *Chou* dynasty commenced in 1122. Wo *Wang's* reign lasted from 1122-1115, *Ch'eng Wang's* from 1115-1078. All these rulers are regarded by the Chinese as true emperors. The interval between 1 u und *T'ang* is about 400 years, that between *T'ang* and *Wen Wang* about 600 years. It is difficult to understand why *Wang Ch'ung* in both cases speaks of a thousand years. The remark of *Mencius* that every five hundred years a true sovereign arises, comes much nearer the truth. About SU0 years in fact after the usual chronology. The Bamboo Annals reduce this space to about 700 years. really the period within which it produces a Sage? If so, why did Heaven not send the Sage forth':'—Because it was not the time for a wise emperor to arise, therefore Heaven did not produce him. Since *Mencius* believes in it nevertheless, he does not know Heaven.

From the commencement of the *Chou* dynasty upwards of seven hundred years had elapsed. "Judging numerically, the date, therefore, was passed, but examining the time, it might be possible." What signifies that the date is passed, and what, that it is possible? Date is equivalent to time, and time to date. The date being passed, five hundred years are passed. From the beginning of the *Chou* epoch up to that time upwards of seven hundred years had elapsed t. e. two hundred years in excess. Should an emperor arise then, he would already have missed the proper time. Yet *Mencius* avers that considering the time, it might be possible. What does that mean '.'

He says that in the course of five hundred years a true Imperial sovereign should arise, and further that during that time there should be some one illustrious in his generation. Is this somebody the same as the emperor or some one else':' If he is, why mention him a second time, if not, what sort of man is

it who is illustrious in his generation? Suppose the answer be:—"men like *Confucius* and scholars like *Mencius,* who will instruct the youth, and awaken the dullards and imbeciles," then *Confucius* has already lived, and *Mencius* himself also has been born. Should we say:— "wise ministers," they must live contemporaneously with a wise ruler, and a wise minister appear, when a wise emperor arrises.

Mencius speaks of five hundred years, but why does he say "during that time?" If he does not mean the space of five hundred years, but the time between, he must think of two or three hundred years. Then a Sage could not work together with a wise emperor arrising after five hundred years, whom then has *Mencius* in view, saying that during that time there should be some one illustrious in his generation? "Heaven," says he, "does not yet wish that the empire should enjoy tranquillity and good order. If it wished this, who is there besides me to bring it about?" By these words *Mencius* does not intend saying that he himself ought to be emperor, but that, if there were an emperor, he would act as his minister. Whether there be an emperor and a minister, depends on Heaven. When fate did not allow the empire to enjoy tranquillity and good order, *Mencius* did not acquiesce with a good grace in *Ch i,* but resented it, and wore a dissatisfied look. That was very wrong of him. *P'eng King* asked *Mencius* saying, "Is it proper that a scholar doing no service should receive support'."'—*Mencius* answered, "If you do not have an intercommunication of the productions of lahour, and an interchange of men's services, so that one from his overplus may supply the deficiency of another, then husbandmen will have a superfluity of grain, and women will have a superfluity of cloth. If you have such an interchange, carpenters and carriage-wrights may all get their food from you. Here now is a man, who, at home, is-filial, and abroad, respectful to his elders; who watches over the principles of the ancient kings, awaiting the rise of future learners— and yet you will refuse to support him.

How is it that you give honour to the carpenter and carriage-wright, and slight him who practises benevolence and righteousness'.'" *P ing King* said, "The aim of the carpenter and carriage-wright is to seek for a living. Is it also the aim of the superior man in his practice of principles thereby to seek for a living'.' "—" What have you to do," returned *Mencius,* "with his purpose? He is of service to you. He deserves to be supported, and should be supported. And let me ask, 'Do you remunerate a man's intention, or do you remunerate his service?'" To this *Ping King* replied, "I remunerate his intention." *Mencius* said, "There is a man here, who breaks your tiles, and draws unsightly figures on your walls;—his purpose may be thereby to seek for his living, but will you indeed remunerate him?"—"No," said *Ping King;* and *Mencius* then concluded, "That being the case, it is not the purpose which you remunerate, but the work done."— *Mencius* referred to the breaking of tiles and disfiguring of walls with the object of impugning the remarks of *P ing King,* knowing very well that he who breaks tiles or disfigures walls does no services, but has a purpose, and that *P eng King* under no eirumstane.es would support him. However, with this reference to the breaking of tiles and disfiguring of walls *Mencius* cannot refute *P ing King,* because people acting in this way do not belong to those who are seeking a living. Such being the case, this argument cannot be put forward against *P eng King.* People who, without a reason, are breaking tiles and disfiguring walls, are either mad, or merely playing. The purpose of madmen is not to seek a living, and those who are disporting themselves, have not this intention either. *Mencius* III, Pt. II, 4.

From those who seek a living a great many persons have no advantage whatever. Therefore those wishing to support themselves sell things in the market as merchants, and live on the price which they receive in exchange for their wares. Now, the breakers of tiles and scribblers profit nobody, and cannot have this intention. Reasonable persons

know that such acts would profit nobody, and consequently desist therefrom. The unreasonable are akin to madmen, and certainly would not have that purpose.

Those who break tiles and disfigure walls, are like boys throwing mud on the road, or is there any difference? When they are dumping mud on the road, have they the intention of seeking a living thereby?—They are still children, and have no purpose.

When old folks are playing, they behave like those who are disfiguring walls. Have players the intention to seek a living? Players rob each-other of their money. When the sums won are very high, they may be used as a livelihood, and eventually there may be this intention.

People who throw stones and leap over them, are also very much alike to those scribblers. Is the intention of those stonethrowers and jumpers directed to their living'.' In short, the criticisms brought forward by *Mencius* against *Ping King* are not very thorough. If *P'ing Keng* trusted in Mencius' words, we may say that the latter "put him off with great smartness of speech." *2K uang Chang Tse* said, "Is not *Chen Chung 1se* a man of true self-denying purity? He was living in *Wu-ling,* and for three days was without food, till he could neither hear nor see. Over a well grew a plum tree, the fruit of which had been more than half-eaten by worms. He erawled to it, and tried to eat some of the fruit, when, after swallowing three mouthfuls, he recovered his sight and hearing." *Mencius* replied, "Among the scholars of *Ch'i,* I must regard *Ch en Chung Tse* as the thumb among the fingers. But still, where A quotation from *Anakct* V, 4, where *Confuting* condemns such smartness of speech. — *Wang Chung* is much smarter here than *Mencius.* The arguments of *Menrius* are quite right, and *Wang Chung* only takes exception at the example adduced by him, which indeed is not very lucky. *Mencius* III, Pt. II, 10. A grandee of the State of *Ch'i.* 4 A recluse. A poor place in modern *Chi-nan-fu (Shantung).* is the self-denying purity he pretends to? To

carry out the principles which he holds, one must become an earth-worm, for so only can it be done."

"Now, an earthworm eats the dry mould above, and drinks from the yellow spring-water below. Was the house in which *Chen Chung Tse* dwelt built by a *Po Yi,* or was it built by a robber like *Che?* Was the millet which he ate planted by a *Po Yi,* or was it planted by a robber like *Chi?* These are things which cannot be known."

"But," said *K'uang Cluing Tse,* "what does that matter'.' He himself weaves sandals of hemp, and his wife twists hempen thread, to barter them." *Mencius* rejoined, "*Cit in Chung Tse* belongs to an ancient and noble family of *Ch'i.* His elder brother *Tea* received from *Ko* a revenue of 10,000 *chung,* but he considered his brother's emolument to be unrighteous, and would not live on it, and in the same way he considered his brother's house to be unrighteous, and would not dwell in it. Avoiding his brother and leaving his mother, he went and dwelt in *Wu-iing.* One day afterwards, he returned to their house, when it happened that some one sent his brother a present of a live goose. He, knitting his brows, said, 'What are you going to use that cackling thing for'.'"—By-and-hy his mother killed the goose, and gave him some of it to eat. Just then his brother came into the house, and said, 'It's the flesh of that cackling thing,' upon which he went out and vomited it.—Thus, what his mother gave him he would not eat, but what his wife gives him he eats. He will not dwell in his brother's house, but he dwells in *Wu-ling.* How can he in such circumstances complete the style of life which he professes'.' With such principles as *Chen Chung Tse* holds, a man must be an earth-worm, and then he can carry them out." *Mencius* in reprehending *Ch'in Chung Tse* does not hit his weak point. When *Ch'in Chung Tse* showed such a disgust for the goose, that he felt like vomiting, was it, because he would eat nothing that came from his mother'.' Previously already he had expressed bis displeasure at the goose saying, "What are you going to use that cackling thing for':'" When, later on, his mother had killed it, and gave him some to eat, and his brother remarked, "It's the flesh of that cackling thing," he felt ashamed that he was acting The exemplar of purity cf. p. 108 Note 2 and below p. 435.

Cf. p. 139. See above p. 419 Note 2. contrary to what he had said before, and vomited it. Had his brother not reminded him, he would not have vomited, and he would then have eaten what his mother offered him. Therefore to say that he would not eat anything coming from his mother conveys a wrong idea. Suppose that Ch'e n Chung Tse was determined not to eat anything from his mother, he ought not to bave eaten of the dish of the goose, when it was brought. Now, after he had eaten it, and learned that it was the goose, he felt so disgusted, that he vomited it. Thus the vomiting was the effect of his being ashamed that he had eaten something in opposition to his determination, it was no want of affection between mother and son, nor a desire to eat nothing that came from his mother.

"But still where is the self-denying purity Ch'hi Chung Tse pretends to? To carry out his nature, one must become an earthworm, for so only can it be done. An earth-worm eats the dry mould above, and drinks from the yellow spring-water below." That would mean that an earth-worm is a paragon of purity, and that, unless he was like an earth-worm, he could not be pure and undefiled. Now, provided the house he was dwelling in was built by Po Yi, and the millet he ate planted by Po Yi, his dwelling and eating would be unstained purity. But perhaps he ate millet sown by robber Chi, or lived in a cottage constructed by robber Che, then this circumstance would contaminate his purity. These strictures on Ch'en Chung Tse are not to the point either.

A house is built for man's sake to be lived in, and sandals and thread are bartered against millet. If it really was planted by a robber, or the house his building, at all events Ch en Chung Tse had no cognisance of it. His brother's unrighteousness, however, was appar-

ent from his conduct. All saw his actions; they were quite notorious and commented upon. Hence Ch'en Chung Tse retired to Wu-ling. He did not stop in his brother's house, and by the weaving of sandals and twisting of thread obviated the necessity of living on his salary. If Ch'en Chung Tse stayed in Wu-ling, he shunned the house of that brother, and vomited his food. Because This seems not to have been the idea of Mencius. The tertium comparationis is not the purity of the earth-worm, but its independence and self-sufficiency. Having its earth to eat and some muddy water to drink, it has no further needs, as man has, who is never quite independent of others. Unless he break off all intercourse with his fellow-creatures, he cannot avoid all pollution. Thus the commentators and Legge understand the passage. Wang Ch'ung's interpretation is forced.

these things could be heard with the ear and seen with the eye, and were so public, that there could be no doubt, it is evident that as a fact Ch'en Chung Tse neither stayed with his brother nor partook of his meals.

Now he had not seen who was the builder of his own house in Wu-ling, nor did he know who planted the millet. But how could he take the house, when it was just completed, or eat the millet, when it was just reaped'.' These criticisms of Mencius go too far.

The house where Ch'in Chung Tse was living, may perhaps have been built by the robber, so that Ch'in Chung Tse would have dwelt there without knowing it. Now Mencius contends that "to carry out the principles which he holds, one must become an earthworm, for so only can it be done." But in the earth underneath the house of the robber there are also earth-worms. They eat the dry mould in the robber's house and drink from the yellow springwater there. How then would an earth-worm meet the requirements? To carry out the principles of Ch'en Chung Tse to the satisfaction of Mencius one ought to be like a fish. A fish swims in the river or the sea, and feeds upon their earth. No robber can dig through the sea, or heap up its earth.

Chin Chung Tse has done a great wrong, but the adverse comments of Mencius do not hit it. Ch en Chung Tse left his mother, and avoided his elder brother, to take up his solitary abode in Wu-ling together with his wife. Because the house of his brother was an unrighteous house, and his income an unrighteous income, he did not care to stay and live with him, which was the height of self-denying purity. However, when after bis emigration to Wu-ling he returned to wait upon his mother, it was his duty to abstain from eating anything and leave again. When the goose was brought in, there must have been other food besides, all prepared by his mother. This food was bought with his brother's money, for it was evident that his mother had not her own private millet which she could have offered him. Then Ch'in Chung Tse partook of his brother's salary. Po Yi rather than eat the millet of Chou died of starvation below Shou-yang. Would a meal of the millet of Chou have defiled his purity? Ch en Chung Tse was not like Po Yi, but he came very The Chou dynasty which Po Fi regarded as usurpers of the throne of the legitimate emperors of the house of Shang. A mountain in Shensi. near him. Saying that one must become an earth-worm to carry out those principles, Mencius uses a comparison which does not justice to Chen Chung Tse at all. Mencius said, "There is a destiny for every thing. Those who act as they ought, receive the natural destiny. Therefore, he who has the true idea of destiny, will not stand beneath a precipitous wall. Death sustained in the discharge of one's duties, is the natural destiny. Death under handcuffs and fetters is not the natural destiny."

The meaning of these words of Mencius is that a man should not run counter to his allotted fate. Through fair conduct he obtains the natural destiny, whereas with recklessness and perversity he does not receive the natural one. Accordingly Heaven's decree would depend on human actions. Confucius did not become an emperor, Yen Yuan died prematurely, Tse Hia lost his eye-sight, Po Niu got leprosy. Was the conduct of these four men not fair? Why did they not receive the right destiny? *Pi Kan1* was disemboweled, *Tse Hsil* was cooked, *Tse Lu* pickled. These were the most cruel modes of death on earth, otherwise painful than handcuffs and fetters. If handcuffs and fetters are really proving that the destiny of the person in question is not the right one, then the conduct of *Pi Kan* and *Tse Hsil* was not fair.

Man receives his destiny, and may be doomed to be crushed to death, or to be drowned, or to be killed in battle, or to be burned. He may be ever so conscientious in his dealings and careful in his doings, it is of no avail. *Ton Kuang Kuo* was sleeping with a hundred persons below a mound of charcoal. The charcoal collapsed, and all the hundred *Mencius* VII, Pt. I, 2. *Legge* understands this passage differently. *Wang Chung* denotes by *natural* destiny something different from what *Mencius* expresses by it, which explains his polemic. *Wang Ch'ung's* natural destiny is not influenced by human actions, whereas the natural, right, or correct destiny of *Mencius* is the upshot of proper conduct. Cf. p. 138. *Vid.* p. 169. Cf. p. 164. On *Yen Yuan* and *Po Kiu* see p. 165.
'Cf. p. 485 Note 6.
Tse Hsu or *Wu Tse Hsu,* the same as *Wu Yuan* p. 140.
» Cf. p. 165.
Vid. p. 179.
people were killed, only *Ton Kuang Kuo* was saved, because it was his destiny to be made a marquis. What difference is there between the heaped up charcoal and the precipitous wall? Provided that one is not doomed to be crushed, there may be a collapse, those who have the fate of *Tou Kuang Kuo* will escape withal. "A man's advancement may be effected by others, and the stopping him may be from the efforts of others." He who is to be crushed, may perhaps be induced to stand below a wall.
The son of the landlord into whose cottage *K'ung Chia2* entered, was predestinated to a premature death and meanness. Though he was introduced into the palace, he still became a doorkeeper.

The not standing below a precipitous wall has the same result as *K'ung Chia's* carrying the child into the palace.
Mencius I, Pt. II, 1G. During a tempest the *H.tia* emperor *K img Chia,* 1879-1848 B.C., sought shelter in a cottage. The landlord imagined that the visit of the son of heaven was a lucky augury for his son, and that no misfortune would befall him in future. Yet this son, later on, doing carpenter's work, accidentally broke his axe, and cut off his two legs. He then became a doorkeeper, the only office for which he was still fit *(Lii Shi ch'w-ch'iu).* CHAPTER XXXV. Strictures on Han Fei Tse *(Fei Han).*
Ran Fei Tse's system consists in propounding the law and making much of success. Worthies who do not benefit the State, he will not reward, and bad characters who do not interfere with the administration, he does not punish. He grants rewards as an incentive to extraordinary actions, and he relies so much on criminal law, that he makes use of capital punishment. When speaking of the Literati, he says that they eat, but do not sow, and likens them to voracious grubs. Discussing the question of usefulness, he compares them with a deer and a horse. A horse resembling a deer fetches a thousand *chin.* There are horses on earth worth so much, but no deer costing a thousand *chin.* Deer are useless, horses are useful. The Literati are like the deer, the active officials like the horse. *ilan Fei Tse* knows very well how to make use of the parable of the deer and the horse, but not that of the cap and the shoe. Provided that *Hon Fei Tse* presented himself at court only in his shoes and without a cap, I would listen to his words. But he will appear at court with his cap on his head. lie uses a useless article of dress, and thereby increases the number of the useless scholars. His words do not agree with his dress, and there is a want of harmony between his theory and his practice. Therefore I condemn his words, and reject his method. There is nothing more trying to the body of an individual and less profitable to it than kneeling and prostrating one's self. If *Han Fei Tse,* when meeting any one, does not make obeisance, and in

the presence of his sovereign or his father does not show his respect, he does not do any harm to his body, but these ceremonies must be gone through out of respect for one's parents.
On the Taoist philosopher *Han Fei Tse* see p. 170. In Chapt. 19, No. 49, p. 1 of *Han Fei Tse's* work. The chapter is entitled the: "Five kinds of voracious grubs. " An ancient coin or a monetary unit whose value is doubtful.
Cf. *Han Fei Tse* XIII, 5v.
Lun-Heng. 28
These rules of propriety are very important and cannot be neglected. While they are being observed by any one, his body does not become fat thereby, and when he disregards them, his body does not become weak nor decay.
If he speaks of utility, then propriety and righteousness are not like eating and drinking. Would *Han Fei Tse,* in case he was granted the previlege of eating in the presence of his sovereign or his father, dare to do so without first bowing'.' Such a homage shown to a superior would be a manifestation of propriety and righteousness, but no benefit to the body. Yet after all *Han Fei Tse* would not do away with it, nor would he reject propriety and righteousness in view of a temporary profit. The Literati are propriety and righteousness, the agriculturists and warriors are eating and drinking. He who exalts agriculture and war, and despises the men of letters, would reject propriety and righteousness, and seek eating and drinking.
When propriety and righteousness are neglected, the moral laws lose their force, there is confusion in the higher and the lower spheres, and the *Yin* and the *Yang* principles become disorganised. The dry and the wet seasons do not come in proper time then, the grain does not grow, and the people die of starvation. The agriculturists have nothing to till, and the soldiers can do no fighting. *Tse Kung* desired to abolish the sacrificial sheep announcing the new moon. *Confucius* said, "*T se,* you care for the sheep, 1 care for propriety." *Tse Kung* disliked to immolate the sheep, whereas *Confucius* apprehended a disregard of propriety.

If old dykes are removed as useless, an inundation will be the necessary consequence, and if the old ceremonies are abolished as good for nothing, one may be sure of a revolution. The Literati ia this world are the old dykes of propriety and righteousness. When they are there, they are of no direct use, but their absence is fatal.

From olden times schools have been erected, where the foundation is laid for power and honour. Officials have been appointed, and officers nominated. The officials cannot be suppressed, and the true doctrine cannot be rejected. The Literati are the officers in charge of the true principles. If they are considered to be useless and therefore suppressed, the true principles are lost simultaneously. These principles bring about no direct results, but man requires them for his achievements.

Analects III, 17.

When the foot walks on a path, this trodden path must not walk itself. The body has hands and feet; to move they require what remains unmoved. Thus things are perhaps useless, but the useful ones require them, they themselves have no direct effect, yet to those which have they are indispensable. Peasants and soldiers stand in need of the Literati, how could they be rejected and not be retained? *Han Fei Tse* denounces the scholars, saying that they are no use, and only do harm. He has in view the vulgar scholars, who do not exert themselves, nor in their dealings take account of propriety. They are scholars by name oulv, but by practice vulgar persons. They profess true science, but what they say is wrong, and they are hunting after official honours and titles. Consequently they cannot be held in esteem. Those who have a pure heart and whose conduct does not shun the light, do not strive for rank and emoluments. They would repudiate the position of a minister or a secretary of State, as if they were throwing away an old boot. Although they have not the same success as those who hold office and fill a post, their domain is propriety and righteousness. That which preserves a State, is propriety and righteousness. If the people do not practice these two virtues, they will overthrow the State and ruin their prince.

Now, the scholars do pay regard to propriety, and love justice. In so far as they become the leaders of those fellows who are devoid of propriety, and incite those lacking justice, people do good, and learn to love their sovereign. That is also an advantage.

Upon hearing of the fame of *l'o Yi* the greedy became disinterested, and the weak, resolute, and hearing of the renown of *Liu Hsia Hui* the narrow-minded became generous, and the mean, liberal. The conversion was more extraordinary than had ever been witnessed by man before. *Tuan Kan Mu* closed his door and did not go out. Prince *Win* of *Wei* used to bow, when passing his house, to show his respect. When the army of *Ch i n* heard of it, they suddenly did not invest *Wei*. Had *Wei* not had *Tuan Kan Mu*, the soldiers of *Ch'in* would have invaded its territory and made a waste of it, for *Ch in* was a powerful country, whose soldiers were ever victorious. Had they been let loose upon *Wei*, Cf. p. 168 Note 2.

The posthumous designation of *Chan Huo*, 6th and 7th cent. B.c., who was magistrate of the *Lw-hsia* district in *Im* and famous for his virtue. *Chin* desisted from its invasion of *Wei* in 399 B.C., hecause the *Wei* State was so flourishing under the Marquis *Wen*, who honoured the worthies and literati. *Vid. Shi-chi* chap. 44, p. 3v. the kingdom of *Wei* would have gone to pieces. Its three armies would have been defeated, and the blood would have run over a thousand Li. Now a scholar closeted in his house and honoured by *Win* of *Wei*, averted the troops of powerful *Ch in* and saved the land of the *Wei* kingdom. His deserts in succouring the three armies could not have been greater, and nobody was worthier of a reward.

In *Ch i* there were living two scholars of the highest standard, called *K'uang Chi-ieh* and *Hua Shiit*, two brothers. In their stern justice they did not bend their will, and refused to serve him whom they did not regard as their master. When *T ai Kung* was invested with *Ch'i*, he had the two men executed at the same time for inveigling the masses in *Ch'i*, setting them the example of not taking service with their ruler. *Han Fei Tse* approves of this on the ground that the two scholars were of no use and doing mischief. However, *K'uang Chiieh* and *Hua Shih* were of the same type as *Tuan Kan Mu*. When *T'ai Kung* put them to death, no disaster had yet happened which they might have averted. The marquis *Win* of *Wei* honoured *Tuan Kan Mu*, and subsequently he warded off powerful *Ch'in* and rescued *Wei*, a deed unparalleled forsooth. If *Han Fei Tse* acknowledges the high standard of *Tuan Kan Mu*, who shut himself up, and also admits that *Win* of *Wei* was justified in honouring him, he is all right. But the conduct of *K'uang Chiieh* and *Hua Shih* was as virtuous as that of *Tuan Kan Mu*. Therefore it is wrong to approve of the penalty inflicted by *T ai Kung* Now, if *Han Fei Tse* disapproves of the conduct of *Tuan Kan Mu*, and objects to the marquis of *Wei* honouring him, it must be born in mind that *Tuan Kan Mu* by his conduct was very useful, and that the marquis of *Wei* honoured him on account of his merit. Thus *Han Fei Tse* would not reward merit, nor give credit to the useful.

Some one might urge that the respect shown by the marquis to the dwelling place of *Tuan Kan Mu* and the subsequent nonarrival of the troops of *Ch'in* is not the result of administration, but of a single act, which cannot be always repeated and which, though instrumental in saving the State, does not deserve so much praise. But what is to be understood by administration? The maintenance of troops, the promulgation of the edicts concerning rewards and punishments, a stern criminal law, a strict discipline, and measures to increase the national wealth and the military strength, all that is administration. Would *Cli'in* with her strength mind it? The Six States were all wiped out hy the troops of *Ch'm*. The soldiers of the Six States were courageous enough, and the onslaught of their armies not without vigour, yet not only did they not vanquish, but were utterly defeated at last, because they were not of equal force and inferior in numbers. Their administration might have been ever so evident, it was of no avail.

If boys annoyed *Ming Pen* and. when he was roused to anger, would fight with him, sword in hand, they would certainly court defeat, being no match for him. Had the boys upon *Meng Pin* becoming angry, soothed him by great politeness and reverence, he would not have been capable of doing harm to them. *Ch'in's* position towards *Wei* is analogous to that of *Meng Pin* and the boys. The administration of *Wei* would certainly not have frightened *Ch in* just as *Ming Pen* would not run away from the boys when wielding their swords. The honour and the respect shown to scholars and to the homes of worthies would be more than the politeness and reverence of the boys.

The weak will have recourse to virtue, whereas those who have a strong army, will use their power. Because *Ch'in* had such a strong army, nothing could withstand her power. If they held back their troops, and recalled their men, and did not infest *Wei,* it was out of respect for *Tuan Kan Mu* and as a mark of esteem for the marquis of *Wei.* The honouring of worthies is an administrative measure of weak States and a means to increase the might of the powerless. How can it be said that this is not the result of administration?

Han Kao Tsn had the intention to depose the heir-apparent. The empress *Lii Hott* in her distress summoned *Chang Tse Fang* to ask his advice. *Chang Tse Fang* suggested that the crown-prince should reverently meet the Four Grey Beards, and present them with rich gifts. When *Kao Tsu* saw this, he changed his mind, and the prince was saved. Had *Han Fei Tse* advised *Lil Hon,* that the best offensive were strong remonstrances, and the best defensive, energy, and that in this manner the prince would be safe, he See p. 278 Note 1.
Cf. p. 380 Note 4.
The same as *Chang Liang,* the helpmate of *Han Kan Tm.* Cf. p. 235. Four recluses, who during the troubles attending the overthrow of the *Ch'in* dynasty had

taken refuge into the mountains near *Hsi-an-fu,* would, on the contrary, have brought about his own death, not to speak of his deposition. The deep reverence of the crownprince towards the four old men changed *Han Kao Tsu's* design. Just so the respect shown by the Marquis *Win* of *Wei* to *Tnan Kan Alu's* home warded off the troops of powerful *Ch'in.*
The government of a State requires the cultivation of two things, of virtue and of strength. Virtue is cultivated by maintaining famous men, whereby one shows one's ability to honour worthies. Strength is developed by keeping strong men, which shows that one knows how to use soldiers. Then we may say that all the civil and military measures are in operation, and that virtue and strength are sufficient. In the international intercourse, a State may win the other side by virtue, or repel it by force. If, in its foreign relations, it makes virtue its basis, and at the same time keeps a strong force, those who esteem virtue, will be on good terms with it without fighting, whereas those who do not care for virtue, will keep aloof for fear of military complications.

King *Yen* of *Hsil* practised benevolence and justice, and thirtytwo States sent envoys to his court overland. When powerful *Ch'u* heard of this, it despatched its troops, and destroyed him. King *Yen* of *Hsi l* possessed virtue, but had no strength in readiness. One cannot solely rely on virtue to govern a State, nor straightway resort to force to ward off an enemy. In *Han Fei Tte's* system there is no room for the cultivation of virtue, whereas King *Yen* of *Hsi l* did not rely on strength. Both their views were one-sided and contradictory. King *Yen* came to grief, because he was powerless, and we may be sure that *Han Fei Tse* would have to suffer for want of virtue.

Human nature is pure or impure, selfish or disinterested, and people act accordingly. In the same manner plants and trees consist of different substances, which cannot change again. *K'nang Cli-iieli* and *Hua Shih* did not take office in *Ch'i,* as *Tnan Kan Mu* did not become

an official in *Wei.* Their nature was pure and unselfish, they did not long for wealth or honour, criticised their times, and disliked this world. Their sense of justice prevented From *Han Fei Tse* chap. 19, p. 2v. we learn that *Yen* was the sovereign of a small State covering f,00 square li in *lian-tung (Ilapei).* King *Wen* of *Ch'u,* 688-675 B.c., fearing the growing power of the virtuous *Yen—Han Fei Tse* speaks of H6 States which were allied to him—destroyed the *Hsu* State. *Huai Nan* 7V XIII, 14v. also refers to *Yen* and mentions that 32 States were his allies.
them from taking office inconsiderately. Even if they had not been executed, they would not have had followers. *T'ai Kung* put them to death, and *Han Fei Tse* thinks him quite right. But that would be denying that men have their special natures, and plants and trees their special substances. *T'ai Kung* beheaded the two scholars. Provided that there were people like them in *Chi,* they would certainly not have desisted from purifying their hearts, because the two were put to death, and if there were none, no training would have made them such. *Yao* did not execute *Hsu Yu,* yet the people of *Tang* did not all live in nests. *Wu Wang* did not kill *Po Yi,* yet the people of *Chou* did not starve in solitude, and, when Marquis *Win* of *Wei* had honoured *Tuan Kan Mus* dwelling-place, the people of *Wei* did not all close their doors. Consequently, even if *T'ai Kung* had not executed the two men, the people of *Ch i* would not all have disdained the official career, for people cannot assume integrity and disinterestedness at will. What people are unable to do, they cannot be induced to do, and all training and exhorting is in vain. Conversely what they can do, they cannot be hindered from doing, even executions are no preventive. Therefore the execution of the two scholars by *T ai Kung* was not calculated to bring about improvement, it was a useless murder of innocent persons. *Han Fei Tse* would not approve of rewards without merit or of death without guilt. *T'ai Kung* killed innocent men, yet *Han Fei Tse* assents to it, ergo his theory admits the assassi-

nation of the innocent. Those who persist in not taking office, have not necessarily some real guilt, yet *T'ai Kung* put them to death. If people, who had become officials, had no merit, would *T'ai Kung* be willing to reward them? Rewards must be given to merit, and punishment meted out to the guilty. If *T'ai Kung* did not reward officials without merit, then his execution of innocent men, who did not want to become officials, was unjust. *Han Fei Tse's* approval is a mistake.

Moreover, people who do not become officials generally have an unselfish character and few desires, whereas those who would like to take office, are greedy of profit. As long as desires and the thought of gain are not ingrafted in one's heart, one looks upon rank and salary as dung and dirt. The disinterested are A legendary hermit of the time of the emperor *Yao*, reported to have lived in a nest in a tree.

Yao's principality. extremely thrifty, the extravagance of the ambitious knows no bounds, and therefore their desires do not even recoil from their sovereign. Among the rebelling officials of ancient times those with pure and unselfish motives have been very few. The ambitious will make themselves conspicuous, and the haughty will risk their lives. For all the laurels won they aspire to a great reward, and in their immoderation covet princely dignity. *T ai Kung* left his system behind, and subsequently *Ch i* was the scene of the violent murder perpetrated by the *Chin* family. *T'ai Kung's* system led to robbery and murder. *Han Fei Tse* praises it, which shows that his own theory is also very dangerous. When *Chou Kung* heard of the execution of the two men by *T ai Kung*, he expressed his disapproval, and did not think him right. Personally he took gifts and condescended to present them to scholars living in poor huts. These scholars living in poor huts were like the two men. *Chou Kung* honoured them, and *T ai Kung* put them to death. Whose action was the right one?

In *Sung* there was a charioteer. A horse refused to go on. He thereupon drew his sword, cut its throat, and threw it in-

to a ditch. He then tried another horse, which also would not go. Again he cut its throat, and threw it into a ditch. This he repeated thrice. It was a very strong measure to break the obstinacy of horses, but it was not the way of *Wang Liang*. When he stepped into a carriage, there was no horse stubborn or restive. During the reign of *Yao* and *Shun,* the people were not rebellious. *Wang Liang* knew how to touch the hearts of the horses, just as *Yao* and *Shun* influenced the popular feelings.

Men have the same nature, but there are different kinds of horses. *Wang Liang* could manage these different kinds, whereas *T'ai Kung* could not get along with scholars, who were all of the same nature. *Chou Kung's* kindness towards the poor scholars corresponds to *Wang Liang's* horse-breaking. *T ai Kung's* execution of the two scholars is like the throat-cutting of the man of *Sung*.

If *Han Fei Tse* were called upon to decide between the methods of *Wang Liang* and the man of *Sung,* he would certainly be in favour of *Wang Liang* and against the man of *Sung*. *Wang Liang* preserved the horses, the man of *Sung* destroyed them. The de In 481 B. c. *Ch'en Hmg* alias *Tien Ch'eng Tse* murdered the sovereign of *Ch'i,* a descendant of *T'ai Kung*. The *Ch'en* family had assumed the name *T'ien* in *Ch'i.* Cf. *Shi-ch!* chap. 32, p. 24v. and chap. 36, p. 7.

Vid. Hun Fei Tse XIII, 5.

» Cf. p. 480.

struction of horses is not as good as their preservation. Thus it is better that people should live than that they should die. Should *Han Fei Tse* be against *Wang Liang*, he would be on a level with the man of *Sung* by destroying good people. If he be against the man of *Sung*, it must be borne in mind that the latter's method is the same as that of *'/' ai Kung*. By condemning the man of *Sung* and upholding *T ai Kung, Han Fei Tse* would show that he cannot discriminate between right and wrong.

The government of a State is like governing an individual. If in governing an individual grace and virtue are seldom

resorted to, but much bodily injury is inflicted, friends and partisans will make themselves scarce, lest disgrace should befall them. If the principles of governing an individual are extended to the government of a State, this government must be based on virtue. *Han Fei Tse* solely relies on criminal law to govern the world. That would mean that he who governs an individual, must trust to the infliction of injuries. Does *Han Fei Tse* not know that to place reliance on virtue is the best way'.'

He holds that the world is depraved, that things have changed for the worse, and that the general feelings are base and mean. Therefore in working out a system his only thought is penal law. However, the world is not deficient in virtue, as a year is not deprived of its spring. Would he who contends that owing to its depravity the world cannot be governed by virtue, assert also that a year full of troubles does not generate in spring?

A wise ruler governs a country as Heaven and Earth create all things. In a year of troubles they do not omit spring, and a wise ruler does not discard virtue, because the world is degenerated. *Confucius* said, "Those people were the cause of the steady progress of the three dynasties!"

The time of King *Mu* of *Chou* can be called one of decay. He attempted to govern with criminal law, but the result was confusion, and no glory was won. The Marquis of *Fu* remonstrated with him, and the king became attached to virtue, and enjoyed

'Analects XV, 24.

The depravity of the people cannot have been as great as *Han Fei Tse* presumed, for otherwise the progress made during the three dynasties:— *Hsia, Shimy*, and *Chou* could not have been accomplished. 1001-946 B.c. his kingdom for a long time. His deeds were handed down to posterity. King *Mn's* administration first led to disorder, but at last to order, not because his mind was beclouded first, and his talents came forth later on, but because he at first relied on *Ch'ih Yus* criminal law, and only subsequently followed the advice of the Marquis of *Fu.* In governing individuals, one cannot do without mercy, in governing a State one cannot neglect virtue, and in creating things spring cannot be left out. Why does *Han Fei Tse* wish to rely on law and capital punishment alone? Duke *Mu* of *Lu* asked *Tse Sse* saying, "I have heard that *I' ang Hsien* is no filial son. How is his unfilial conduct?" *Tse Sse* replied, "A prince honours the virtuous to exalt virtue, and raises the good to admonish the people. As regards faults, only common people know about that, not I."

When *Tse Sse* had left, *Tse Fu Li Po* saw the prince, who questioned him about *P'ang Hsien s* filial conduct also. *Tse Fu Li Po* rejoined, "Your Highness has not yet heard about all his misdeeds."

Afterwards the prince held *Tse Sse* in esteem and despised *Tse Fu Li Po.* When *Han Fei Tse* heard of it, he censured duke *Mu* on the ground that a wise ruler ought to search for scoundrels and punish them. *Tse Sse* would not speak about rascality, which *Tse Fu Li Po* did. Therefore, in *Han Fei Tse's* belief, the latter deserved honour, and the former contempt. Since Duke *Mu* esteemed *Tse Sse* and despised *Tse Fu Li Po,* he did not divide honour and contempt in the right way, hence *Han Fei Tse's* adverse criticism.

Han Fei Tse lays the greatest stress upon administration. If a man does good, the administration rewards him, if he does evil, it punishes him. Even if good and evil do not transpire, they fall under strict rules. Yet merely hearing of a bad deed, one cannot punish at once, as hearing of a good one, one cannot rashly reward it. It is therefore not in keeping with the theory' of *Han Fei Tse* to blame a man for not having denounced wickedness. A legendary person said to have lived at the time of the Emperor *Hnang Ti.* He rebelled against the latter, and was defeated. Some say that he was a prince, who terrorised the people, others that he was a minister of *Huang Ti.* -Quoted with some slight alterations from *Huai Nan Tse* chap. 16, p. 1. 408- 375 B.c. His full name is *JVumj Tse Sse* or *K'ung Citi,* the grandson of *Confucius,* to whom the *Chmig-gung,* the

"Doctrine of the Mean" is ascribed. Suppose *Han Fei Tse* heard of a good action, he would certainly make investigations first and, in case some merit were brought to light thus, he would grant a reward. Upon the mere news of some good deed, one does not reward indiscriminately, for not every remark is reliable. Therefore it makes no difference, whether we hear of good actions or not. Hearing of goodness, one does not rashly reward, and upon hearing of wickedness, one does not punish forthwith. Hearing of goodness, one must first investigate, and hearing of badness, one must make inquiries. Provided some merit is discovered, then a reward may be given, and, if there is evidence, a penalty may be determined. Rewards and punishments are not given upon mere hearsay or vague appearances, before the truth is found out, and as long as they are not given, goodness and badness are not determined. Therefore there must be a method to establish them, and it is not right to require that one must have heard the thing with one's own ears.

Tse Ch'an of *Ching2* went out one morning, and passed the house of *Tung Chiang,* where he heard the cries of his wife. He grasped the hand of his attendant, and listened. After a while, he directed his officers to arrest the woman, and sue her for having murdered her husband with her own hand.

The next day his attendant asked him, "Sir, how did you know all this?" *Tse Ch an* replied, "Her voice was not moved. When people learn that those they love dearly are sick, they become depressed, when death approaches, they get alarmed, and, after death, give vent to their grief. This woman bewailed her dead husband, but in lieu of being grieved she was frightened. Thence I knew that she had committed a crime." *Han Fei Tse* expressed his disapproval and said, "Was not *Tse Chan* a busy body?"

If a crime could only be known, when we perceive it with our own eyes or ears, very few cases would be disclosed in *Cheng.* And would it not be a lack of method, if the city police could not be trusted to possess the necessary insight

for examining the conduct of the smaller congregations of the community, and if one had to use all owns intelligence and mental power to discover such cases? " *Han Fei Tse* chap. 16, p. 5. The text slightly differs.

Tse Chan is the style of *Kung Sun Chiao,* a famous minister of the *Cheng* State, 581-521 n.r., who compiled a penal code. *Luc. cit.* p. 5v, *Han Fei Tse* is justified in blaming *Tse Ch'an,* but he is wrong in his adverse comments on Duke *Ma.* The lack of grief of the woman is like the unfilial conduct of *Pang Hsten. Han Fei Tse* objects to *Tse Ch an* relying merely on his eyes and ears to get information about crimes, but, on the other hand, wishes that Duke *Mu* should have made inquiries to determine the guilt of *P ang Hsien. Tse Ch'an* had no recourse to the city police, and determined the truth from what he heard. Duke *Mu* did not place confidence in the police either, and attained the same result by his inquiries. Hearsay and inquiries are about the same thing. Neither trusted the police, or made investigations among the citizens. From *Tse Fa Li Po's* answer it is impossible to learn the truth, just as from the crying of the womau one cannot arrive at a cogent conclusion. If under such circumstances one orders the officers to arrest and try a person, one cannot find out the truth thereby. But how is it possible not to order the officers to make investigations and to cbarge a person with a crime without any inquiries merely upon the word of *Tse Fu Li Po' Han Fei Tse* says', *Tse Sse* did not mention faults, and Duke *Mu* honoured him. *Tse Fu Li Po* spoke of crimes, and Duke *Mu* despised him. Human nature is such, that all people like honour and are displeased with contempt.

When the *Chi* family made trouble, it was not brought to the knowledge of the sovereign, and consequently the princes of *Lu* were robbed of their power. Were they robbed, because they did not make a wise use of the laws and administration or, because they did not hear of the wicked designs in time? If the administration is wisely organised, wickedness has no field where it might grow, although it be not beard of, whereas in case the administration is not wise, the searching after criminals is like digging a well, and then trying to stop it with one hand.

If a chariot-driver without a bridle sees a horse, it will run away, and he has no coercive means. Should, however. *Wang Liang* have come near with reins in his hand, no horse would have had the desire to bolt. He knew the method of driving horses. Now, nothing is said about the princes of *Lu* having no method, but it is mentioned that they did not hear of the treason *Han Fei Tse* chap. 16, p. 1.

During the 6th cent. B.C. the *Chi* family, a side branch of the ducal house of *Lu,* engrossed the power in *Lu* and almost superseded the reigning princes. *Confucius* openly condemned their usurpation. Cf. p. 305. See above p. 440. able designs, nothing is said about their looking after the government, but it is emphasized that they did not understand the feelings of the people. *Han Fei Tse's* attack on Duke *Mu* does not tally with the tendency of his theory. *Tse Sse* did not speak of *Pang Hsien's* unfilial conduct, therefore Duke *Mu* honoured him. *Han Fei Tse* blames him, saying that "a wise ruler looks out for the good to reward and for rascals to punish them." '—Unfilial persons have a very limited intellect. For want of insight, they know no propriety, and follow their desires and propensities just like beasts and birds. One may call them bad, but to call them rascals is not correct. Rascals are good in outward appearance, but bad inwardly, or "they show a stern exterior, and are inwardly weak," and in their doings imitate the good to get on in their career. They smile to their superiors— how could they be unfilial'.'—but they do wicked things, which make them worthy of capital punishment. *P ang Hsien* can be said to have been unfilial, but not a rascal. If *Han Fei Tse* calls him so, he ignores the true meaning of this word. *Han Fei Tse* says:—"If silk fabrics are so common, that ordinary people do not desire them, and if gold can be cast into a hundred coins without robber *Che*

snatching it away, then we can speak of a manifestation of law." People do not dare to infringe it. If the law is manifest in a State, robbers are afraid to break it, and do not venture to bring about unforeseen calamities. They hide their vicious thoughts in their hearts, and dare not transgress the penal law, being in awe of it. If the law is known and dreaded, there is no need for investigating rascality, or inquiring after wickedness among the citizens. If the law is imposing, people are not vicious, if it is not, they commit many a felony. Now *Han Fei Tse* does not speak of the severe penalties and the awe-inspiring law of a wise sovereign, but that he is on the look-out for miscreants to punish them. If he says that he looks out for miscreants, the law is not awe-inspiring, so that people offend against it. In the world much more attention is paid to the persecution of criminals than to upholding the respect of the law. Therefore *Han Fei Tse's* remarks do not agree with the law.

When the water of a creek is let out, those who know that it can drown a man, do not attempt to stop the current, but they *Han Fei Tse loc. cit. Analects* XVII, 12.

Han Fei Tse chap. 19, p. 4. keep boats and oars in readiness. They know the nature of the water, that its rush cannot be checked, and that it would certainly drown a man. When a subject or a son is bent upon committing a misdeed against his sovereign or his father, they are like the water which drowns a man. Now, *Han Fei Tse* does not inform us, which precautions might be taken against the crime, but takes exception that it is not known or heard of. This would be nothing else than not to prepare the necessary implements for the water, and merely to wish to learn, as soon as possible, that the water is drowning somebody. Being drowned by water one cannot hold the water accountable, but is oneself guilty of having neglected the necessary precautions. When a sovereign is robbed by a subject, he himself has neglected the law. Preparing against drowning, one does not dam in the fountain-head, and in

guarding oneself against an attack, one does not look out for the misdemeanours of the subjects. *Han Fei Tse* stands in need of self-instruction on these points.

The nature of water is stronger than fire, but pour the water into a kettle, it will boil, but not gain the upper hand. A sovereign is like fire, a subject like water, administration is the kettle. Fire does not seek the misdeeds of water. Thus a prince ought not to search l'or the faults of his subjects.

CHAPTER, XXXVI.

Statements Corrected *(Ching-shuo),*

The researches of the Literati into the Five Canons for the most part miss the truth. The former scholars, unable to distinguish between essential and accidental points, indulged in fanciful inventions, and their successors, relying on the words of old teachers, stuck to the old traditions and walked in the old grooves. SoOn well versed in quibbling, they would thoughtlessly uphold the doctrine of one master and follow the teachings of their professor. When the time had come, they quickly tools office, and in their eagerness for promotion, they had no time left to devote their faculties to the handling of such problems. Consequently an unbroken chain of false theories has been handed down, and truth has hid her face.

The truth about the Five Canons has been equally obscured, but compared with the *Viking,* the statements about the *Shuking* and the *"Spring and Autumn"* are still tolerably correct.

This rough theme may serve as an introduction into the minor details of this essay.

Some of the critics of the *Shuking* are of opinion that originally it consisted of one hundred and two chapters, and that afterwards, when *Chin* burned the books of poetry and history, twenty-nine chapters were preserved. The statement that *Chin* burned the books of poetry and history is correct, but the assertion that originally there were one hundred and two chapters is erroneous.

The *Shuking* consisted of one hundred chapters first, which were transmitted by *Confucius.* When, by the ad-

vice of *Li Sse, Chin* burned the Five Canons, *Fu Shing2* of *Chi-nan* took the hundred chapters and concealed them in a mountain. Under the The Five *King* or ancient Classics: *Yiking, Shiking, Shaking, Liki,* and (*'h'un-ch'iu.* A scholar of great learning.
The capital of *Shantung.*
The *Shi-chi* chap. 121, p. 8 says "in a wall." reign of the Emperor *Hsiao Ching Ti* the *Shaking* was saved. *Fa S/ting* had taken it out from the mountain. *Ching Ti* sent *Ch ao Tso* to him. He received from *Fu Shing* twenty odd chapters of the *Shuking. Fu Sheng* died as a very old man. His book was greatly damaged. *Ch ' ao Ts o* handed it over to *Ni K'uan.*

During the time of the Emperor *Hsiao HsOan Ti* a young woman in *Honei,* while opening an old room, discovered a chapter of a preserved *Yiking, Liki,* and *Shuking.* The books were presented to the emperor, who communicated them to the principal men of learning. Subsequently the *Yiking,* the *Liki,* and the *Shaking* had each one chapter added. It was then that the number of the chapters of the *Shuking* was brought up to twenty-nine.

When *Hsiao Cliing Ti* had ascended the throne, I'rince *Kung* of *Lu,* while demolishing the school of *Confucius* for the purpose of building a palace there, found a copy of the *Shuking* in one hundred chapters in the wall. The Emperor *Wa Ti* sent messengers to fetch the books for him to see, but there was nobody who could read them, whereupon he stored them away in the palace, so that no one outside could see them.

Under the Emperor *Hsiao Ch fag TV* the study of the *Shuking* in ancient characters received a new impetus. *Chang Pa* of *Tung-hai* concocted a *Shuking* of one hundred and two chapters, following the order of the hundred chapters, and presented it to the emperor. The emperor produced the concealed hundred chapters for comparison, but it was found out that they did not agree at all. Upon this the emperor handed *Chang Pa* over to the court. The judges declared that his crime deserved death, but the emperor, who had a very high opin-

ion of his talents, did not put him to death, nor did he destroy his writings, for which he had a certain weakness. Thus the one hundred and two chapters were handed down to posterity, and people who saw them imagined that the *Shuking* had one hundred and two chapters first.

'150-141 B.r. 73 49 B.c. A city in *Iluai-ch'ing-fu (Hoaan).* In 156 B.c. A son of the Kmperor *Ching Ti,* who in 154 B.c. was made Prince of *Lu.* In addition to these hundred chapters of the *Shaking,* a *Li(k!)* in 3'X) chapters, a *Ch'un-ch'iu* in 300 chapters and a *Lun-gu* in 21 chapters were brought to light. Cf. *Lun-heng* XX, 4 v. *(i i-wi'n).* 32-7 B.c. A place in *Huai-an-fu (Kiangsu).*

Some hold that, when *Ch'in Shih Huang Ti* burned the "poetry (and the) books," he burned the Book of Poetry, but not the Canons. Thus the *Shiking* would alone have been committed to the flames. However, the term "poetry and the books" is a general designation of the Five Canons.

There is a common saying to the effect that a lad who does not read the Canons is bent on plays and amusements. "*Tse 1m* got *Tse Kao*" appointed governor of *Pi.* The Master said, 'You are injuring a man's son.'—*Tse Lu* replied, "There are the people, and there are the spirits of the land and grain. Why must one read *books,* before he can be considered to have learned?"

A general term for the Five Canons is "the books." Those who have recorded the burning of the books by *Ch'in* do not know the reason for this measure, therefore they do not understand its meaning.

In the 24 th year of *Ch'in Shih Huang Ti's* reign," a banquet was given in the *Hsien-yang* palace. Seventy great scholars wished the emperor long life, and the *Pu-yeh' Chou Ching Chen* made a eulogistic speech. When the emperor had gathered all the people around him, *Shun Yil Yileh* remonstrated with him. He was of opinion that, because the emperor did not grant fiefs to the sons of the nobility, a catastrophe like that of *T ien Chang* and the six ministers was unavoidable. Besides he stigmatised *Chou*

Ch'ing Ch en's panegyric as a flattery of the emperor.
Cliin Shih Huang Ti handed over his memorial to the premier. The premier, *Li Sse,* regarded the remarks of *Shun Yil Yileh* as quite unfit to be taken into consideration. For this reason he denounced the speeches of the literati as inveigling the black haired people. Then the officials were ordered to completely destroy the Five *Tse Lai* and *Tse Kao* were both disciples of *Confucius.* A place in *Shantung.*
Analects XI, 24.
On the burning of the books cf. p. 490. This is a misprint. It was the 34th year (213 B.C.). See the *Shi-chi* chap. 6, p. 21v. and p. 490. An official title under the *Ch'in and Han* dynasties. A noble of the State of *Ch'i,* who in 481 B.C. put to death the reigning sovereign Duke *Chien,* and usurped the government of the State with the title of chief minister. The chiefs of the six powerful families in *Chin* who struggled for supremacy. Three of these families were destroyed during these straggles, the remaining three: *Chao, Han* and *Wei* in 403 B.C. divided the *Chin* State among them.
Lun-Hcng. 29

Canons by fire. Those who dared to conceal books or writings of the hundred authors should be severely dealt with. Only members of the academy were allowed to keep books. Thus the Five Canons were all burned, and not merely the books of the various schools of thought. In this the writers on this epoch believe. Seeing that poetry and "books" are mentioned we can only say that the Canons are here termed "books."

Some writers on the *Shuking* are aware of the fact that it was burned by *Ch'in,* but urge that twenty-nine chapters were saved and left unscathed.. If this was the case, then were the twenty-nine chapters of the *Shuking* left by the fire, and did the seventy-one chapters become coal and ashes, whereas the twentynine remained?

When *Fu Shing* was old, *Ch'ao T'so* studied under him and just, when he had received twenty odd chapters, *Fu Sheng* died. Therefore these twenty-nine chapters alone came forth, and the seventy-one had been saved. Seventy-one chapters had been saved, and they conversely state that twenty-nine chapters were saved.

Some say that the twenty-nine chapters of the *Shuking* are an imitation of the Dipper and seven zodiacal constellations. Four times seven gives twenty-eight chapters, and the one is the Dipper, so that there would be the number of twenty-nine. However, when the *Shuking* was destroyed in *Chin,* only twenty-nine chapters remained, how could there be any imitation? During the reign of the emperor *Hsilan Ti* one chapter was found of the lost *Shuking,* the *Yiking,* and the *Liki* each. The number of the chapters of the *Yiking* and the *Liki* became complete then. How could any imitation find its way? Out of the series of the hundred chapters of the *Shuking,* seventy-one were missing, and no more than twentynine still extant. How should the imitation have taken place then':'

Others hold that *Confucius* selected twenty-nine chapters, and that these alone were up to the standard. Only common scholars can speak so, and it does not show much wisdom in the writers Writers on philosophy and science.

There are 28 stellar mansions in all, 7 for each quadrant. on these subjects. The twenty-nine chapters were a fragment and incomplete, and just on account of this difficiency the writers conceived the idea of the imitation. They misunderstand the sage, and their opinion disagrees with the facts now and formerly.

The chapters of a Classic correspond to the periods and clauses. Periods and clauses still consist of words. Words giving a sense form a clause, and a certain number of clauses is combined into a period. A complex of periods gives a chapter. A chapter therefore is a combination of periods and clauses. If one maintains that the chapters imitate something, then he must admit that periods and clauses have their prototype likewise.

In ancient times the *Shiking* also con-

sisted of several thousand chapters. *Confucius* expunged a great many and made a revised edition, retaining but three hundred chapters. They are like the twenty-nine chapters of the *Shuking.* Provided that the letter had their model, the three hundred and five chapters must have had theirs likewise.

Some one might suggest that the *Ch'un Ch'iu* is a reproduction of the twelve months. The twelve dukes of the *Chun Ch'iu* are like the hundred chapters of the *Shuking.* Since these chapters are not modelled after anything, the twelve dukes cannot be such an imitation either.

Discussing the " Spring and Autumn," people have put forward the following theory. During the two hundred and forty-two years of the "Spring and Autumn" period, the people had excellent principles, and those of the emperor were perfect. The good were liked, and the wicked detested. Revolutionists were led back to the right path. Nothing could be like the "Spring and Autumn" period in this respect. Thus the principles of the people and of the emperor just happened to be perfect.

Three armies forming six divisions, of 12,000 men, suffice to crush an enemy, to defeat brigands, and to put a stop to their attacks on the empire, but it is not necessary that they should be an imitation of any standard.

When *Confucius* composed the "Spring and Autumn," the chronicle of the twelve dukes of *Lu.* it was like the three armies forming six divisions. The number of soldiers, 12,000 in all, would correspond to the two-hundred and forty-two years. Six divisions consisting of 12,000 soldiers would suffice to form an army, and twelve dukes comprising two hundred and forty-two years would

'The twelve dukes of *Lu,* whose history is given in the *Ch'un-ch'iu.* be sufficient to establish a moral system. But those who concern themselves with these questions, are very partial to extravagant theories and imposing doctrines. In their opinion, the reckless meet with misfortune, therefore the number of the chapters of the classical writings has always a certain sense.

Let us get to the bottom of the thing, and see what these writings are meant to be, and I am sure that our ideas will represent the view of the venerable men who wrote those books and poetries. The sages are tln; authors of the Canons, the worthies of the Classics. Having exhausted a theme and said all they could about it, they made a chapter of it. The subjects were cognate, and the various paragraphs homogeneous. In case the subjects were heterogeneous, and the diction not uniform, they formed a new chapter. The sense being different, the words differed too. Thus, when a new theme was treated, another chapter had to be commenced. All depended on the subject, how could the number of stars be imitated?

Concerning the two hundred and forty-two years of the "Spring and Autumn" there are some who say that the longest life lasts ninety years, a medium long one eighty, and the shortest long life seventy years. *Confucius* took three generations of a medium long life for his work. Three times eight gives twenty-four, ergo there are two hundred and forty years. Others urge that this is the mean number of the days of pregnancy. Others again contend that during two hundred and forty-two years the ways of the people were excellent, and those of the emperors perfect.

Now, if we accept the three generation theory, the statement about the excellent conduct must be wrong,, and, if we declare the latter view to be correct, then we must dismiss the theory about the three generations as erroneous, for both are contradictory. How could we be sure to be in accordance with the views of the sage, if we decide in favour of either of these opinions?

The addition of years, months, and days to a record will always increase its accuracy. The Five Timekeepers of the *Hung-fan,'* This translation is a mere guess, might mean "rule for the new born." According to Chinese ideas pregnancy lasts 7-9 months or 210-270 days, whereas we reckon 182-300 days. The mean number would be 240 or 241 days. The dictionaries do not explain the expression.

These Five Timekeepers of the *Hung-fan* chapter are: the year, the mouth, the day, the stars, and the dates of the calendar. *Shuking, Hung-fan,* Pt. V, Bk. IV, 8 *Legge* Vol. III, Pt. II, p. 327). the years, months, days, and stars serve to describe events, but have no reference to any outwards signs. It is on record that the years during which the twelve" dukes enjoyed the possession of their State were two hundred and forty-two altogether. These, at all events, have given rise to the three generation theory. As a matter of fact, *Confucius* in writing the history of the twelve dukes, either was of opinion that the events which happened under their reigns were sufficient to illustrate the principles of a sovereign, or he took three generations, and these three generations just happened to embrace the time of the twelve dukes. If he took the twelve dukes, then the two hundred and forty-two years were not regarded as three generations, and if he took three generations, so that eight were multiplied by three, this would give two hundred and forty, why then did he add two?

I shall receive the answer that he wished to include the first year of Duke *Yin,* and did not add two years. Had these two years not been included, the first year of Duke *Yin* would have been omitted in the Classic. Provided that in the composition of the *Ch'un-chiu* the time for three generations was chosen on purpose, wherefore was it necessary to begin the narration from the events which happened during the first year of Duke *Yin's* reign? If, conversely, these events were required for the beginning, then only completeness was aimed at, and it would be no use speaking of three generations. They say that Duke *Yin* reigned fifty years. Now, should a complete record be given from the first year, or should it be cut in two to have the number of three times eight? If a complete record from the first year was given, the number of three times eight did cut it in two, and, if it was cut in two with the object of obtaining the full number of years for three generations, then the first years of Duke *Yin* were superfluous.

Furthermore, a year differs in length from months and days, but the events, which they embrace, have all the same purport. Since the two hundred and forty-two years are believed to represent three generations, the days and months of these two hundred and forty-two years ought to have a fixed number likewise. The years represent three generations, but how many months and days are there, and what do they represent? The years of the "Spring and Autumn" are like the paragraphs of the *Shuking.* A paragraph This would seem a misprint. Duke J *in* of *Lm* reigned from 721-711 B.C. f. e. 10 years, not 50. serves to bring out a meaning, and a year to chronicle events. He who holds that the years of the *Chun-ch'iu* have a prototype, must admit that the paragraphs of the *Shuking* have a prototype also.

Writers on the *Yiking* all state that *Fu Hsi* made the Eight Diagrams, and that *Win Wancl* increased them to sixty-four. Now, because a wise emperor rose, the *Yellow Hiver* produced the Plan and the *Lo* the Scroll. When *Fu Hsi* was emperor, the Plan of the *River* put forward the diagrams of the *Yiking* from the water of the *River,* and during *Yils* time the Scroll of the *Lo* was obtained. It emerged from the *Lo,* putting forward the nine paragraphs of the "Flood Regulation." Thus by means of the diagrams *Fu Hsi* governed the empire, and *Yii* put the "Flood Regulation" into practice to regulate the great flood.

Of old, when *Lieh Shan2* was on the throne, he obtained the Plan of the *River.* The *Hsia* dynasty took it over and called it *Lien-shan.* The Plan of the *River* obtained by the Emperor *Lieh Shan* also went over to the *Yin* dynasty, which styled it *Kuei-tsang. Fu Hsi* came into possession of the plan during his reign, and the people of *Chou* denoted it as *Chou-Yi.* The diagrams of this Classic were sixty-four in all. *Wen Wang* and *Chou Kung* made a summary of them in eighteen paragraphs and explained the six lines.

The current tradition on the *Yiking* is that *Fu Hsi* made the eight diagrams. Only he who keeps on the surface, can say that *Fu Hsi* really composed the eight diagrams. *Fu Hsi* obtained the eight diagrams, but did not make them, and *Wen Wang* received the sixty-four quite complete, and did not increase them. These words: to make and to increase, have their origin in the common tradition. People lifjhtly believe in this statement, and consider it The chapter of the *Shuking* entitled "*Hung-fan.*" The Emperor *Shen Nung.* The *Yiking* of the *Chou* Dynasty, the only one which has come down to us.

We learn from the *Ti-wang-slUh-chi* (3d cent, A.d.) that *Fu Hsi* made the eight diagrams, and that *Shi'n Nung* increased them to sixty-four. *Huang Ti, Yao,* and *Shun* took them over, expanded them, and distinguished two *Yikings.* The *Hia* dynasty adopted that of *Shen Nung,* and called it *Lim-.,han,* the *Yin* dynasty took the version of *Huang Ti,* and called it *Kuei-tsang. Wen Wang* expanded the sixtyfour diagrams, composed the six broken and unbroken lines of which they were formed, and called it *Chou Yi.*

Others think that *Lien-shan* is another name of *Fu Hsi,* and *Kwi-Umg* a designation of *Huang Ti.* as true, whereas the truth is nearly forgotten. Not knowing that the *Yiking* is the Plan of the *River,* they are not aware either to which dynasty the different *Yikings,* still extant, belong. Sometimes it is the *lAen-shan* or the *Ktm-tsang Yiking,* and sometimes the *Yiking* of the *Chou* dynasty.

The amplifications and abridgements which the Books of Rites underwent under the *Hsia, Yin,* and *Chou* dynasties vary very much. If, because the *Chou* dynasty is the last of the three, our present *Yiking* is regarded as that of the *Chou* dynasty, then the *Liki* ought to be from the *Chou* time also. But, since the "Six Institutions" do not tally with the present *Liki,* the latter cannot be that of the *Chou* dynasty. Thus it becomes doubtful too, whether our *Yiking* dates from the *Chou* epoch.

Since *Tso Ch'iu Ming,* who in his commentary quotes the authors of the *Chou* dynasty, uses diagrams which agree with our modern *Yiking,* it is most likely the *Yiking* of the *Chou* period.

The writers on the *Liki* all know that the *Liki* is the *Liki*, but to which dynasty does it belong?

Confucius says, "The *Yin* dynasty continued the Rites of the *Hsia;* wherein it amplified or abridged them, may be known. The *Chou* dynasty has continued the Rites of the *Yin;* wherein it amplified or abridged them, may be known." Accordingly the *Hsia* as well as the *Yin* and *Chou* all had their own *Liki.* Now is our own the *Chou Liki* or that of the *Hsia* or *Yin* dynasties?

If they hold that it is the *Chou Liki,* one must object that the Rites of the *Chou* had the Six Institutions, whereas our *Liking* does not contain them. Perhaps at that time the *Yin Liki* was not yet extinct, and the *Liki* with the Six Institutions was not handed down. Consequently ours has been regarded as the *Chou Li.* The Official System of the *Chou* does not agree with the present *Liki*, it must be the *Chou Liki* with the Six Institutions therefore, but it is not being handed down, just as the *Shuking,* the *Ch'un-ch'iu,* and the *Tso-chuan* in ancient characters are not much in vogue. The tradition about the Plan of the River and the Scroll of the Lo is very old. We find traces of it in the *Yiking,* the *Liki,* the *Shuking,* and the *Analects.* Cf. *Legge's translation of the Yiking,* p. 14. The author of the *Tso-chuan. Analects* II, 23, 2. The Six Institutions or departments of the *Chou*: administration, instruction, rites, police, jurisdiction, and public welfare. Cf. *Chou-li,* Bk. II, *T ien-kuan. (Biot's translation,* Vol. I, p. 20.) Now known as the *Chou-li.*

Those who treat of the *Analects* merely know how to discourse on the text, and to explain the meaning, but they do not know the original number of the books of the *Analects.* During the *L'hou* time eight inches were reckoned to one foot. They do not know for what reason the size of the *Analects* was only one foot. The *Analects* are notes on the sayings and doings of *Confucius,* made by his disciples. It happened very often that he corrected them. Many tens of hundreds of books thus originated. For writing them down the size of one foot of eight inches was chosen, as it was more

economical, and the books could be kept in the bosom more conveniently. Because the sayings left by the sage were not to be found in the Classics, the pupils were afraid lest they should forget them, when recording from memory, therefore they only used books of one foot like eight inches, and not of two feet four inches.

At the accession of the *Han* dynasty the *Analects* had been lost. When under *Wu Ti's* reign the wall of the house of *Confucius* was pierced, twenty-one books in ancient characters were brought to light. Between the two rivers of *Ch i* and *Lu* nine books were discovered, which makes thirty together. The daughter of the Emperor *Chao Ti* read twenty-one books. When the Emperor *Hsilan 7«* sent them down to the scholars of the court of sacrificial worship, they still declared that the work was hard to understand, and called it a record. Afterwards it was transcribed in *Li* characters" to give it a wider publicity. First the grandson of t*anfucius, K una An Kuo,* explained it to *Fu Ching,* a native of *Lu.* When the latter became governor of *Ching-chou,* he first called it *Analects.* Now we speak of the twenty books of the *Analects.* Under the *Hsia* dynasty the foot had ten inches, under the *J 'in* nine, under the *Chou* eight. Now it has ten inches again The foot of the *Chou* time measured but about 20 cm., whereas the modern foot is equal to 35 cm.

By Prince *Kung. Vid.* above p. 448. It is not plain which rivers are meant. They must have been at the frontier of the two conterminous States. There was the *Chi* River, which in *Chi* was called the *Chi* of *Ch'i,* and in *Lu* the *Chi* of *Lu.* 86-74 B.c.

73-49 B.c.

The massive *IA* characters were invented during the *Han* time and form the link between the ancient seal characters and the modern form of script. A place in *Hupei* province. *Analects — Lun-yu.* 'Our text of the *Lwn-yH* consists of twenty books. In the *Hun* time there were two editions of the Classic, one of *Lu* in twenty books and one of *Ch'i* in twenty-two.

The nine books found between the rivers of *Chi* and *Lu* have again been lost. Originally there were thirty, but by the transmission of separate books, some have disappeared. Those twenty-one books may be too many or too few, and the interpretation of the text may be correct or erroneous, the critics of the *Lun-yll* do not care, they only know how to ask knotty questions concerning the explanation of ambiguous passages, or find difficulties in all sorts of minutiae. They do not ask about the orig1n of the work, which has been preserved, or the number of its books or its chapters. Only those well versed in antique lore, who also understand the present time should become teachers, why do we now call teachers men who know nothing about antiquity?

Mencius said, "The traces of the old emperors were obliterated, and the Odes forgotten, when the *Ch'un-ch'iu* was composed. The *Ch eng* of *Chin* and the *T ao-wu* of *Ch'u* correspond to the *Ch'unch'iu* of *Lu."*

As *Mencius* states, *Ch'un-ch'iu* was the name of the history of *Lu* like the *Ch eng* and the *T ao-wu. Confucius* preserved the old name and styled it the *Ch'un-ch'iu* Classic. This is by no means a queer expression, nor has it any other sense or any deep and excellent meaning. The ordinary scholars of the present day contend with reference to the *Ch un-ch'iu,* that *Ch'nn* (Spring) is the beginning and *ch iu* (Autumn) the end of the year. The *Ch'un-ch'iu* Classic can feed the young and afford nourishment to the old, whence the designation *Ch'un-ch'iu* (Spring and Autumn). But wherein does the *Ch'un-ch'iu* differ from the *Shuking*? The *Shuking* is regarded as the book of the emperors of remotest antiquity, or people think that it contains the deeds of the ancients, which were written down by their successors. At all events, the facts and the mode of transmission are both in accordance with truth, and so is the name. People were not at a loss what to say, and then concocted a meaning, so that the expression seemed strange. Those dealing with the *Shuking* speak the truth about it, whereas those concerned with the *Ch'un-ch'iu,* have missed the meaning of the Sage.

We read in the commentary of the *Ch'un-ch'iu.* the *Tso-chuan,* that during the seventeenth year of Duke *Huan's* reign, in winter, i *Mencius* Bk. IV, Pt. II, chap. 21.

The meaning of the names of these old chronicles, *Ch'eng* and *T'ao-uru,* is as obscure as that of the *Ch'un-ch'iu.* 710-693 B.c. in the tenth month, the first day of the moon, the sun was eclipsed. The day is not mentioned, because the responsible officer had lost it.

The idea that the official had lost the day is correct, I dare say. The historiographer had to record the events, as in our times the district magistrates keep their books. Years and months are long and difficult to be lost, days are short and may easily be forgotten. Good and bad actions are recorded for the sake of truth, and no importance is attached to days and mouths.

In the commentaries of *Kung Yang* and *Ku Liang* days and months are not mentioned at all. That is on purpose. To omit usual things and use queer expressions, and to give an ambiguous meaning to straightforward words would not be to *Confucius* mind. In reality *Ch'un-ch iu* (Spring and Autumn) refers to the Summer also. That it is not mentioned is like the omission of days and months.

T ang, Yil, Hsia, Yin, and *Chou* are territorial names. *Yao* ascended the throne as marquis of *T'ang Shun* rose to power from the *Yil* territory. *Yil* came from *Hsia"* and *T'ang* from *Yin,* when they began their brilliant careers. *Wu Wang* relied on *Chou* to fight his battles. They all regarded the country, from which they had taken their origin, as their basis. Out of regard for their native land, which they never forgot, they used its name as their style, just as people have their surnames. The critics on the *Sliuking,* however, assert that the dynastic names of the ruling emperors, such as *T ang, Yil, Hsia, Yin,* and *Chou,* are expressive of their virtue and glory, and descriptive of their grandeur. *T'ang* means majesty, they say, *Yil* joy, *Hsia* greatness, *Yin* to flourish, and *Chou* to reach. *Yao's* majesty was such, that the

people had no adequate name for it, *Shun* was the joy and the bliss of the world, *Yil* got the heritage of the two emperors, and once more *C'h'un-ch'iu* II, 17, 8. *I. e.* the day of the sexagenary cycle, for the day of the month is mentioned. Two other commentaries to the *Ch'un-ch'iu,* less important than the *Tso-chuan. T'ang* was situated in *Pao-ting-fu (Chili).* In *Shawn. '* In *K'ai-feng-fu (Honan). Ch'cng T'ang,* the founder of the *Yin (Shang)* dynasty. A principality in *Honan.* The kingdom of *Chou* in *Shen&i.* established the majesty of the moral laws, so that the people had no adequate name for him. Under *Tang* of the *Yin* morality nourished, and the glory and virtue of *Wu Wang* of *Chou-* reached everywhere. The scholars have found very nice meanings, indeed, aud bestowed great praise on these five reigning houses, but they arc in opposition to the real truth, and have misconceived the primary idea. The houses of *T'ang, Yil, Hsia, Yin* and *Chou* bear their names just as the *Chin* and *Han* do theirs. The *Ch'in* rose from *Chin,* and the *Han* started from *Han-chung.* Therefore they still kept the names of *Ch'in* and *Han.* Similarly *Wang Mang* seized the supreme power as a marquis of *Hain-tu,3* and for this reason was called doomed *Hsin.* Had the *Ch'in* and the *Han* flourished anterior to the classical writings, the critics would surely have explained the words *Ch'in* and *Hun* as meaning morality and virtue.

When *Yao* was old and wished to yield the throne, the Chief of the Four Mountains recommended *Slntn. Yao* said, "1 will try him." The commentators of the *Shuking* maintain that this signifies, "I will use him, namely: — I will use him and make him emperor." To make him emperor, is to be understood.

The text goes on, "I will wive him, and then observe his behaviour with my two daughters." To observe means nothing more than that *Shun* is to show himself to the world, they say, it does not imply that *Yao* himself is going to observe him. Two such extraordinary men like *Yao* and *Shun,* who are regarded as sages, must have known one another at first sight. There was no need

for any trial or observation. The flashes of their genius meeting, they felt an unlimited confidence in each other.

We read further on:—" The four quarters of the empire were all submissive. Being sent to the great plains at the foot of the mountains, amid violent wind, thunder and rain, he did not go astray."" *7a W* (the great plains at the foot of the mountains) is the office of the three prime ministers, they say. Filling the post of The kingdom of *dim* in *Shensi.* In *Shensi.* Principality in *Nan-yang-fu (Honari).* The president of all the nobles of the empire.

Shaking Yao-tien, Pt. I, Bk. lll, 12 *(Legge* Vol. lll, Pt. I, p. 26). *Shuking Shun-tien,* Pt. II, Bk. I, 2 *(Legge* Vol. lll, Pt. I, p. 31). one minister, *Shun* had to act as registrar-general, the duties of the two other ministers were manifold, but in all he was equally successful like violent wind and powerful rain-showers. Now, inspite of their great ability sages do not always know each other, although they be sages in fact. *Shun* found it difficult to know the cunning, wherefore he employed *Kao Yao* who showed a great knowledge of men. Cunning people are hard to know, and sages are difficult to find out. *Yao's* genius was like *Shuns* knowledge; *Shun* knew cunning people, and *Yao* knew sages. When *Yao* had heard of *Shuns* virtue, and that he was recommended by the Chief of the Four Mountains, he knew that he was an extraordinary man, but he was not yet sure of his ability. Therefore he said, "I will try him," and he tried him in an office and gave him his two daughters in marriage to see, how he would behave as husband. He filled his posts irreproachably, nor did he deviate from the right path of matrimony. Then *Yao* again bade all the people go into the country and observe his sagehood. *Shun* braved storm and rain-showers, and did not go astray. Then *Yao* knew that he was a sage and entrusted him with the empire. If the text speaks of observing and trying, it means to observe and to try his ability.

The commentators regard this expression as figurative and by adding to and embellishing the text they distort everything, and do not preserve the true sense. Their misinterpretations quite spoil the meaning. Thus the wrong explanations are transmitted to posterity uninterruptedly, and fanciful comments obscure the truth ever since.

Intelligent persons wishing to understand the Canons do not go back to the original meanings, and even if they do, they still compare the old commentaries, and adopt the old explanations, which have been several times repeated, and look upon them as proofs. What has been handed down about the Canons cannot be relied upon, for the erroneous statements about the Five Canons arc very numerous. The facts and the texts of the *Shuking* and the *Ch'un-ch iu* are comparably plain and intelligible, therefore my remarks apply especially to them.

Minister of Crime under *Shun*. CHAPTER XXXVII.

Critical Remarks on Various Books *(An-shu).*

The-Confucianists look up to *Confucius* as the founder of their school, whereas the Mehists regard *Mi Ti* as their master. The Confucian doctrine has come down to us, that of *Mi Ti* has fallen into desuetude, because the Confucian principles can be put in use, while the Mehist system is very difficult to practise. How so?

The Mehists neglect the burials, but honour the ghosts. Their doctrine is abnormal, self-contradictory, and irreconcilable with truth, therefore it is hard to practise. Which are its anomalies?

Provided that ghosts are not the spirits of the departed, then they can have no knowledge of the honour shown them. Now the Mehists aver, that the ghosts are indeed the spirits of the dead. They treat the souls well, and neglect the corpses. Thus they are generous to the spirits and mean with reference to their bodies. Since generosity and meanness do not harmonize, and the externals and internals do not agree, the spirits would resent it, and send misfortunes down upon their votaries. Though then' might be ghosts, they would, at any rate, be animated by a deadly hatred. Human nature is such, that it likes

generosity, and detests meanness. The feelings of the spirits must be very much the same. According to *Me Tse's* precepts one would worship the ghosts, aud pray for happiness, but the happiness obtained thereby would be very scarce, and misfortune on misfortune would be the result. This is but one instance among a hundred, but the entire Mehist system is like that. The cause that it has lost its ground, and is not being handed down, is contained therein. *Me Ti*, the philosopher of universal love, a younger contemporary of *Confuciax*, 5th or 4th cent. B.c. Cf. *E. Faber, Lehre des Philosophen Miciiu*, Elberfeld 1877 (Extracts from his works).

The *Tso-chuan* of the *Ch'un-chiu* was recovered from the wall of the house of *Confucius*. Under the reign of the emperor *Hsiao Wu Ti*, Prince *Kung* of Lu demolished the school of *Confucius* for the purpose of building a palace. There he found thirty books of the *Chun-ch in*, which had been concealed. These were the *Tso-chuan. Kung Yang Kao, Ku Liang Ch'ih3* and *Hu Mu* all transmitted the *Ch nn-ch'iu*, representing different schools, but the commentary of *Tso Ch'iu Ming* alone was in time the nearest to *Confucius* and did embody the right views:

The *Liki* was composed in the school of *Confucius*. The Grand Annalist (the author of the *Shi-chi*) was a man of great talents in the *Han* time. Now the statements of *Tso Ch'iu Ming* are in accordance with these two books, whereas the writings of *Kung Yang Kao, Ku Liang Ch'ih* and *Hu Mu* differ very much. Besides these writers are too far remote from *Confucius*. It is much better to be near, than to be distant, and better to see, than to know by hearsay.

Liu Tse Cheng mocked at the *Tso Chuan*, whereas his servants, his wife, and his sons used to recite it. At *Kuang Wu lls* time *Ch en Yuan* and *Fan Shu* reported to the throne on the *Tso-chuan*, collecting all the facts and giving their opinions on the pros and cons. Then the fame of *Tso Ch'iu Ming* became established. *Fall Shu* soon after was dismissed for an offence. CH *en Yuan* and *Fan Shu* were the most talented men of

the empire. In their arguments on the merits of the *Tso Chuan* they display a remarkable vigour. *Chen Yuan* used to express himself very cautiously and *Fan Shu's* criticisms were silenced." Hence it became evident that *Tso Ch'iu Ming* gives us the truth. In the opinion of most Chinese critics the *('hun-ch in*, as we have it, has not been preserved, but was reconstructed from the *Tso-chuan* or from the other commentaries. This view is supported by what *Wang ('h'ung* says here. See on this question *Legge, Prolegomena to hi translation of the t'h'un-ch'iu*, p. 16 seq. Cf. above pp. 448 and 456. *Kung Yang* and *Ku Liang* are the surnames, *Kao* and *Ch'ih* the personal names. *Hu Mu's* commentary is not mentioned in the Catalogue of the *Han-shu*. To wit the *Liki* and the *Shi-cM. Liu Tse Clumg " -Liu Hsiang*, 80-9 B.c, was an admirer of the commentary of *Ku Liang*, whereas his son *Liu Ilsin* stood up for the *Tso-chuan*. 25-57 A.d. *Fan Slm* alias *Fan Sheng. Fan Shu* in his report to the throne had attacked the *Tso-chuan* on fourteen points.

To relate marvellous stories is not at all in the style of *Confucius*, who did not speak of strange things. The *Lii-shih-ch1m-chiu e. g.* belongs to this class of works. The *Kuo-yil* is the exoteric narrative of *Tso Ch iu Ming*. Because the text of the *Tso-chuan* Classic is rather concise, he still made extracts and edited the text of the *Kuo-yil* to corroborate the *Tso-chuan*, Thus the *Kuo-yil* of *Tso Ch'm Ming* is a book which the Literati of our time regard as genuine.

Kung Sun Lung wrote a treatise on the hard and white. He split words, dissected expressions, and troubled about equivocal terms. His investigations have no principles and are of no use for government. *Tsou Yen in Chi* published three works which are vague and diffuse; he gives very few proofs, but his words startle the reader. Men of great talents are very often led astray by their imagination and show a great lack of critical acumen. Their style is brilliant, but there is nothing in it. and their words are imposing, but their researches are conspicuous by the absence of sober judgment.

When *Shang Yang3* was minister of *Ch' in*, he developed the system of agriculture and fighting, and, when *Kuan Chung* held the same position in *Ch i*, he wrote the book on weight. He made the people wealthy, the State prosperous, the sovereign powerful, and the enemies weak, and adjusted rewards and punishments. His work is classed together with that of *Tsou Yen*, but the Grand Annalist has two different records about them. People are perplexed thereby, and at a loss, which view to take.

An important work on antique lore composed under the patronage of Prince *Lu Pu Wei* in the 3d cent. B.C. Works relating marvellous stories. Cf. my paper on the *Chinese Sophists, Journal of the China Branch of the K. As. Soc*, Shanghai 1809, p. 29 and appendix containing a translation of the remains of this philosopher. Cf. p. 25:5. *Wei Yang*, Prince of *Shang*, a great reformer of the civil and military administration of the *Chin* State, which he raised to great power. Died 338 B.c. One of the most celebrated statesmen of antiquity, who died in (45 K.c A speculative work which passes under the title of *Kuan Tse*. The one still in existence is perhaps a later forgery. *Sse Ma Ch'ien* extols *Kuan Chung* (Shi-chi chap. 62, p. 2v) and finds fault with *Slumg Yang (Shi-chi* chap. tiS, p. 9), although, in *Wang Ch'ung's* opinion, their deeds and their theories are very similar. It must be noted, however, that *Shang Yang's* criminal laws were very cruel. *Wang Ch'ung*, who is to a certain extent imbued with Taoist ideas, feels a natural aversion to all forms of government, and to legislation in particular. *Cliang Yi* was a contemporary of *Su Ch'in*. When the latter died, *Chang Yi* was certainly informed of it. Since he must have known all the details, his words ought to have served as basis to fix the thruth. However, the reports are not clear, there being two versions. *Chang Shang* of *Tung-hai* also wrote a biographyWas *Su Ch'in* an invention of *Chang Shang*, for how is it possible that there is such a discrepancy between the two versions?

In the Genealogical Tables of the Three Dynasties it is said that the Five Emperors and Three Rulers were all descendants of *Huang Ti*, and that from *Huang Ti* downward they were successively born without being again informed by the breath of heaven. In the special record of the *Yin* dynasty we read, however, that *Chien Ti*, the mother of *Hsieh5* while bathing in a river, met a black bird, which dropped an egg. She swallowed it, and subsequently gave birth to *Hsieh*.

In the special record of the *Chou* dynasty we find the notice that the mother of Lord *Chi, Chiang Yuan3* while going into the country, saw the footprints of a giant. When she stept into them, she became with child, and gave birth to Lord *Chi*.

Now we learn from the Genealogical Tables that *Hsieh* and Lord *Chi* were both descendants of *Huang Ti*, whereas we read in the records of the *Yin* and *Chou* dynasties that they were conceived from the sperm of the black bird and the giant. These two versions ought not to be transmitted simultaneously, yet the Great Annalist recorded them both indiscriminately. The consorts of emperors should not stroll into the country or bathe in a river. Now the one is said to have bathed in a river, and to have swallowed the egg of a black bird, and. the other went into the country, and there walked in the footprints of a giant. That is against all the laws of decorum and a mixing up of the distinctions between right and wrong.

A place in *Kiangm. Shi-chi* chap. 13. *Shi-chi* chap. 3. Second wife of the Emperor *K u.* The first ancestor of the *Yin* dynasty. *Shi-chi* chap. 3, p. 1. *Shi-chi* chap. 4, p. 1. First wife of the Emperor *Ku*.

» *Hon Chi* — "Lord of the Soil," the ancestor of the *Chou* dynasty.

The "New Words " is the work of *Lu Chia*, which was appreciated very much hy *Tung Chung Shu*. It deals with sovereigns and subjects, good and bad government, the words are worth remembering, the facts related, excellent, and show a great amount of knowledge. They may supplement the Classics; although there is not much to be added to the words of the old sages, at all events there is nothing amiss with *Lu Chia's* words. The utterances of *Tung Chung Shu*, on the other hand, about the rain sacrifices responding to heaven and the earthen dragon attracting the rain are very obscure.

Droughts will happen in consequence of the rain sacrifices (being in disorder), but have nothing to do with the state sacrifices of the *Hsia* dynasty. Was the marquis of *Chin* responsible, or was his administration defective, so that the *Yang* and the *Yin* were not in harmony? *Chin* had dropped the state sacrifices of the *IMa*. When the marquis of *Chin* was laid up with sickness, he took the advice of *Tse Chan* of *Ching* and instituted the *Hsia* sacrifices, whereupon he recovered from his disease. Had in fact the rain sacrifices not been in order, or the dragon neglected, the same misfortune would have befallen *Cliin* again. Provided the drought was attracted by the administration, the latter should have been reorganised, but what would be the use of making provisions for the rain sacrifices or the dragon, if the administration was defective?

Kung Yang in his commentary on the *Ch'un-ch iu* says that during the time of extraordinary heat, it suffices to reform the government, when the *Yin* and the *Yang* fluids mix, and dryness and moisture unite; such being the law of nature. Wherefore must the rain sacrifices still be prepared then, and the dragons be put up? Do the spirits delight in these offerings? If, when the rain comes, the broiling heat did not relax, nor the disastrous drought cease, where would be the effect of the changes and reforms? Moreover heat and cold are the same as dryness and moisture; all are the results of government, and man is responsible for them. It is difficult therefore to see the reason, why in time of drought people pray for happiness, but not in cold or hot weather. In case *Hrin-yii*. The work still exists.

Lu Chia lived in the 2nd cent. B.c. at the beginning of the *Han* dynasty. Twice he was sent as envoy to the southern *Yiieh*. Cf. I, p. 304. An author of the 2nd cent.

B.c. He wrote the *Chun-chist-fan-lu,* the "Rich Dew of the Spring and Autumn," which has come down to us. Cf. p. 206. » Cf. p. 214.

Lud-Heng. 30 that there is a retribution, we ought to have recourse to the rain sacrifices and to the dragon for heat and cold as well. Men of superior intellect and great knowledge, however, do not believe in either of these theories.

Tung Chung Shu does not call himself a scholar in his books, probably thinking that he surpassed all the others. Among the prolific, writers of the *Hun* time *Sse Ma Ch urn* and *Yang Tse Yiin* are the *Yellow River* and the *Han,* all the rest like the *Ching* and *Wei* rivers. Yet *SseMaCh'ien* gives us too little of his own judgment, *Yang Tse Yiin* does not speak on common topics, and *Tung Chung Shu's* discussions on the Taoist doctrines are very strange. These are the three most famous men of the north.

The *Chan-shu* states that *Tung Chung Shu* disturbed their books, which means the sayings of *Confucius.* The readers either hold that "to disturb our books" means that he throws the works of *Confucius* into disorder, or they suppose that "*luan*" is equivalent to "adjust," and that he adjusts the writings of *Confucius.* In both cases it is the same word "*luan*" but between order and disorder there is a great distance. Yet the readers do not equally apply their minds, nor thoroughly study the question, hence their wrong statements. To say that *Tung Chung Shu* carried disorder into the writings of *Confucius,* would imply an extraordinary talent, and to say that he adjusted these writings, would likewise imply a wonderful knowledge. Nobody ever said of *Sse Ma Chien* or *Yang Tse Yun* that they belonged to the school of the Sage or not, or that they disturbed or adjusted the works of *Confucius.* Most people now-adays do not think enough and, when treating a problem, lose sight of the principal facts. Therefore we have these two doubtful views, between which the scholars are vacillating.

The work of *Tung Chung Shu* is not antagonistic to the Confucian school, neither does it equal the writing of *Con-*

fucius. Therefore the statement that it invalidates those writings is preposterous. On the other hand the writings of *Confucius* are not in confusion, consequently the assertion that it brings these writings into good order is wrong likewise.

The philosopher *Yang Hsiung.* Cf. p. 124. The largest affluent of the *Yangtse.* Both tributaries of the Yellow River in *Kan-vu* and *Shensi,* which joined together, fall into the *Huang Ho* near its elbow in *Shensi. Vid.* p. 319. *Confucius* said, "When the music-master *Chih* began and then came the finish (luan) of the *Kuan-chil,* how magnificent it was and how it filled the ears!"

The finish (luan) in our case refers to the sayings of *Confucius. Confucius* lived under the *Chon* and laid the foundation (of the Confucian doctrine); *Tung Chung Shu* under the *Han* finished it, in so far as it was not yet complete, and *Sse Ma Ch'ien* supplemented it here and there. That is the idea. In the collections of irregular verse and dithyrambs every song has a refrain (luan), which amounts to the same. Since it was *Tung Chung Shu* who gave the last touch to the *Analects* of *Confucius,* we should not be surprised that his remarks on the offering of the rain sacrifice and the use of dragons have some meaning.

Yen Yuan said, "What man is *Shun,* and who am I?"— Among the Five Emperors and Three Rulers *Shun* was his only ideal. He knew that he was pursuing the same goal. The ideals of the wise and virtuous and the aims of the silent scholar are in fact identical.

What *Tung Chung Shu* says about morals, virtue, and government deserves the highest praise, but as regards researches into every day life and discussions of the most common errors, *Huan Chiln Slum* stands unrivalled. *Tung Chung Shu's* writings may be equalled, but it would be very difficult to challenge *Huan Chiln Shan.*

A Bayardo has his special features distinguishing him from other horses, or is a noble steed with a peculiar gait. There may be horses capable of running a thousand li, they will never be called Bayardos, because the colour of their

hair differs from that of Bayardo. There may be men whose writings could be compared with those of *Tung Chung Shu,* or whose essays would rank close ofter those of *Huan Chiln Shan,* yet they would not be like 1 *Analects* VIII, 15. 'fl

The music-master of *Lu.* The first Ode of the *Shiking.* Cf. the great number of such collections enumerated in the Catalogue of the *Han-shu,* chap. 30.

Quotation from *Mencius* III, Pt. 1,1 (*Legge* Vol. II, p. 110). *Huan Chiin Shan = Huan Tan,* a great scholar of the 1st cent. B.c. and A.d. People admired his large library. He incurred the displeasure of *Kuang Wu Ti,* whom he rebuked for his belief in books of fate, and was sentenced to banishment. the two scholars, their names would always be different. A horse might learn to make a thousand li, it would not become a Bayardo or a Bucephalus thereby, and a man might aspire to sagehood and knowledge, he would not become a *Confucius* or a *Mi Ti* for the following reason:

It is very difficult to ecp1al *Huan Chun Shan's* writings. When two blades cut one another, we see, which is sharp and which blunt, and, when two treatises are compared together, one finds out, which of the two is right and which wrong. This is the case of the " Four Difficulties " by' *Han Fei Tse,* the treatise on " Salt and Iron by *Huan K uan,* and the " New Reflections " by *Huan Chiin Shan.*

The statements of the people are often doubtful and untrue, yet some mistaken critics regard them as true, which leads to great dilemmas. If a judge deciding a case has his doubts about it, so that though giving his judgment he would hesitate to inflict a punishment, truth and untruth would not be determined, and right and wrong not established. Then people would be entitled to say that the talents, of the judge were not sufficient for his post. If in ventilating a question one does not do it thoroughly, merely noting two doubtful opinions and transmitting them both, one does not do much to settle the question. Would it not be better then to break through the confusion and cut the Gordian knot, for words must be intelligible, and expressions convey a meaning? *Confucius* wrote the *Chun-ch'iu* in such a way that he recommended the slightest good thing and blamed the smallest evil. Whenever there was anything praiseworthy, his words served to set forth its excellence, and whenever there was anything open to blame, he pointed out its badness with a view to stigmatise the action. The "New Reflections" fall in with the *Ch'un-ch tu* in this respect. But the public prizes antiquity, and does not think much of our own times. They fancy that the modern literature falls short of the old writings. However, ancient and modern times are the same. There are men of great and of small talents, and there is truth and falsehood. If irrespective of the intrinsic value they only esteem what is old, this would imply that the ancients excelled our moderns. Yet men like *Tsou Po Ch i* of *Tung* Four chapters of *Hun Fei Tse's* work, forming chap. 15 and 16, Nos. 36-39. *Yen-t'ieh-lun,* a treatise on questions of national economy. *Huan K'nan,* also called *Chen Shan Tse,* lived in the 1st cent. B.C. *Hsin-lun. fan, Yuan T'ai Po* and *Yuan Wbi Shu* of *Lin-hum,1 Wu Chun Kao* and *Chou Ch ang Sheng* of *K'uei-chi,*-though they never attained the dignity of state-ministers, were all men of stupendous erudition and abilities and the most elegant and dashing knights of the pen.

The *Yuan-sse* of *Tsou Po Ch'i,* the *Yichang-chil* of *Yuan T'ai Po,* the *Hsienming* of *Yuan Wen Shu,* the *Yileh-go* of *Wu Chun Kao,* and the *Tung-li* of *Chou Ch ang Sheng* could not be surpassed by *Liu Tse Cheng* or *Yang Tse Yiln.* Men of genius may be more or less gifted, but there are no ancients or moderns; their works may be right or wrong, but there are no old or new ones. Although no special works have been written by men like *Ch'en Tse Hui* of *Kuang-ling, Yen Fang, Pan* Am, at present clerk of a board, the officer of the censorate, *Yang Chung,* and *Chuan Yi,* their verses and their memorials are written in the most fascinating and brilliant style. Their poetry resembles that of *Ch'il Yuan* and *Chia,* their memorials those of *T'ang*

Lin and *Km Yung.* Placed side by side, the beauty of their compositions proved to be the same. At present they are not yet illustrious, but after a hundred generations they will be on a par with *Liu Tse Cheng* and *Yang Tse Yiin. Li Sse* freely culled from the works of *Han Fei Tse,* and *Hou P'u Tse* did much to divulge the *Tai-hsiktn-ching* of *Yang Tse Yiln. Han Fei Tse* and *Li Sse* belonged to the same school, and *Yang Tse Yiln* and *Hou P'u Tse* lived at the same court. They had an eye for what was remarkable and useful, and were not intluenced in their opinions and judgments by considerations of time. Searching truth and seeking whatever was good, they made it their principle not to look too far for it, and not to despise those with whom A region in *Anhui,* A city in *Chekiang.* Nothing is known of these authors or their writings. The cyclopedias do not even mention their names. A place in *Kiangsu.* The historian *fan Ku,* author of the *Honshu* "History of the Former *Han* Dynasty," who died 92 A.d. Who wrote the famous poem *Lisao* cf. p. 113.

'*Chia* J'ti.

A« Yung lived in the 1st cent. B.c. As censor he remonstrated against the abuses of the court, and presented over forty memorials upon divine portents. *Liu Txe Cheng* = *Liu Hsiung,* NO-9 B.c. , is a celebrated writer of the *Han* time, who did much for the preservation of ancient literature. Besides he wrote works on government and poetry. *Wang Chung's* prediction has not proved true. The authors of his time, whom he praises so much, are all forgotten, *Pan Ku* alone excepted. At the court of the Emperor *Cheng Ti* 32-7 B.c. they were working shoulder to shoulder. They had a great partiality for everything uncommon, and quite uncommon was the fame which they won thereby. *Yang Tse Ytin* revised the *Li-sao.* He could not completely change a whole chapter, but whenever he found anything wrong, he altered it. Though it be impossible to read all the thirteen thousand chapters contained in the list of the Six Departments of Literature, one may know at least their purport and take up for dis-

cussion some of those passages which give no proper sense. In the Catalogue of Literature, forming chapter 30 of the *Hon-shu, Liu HMn* divided the tlen existing body of literature under 7 heads: Classics, works on the six arts, philosophy, poetry, military science, divination, and medicine. Owing to the decline of the healing art under the *Han* dynasty, the last division was dropped, and no titles of medical books are given. There remained but the six divisions, mentioned in the text. Under these divisions were comprised 38 subdivisions with 596 authors, whose names and works are given in the Catalogue. Their writings contain 13,209 chapters or books. CHAPTER XXXVIII.

The Equality of the Ages *(Ch'i-shih).*

There is a saying that in ancient times people were tall, good-looking, and strong, and lived to become about a hundred years old, whereas in modern times they are short, ugly, cut off in their prime, and short-lived. The following cause is given:—In ancient times the harmonious fluid was in abundance. People married at the proper time. At their birth they received this good fluid, and therefore suffered no injuries afterwards. Their hones and joints being strong and solid, they grew tall, and reached a high age, and their outward appearance was beautiful. In later generations all this was reversed, therefore they were small, died young, and looked nasty.

This statement is preposterous. In olden days the rulers were sages, and so they are in modern times. The virtue of the sages then and now does not differ, therefore their government in ancient and modern times cannot be different. The Heaven of antiquity is the Heaven of later ages. Heaven does not change, and its fluid has not been altered. The people of former ages are the same as those of modern times. They all are filled with the original fluid. This fluid is genuine and harmonious now as well as in days of yore, why then should their bodies, which are made of it, not be the same? Being imbued with the same fluid, they have the same nature, and their nature being the same, their physical frames must be alike. Their physical frames being alike, their outward appearance must be similar, and this being the case, their length of life cannot but be equal. One Heaven and one Earth conjointly produce all beings. When they are created, they all receive the same fluid. Its scarcity and abundance varies in all ages equally. Emperors and kings reign over successive generations, and all the different ages have the same principles. People marry at the same time and with similar ceremonies, for although it has been recorded that men married at the age of thirty, and women at that of twenty, and though there has been such a rule for marriages, it is not certain that it really has been observed. We can infer this from the fact that it is not observed now either. The rules for ceremonies and music have been preserved up to our days, but are the people of to-day willing to comply with them? Since they do not like to practise them, people of old have not done so either. From the people of to-day we learn to know the people of old.

Creatures are creatures. Man can live up to one hundred years, but very often we see b,oys who only reach the age of ten years. The lives of the creatures living on earth and their transformations at the utmost last one hundred years. When they approach this period, they die, which can always be observed. Between all these creatures and those who do not become older them ten years is no fundamental difference. If people of ancient and modern times do not differ, it must be possible to predetermine the length of their lives within the limit of one hundred years by means of divination.

In the height of the domestic animals, the size of the various kinds of grain, the reptiles, plants, trees, metals, stones, pearls, and jewels as well as in the creeping, wriggling, crawling, and panting of the various animals there is no difference, which means that their shape is identical. The water and the fire in olden days are the present water and fire. Now, the fluid changes into water or fire. Provided that there be a difference in the fluids, was the water pel-

lucid, and the fire hot formerly, and is now the water opaque, and the fire, cold?

Man grows six to seven feet high, measures three to four spans in circumference, his face has five colours, and his greatest age is one hundred years. During thousands and thousands of generations there is no change. Let us suppose that in ancient times men were tall, good-looking, strong, and long-lived, and that in later generations all this was reversed. Then, when Heaven and Earth were first established, and the first men were created, could they be as tall as the Prince of *Fang-feng,* as handsome as This seems to have been the rule under the *Chou* dynasty. Cf. *Liki,* Alette' Sect. II *(Lsggs, Sacred Books* Vol. XXVII, p. 478).

The complexion is yellowish, the lips are red, the teeth white, the hair black, and the voins are bluish. Cf. p. 486. Prince *Chao* of *Sung* and as long-lived as *Peng Tsu?* And after thousand generations hence, will they be as small as flower-seeds, as ill-favoured as *Mu Mu,* and as short-lived as an ephemeral fly?

Under the reign of *Wang Mang* there was a giant ten feet high, called *Pa Chu,* and during the *Chien-wu* period *Chang Chung Shili* in *Ying-ch'uan* measured ten feet, two inches, and *Chang T ang* over eight feet, whereas his father was not quite five feet high. They all belong to the present generation, and were either tall or small. The assertion of the Literati is wrong therefore and a mistake.

They say that in times of yore people were employed, as befitted them. Hunchbacks were used as gate-keepers, and dwarfs as actors. But, if all were tall and good-looking, where did the hunchbacks and the dwarfs come from?

It is further alleged that the natures of the people of the past were honest and easily reformed, whereas the culture of later ages is superficial, so that they are difficult to be governed. Thus the *Yiking* says that in the remote past, cords were knotted as a means of governing the people, which knots in later ages were replaced by books. First knots were used, because reforms were

easy, the books afterwards prove the difficulty of government. Prior to *Fu Hsi,* the characters of the people were of the plainest kind:—They lay down self-satisfied, and sat up perfectly pleased. They congregated, and flocked together, and knew their mothers, but not their fathers." At *Fu Hsi's* time people had attained such a degree of refinement, that the shrewd attempted to deceive the simple-minded, the courageous would frighten the timid, the strong insult the weak, and the many oppress the few. Therefore *Fu Hsi* invented the eight diagrams for the purpose of restraining them. At the *Chou* epoch, the state of the people had A contemporary of *Confucius,* famous for his beauty (cf. *Analects* VI, 14), but of a perverse character. He committed incest with his half-sister *Kan Tse,* the wife of Duke *Ling* of *Wei.* The Chinese Methusaleh. The fourth wife of *Huang Ti,* an intelligent, but very ill-favoured woman. 4 9-23 A.d. 25-56 A.d. A circuit in *Anhui. Yiking,* CM-t'se II *(Legge'x* translation p. 385). The most ancient mythical emperor. Does that mean that the pre-historic Chinese lived in a state of matriarchate or in polyandry like the Tibetans? We find the same notice in *Chuang Tse* chap.20, p. 22 v. become very degenerate, and it was difficult to raise the eight diagrams to their former importance. Therefore King *Win* increased their number to sixty-four. The changes were the principill thing, and the people were not allowed to flag. When, during the *Chou* epoch, they had been down for a long while, *Confucius* wrote the "Spring and Autumn," extolling the smallest good, and criticizing the slightest wrong. He also said, *"Chou* had the advantage of viewing the two past dynasties. How complete and elegant are its regulations. I follow *Chou."*2 *Confucius* knowing that the age was steeped in sin, ill-bred, and hard to govern, made the strictest rules, and took the minutest preventive measures to repress the disrespectful, and everything was done in the way of restrictions.

This is absurd. Of old, people were imbued with the Five Virtues, and later generations were so likewise. They all had the principle of the Five Virtues in their hearts, and at birth were endowed with the same fluid. Why shall the natures of the former have been plain and honest, and the latter unmannerly'.' The opponents have noted that in olden times people drank blood, and ate herbs, as they had no grain for food. In later ages they dug up the earth for wells, tilled the ground, and sowed grain. They drank from the wells, and ate grain, which they had prepared with water and fire. They also note that in remote antiquity people were living high up in caverns, and wrapt themselves in skins of wild beasts and birds. Later generations changed the caverns into houses and palaces, and bedecked themselves with cloth and silk fabrics. It is for this reason that they regard the natures of the former as plain and honest, and the later as ill-bred. The tools and the methods have undergone a change, but nature and its manifestations have continued the same. In spite of that, they speak of plainness of nature and the poorness of culture.

In every age prosperity alternates with decay, and, when the latter has gone on for a long time, it begets vices. That is what happens with raiment and food used by man. When a garment has just been made, it is fresh and intact, and food just cooked is clean and smells good. After a while, the garment becomes worn out, and after some days, the food begins to smell bad. The laws by which nature and culture were governed in the past and at the present, are the same. There is nature, and there is culture, sometimes there is prosperity, and sometimes decay. So it has been of yore, not only now. How shall we prove that?
The *Chou* dynasty.
Analects 111, 14.
It has been put on record that the kings of the house of *Hsia* taught faithfulness. The sovereign teaching faithfulness, good men were faithful, but, when the decline set in, common people became rude. To combat rudeness nothing is better than politeness. Therefore the

kings of the *Yin* dynasty-taught politeness. The sovereign inculcating politeness, good men were polite, but when the decline began, common people became rogues. To repress roguishness nothing is better than education. Therefore the kings of *Chcrn* taught science. The sovereign teaching science, good men were scholarly, but then came the decline, and common people became narrow-minded. The best antidote against narrow-mindedness is faithfulness, therefore the rulers succeeding the *Chou* dynasty ought to have recourse to faithfulness. The reforms of *Yil* continued by the *Hsia* dynasty, were labouring under narrow-mindedness, therefore it inculcated faithfulness. Since *Yii* based his reforms on science, roguishness must have been the defect of the people under his predecessors. Our contemporaries viewing the narrowmindedness of our present culture, despise and condemn it, and therefore they say that in old times the natures of people were plain and honest, whereas the culture of later ages is narrowminded. In the same manner, when the members of one family are not zealous, people will say that the members of other families are diligent and honest.

It has been asserted that the ancients set high store in righteousness, and slighted their bodies. When an event happened that appealed to their sense of loyalty and justice, so that they felt it their duty to suffer death, they would jump into boiling water, or rush into the points of swords, and die without lament. Such was the devotion of *Hung Yen5* and the honesty of *Pu Chan* of *Chen* who acted like this. Similar instances have been recorded in books. The cases of voluntary deaths, and self-sacrifices are very numerous, and not scarce. The people now-a-days, they believe, are struggling for gain only, and leading a wild life. They have discarded justice, and are not scrupulous as to the means 2205-1766 B.c.
» 1766-1122 B.c.
» 1122-249 B.c.
People like to contrast, even though there be little difference between the things thus contrasted.

A faithful minister of Duke / of *Wei.* Cf. p. 496. When in 546 B.c. *Chiang,* Duke of *Ch'i,* was murdered, *Pu Chan* drove to his palace and on hearing the affray, died of fright. they employ in obtaining their ends. They do not restrain one another by righteousness, or vie in doing good. The disregard of justice they do not consider a source of danger, nor are they afraid of the consequences of their wrong doing.

This is nonsense. The heroes of ancient times are the heroes of the present age. Tbeir hearts are equally sensible to benevolence and justice, and in case of any emergency they will be roused. In the past, there have been unprincipled characters, and at present there are persons with the keenest sense of honour. Goodness and badness are mixed, why should one age be devoid of either? The story-tellers like to extol the past, and disparage the present time. They make much of what they know by hearsay, and despise what they see with their own eyes. The disputants will discourse on what is long ago, and the literati write on what is far away. The curious things near at hand, the speakers do not mention, and the extraordinary events of our own time are not committed to writing.

When during a famine starved people were going to eat the elder brother of *Tse Ming,* a young man of *Lang-geh.* he bound and prostrated himself, and asked to be eaten in lieu of his brother. The hungry people so much admired his generosity, that they set them both free, and did not eat them. After the elder brother had died, he took his orphan son, and brought him up, and loved him as much as his own son. At a time of scarcity, when no grain was left, so that both boys could not be kept alive, he killed his own son by starvation, and preserved the life of the son of his elder brother. *Hsii Shu* of *Lin-hum* also brought up the orphan son of his elder brother, and at a time of dearth allowed his own son to die of hunger in order to keep his brother's son alive. His magnanimity was like that of *Tse Ming.*

The father of *Ming Chang* in *Kuei-chi? Ying,* was judicial secretary of the prefecture. When the general of the prefecture had beaten an innocent man to death, and the case came up for revision, *Ying* took the guilt upon himself, offered himself for punishment, and at last suffered death for the general. *Ming Chang* later on became civil secretary of a prefecture. He took part in a campaign against insurgents, but the soldiers were routed, and shot by the rebels. Thereupon he took the place of the commander, which he did not leave, until he was killed. Is there any difference from A place in *Shantung.* A circuit in *Anhui* province.

A city in *Chckiang.*

the faithfulness of *Hung Yen* or the righteousness of *Pu Chan* of *Ch'in?* But would the writers of our own time deign to use these cases as examples? For illustrations in proof of their views they go up to *Yu* and the *Hsia* period, and down as far as the *Yin* and *Chou* dynasties. The exploits and remarkable feats of the *Chin* and *Han* epoch are already too modern for them, and fancy our own time, which comes after all the other ages, and what the narrators have seen with their own eyes! The painters like to paint men of ancient dynasties, and reject heroes of the *Ch in* and *Han* epoch, however wonderful their deeds may have been. The scholars of the present age prize antiquity, and scorn the present. They value the snow-goose and disdain the fowl, because the snow-goose is from afar, and the fowl is near.

Provided that there were a moralist now more profound than either *Confucius* or *Mi Ti,* yet his name would not rank as high as theirs, and, if in his conduct he should surpass even *Tseng Tse* and *Yen Hiii,* he would not be as famous as they. Why? Because the masses think nothing of what they see, but esteem what they know only by hearsay. Should there be a man now, just and generous to the highest degree, and should an inquiry into his actions prove that he is not outvied by anybody in the past, would the writers mention him in their works, showing that they give him credit for what he has done? Narrating marvellous stories, they would not wrong the ancients by taking their subjects from modern times, but would those who are fond of these stories put aside those books on antique lore and things far off, and take an interest in modern writings? *Yang TseYiln* wrote the *T'ai-hsilan,* and composed the *Fagen,* but *Chang Po Sung* did not deign to cast a look upon these books. As he was living with *Yang Tse Yun* shoulder to shoulder, he had a poor opinion of what he said. Had *Yang Tse Yun* lived prior to him, *Chang Pu Sung* would have looked upon him as a gold safe.

One hears people say that the sages of old possessed most brilliant qualities, and accomplished wonderful works. Hence *Confucius* said, "Great indeed was *Yao* as a sovereign! How majestic was he! It is only Heaven that is grand, and only *Yao* corresponded to it. How vast was his virtue! The people could find no name for it. How majestic was he in the works which he accomplished! How glorious in the elegant regulations which he These two works of the philosopher *Yang Tse Yun* have come down to us. The more celebrated of the two is the *Fa-gen,* the *T'ai-hsiian,-soi-disanl* an elucidation of the *Yikmg,* is very obscure.

instituted!" *Shun* followed *Yao,* and did not impair his grand institutions, and *Yil* succeeded *Shun,* and did not mar his great works. Subsequently we come to *T'ang.* He rose in arms, and defeated *Ohieh,* and *Wu Wang* took the battle-axe, and punished CAom. Nothing is said about majesty or glory, we hear only of f1ghting and defeating. The qualities of these princes were bad, therefore they appealed to arms. They waged war, and neglected the arts of peace. That explains why they could not get along together. When the *Chin* and *Han* period arrived, swords were drawn, and conclusions tried everywhere. Thus *Chin* conquered the empire. When *Ch in* was in possession of it, no felicitous omen appeared as the phoenix *e. g.,* which comes, when all the States are at peace. Does that not show their moral impotence and the poorness of their achievements?

This statement is unreasonable. A sage is born by a fusion of the fluids of Heaven and Earth: he does great things, when he takes the reins of government. But this fusion of the fluids does not only take place in the past and formerly in few instances; why then should a sage alone be good? The masses are inclined to cherish the past, and decry the present, to think nothing of what they behold, and very much of what they have heard. Besides, they see that in the Classics and other works the excellence of sages and wise men is painted in the most vivid colours, and that *Confucius* extols the works of *Yao* and *Shun* still more. Then they have been told that *Yao* and *Yil* abdicated, and declined the throne, whereas *T'ang* and *Wu* fought for it, and snatched it from their predecessors. Consequently they think that in olden times the sages were better than now, and that their works, and their civilizing influence was greater than in later times. The Classics contain highly coloured reports, and extravagant and exaggerated stories are current among the people. Those who study the Classics and read books all know this.

Confucius said, "*Chou's* wickedness was not so very great. Therefore the superior man hates to consort with base persons, for the faults of the whole world are laid to their charge." People always will contrast *Chieh* and *Chou* with *Yao* and *Shun.* When they have any praise to bestow, they give is to *Yao* and *Shun, Analect* VIII, 19. When *Chou* was defeated, he burned himself on the "Deer Terrace." Afterwards *Wu Wanj* shot three arrows at the corpse, struck at it with his sword, and with his battle-axe severed the head from the body. Cf. *Shi-chi* chap. 4, p. 11. *Analects* XIX, 20. and, when they speak of any wickedness, they impute it to *Chou* and *Chieh.* Since *Confucius* says that the wickedness of *Chou* was not so very great, we conclude that the virtue of *Yao* and *Shun* was not so extraordinary either. The resignation of *Yao* and *Shun* and the overthrow of the preceding dynasties by *T'ang* and *Wu* were predetermined by the fate of Heaven. It could not be achieved by goodness or badness, or be brought about by human actions. If *T ang* and *Wu* had lived in the time of *Yao* and *Shun*, they would also have abdicated the throne instead of defeating their predecessors, and had *Yao* and *Shun* lived in the *Yin* and *Chou* dynasties, they would likewise have overthrown their opponents, and not have declined the throne. What has really been fate, is by people thoughtlessly described as goodness or wickedness. At the period, when according to the Classics all the States were living in harmony, there was also *Tan Chu*, and when the phoenix made its appearance, there were at the same time the *Yu Miao*, against whom every one had to take up arms and fight continually. How did goodness and wickedness or great and small virtue come in?

They say that the wickedness of *Chieh* and *Chou* was worse than that of doomed *Ch'in*, but, as a matter of fact, we must admit that as for wickedness doomed *Ch'in* was ahead of *Chieh* and *Chou*. There is the same contrast between the excellence of the *Han* and the depravity of the *Ch'in* dynasty as between *Yao* and *Shun* on the one, and *Chieh* and *Chou* on the other side. Doomed *Ch'in* and *Han* belong both to the later generations. Since the wickedness of doomed *Ch'in* is worse than that of *Chieh* and *Chou*, we may infer that in virtue the great *Han* are not outrivalled by *Yao* and *Shun*. *Yao* consolidated the various States, but his work did not last. The phoenix which appeared under the reign of *Shun* was five times attracted by *Hsikm* 7V. Under the reign of *Ming Ti* lucky omens and portents were seen in great numbers. Omens appear, because there is high virtue. When the omens are equal, the achievements must be on a level too. Should *Hsikm Ti* and *Hsiao Ming Ti* be inferior and not come up to *Yao* and *Shun*, how could they evoke the omens of *Yao* and *Shun?* The degenerate son of virtuous *Yao*. Aboriginal tribes, against which *Shun* had to fight. *Vid.* p. 494.

The hatred of the scholars of the *Han* time towards *Chin Shih Huang Ti* was still fresher and therefore more intense than their aversion to *t hish* and *Chou*. Cf. p. 359. Cf. p. 372.

Under *Kuang Wu Ti* dragons rose, and phoenixes came forth. If, when he got the empire, things left in the street were picked up, did he not equal *T'ang* of the *Yin* and *Wu* of the *Chou* dynasty at least?

People say that *Ching* and *K'ang* of *Chou* did not impair the imposing works of *Win Wang*, and that *Shun* in his glory did not mar the brilliant achievements of *Yao*. Our present sage and enlightened sovereign is continuing the blessings and the prosperity of the reigns of *Kuang Wu Ti* and *Hsiao Ming Ti*, without the slightest symptom of a decline. Why should he not rank with *Shun* and *Yil* in remote antiquity, and be on a par with *Ching* and *K'ang* later on? It is because the Five Emperors and the Three Rulers lived previous to the classical writings, that the chronicles of the *Flan* time look up to them, and that the writers imagine that in ancient times there were sages and excellent men, who accomplished great works, whereas later generations have declined, and that their culture is low.

Cf. p. 3(i5. The Emperor *Ch'eng* reigned from 1115 to 1078, *Hang* from 1078 to 1052. The Emperor *Chang Ti*, 76 89 A.d., who succeeded *Ming Ti*. Under his reign the *Lun-hiing* seems to have been written. *Vid.* p. 372 Note 3. The reigns of these three first sovereigns of the later *Han* dynasty were prosperous indeed. CHAPTER XXXIX.
Exaggerations (*Yu-tseng*).
The Records say that Sages toil and trouble for the world, devoting to it all their thoughts and energies, that this harasses their spirits, and affects their bodies. Consequently *Yao* is reported to have been like shrivelled flesh, and *Shun* like dried food, whereas *Chieh* and *Chou* had an *embonpoint* over a foot thick. One may well say that the bodies of Sages working hard for the world, and straining their minfls for mankind, are weakened, and that they do not become stout or fat, but to say that *Yao* and *Shun* were like dried flesh or food, and that the *embonpoint* of *Chieh* and *Chou* measured over a foot is exaggerating.

Duke *Huan* of *Chi* said:—" Before I had got hold of *Kuan Chung*, I had the greatest difficulties, after I had got him, everything was easy." Duke *Huan* did not equal *Yao* and *Shun*, nor was *Kuan Chung* on a par with *Yu* and *Hsieh*. If Duke *Huan* found things easy, how could they have been difficult to *Yao* and *Shun?* From the fact that Duke *Huan*, having obtained the assistance of *Kuan Chung*, went on easily, we may infer that *Yao* and *Shun* after having: secured the services of *Yu* and *Hsieh* cannot have been in difficulties. A man at ease has not many sorrows. Without sorrows he has no troubles, and if he is not troubled, his body does not wither. *Shun* found perfect peace brought about by *Yao*, both carried on the virtues of the preceding generation and continued the pacification of the border tribes. *Yao* had still some trouble, but *Shun* could live at ease and unmolested. The *Book of History* says that the Supreme Ruler gave repose, which refers to *Shun*, for *Shun* found peace everywhere, he continued the government, appointed intelligent officers, employed able men, and enjoyed a dignified repose, while the Empire was well administrated. Therefore *Con Yu* and *Hsieh* were both ministers of *Yao* and *Shun*. *Yii* became emperor afterwards.

« *Shutting* Part V, Bk. XIV, 5 *(Legge, Classics* Vol. Ill, Pt. U, p. 455). The passage has been variously explained.

Lun-Heng. 31 *fucius* exclaims:—"Grand were *Shun* and *Yil* who, possessing the Empire, did not much care for it." In spite of this *Shun* is said to have been dried up like preserved meat, as though he had been lacking in virtue, and had taken over a state in decay like *Confucius*, who restlessly wandered about seeking employment, having no place to rest in, no way to walk, halting and tumbling down on the roads, his bones protruding.

Chou passed the whole night drinking. Sediments lay about in mounds, and there was a lake of wine. *Chou* was swimming in wine, stopping neither by day nor by night. The result must have been sickness. Being sick, he could not enjoy eating and drinking, and if he did not enjoy eating and drinking, his fatness could not attain one foot in thickness.

The *Book of Historg* remarks that debauchery was what they liked, and that they could not reach a great age. Prince *Wu Chi* of *Wei* passed his nights feasting, but these excesses proved such a poison to him, that he died. If *Chou* did not die, his extravagance ought at least to have shattered his system. *Chieh* and *Chou* doing the same, ought to have contracted the same sickness. To say that their *embonpoint* was over a foot thick is not. only an exaggeration, but an untruth.

Of *Chou* there is further a record that his strength was such, that he could twist iron, and straighten out a hook, pull out a beam, and replace it by a pillar. This is meant to be illustrative of his great strength. Men like *Fei Lien* and *0 Lai* were much liked by him, and stood high in his favour, which is tantamount to saying that he was a sovereign very fond of cunning and strength, and attracted people possessing those qualities.

Now there are those who say that, when *Wu Wang* defeated *Chou,* the blades of his weapons were not stained with blood. When a man with such strength, that he could twist iron and *Analects* VIII, 18.

The last emperors of the *Hsia* dynasty. Quoted from the *Shaking* Part V, Bk. XV, 7 *(Legge, Classics* Vol. III, Pt. II, p. 408). Died 244 B.c. *Wu Chi* was a famous general of the *Wei* State, who inflicted some crushing defeats upon the armies of *Chin*. For some time he succeeded in checking the encroachments of *Chin*. It was not, until his later years, that he retired from public life, and gave himself up to debauchery. The *Shi-chi* chap. 8, p. 10 likewise ascribes superhuman forces and extraordinary natural endowments to the last ruler of the *Hsia* dynasty. *Fei Lien* and *0 Lai* were two clever, but wicked consellors of King *Chou*. In the *Shi-chi* chap. 3, p. llv. *Fei Lien* is called *Fei Chung*. L straighten out hooks, with such supporters as *Fei Lien* and *0 Lai* tried issues with the army of *Chou, Wu Wang,* however virtuous he may have been, could not have deprived him of his natural abilities, and

Chou, wicked though he was, would not have lost the sympathy of his associates. Although he was captured by *Wu Wang,* some ten or hundred people must have been killed or wounded at that time. If the blades were not stained with blood, it would contradict the report of *Chou's* great strength and the support he received from *Fei Lien* and *0 Lai2*

The auspicious portents of *Wu Wang* did not surpass those of *Kao Tsu. Wu Wang* saw a lucky augury in a white fish and a red crow, *Kao Tsu* in the fact that, when he cut a big snake in two, an old woman cried on the road. *Wu Wang* had the succour of eight hundred barons, *Kao Tsu* was supported by all the patriotic soldiers of the Empire, *Wu Wang's* features were like those of a staring sheep. *Kao Tsu* had a dragon face, a high nose, a red neck, a beautiful beard and 72 black spots on his body. When *Kao Tsu* fled, and *Lu Hou* was in the marshes, she saw a haze over his head. It is not known that *Wu Wang* had such an omen. In short, his features bore more auspicious signs than *Wu Wang's* look, and the portents were clearer than the fish and the crow. The patriotic soldiers of the Empire assembled to help the *Han,* and were more powerful than all the barons. *Wu Wang* succeeded King *Chou,* and *Kao Tsu* took over the inheritance of *Erh Shih Huang Ti* of the house of *Chin,* which was much worse than that of King *Chou*. The whole empire rebelled against *Ch in,* with much more violence than under the *Yin* dynasty. When *Kao Tsu* had defeated the *Ch in,* he had still to destroy *Hsiang Yii*. The battle field was soaked with blood, and many thousands of dead bodies lay strewn about. The losses of the The *Chou* dynasty which overthrew the *Shang* or *Yin* dynasty. The name of King *Chou Hsin* of the *Shang* dynasty has the same sound, but is quite a different character. According to the *Shi-chi* and the *Shutting* King *Chou* (led, when his troops had been routed by *Wu Wang,* and burned himself, dressed in his royal robes, in the palace. He was not caught by *Wu Wang.*

» Cf. p. 130.

Cf. p. 178.

Wu Wang had large, staring sheep's eyes.

8 Cf. p. 305.

The wife of *Han Kao Tsu*. Cf. p. 178.

The *Han* dynasty. defeated army were enormous. People had, as it were, to die again and again, before the Empire was won. The insurgents were exterminated by force of arms with the utmost severity. Therefore it cannot be true that the troops of *Chou* did not even stain their swords with blood. One may say that the conquest was easy, but to say that the blades were not stained with blood, is an exaggeration.

When the *Chou* dynasty conquered the empire of the *Yin,* it was written in the strategical book of *L' ai Kung2* that a young boy brought up in the camp *Tan Chiao* had said:—"The troops which are to destroy *Yin* have arrived in the plain of *Mu*. At dawn they carry lamps with fat." According to the *"Completion of the War* " the battle in the plain of *Mu* was so sanguinary, that the pestles were swimming in the blood, and over a thousand Li the earth was red. After this account the overthrow of the *Yin* by the *Chou* must have been very much like the war between the *Han* and *CHin* dynasties. The statement that the conquest of the *Yin* territory was so easy, that the swords were not stained with blood is meant as a compliment to the virtue of *Wu Wang,* but it exaggerates the truth. All things of this world must be neither over-nor under-estimated. If we examine, how the facts follow one another, all the evidence comes forth, and on this evidence the truth or the untruth can be established.

People glorify *Chon's* force by saying that he could twist iron, and at the same time praise *Wu Wang,* because the weapons, with which he destroyed his opponent, were not blood-stained. Now, if anybody opposed his enemies with a strength that could twist iron and straighten out a hook, he must have been a match for *Ming Pin* and *Hsia Yii,* and he who managed to defeat his adversary through his virtue without staining his swords with blood, must have belonged to the *Three Rulers* or to the *Five Emperors.1* Endowed with sufficient strength to twist iron, the one could not be compelled to submission, whereas the other, possessing such The *Chou* dynasty.

T'ai Kung Waxy, the counsellor of *Wu Wang*, laid the plans of the campaign against the *Tin* dynasty. This plain was situated in *Honan*. This is the title of the 3d Book of the 5th Part of the *Shuking*. (Cf. *Legge*, Classics Vol. lll, Pt. ll, p. 315.) With which the soldiers were pounding their rice. *Meng Pin* and *Hsia Yu* are both famous for their gigantic strength. The one could tear off the horns, the other the tail from a living ox. Both lived in the *Chou* epoch. The legendary rulers accomplished everything by their virtues. virtue that his weapons were not reddened with blood, ought not to have lost one soldier. If we praise *Chou's* strength, *Wu Wang's* virtue is disparaged, and, if we extol *Wu Wang*, *Chou's* strength dwindles away. The twisting of iron and the fact that the blades were not covered with blood are inconsistent, and the praise bestowed simultaneously on the *Yin* and the *Chou* mutually clashes. From this incompatibility it follows that one proposition must be wrong. *Confucius* said:— "*Chou's* wickedness was not so very great. Therefore the superior man hates to consort with base persons, for the faults of the whole world are laid to their charge." *Mencius* said: —" From the '*Completion of the War*' I accept but two or three paragraphs. If the most humane defeated the inhumane, how could so much blood be spilt, that clubs swam in it?" The utterance of *Confucius* would seem to uphold the swimming of clubs, whereas the words of *Mencius* are very much akin to the assertion that the weapons were not stained with blood. The first overshoots the mark, the second falls short of it. Thus a Sage and a Worthy pass a judgment on *Chou*, but both use a different weight, and one gives him credit for more than the other. *Chou* was not as depraved as *Wang Mang*. *Chou* killed *Pi Kan*, but *Wang Mang* poisoned the emperor *P'ing Ti*. *Chou* became emperor by succession, *Wang Mang* usurped the throne of the *Han*. To assassinate one's sovereign is

infinitely worse than the execution of a minister, and succession to the throne is quite different from usurpation. Deeds against which the whole people rose up, must have been worse than those of *Chou*. When the *Han* destroyed *Wang Mang*, their troops were exhausted at *K'un-gang*, the deaths numbering ten thousand and more.. When the forces reached the *Analects* XIX, 20. In our text of the *Lun-gu* these words are not spoken by *Confucius* himself, but by his disciple *Tse Kung*. A good man avoids the society of disreputable people, for everviwickedness is put to their account, even if they be innocent. Thus King *Chou* has been better than his name, which has become a by-word for every crime. Cf. p. 478.

'*Mencius* Hook VII, Pt. II, chap. 3. The most humane was *Wu Wang*. In the estimation of the Confucianists *Mencius* is only a Worthy, not a Sage like *Confucius*. *Wang Mang* the usurper reigned from *9* to 23 A.d. *Pi Kan* was a relative of *Chou*. When he remonstrated with him upon his excesses, *Chou* caused him to he disembowelled.

1-0 A.d. A city in southern *Hunan*. *Chien* terrace, the blood made all the foot-prints and ruts invisible. Consequently it cannot be true that, when the *Chou* conquered the Empire, the weapons were not even stained with blood.

It is on record that *Win Wang* could drink a thousand bumpers of wine and *Confucius* a hundred gallons. We are to infer from this, how great the virtue of these Sages was, which enabled them to master the wine. If at one sitting they could drink a thousand bumpers or a hundred gallons, they must have been drunkards, and not sages.

In drinking wine there is a certain method, and the chests and stomachs of the Sages must have been of nearly the same size as those of others. Taking food together with wine, they would have eaten a hundred oxen, while drinking one thousand bumpers, and ten sheep would correspond to a hundred gallons. If they did justice to a thousand bumpers and a hundred oxen, or to a hundred gallons and ten sheep, *Wen*

Wang must have been as gigantic as the Prince of *Fang-fing* and *Confucius* like a *Great Ti*. *Win Wang* and *Confucius* did not equal the Prince of *Fang-fing* or the *Great Ti* in length. Eating and drinking such enormous quantities with small bodies would be derogatory to the grandeur of *Win Wang*, and undignified in *Confucius*. According to the Chapter "*Chiu Kao*" *Win Wang* would say morning and evening:—"pour out this wine in libation." This shows how careful *Wen Wang* was about wine. Because he was so careful morning and evening, the people were converted thereby. Had his advice to be careful only been for outside, while he himself emptied a thousand bumpers at home, the efforts to educate the people and his subjects would have been in vain. And how would he have distinguished himself from the depravity of *Chou*, whose successor he was?

Moreover, at what time should the thousand bumpers and the hundred gallons have been drunk? When *Win Wang* and *Con* A terrace near *t'hang-an-fu*, where *Wang Mang* made his last stand. A feudal prince of gigantic size said to have lived under the Emperor *Yu*, who put him to death. Of. *Han Fei Tse* chap. 19, p. llv. *Ti* is a general name for northern barbarians. The *Shutting, Hung-fan*, j", speaks of a *Ti* measuring over 50 feet, *Ku Liang* of three *Ti* brothers, of which one was so enormous, that his body covered 9 *Mou. fucius* offered wine in sacrifice? Then the sacrificial meat would not have sufficed to satiate them. At the shooting-feast? At the shooting-feast there were certain recognised rules for drinking wine. If at a private banquet they gave their guests wine to drink, they must have given to all their inferiors equally. The emperor would first take three cups, and then retire. Drinking more than three, he would have become intoxicated, and misbehaved himself. But *Win Wang* and *Confucius* were men to whom propriety was everything. If they had given so much to their attendants, that they became drunk and disorderly, they themselves taking a thousand bumpers of wine or a hundred gallons, they would have been like

Chieh and Chou or, to say the least, drunkards. How could they then have manifested their virtues and improved others, how acquired a name still venerated by posterity?

There is a saying that the virtuous do not become intoxicated. Seeing that the Sages possess the highest virtue, one has wrongly credited Win Wang with a thousand bumpers and foolishly given a hundred gallons to Confucius. Chou is reported to have been an incorrigible tippler. The sediments lay about in mounds. He had a lake full of wine, and filled three thousand persons with liquor like cattle. Carousing he made night day, and even forgot the date.

Chou may have been addicted to drink, but he sought pleasure. Had his wine-lake been in the court-yard, then one could not say that in carousing he made night day. This expression would only be correct, if he shut himself up in his rooms behind closed windows, using candle-light. If he was sitting in his rooms, he must have risen and gone to the court-yard each time he wished to drink, and then returned to his seat, an endless trouble, which would have deprived him of all enjoyment. Had the wine-lake been in the inner apartments, then the three thousand people must have been placed close to the lake. Their amusement would have consisted in bowine down to drink wine from the lake, and in rising to taste the dainty dishes, singing and music being in front The shooting-feasts referred to are the competitions of archery, held in ancient times at the royal court, at the feudal courts, and at the meetings in the country. A banquet was connected with these festivities. Cf. Legge, The Li Ki (Sacred Books of the East Vol. XXVII) p. 57. This wine-lake is mentioned in the Shi-chi chap. 3, p. 1Ov, of them. If they were really sitting quite close to the lake, their drinking in front would have interfered with their dining, and the concert could not have been in front. Provided that at the banquet they had thus unmannerly sucked wine from the lake like oxen, they would not have required any cups during the dinner, and would also have gulped down and devoured the

food like tigers. From this we see that the wine-lake and the drinking like cattle are mere stories.

There is another tradition that Chou had made a forest by hanging up meat, and that he caused naked males and females to chase each other in this forest, which would be drunken folly, and unrestrained debauchery. Meat is to be put into the mouth. What the mouth eats, must be clean, not soiled. Now, if, as they say, naked males and females chased each other among the meat, how could it remain clean? If they were drunk, and did not care, whether it was clean or not, they must have bathed together in wine, and then run naked one after the other among the meat. Why should they not have done this? Since nothing is said about their bathing in wine, we may be sure that neither did they chase each other naked among the meat.

There is another version to the effect that wine was being carried about in carts and roast-meat on horseback, and that one hundred and twenty days were reckoned one night. However, if the account about the wine-lake is correct, it cannot be true that the wine was transported in carts, and if the meat was suspended so, as to form a forest, the statement that roast-meat was carried about on horseback must be wrong.

It may have happened that, when Chou was flushed with drink, he overturned the wine, which spread over the floor, whence the story of the wine-lake. When the wine was distilled, the sediments were heaped up, therefore the tale that the sediments lay in mounds. Meat was hung up in trees, thence the report that a forest was made of meat. The shade and darkness of this forest may sometimes have been visited by people with the intention of doing things shunning the light of day, which led to the belief that they chased each other naked. Perhaps wine was transported once on a deer-carriage, which would account for the story that wine was being

Quoted from the Shi-chi chap. 3, p. 11.

A royal carriage ornamented with deers.

carried about in carts, and roast-meat on horseback. The revelry may have extended once over ten nights, hence the hundred and twenty days. Perhaps Chou was intoxicated and out of his mind, when he inquired, what day it was. Then people said that he had forgotten dates altogether.

When Chou Kung invested Kang S/m he spoke to him about Chou's wine drinking, wishing that he should know all about it, and take a warning, but he did not mention the mounds of sediments, or the wine-lake, or the forest made of meat, or the revelries lasting far into the morning, or the forgetting of dates. What the Sages do not mention, is most likely unfounded.

As an instance of Chou's perversity it is recorded that he sucked wine from the wine-lake like an ox, together with three thousand people. The Hsia dynasty had a hundred (metropolitan) officials, the Yin two hundred, the Chou three hundred. The companions of Chou's Bacchanals were assuredly not common people, but officials, and not minor officials, but high ones. Their number never could reach three thousand. The authors of this report wished to disparage Chou, therefore they said three thousand, which is a gross exaggeration.

There is a report that the Duke of Chou was so condescending that with presents he called on simple scholars, living in poor houses, and inquired after their health. As one of the three chief ministers, a prop to the imperial tripod, he was the mainstay of the emperor. Those scholars were persons of no consequence in their hamlets. That a prime minister should have flung away his dignity as supporter of the dynasty in order to do homage to common scholars, cannot be true. May be, that he treated scholars with courtesy and condescension, and was not haughty towards Tan, Duke of Chou, a younger brother of Wu Wang. K'ang Shu was the first prince of the Wei State (Honan), which he governed until 1077 B.c. Cf. Shaking Part V, Book X, 11 (Legge, be. cii. p. 408).

Chou Kung.

The sacrificial tripod is the emblem of

Shuking [Shiking (see p 24)

royalty. The three chief ministers are likened to its three feet.

poor people, hence the report that he waited upon them. He may have raised a scholar of humble origin, and received him with his badge in hand. People then said that he came with presents and waited upon his family.

We have a tradition that *Yao* and *Shun* were so thrifty, that they had their thatched roofs untrimmed, and their painted rafters unhewn. Thatched roofs and painted rafters there may have been, but that they were untrimmed or un-hewn, is an exaggeration. The Classic says, "I assisted in completing the Five Robes." Five Robes means the five-coloured robes. If they put on five-coloured robes, and at the same time had thatched roofs and painted rafters, there would have been a great discrep-ancy between the palace buildings and the dresses. On the five-coloured robes were painted the sun, the moon and the stars. Consequently thatched roofs and painted rafters are out of the question.

It is on record that *Chin ShiJi Huang Ti* burned the Books of Poetry and His-tory, and buried the Literati alive. This means that by burning the Books of Poetry and History he eradicated the Five Classics and other literary works. The Literati thus thrown into pits were those, they say, who had concealed the Classics and other works. When the books were burned, and the men thrown into pits, Poetry and History were ex-tinguished. The burning of the Books of Poetry and History and the assassi-nation of the Literati are indisputable. But the allegation that, for the purpose of destroying those books, the men were put to death, is not correct, and an exag-geration.

In the 34th year of his reign *Chin Shih Huang Ti* gave a banquet on the terrace of *Hsien-iiang.*' Seventy Literati came to wish him long life. The *Pu-gehR Chou C/ting Ch' in,* delivered a The Emperor *Tii.* Quotation from the *Shuking, Yi Chi* Pt. II, Bk. IV, 8 *(Legge* Vol. HI, Pt.I, p. 85). Modern commen-tators and *Legge* explain *ff* JjjJ "& l" tenures," *Wang Ch'ung* as the Five State Robes worn by the Emperor and the of-

ficials, which are mentioned a few para-graphs before our passage *(Leggr, he. cit.* p. 80).

The *Shitting* and the *Shaking.*

213 B.c.

Near *IIsi-an-fu* in *Shensi.*

An official title.

speech, enlogising the emperor's excel-lence, whereupon *Shun Yii Yileh* of *Chi* stepped forward, and reproached *Ch'in Shih Huang Ti* for not having invested his kinsmen and meritoriouu officials, to use them as his assistants. He accused *Chou Ch'ing Ch'en* of open flattery. *Ch'in Shih Huang Ti* directed the *premi-er Li Sse* to report on the matter. *Li Sse* blamed *Shun Yil Yileh,* saying that the scholars did not care to learn the exigen-cies of modern times, but were studying antiquity with a view to condemn every-thing new, and to excite the masses. *Li Sse* proposed that the Historiographers be authorized to burn all the books ex-cept the Annals of *Ch'in,* and also to make an exception in favour of the offi-cials in charge of the Imperial College. All the books on poetry, history, phi-losophy, and jurisprudence, which peo-ple had dared to conceal, were to be brought to the governors and burned to-gether. Those who perchance should dare to discourse on poetry and history, would be executed and publicly ex-posed. Should anybody hold up antiq-uity and decry the present time, he was to be destroyed together with his clan. Officials who saw or knew of such cas-es without interfering, were to suffer the same penalty. *Ch'in Shih Huang Ti* ap-proved of it.

The next year, which was the 35th of the emperor's reign, the scholars in *Hsien-yang* spread all kinds of false rumours. *Ch'in Shih Huang Ti* had them tried by the censors. Those who gave informa-tion about their accomplices, and de-nounced others, got free themselves. 467 delinquents were all thrown into pits.

The burning of the Books of Poetry and History was the consequence of *Shun Yii Yiieh's* recriminations. The deaths of the literati were due to the ru-mours divulged by the scholars. Seeing 467 men perish in pits the chronicler

went a step farther, stating that the literati were murdered for the purpose' of doing away with poetry and history, and even saying that they were all thrown into pits. That is no true report but also a highly coloured one.

The abilition of feudalism was much disliked by the Literati. The text says, the "discussions of the hundred au-thors," which means the writers on phi-losophy and science. Various transla-tions of this last passage have been pro-posed. Cf. *Chavannes, Mim. Hist.* Vol. II, p. 181 Note 2.

The foregoing narration is abridged from *Shi-cln* chap. 6, p. 21v et seq. Our text speaks of 4G7 scholars, whereas the *Shi-chi* mentions but 460 odd, and it uses the word "to throw into a pit" instead of the vaguer term So perhaps *Wang Ch'nng* has not culled from the *Shi-chi,* hut both hav e used the same older source.

There is a tradition to the effect that "field by field were treated as *Ching K'o's* hamlet." They say that at the insti-gation of Prince *Tan* of *Yen, Ching K'o* made an attempt on the life of the King of *Chin* The latter afterwards caused the nine relations of *Ching K'o* to be put to death. But his vindictive wrath was not yet appeased thereby, and he subse-quently had all the inhabitants of *Ching K'o's* village killed, so that the whole village was exterminated. Therefore the expression "field by field." This is an exaggeration.

Although *Ch'in* was lawless, the king had no reason to exterminate the entire village of *Ching K'o. Ch in Shih Huang Ti* once visited his palace on the *Liang-shan.* From its height he perceived that the carriages and the horsemen of his prime-minister *Li Sse* were very gor-geous. This made him angry, and he gave utterance to his disapproval. The attendants informed *Li Sse,* who forth-with diminished his carriages and men. *Ch in Shih Huang Ti* thus became aware that his words had leaked out through the servants, but did not know who the culprit was. Thereupon he had all the persons near him arrested, and put to death. Later on, a meteor fell down in *Tung-chiin* and when it touched the earth, became a stone. Some one engraved upon the stone the inscription:— "When *Ch'in Shih Huang Tvs* dies, the territory will be divided." When the Emperor heard about it, he ordered the censors to ask the people one by one, but nobody confessed. Then all persons found near the stone were seized and executed.

If the Emperor executed his attendants in the Palace on the *Liang* Mountain and all the persons near the stone, he destroyed them all, because he wished to find those who had divulged his words, or engraved the stone, but could not discover them. But what had the village of *Ching K'o* done to *Ch'in* to be exterminated? If the King of *Chin* had been stabbed in the village, and the assailant was unknown, there might have been a wholesale exeeu A State in Chili.

In 227 B.c. *Ching K'o* made an unsuccessful attempt on *Ch'in Shih Huang Tix* life, who at that time was still king of *Chin.* It was not before 221 that, having vanquished all the rival States, he assumed the imperial title. All the ascendants and descendants from the great-great-grandfather to the great-great-grandson. A mountain in the province of *Shensi.* Quoted from *Shi-chi* chap, 6, p. 24. A circuit or province comprising the south of Chili. A quotation from *Shi-chi* chap, ti, p. 25 v. Cf. p. 231. tion. But *Ching K'o* was already dead, the would-be-assassin found, why then should all the villagers suffer for him?

During the 20th year of *Ch'in Shih Huang Ti's* reign *Ching K'o,* the envoy of *Yen,* attempted to assassinate him, but the King of *Ch'in* got wind of it, and caused *Clang K'o* to be torn to pieces as a warning. There is no mention of the entire destruction of his village. Perhaps he gave orders to behead the nine relations of *Ching K'o.* If these were many, and living together in one hamlet, this hamlet may have been wiped out by their execution. People fond of exaggerations then said: — "field by field." The *Shi-chi* does not mention it.

CHAPTER XXXX.

Exaggerations of the Literati *(Ju-tseng).*

In the books of the Literati we find the statement that the virtue of *Yao* and *Shun* was so great and wonderful, that perfect peace reigned on earth, and not a single person was punished; and further that, since *Wbi Wang* and *Wu Wang* bequeathed their greatness to *tJh'eng* and *K'ang,* the instruments of punishment were laid aside, and not used for over forty years. The idea is to praise *Yao* and *Shun,* and to extol *Win Wang* and *Wu Wang.* Without high-flown words one deems to be unable to applaud greatness, as it deserves, and without some figures of speech, to do justice to what has been achieved. But however excellent *Yao* and *Shun* have been, they could not manage that nobody was punished, and with all their superiority *Win Wang* and *Wu Wang* could not do without punishments. That there were few offences committed, and punishments seldom, may be true. But that nobody was punished, and that the instruments of punishment were not used, is an exaggeration.

If it could be contrived, that nobody was punished, it could be brought about also, that no State was attacked. If the instruments of punishment were put aside and not used, arms also could be laid down, and would not be required. However, *Yao* attacked *Tanshui,* and *Shun* fought against the *Yu Muio.* Four nobles had to submit, and instruments of punishment as well as weapons were resorted to. At the time of *Cheng Wang* four States rebelled:—the *Huai, I, Hsu,* and *Jung* all brought misfortune upon themselves. To punish a man, one uses a sword, to exterminate *Ch'eng* was the successor of King *Wu Wang.* He reigned from 1115-1078 B.c., and was succeeded by *K'ang* 1078-1052. a Cf. *Shi-chi* chap. 4, p. 17.

A place in *Honan.* The aboriginal *Miao* tribes which exist still to-day. *Shun* banished *Kung Kung, liuan Ton,* the prince of the *San Aliao* and *K'un.* Cf. *Mencim* V, Pt. II, 3 and *Shaking* Pt. II, I, 12. The *Huai, I,* and *Jung* were non-Chinese tribes; *Hxii* is the name of one of the Nine Provinces of FtJ, in modem *Shantung.* him, arms. The punishment is a matter of criminal law, the extermina-

tion of fighting. Fighting and criminal law do not differ, weapons and swords are the same. Even an able dialectician could not discover a difference. Against depravity arms are used, against lawlessness instruments of punishment. These latter bear the same relation to weapons as feet do to wings. Walking, one uses one's feet, flying, one's wings. Though different in shape, both of them equally move the body: in the same manner instruments of punishment and weapons combined serve to check the evil. Their effect is the same.

The allegation that no arms were used implies the idea, that no penalties were meted out. Should a man with defective ears, but intact eyes be said to be in possession of a perfect body, we would not admit that, and if some one being an excellent tigerhunter, but afraid of striking a man, were called brave by reason of this tiger-hunting alone, we would not agree to it. Only in case of the body having no defects and the courage facing whomsoever, there is perfection. Now, they say that nobody was punished, but not that no weapon was used. Much fuss is made about the fact, that instruments of punishment were put aside, and not used, but no mention made, that nobody rebelled. Therefore, we cannot speak of wonderful virtue or greatness.

The books of the Literati tell us that *Yang Yn Chi* of *Ch'a* was very remarkable at archery. Shooting at an aspen leaf, with a hundred shots he hit it a hundred times. This is of course said in praise of his brilliant shooting. That, whenever he aimed at an aspen leaf, he hit it, may be so, but to say, that out of a hundred shots a hundred hit the mark, is an exaggeration.

An aspen leaf hit by an arrow over and over again, would soon be so perforated, that it could no more serve as a target. If *Yang Yu Chi* had shot at an aspen leaf, as it was hanging on the tree, he would always have bit one, though not that which he wanted, there being such a multitude of them. Consequently he would be obliged to take the leaves down, and place them one by one on the earth to shoot at them. After several ten shots, his dexterity would have been seen. The spectators would all have become aware of his skill at archery, and would not have required a hundred shots.

A minister of the *Ch'u* State in the *thou* epoch.

Narrators are fond of adorning dexterity and other accomplishments. If any one hit thirty and more times, they say a hundred. A hundred and a thousand are big numbers. Wishing really to say ten, they say a hundred, and in lieu of a hundred, a thousand. The meaning is the same as, when the *Shuking* speaks of the "harmony of the ten thousand countries" or the *Shiking* of the "thousand and hundred thousand descendants."

We learn from the writings of the Literati that there was a loyal official in *Wei:—Hung Yen,* who was sent abroad as envoy of Duke *Ai* of *Wei.* Before he returned, the 7P had attacked, and killed the duke, and eaten his flesh, leaving only the liver. When *Hung Yen* returned from his mission, he reported himself to the liver. Out of sorrow, that Duke *Ai* had died, and was eaten up, so that his liver had no resting-place, he took a knife, ripped up his stomach, took all its contents out, put the liver of Duke *Ai* in, and expired. Those telling this story intend to praise his loyalty. It is possible that he ripped himself open, put Duke *Ai's* liver in, and died. To say that he took out all the contents of the stomach, and put in the liver of Duke *Ai,* is an exaggeration.

If people stab one another with knives, and hit the Five Intestines, they die. Why? Because the Five Intestines regulate the Vital Fluid, just as the head is the centre of all the arteries. When the head has been cut off, the hands cannot take another man's head, and put it on the neck. How then should *Hung Yen* be capable of first emptying his own stomach, and then putting in the liver of Duke *Ai?* When the contents of the stomach have been taken out, death ensues. Then the hands can no more grasp. If he first put in the liver of Duke *Ai,* and then took out the contents of the stomach, then it ought to be said, that he put in the liver of Duke *Ai,* and emptied his stomach. But now it is first mentioned that the contents of the stomach were completely taken out, and that the liver of Duke *Ai* was put in, which is a gross exaggeration of truth.

This must be a misprint, for no Duke of this name is known. The *Lii shih ch'un ch'iu,* which mentions the story, speaks of Duke / of *Wei,* 667-659 B.c. The northern barbarians.

We read in the books of Literati, that, when *Hsiung ChUl Tse* of *Cliu* once went out, he saw a stone lying on the ground, which he took for a crouching tiger. He grasped his bow, and shot at it. The arrow disappeared up to the feathers. Others relate that *Yang Yu Chi* saw a stone stretched like a rhinoceros. He shot at it, and the arrow was absorbed with the plumes. Some hold that *Hsiung Ch'ii Tse* is *Li Kuang Yang Yu Chi* and *Li Kuang* must give their names, and one does not discover, that the story is not true.

Some speak of a tiger, some of a rhinoceros. Both being fierce animals, it amounts to the same. Some say, that the feathers disappeared, some, that the plumes were absorbed. Plumes are feathers, only the wording is a little different. The chief idea is that a stone resembled a tiger or a rhinoceros, and that out of fright the arrow was shot with such force, that it entered deep. One may say, that a stone resembled a tiger, and that, when shot at, the arrow entered deep. But to maintain that it disappeared up to the feathers is going too far. Seeing something like a tiger, one regards it as such, draws the bow, and shoots at it with the utmost force and energy. The aspect of a real tiger would have quite the same effect. Upon shooting a stone resembling a tiger the arrow should enter so completely, that nothing of the feathers could be seen. Would then, when hitting a real tiger, the arrow pass straight through its body? It is difficult to pierce a stone, whereas with flesh it is very easy. If the feathers vanished in a substance difficult to be pierced, there could be no doubt that an arrow must traverse a stuff affording no obstacle.

A good marksman can shoot at great distances, and hit the smallest object,

not missing one line. But how could he give greater force to the bow or the cross-bow? *Yang Yu Chi* shot at the Marquis of *Chin* in a battle, and hit him in the eye. A commoner aiming at a ruler of ten thousand chariots would certainly strain his nerves to the utmost, and double his forces, not less *Hsiung Ch'ii Tse* lived during the *Chou* dynasty. This story is told in the *Hsin-hm* of *Liu Hsiang.*

Cf. above p. 495.

A general of *Han Wu Ti,* cf. p. 168. The *Tso-chuan,* Duke *Cheng* 16th year *(Lrgge, Classics* Vol. V, Pt. I, p. 397) informs us that in a battle fought by the Marquis of *Chin* against King *Kung* of *Ch'u* in 574 B.c. / of *Lu,* an archer of *Chin,* shot at King *Kung* of *Ch'u* and hit him in the eye. The king thereupon ordered his own archer, *Vang Yu Chi,* to revenge him, handing him two arrows. With the first arrow *Yang Yu Chi* killed /.

According to this account it was not the Marquis of *Chin,* who was hit in the eye, but the King of *Ch'u,* and not *Yang Yu Chi* shot the arrow, but *I* of *Lu. hun* -Heng. 3'2 than, when shooting at the stone. Could then the arrow hitting the eye of the Marquis pass through to the neck? If it had done, the Marquis of *Chin* would have died on his chariot.

I presume that an arrow projected from a ten stones ballista, would not enter one inch into a stone, and split into three pieces. Now, should a weak bow be drawn with human force, how could the feathers disappear in the stone, though the bowman used all his strength?

Human energy is a fluid, and this fluid a force. When in distress of fire or water people are very fluttered and frightened, and carry away their belongings, their energies reach their maximum. If, at ordinary times, they could carry one picul, they then carry two. Now, provided that, when shooting at the stretched out stone, the energy is doubled, the arrow nevertheless could not enter deeper than one inch. The disappearance of the feathers is out of the question.

Let is suppose that a good swordsman

beholds a stone lying on the ground, gets frightened, and strikes it. Could he cut it asunder? Or let a brave man, who would tackle a tiger with his unarmed fist, unexpectedly catch sight of such a stone, and hammer down on it with his hand. Would he leave any trace on the stone?

The strength of clever people is equal to that of the stupid, the earnestness of purpose of the ancients like that of the moderns. If now-a-days an archer shoots animals and birds in the country, he spares no force to get them. Yet, when he hits an animal, the blow enters only some inches. If it slips and hits a stone, the sharp point does not enter, and the arrow breaks to pieces. Accordingly the statements in the books of the Literati to the effect that *Hsiung Ch'u Tse* of *Ch'u, Yang Yu Chi*, and *Li Kuang* shot at a stone lying on the ground, and that the arrow disappeared up to the feathers, or was engulfed together with the plumes, are all exaggerations.

In the writings of the Literati we find the notice that *Lu Pan* was as skilful as *Mi Tse*. From wood he carved a kite, which The force of a bow, a cross-bow, or a ballista is measured by the weight required to draw them.

One stone or one picul in ancient times amounted to 120 pounds.
A celebrated mechanic of the *Lu* State, who lived contemporaneously with *Confucius. Lu Pan* is his sobriquet, his proper name being *Kung Shu Tse*. He has become the tutelary god of artisans. The philosopher *Me Ti* has been credited with mechanical skill, erroneously I presume. could fly three days without coming down. It may be, that he made a kite of wood, which he flew. But that it did not alight for three days, is an exaggeration. If he carved it from wood, he gave it the shape of a bird. How then could it fly without resting? If it could soar up, why did it do so just three days? Provided there was a mechanism, by which, once set in motion, it continued flying, it could not have come down again. Then people ought to say that it flew continually, and not three days.
There is a report that *Lu Pan* by his skill lost his mother. That is to say, the clever

artisan had constructed a wooden carriage and horses with a wooden charioteer for his mother. When the mechanism was complete, he put his mother in the carriage, which drove off to return no more. And thus he lost his mother. Provided the mechanism in the wooden kite was in order, it must have been like that of the wooden carriage and horses. Then it would have continued flying without rest. On the other hand, a mechanism works but for a short while, therefore the kite could not have continued flying much longer than three days. Then the same holds good with regard to the wooden carriage, it also ought to have stopped after three days on the road, and could not go straight on, so that the mother was lost. Both stories are apparently untrustworthy.

In some books the statement is made that *Confucius* had no resting-place in this world. Wandering about he visited over seventy States, where he attempted to gain influence, but nowhere he found repose. One may well say, that he wandered about, and found nothing, but to say, that he came to seventy States, is going too far. According to the *Analects* and the works of other philosophers he returned from *Wei* to *Lu*. In *Ch en* his supplies were exhausted, in *Wei* his traces were obliterated. He forgot the taste of food in *Ch'i* a tree was felled over him in *Sung5* and besides there are A State in northern *Honan. '* A State comprising the southern part of *Honan.* » Cf. p. 155.
"When the Master was in *Ch'i,* he heard the *Sliao* music, and for three months he did not know the taste of flesh," so engrossed was he was this music, that he did not taste what he ate *Legge, Analects* p. 199; *Analects* VII, 13).
The emissaries of a high officer of *Sung* tried to kill *Confucius* by pulling down the tree under which he was practising ceremonies. Cf. *Legge, Analects* p. 202 Note 22.
K *Tun,* and *Mou.* These States, which he visited, do not even amount to ten. The statement about seventy States is therefore unreliable. Perhaps he went to more than ten States. Then the report about seventy States was spread in

books, and people now talk of seventy States.

We read in the *Analects* that *Confucius* asked *Kung Ming Chia* about *Kung Shu Win Tse* saying, "Is it true that your master does not speak, nor laugh, nor take anything?"—*Kung Ming Chia* replied, "That is a misrepresentation. The Master speaks, when it is time, and people do not dislike his words. He laughs, when he is merry, and people are not displeased with his laugh. He takes things, when he has a right to do so, and people are not dissatisfied." *Confucius* exclaimed, "How is it possible! How is it possible!" In fact *Kung Shu Win Tse* spoke at the proper time, laughed when pleased, and took what he was entitled to. Out of this fact, which became known, people made the story that *Kung Shu Win Tse* did neither speak, nor laugh, nor take anything. When common people tell a thing, they always like to overdo it.

We read in some books that when Duke *Mu* of *Ctiin6* invested *Ching,* he passed through *Chin* without borrowing a passage. Duke *Hsiang* of *Chin'* therefore intended to strike a blow at him with the help of the *Chiang Jung* in the *Yao* passes. When no horses nor carriages came back, *Ch'in* sent out three high officers: *Ming Ming Shih, Hsi Ch i Shu,* and *Po Yi Ping,* who all returned. Since they came back, the horses and carriages must have come back likewise. The report to the contrary is an exaggeration. A city in southern *Shantung.*
A territory in *Ch'en.*
A princedom in *Shantung.*
4 *Analects* XIV, 14.
Kung Shu Wen-Tse was a high officer in the State of *Wei,* and *Kung Ming Chia* would seem to have been his disciple. 658-619 B.c. '626-619 B.c. Western barbarians.
A dangerous defile in the district of *Yung-ning, Honan.* According to the *Ch'un-ch'iu,* Duke *Hsi* 33d year, the army of *Chin* was defeated at *Yao* in 62G B.c. The *Tso-chuan* narrates the campaign in detail, and relates that the three officers were first taken prisoners, but afterwards released by the interces-

sion of the mother of the Duke of *Chin,* who was a princess of the ducal house of *Ch'in.*

We are told in several books that the Princes of *Ming Ch ang* in *Ch i,1 Hsin Ling* in *Wei, Ping Yuan* in *Chao,* and *Chun Shfoi* in *Ch'u* treated their retainers with great kindness, and attracted them from everywhere, each 3000 men. This is meant to illustrate their kindness and the great conflux. That the number of retainers was very great, is possible, but that they amounted to 3000,-an exaggeration. For, although the four princes had a partiality for retainers, and though the latter assembled in great numbers, yet each one could not have more than about a thousand. Then the books made it three thousand. For a great many, people will say a thousand, and in case of a small number, not a single one. That is the common practice, and thus misstatements originate.

There is a tradition, that *Kao Tse Kao* mourning his father, shed bloody tears, and that for three years he did not show his teeth. To an honest man this would seem to be rather difficult; for it is not easily done. He would not consider it untrue, but only difficult, and therein he is mistaken.

That *Kao Tse* shed bloody tears, is probably true. *Ho of Ching* offered a precious stone to the Prince of *Ch u,* who cut off his foot. Distressed that his jewel did not find favour, and that his feelings were not appreciated he wept, until his tears were dried up, when he continued weeping with tears of blood. Now *Kao Tse* bewailed the death of his father. His grief was extreme. It must be true that, when his tears ceased, blood came out, but the saying that for three years he did not show his teeth, is an exaggeration.

These words mean that *Kao Tse* did not speak nor laugh. That a filial son, while mourning his parents, should not laugh, is only natural, but how can he avoid speaking, and when speaking, avoid showing his teeth?

Confucius said: "What he said, was not elegant, and at times he did not speak at all." Then it was reported, that he did not show his teeth, or even, that for

three years he did not show his Cf. p. 161. These four princes are known as the "Four Heroes," living at the end of the *Chou* epoch, during the time of the "Contending States," the 3rd century B. c. *Kao Ch'ai* or *Kao Tse Kao,* was a disciple of *Confucius,* noted for his filial piety. Quotation from the *Li-ki, Tan Kung* Sect. I, II, 14. *Ho of Ching* i. e. of *Ch'u,* known as *Pien Ho viz Ho* of the *Pien* district. Cf. p. 113. teeth. *Kao Tsung* while in the mourning shed did not speak for three years. He enjoyed imperial majesty. That he did not speak means to say, that he did not use elegant expressions, and even that seems doubtful, and is perhaps an exaggeration. On the other hand *Kao Tse Kao* held a very humble position, yet he is believed not to have shown his teeth, which is certainly still more exaggerated.

The Literati write in their books that *Ch'in Hsi* recommended *Po Li Hsi* to Duke *Mn* who, however, did not pay attention to it. Then *Ch'in Hsi* went out of the front door, bowed down his head, and knocked it on the ground, so that it broke to pieces, and died. This affected Duke *Mu* so deeply, that he took *Po Li Hsi* into his service. The meaning of this story is that a worthy in recommending a good man did not spare his own life, knocking his head on the ground, that it broke, and died, all with the object to further his friend.

With this story scholars use to exhort one another, and it is handed down in their books. Nobody discredits it. That somebody kotows, while recommending a good man, has happened of old, as it happens now. It is true that *Ch'in Hsi* knocked his head, but the allegation that he broke it, and expired is an exaggeration.

When a man kotows, that his head aches, and the blood comes out, he cannot fracture his skull, however angry and agitated he may be. I do not maintain, that the skull cannot be broken, but man has not sufficient strength to do it alone. With a knife one may cut one's throat, or with a blade pierce one's bosom. By means of the knife or the blade the hand acquires the necessary strength. If *Ch'in Hsi* had taken a ham-

mer, and smashed his skull, there would be nothing wonderful in it. To fall down, and smash his skull *Ch'in Hsi* would not have had the necessary strength. There have been people who died while prostrating themselves, but none who broke their heads oc smashed their skulls. Perhaps *Ch in Hsi* performed the kotow, while recommending *Po Li Hsi,* which gave rise to the story of his death, or he really died, while kotowing, hence the idle talk of people that he broke his head.

Posthumous title of the *Shang* emperor *Wn Ting.* See p. 328. Quoted from the *Sfmking,* Wit *Yi* Pt. V, Bk. XV, 5 *(Leggs* Vol. Ill, Pt. II, p. 466). Duke *Mu* of *Ch'in,* 658-619 B.c.

The books of the Literati tell us that for the Prince of *Yen, Ching K o* attempted to assassinate the King of *Ch'in.* He struck him with a stiletto, but did not hit. The King of *Ch'in* then drew his sword and struck him. When *Ching K'o* assaulted the King of *Ch'in* with a stiletto, he did not hit his adversary, but a copper pillar, into which the dagger entered a foot deep. With these words one wishes to emphasize the sharpness of the stiletto.

Ching K'o was a powerful man. He thrust the sharp blade, so that it penetrated into the hard pillar. In order to exalt *Ching K'o's* courage people have coloured the real facts. It is true that the stiletto went into the copper pillar, but the assertion that it entered a foot deep, is an exaggeration, for, although copper does not possess the hardness of a dagger, the latter cannot penetrate deeper than some inches, but not one foot.

Let us consider the question, in case he had hit the King of *Ch'in,* would he have run the dagger through him? Pulling a ten stones ballista with a windlass and shooting at a wooden target in a wall, one would not perforate it to the extent of one foot. With force of hand *Ching A"o* thrust a small stiletto. While he himself was struck by the *Lung-yuan* sword, the dagger entered into the hard copper pillar. Then *Ching K'o's* force was stronger than that A famous sword forged by *On Yeh* and *Kan Chiang,* in later times a term for a good blade in general. Cf. p. 377.

The *Shi-chi* chap. 86, p. 16v. gives us a graphic description of the assault of *Ching K'o* on *Shih Huang Ti.* When at a reception the envoy of *i en* presented a map to the king, the latter caught sight of the dagger, which *(hing K'o* had concealed. Then *Ching K'o* "with his left hand grasped the sleev e of the King of *t'h'in,* and with his right hand the dagger, and was going to strike the king, but, before he touched his body, the king frightened, retreated, and rose, tearing off his sleeve. He tried to draw his sword, but the sword was very long, and while engaged with the scabbard, he was so excited, and the sword was so hard, that he could not draw it out at the moment. *Chiag Ko* chased the king, who ran round a pillar. The assembled officers were thunderstruck. They all rose in a body, but were so much taken by surprise, that they completely lost their heads. By the rules of *Ch'in* the officers, waiting upon the king in the palace hall, were not allowed to carry the smallest weapon with them. The armed guards were all stationed below the hall, but, without a special order, they were not permitted to walk up. At the critical moment there was no time to summon the soldiers below. This is the reason, why *Ching K'o* could pursue the king, and that his attendants, though startled, did not strike the assailant. They all seized him with their hands, however, and the royal physician *Hsia Wu Chu* flung his medicine bag, which he was presenting, against him. While the King *of Ch'in* was thus fleeing round the pillar, all were alarmed, but did not know what to do. The attendants only shouted, 'Push your sword backwards, King! Push your sword backwards!' The king then drew his sword, and hit *Ching K'o,* cutting his left leg. *Ching K'o* maimed then lifted his dagger and thrust it at of the ten stones ballista, and the copper pillar softer than the wooden target. The courage of *Ching K'o* is made much of, but there is no mention that he possessed great strength. Of strong men there is none like *Ming Pen.* Would *Meng Pen,* if he had struck a copper pillar, have cut it

one foot deep? Perhaps the stiletto was as sharp as the famous swords *Kan-chiang* and *Mo-ga,* whose thrusts and blows nothing could withstand, and that therefore it really penetrated one foot deep. Unfortunately the praise bestowed on *Kan-chiang* and *Mo-ga* also overshoot the mark, and are much akin to the foot deep cutting of the copper pillar.

We learn from the works of the Literati that *Tung Chung Shu* while reading the *Ctiun-cKiu* was so absorbed in his study, that he did not think of anything else, and for three years did not cast a look at the greens in the garden. That he did not look at the greens in the garden may be true, but the three years are an exaggeration. Although *Tung Chung Shu* was very industrious, yet he must have relaxed from time to time, and at such moments he also would have sauntered about his court-yard. Strolling out into the court-yard, why should he have disdained to gaze at the greens in the garden?

1 have heard that persons engrossed in some idea, and studying some question, do not appear in public, and that for a principle some have lost their lives, but I never heard, that they did not go into the court-yard, and were sitting rapt in thoughts for three years, without ever looking at the garden. In the *Wu-gi* Chapter of the *Shuking* it is said that the good man does not find repose, because he foresees the troubles of the harvest. If he reposes nevertheless, it is because his nerves and bones are not of wood or stone, and must be unstrung from time to time. Hence *Whi Wang* never strained his nerves without slackening them again, nor did the king, but missed him, and instead hit the copper pillar. Then the King of *CHin* dealt him another blow, and thus *t'hing lCo* received eight wounds. Seeing that his scheme had failed, he leant against the pillar. Weeping, he squatted down, and said.... At that moment the attendants came forward, and killed *Ching lCo.*" Two swords wrought by the noted swordcutler *Kan Chiang* for *Ho Li,* king of *Wu* 513-404 B.c. *Mo-ga* was the name of his wife. The *Kan-chiang* sword was regarded as the male, the *Mo-ga* as the

female sword. An author of the 2nd century B.c.

» Quotation from the *Shuking, Wu-gi* Pt. V, Bk. XV, 1 *(Legge* Vol. III, Pt. II, p. 464).

he slacken without subsequent straining. An interchange of activity and passivity was in his eyes the right thing. If even the brilliant mental faculties of the Sages had to relax after an effort, *Tung Chung Shu,* whose strength was much less than that of those men, could not well concentrate his thoughts for three years without repose.

The books of the Literati contain a statement to the effect that at the time when the *Hsia* Dynasty had reached its prime, distant countries sent pictures of their products, and the nine provinces metal as tribute. From this tripods were cast, on which all kinds of objects were represented. The consequence was, that, when people went into forests or to lakes, they did not meet spectres, and they could thereby ward off the influences of evil spirits. The Emperor and his subjects being in harmony, heaven gave its protection.

Metal is by nature a thing. The tribute metal from distant places was thought very beautiful, and therefore cast into tripods, on which all sorts of curious objects were depicted. How could this have the effect that people in forests or by lakes did not meet with spectres, and could ward off the evil influences of spirits? During the *Chou* time there was universal peace. The *Yiteh-shang* offered white pheasants to the court, the *Japanese* odoriferous plants. Since by eating these white pheasants or odoriferous plants one cannot keep free from evil influences, why should vessels like bronze tripods have such a power?

The appearance of the Nine Tripods was an auspicious sign of high virtue. Yet the wearing of a felicitous object does not attract happiness. Boys use to wear jade-stones, girls pearls, yet neither pearls nor jewels can guard mankind against evil. Precious and rare things are used as excellent charms and amulets, and they are regarded by some as very useful. The same is maintained in regard to the Nine Tripods. They cannot ward off evil in Abridged from the *Tso-chuan,* Duke *Hsiian* 3rd year.— From the *Hsia* dynasty these tripods came down to the *Shang* and the *Chora* dynasties, and in 605 B.C. were still in existence.

A people in the southern part of *Kuangtung* province, near the *Annamese* frontier. The *Wu,* an old name for the Japanese, which Chinese authors have explained to mean "Pygmies." The virtue of the Emperor *Yii.* fluences, the report to the contrary is an exaggerated statement in the afore-mentioned books.

There is a popular tradition that the tripods of *Chou* boiled of themselves without fire, and that things could be taken out of them, which had not been put in. That is a popular exaggeration. According to the exaggerated statement in the books of the Literati the Nine Tripods, having nothing peculiar, would possess supernatural powers without any reason.

What proof would there be for this assertion? The metal of the *Chou* tripods came from afar as tribute. *Yil* obtained it and caused it to be wrought into tripods. On the tripods a great many things were represented. If as a tribute from distant lands they were spiritual, why should things from distant countries be spiritual? If they were so, because *Yil* cast them, *Yil* himself, though a.Sage, could not be a spirit, how then should cast vessels be? If they were, because they were made of metal, metal is like stone, but stone cannot be spiritual, why then should metal be? If they were spirits, because they were covered with pictures of all kinds of things, these pictures are like the lightning of the Thunder Goblet. On this goblet were carved clouds and thunder. They are in the sky and much more spiritual than ordinary things. Since the representations of clouds and lightning are not spirits, the pictures of various things cannot be either.

It is on record that, when *Ch'in* extinguished *Chou,* the Nine Tripods of *Chou* fell into the power of *Ch in.* In fact, during the reign of King *Nan,* King *Chao* of *Ch in* sent his general *Chin* to attack AW *Wang.* The latter terrified,

hastened to *Ch'in,* prostrated himself, confessed his guilt, and ceded all his cities, 36 with 30,000 souls. *Ch'in* accepted the gift, and allowed King AW to go home. At his death the king of *Ch'in* seized the Nine Tripods and other precious utensils. Thus the tripods came to be in *Ch in.* In the 28th year of his reign *Ch in Shih Huang Ti* travelled north A sacrificial vessel nsed during the *Hsia* dynasty.

314-255 B.c. 305-249 B.c. The full name of this king is *Chao Ilsiang.* Cf. the parallel passage in *Shi-chi* chap. 4, p. 39 where, however, not *Kan Wang,* but the Prince of the Eastern *Chou* submits to *Ch'in* and cedes his territory. In 255 B.c. *Vid. Shi-t/d* chap. 28, p. 8. ward to *Lang-geh.* On his return he passed *P'eng-ch'ing,* and by feasting prepared himself for a sacrifice. Wishing to get the Tripods of *Chou* out, he sent a thousand men to plunge into the *Sse* River, but'all searching was in vain. *Ch'in Shiit Huang* 7 came three generations after King *Cliao.* At that time there was neither disorder nor rebellion in *Cliin,* and the tripods ought uot to have disappeared. That they might have done perhaps during the *Chou* time. The report says that King *Nan* hurried to *Ch in,* and that *Ch'in* seized the Nine Tripods. Perhaps there is a mistake in time.

There is another tradition that when the *Iai-cKht* altar to the spirits of the land disappeared in *Snng,* the tripods went down in the river below the city of *P eng-cKing.* Twenty-nine years later *Ch'in* united the Empire. Such being the case, the tripods would not have come into the possession of *Ch'in,* and must have been lost from the *Chou* already.

They were not spirits. During the "Spring and Autumn" period, five stones fell down in *Sung.* These five stones were stars. The separation of stars from heaven is like the disappearance of the tripods from earth. The stars falling down from heaven did not thereby become spirits, why then should the tripods vanishing from earth, acquire spiritual powers? In the "Spring and Autumn" time, three mountains vanished in the same manner as the *T'aich'iu* altar disappeared. Five stars de-

scended from heaven in *Sung,* three mountains vanished, five stones fell down, and the *T'ai-ch'iu* altar disappeared. All these events were brought about by causes residing in these things. The loss of the tripods was also the effect of some cause. One must not regard them as spirits merely on account of their disappearance. If the tripods resembled the three mountains of *Ch'in,* their disappearance is no sufficient reason, why they should be spirits. If they really possessed knowledge, and wished to avoid the disastrous revolution, the reigns of *Chieh* and *Chou* would have been the proper time for that.

The disorganisation and lawlessness were never worse than under *Chieh* and *Chou,* but at that time the tripods did not dis The eastern part of *Shantung* under the *Ch'in* dynasty.

A city in *Kianggu,* the modern *Hmchou-fu.* A river in *Shantung.* Quotation from the *Shi-chi* chap. 6, p. 18. *T ai-chiu* was a place in the *Yung-ch'cng* district, *Honan.*

"*Veng-clu'ng* does not lie on the *Sse* River, but on another small river.

In 221 B.c. Then the tripods would have been lost in 250 B.c. appear. The decadence of the kings of *Chou* was far from that of *Chieh* and *Chou.* Yet the tripods remained with the dissolute *Chieh* and *Chou,* and left the declining *Chou.* They did not stay nor leave at the proper time, and gave no sign of being spirits, endowed with knowledge.

It is possible that, at the collapse of the *Chou,* the men of General *Chiu,* who were in great number, saw the tripods, and stole them, and that some miscreants melted them, and made them into other objects, so that, when *Ch'in Shih Huang Ti* searched for them, he could not find them. Subsequently they were called spirits, which gave rise to the story that they were sunk in the *Sse* River.

Under the reign of the Emperor *Hsiao Win Ti* a man of *Chao, Hsin Yuan P'ing* addressed a memorial to the throne saying, "The *Chou* tripods are lost in the midst of the *Sse* River. Now the *Huangho* overflows, and communicates with the *Sse.* In a northeasterly direction near *Fin-gin* I perceive a metallic fluid. I presume it to be an angury of the *Chou* tripods' return. But unless fetched, they will not come out."

Thereupon *Hsiao Win Ti* sent a special envoy to superintend a temple south of *Fin-yin* near the River, in the hope that a spirit would bring the *Chou* tripods. Others denounced *Hsin Yuan P'ing,* showing that, what he had said about the supernatural vessels, was an imposture. Then *Hsin Yuan P'ing* was delivered to a tribunal, which sentenced him to death. The statement that the tripods are in the *Sse* is like the imposture of *Hsin Yuan P'ing* that he saw the spiritual fluid of the tripods.

Viz. the *Chou* dynasty. 179-156 B.c. A place in *Sharvrt,* in the present *Wan ch'iian hsien.* Quotation from the *Shichi* chap. 28, p. 20. CHAPTER XLI.

Sacrifices to the Departed *(Sse-yt).*

The world believes in sacrifices, imagining that he who sacrifices becomes happy, and he who does not, becomes unhappy. Therefore, when people are taken ill, they first try to learn by divination, what evil influence is the cause. Having found out this, they prepare sacrifices, and, after these have been performed, their mind feels at ease, and the sickness ceases. With great obstinacy they believe this to be the effect of the sacrifices. They never desist from urging the necessity of making offerings, maintaining that the departed are conscious, and that ghosts and spirits eat and drink like so many guests invited to dinner. When these guests are pleased, they thank the host for his kindness.

To prepare sacrifices is quite correct, but the belief that spirits can be affected thereby is erroneous. In reality the idea of these oblations is nothing else than that the host is anxious to manifest his kindness. The spirits are not desirous of tasting the offerings, as I am about to prove.

Our sacrifices are for the purpose of showing our gratitude for benefits enjoyed. In the same manner we are kind to living people, but would the latter therefore wish to be treated to a dinner? Now those to whom we present sacrifices are dead; the dead are devoid of

knowledge and cannot eat or drink. How can we demonstrate that they cannot possibly wish to enjoy eating and drinking?

Heaven is a body like the Earth. Heaven has a number of stellar mansions, as the Earth has houses. These houses are attached to the body of the Earth, as the stellar mansions are fixed to the substance of Heaven. Provided that' this body and this substance exist, then there is a mouth, which can eat. If Heaven and Earth possess mouths to eat, they ought to eat up all the food offered them in sacrifice. If they have no mouths, they are incorporeal, and being incorporeal, they are air like clouds and fog. Should the spirit of Heaven and Earth be like the human spirit, could a spirit eat and drink?

A middle-sized man is seven to eight feet high and four to five spans in girth. One peck of food and one peck of broth are enough to satisfy his appetite and his thirst. At the utmost he can consume three to four pecks. The size of Heaven and Earth is many ten thousand Li. Cocoon millet, ox rice cakes, and a big soup are offered them on round hills, but never more than several bushels. How could such food appease the hunger of heaven and earth?

Heaven and Earth would have feelings like man. When a man has not got enough to eat, he is vexed with his host, and does not requite him with kindness. If we hold that Heaven and Earth can be satiated, then the sacrifices presented to them in ancient times were derogatory to their dignity.

Mountains are like human bones or joints, Rivers like human blood. When we have eaten, our intestines are filled with food, which forms abundance of bones and blood. Now, by the oblations made to Heaven and Earth, Mountains and Rivers are also satiated along with Heaven and Earth, yet Mountains and Rivers have still their special sacrifices, as if they were other spiritual beings. That would be like a man who, after having eaten his fill, would still feed his bones and his blood.

We thank the Spirits of the Land and Grain for their kindness in letting grain

and other organisms grow. The ten thousand people grow on earth, as hair does on a body. In the sacrifices to Heaven 'and Earth the Spirits of the Land and Grain are therefore included. Good men revere them, and make to them special offerings. They must hold that they are spirits. In this manner man ought to specially feed his skin and flesh likewise.

The origin of the Five Sacrifices is the Earth. The Outer and Inner Doors arc made of wood and earth, both substances growing from earth. The Well, the Hearth, and the Inner Court of the house all depend on earth. In the sacrifice to the Earth, these Five Sacrifices are therefore comprised. Out of veneration a good man prepares special oblations for them, being convinced undubitably that they are spirits. But that would be, as if a man. after having appeased his appetite, were still specially feeding his body.

Ancient Chinese feet, which are much smaller than the modern. Large kinds of rice and millet. The Five Sacrifices of the house often mentioned in the *Liki.*

The Gods of Wind, Rain, and Thunder' are a special class of spirits. Wind is like the human breath, rain like secretions, and thunder like borborygmus. These three forces are inherent in heaven and earth, therefore they partake of the sacrifices to the latter. Pious men make special offerings to them as a mark of respect, regarding them as spiritual beings. Then a man ought to feed still his breath, his secretions, and his borborygmus.

The Sun and the Moon are like human eyes, the Stars like human hair. These luminaries being attached to heaven, they are included in Ihe sacrifices presented to the latter. Out of piety good men honour them with special sacrifices regarding them, no doubt, as spirits. That would be tantamount to our still feeding our eyes and hair after having satisfied our appetite.

The ancestral temple is the place of one's forefathers. During their life-time they are diligently and reverently maintained and nourished by their children, and after their deaths the latter dare not become unfaithful, and therefore prepare sacrifices. Out of consideration for their ancestors they attend their dead to show that they have not forgotten their forefathers. As regards the sacrifices to the Five Emperors and the Three Rulers like *Huang Ti* and *Ti K'u,* they were offered in appreciation of their mighty efforts and great accomplishments, for people did not forget their virtues. This, however, is no proof that there really are spirits, who can enjoy offerings. Being unable to enjoy, they cannot be spirits, and not being spirits, they cannot cause happiness nor unhappiness either.

Happiness and unhappiness originate from joy and anger, and joy and anger proceed from the belly and the intestines. He who possesses a belly and intestines, can eat and drink, and he who cannot eat and drink, has no belly and no intestines. Without a belly and intestines, joy and anger are impossible, and in default of joy and anger, one cannot produce happiness and unhappiness.

Somebody might object that odours cannot be eaten. I reply that smelling, eating, and drinking are very much the same. With the mouth one eats, and with the mouth one likewise smells. Unless there be a belly and intestines, there is no mouth, and without a mouth one cannot eat nor smell either.

How can we demonstrate that smelling is out of the question?

When some one offers a sacrifice, and others pass by, they do not immediately become aware of it. Unless we use the mouth, *Fmg Po,* the Prince of the Wind, *Yu Shih,* the Master of Rain, and *Lei Kimg,* the Thunderer. Their sacrifices are determined in the *Citon* ritual.

we must use the nose for smelling. When with the mouth or the nose we smell something, our eyes can see it, and what our eyes perceive, our hands can strike. Now, in case the hands cannot strike, we know that the mouth and the nose cannot smell.

Another objection might be raised. When Duke *Pao* of *Sung'* was sick, the priest said, " *Yeh Ku* will direct the service of the discontented spirit." The ghost leaning on a pole addressed *Ydi*

Ku saying, "Why are my vessels not filled with plenty of rice? Why are the grazing animals for the sacrifice not big and fat? Why are the sceptres and badges not of the proper measure? Is it your fault or *Pao's?*"

"*Pao* is still an infant in swathing cloth," replied *Yeh Ku* with a placid face, "who understands nothing about this. For how could he know or give any directions?"

The angry spirit lifted his pole and struck *Yeh Ku* dead on the steps of the altar.—Can this not be considered a proof of his having been able to use his hand?

It is not certain that *Yeh Ku's* death was caused by the blow of a discontented ghost. Just at that moment he was doomed to die; an apparition took the shape of a malignant ghost, and being shaped like a ghost, it had to speak like a ghost, and it also dealt a blow like a ghost. How do we know?

A ghost is a spirit, and spirits are prescient. Then after having remarked that the sacrificial vessels were not full of rice, the sceptres and badges not of the proper size, the victims lean and small, the ghost, being prescient, ought to have reproached *Yeh Ku* and struck him with the pole. There was no need to first ask him. The fact that he first asked, shows that he was not prescient, and, if he was not prescient, it is plain that he was not a spirit. Being neither prescient nor a spirit, he could not appear with a body, nor talk, nor strike a man with a pole.
Yeh Ku was an honest official who took the guilt upon himself, and offered himself for punishment, so that the ghost struck him. Had he been dishonest and inculpated *Pao,* the ghost would have hit *Pao* with his pole.
Furthermore, provided that the spirit resented the laxity in the performance of his sacrifice, and therefore made his appearance, and killed the superintendent of the sacrifice, then would he, in case all the rites were duly fulfilled, be pleased and appear, and as a favour present the sacrificer with some food? Men have joy and anger, and spirits should have these sensations likewise. A man who does not rouse another's anger,

preserves his life, whereas he who displeases him, loses it. The malignant ghost in his wrath made his appearance, and inflicted a punishment, but the sacrifices of the *Sung* State have certainly often been according to the rites, wherefore did the ghost not appear then to reward?

Joy and anger not being like the human, rewards and punishments are not like those dealt out by man either, and owing to this difference we cannot believe that *Yeh Ku* was slain by the spirit.

Moreover, in the first place, for smelling one takes in air, and for speaking one breathes it out. He who can smell, can talk likewise, as he who inhales, can exhale too. Should ghosts and spirits be able to smell, they ought to speak about the sacrifices. Since they are incapable of speech, we know that they cannot smell either.

Secondly, all those who smell, have their mouths and their noses open. Should their noses be stopped up by a cold, or their mouths gagged, olfaction becomes impossible. When a man dies, his mouth and his nose putrefy, how could they still be used for smelling?

Thirdly, the *Liki* has it that, when men have died, they are dreaded. They then belong to another class of beings than man, hence the dread. As corpses they cannot move, they decay, and are annihilated. Since they do not possess the same bodies as living people, we know that they can have no intercourse with the living. As their bodies are dissimilar, and as we know that there can be no intercourse, their eating and drinking cannot be like that of man. The Mongols and the Annamese are different nations, and in the matter of eating their tastes widely differ. Now, the difference between the departed and the living is not merely like that between the Mongols and the Annamese. Hence we infer that the dead cannot smell.

Fourthly, when a man is asleep, we may put some food near him, he does not know, but. as soon as he awakes, he becomes aware of it, and then may eventually eat it. When a man is dead, however, and sleeps the long sleep, from which there is no awakening, how could he know anything or eat then? This shows that he is unable to smell. The *Hu* in the north, and the *Yiieh* in the south of China.

I.un-Heng. 33

Somebody might raise the question, what it means that the spirits partake of a sacrifice, as people say. It means that people conscientiously clean the sacrificial vessels, that the rice is fragrant, and the victims fat, so that persons coming near and perceiving all this would feel inclined to eat and drink. With these their feelings they credit the ghosts and spirits, which, if they were conscious, would decidedly enjoy the offerings. Therefore people speak of the spirits, as though they were partaking of the sacrifice.

Another objection is the following:— The *Yiking* says that an ox killed by the eastern neighbour, is not like the humble oflering of the western neighbour. . This assertion that the eastern neighbour does not come up to the western, signifies that the animal of the eastern neighbour is big, but his luck small, whereas the fortune of the western neighbour is great, though his sacrifice be poor. Now, if the spirits are denied the faculty of enjoying the oflering, how can we determine the amount of happiness?

This also depends on the question, whether a sacrifice is carefully prepared, so that everything is clean, or not. *Chou* had an ox immolated, but he did not fulfill all the rites. *Win Wang*, on the other hand, made only a small offering, but did his utmost to show his devotion. People condemn a lack of ceremonies, and are full of praise for a pious fulfilment of all the rites. He who is praised by the people, finds support in all his enterprises, while the one who is disliked, meets with opposition, whatever he says or does. Such a resistance is no smaller misfortune than the rejection of a sacrifice by the spirits, and the general support is a happiness like that experienced, when the spirits smell the oblation.

Ghosts cannot be pleased or angry at a sacrifice for the following reason. Provided that spirits do not require man for their maintenance, then, in case they did need them, they would no more be spiritual. If we believe in spirits smelling the sacrifices, and in sacrifices causing happiness or misfortune, how do we imagine the dwelling places of the ghosts? Have they their own provisions stored up, or must they take the human food to appease their hunger? Should they possess their own stores, these would assuredly be other than the human, and they would not have to eat human food. If they have no provisions of their own, then man would have to make offerings to them every morning and every evening. According as he had sacrificed to them or not, they would be either satiated or hungry, and according as they *Yiking,* 03d diagram *(Chi-chi), Legge's* translation p. 206.

had eaten their fill or were hungry, they would be pleased or vexed.

Furthermore, sick people behold ghosts, and, while asleep, people meet with the departed in their dreams. They are shaped like men, therefore the sacrifices presented to them are like human food. Having food and drink, the spirits must be provided with raiment too, therefore one makes silken clothes for them after the fashion of the living. Their sacrifices are like dinners for the living. People desire to feed them, and hope that the ghosts will cat their offerings. As regards the clothes, however, they are not larger than from five or six inches to one foot. Now, supposing that tall and big spirits, which have been observed, are to don garments of a foot in length, would they be very pleased, and bestow happiness on the donors?

Should the ghosts, which have been seen, be really dead men, then the clothes made for them ought to be like those of the living, if, however, those garments are really put on by the ghosts, they must be shaped like dolls. Thus the question about ghosts and spirits remains an open one. How is it possible then to secure their protection and happiness by means of abundant offerings, and how can people firmly believe in this?

CHAPTER XLII.
Sacrifices *(Chi-yi).*

According to the *Liki* the emperor sacrifices to Heaven and Earth, the feudal princes to the Mountains and Rivers, the ministers, and high dignitaries to the Five Genii, the scholars and the common people to their ancestors. From the offerings to the spirits of the Land and Grain down to those in the ancestral hall there is a gradation from the son of heaven down to the commoners.

The *Shutting* says that a special sacrifice was made to *S/iangti,* a pure one to the Six Superior Powers, a sacrifice on high to the Mountains and Rivers, and a sacrifice to the various spirits round about. *Shun,* says the *Liki,* offered the imperial sacrifice to *Huang Ti,* the suburban sacrifice to *Ti K'u,* the patriarchal to *Chuan Hsil,* and the ancestral to *Yao.* The *Hsia* dynasty likewise presented the imperial sacrifice to *Huang Ti,* but the suburban to *K'un,* the patriarchal to *Chuan Hsil,* and the ancestral to Yii. The *Yin* dynasty transferred the imperial sacrifice to *Ti K'u,* the suburban to *Ming,* the patriarchal to *Hsieh,* and the ancestral to *T ang.* The *Chou* dynasty made the imperial sacrifice to *Ti K'u,* the suburban to *Chi,* the patriarchal to *Wen Wang,* and the ancestral to *Wu Wang. '*

Wood was burned on the big altar as a sacrifice to Heaven, a victim was buried in the big pit as a sacrifice to Earth. A red The mountains and rivers of their territory.

The five genii of the house to whom the Five Sacrifices were offered. See further on.

» Cf. *Liki, Ch'u-ti (Legge, Sacred Books* Vol. XXVII, p. 116).

Shuking, Shun-tien Pt. II, Bk. I, 6 *(Legge* Vol. III, Pt. I, p. 33). *Huang Ti, Ti K'u* and *Chuan Hsu* are mythical emperors. *Ti K'u* is said to have been the father of *Yao. K'un,* the father of *Yii. Ming* was a descendant of *Hsicit,* who was a son of *Ti K'u. Chi = Hou Chi,* the ancestor of the *Chou* dynasty. 9 The four sacrifices here mentioned were presented by the sovereigns of the ancient dynasties to the founders of their dynasties, their ancestors, and predecessors. calf was immolated, and a sheep buried in bright daylight as a sacrifice to the Seasons, and they approached the sacrificial pits and altars to offer sacrifice to the Heat and the Cold. In the imperial palace a sacrifice was made to the Sun, and in clear night they sacrificed to the Moon. Oblations were made to the Stars in the dark hall, to Water and Drought in the rain hall, and to the Four Cardinal Points at the four pits and altars.

The mountain forests, the valleys of the rivers, and the hills and cliffs can emit clouds and produce wind and rain. All these curious phenomena are regarded as spirits. The ruler of the world sacrifices to all the spirits, the princes only as long as they are within their territories, but not, when they have left them.

Such are the official sacrifices according to usage and the prescribed rites. The emperor treats Heaven like his father and Earth like his mother. Conformably to human customs he practises filial piety, which accounts for the sacrifices to Heaven and Earth. In the matter of Mountains and Rivers and the subsequent deities the offerings presented to them arc in appreciation of their deserts. A living man distinguishing himself is rewarded, ghosts and spirits which are well-deserving have their sacrifices. When mountains send forth clouds and rain, the welcome moisture for all the organisms, and when the Six Superior Powers keep in their six spheres, and aid Heaven aud Earth in their changes, the emperor venerates them by sacrifices, whence their appellation the "Six Honoured Ones."

The spirits of Land and Grain are rewarded for their kindness in letting all the things grow, the spirit *Shi* for all the living and growing things, the spirit *Chi* for the five kinds of grain.

The Five Sacrifices are in recognition of the merits of the Outer and Inner Doors, the Well, the Hearth, and the Inner Hall. Through the outer and inner doors man walks in and out, the well and the hearth afford him drink and food, and in the inner hall he finds a resting-place. These five are equally meritorious, therefore they all partake of a sacrifice.

Quotation from the *Liki, Chi-fa* (Law of sacrifices). The commentators, whom

Legge follows in his translation *(Sacred Books* Vol. XXVIII, p. 201), read much between the lines, which appears rather problematic. What the "Six Honoured Ones" are, is disputed. Some say:—water, fire, wind, thunder, hills, and lakes; others explain the term as signifying:—the sun, the moon, the stars, rivers, seas, and mountains. The Spirit of the Land or the Soil.

The Spirit of Grain.

Ch'i of *Chou* was called *Shao Hao.* He had four uncles of the names of *Chung, Kai, Hsiu,* and *Hsi* who could master metal, fire, and wood, wherefore he made *Chung* the Genius of Spring, *Kou Mang, Kai* the Genius of Autumn, *Ju Shou,* and *Hsiu* and *Hsi* Gods of the Winter, *Hsuan Ming.* They never neglected their office, and assisted *Ch'kmg-sang.*5 To these the Three Offerings are made. *Chuan Hsil* had a son called *Li,* who became the God of Fire, *Chu Yung.1 Kung Kung's3* son was named *Kou Lung.* He was made Lord of the Soil, *Hon Tu.* The Two Sacrifices refer to these two personages.

The Lord of the Soil was the spirit of the land and grain in charge of the fields. The son of *Lieh Shan, Chu,* was the spirit of the grain and from the *Hsia* dynasty upwards worshipped as *Ch'i,* the first ancestor of the *Chou* dynasty, venerated as the Spirit. of Grain under the title *Hou Chi* "Lord of the Grain." On his miraculous birth *vid.* p. 174.

By other authors *Ch'i* is not identified with the legendary emperor *Shao Hao,* whose birth was miraculous also. His mother was caused to conceive by a huge star like a rainbow *(T'ai-p'ing-yu-lan).* According to the commentary of the *Liki* these were not uncles, but sons of *Shao Hao.* The names of these deities or deified men correspond to their functions:— *Kou Mang* = "Curling fronds and spikelets," *Ju Shou* "Sprouts gathered," and £ *Hsuan Ming* = " Dark and obscure." According to the *Liki (Yueh-ting)* these three deities were secondary spirits, each presiding over three months of spring, autumn, and winter. Some say that *Hsuan Ming* was a water spirit. As the spirit of summer jjjJ *Chu Yung,* who is related to fire, is vener-

ated. There being a fixed relation between the four seasons, the four cardinal points, and the five elements we have the following equations:— *Kou Mang,* Genius of Spring, the east, and wood. *Chu Yung,* Genius of Summer, the south, and fire. *Ju Shou,* Genius of Autumn, the west, and metal. *Hsiian Ming,* Genius of Winter, the north, and water. I suppose that in the clause "who could master metal, *Jire* and wood" we ought to read *uatcr* in lieu of *Jire,* for the gods there enumerated are those of wood, metal and water. The spirit of fire follows in the next clause.

In the *Liki, Hou Tu,* the Lord of the Soil is made to correspond to the middle of the four seasons—in default of a fifth season-to the centre, and to earth. (Cf. *Legge, Sacred Booh* Vol. XXVII, p. 281 Note.) Thus we have:— *Hou Tu,* Genius of Mid-year, the centre, and earth. These Five Spirits are called the *Wu Slten.* They were worshipped during the *Chou* dynasty and are mentioned in ancient works *(Liki, Tso-chuan, HuaiKan* 7'e). Another name of *Shao Hao,* who was lord of *Ch'iung-mng.* A legendary emperor. 'Cf. Note 4.

See p. 250. Personal name of the emperor *Shen Nung,* who was lord of *Lieh-shan,* such. *Chi* of *Chou* was likewise spirit of the grain. From the *Shang* dynasty downwards people sacrificed to him.

The *Liki* relates that, while *Luh Shan* was swaying the empire, his sou of the name of *Cliu* could plant all the various kinds of grain, and that after the downfall of the *Hda* dynasty, *Ch'i* of *Chou* succeeded him, and therefore was worshipped as Spirit of the Grain. While *Kung Kung* was usurping the power in the nine provinces, his son, called Lord of the Soil, was able to pacify the nine countries, and therefore was worshipped as Spirit of the Land.

There is a tradition to the effect that *Yen Ti* produced fire and after death became the tutelary god of the Hearth, and that *Yd* having spent his energy on the waters of the empire, became Spirit of the Land after death.

The *Liki* says that the emperor institutes the Seven Sacrifices as representative of his people, namely for the arbiter of fate, for the inner court, for the gates of the capital, for its high-ways, for the august demons, for the doors, and for the hearths. The princes on their part institute the Five Sacrifices for their States, namely for the arbiter of fate, for the inner court, for the gates of their capital, for its high-ways, and for the illustrious demons. The high dignitaries present the Three Sacrifices for the demons of their ancestors, for their doors, and for their roads. The ordinary scholars make Two Offerings, one for the door and one for their roads, and the commoners only one, either for their inner doors or for the hearth.

There are no fixed rules for the oblations to be made to the spirits of the Land and Grain or for the Five Sacrifices, but they are all expressions of gratitude for benefits received from the spirits, whose goodness is not forgotten.

If we love somebody in our heart, we give him to eat and to drink, and, if we love ghosts and spirits, we sacrifice to them. With Yü the worship of the spirits of the land and grain, and the sacrifices to the lord of the grain commence. Subsequently they fell into desuetude, until in the 4th year of the emperor Kao Tsu The Liki in the current edition writes:— Li Shun. The Liki has:— Nung. Liki, Chi-fa (end).
Dynastic appellation of Shot Aung.
The fourth star in Ursa major.
The discontented and mischievous spirits of former sovereigns without children, who must be propitiated. Quotation from the Liki, Chi-fa (Legge, loc. cit. p. 206). s In 203 B.c. the world was called upon to sacrifice to the Ling constellation, and in the 7th year people were enjoined to sacrifice the spirits of the land and grain.
The offerings to the Ling constellation are for the sake of water and drought. In the Liki their ancient name is rain sacrifices. They are being performed for the people praying for grain rain and for grain ears. In spring they sue for the harvest, and within one year's time they sacrifice again, because grain grows twice a year. In spring this is done in the second moon, and in autumn in the

eighth. Therefore we read in the Analects: "About the end of spring, when the spring robes are all complete, along with five or six young men who have assumed the cap, and six or seven boys, I would wash in the Yi, enjoy the breeze among the rain altars, and return home singing."

The end of spring is the fourth month, but the fourth month of the Chou dynasty corresponds to our first and second months. During the time of the second month, the Dragon Star rises, whence it has been observed that, when the dragon appears, the rain sacrifice takes place. When the Dragon Star becomes visible, the year has already advanced as far as the time, when the insects begin to stir.

The vernal rain sacrifice has fallen into oblivion, while the autumnal one is still observed. Yet during all the ages the sacrifices to the Ling Star have always been prepared until now without interruption, only the ancient name has been changed, therefore the people of our time do not know it, and, since the ceremony has been abolished, the scholars are not cognisant of the fact. Finding nothing about the sacrifice to the Ling Star in the Rites, our literati could not form an opinion about it, and declare that the emperor ' had the Ming Star in view. Now the Ming Star is identified with the planet Jupiter. Jupiter stands in the east, the east rules over the spring, and the spring over all things that grow. Consequently one sacrifices to the planet Jupiter, they say, with the purpose of praying for The constellation T'ien-t'ien "Heavenly field" in Virgo. According to the Shi-chi chap. 28 (Chavannes Vol. HI, p. 453) Han Kao Tsu instituted these sacrifices in the Oth and 10th years of his reign. Analects XI, 25, VII. River in the south-east of Shantung. Kao Tsu.
9j 'Ti i "bright " ' generally regarded as another name of Venus. Cf. Shi-chi chap. 27, p. 22. vernal bliss. However all the four seasons affect the growth of things. By imploring the spring only, one lays great stress on the outset and emphasizes the beginning. Provided that in fact, according to the opinion of

the scholars, the happiness of spring be sought, then by the autumnal sacrifice spring could not well be implored. In conformity with the Yileh-ling one sacrifices to the inner door in spring, and to the outer door in autumn, all in accordance with the proper time. If the offerings made to the outer door in autumn were considered to be those to the inner door, would this be approved of by the critics? If not, then the Ming Star is not the planet Jupiter, but the "Dragon Star. "

When the Dragon Star becomes visible in the second month, one prays for grain rain at the rain sacrifice, and, when in the eighth month it is going to disappear, one sues for the grain crop at the autumnal rain sacrifice. The literati were probably aware of this, and what they say is not quite unreasonable. The vernal sacrifice for rain has been abolished, and only the autumnal one has survived. This explains why they termed the star corresponding to the autumnal sacrifice the Ming Star. The correct name however is the Ling Star.

The Ling Star means a spirit, and this spirit is the Dragon Star, as under the various spirits the wind god Feng Po, the rain god Yü Shih, the god of thunder, Lei Kung, and others are understood. Wind produces a wafting, rain a moisture, and thunder a concussion. The four seasons, the growing, heat and cold, the natural changes, the sun, the moon, and the stars are what people look up to, inundations and droughts are what they dread. From the four quarters the air pours in, and from the mountains, the forests, the rivers, and valleys people gather their riches. All this is the merit of the spirits.

Two motives are underlying all sacrifices: gratitude for received benefits and ancestor worship. We show our gratitude for the efforts others have take on our behalf, and worship our an Thus Jupiter, which rules over spring only, could not well be sacrificed to at the rain sacrifice in autumn. A chapter of the Liki. Cf. Lcgge's translation of the Liki Sacred Books Vol. XXVII, p. 251 and 283).

The Dragon Star occurs in the Tsoehuan, Duke *Rsiang* 28th year, as the star of *Sung* and *Cheng*. The commentary explains it as a synonym of *Jupiter*. The *Ming* Star = *Venus* governs the west and autumn, whereas *Jupiter* reigns in the east and in spring. cestors out of regard for their kindness. Special efforts, extraordinary goodness, merits, and universal reforms are taken into consideration by wise emperors, and it is for this reason that they have instituted sacrifices. An oblation is offered to him who has improved the public administration, who for the public welfare has worked till his death, who has done his best to strengthen his country, wlio has warded off great disasters, or prevented great misfortunes. 7V *K'u* could fix the courses of the stars and enlighten the world. *Yao* knew how to reward, and equitably mete out punishments, so that justice reigned supreme. *Shun* toiled for his people, and died in the country, *K'un* laboured to quell the flood, and was banished for life. *Yil* could take up his work. *Huang Ti* gave things their right names to enlighten people about the use to be made of them. *Chium Hsil* still further developed this system. When *Hsieh* was minister of education, the people flourished. *Ming* fulfilled his official duties with the greatest diligence, and found his death in the water. *T'ang* inaugurated a liberal government, and delivered the people from oppression. *Win Wang* relieved the misery of the people by culture and science, *Wu Wang* by his military exploits. By all these glorious deeds the people were benefitted. They rely on the strength of men like those, and show their gratitude by sacrifices.

The ancestors in the ancestral temple are our own kindred. Because, while they are alive, it is customary to maintain our parents, this duty cannot be shirked, when they are dead. Therefore we sacrifice to them, as though they were still alive. Ghosts are treated like men, for it is the living who attend the dead. For man it is usual to reward good deeds, and to maintain the nearest relatives, whence the duty to requite the kindness of the ancestors and to sacrifice to them has been derived.

When the dog which *Confucius* had bred was dead, he requested *Tse Kung* to bury him. "I have been told, quoth he, that one does not throw an old curtain away, but uses it to bury a horse, and that an old cart-cover is not thrown away, but used to bury a dog. I am poor, and have no cover to wrap him in." Then he gave him a mat, and bade him not to throw the dog down with his head first. About the prognostics furnished by the stars.
Quoted from the *Liki, Chi-fa (Legge, he cit.* p. 208). Quotation from the *Liki, T'an-kung (Legge, lo: cit.* p. 196). *Chi Tse of Yen-ling* passed through *Hsil*. The prince of *Hsil* was very fond of his sword, but, because *Chi Tse* had to go as envoy to a powerful State he, at that time did not yet consent to give it him. When *Chi Tse* came back from his mission, the prince of *Hsil* had died in the meantime. *Chi Tse* unbuckled his sword and hung it up on a tree over the grave. His charioteer asked for whom he did so, since the prince of *Hsil* wa-s already dead. "Previously, replied *Chi Tse,* I have made this promise in my heart already. Shall I become unfaithful, because the prince of *IlsO* has died?"— Whereupon he hung up his sword and went away.
Those who make offerings in recognition of special merits, are animated by the same sentiment as *Confucius,* when he interred his pet dog, and those who sacrifice, lest they should evade a former obligation, have the same tenderness of heart as *Chi Tse,* who hung up his sword on a tree over a tomb.

A sage knows these facts, and yet while sacrificing he will fast, and show such respect and devotion, as if there were really ghosts and spirits, and reform without cease, as if happiness and unhappiness depended thereon. But though people thus appreciate goodness, and honour merit, and take such pains to manifest their gratitude, it is not necessary that there should be really ghosts to enjoy these manifestations. We see this from the sacrifice offered to Earth at the meals. When people are going to eat and drink, they respectfully retire, as if they were giving precedence

to somebody. *Confucius* says: —" Although the food might be coarse rice and vegetable soup, one must offer a little of it in sacrifice with a grave, respectful air."6
The *Lite* tells us that, when subjects are invited to dine with their prince, he first calls upon them to sacrifice, before they receive their rations.

These oblations are like the various sacrifices of the *Liki*. At a meal one also may omit the offering, and though venerating the spirits one may forego a sacrifice. The same principle holds good for all the sacrifices, which invariably consist in giving *Chi Cha,* fourth son of King *Shou Mi'ng* of *Wu,* who died in 561 B.c.
A territory in *Kiangsu,* the appanage of Prince *Chi Tse.* A State in *Anhni.* He was on an embassy to *Lu, Ch i, Cheng, Wei* and *Chin,* and passed through *Hsil* in 544 B.c. .Se a parallel passage in the *Shi-chi* chap. 31, p. 9 v.
« *Analects X,* 8, X.
something as an offering. He who knows that at the sacrifice to Earth no spirit is present, and still maintains that ghosts attend the various sacrifices, ignores how to reason by analogy.

In the text of the Classics and the writings of the worthies nothing is said yet about ghosts and spirits, nor did they compose special works on this subject. The unauthorized sacrifices offered by the people are not enjoyed by any ghosts, but people believe in the presence of spirits, who can cause either happiness or misfortune.

The votaries of Taoism studying the art of immortality abstain from eating cereals and take other food than other people with a view to purifying themselves. Ghosts and spirits, however, are still more ethereal than immortals, why then should they use the same food as man?

One assumes that after death man loses his consciousness, and that his soul cannot become a spirit. But let us suppose that he did, then he would use different food, and using different food, he would not like to eat human food. Not eating human food, he would not ask us for it, and having nothing to ask at the hands of man, he could not give luck or mishap.

Our joy and anger depend on the fulfilment of our wishes. When they are satisfied, we are pleased, when not, irritated. In our joy we are generous and cause happiness, when we are sulky, we give vent to our anger and make others unhappy. Ghosts and spirits are insensible of joy and anger. People may g6 on sacrificing to them for ever, or completely disregard and forget them, it makes no difference, how could they render man happy or unhappy?

This is not quite true. The *Liki*, the *Tao-chuan,* and the *Shi-chi* treat of ghosts and spirits in many places, as we have seen. CHAPTER XLHI.

Criticisms on Noxious Influences *(Pien-sui).*

It is a common belief that evil influences cause our diseases and our deaths, and that in case of continual calamities, penalties, ignominious execution, and derision there has been some offence. When in commencing a building, in moving our residence, in sacrificing, mourning, burying, and other rites, in taking up office or marrying, no lucky day has been chosen, or an unpropitious year or month have not been avoided, one falls in with demons and meets spirits, which at that ominous time work disaster. Thus sickness, misfortunes, the implication in criminal cases, punishments, and even deaths, the destruction of a family, and the annihilation of a whole house are brought about by carelessness and disregard of an unfortunate period of time. But in reality this idea is unreasonable.

In this world men cannot but be active, and, after they have been so, they become either lucky or unlucky. Seeing them lucky, people point at this happiness and regard it as the happy result of their previously having chosen a lucky day, and seeing them unlucky, they look at their misfortune as the fatal consequence of their former inattention to an ill-timed hour. However, there are many persons who become unhappy, although they have chosen their day, and others who obtain happiness in spite of their neglect. The horoscopists and seers, de-

sirous of propagating their mystical theory, are silent upon such misfortunes, when they observe them, and hush up those cases of happiness. Contrariwise they adduce abundance of misfortunes with a view to frighten people, lest they should be careless in electing a day, and give many instances of happiness to induce them to be cautious in observing the proper time. Consequently all classes of people, no matter whether they be intelligent or feeble-minded, virtuous or depraved, princes or common citizens, believe in this from fear, and dare not make any opposition. They imagine that this theory is of high antiquity,

Not a moral offence, but a disregard of noxious influences.

and make the nicest distinctions, regarding it as a revelation of Heaven and Earth and a doctrine of wise and holy men. The princes are anxious for their throne, and the people love their own persons, wherefore they always cling to this belief, and do not utter any doubts. Thus, when a prince is about to engage in some enterprise, the horoscopists throng his halls, and, when the people have some business, they first ask for the proper time to avoid collision and injury. A vast literature of sophistic works and deceitful writings has appeared in consequence. The writers are very clever in passing their inventions off as knowledge for their own profit, winning the stupid by fear, enticing the rich, and robbing the poor.

This is by no means the method of the ancients or conformable to the intentions of the sages. When the sages undertook something, they first based it on justice, and, after the moral side of the question had been settled, they determined it by divination to prove that it was not of their own invention, and showed that ghosts and spirits were of the same opinion, and concurred with their view. They wished to prevail upon all the subjects to trust in the usefulness of divination and not to doubt. Therefore the *Shnking* speaks of the seven kinds of divination by shells and the *Yiking* of the eight diagrams. Yet those who make use of them, are not necessarily happy, or those who neglect them,

unhappy.

Happy and unhappy events are determined by time, the moments of birth and death, by destiny. Human destiny depends on Heaven, luck and misfortune lie hidden in the lap of time. If their allotted span be short, people's conduct may be ever so virtuous. Heaven cannot lengthen their span, and, if this span be long. Heaven cannot snatch it away from them, though their doings be evil.

Heaven is the master of the hundred spirits. Religion, virtue, kindness, and justice are the principles of Heaven, trembling and fear, heavenly emotions. The destruction of religion and the subversion of virtue are attacks upon the principles of Heaven: menaces and angry looks are antagonistic to the mind of Heaven.

'Shaking, Hang-fan Pt. V, Bk. IV, 23 (*Legge* Vol. lll, Pt. II, p. 335). By another punctuation the commentators bring out another meaning *viz.* that there are seven modes of divination in all, five given by the tortoise and two by milfoil. We must not suppose that Heaven can fear and tremble, for, as *Wang Ch'ung* tells us over and over again, Heaven is unconscious and inactive. It possesses those qualities ascribed to it only virtually. They become actual and are put into practice by man, who fulfils the commands of Heaven with trembling awe. Its moral feelings are heavenly principles and heavenly emotions. Cf. p. 129. Among the irreligious and wicked none were worse than *Chieh* and *Chou,* and among the lawless and unprincipled of the world none were worse than *Yu* and *Li.* Yet *Chieh* and *Chou* did not die early, and *Yu* and *Li* were not cut off in their prime. Ergo it is evident that happiness and joy do not depend on the choice of a lucky day and the avoidance of an unpropitious time, and that sufferings and hardships are not the result of a collision with a bad year or an infelicitous month.

Confucius has said, "Life and death are determined by fate, wealth and honour depend on Heaven." In case, however, that certain times and days are to be observed, and that there are really noxious influences, wherefore did the sage hesitate to say so, or why was he afraid to mention it? According to the ancient writings scholars have been enjoying peace or been in jeopardy, thousands of princes and ten thousands of officials have either obtained or lost luck or mishap, their offices have been high or low, their emoluments have increased or diminished, and in all this there have been many degrees and differences. Taking care of their property, some people have become rich, others poor, they have made profits, or suffered losses, their lives have been long or short, in brief, some have got on, while others remained behind. The exalted and noble have not selected lucky days in all their doings, nor have the mean and ignoble chosen an unlucky time.

From this we learn that happiness and unhappiness as well as life and death do not depend on the lucky auguries which people encounter, or on the time of ill omen or dread, whith which they fall in. While alive, men are nurtured by their vital fluid, and, when they expire, their life is cut off. During their lives people do not meet with a special luck or joy, nor can it be said that at their deaths they fall in with an ominous time of dread. Taking *Confucius* as a witness and basing our arguments on life and death, we come to the conclusion that the manifold misfortunes and calamities are not brought about by human actions. *Confucius* is a sage and a store of knowledge. Life and death are the greatest events. These great events prove the justness of our theory. *Confucius* has declared that life and death are determined by destiny, and that wealth and honour depend on Heaven. All the writings and covert attacks cannot invalidate this dictum, and common and weak-minded people cannot controvert it. Our Two emperors of the *Chou* dynasty of bad repute. *Yu Wang* reigned from 781 to 771 B.c., *Li Wang* from 878 to 828 B.c. Cf. p. 136. happiness and unhappiness in this world are fixed by fate, but we can attract them ourselves by our actions. If people lead a tranquil and inactive life, happiness and misfortune arrive of their own accord. That is fate. If they do business and work, and

luck or mishap fall to their lot, they have themselves been instrumental.

Very few of the human diseases have not been caused by wind, moisture, eating or drinking. Having exposed themselves to a draught, or slept in a damp place, people spend their cash to learn. which evil influence has been at play. When they have overeaten themselves, they rid their vital essence from this calamity by abstinence, but, in case the malady cannot be cured, they believe that the noxious influence has not been detected, and, if their life comes to a close of itself, they maintain that the divining straws have not been well explained. This is the wisdom of common people.

Among the three hundred and sixty naked animals man ranks first; he is a creature, among the ten thousand creatures the most intelligent. He obtains his life from Heaven and his fluid from the primordial vapours in exactly the same manner as other creatures. Birds have their nests and eyries, beasts their dens and burrows, reptiles, fish, and scaly creatures their holes, just as man has cottages and houses, high-storied buildings and towers.

Those moving creatures die and suffer injuries, fall ill and become worn out, and the big and the small ones prey upon one another, or man hunts and seizes them as a welcome game for his mouth and belly. They do not miss the proper time in building their nests and burrowing their hollows, or fall in with unlucky days in rambling east and west. Man has birth and death, and so other creatures have a beginning and an end. He is active, and so other creatures have their work likewise. Their arteries, heads, feet, ears, eyes, noses, and mouths are not different from the human, only their likes and dislikes are not the same as the human, hence man does not know their sounds, nor understand their meaning. They associate with their kindred and consort with their flock, and know, when they can come near, and when they must keep away just like man. They have the same heaven, the same earth, and they look equally up at the sun and the moon. There Even in

that case there is fate, which includes human activity.

Snakes, reptiles, and worms which like man have no scales, fur, or feathers. i fore one does not see the reason, why the misfortune caused by demons and spirits should fall upon man alone, and not on the other creatures. In man the mind of Heaven and Earth reach their highest development. Why do the heavenly disasters strike the noblest creature and not the mean ones? How is it that their natures are so similar, and their fates so different?

Punishments are not inflicted upon high officials, and wise emperors are lenient towards the nobility. Wise emperors punish the plebeians, but not the patricians, and the spirits visit the noblest creature with calamities and spare the mean ones? This would not tally with a passage in the *Yiking* to the effect that a great man shares the luck and mishap of demons and spirits.

When I have committed some offence and fallen into the clutches of the law, or become liable to a capital punishment, they do not say that it has been my own fault, but that in my house some duty has been neglected. When I have not taken the necessary precautions for my personal accommodation, or when 1 have been immoderate in eating or drinking, they do not say that I have been careless, but discover some impordonable disregard of an unlucky time. In case several persons die shortly one after the other, so that there are up to ten coffins awaiting burial, they do not speak of a contagion through contaminated air, but urge that the day chosen for one interment has been unlucky. If some activity has been displayed, they will talk about the non-observance of lucky or unlucky days, and, if nothing has been done, they have recourse to one's habitation. Our house or lodging being in a state of decay or delapidation, flying goblins and floating spectres assemble in our residence, they say. They also pray to their ancestors for help against misfortunes and delivery from evil. In case of sickness, they do not ask a doctor and, when they are in difficulties, they do not reform their conduct.

They ascribe everything to misfortune and call it offences or mistakes. Such is the type of the ordinary run: their knowledge is shallow, and they never get at the bottom of a thing.

When delinquents are employed by the Minister of Works for hard labour, it does not follow that the day, when they appeared before the judge, was inauspicious, or that the time, when they were condemned to penal servitude, was one of ill omen. If a murderer selects an auspicious day to go out and meet the judge, who inflicts his punishment, and if he chooses a good time for r entering the prison, will the judgment then be reversed, and his pardon arrive?

A man is not punished, unless he has met with mishap, nor thrown into jail, if not punished. Should oneday a decree arrive, in consequence of which he could walk out released from his fetters, it would not follow that he had got rid of evil influences.

There are thousands of jails in the world, and in these jails are ten thousands of prisoners, but they cannot all have neglected the precarious time of dread. Those who hold office and have their revenues, perhaps from special towns and districts, which have been given them in perpetual fief, number thousands and tens of thousands, but the days, when they change their residences, are not always lucky.

The city of *Li-yang* was flooded during one night and became a lake. Its inhabitants cannot all have been guilty of a disregard of the year and the months. When *Kao Tsu* rose, *FSng* and *P'ei* were recovered, yet their inhabitants cannot be said to have been particularly cautious with reference to times and days. When *Hsiang Yii* stormed *Rsiang-an,* no living soul was left in it. This does not prove, however, that its people have not prayed or worshipped. The army of *Chao* was buried alive by *Ch in* below *Ch angping.* 400,000 men died at the same time together. When they left home, they had surely not omitted to choose a propitious time.

On a *shin* day one must not cry, for crying entails deep sorrow. When some one dies on a *wu* or a *chi* day, other deaths will follow, yet in case an entire family dies out, the first death did not of necessity take place on a *shin, wu,* or *chi* day. On a day, when blood-shed is forbidden, one must not kill animals, yet the abattoirs are not scenes of more misfortunes than other places. On the first day of the moon, people should not crowd together, yet shops are not especially visited with disasters. When skeletons become visible on the surface of the soil, they have not necessarily come out on a *Wang-wang* day, and a dead man, whose coffin is standing in a house, must not just have returned on a *Kuei-chi* day. Consequently *Vid.* p. 136. Cf. p. 185. The *Shi-chi* chap. 8, p. 11 v., where this passage occurs *(Chavannes, Mim. Hist.* Vol. II, p. 343), speaks of the city of *Hsiang-ch'e'ng* in *Honan,* whereas *H/dang-an* is situated in *Anhui.* Cf. p. 136. Three cyclical numbers. On a *Wang-uiang* day one must not go out, and on a *Kuei-chi* day returning home is desastrous. those who interpret evil influences cannot be trusted, for if they are, they do not find the truth.

Now, let us suppose that ten persons living and eating together in the same house do not move a hoe or a hammer, nor change their residence, that in sacrificing and marrying they select but lucky days, and that from Spring to Winter they never come into collision with any inauspicious time. Would these ten persons not die, when they have attained a hundred years?

The geomancers will certainly reply that their house would either be in good repair or commence to decay, and that, on the *Sui-po* or *Chih-fu* days they would not think of leaving it. In that case they might every now and then ask the soothsayers about the state of their house and remain in it, as long as it is in good repair, but leave it, when it begins to delapidate, and, on the *Suipo* and *Chih-fu* days, the whole family might move. But would they not die then at the age of a hundred years?

The geomancers would again object that while changing their residence they would hit upon an unlucky time, or that their moving to and fro might be unpropitious. Then we would advise them to consult the seers and not to move, unless they can safely go, nor revert, unless their coming is without danger. But would they remain alive then after having reached a hundred years?

The geomancers would not fail to reply that life stops and that age has a limit. Ergo human life and death solely depend on destiny; they are not affected by unlucky years and months, or influenced by a disregard of fatal days of dread.

Wang-wang, Kuei-chi, Sui-p'o, and *Chih-fu* jftjj Jjjr . c are technical terms used by geomancers and in calendars to designate certain classes of unlucky days. CHAPTER XLIV.

On Exorcism *(Chieh-chu).*

The world believes in sacrifices, trusting that they procure happiness, and it approves of exorcism, fancying that it will remove evil influences. Exorcism begins with the ceremony of presenting an offering. An offering is like a banquet given by the living to their guests. First the ghosts are treated like guests and given a meal, but, when they have eaten it, they are expelled with swords and sticks. Provided that ghosts and spirits possess consciousness, they would undubitably resent such a treatment, offering resistance and fighting, and would refuse to leave forthwith. In their anger, they would just cause misfortune. If they are not conscious, then they cannot do mischief. In that case exorcising would be no use, and its omission would do no harm.

Moreover, what shape do people ascribe to ghosts and spirits? If they believe them to have a shape, this shape must be like that of living men. Living men in a passion would certainly make an attempt upon the lives of their adversaries. If they have no shape, they would be like mist and clouds. The expulsion of clouds and mist, however, would prove ineffectual.

As we cannot know their shapes, we can neither guess their feelings. For what purpose would ghosts and spirits gather in human dwellings? In case they earnestly wish to kill people, they would avoid their aggressors, when they drive them out, and abscond, but, as soon as the expulsion ceases, they would return, and re-occupy their former places. Should they have no murderous intentions, and only like to dwell in human houses, they would cause no injury, even if they were not expelled.

When grandees go out, thousands of people assemble to have a look at them, thronging the streets and filling the alleys, and striving for the places in front. It is not before the soldiers repel them, that they go away, but no sooner have the soldiers turned their back, than they return to their places. Unless the soldiers kept watch the whole day without leaving their post, they could not restrain them, because they are bent on having a look and would not go home on account of having-been driven back once. Provided that ghosts and spirits resemble living men, they would feel attracted to their homes in the same way as those thousands are determined on sight seeing. If the soldiers repelling them do not keep watch for a long while, the lookers-on do not disperse, and unless expelled during a whole year, the ghosts would not leave. Now, being expelled, after they have finished their meal, they would retire, but having retired, come back again, for what could prevent them?

When grain is being dried in a courtyard, and fowls and sparrows pick it up, they escape, when the master drives them off, but return, when he relaxes his vigilance. He is unable to keep the fowls and sparrows at bay, unless he watches the whole day. If the ghosts be spirits, an expulsion would not induce them to retreat, and if they be not spirits, they would be like fowls and sparrows, and nothing but a constant repulse could trighten them away.

When tigers and wolves enter into a territory, they are pursued with bows and cross-bows, but even their deaths do not do away w ith the cause of those terrible visits. When brigands and insurgents assault a city, the imperial troops may beat them, but notwithstanding this rebuff, the cause of their frightful incursions is not removed thereby. The arrival of tigers and wolves corresponds to a disorganised government, that of

rebels and bandits, to a general disorder. Thus the gathering of ghosts and spirits is indicative of the sudden end of life. By destroying tigers and wolves and by defeating insurgents and bandits one cannot bring about a reform of the government or re-establish order, neither is it possible to remove misfortune or prolong life by ever so much exorcising or expelling ghosts and spirits.

Sick people see ghosts appear, when their disease has reached its climax. Those who are of a strong and violent character will grasp the sword or the cudgel and fight with the ghosts. They will have one or two rounds, until at last, having missed a thrust, they are forced to surrender, for, unless they surrender, the duel will not come to a close. The ghosts expelled by exorcism are not different from those perceived by sick people, nor is there any difference between expelling and fighting. As the ghosts will not withdraw though assailed by sick people, the conjurations of the master of the house will not prevail upon the ghosts and spirits to leave. Consequently of what use would be such conjurations for the house? Therefore we cannot accept the belief that evil influences might thus be neutralised.

Furthermore, the ghosts which are expelled from the house live there as guests. The hosts are the Twelve Spirits of the house, such as the Blue Dragon and the White Tiger, and the other spirits occupying the Twelve Cardinal Points. The Dragon and the Tiger are fierce spirits and the chief ghosts of heaven. Flying corpses and floating goblins would not venture to gather against their will, as, when a host is fierce and bold, mischievous guests would not dare to intrude upon him. Now the Twelve Spirits have admitted the others into the house, and the master drives them away. That would be nothing less than throwing out the guests of the Twelve Spirits. Could such a hatred against the Twelve Spirits secure happiness? If there are no Twelve Spirits, there are no flying corpses or goblins either, and without spirits and goblins exorcism would be of no avail, and the expulsion have no sense.

Exorcism is an imitation of the old ceremony of the expulsion of sickness. In ancient times-Chuan Hsu had three sons, who vanished, when they had grown up. One took up his abode in the water of the Yangtse and became the Ghost of Fever, one lived in the Jo River and became a Wafer Spirit, and one in damp and wet corners as the arbiter of sickness. At the end of the year, when all business had been finished, sick people used to drive out the Spirit of Sickness, and believed that by seeing off the old year and going to meet the new one they would obtain luck. The world followed this example, whence originated exorcism. But even the ceremony of driving out sickness is out of place.

When Yao and Shun practised their virtue, the empire enjoyed perfect peace, the manifold calamities vanished, and, though the diseases were not driven out, the Spirit of Sickness did not make its appearance. When Chieh and Chou did their deeds, everything within the seas was thrown into confusion, all the misfortunes happened simultaneously, and although the diseases were expelled day by day, the Spirit of Sickness still came back. Declining ages have faith in ghosts, and the unintelligent will pray for happiness. When the Chou were going to ruin, the people believed in ghosts, and prepared sacrifices with the object of imploring happiness and the divine help. Narrow-minded rulers fell an easy prey to im In addition to the Blue Dragon and White Tiger Wang Ch'ung mentions the £ T'ai-sui, EJJJ Teng-ming and Tsung-k'usi as such spirits. Cf. Lun-heng, chap. 24, 13 (Xansui). The Blue Dragon and the White Tiger are also names of the eastern and western quadrant of the solar mansions. Comp. p. 106 and p. 352.
Cf. p. 242. posture, aud took no heed of their own actions, but they accomplished nothing creditable, and their administration remained unsettled.
All depends upon man, and not on ghosts, on their virtue, and not on sacrifices. The end of a State is far or near, and human life is long or short. If by offerings, happiness could be obtained, or if misfortune could be removed by ex-

orcism, kings might use up all the treasures of the world for the celebration of sacrifices to procrastinate the end of their reign, and old men and women of rich families might pray for the happiness to be gained by conjurations with the purpose of obtaining an age surpassing the usual span.

Long and short life, wealth and honour of all the mortals are determined by fortune and destiny, and as for their actions, whether they prove successful or otherwise, there are times of prosperity and decline. Sacrifices do not procure happiness, for happiness does not depend on oblations. But the world believes in ghosts and spirits, and therefore is partial to sacrifices. Since there are no ghosts and spirits to receive these sacrifices, the knowing do not concern themselves about them.

Sacrifices are meant as a kindness done to the ghosts and spirits, and yet they do not bring about luck and happiness. Now fancy that these spirits are expelled by brute force. Could that bring any profit?

The sacrificial rites and the methods of exorcism are very numerous. We will prove their uselessness by one example, for from a small sacrifice one may draw a conclusion to the great ones, and from one ghost learn to know the hundred spirits.

When people have finished the building of a house or a cottage, excavated the ground, or dug up the earth, they propitiate the Spirit of Earth, after the whole work has been completed, and call this appeasing the earth. They make an earthen figure to resemble a ghost. The wizards chant their prayers to reconcile the Spirit of Earth, and, when the sacrifice is over, they become gay and cheerful, and pretend that the ghosts and spirits have been propitiated, and misfortunes and disasters removed. But if we get to the buttom of it, we find that all this is illusive.

Why? Because the material earth is like the human body. Everything under heaven forms one body, whose head and feet are tens of thousands of Li apart. Mankind lives upon earth as fleas and lice stick to the human body. Fleas

and lice feed upon man, and torment his skin, as men dig up the earth, and torment its body. Should some among the fleas and lice, being aware of this, wish to appease man's heart, and for that purpose assemble to propitiate him near the flesh, which they have eaten, would man know about it? Man cannot comprehend what fleas and lice say, as Earth does not understand the speech of man.

The *Hu* and the *Yileh* have the same ears and mouths, and are animated by similar feelings, but even if they speak mouth to mouth, and ear to ear, they cannot understand each other. And there should be a communication between the ears and the mouth of Earth and man, who does not resemble her?

Moreover, who is it that hears what man says? Should it be Earth, her ears are too far away to hear, and if it be the earth of one special house, this earth is like an atom of human flesh, how could it understand anything? If the spirit of the house be the hearer, one ought to speak of appeasing the house, but not of appeasing Earth.

The Kites prescribe that entering into the ancestral hall one must not find a master there. One has made the device of cutting a wooden tablet, one foot and two inches long, and calling it the master, and serves it in the spirit, but does not make a human likeness. Now at the propitiatory sacrifices to Earth, they make an earthen human figure resembling the shape of a ghost. How could that have a propitiatory effect? Spirits are diffuse, vague, and incorporeal: entering and departing they need no aperture, whence their name of spirits. Now to make a bodily image is not only in opposition to the Rites, but also reveals a misapprehension of the nature of spirits. We know that they have no likeness, therefore, when the mats are spread for sacrifice, no figures of ghosts are put up.

If at the propitiatory service for Earth they set up human figures, could a stone effigy be used at the sacrifice to the Mountains, or could a wooden man be made for the sacrifice to the Gates and Doors?

When *Ch'ung Hang Yin* of *Chin* was near his end, he summoned his highpriest, wishing to punish him. "The victims." said he, "which you have immolated for me, have not been fat and glossy. You have not observed the rules of fasting with reverence, and thus have caused the ruin of my State. Is it not so?" The image of the departed, who as master dwells in the ancestral hall.

No figures are used at the sacrifices to those deities. A nobleman, related to the ducal house of *Chin,* of the 5th cent. B. c. The *Ch'ung Hang* family possessed large domains in *Chin.*

The priest replied in plain terms, "Formerly, my old lord, *Chung Hang Mi Tse,* possessed ten chariots, and did not feel grieved at their small number, but at the insufficiency of his righteousness. Your Lordship has a hundred warchariots, and does not feel distressed that your justice is so imperfect, but merely regrets that your chariots do not sufflce. When vessels and chariots are well equipped, the taxes must be high, and the taxes being heavy, the people defame and curse their sovereign. If he then offers sacrifices, of what use, can it be to his State? These curses must also ruin the State. —One man prays for him, and the whole State curses him. One prayer cannot overcome ten thousand curses. Is it not quite natural that a State should perish thus? What is the guilt of the priest?" — *Ch'ung Hang Yin* then felt ashamed.

The people of to-day rely on sacrifices like *Ch'ung Hang Yin.* They do not improve their conduct, but multiply the prayers, do not honour their superiors, but fear the ghosts. When they die, or misfortune befalls them, they ascribe it to noxious influences, maintaining that they have not yet been regulated. When they have been regulated and offerings prepared, and misfortunes are as numerous as before, and do not cease, they make the sacrifices answerable, declaring that they have not been performed with sufficient reverence.

As regards exorcism, exorcism is of no use, and as regards sacrifices, sacrifices are of no avail. As respects wizards and priests, wizards and priests have no power, for it is plain that all de- pends upon man, and not on ghosts, on   his virtue, and not on sacrifices.

Lightning Source UK Ltd.
Milton Keynes UK
UKOW02f1915020414

229314UK00007B/441/P